MANAGEMENT & ORGANIZATIONAL BEHAVIOR

The Wiley Series in Management

MANAGEMENT & ORGANIZATIONAL BEHAVIOR

SECOND EDITION

Burt Scanlon
University of Oklahoma

Bernard Keys
Memphis State University

John Wiley & Sons

New York · Chichester · Brisbane · Toronto · Singapore

Production Supervised by Cathy Starnella.
Cover and text design by Laurie C. Ierardi.
Cover Photo by Ted Horowitz.

Copyright © 1979, 1983 by John Wiley & Sons, Inc.

All rights reserved. Published simultaneously in Canada.

Reproduction or translation of any part of
this work beyond that permitted by Sections
107 and 108 of the 1976 United States Copyright
Act without the permission of the copyright
owner is unlawful. Requests for permission
or further information should be addressed to
the Permissions Department, John Wiley & Sons.

Library of Congress Cataloging in Publication Data:

Scanlan, Burt K.
  Management and organizational behavior.

  (The Wiley series in management, ISSN 0271-6046)
  Includes bibliographical references and indexes.
  1. Management. 2. Organization. I. Keys, Bernard.
II. Title.   III. Series.
HD31.S3256   1983   658.4   82-13536
ISBN 0-471-86183-9

Printed in the United States of America

10 9 8 7 6 5 4 3 2 1

To Henry and Dorothy Paul with Love—BKS
To Louise, Kim, Kristie, and Ted with Love—BK

ABOUT THE AUTHORS

Burt Scanlan is Professor of Management in the College of Business Administration at the University of Oklahoma. He received his bachelor's degree from Carroll College, his M.B.A. from the University of Wisconsin and his Ph.D. from the University of Nebraska. In addition to teaching at both of the above universities, he has taught at Drake University and the University of Wisconsin's Management Institute where he was involved in planning, developing, and conducting executive and management development programs.

Professor Scanlan has also authored *Results Management In Action* and *Management 18: Results Management in Practice*. The latter is published by John Wiley's Professional Development Programs and appeared in a second edition in January 1982. His books have been translated into German, Dutch, Portuguese, and Spanish. He has written over 80 articles for journals and business publications.

Dr. Scanlan has an extensive background in consulting and conducting management development programs in addition to his academic teaching. He has worked for a wide variety of profit and nonprofit organizations specializing in the areas of motivation, leadership, organizational effectiveness, planning, and objective setting and productivity achievement.

Bernard Keys is Associate Dean and Professor of Management at the Fogelman College of Business and Economics, Memphis State University. He received his B.S. from Tennessee Technological University, his M.S. from the University of Tennessee, and his Ph.D. from the University of Oklahoma. In addition to his academic duties, Dr. Keys is a consultant in management development programs for nationally known firms. For three years he conducted supervisory training for the Oklahoma City Municipal Government, and he is presently an adjunct faculty member for the U. S. Office of Personnel Management, Executive Seminar Center, at Oak Ridge, Tennessee.

Dr. Keys has been vice-president of the Oklahoma City Society for Advancement of Management, a director of the Oklahoma City American Society of Training Directors, placement director for the Academy of Management, and president of The Association for Business Simulation and Experiential Learning. He is presently secretary-treasurer for The Foundation for Administrative Research. Dr. Keys is Business Games Editor for the journal of *Simulation and Games*. He has published numerous journal articles and is the author of six books, including *The Executive Simulation*, Kendall/Hunt and *The Multinational Management Game*, Business Publications Inc.

PREFACE

This book is devoted to the study of management thought. It is designed for undergraduate and graduate students taking basic management courses, as well as for individuals who may wish to crystallize previously acquired knowledge or experience. It provides a complete foundation to principles of management, organizational behavior, and operations management in a straightforward manner.

In this edition we have once again tried to provide a text that offers the instructor and student considerable flexibility in approaching the teaching and study of management thought. This is done recognizing the fact that different environments and individual preferences dictate the need for a variable course structure.

The book is built around the fields of management, beginning with a solid management foundation in the classical functions of management (the control function is integrated into operations management). This is followed by an integrated and coordinated view of two fields: the fast-growing and popular field of organizational behavior and the field of operations management as it related to all types of organizations including production, health care, education, government, and the service sector. Part Six includes the development areas of social responsibility and international management plus an integrative chapter—management by objectives.

The flexibility of the text allows concentration on those chapters or parts that fit the structure of a given course outline while omitting others. Building in this potential for flexibility was one of our objectives in compiling the manuscript. Thus, the text allows the instructor and student considerable latitude in their individual approach to study.

While organized around the fields of management, the text is not based on any single viewpoint or theory. It includes a balanced coverage of normative and contingency theory and interpersonal, group, and organizational concepts. The text is based on an extensive review of professional literature from a wide variety of journals. Each chapter includes from 20 to 40 references from classical and recent publications. As in the first edition, the text provides particularly strong coverage of results-oriented management and leadership. This edition includes stronger coverage of the developing areas of human resource development, quality of work life, and organizational development—especially Japanese management.

Behavioral and organizational concepts are integrated into the other chapters where possible. For example, the subject of quality circles is covered in Chapter 17, Operations Management. In that same chapter the job design concept is tied to Wickham Skinner's focused factory idea.

Each chapter begins with a short vignette taken from current publications in the field of business and management. These vignettes are designed to spark the reader's interest and also highlight the operational significance of the material being presented. Each chapter is followed by a written summary, a unique summary chart, review questions, and application exercises and cases. Both the review questions and the application exercises and cases can be used as a source for essay-type examinations or quizzes.

A new feature of this edition is the use of marginal notes in the individual chapters. These call the reader's attention to specific key concepts and material that is being discussed and furnish a good basic guide to the key ideas in the chapter.

Most of the application exercises and cases at the end of each chapter have been updated and all are of a high quality. The questions for study that follow provide an excellent vehicle for a class discussion promoting an application of the material. The questions may also be used for examination purposes because of the direct and specific link to the chapter content.

Another new feature of this edition involves the inclusion of two integrative but very manageable cases at the conclusion of each part. As above, these cases and the study questions that accompany them are designed to require the application of specific principles and concepts contained in each respective part. The cases are also sufficiently varied to allow the instructor flexibility in terms of choosing which material he or she wishes to highlight.

This edition is accompanied by an expanded teaching/learning aid—*Practice in Management*. This is a combination study guide, reading selections, and experiential exercises for each of the six parts. Each chapter of the book has a parallel section in *Practice in Management*. It includes a brief summary of the chapter and true-false, multiple choice, and matching self-evaluation questions. Each chapter also includes a reading selected especially to stimulate the reader's interest and to expand the reader's understanding of the various subject areas. Each part of the text includes one or more managerial exercises, most of which can be completed as an independent or group activity. A few are included for possible group activities only.

A comprehensive instructor's manual is also available. For each chapter we have provided a suggested possible introduction to the chapter, a complete lecture outline, answers to end-of-chapter discussion questions, notes on the application exercises and cases, suggested readings to supplement the chapter material, and films and film summaries that complement the chapter. Also included are several transparency masters for use with each chapter. A separate test bank of over 1000 true-false and multiple-choice questions organized by chapter and subject matter is included. These materials can be obtained by contacting Wiley's representative or writing to them directly.

We hope you will find this edition with its updating and improvements to be of great value in providing meaningful insight into the field of management thought. Once again we have tried to provide a text that offers considerable flexibility for the instructor and reader in approaching the study of management.

We acknowledge the following people for their help in reviewing the book: Dr. James Gatza, Insurance Institute of America; Professor Michael Alford, The Citadel; Professor John Miller, Bucknell University; and Professor John Dunkelbury, College of Charleston.

BURT SCANLAN
BERNARD KEYS

CONTENTS

PART ONE INTRODUCTION / 1

1. Management in Perspective / 3
The Functions of Management / 6
How Managers at Different Levels Perform the Functions of Management / 8
Management as a Distinctive Activity / 11
Managing and Human Resources / 12
Contingency Nature of Management / 13
The Motivation to Manage / 13
The Nature of the Managerial Job / 14
Universality of Management / 16
Application Exercises and Cases / 20
   Utilizing Your Understanding of Management / 20
   Importance of the Management Job / 21

2. Historical Development of Management Thought / 23
Early Development of Management Thought / 25
Scientific Management Era / 26
Human Relations Era / 32
Organization and Management Principles Era / 34
Modern Management Era / 37
Application Exercises and Cases / 45
   Utilizing Management Concepts / 45
   Efferson Associates, Consultants / 45

INTEGRATIVE CASES / 47

The Function of the Chief Executive / 47

The Wilson Bindery—Application of Scientific Management to a Small Business / 48

PART 2 CLASSICAL MANAGEMENT CONCEPTS / 51

3. Managerial Planning and Strategy / 53
Managerial Orientations Toward Planning / 54
Importance of Planning / 55
What Planning is Not / 57
The Four Phases of the Planning Function / 58
Some Positive Payoffs of Long-Range Planning / 76
Key Elements and Benefits of Successful Planning / 77
An Integrative View of Planning / 77
Application Exercises and Cases / 82
    Planning for Home Improvements / 82
    Pitt Foundry / 83

4. Managerial Problem Analysis and Decision Making / 84
The Decision-Making System / 86
Decision Making—Four Essential Phases / 88
Participation in Decision Making / 97
Group Decision Making / 100
Group Decision-Making Techniques / 102
Barriers to Effective Decision Making / 104
Application Exercises and Cases / 107
    Industrial Scale Company / 107
    Foster Chemical, Inc. / 108

5. Organization Through Departmentation / 110
Elements and Functions of Organization / 112
The Development of an Organization / 115
The Growth of Staff in the Organization Structure / 118
Types of Staff Authority / 120
Dividing Work and Grouping Jobs / 125
Responsibility, Accountability, and Authority / 128
The Steps in Organizing / 130
Limitations to the Structural Study of Organization / 132
Application Exercises and Cases / 136
    Forming a New Company / 136
    Douglas Fowler's Dilemma / 137

6. The Organization in Operation—Some Critical Issues / 138
Managerial Delegation in Perspective / 139
A Positive Management Philosophy—Key to Effective Delegation / 140
Advantages of Delegation / 141
Authority and Power / 143
The Effective Use of Power and Authority / 148
The True Meaning of Managerial Delegation / 151

                What Delegation is Not / 153
                Span of Control / 154
                Review of Organization Structure / 159
                Application Exercises and Cases / 164
                    Importance of Management Philosophy / 164
                    Central High School / 165

7. Organizational Dynamics / 166
    Scientific Management and Human Relations / 168
    Principles of Management / 168
    Life Cycle of an Organization / 171
    Bureaucracy / 174
    A Balance Between Bureaucracy and Enterprise / 178
    Decentralization and the Profit Center Concept / 179
    Management by Objectives / 184
    Application Exercises and Cases / 188
        Research Coordination in the Pharmaceutical Industry / 188
        Naylor Corporation / 189

INTEGRATIVE CASES / 191

The Stellar Steel Products Company / 191
The Harder Company / 193

PART 3 ORGANIZATIONAL BEHAVIOR AND DESIGN / 195

8. Organizational and Interpersonal Communications / 197
    The Communication Problem in Perspective / 199
    Importance of the Top-Level Commitment / 199
    Communication Defined and an Overview of The Manager's Communication Environment / 201
    Information Side of the Communication Process / 202
    Interpersonal Behavior and Communication / 205
    Establishing a Management Approach / 206
    The Importance of Listening / 211
    Barriers to Creating Understanding and How to Overcome Them / 212
    Organizational Problems in Establishing Effective Communication / 214
    Application Exercises and Cases / 218
        C. I. T. Financial Corporation / 218
        Adleson Sales / 219

9. Human Motivation / 221
    Content Theories / 224
    Process Theories / 229

Herzberg's Dual Factor Theory / 235
The Porter and Lawler Motivation Model / 241
Systematic Approaches to Incentive Application / 243
Some Concluding Notes on Motivation / 246
Application Exercises and Cases / 250
   Analyzing Motivational Patterns / 250
   Dr. Holt's Dilemma / 251

10. Job Design—Creating More Meaningful Work / 252
Historical Approach to Designing Jobs / 254
Job Design and Motivation / 259
Job Enrichment / 264
Research on Job Enlargmeent and Job Enlargement / 269
A Contingency Approach to Job Design / 270
Application Exercises and Cases / 277
   Implementing Concepts in Job Design / 277
   Turning People On / 278

11. Role and Function of the Group in Organizations / 280
A Small Group Defined / 282
Types of Groups / 283
Factors in Group Formation / 284
A Model of Intragroup Behavior / 288
Intergroup Behavior / 294
Managerial Implications of Group Behavior / 298
Application Exercises and Cases / 301
   The Plating Room Group / 301
   River Glen Manufacturing Plant / 302

12. Contingency Approaches to Organizations / 303
Patterns of Organizing / 306
Choosing the Appropriate Organizational Form / 307
Organization Structure / 308
The Functional Organization / 311
Design Principles / 313
Design Logic / 313
Organizational Adaptations / 314
Application Exercises and Cases / 323
   Free Form Chaos / 323
   The Office of the President / 324

INTEGRATIVE CASES / 326

Kentown Corporation / 326

The Creative Organization—A Japanese Experiment / 329

PART 4 THE MANAGEMENT OF HUMAN RESOURCES / 335

13. Developing an Organizational and Leadership Philosophy / 337
Concepts About People and the Approaches to Management They Suggest / 339
Organizational Philosophy—a Concluding Note / 342
How Organizations Get Results Through People / 343
The Work of a Leader / 344
Leadership Skills / 348
The Activities of Successful Leaders / 349
Some General Observations Concerning Leadership / 355
Application Exercises and Cases / 358
   One Out of Three / 358
   Communication at the James River Plant / 360

14. Leadership Styles / 361
Normative Theories of Leadership / 363
Contingency Approaches to Leadership / 373
Application Exercises and Cases / 387
   Identifying Leadership Styles / 387
   Can One Learn to Manage Subordinates? / 388

15. Human Resource Development and Quality of Work Life / 390
Human Resource Planning and Development—An Overview / 391
Human Resource Development—Quality of Work Life / 400
Behavior Modification / 401
Performance Appraisal / 403
An Integrated Goal Setting, Appraisal, and Coaching System / 405
Management Development / 407
Developing a Career Plan / 410
Application Exercises and Cases / 415
   Talent Hunt / 415
   A Novel Approach to Management Development / 416

16. Organization Development / 418
The Management of Change / 420
Total Organizational Development (OD) / 421
Current Insights into Management Philosophy / 426
Initiating Changes in the Structural Environment / 426
Initiating Changes in the Behavioral Environment / 428
Methods of Behavioral Intervention / 429
Steps in Behavioral Intervention / 430
The Grid Approach to Organizational Development / 431
An Integrative View of OD Implementation / 439
Application Exercises and Cases / 442

Planning to Introduce Change / 442
A Case Incident From Germany / 443

INTEGRATIVE CASES / 445

South Pacific Hotel / 445

John Anderson / 448

PART 5 MANAGEMENT OF OPERATIONS / 453

17. Operations Management / 455
An Overview of Operations or Production Systems / 457
Operations Management Activities and Decisions / 459
Facilities Layout / 463
Production Plans, Scheduling, and Dispatching / 466
Product Life Cycle Approach / 468
Quality Circles / 474
Issues in Operations Management / 476
Application Exercises and Cases / 478
   Sebastian's—Layout of a Restaurant Kitchen / 478
   Workers are Experts—Quality Circles in Breakthrough / 479

18. Quantitative Decision Making and Operations Research / 481
Models / 483
The Management Decision Environment / 484
Decision Support and the Computer / 485
Product Design and Development, Using Cost-Volume-Profit Models / 485
Forecasting / 488
Resource Allocation with Linear Programming / 490
Decision Trees / 493
Operational Planning Activities / 495
The Managerial Role / 497
Advantages and Limitations of Quantitative Models / 498
Application Exercises and Cases / 501
   Retirement Hotel / 501
   Long-Term Health Facility / 501
   Catch a Falling Tristar / 502

19. Management Information Systems and the Computer / 503
The Evolution of Management Information Systems / 505
The Developing Uses of MIS / 506
Elements in an Effective MIS / 508
The Use of Computers in MIS / 510

Organizational Problems Created by MIS / 514
Behavioral Problems in MIS / 518
Preventing Dysfunctional Behavior in MIS / 521
Application Exercises and Cases / 525
  Needed: Business-Oriented Systems Analysts / 525
  We Have Play-Offs, Bake-offs; Now a Compute-off / 526

20. Controlling Operations / 529
Definition and Purpose of Control / 531
Elements of Control / 531
Control in the Operations of Productive Systems / 535
Budgeting / 543
Project and Scheduling Control Devices / 546
Human Aspects of Managerial Control / 548
Fundamental Guidelines of Effective Control Administration / 550
Application Exercises and Cases / 553
  The Sirocco Company—Introduction of a Budgetary Control Plan / 553
  Hell Week / 555
  Faulty Light Bulbs / 557

INTEGRATIVE CASES / 559

McCall Diesel Motor Works / 559
The Home Equipment Company / 561

PART 6 GOAL-ORIENTED MANAGEMENT SYSTEMS / 565

21. Social Responsibilities of Management / 567
What is Corporate Social Responsibility? / 569
Research Findings Regarding Social Responsibility of Business / 574
Developing a Strategic Posture Toward Social Responsibility / 576
Areas of Managerial Response to Social Responsibility / 579
Patterns of Social Action Programs / 581
The Social Audit: A Strategy for Defining and Implementing Social Responsibility / 583
Application Exercises and Cases / 587
  A Matter of Priority / 587
  The Xerox Experiment / 589

22. MBO—An Integrative System of Management / 591
A Systems Approach to MBO / 595
Setting Objectives and Developing Strategic Plans / 595
Assessing the External Environment / 597
Developing Action Plans / 597
Implementing Plans Through Leadership and Delegation / 599
Measuring and Rewarding Performance, In View of the Objectives / 602

Budgeting and Control / 604
External Inputs from Managerial and Organizational Development / 606
Application Exercises and Cases / 613
   MBO or Something Else? / 613
   Choose a Leadership Style / 614

23. International Management and Management in the Future / 616

Multinational Corporations / 617
The Organization and the Manager in the Twenty-First Century / 624
Changing Social Needs / 628
Management Practices of the Future / 634
Application Exercises and Cases / 643
   Success in the Small Multinational Corporation / 643
   The Nonconformists / 644

INTEGRATIVE CASES / 646

Union Carbide and Vienna, West Virginia / 646

Consolidated Instruments—B / 647

INDEX / 655

PART ONE
INTRODUCTION

CHAPTER 1
MANAGEMENT IN PERSPECTIVE

CHAPTER 2
HISTORICAL DEVELOPMENT OF MANAGEMENT THOUGHT

INTEGRATIVE CASES

THE FUNCTION OF THE CHIEF EXECUTIVE

THE WILSON BINDERY— APPLICATION OF SCIENTIFIC MANAGEMENT TO A SMALL BUSINESS

Part One sets the stage for our study of management thought. Specifically, we have four objectives; the first is to develop an appreciation for the part of a manager's job that consists of achieving results through others.

The second purpose is to develop an initial overview and understanding of the functions a manager performs. We have chosen as the basis for our approach the four functions that traditionally are included by all authors: planning, organizing, directing, and controlling. A fuller appreciation of the significance and dynamics of the four basic functions will be realized as we progress through the book.

Third, Chapter 1 addresses material relating to the motivation to management and some facts about managerial life. Chapter 1 briefly outlines the plan of this book. We hope that this summary will give you a bird's-eye view of the entire profession of management.

The fourth objective of Part One is to present the historical development of management thought. To better appreciate where we are today it helps to know from where we have come. Put another way, an appreciation for the past helps us to better understand the present. Thus the historical overview of management thought contained in Chapter 2 was included to help you develop perspective in this area.

Good management is the primary determinant of the success of any organization, whether it is a service club, hospital, school, agency of the federal or state government, museum, or business. Although much of our discussion may be couched in business terms, we have attempted to reinforce this universality concept at numerous points throughout the book. You must, however, bear some of the burden for applying the principles of good management to many types of organizations.

At several points in the text we will be stressing that there is not just "one best way" that fits all situations and solves all problems. Instead a myriad of factors needs to be given consideration when making decisions regarding organizational design, leadership style, and a host of other key issues.

CHAPTER 1
MANAGEMENT IN PERSPECTIVE

THE FUNCTIONS OF MANAGEMENT
AN OVERVIEW OF PLANNING
AN OVERVIEW OF ORGANIZING
AN OVERVIEW OF DIRECTING
AN OVERVIEW OF CONTROLLING

HOW MANAGERS AT DIFFERENT LEVELS PERFORM THE FUNCTIONS OF MANAGEMENT
PLANNING
ORGANIZING
DIRECTING
CONTROLLING

MANAGEMENT AS A DISTINCTIVE ACTIVITY
MANAGING AND HUMAN RESOURCES
CONTINGENCY NATURE OF MANAGEMENT
THE MOTIVATION TO MANAGE
THE NATURE OF THE MANAGERIAL JOB
UNIVERSALITY OF MANAGEMENT
PLAN OF THIS BOOK
PART ONE: INTRODUCTION
PART TWO: CLASSICAL MANAGEMENT CONCEPTS
PART THREE: ORGANIZATIONAL BEHAVIOR AND DESIGN
PART FOUR: THE MANAGEMENT OF HUMAN RESOURCES
PART FIVE: MANAGEMENT OF OPERATIONS
PART SIX: GOAL-ORIENTED MANAGEMENT SYSTEMS

APPLICATION EXERCISES AND CASES
UTILIZING YOUR UNDERSTANDING OF MANAGEMENT
IMPORTANCE OF THE MANAGEMENT JOB

MANAGERIAL TALENT—A CRITICAL NEED FOR ORGANIZATIONS

One of the biggest jobs in Union Pacific's reorganization, Evans allows, has been getting management in place. When Champlin and Rocky Mountain Energy came aboard, he explains, "We had the balance sheet and the physical resources, but we didn't have the in-house people to manage them. We had to make a strong commitment to building a top management team."[1]

During the 1980s, an entire generation of senior executives who entered business after World War II will be retiring. But instead of having an abundant pool of talent to fill these vacancies, American industry is faced with a crucial shortage of management leaders in the decade ahead. The primary reason is that many of the management succession programs so widely heralded in the 1970s have not worked out. Hundreds of large corporations in those days bragged about their plans to groom young executives in broad-based responsibilities that would guarantee corporate continuity. Instead, far too many of these managers have ended up sidetracked in specialized jobs or single-function careers.

Some of the skills needed vary from company to company. But personnel managers generally agree that basic management experience in the fundamental functions of manufacturing, marketing, and finance are essential. On top of that, they see a strong need for grounding in such strategic skills as planning and control, problem solving and the management of people. And because they expect the business environment of the 1980s to be far more complex than in recent decades, they foresee a need for top-echelon generalists who are knowledgeable about international business affairs, government regulation, economics, and the uses of the computer. Personnel executives agree that formal development programs are required. "It can't be done hit or miss or on the hope that the cream will automatically rise to the top," says a U.S. Steel Corp. personnel manager.[2]

---

[1]"The Five Best Managed Companies, Union Pacific's New Eminent Domain," *Dun's Review,* December 1979, Vol. 114, No.16, p. 54.
[2]"Where Are Tomorrow's Top Managers?" *Dun's Review,* December 1979, Vol. 114, No. 6, p. 98.

Moving into a position of management will present a new challenge.

Some years ago two engineers with essentially the same educational backgrounds, experiences, and tenure in a large organization were placed simultaneously in management positions. Instead of being paid for performing their technical specialties, they were being paid as managers of departments in which engineering work was performed. At the end of the first six months Manager A was experiencing considerable success and enjoying the new managerial job, but Manager B was less successful. Problems were being experienced in meeting schedules and project deadlines, there was unrest among the engineers in the department, and Manager B was becoming discouraged, disillusioned, and frustrated. Higher-level management was also becoming very concerned about this situation.

The successful Manager A had obviously adapted very well to the new managerial role, because he realized he was embarking on a new and different career with the organization and had adjusted accordingly. More specifically, he perceived his role and function to be different from what it previously had been. After his appointment as manager, Manager A initially inventoried the department to determine both the work that had to be accomplished and the personnel that were available to do it. In the latter area his concern was not only with the number of people available, but also with their individual skills, abilities, strengths, and weaknesses. The current status of work in the department was reviewed. Then, using this as a base, priorities and completion schedules for the various projects were formulated.

Through individual and department meetings Manager A communicated to employees the position and importance of the department as a whole in the total organization, as well as the purposes and objectives of the various projects in which they were involved. In addition, his engineers were given a clear picture of where the total department stood with respect to what was expected and the present status of work completion. Manager A shared and discussed with them his perception of some of the problems inhibiting better departmental performance and obtained their suggestions for improving things. Beyond this, an active interest was taken in each person individually and the new manager worked with them in a coaching capacity to set goals, improve performance, and gain more satisfaction from the job. In other words, Manager A managed, planned, organized, directed, and controlled.

> Total accomplishment is the result of effectively integrating the human assets of the organization around the task at hand.

Manager B grew frightened by the new role. When he realized he was no longer expected to do actual engineering work, he became confused. Time had to be spent some way so he made a point of checking everything every engineer did before it left the department. When an error was found, he quickly called it to the attention of the engineer responsible. The corrections Manager B made himself. After finding a few such cases he concluded that more checking of work was needed; it almost became a challenge to find something wrong. He began to spend more and more time watching over employees' shoulders to make sure things were done right. There were also projects in his department that the organization considered very strategic as well as high priority. Manager B felt these projects demanded his personal attention, so a drafting table was moved into the office and he worked on them himself, very often until late at night and on weekends.

Because his involvement in these special projects was so heavy, certain other things did not get done. Progress reports on other projects were not filed on time. At a central unit meeting with other managers, Manager B was unable to give an adequate breakdown of the status of the total department effort and the projected completion dates for various jobs. In addition, the people in his department progressively assumed less responsibility for their work. They became passive. One of the more experienced engineers resigned and two others filed transfer requests.

Management was not being practiced; Manager B was doing what he had always done—practicing his technical specialty. As a manager, he encountered something unfamiliar and different, but did not make the necessary adjustment.

INTRODUCTION

> To be an effective manager requires a unique set of skills, abilities, knowledge and attitudes.

He was not able to become a supervisor and gain satisfaction in the accomplishments of others. He could not let go of the slide rule, the T square, and all the other tools of the trade. Eventually he failed as a manager of others, and returned to his specialty.

Whether such problems lie in bad selection or in inadequate training is not our concern here. The point is that managing is a distinct activity that requires a specific set of skills, abilities, knowledge, and attitudes. Not everyone can be successful at managing. Performing the operational aspects of a job and managing are different activities.

THE FUNCTIONS OF MANAGEMENT

Management may be defined as the *coordination and integration of all resources (both human and technical) to accomplish various specific results*. According to this definition, management is viewed in terms of the functions that a manager performs. The four basic functions that have historically formed the core for studying management are planning, organizing, directing, and controlling. In this section we very briefly examine each of the functions and develop an overall picture of what they involve (see Figure 1-1).

> Management involves the coordination and integration of all resources to accomplish specific results.

FIGURE 1-1

The Functions of Management in Perspective

Planning
1. Establishing the mission or overall long-range direction of the organization.
2. Establishing specific shorter-range objectives.
3. Determining policies and procedures.
4. Developing operational plans.

Organizing
1. Developing a formal structure.
2. Grouping activities into departments.
3. Specifying relationships between departments and operating units: lines of authority, responsibility, accountability, communications, decision making.
4. Delegation of authority and responsibility.

Directing
1. Developing a total organizational philosophy about people.
2. Integrating the needs of individuals with those of the organization: creating a motivational climate.
3. Creating a result-producing leadership climate: effective communication, job design, small groups, coaching, and developing.

Controlling
1. Developing standards and objectives.
2. Deciding on measures or criteria of successful performance.
3. Designing a system of status reporting.
4. Taking corrective action when and where needed.

AN OVERVIEW OF PLANNING

The planning function can be divided into two essential phases. The first phase is determining the overall long-range direction or mission of the organization. This requires considerable analysis and thought. Is the industry in which the organization is centered growing and expanding, declining, or one which is relatively static? If either of the latter two situations pertains, decisions must be made regarding what strategy should be undertaken to insure the organization's continued health and perhaps even survival. If it is a growing and expanding industry, plans must be made for the organization to keep pace. Determining the mission also involves decisions about the long-range size of the organization, where growth potential exists, the degree and extent to which the organization wants to expand in those areas, and the consideration of the advantages, disadvantages, and consequences of taking or not taking certain actions. Only after decisions are made about these and similar long-range goals can the shorter-range specific objectives be developed.

The second phase of planning is the formation of these specific shorter-range objectives to insure that the longer-range missions are realized. Part of this objective-setting process involves both the determination of overall policies and procedures and devising the operational or "how to" aspects of accomplishing the objectives. These plans should be designed both to take maximum advantage of the strengths of the organization and to overcome or compensate for any weakness or shortcomings.

The first phase of planning involves determining the overall mission of the organization.

The second phase of planning involves determining shorter-range specific objectives and developing operational plans.

AN OVERVIEW OF ORGANIZING

Organizing involves developing a formal structure that will facilitate the coordination and integration of resources. Viewed another way, the organization structure should contribute to the efficient accomplishment of both the long-range mission and the shorter-range objectives and plans. The process of organizing proceeds with the concept of division of work. Accordingly, a series of operating units or departments is formed, with each being responsible for a particular phase of the operation. Once this division of work for departmentation is complete, managers must then concern themselves with specifying the relationships among the various operating units. These relationships may take many forms, including authority relationships among people and departments, lines of responsibility and accountability, channels of communication, lines of decision making, and the complete spectrum of interrelationships that exists among the various parts. The manager's delegation of authority and responsibility is one of several other key issues involved in organization.

Organizing results in a formal structure.

AN OVERVIEW OF DIRECTING

The function of directing is primarily concerned with the questions of motivation and leadership. Management should first develop an appreciation about the fundamentals of human motivation, and then promote an overall organizational philosophy about people conducive to creating a motivational climate. The issue at hand is essentially one of creating a climate where the needs of the individual are integrated with the needs of the organization; that is, a climate in which individuals can best satisfy their own goals by working toward the goals of the organization. Of particular significance in leadership is the quality of face-to-face and day-to-day interaction that a manager has with people. Although many factors are involved in creating a result-producing climate, effective communication, job design, and management of groups are key concerns. Also, the extent and degree to which a manager works with people in a coaching capacity, to help them accomplish their specific job objectives and perform at their maximum level of capability, determines how successful she will be in efforts at direction and leading.

The directing function involves integrating the needs of the individual with those of the organization.

AN OVERVIEW OF CONTROLLING

The purpose of the controlling is to make certain that events conform to plans. Control is concerned with the present, with what is happening now. As a result of planning, specific objectives have been set in all important phases of the operation. The control function, if effectively carried out, will provide the manager with continual feedback on exactly where the operation stands at any time with respect to achieving these objectives. This information feedback should not only deal with the general picture, but will ideally pinpoint some of the specifics. If objectives are not being achieved or if their accomplishment is behind schedule, the manager must identify the areas that are causing problems and develop alternatives to overcome them. Thus, control is a four-phase process involving the presence of standards and objectives, the determination of how performance in each area is to be measured (criteria of successful performance), developing a status reporting system, and finally taking corrective action when and where needed. Figure 1-1 summarizes the four basic functions of management.

The purpose of control is to insure that events conform to plans.

HOW MANAGERS AT DIFFERENT LEVELS PERFORM THE FUNCTIONS OF MANAGEMENT

Further insight and understanding of the functions of management can be provided by comparing how managers at different levels in the organization perform these five basic managerial functions. The farther apart the various management levels, the more dramatic the difference. For this reason we compare the executive, or very top-level manager with the first-line supervisor, who is at the bottom of the managerial ladder. Figure 1-2 summarizes these differences.

PLANNING

As indicated in Figure 1-2, planning at the executive level is long range. Such questions as the extent and degree of diversification, expansion by either growth or acquisitions, and capital procurement and mergers are significant. These issues and the decisions that are made concerning them will have an important impact over an extended period of time. Planning at this level of management is

Planning at the executive level is long range, deals with broad overall goals, and is originating in nature.

FIGURE 1-2

How Managers at Different Levels Perform the Managerial Functions

Executive Level	*Supervisory Level*
Planning	
A. Long range	A. Short range
B. Broad overall goals	B. Specific and precise
C. Originating	C. Derivative
Organizing	
A. Overall formal structure	A. Coordination of people, machines, and materials on short range basis
B. Lines of authority, responsibility, and accountability	
C. Lines of communication and decision making	
D. Degree of decentralization	
E. Relationships between departments	
Directing	
A. Establish total organizational philosophy and approach toward managing people	A. Deal with operational employees
	B. Emphasis on getting the work out
B. Long range development of people	C. Overall leadership style and specific leadership techniques important
C. Organize wide programs to motivate the human element	
Controlling	
A. Long range overview	A. Specific day-to-day factors affecting results
B. Setting overall requirements	B. Removing immediate obstacles to accomplishment
C. Scope broader	C. More immediate in scope

usually concerned with broad overall goals. It concentrates on such things as return on investment, sales-earnings ratios, share of the market, and product mix. Finally, executive planning is originating in nature. By this we mean that the decisions made and the plans formulated at this level serve as a basis for planning at each successive level in the organization.

In contrast, planning at the supervisory level is shorter range in nature. It is more likely to be on a day-to-day or week-to-week basis and carried out in a more informal way. Indeed, many aspects of the planning function are performed for the supervisor by any number of centralized planning departments.

Accordingly, in a production operation a centralized production planning and control department may predetermine the supervisor's production schedule to the point of specifying which equipment will be used to perform various jobs. The supervisor's responsibility is to see that the schedule is met. Also, there may be a plan to carry out equipment maintenance work on a periodic schedule. The supervisor becomes involved only in emergencies. Similarly, a centralized cost control unit may plan and predetermine a cost budget for the department. The cost control unit keeps the necessary records and provides feedback, and the supervisor is charged with making needed adjustments to meet the budget. These phenomena lead to our second observation that the further down in the organization the more specific and precise planning tends to become. Plans at lower levels necessarily must be concerned with the details that affect accomplishment of broader goals. Thus, planning at these levels is derivative rather than originating in nature. They are an outgrowth of decisions made at higher levels. They deal more with the "how to" as opposed to the "what."

ORGANIZING

Decisions involving organization at the top level are directed toward determining what the overall formal organization structure should be. The executive level must consider the following questions. What will the basis for departmentalizing work be? Should activities be grouped on a functional basis such as production, marketing, and personnel management, or should the basis for organizing be in terms of products, territory, or types of customers? Also, how much decentralization should exist? The decentralization issue includes the question of facilities or physical decentralization as well as decentralization of decision making. Finally, a part of developing an overall organization structure involves establishment of lines of authority, responsibility, accountability, communications, and decision making. Of critical importance will be the relationships between line and staff departments, particularly in terms of the provisions for integration and coordination of effort between them.

The executive level is concerned with the overall formal organization structure.

Organization at the supervisory level deals almost exclusively with the day-to-day coodination of people, machines, and materials to accomplish specific results. In an organizational sense, the supervisor is more concerned with the relationships among things than he is with relationships among people. His place in the total structure has been determined from above and he must operate within that framework.

At the supervisory level organization deals with the day -to -day coordination of people, machines, and materials.

DIRECTING

As in the functions of planning and organizing, the executive-level manager's concern with the directing function is broader in scope than that of the first-line supervisors. It is the responsibility of the top-level administrators to develop and promote an overall positive philosophy and approach to the directing funcction. Beyond this, the executive level must see to it that managers at all levels receive training necessary to make them effective leaders and developers of men and women. It is not enough simply to verbalize what should be. The example must be set from above. To a degree, how a manager directs her people in general and her specific approach to leadership is a mirror of her superior. Managers tend to manage as they themselves are managed. Beyond the issue of laying the groundwork for effective approaches for day-to-day supervision, the executive level will also become involved in developing organizational wide motivation programs. Also of concern to the higher-level executive is the longer-range development of people in the enterprise to insure a continued supply of qualified personnel.

Top management's responsibility in directing consists of developing and promoting an overall philosophy.

Instead of managing other managers, the first-line supervisor is responsible for the efforts of operative employees. Although his ultimate goal is to get the work out, he must be particularly concerned about his overall style of leadership and the specific leadership techniques that he uses to create a motivational climate. To the operative employee the first-line supervisor represents the total organization and his perception of that organization is a reflection of his perception of his supervisor. The abilities to relate to people individually and to be sensitive to them as individuals are key elements of effective first-line supervision.

CONTROLLING

Like planning, top management centers control efforts on longer-range issues that are broader in scope.

Because of the very close tie among the functions of planning and controlling, the distinction between the executive and supervisory levels in terms of performance of these functions is very similar to those cited earlier. The executive level is more likely to focus on the longer-range issues that are somewhat broader in scope. The executives will be more concerned with setting forth standards or goals to be achieved and reviewing information to assess where the organization as a whole stands. Unless high-level issues are involved, they will leave the details of corrective action to lower-level administrators. Their emphasis will focus on the major functional areas of the organization such as production, marketing, and finance. The supervisor will center control efforts on specific factors that influence day-to-day results and removal of immediate obstacles. Although not always true, the supervisor is more likely to become involved with immediate crisis.

MANAGEMENT AS A DISTINCTIVE ACTIVITY

Prior success as an operative employee in a specialized area does not insure that one will be successful as a manager.

In times past, when a manager was needed, the common practice was to look around the organization or department and spot the best operative employee. She was then appointed as a supervisor. The assumption was that since she was good at whatever operative job she held, she would automatically make a good manager. Accordingly, the best office worker, accountant, medical technician, or salesperson was the prime candidate for the management position. There were undoubtedly many employees desiring to move into management who believed that superior performance and competence on their present jobs was the key to the door.

Many of the skills and abilities needed can be developed.

But being a manager requires a very specialized set of knowledge, skills, abilities, and attitudes. If she is to be successful, these attributes must be acquired. It is certainly true that some people have more innate or inborn talent to be effective managers than others, but it is also true that these skills and abilities can be learned and developed. This point is evidenced by the fact that organizations are spending millions of dollars each year on various types of management development programs. One recent, study estimated that there are between 30,000 and 40,000 public management seminars conducted annually and that over 750,000 people attend these seminars at a total cost of $1 billion.[3]

---

[3]"Public Seminar Business May Exceed $1 Billion," *Training*, May 1981, p. 94.

There are few organizations of any size that do not either have a separate management development department, or one person who devotes a major share of time to these activities. In addition, many national organizations, such as the American Bankers Association, the U.S. Postal Service, the Federal Aviation Administration, American Society of Personnel Administrators, and the American Society of Training and Development, sponsor extensive management development programs.

In spite of all that has been and is being done in this area, there are still many organizations who need to get a start on management development activities or expand the scope of efforts that have already begun. Many examples of this may be found in the health sciences, education, government, and others. The incident that opened the chapter highlights the important need to develop future managers as does the following: "Corporate personnel chiefs are pressing hard to get their companies' management succession programs beefed up. In a survey of 330 personnel officers last summer, Haskell & Stern found that the vast majority named management succession planning as the most important issue facing them in the 1980s.[4]"

MANAGING AND HUMAN RESOURCES

Imagine that you have been an operative employee for a period of three or four years.

One day your superior calls you into the office and explains that because of expansion and other changes that will be in effect shortly, a new supervisory position has been created. Your superior further explains that over the past few years your general work and other aspects of your overall job performance have been very good, and you have been selected to fill the new position if you wish to accept it.

Assuming that you are a typical employee, the opportunity to move into a management position is something that you have aspired to as a distinct step in your career development. Let us assume that you accept the new job and the challenge that accompanies it. As you begin to function as a manager, several things will happen. First, you will notice that things look much different from the way they used to: your promotion may have seemed at the time to be a small step but it was a giant leap. You will discover that there is a big difference between being one of several operative employees in a department and being the supervisor of that department. Your perspective broadens; your outlook and perhaps your attitude also change.

Second, the distinction between *doing* versus *managing* will come into sharper focus. As an operative employee you were expected to perform a series of activities or tasks and meet certain basic performance standards. As a manager you no longer ply your trade in a direct sense. If you were a supervisor of production workers in a unionized plant, there probably would be specific prohibitions against you or any other supervisor doing any *physical* work. Your job is now that

<small>Management involves getting things done by, with, and through people.</small>

---

[4]"Where Are Tomorrow's Top Managers?" *Dun's Review*, December 1979, Vol. 114, No. 6, p. 98.

of a manager who is responsible both for the operation of the entire department and for the direction of other people in their work.

Finally, if you did not realize it when you started your new job, *you will be successful if your employees, individually and as a group, are successful in their jobs.* Your performance will be a reflection of their performance, and you will be judged largely by what they accomplish.

To a large degree, a manager's success is determined by the success of her people.

The above example serves to illustrate three important points. First, it stresses the *human element* in management. Managers do not get things done by themselves. If they try to do everything alone, their accomplishment will be limited to their individual talents and energies.

Second, a manager's job is to *make things happen.* If quality is bad, the manager takes steps to improve it. If sales are down, he develops new customers and markets. If costs are high, he takes the initiative to find out how to cut them. Thus, management is active rather than passive; it is causal, not effect oriented. Managers do more than react to what is happening—they take positive action.

A manager's job is to make things happen.

Third, management is a *dynamic process.* Managers transform potential into reality. They must be innovators and agents for change, progress, and growth, as opposed to merely responding or adapting passively to what is happening around them. The manager's job is to insure that results are achieved.

CONTINGENCY NATURE OF MANAGEMENT

Many organizations, individual managers, and writers have historically searched for the one best way to manage. Accordingly, they sought definitive answers as to how an organization or individual should carry out the planning, organizing, leading, and controlling functions.

More recently we have come to recognize the contingency nature of management. In fact, *contingency theory,* as it relates to a number of specific factors such as organization structure, leadership, and participation, has occupied a prominent role in the literature of recent years.

Briefly, contingency theory states that the proper approach to a management function such as leadership, is contingent or dependent on forces in the manager, the people being supervised, and the situation. Each of these major areas would have several associated subconsiderations, and together they would suggest an appropriate leadership style (one most likely to yield best results). We will be introducing contingency aspects of management throughout the book when they relate to specific topic areas, after certain preliminary concepts have been established.

The proper approach to management is dependent on the situation, the people involved, and the manager.

THE MOTIVATION TO MANAGE[5]

In addition to recognizing the importance of the human element and developing skill in the performance of the various managerial functions, success in man-

---

[5] John B. Minor, *The Human Constraint: The Coming Shortage of Managerial Talent*, Washington D.C., Bureau of National Affairs, 1974.

agement requires that an individual wants to manage, or more specifically, possesses the motivation to manage. The following list gives six ingredients that comprise the motivation to manage.

1. Favorable attitude toward those in positions of authority. A manager must be able to gain support at higher levels in the organization and represent his group upward. To do this requires a positive attitude toward those in positions of authority so as to elicit positive responses from superiors.
2. Desire to engage in competition. Managers must be prepared to accept challenges and must strive to win for themselves and their group. They must be inclined to compete for available rewards or face continually declining achievement levels. The very nature of the job has a strong competitive element built into it.
3. Desire to assert oneself and take charge. As pointed out earlier, the manager must transform potential into reality. It is a dynamic job that requires exercising initiative to make things happen as opposed to just reacting to what has already happened. A certain amount of assertive behavior is critical to success.
4. Desire to exercise power and authority. Leadership involves influencing others toward specific goals and this requires skill in the effective use of authority. A person who is not comfortable exercising authority is not likely to be successful or comfortable in a managerial role.
5. Desire to be visible. As soon as a person accepts a managerial job they put themselves in a position that sets them apart from the larger group. Behavior must change and this will inevitably invite attention and even sometimes criticism.
6. Sense of responsibility. Management requires getting work out and meeting many routine demands. Among these demands is a great deal of administrative work. At a minimum the manager must be willing to complete this type of work and ideally receive a certain amount of self-satisfaction in actually doing it.

THE NATURE OF THE MANAGERIAL JOB

The Center for Creative Leadership has published the results of research studies designed to determine the nature of the managerial job. The results of some of their work regarding what managers do are summarized as follows and provide insight for any prospective manager.[6]

1. Managers work long hours. The typical manager will work a minimum of fifty hours per week and estimates range upward from that point. The higher one goes the longer the number of hours of work tend to grow.
2. Managers are busy. A manager may face as many as 200 different incidents in

---

[6]Morgan W. McCall, Jr., Ann M. Morrison, and Robert L. Hannan, *Studies of Managerial Work: Results and Methods,* 9, Greensboro North Carolina, Center for Creative Leadership, 1978.

a single day. This means that the amount of uninterrupted time that is available in any one day is very restricted.

3. The management job is fragmented and varied. Paperwork, phone calls, scheduled meetings, unscheduled meetings, and inspection tours are common activities in the day of every manager. At the middle management level, unscheduled meetings and informal interactions account for 43 percent of the manager's time.

4. Managers tend to stay in their own departments. The higher up one goes the more time that is spent at one's own desk. This partially explains why managers must be willing to do administrative work and receive a certain amount of self-satisfaction from completing it.

5. Management requires a lot of interpersonal contact and oral communications. Most interaction is with subordinates and with peers as opposed to superiors. In addition, managers tend to supervise others more than they are supervised. At all levels, face-to-face communication occupies a great deal of time and predominates over other forms of communication.

6. There is little time spent in reflective thinking and planning. In spite of the fact that we know planning is one of the key and most important managerial functions, most managers spend a minimum of time doing it. This can be accounted for by the weight of administrative paperwork and other factors discussed above. Increasingly, however, planning is becoming an absolute necessity and the consequences of not doing it are becoming too expensive to bear.

7. Managers find it difficult to account for their time. Rather consistently managers underestimate the amount of time spent in personal contacts and overestimate that spent on production, reading, writing, and on the phone. This inability to account for time is a serious handicap to managers who are concerned about increasing their personal effectiveness. Insight into the sum of the nature and requirements of the managerial job can be summarized as follows:

The manager we have described is hard working, spends very long hours at his or her job, and, therefore, must be highly motivated. The demands on the manager require special perceptual and personality characteristics, particularly since so much time is spent in interaction with others. Of necessity, the manager must engage in decision making, and must understand the dynamics of being an effective leader. Considering the substantial amount of time the manager spends interacting with others, frustration, conflict, and stress are inevitable at times. The manager must influence other people and must understand how others are influenced and affected by persons around them. This in turn requires that the manager understand the various norms of the group he or she works with, and the forces that encourage conformity or deviance from these norms. Finally, the manager is a product and a prisoner of the organization, and must work effectively within the organizational concept.[7]

The demands on a manager are many and varied.

---

[7]Thomas V. Bonoma, and Gerald Zaltman, *Psychology for Management*, Boston, Kent Publishing Company, 1981 pp. 9–10.

UNIVERSALITY OF MANAGEMENT

The word management usually evokes the thought of profit-making business and industry. Much of the impetus for developing a unified body of knowledge about management and a professional approach to performing the management function has come from the needs created by our free enterprise system. But it would be a mistake to assume that the only place that management skills are needed is in a profit-making enterprise.

If two or more people are involved in a joint effort, management is required. The activity being undertaken may be as informal as a bowling team, or three or four people going on a hunting trip, or as highly formal as a business. Whether it be a hospital, a university, the military, a health clinic, a branch of the federal government, a museum, a church, or a volunteer organization, the management functions, principles, and concepts discussed in this text must be performed effectively if the group's objectives are to be successfully achieved.

Universality refers to the idea that the management functions must be performed regardless of the type organization.

PLAN OF THIS BOOK

PART ONE: INTRODUCTION

This book is divided into six parts with a total of twenty-three chapters. It is designed to provide you with an integrated and comprehensive view of the practice of management. Part One and Chapter One presents a broad perspective of management. Chapter Two, "Historical Development of Management Thought," traces management from the scientific and classical eras through the human relations era to modern management. This total discussion should provide you with a comprehensive perspective of much of what will be covered in later parts.

PART TWO: CLASSICAL MANAGEMENT CONCEPTS

Early management practitioners tended to view the route to success in organizations as that of finding more efficient ways to do things. Accordingly, they emphasized the concepts of specialization and methods analysis. Classical theorists also looked for the answers to achievement in the structure of the organization itself. These theorists examined such factors as formal organizational relationships (including authority), delegated activities, the number of persons reporting to an individual, and similar phenomena.

The five chapters that comprise Part Two are devoted to exploring the managerial functions of planning and organizing from a classical viewpoint. The related areas of the organization in operation, delegation, managerial decision making, and organizational dynamics are also covered. The material examined in these early pages are a strong foundation on which to build your understanding and appreciation for the entire process of management.

PART THREE: ORGANIZATIONAL BEHAVIOR AND DESIGN

Part Three looks both vertically and horizontally at the interrelationships of certain roles within the organization. More specifically, organizational behavior concerns itself with the individual needs of men and women in the organization, communication processes, the behavioral aspects of job design, small-group behavior, and intradepartmental and interdepartmental relationships. In short, organizational behavior views the organization while key participants are moving and interacting in the most complex fashion, much in the same way that airplanes are tested in wind tunnels to examine flight characteristics and stresses that might occur during flight. Organizational behavior attempts to bridge the gap in the early classical approaches to management by providing tools of analysis that allow the manager to tie together individual tasks, human needs, and motivational factors with the proper organizational structure.

PART FOUR: THE MANAGEMENT OF HUMAN RESOURCES

There is a very close relationship between the material in Part Three and that in Part Four. Leadership has been defined as "getting other people to accomplish the objectives of the organization *because they want to.*" The key elements of leadership include the superior, the subordinate, the task to be accomplished, and the organizational climate. All of the concepts discussed in organizational behavior, as well as those covered under formal organization in the classical section, build a framework for the understanding of leadership. In moving from classical theories of leadership to contingency approaches, the leader is required to have a great deal of knowledge and understanding of human relationships. Leadership styles have changed significantly in our society as a reflection of the less authoritarian norms expected in all social relationships, including the church, the family, the school, and work institutions. Where once the organization and the task was accepted as given, with most change expected to come from the worker, now organizations are being modified to accommodate individual needs, and jobs are being redesigned to make them more compatible with human beings. Today's leader must be more adaptable than was once the case; hence the need to study contingency approaches to leadership.

PART FIVE: MANAGEMENT OF OPERATIONS

The units on organizational behavior and managing human resources consider the needs of the worker, her organizational setting, and management's attempts to optimize these factors. The implicit assumption is that if the organization climate and needs satisfaction of the worker are optimized and made as coincident with organizational objectives as possible, the worker will find a way to accomplish these objectives. This may be an idealistic viewpoint. Part Five focuses primarily on this task by asking the question, "What is the best way to allocate the available resources of a productive system in order to most effectively meet a demand forecast, at the lowest possible costs?" The following quote from Buffa reveals the emphasis of operations management:

In attempting to meet the objectives of a plan, certain realities interfere, such as equipment failure, human error, discrepancies in the timing of order flow, quality variation, and so on. Therefore systems for scheduling maintenance, quality control, and cost control are invented to help retain order where otherwise the system would naturally tend toward chaos.[8]

While Buffa fully realizes that there are other limitations to optimizing operations management, notably those of motivation and morale of workers, his emphasis is on the physical elements rather than the psychological factors.

It is important to note that production, or industrial enterprise, is not dealt with exclusively in the operations management part. The operations phase of any organization or institution which processes either a product or information can utilize similar tools of analysis and quantitative decision-making techniques.

PART SIX: GOAL-ORIENTED MANAGEMENT SYSTEMS

Finally, in Part Six, we examine management by means of the systems approach. This approach recognizes the fact that management is a complex set of relationships between people and is systematically organized with inputs, interaction, and outputs. The efficiency of the organization is a function of the ratio and quality of inputs to outputs. The three chapters in this part examine the issues of the management of social responsibility, management by objectives as an integrative system of management, and the future of management. The summary chart at the end of this chapter provides an overview of the evolution of management and the sequential development of the total text.

SUMMARY

The Summary Chart depicts the functions and process of management. Notice that movement from left to right denotes chronology. Over the past seventy-five years the fields of operations management and organizational behavior have evolved out of what were at first areas of inquiry and later became well-defined elements of management.

In this chapter, management was examined by looking at the four basic managerial functions: planning, organizing, directing, and controlling.

---

[8]Elwood S. Buffa, *Basic Production Management*, 2nd ed., New York, Wiley, 1975, p. 6.

MANAGEMENT IN PERSPECTIVES   19

Planning involves establishing overall direction of the organization, and then determining shorter-range objectives, which includes developing policies and procedures and devising day-to-day operational plans.

The function of organizing encompasses the creation of a formal structure within which the actual work will take place. The matters of departmentalizing the work, determining the relationships between departments, chain of command, and delegation of authority are all significant issues in organizing.

The directing function is concerned with managing the human assets of the organization. Development of a management philosophy about people, the creation of a motivational climate, and leadership strategies are significant aspects of direction.

SUMMARY CHART

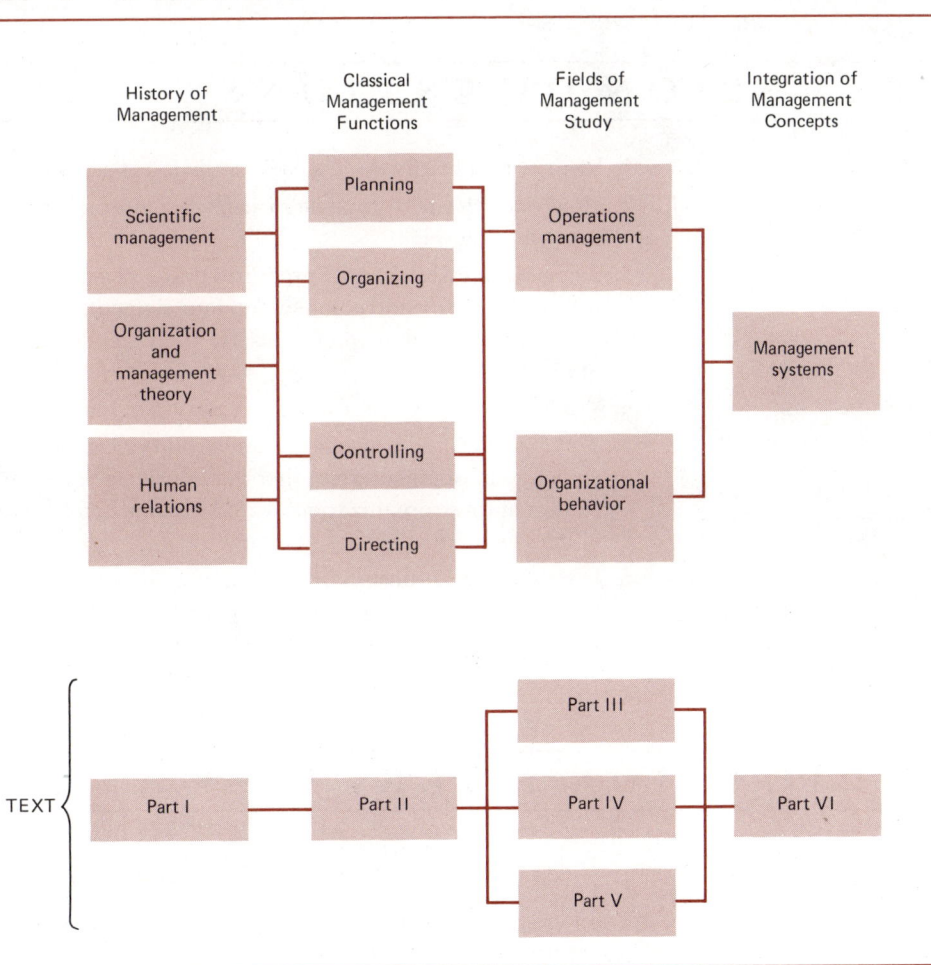

History of Management	Classical Management Functions	Fields of Management Study	Integration of Management Concepts
Scientific management	Planning	Operations management	
Organization and management theory	Organizing		Management systems
Human relations	Controlling	Organizational behavior	
	Directing		

TEXT: Part I → Part II → { Part III, Part IV, Part V } → Part VI

Finally, the objective of managerial control is to insure that events conform to plans. Standards must be set, measures of successful performance must be developed, a system of reporting events as they occur must be established, and provision must be made for corrective action, if needed.

The idea that management is a distinct activity requiring specialized knowledge, skills, abilities, and attitudes was stressed, as was the job of a manager as it relates to working with and through others to achieve results. To be successful in management requires that a person possess the motivation to manage and also understand and be able to cope with the unique nature of the job. We recognized that effective management is a universal process in that it is a key determinant for any successful organization, whether it be a business, a sorority, or a church or synagogue. We also pointed out the contingency nature of management, which stresses that there is no one best way or one best answer to all management issues and problems.

DISCUSSION QUESTIONS

1. Identify and briefly discuss each of the four basic managerial functions.
2. How does the performance of each function differ at the executive versus supervisory level?
3. Being a successful manager requires that a person possesses the motivation to manage. Identify and comment on four elements of the motivation to manage and cite four of what you feel are the more significant facts about managerial life.
4. What is meant by the contingency nature of management?
5. To what does the concept of "universality of management" refer? Give two examples of organizations other than business types, and cite areas where the leaders of those organizations would become involved in each of the functions of management.
6. Discuss the relationship between managing and operating work by pointing out the differences between being one of several operative employees and being the manager of a department or unit.

APPLICATION EXERCISES AND CASES

UTILIZING YOUR UNDERSTANDING OF MANAGEMENT

Upon graduation from school you accepted a position with a medium- to large-sized company in their general management training program. The program was structured so that every few months you received an assignment in a different department such as production, marketing, or accounting.

Currently you are working in the Personnel Department. For some time the company has been contemplating the development of a presupervisory training program. This program is designed to provide hourly employees who have expressed an interest in becoming supervisors with some background information about management as well as expose them to specific subject areas where they will need to develop certain skills and abilities.

You have been asked to formulate an outline for an initial orientation session. The overall purpose of this session is to provide participants with a better understanding of what the job of a manager involves from a conceptual standpoint, some of the specific activities of functions a manager performs and other information that is pertinent to anyone contemplating a move from the ranks of the operative employee to those of management.

Assignment:

Based on what you have learned from your study of Chapter One prepare an outline of what your orientation session would include in terms of subject matter. In addition to setting forth the major topic areas you would cover, include specific subpoints and key thoughts that you would place emphasis on. Since working in personnel is one of your higher preferences for a permanent assignment after the two-year management training program, you wish to really excel at this assignment.

IMPORTANCE OF THE MANAGEMENT JOB[9]

Arnold Hodge has recently been promoted to the position of sales manager of the eastern division of Alco Products, Inc. Before his promotion Arnold had spent twelve years as a highly successful salesperson for the company. He seemed to have a knack for talking to people, and many of his clients thought of him as a close personal friend.

In his new job Arnold spent his time in hiring and firing salespeople, in setting up sales programs for his division, in reviewing the daily reports of his twenty salespeople, and in supervising the activities of his office staff. Sales in the eastern division had risen 10 percent since Arnold had become manager, while no similar improvement had occurred in the other divisions.

One evening Arnold was talking to his friend Ray Bower about his new job. "It just seems like I never get anything done in the office. It's just a constant stream of other people's problems. I wish I were back on the road where I was doing some real work. I feel like all I'm doing in the office is pushing paper."

---

[9]Herbert G. Hicks, *The Management of Organizations: A System and Human Resources Approach*, 2nd ed., New York, McGraw-Hill Book Co., 1972, p. 196.

Questions
1. Why did Arnold feel that his selling job was more important than his managing job? Do you agree? Why?
2. Arnold had never studied anything about organizations and management. What information about the job of management is needed so Arnold will have a better appreciation of his managerial job?

CHAPTER 2
HISTORICAL DEVELOPMENT OF MANAGEMENT THOUGHT

EARLY DEVELOPMENT OF MANAGEMENT THOUGHT
ROBERT OWEN (1771–1858)
CHARLES BABBAGE (1792–1871)
SCIENTIFIC MANAGEMENT ERA
FREDERICK W. TAYLOR (1856–1915)
FRANK AND LILLIAN GILBRETH (1868–1924)
HENRY L. GANTT (1861–1919)
HARRINGTON EMERSON (1853–1931)
RESULTS OF SCIENTIFIC MANAGEMENT
HUMAN RELATIONS ERA
HAWTHORNE STUDIES
RESULTS AND IMPACT OF THE HUMAN RELATIONS ERA
ORGANIZATION AND MANAGEMENT THEORISTS ERA
HENRI FAYOL (1841–1925)
JAMES D. MOONEY (1884–1957)
MARY PARKER FOLLETT (1868–1933)
CHESTER I. BARNARD (1886–1961)
MODERN MANAGEMENT ERA
ORGANIZATIONAL BEHAVIOR
OPERATIONS MANAGEMENT
MANAGEMENT SCIENCES DEFINED
APPLICATION EXERCISES AND CASES
UTILIZING MANAGEMENT CONCEPTS
EFFERSON ASSOCIATES, CONSULTANTS

HISTORY REPEATS ITSELF[1]

In 1940, when labor relations in the steel industry were still in a primitive state, steel union leader Philip Murray proposed an idea that was daring for the time. Instead of perpetuating conflict, labor and management should collaborate on the shop floor, Murray said. By "tapping labor's brains"—that is, seeking workers' advice on how to improve production processes—management could make labor an "active participant" in managing the workplace and thus increase productivity. But except for brief periods in the 1940s and the 1970s, steel labor and management have largely ignored Murray's idea for forty years. Now, as the industry faces a bleak future, the two sides feel they must revive the concept to insure the industry's survival.

The United Steel Workers and nine major companies that bargain as an industrywide group are now preparing to establish "labor-management participation teams" at the mill-floor level to implement, finally, the concept proposed forty years ago by Murray, the USW'S first president. Indeed, some companies—including Jones and Laughlin Steel Corp. and Bethlehem Steel Corp.—have already adopted innovative programs at two small plants and can point to fairly dramatic productivity gains.

This idea is at least as old as the "suggestion box" system, which was introduced in some industries in the early 1900s.

[1]"Steel Seeks Higher Output via Workplace Reform," *Business Week*, August 18, 1980, p. 98.

The development of management thought has been evolutionary in nature.

As in all fields of study, the development of management thought has been evolutionary in nature. Therefore, in order to better understand and appreciate where we are today, it helps considerably to know from whence we have come. While the purpose of this chapter is to explore the historical development of management thought, our objective is not to expose the reader to a vast amount of detailed material but to provide an overview. Indeed, the history of management thought is of such magnitude that numerous books have been written about it, and complete courses are taught that deal with nothing else.[2]

Specifically, we concern ourselves with building a foundation to provide an appreciation of how we arrived at where we are today, as well as the evolutionary nature of management. The following four principle eras are covered, as well as some of the more significant contributions in each period.

1. Scientific management era.
2. Human relations era.
3. Organization and management theorists era.
4. Modern management era.

[2]See, for example, Dan Wren, *The Evolution of Management Thought*, New York, Wiley, 1979.

This discussion serves two purposes. First, it should at least partially illustrate that modern management thought has been, is now, and will continue to be evolutionary in nature. Historians can trace the beginnings of the application of management principles and concepts back to Babylonian, Roman, and other early cultures. Second, this chapter should make you aware of the fact that while each of the major eras emphasized a different central theme, they were all stages in forming a unified and comprehensive body of knowledge about the total process of management. The part and chapter structuring of this book also parallels this evolution.

Before launching into a discussion of each of these eras we want to set the stage by presenting some of the developments in management thought that occurred even prior to the scientific management era.

EARLY DEVELOPMENT OF MANAGEMENT THOUGHT

As early as 1800, developments were occurring that signaled the advent of what historians label as scientific management.

Before what historians label as the scientific management era, developments were occurring in our emerging industrial society that were forerunners of modern management thought. As early as 1800, several innovations were introduced at the foundry operation of Boulton, Watt and Company in England. Among these developments were the following:

1. Based on information supplied in market forecasts, the company developed a simplified inventory-production system.
2. A study of the flow of work was used to arrange the workplace, facilitate flow of materials, and increase the efficiency of human effort by specializing jobs.
3. Work standards were established, and a bonus system based on piece rates was used.
4. Various types of record-keeping systems were established. These systems were designed to generate information on productivity with the objective of increasing efficiency.

All of these ideas are related in one way or another to some of the developments discussed later.

ROBERT OWEN (1771–1858)

In the early 1800s Robert Owen, who was a self-made entrepreneur in the cotton-spinning industry, was stressing the importance of the human element in production. He was critical of manufacturers for their preoccupation with improving machines, specializing labor, and cutting costs yet neglecting to understand and invest in the human element. Owen's philosophy is exemplified by the following quote.

Robert Owen was one of the very early pioneers who stressed the need to understand and invest in the human resources of the organization.

> . . . *you will find that from the commencement of my management I viewed the population (the labor force) . . . as a system composed of many parts, and which it was my duty and*

interest so to combine, as that every hand, as well as every spring, lever, and wheel, should effectually cooperate to produce the greatest pecuniary gain to the proprietors . . . Experience has also shown you the difference of the results between a mechanism which is neat, clean, well-arranged, and always in a high state of repair; and that which is allowed to be dirty, in disorder, without the means of preventing unnecessary friction, and which therefore becomes, and works, much out of repair . . . If, then, due care as to the state of your inanimate machines can produce such beneficial results, what may not be expected if you devote equal attention to your vital machines (the human resource), which are far more wonderfully constructed?[3]

CHARLES BABBAGE (1792–1871)

Another early pioneer in the evolution of management thought was Charles Babbage. His contributions came long before those of Frederick Taylor, who will be discussed later as a major figure in the scientific management era. For this theorizing and application of the scientific approach, Babbage earned a place in history as the patron saint of operations research and management science. Among other things, Babbage did the following:

Charles Babbage is known as the patron saint of operations research and management science.

1. Demonstrated the first practical mechanical calculator, which had all the basic ingredients of a modern computer.
2. Developed gaming programs for his computer, which were a forerunner to modern business gaming techniques.
3. Invented his own engine, and its manufacture got him interested in management.
4. As an operations research man, he analyzed operations, the kinds of skills involved, the expense of each process, and made suggestions for process improvement.
5. Was a strong proponent of the division of labor through specialization.
6. Advocated the mutuality of interests between workers and factory owners, (similar to what Taylor would do seventy-five years later).
7. Devised a profit-sharing scheme.

Without question Babbage was a man of vision in management.

SCIENTIFIC MANAGEMENT ERA

The scientific management era was marked by the contributions of Frederick W. Taylor, Frank and Lillian Gilbreth, Henry L. Gantt, and Harrington Emerson. There were others, of course, but in keeping with our overall purpose, we will limit our attention to those named.

---

[3]Robert Owen, *The Life of Robert Owen*, London, Effingham Wilson, 1857, Appendix B, p. 260.

FREDERICK W. TAYLOR (1856–1915)

Frederick Taylor is considered "the father of scientific management."

For his original work in the early 1900s, Taylor is considered "the father of scientific management."[4] Taylor originally received training as a machinist in the early 1870s, and eventually became a machinist foreman. Young and ambitious, he wished to establish his department as highly productive. Thus Taylor was very much concerned with the efficiency with which machinists performed their jobs. He felt that the key to better productivity was greater efficiency. Having been a machinist himself, he was convinced that there was substantial amount of inefficiency present in the performance of all tasks at the shop level.

Taylor believed that the remedy for curing this inefficiency lay in scientifically designing jobs. Under Taylor's approach each job, operation, or process was studied to determine the one best way of completing it. "Best" meant requiring the least number of motions on the part of the worker and the least amount of time. Then workers were thoroughly trained to follow this method. According to Taylor's thinking there were certain laws, principles, rules, and concepts that could be applied to designing all jobs, thereby increasing the efficiency of the person doing it.

Taylor's approach emphasized the "one best way" of doing a job.

To actually determine what constituted the one best way, Taylor broke down each job or task into sets of individual elements. Then with a stopwatch he timed how long it took a worker to complete each element of the job. Making some allowances for unavoidable delays and brief rests, as well as a judgment about how much effort the worker was expending, he could then add the individual element times to arrive at the total time that the job should take. It was thus possible to scientifically determine a standard of worker performance that constituted a fair day's work.

An integral part of Taylor's approach was also to study the worker's motions and how the tools were used, with a view toward simplification. He found that in most cases the same result could be achieved with fewer or shorter motions. Taylor provided the impetus for the growth of time and motion study.

To promote worker cooperation in increasing efficiency Taylor advocated the use of incentive systems.

One of Taylor's assumptions was that the worker was paid to produce and should be willing to follow the instructions and methods that were specified by those in authority. To promote this cooperation, he introduced the concept of a differential piecework plan for payment of wages. Under this plan, two piece rates were established. If a person produced at the standard pace, he would receive one rate for each piece he produced; say 20¢ per piece. If the worker exceeded the standard pace, he would receive 25¢ per piece, and this higher rate would apply to everything he produced, not just those pieces that were produced above the standard. Taylor believed management could afford this arrangement because of higher productivity, and the wage incentive would encourage workers and management alike to respond positively.

Industrial engineering was not Taylor's only concern. He was an advocate of drawing a sharp line between the responsibilities of a supervisor and an operative

---

[4]Frederick Winslow Taylor, *Scientific Management*, New York, Harper & Row, 1947. First published in 1911.

employee. The supervisor should plan, organize, and control the work, while the operative employee should concern himself with physically performing it. Heretofore it had been common practice for each person to plan his own work. Through observation and experience each employee developed his own approach to the job on a hit-or-miss basis. The supervisor had told him *what* to do but not *how* to do it.

Taylor also advanced an organizational concept of functional foremanship. Under this plan a worker would have several supervisors, each a specialist in a given line of work. If the job required drilling, grinding, and lathe work, the worker would get three sets of "how to" instructions, from each of three supervisors regarding their specialized areas. Thus, he would have three different supervisors.

What Taylor sought was a reshuffling of both management and worker thinking. He believed that there was no reason why management and workers could not work together cooperatively toward the achievement of common goals. Taylor further believed that the key to achieving this cooperation was to offer incentives for superior production. With this motivation, the worker would be willing to follow management's methods and directives. For management's benefit, he argued that the increased productivity would more than offset the cost involved.

In essence, what Taylor was trying to say was as follows:

1. The objectives of good management were to pay high wages and have low unit production costs.
2. To achieve this objective, management had to apply scientific methods of research and experiment to its production methods in order to formulate principles and standard processes that would permit control of the manufacturing operations.
3. Employees had to be systematically placed on jobs where materials and working conditions were scientifically selected so that standards could be met.
4. Employees should be trained to improve their skills in performing a job so that the standard of output could be met.
5. An air of close and friendly cooperation would have to be cultivated between management and workers to insure the continuance of this psychological environment and the application of the other principles Taylor had mentioned.

Although scientific management was a popular movement of the time, Taylor's ideas were subject to considerable resistance from unions.[4a]

FRANK AND LILLIAN GILBRETH (1868–1924)

The second major contributors to the scientific management era that we are considering were Frank and Lillian Gilbreth. After completing high school,

---

[4a]Claude S. George, Jr., *The History of Management Thought*, Englewood Cliffs, N.J., Prentice-Hall, 1968, p. 89.

Gilbreth became a bricklayer's apprentice. Like Taylor, he was very much interested in his career development. He began by developing a series of shortcut motions for laying bricks. While Taylor was concerned with both the time it took to do the job and the method of doing it, Gilbreth concentrated primarily on the latter area. He went beyond Taylor in that he concerned himself not only with the method requiring the fewest and simplest motions but also had placed considerable emphasis on the work area and the positioning of the tools and workers themselves. As he applied his ideas to the bricklaying trade, he designed better rigging and scaffolding and positioned things to eliminate excessive stooping, bending, and wasted time out. Eventually the Gilbreths went into business for themselves and later became consultants.

The Gilbreths concentrated more of their attention on work methods.

While Taylor did much to stimulate interest in the application of principles of motion economy, the Gilbreths refined the entire concept. The system they developed broke the job motions down into seventeen basic elements. These elements were called *therbligs* (Gilbreth spelled backward, with the "th" transposed), and together they furnished a basis for a very detailed breakdown of work for purposes of studying and then simplifying it. The seventeen elements were (1) search, (2) find, (3) select, (4) grasp, (5) position, (6) assemble, (7) use, (8) disassemble, (9) inspect, (10) transport, (11) preposition, (12) release, (13) empty, (14) wait, (15) avoidable and unavoidable delays, (16) rest, and (17) plan. Using these elements, a thorough "therblig analysis" could be made of any job.

The breaking down of motions into seventeen separate elements called "therbligs" represented a refinement of motion study.

Another of the Gilbreths' contributions was the introduction of process flowcharting, which enabled one to scientifically study a whole operation as opposed to a single task or one operator. The process flowchart provides a written record of what is done in producing or processing something. The various steps are diagrammed in terms of operations, transportation, inspection, delays, and storage. The total can then be studied with the objective of eliminating, shortening, or combining some steps. George summarizes the essence of Gilbreths' work and sets the stage for understanding scientific management with the following remark.

The introduction of process flowcharting enabled the Gilbreths to study a whole operation.

> *The Gilbreths' legacy to the development of management thought is the inculcation in the minds of managers that any and every thing should be questioned as to its feasibility and applicability, and that even the new should be discarded if an improvement is in the offering. It is a legacy of the questioning frame of mind, the quest for a better way.*[5]

HENRY L. GANTT (1861–1919)

Gantt was a protege of Frederick Taylor. Like Taylor he promoted the ideas of (1) mutual cooperation between labor and management, (2) scientific selection of workers, (3) financial incentives to stimulate productivity, and (4) use of detailed work instructions. Gantt devised a bonus system that guaranteed the worker a given rate for meeting the day's standard and then paid a bonus for exceeding that standard. This was a departure from Taylor's differential piecework plan. His plan also provided for a bonus to the supervisors, based on how many of their

Gantt promoted many ideas similar to Taylor and also introduced the bonus system concept.

---
[5]Ibid., p. 99.

workers reached standard. Gantt was a strong proponent of teaching. He saw the job of the supervisor as an instructor. In his own words: "Whatever we do must be in accord with human nature. We cannot drive people; we must direct their development."[6]

Gantt is best known for his development of graphic aids to management planning, coordination, and control of production. His Gantt Chart, which first appeared while he was working to aid the World War I effort was revolutionary. The essential element of his thinking was scheduling around time instead of around quantities, which up to then had been the practice. For his work he received the government's Distinguished Service Medal, and his Gantt Charts were eventually used the world over, even by the U.S.S.R. central planners in controlling their five-year plans. Our modern production planning and control devices, as well as the computerized Program Evaluation and Review Technique (PERT), are founded on the principles of planning and controlling times and cost that Gantt pioneered.

Gantt developed charts for scheduling around time instead of quantities.

HARRINGTON EMERSON (1853–1931)

Waste and inefficiency were the problems Emerson saw as plaguing the industrial system, and he attributed these to lack of organization. He advocated a *chief of staff*, with four heads reporting to him or her. Each head would plan and advise in a special area. One, for example, would be responsible for everything relating to the well-being of employees, a second for equipment, a third for materials, and a fourth, standards and accounting. Their advice would be available to all levels in the organization. Emerson advocated leaving supervision and authority with those directly responsible, but they would operate on the basis of the planning and advice by the specialists.

Emerson advocated a "chief of staff" concept.

Emerson is best known for his *Twelve Principles of Efficiency*,[7] summarized as follows.

1. Clearly defined ideals—agreement among all involved as to the objectives of the organization.
2. Common sense—managers taking a larger view of problems and seeking knowledge and advice wherever it can be found.
3. Competent counsel—building a competent staff.
4. Discipline—adherence to organizational rules.
5. Fair deal—fairness in dealing with workers.
6. Reliable, immediate, accurate, and permanent records—information and accounting systems.
7. Dispatching—planning and routing work.

---

[6]H. L. Gantt, *Work, Wages, and Profits*, 2nd ed., New York, Engineering Magazine Company, 1916, p. 124.
[7]Harrington Emerson, *Twelve Principles of Efficiency*, New York, Engineering Magazine Company, 1913.

HISTORICAL DEVELOPMENT OF MANAGEMENT THOUGHT 31

8. Standards and schedules—methods and times for tasks.
9. Standardized conditions.
10. Standardized operations.
11. Written standard practice instructions.
12. Efficiency reward—incentive plan.

RESULTS OF SCIENTIFIC MANAGEMENT

As we noted in our earlier discussion the development of management thought has been and will continue to be evolutionary in nature. For purposes of clarity we are discussing each era separately but in fact these eras blend into one another. The division into historical eras recognizes that management thought experienced a shift of emphasis in terms of the overall issues. It is also important to note that the contributions of the thinkers in one era did not suddenly cease to be of significance and lose their validity in the next era. Just as Taylor's work was a stepping stone for the Gilbreths, the scientific management era was the forerunner of the human relations era, and both of them together provided the foundation for the organization and management theorists era. In the future we will find another distinguishable development appearing on the horizon.

Scientific management emphasized the need to increase productivity by scientifically designing jobs.

The student of management must also realize that because the application of any individual's ideas, or even those of an era, were not all successful, or did not in practice turn out the way they were conceptualized, it does not mean that they were unsound. As conditions change, approaches to management must necessarily change. Experience should furnish us with the knowledge for evolving a more productive future. Thus, we can list some of the results and impacts of the scientific management era as follows.

1. Considerable new emphasis was placed on achieving increased output and efficiency. In a sense these two things became the bywords of industry.
2. There was a move toward reducing jobs to their least common denominators. It was believed that the more a job could be specialized and routinized, the greater would be the worker's productivity. Accordingly, what had been done by one worker was now done by two or three: each one performed only a small part of the total. The idea was that if a person repeated only one small segment of work, over and over again, he or she would become proficient at it.
3. Scientific management sought to reduce fatigue, improve tools, methods and conditions of work, match employee skills to jobs, and provide monetary rewards.
4. The belief that money alone was the worker's reward for compliance, and that incentive would stimulate the worker to higher production to get it, fell short of the mark. In many cases there was open resistance to incentive systems. This resistance sometimes took the forms of restriction of output and sabotage of equipment.

In spite of scientific management, the cooperative revolution that Taylor had envisioned between labor and management never materialized. The reasons for this are not necessarily related to the scientific management era itself. Instead, numerous changes were taking place in society in general and in our industrial development in particular, which caused the gap between labor and management to grow larger. Nevertheless, the developments of this era are still with us today and we are still benefiting from some of its ideas.

HUMAN RELATIONS ERA

The Hawthorne experiments at Western Electric Company were originally designed to assess the impact of changes in working conditions on productivity.

Beginning in the early 1920s the human relations era was beginning to take shape. The principal people involved were Elton Mayo, a psychologist, and Fritz Roethlisberger, a sociologist.[8] They were primarily concerned with the link between the physiological aspects of work and productivity, or more specifically the effect of working conditions on productivity.

HAWTHORNE STUDIES

Beginning in 1924, a series of experiments was begun at the Hawthorne branch of the Western Electric Company in Cicero, Illinois. The experiments continued over many years, lasting into the early 1930s and took on many aspects. The results of the total study are best summarized by the findings related to the assembly of telephone relays by a group of women. Each relay consisted of a number of parts that the women assembled into the finished product. Output depended on the speed and continuity with which the women worked.

At the beginning of the experiments, the operators worked together in groups of about 100, and incentive pay was awarded to individuals on the basis of the entire group's performance. With their consent, 5 women were selected to participate in the experiment. For a period of time before the experiment began, production records were kept so that the effect of various changes on subsequent productivity could be assessed. Over a period of time, and with adequate controls and precise record keeping, the following changes were introduced in sequence.

1. The five women were moved off the main assembly floor and into a separate assembly room by themselves.
2. The incentive was changed so that each woman's extra pay was based on the output of the 5 rather than on the output of about 100 as before.
3. Two rest periods (one in the morning and one in the afternoon) of five minutes each were introduced.
4. The rest periods were later extended to ten minutes.
5. Later, the rest periods were again reduced to five minutes, but the number of such periods were extended to six.
6. There was reduction to two rest periods each, but in the morning coffee or soup was furnished with a sandwich; an afternoon snack was also provided.

---

[8] For a classical rendering of this study see F. J. Roethlisberger and William J. Dickson, *Management and the Worker*, Cambridge, Mass., Harvard University Press, 1939.

7. The morning period was extended to fifteen minutes with the same arrangement as above.
8. Changes in the workday were introduced at various times, such as cutting an hour off the end of the day, or eliminating Saturday work.
9. Lighting, ventilation, and similar things were changed.

Before each change was introduced, the operators were consulted and it was discussed with them. They had an opportunity to express their viewpoints and concerns with the supervisor; their ideas and suggestions were sought, and in some cases they were actually allowed to make decisions concerning the equipment. The supervisors of the women were involved with the experimental team, and tended to take more of a personal interest in the women than did the previous supervisors.

As each change was introduced during the course of the experiment, an increase in productivity occurred. It was found that absenteeism was much lower than on the main assembly floor, less actual supervision was required, and morale was generally higher. After several weeks had elapsed and everyone was fairly well convinced that there was a definite link between productivity and the various physical factors being adjusted, the experimenters decided to return everything to its original status. In other words, no breaks, no coffee, and poor lighting. Much to their surprise, productivity once again took an upward jump and remained there. The anticipated direct link was not substantiated.

RESULTS AND IMPACT OF THE HUMAN RELATIONS ERA

This development caused a considerable amount of redirection in thinking. The Hawthorne studies pointed out the fact that there was more to productivity than just money and working conditions. The type of supervision given was important. The effect and influence of the informal group on the individual appeared to be significant, and group solidarity and cohesiveness were also found to be important, as was the opportunity to be heard and to participate. These findings served to refocus attention on the social side of work and man, as opposed to just the economic and technical aspects. Later authors questioned the rejection of the idea that wages were not a motivator as advanced by the Hawthorne researchers.

The human relations era began to bring into focus elements of the work environment.

At the same time that these discoveries were being unveiled, other developments were emerging on the industrial scene. Principal among these was the powerful move toward extensive unionization, followed by a great deal of resultant strife between labor and management. While supervision before and during the 1920s could be characterized as primarily authoritarian in nature, in the 1930s it began to swing in the opposite direction. More of the "be nice to people" and "keep them happy" management techniques began to appear. But the latter was as ineffective as the former.

Increased emphasis was placed on people and their reaction to the work environment.

The findings of the Hawthorne studies in conjunction with the economic and social developments taking place helped to bring about a a switch in management strategy. But these human relations techniques failed, because of a misinterpretation of what good human relations really involve. Management read the findings of the Hawthorne studies and drew overly simplistic conclusions. This may be understandable considering the pressures many firms were under in their desire to find ready answers to labor problems. By the middle 1940s the words "human relations" were capable of eliciting some strong negative responses from practicing managers. Since then we have considerably refined our insights Hawthorne, and we have also improved our application of these ideas.

ORGANIZATION AND MANAGEMENT THEORISTS ERA

HENRI FAYOL (1841–1925)

Henri Fayol was a French mining engineer who retired from a brilliant career in French industry in 1918 to spend seven years popularizing his theory of administration. In 1925, he published his classic book, *The Theory of the Administration of the State*, in which he outlined the five *elements of management*. These elements, along with Fayol's explanation of them are paraphrased as follows. Note their similarity to the functions of management discussed in Chapter 1.

Fayol is most noted for his formulation of five elements of management.

1. Planning—to foresee and provide means of examining the future in drawing up plans of action.
2. Organizing—building up the dual structure, material and human, of the undertaking.
3. Commanding—maintaining activities among the personnel.
4. Coordinating—binding together, unifying, and harmonizing all activities and efforts.
5. Controlling—seeing that everything occurs in conformity with the established rules and expressed commands.[9]

Nowhere is the difference between the scientific management influence and the functional or classical writers highlighted more than in Fayol's disagreement with Frederick Taylor. Taylor had argued that the military type of organization, with one foreman over the entire shop was inefficient because no one could be expected to understand all of the specialized jobs in the shop. The work of the "single-gang boss" should be subdivided among eight workers—route clerks, instruction card clerks, cost and time clerks, gang bosses, speed bosses, inspectors, repair bosses, and shop disciplinarian. But Fayol argued that multiple bosses for an individual workman negated his principle of unity of command.

Fayol argued for the concept of the general manager and the use of sound organizational principles.

Here we have a clear example of scientific management arguing for intense specialization, even at the supervisory level, while the classical or functional manager argues for sound organizational principles and more general knowledge

---
[9]Henri Fayol, *General and Industrial Management*, London, Sir Issac Pitman and Sons Ltd., 1965, pp. 5–6.

on the part of the supervisor. One of Fayol's stipulated qualities desirable for higher managers is that of "sound general education." Although Fayol recognized the need for the widest possible competence in specialized activities, the following quote from him is noteworthy: "Notwithstanding, the most brilliant specialized ability is not enough to make a good manager of an industrial concern."[10]

In addition to the preceding list of elements, which have become known as the classical functions of management, Fayol also listed and explained fourteen principles of management, many of which are still valid today. Most of these principles will be discussed later in this text from an operational point of view where they will have greater meaning for the reader. For reasons cited above the organization and management theorist era is often called the *classical management era*.

> Fayol's elements of planning, organizing, commanding, coordinating and controlling have become known as the classical functions of management.

JAMES D. MOONEY (1884–1957)

Just as Fayol had done, Mooney, a General Motors executive, categorized certain principles of management that he considered to be fundamental. Mooney derived his principles from an empirical examination of organizations—in this case, government, the Catholic Church, and military organizations. By examining large mature organizations, Mooney was able to anticipate the principles necessary for industrial organizations that were growing rapidly in size during his lifetime.

Mooney defined an organization as any group of two or more persons combining for a given purpose. He proceeded from this point to examine the fundamental or natural laws on which organization is built. These are more universal or perhaps more philosophical laws than Fayol's. He defined them in the following manner.

> Organization and management theorists extended their outlook beyond managing work at the individual level.

1. Coordination—the orderly arrangement of group effort, to provide unity of actions and the pursuit of common purpose. Mooney defines the prerequisites to coordination to be (1) authority, (2) mutual service or mutuality of interest, (3) doctrine, defined as definition of objectives, and (4) discipline.
2. The Scalar Principle—according to Mooney the Scalar Process has its own principle, process, and effect. These are (1) leadership, (2) delegation, and (3) functional definition.[11]
3. The Functional Principle—Mooney means by functionalism the distinction between kinds of duties, illustrated by the difference between an officer of infantry and an officer of artillery as opposed to the Scalar Principle, illustrated by the difference between the general and the colonel.[12]
4. The Principle of Staff—here Mooney lays down one of the first clear distinc-

---

[10]Ibid., p. 74.
[11]James D. Mooney, *The Principles of Organization*, rev. ed., New York, Harper and Brothers Publishers, 1947, p. 15.
[12]Ibid, p. 25.

tions between persons delegated to provide advice or counsel as distinguished from those who have line authority or command.

The transition from the classical management era to the modern management era, to be discussed in the next section of this chapter, came with the writings of two very provocative thinkers: Mary Parker Follett, a British social worker turned management consultant and labor arbitrator, and Chester Barnard, President of the New Jersey Bell Telephone Company.

MARY PARKER FOLLETT (1868–1933)

Mary Parker Follett was a Bostonian who lived and worked in England during much of the early part of her career. She became involved in vocational placement work in industry and developed a lifelong interest in industrial psychology and sociology, in which she pioneered. She ultimately became a world-renowned labor arbitrator and management consultant.[13]

Follett developed a better understanding of the concepts of authority and motivation.

Follett applied her strong background in psychology and social work to the understanding of concepts of authority and motivation in industry. She advocated the use of reason and explanation rather than sheer power in organizations, and argued that real authority rested with *the law of situation*. She felt that reasonable people should be able to resolve conflicts by integration of ideas, not domination or compromise. In the words of one management historian, she "was a true management philosopher, a pioneer who helped span the gap between the mechanistic approach of Taylor and our contemporary approach emphasizing human behavior. More than any other individual, she is responsible for the group process approach to solving managerial problems."[14]

CHESTER I. BARNARD (1886–1961)

Barnard contended that ultimate authority rested with the acceptance or rejection of orders by subordinates.

In addition to his eminent career culminating as president of New Jersey Bell Telephone, Barnard is perhaps best known for his 1938 publication, *The Functions of the Executive*.[15] In this book he defined, in precise terms, the nature of formal organization and the way in which cooperation is achieved in modern industry. Instead of defining organization as consisting of persons, as did Mooney, Barnard defined it as "a system of consciously coordinated activities or forces of two or more persons."[16] He said that since formal organization is comprised of these consciously coordinated activities it behooves the executive to put into practice those things that will elicit the conscious coordination of the participants. It was at this point that Barnard presented his view of authority known as the *acceptance theory*. According to Barnard, authority is the character of the communication

---

[13]Henry C. Metcalf, and L. Urwick, *Dynamic Administration—The Collected Papers of Mary Parker Follett*, New York, Harper and Brothers Publishers, 1940.
[14]George, *History of Management Thought*, p. 132.
[15]Chester I. Barnard, *The Functions of the Executive*, Cambridge, Mass., Harvard University Press, 1938, p. 4.
[16]Ibid, p. 61.

(order) in a formal organization, which causes it to be accepted by a contributor to or member of the organization as governing his or her contributing action.[17]

Mary Parker Follett's admonitions that workers should be treated in industry in much the same way as they are treated in their personal lives, and Barnard's theory that ultimate authority rested with the acceptance or rejection of orders by those being governed, helped spawn the modern field of organizational behavior.

MODERN MANAGEMENT ERA

The modern management era has taken two distinct paths: the one developing from the human relations school is known as organizational behavior; and the other, building upon scientific management, has become known as operations management.

ORGANIZATIONAL BEHAVIOR

Organizational behavior is examined extensively in two units of the text: Part Three, Organizational Behavior and Design, and Part Four, the Management of Human Resources. In keeping with our stated objectives for this chapter, we will provide only an overview of the field at this point. Organizational behavior builds strongly on the behavioral sciences and can be divided into two phases, the human behavior school and the social system school.

The human behavior school has drawn heavily on the work of Abraham Maslow and his development of a need hierarchy, to explain human behavior and the dynamics of the motivation process.[18] Maslow identified five levels of human needs, which operate in a descending order of importance. Not until the lower-level physiological and security needs are reasonably well satisfied do the higher-level social, psychological, and self-actualization needs come into serious play. Maslow's total theory, with a full explanation of its implications for understanding motivation, is discussed in detail in Part Three.

Abraham Maslow formulated a hierarchy of human needs to explain human behavior.

Douglas McGregor[19] built on Maslow's work in explaining two polarized sets of assumptions about people and their reaction to work as well as the management strategy suggested by each set. He labeled the negative set of assumptions Theory X and the positive set Theory Y. It was McGregor's view that many of our traditional management practices are based on Theory X negative assumptions about human nature, and this has resulted in organizations not realizing the full potential represented by their human resources. McGregor's Theory Y not only presents a more positive set of assumptions, but challenges many of the traditional methods of management organization, control, and leadership.

McGregor's Theory X and Theory Y presented two alternative sets of assumptions about people.

---

[17]Ibid, p. 65.

[18]For a later work of Maslow's in which the theory is reviewed, see Abraham Maslow, *Eupsychian Management*, Homewood, Ill., Richard Irwin, Inc., 1965.

[19]Douglas McGregor, *The Human Side of Enterprise*, New York, McGraw-Hill Book Co., 1960.

38 INTRODUCTION

Frederick Herzberg,[20] another of the behaviorists we will study, developed a two-factor theory of motivation. Herzberg makes a distinction between factors that either cause or prevent job dissatisfaction, depending on their presence or absence, and those factors that, if present, actually lead to motivation. His motivational factors relate closely to Maslow's psychological and self-actualization needs, while the factors that he associates with job dissatisfaction (hygiene factors) relate to the physiological and security needs. Herzberg has also made pioneering contributions in the area of job enrichment, which he sees as the ultimate solution to creating more meaningful work, and thereby not only triggering the motivation potential in people but also gaining maximum value from the human assets of the organization. In addition, he emphasizes the human aspects of making work more psychologically meaningful.

> Herzberg's theory maintained that the job factors associated with dissatisfaction and those related to motivation were completely different.

In the area of leadership we will examine the behaviorally oriented conceptual frameworks of several theorists. Robert Blake and Jane Mouton[21] developed and popularized the *managerial grid*. Their grid concentrates on five styles of leadership, which emphasize varying degrees of concern for production versus concern for people. The grid is designed to help managers identify their own styles of leadership, to understand why they get the reactions from people that they do, and to suggest alternative leadership styles.

Rensis Likert[22] has identified and extensively researched four management systems, ranging from System 1: Exploitive-Authoritative to System 4: Group Participative. Each system characterizes an organizational climate by employing several key dimensions of effectiveness, such as communications, motivation, goals, leadership, and others. Likert asserts that a participative approach to management will yield the best long-term results. He identifies the three key ingredients of the successful group participative manager as having high performance standards, exhibiting supportive relationships, and involving people in decision mauing.

Contingency Approaches. Fred Fiedler[23] has suggested a contingency approach to leadership. According to Fiedler's theory, the proper approach to leadership is contingent on the situational forces of leader-member relations (do followers accept or endorse their leader?), task structure (whether or not the task is a well-defined one), and position power (the degree to which supervisor can influence such things as promotion). The supervisor then develops a situational favorableness scale, and emphasizes the idea that there is no one best leadership style that fits all situations and all people.

> Some researchers suggest there is a best or preferred leadership style while others claim it is contingent on the situation.

Paul Hersey and Kenneth Blanchard developed a situational leadership theory that suggests that the appropriate blend between task and relationship

---

[20]Frederick Herzberg, "One More Time: How Do You Motivate Employees?" *Harvard Business Review* (January–February 1968).
[21]Robert R. Blake and Jane S. Mouton, *The Managerial Grid*, Houston, Gulf Publishing Co., 1964.
[22]Rensis Likert and Jane Gibson Likert, *New Ways of Managing Conflict*, New York, McGraw-Hill Book Co., 1976.
[23]Frederick E. Fiedler and Martin M. Chemers, *Leadership and Effective Management*, Glenview, Ill., Scott, Foresman and Co., 1974.

orientation should be a function of the maturity level of the people being supervised.

Social Systems School. A later development in the modern management era was the social systems school of thought. According to this view, organizations are seen as a social system or a system of cultural interrelationships. This view of organizations leans heavily on principles of sociology and emphasizes groups, their interrelationships, and the need to build a total integrated system. Such men as Chris Argyris and Edgar Schein have been significant contributors.

The social systems school sees the organization as a system of cultural interrelationships.

Chris Argyris is one of the most widely published authors in organizational behavior literature, and several of his works are referred to and referenced in Chapter 16, Organizational Development. The primary thrust of Argyris's efforts has been in developing a better understanding of the interpersonal aspects of organizational dynamics as well as popularizing techniques designed to increase effectiveness by improving the quality of interpersonal relations and interactions. He was one of the pioneers in the use of training groups (T-groups) or learning groups (L-groups). The purpose of these groups, when used in an organization development context, is to help an individual manager to see and understand the impact that their behavior has on others, as well as to help groups of managers develop insights into how they operate as a group, with particular attention to those things that are interfering with or hindering maximum effectiveness.[24] More recently Argyris has been studying the learning and conditioning processes people in organization go through and how these processes inhibit effective decision making.

Arygis' work has concentrated on understanding the interpersonal aspects of organizational dynamics.

Like Argyris, Edgar Schein[25] has conducted research and written in a variety of areas related to organization behavior. One such area is small-group dynamics, which is discussed in Chapter 11, Role and Function of the Group in Organizations. Schein has studied factors that influence group formation, the operational dynamics of small-group behavior, the functions groups perform for members, group cohesiveness, intragroup and intergroup competition, and other areas of importance to managers and organizations.

Schein has studied factors that influence group formation.

Fundamental Principles of Organizational Behavior. As contrasted with some of the earlier thinking, the work of the behavioral sciences has pointed up all of the following.

1. Management cannot be viewed as a strictly technical process (rules, procedures, principles).
2. Management must be systematic, and the approach used should be given careful consideration.
3. The organization as a whole and the individual manager's approach to supervision must both fit the situation.

---

[24]Chris Argyris and Donald A. Schon, *Theory in Practice: Increasing Professional Effectiveness*, San Francisco, Jossey-Bass, 1977.
[25]Edgar H. Schein, *Organizational Psychology*, Englewood Cliffs, N.J., Prentice-Hall, 1970.

4. Although the job must be done, it does not get done by means of exercising pure authority over people. A motivational approach, which results in the worker's commitment to the goals of the organization, is needed.

In addition to these findings, some of the more specific ideas that have come out of behavioral research are as follows.

1. The human element is the key factor in determining the success or failure of achieving objectives.
2. Today's manager must be thoroughly trained in the principles and concepts of management.
3. The organization must provide a climate that is conducive to offering people an opportunity to satisfy their full range of needs.
4. Commitment can be fostered through participation and involvement on the part of employees.
5. A person's job must be structured in such a way that it is meaningful and significant. He or she must be able to get a sense of achievement and self-satisfaction from work.
6. Patterns of supervision and management control must be built on the basis of an overall positive philosophy about people and their reaction to work.

OPERATIONS MANAGEMENT

The operations management field of study is linked closely with the early writers in scientific management as well as the later developments in operations research. Many of the principles of operations management have been derived from a school of management thought known as *management science.*

At about the same time that the behavioral scientists were making their contributions, the management scientists appeared on the scene. While the behaviorists were concerned primarily with the human aspects of organization and management, the management scientists concentrated on the need for a more scientific approach to analyzing the complicated physical problems of management. Although operations research techniques can be used to solve human problems, these techniques have most often been applied in plant operations, physical distribution, and project management.

The management scientists had their beginning during World War II. Since then, there has been a great increase of interest in applying the scientific method to management problems in all types of organizations, including banks, hospitals, the delivery of services, and others.

The management sciences concentrate on the need to more scientifically analyze and solve physical problems of management.

MANAGEMENT SCIENCE DEFINED

The term "management science" can be best defined by describing the approach to problem solving used by this school of thought. The approach consists of the following steps.

1. *Formulating the problem.*
   This refers to both the consumer's (decision maker's) problem and the researcher's problem.

FIGURE 2-1

Summary of Quantitative Techniques

Technique	Area of Application
Game theory	Timing and pricing in a competitive market, military strategy
Information theory	Data Processing system design, organization analysis, advertising effectiveness in market research
Inventory control	Economic lot size and inventory control
Linear programming	Assignment of equipment and personnel, scheduling, input-output analysis, transportation routing, product mix, allocation processes
Queuing theory	Inventory control, traffic control, telephone trunking systems, scheduling of patients at clinics, radio communications, etc.
Replacement theory	Replacement of equipment through failure and deterioration
Sampling theory	Quality control, simplified accounting and auditing, consumer surveys and product preferences in marketing research
Simulation theory (including Monte Carlo methods)	System reliability evaluation, profit planning, logistic-system studies, inventory control, and manpower requirements
Statistical decision theory	Estimation of model parameters in probabilistic models

Source: Adapted from Claude S. George, Jr., *The History of Management Thought,* Englewood Cliffs, N.J.: Prentice-Hall, 1968, pp. 157–159.

2. *Constructing a mathematical model.*
   This model expresses the effectiveness of the system as a function of a set of variables, at least one of which is subject to control. Either controlled or uncontrolled variables may be subject to random fluctuations, and one or more may be under control of a competitor or other "enemy."
3. *Deriving a solution from the model.*
   This involves finding the values of the "control variables" that maximize the system's effectiveness.
4. *Testing the model and the solution derived from it.*
   This involves evaluating the variables, checking the model's predictions against reality, and comparing actual and forecasted results.
5. *Establishing controls over the solutions.*
   This involves developing tools for determining when significant changes occur in the variables and functions on which the solution depends, and determining how to modify the solution in light of such changes.
6. *Putting the solution to work—implementation.*[26]

The pioneers in operations management and management science are too numerous to mention. No one person is considered the originator of these sys-

---

[26] Russel L. Ackoff, "The Development of Operations Research as A Science," *Operations Research,* June 1956, pp. 265–266.

tems. Figure 2-1 itemizes a few of the quantitative techniques that have contributed to the development of the field. These techniques and their application to a variety of types of problems are explored fully in Part V, Management of Operations.

The field of operations management includes the following things. First, it relies heavily on the management scientist's belief that decision making should be as precise as possible. Second, a heavy reliance is placed on the use of mathematical and statistical techniques, to quantify as many of the variables involved in a decision as possible. Third, because of the heavy use of quantitative techniques, extensive use is made of computer programming and data processing in the field of operations management. Fourth, operations management stresses the need for viewing any situation in its entirety rather than in a series of individually segmented parts. In other words, the emphasis is on the interrelationship between all the elements of a problem, of the total organization, or a particular segment of the organization.

SUMMARY

The development of management thought has been and will most likely continue to be evolutionary in nature. In this chapter we have discussed four principal eras as they relate to the evolution of management thought. These four eras were scientific management, human relations, organization and management theorists, and modern management.

The scientific management era emphasized the application of the principles and concepts of industrial engineering to design and structure work. Through the use of time and motion study, as well as other techniques, the best way of performing various jobs was determined and workers were then trained accordingly. it was anticipated that since management was willing to pay incentive wages for above-average production there would be a cooperative effort between labor and management. Taylor described this anticipated cooperative effort as a mental revolution, but, in fact, it never occurred.

The human relations era emerged as a result of the Hawthorne studies, conducted at the Hawthorne branch of the Western Electric Company in Cicero, Illinois. Originally these studies were designed to investigate the effect of working conditions on productivity. But the result was to focus attention on the importance of the social aspects of work, as well as the influence of the group; the role of supervision, and the importance of both communication and the opportunity to participate; and the relationship of these factors to productivity.

Organization and management theorists concerned themselves primarily with the analysis and conceptualization of the principles and functions of management in large organizations. Writers in this field such as Fayol, Mooney, Barnard, and Follett concentrated their attention on the nature of authority in organizations and the way they should be structured. Their principle tool of analysis was observation, but observation built on vast experience. They concerned themselves mainly with the formal organization, although the more perceptive writers in the field also touched on the importance of the informal organization and the effect of human relations on management principles.

Beginning in the early 1940s the modern management era began to evolve. Two fields of emphasis were developing rapidly—organizational behavior and operations management. The human behavior school initially placed emphasis on the psychology of the individual as related to personal needs and motivations. This was followed by research and investigations as to how the organization and

SUMMARY CHART

The History of Management Thought

Time Period	Era	Representative Contributors
1940–Present	Modern Management Era	
	1. Needs of individual and motivation emphasized	Abraham Maslow Frederick Herzberg
	2. Social systems explored	Douglas McGregor Chris Argyris Edgar Schien Rensis Likert
	3. Job design emphasized	Frederick Herzberg Chris Argyris
	4. Managerial leadership	Robert Blake and Jane Mouton Fred Fiedler W. J. Reddin Paul Hersey and Kenneth Blanchard
	5. Quantitative decision making developed	Numerous Quantitative Theorists
1900–1940	Organization and Management Theorists Era	
	1. Functions of management defined	Henri Fayol
	2. Principles of management defined	James D. Mooney
	3. Managerial problem solving examined	Mary Parker Follett Herbert Simon
	4. Formal organization and its coordination explored	Chester I. Barnard
1930–1940	Human Relations Era	
	1. Type of supervision given important	Hawthorne Studies
	2. Social side of work—the group important	Elton Mayo
	3. Participation is effective	Fritz Roethlisberger
1870–1930	Scientific Management Era	
	1. Planning separated from operations	Frederick W. Taylor
	2. Search for one best way	Frank and Lillian Gilbreth
	3. Efficiency increased through specialization	
	4. Scientific motion study	Henry Gantt

the individual manager could trigger the motivational potential in people. A social systems school of thought followed, which viewed organizations as systems of cultural interrelationships. These theories lean heavily on the field of sociology, and focus on groups and the need to build a total integrated system. These two streams of thought have led to a modern field of management study known as organizational behavior. So far this era has placed more emphasis on the human element in organizations.

The management sciences began during World War II. They are concerned with the application of mathematics and the use of scientific methods in making managerial decisions. Over the past twenty years, approaches to solving management problems have become much more sophisticated, with the development of large-scale computers and more refined statistical and mathematical techniques. This development has led to the field of management study known as operations management.

DISCUSSION QUESTIONS

1. Applying your knowledge of U. S. history and the information given in this chapter, discuss some of the reasons Taylor felt that people are motivated primarily by economic (financial) incentives. Does this type of motivation exist today? If so, cite examples of situations where Taylor's assumptions of worker motivation might apply.

2. Why do you think the human relations era failed to provide management with a sound theory of worker motivation? From your own experience, cite examples where you did not necessarily work hard for a supervisor or teacher who was just "nice" to you. Why did you fail to respond to this "be nice" treatment? Do you think that your reasons would apply to other people if they were in your situation? Is it possible that the findings of such people as Mayo and Roethlisberger were misinterpreted? What were the really important ideas that they uncovered?

3. Two basic concepts of organizational behavior are as follows:
    (a) Employee commitment can only be achieved through employee participation and involvement.
    (b) A person's job must be structured in such a way that it is meaningful and significant.

    What is meant by *commitment, involvement,* and *structured* in these concepts? How are each of these concepts applied? Be specific and illustrate with examples.

4. Discuss what is meant by management and organization theory. In terms of its point of emphasis, how does this differ from the other three eras of management thought which were discussed?

5. In a short paragraph identify and describe each major era in the development of management thought.

APPLICATION EXERCISES AND CASES

UTILIZING MANAGEMENT CONCEPTS

In Chapter 1 it was pointed out that management is a universal discipline, that is, the principles and concepts of management apply to the effective functioning of any organization. Select an organization of your choosing other than a traditional business and complete the following.

Questions
1. Identify, explain, and discuss how at least three of the concepts that were part of the scientific management era would apply and have significance for the organization you chose.
2. Do the same as (1) above for the human relations era.
3. Several management and organization theorists were discussed. Select two of them, summarize the major thrust of their ideas, and explain why and how they would have significance for your organization.
4. From the modern management era identify at least three areas of thrust, summarize their major point of emphasis, and explain their significance to the organization you selected.
5. What is the personal significance of the organization you chose to work with? In other words, why did you choose the one you did?

Some examples of typical organizations might be a hospital, service club or group, volunteer organization or a student group to which you belong including a fraternity or sorority.

EFFERSON ASSOCIATES, CONSULTANTS[27]

Efferson Associates, industrial efficiency consultants, had been retained to study the work methods of Striker Products Co., a large fabricator of aluminum doors and windows. The consultants planned to do a motion-and-time study of each production job. For their pilot study in the plant the consultants planned to study a punch-press operation.

When the consultants tried to start their pilot study, every man in the plant shut down his machine and walked out. Frank May, the shop steward (union representative), went to the office of Mr. Brown, the production manager, and handed him the following statement:

"We, the production employees of Striker Products, represented by Local 1077, refuse to work in a sweat shop. The present plan of management to make a scientific study of the plant is nothing more than an old-fashioned speedup. We

---
[27]Herbert G. Hicks, *The Management of Organizations: A System and Human Resources Approach*, 2nd ed., McGraw-Hill Book Co., New York, 1972, p. 383.

will not be a party to throwing some of our members out of work by permitting other of our members to break their backs trying to reach arbitrary work standards. The proposed motion-and-time study cannot succeed because it would reduce all our members to nothing more than machines. We demand that the program be eliminated before we will resume work."

Mr. Brown was deeply concerned about the effects of the work stoppage; yet he felt that management must retain the right to make decisions.

Questions

1. What caused the resentment of the workers to the motion-and-time study?
2. Do you agree that the results of such a study could, in effect, turn the workers into machines?
3. How could Mr. Brown approach implementing the plan and at the same time gain cooperation from the workers?

PART ONE
CASES

THE FUNCTION OF THE CHIEF EXECUTIVE[28]

Although the mandatory retirement age at this company was 65, John Neyland, the president, decided to retire at 62. He was 60 when he made this decision. He had come in as chief executive officer of the company twenty-one years earlier. During his tenure the company had grown and prospered. He enjoyed his work, but lately he had noticed a tendency to tire more rapidly than in the past. Also Neyland, a devoted churchman, felt that he could contribute a good deal to his church, and especially to the colleges affiliated with it. For the last five years, he had served on the board of advisers for higher education of his church. He had greatly enjoyed the work and had felt that he was not really doing as much as was needed—especially at a time when the colleges were faced with tremendous demands for money, facilities, and faculty, let alone with serious questions regarding their educational policy.

But what convinced John Neyland to step out earlier than he had to was the fact that he felt sure of having a first-rate successor. When Neyland had joined the company, Bill Strong was a very young accountant, fresh out of college. He was, however, already considered a very able man. When Neyland needed a young analyst to help him with a difficult tax negotiation during the Vietnamese war, Strong had been put on his staff. Shortly thereafter Strong became assistant to the president and, three years ago, vice-president in charge of administration. Neyland felt certain that Strong could easily step into his job, felt indeed that Strong was likely to do a better job than he himself had done.

Before Neyland announced his intention to the board, he thought it best discuss it with his closest and oldest friend on the board, the man who, many years earlier, had brought him to the company and who represented the largest and most influential group of shareholders. This friend agreed with Neyland's decision to retire early. But he disagreed violently with Neyland's nomination of Strong as his successor. "You know," he said, "that I have never voted against management, and that it is against my principles to do so. But if you propose Strong as your successor, I will vote against him and will make an issue of it. There is a capable successor in the company, but it is not Strong. It is Margaret Wetherall, your vice-president of manufacturing. Strong has never in his life done any operating work. He has been a staff man all along. His only experience is in finance. Wetherall on the other hand started out as a design engineer, has been a sales manager, and has now run manufacturing for ten years. She really knows the business. And also, Strong has never had an independent responsibility. He has always been an assistant to you rather than responsible for results himself."

Neyland protested. "But look at the jobs Strong has done. You yourself have considered them outstanding. Strong did most of the thinking behind the basic change in our direction fifteen years ago to which we owe our growth. He does all the thinking behind our financing. And he has really been the one who has

---

[28]From Peter F. Drucker, *Management Cases*, New York, Harper's College Press, 1977, p. 44.

developed people and made the decisions whom to put where. It was his courage that shifted Margaret Wetherall out of the sales job into manufacturing management. He is by far the best thinker we have. And you yourself have stressed often enough that he is a man of courage and integrity. Wetherall is a perfectly fine operating manager. But she has neither the imagination nor the ability to think that is needed for the top job."

"I don't think, John," his friend answered, "we will get anywhere on this by discussing people. You have made up your mind for Strong; I have made up my mind against him. But we ought not to talk people. We ought to talk about the function of the chief executive and the job to be done. It is there, I think, that we disagree. I think we agree on the qualities of the individuals. Why don't you go back and think through what, in your mind, the chief executive of this company has to do, what he is responsible for, what his function is and what his qualification ought to be. I'll do the same. I'm sure we won't agree—otherwise we would have agreed on the candidate. But at least after we have done this, we will be able to find out why we disagree. And I think you and I better agree before we bring this up with our colleagues on the board."

Questions
1. What do you think is John Neyland's concept of the functions of the chief executive?
2. How does his friend see the job?
3. Do you think the friend is right in starting out with an objective idea of the function? Or do you think it would be better to begin with an outstanding candidate—or candidates—and then adapt the job to what he or she is and how he or she does the work?

THE WILSON BINDERY—
Application of Scientific Management to a Small Business [29]

The Wilson Bindery was located in Boston, Massachusetts, and specialized in the printing and binding of fine books. It had fifty employees, the vast majority of whom were skilled artisans—leather crafters, gilt workers, artists, makeup people, and typesetters. The company had been located in the same building for over fifty years and enjoyed the reputation for producing higher quality work than any other bindery in New England. It served customers throughout the eastern part of the United States.

Runs varied from 1 to 2000 units. The smaller runs ordinarily involved binding only and were performed for libraries, museums, and individuals. The larger orders were ordinarily for universities or business concerns, and occasionally for individuals. These included limited editions of company histories, research projects, gift editions of various kinds, and private collections or writings. Such books were seldom intended for commercial distribution. An extreme example of the precision and care that such projects might involve is one recently completed by the company, the printing and binding of 100 copies of "the smallest book in the world." This book, *The Rubaiyat of Omar Khayyam*, did not measure more than one-quarter of an inch in any dimension. The printing on this project involved such great precision that it was done after midnight to avoid the vibrations of passing trucks that might have blurred the minute letters. This order also involved the fabrication of a tooled leather case to contain each book and a magnifying glass to read it.

[29] From Paul E. Holden, Frank K. Shallenberger, and Walter A. Diehm. *Selected Case Problems in Industrial Management*, Englewood Cliffs, N.J., Prentice-Hall, 1962.

Almost all of the binding and artwork and much of the typesetting, printing and trimming were performed by hand. There were two working foremen, one in charge of the bindery, the other in charge of the print shop. The foremen generally produced designs prepared by the art department, but occasionally they also conferred with customers in the development of designs or specifications. They were virtually autonomous in their own departments—scheduled the work, determined methods, hired and fired and promoted workers, controlled quality, and frequently purchased materials. The foremen also performed productive work when their administrative duties permitted. Emphasis on quality of production was paramount at all times—there was little pressure for speed. The outstanding reputation of the company protected it from serious competition in its chosen sector of the industry.

In general the foremen made suggestions as to method, but for the most part this was left up to the judgment of the worker. Most workers owned their hand tools, a custom of the profession.

Employee relations were excellent. The company respected the skills of the workers, who in turn took a great professional pride in their work. Only very rarely did the foreman find it necessary to return work to the employee because the quality was not acceptable. Many of the workers had been with the company for more than twenty-five years, some for more than forty years.

Question

1. Are the principles of scientific management applicable to the operation and management of this company? Explain.

PART TWO
CLASSICAL MANAGEMENT CONCEPTS

CHAPTER 3
MANAGERIAL PLANNING AND STRATEGY

CHAPTER 4
MANAGERIAL PROBLEM ANALYSIS AND DECISION MAKING

CHAPTER 5
ORGANIZATION THROUGH DEPARTMENTATION

CHAPTER 6
THE ORGANIZATION IN OPERATION— SOME CRITICAL ISSUES

CHAPTER 7
ORGANIZATIONAL DYNAMICS

THE STEELAR STEEL PRODUCTS COMPANY
THE HARDER COMPANY

Part Two investigates the classical managerial functions of planning and organizing. After establishing the importance of planning and what planning is not, Chapter 3 explores in detail each of the major phases involved in planning. Some of the key elements in successful planning and an example of the total process will then be presented.

Chapter 4 investigates the dynamics of managerial problem analysis and decision making. A four-phase analytical framework is outlined and discussed. The use of participation in decision making and the dynamics of groups and consensus decision making are explored.

Chapter 5 introduces the process of organization through departmentation. In addition to tracing both the vertical (line) and horizontal (staff) growth of an organization, the chapter delves into such areas and issues as the line organization structure, the introduction of staff into the organization, types of staff authority, scalar chain of command, various bases for departmentation, and defines the relationship between authority, responsibility, and accountability.

Chapter 6 deals with the organization in operation. The process of managerial delegation is developed and explored in detail as are the concepts of authority and power and span of control. The chapter concludes with a review of organization structure.

Chapter 7 discusses some aspects of organizational dynamics. After tracing the development of certain principles of management, and the life cycle of an organization, the concepts of bureaucracy and enterprise are developed, and the need for blending the two are emphasized. The use of decentralization, profit centers, and a brief introduction to management by objectives (MBO) are discussed, as a means to achieve this blending process.

CHAPTER 3
MANAGERIAL PLANNING AND STRATEGY

MANAGERIAL ORIENTATIONS TOWARD PLANNING
IMPORTANCE OF PLANNING
WHAT PLANNING IS NOT
THE FOUR PHASES OF THE PLANNING FUNCTION
ESTABLISHING THE MISSION AND OBJECTIVES OF THE ORGANIZATION
FORMULATING STRATEGIES AND POLICIES TO CARRY OUT OBJECTIVES
DEVELOPING INTERMEDIATE AND SHORT-RANGE PLANS
STATING DETAILED PROCEDURES FOR IMPLEMENTING EACH PLAN
SOME POSITIVE PAYOFFS OF LONG-RANGE PLANNING
KEY ELEMENTS AND BENEFITS OF SUCCESSFUL PLANNING
AN INTEGRATIVE VIEW OF PLANNING
APPLICATION EXERCISES AND CASES
PLANNING FOR HOME IMPROVEMENTS
PITT FOUNDRY

THE NEED FOR LONG-RANGE PLANNING

The events that led to the ousting of Edgar H. Griffiths and the appointment of Thornton F. Bradshaw as RCA Corporation's chairman and chief executive, provides a rare view into the inner workings of a board when it is dissatisfied with its chairman's performance. But the problems facing Bradshaw are clear. He must establish long-range plans for each of the company's businesses. Almost since Griffiths took over as chief executive in 1976, the board sought long-range plans from Griffiths for each of RCA's operations. Instead it got an emphasis on short-term earnings. Says one source close to the board: "Long-range planning at RCA meant, 'What are we going to do after lunch?'"[1]

"Why Griffiths Is Out As RCA Chairman," *Business Week*, February 8, 1981, pp. 22-23.

Planning enables us to have some assurance that desired goals will be achieved.

Before any other managerial function can be undertaken, the direction, objectives, and means for achieving them must be determined. This is true whether the organization be a business, agency of the federal or state government, or has a service or social orientation. Planning enables us to design for an uncertain tomorrow with some assurance of meeting our goals. This assurance has been described as "bridging the gap" between what is desirable and what can be accomplished.

MANAGERIAL ORIENTATIONS TOWARD PLANNING

The management of most organizations can be divided into one of three groups according to the amount of initiative they take in trying to achieve excellence and become the pacesetters in their particular field of endeavor. The three groups are the complacent, the efficiency oriented, and the dynamic organization.

Complacent organizations operate on a day-to-day basis.

The management of the complacent organization operates pretty much on a day-to-day basis under the mistaken assumption that today and tomorrow are reflections of the past. They are content to ride the waves and follow the progressive lead of others only after potential success is reasonably well assured. Its business-as-usual approach results in minimum achievement and little enthusiasm among members of the organization. Opportunities are missed or not seen at all because the organization's capabilities and resources are neglected. The complacent management is convinced that it can meet tomorrow's challenges with yesterday's talent, resources, commitment, and approaches. Change has little meaning to this group and the byword is don't rock the boat. Needless to say they are relatively static.

The efficiency-oriented organization takes positive initiative.

The efficiency-oriented managements have shed some of this complacency. They realize that no one can stand still and long survive and that the past is not just a mirror of the future. This realization leads to some positive initiative in terms of expanding the capabilities represented by the organizations present resources. The efficiency oriented organization will not add to present resources but will make what they have work harder. They are still content however, to follow the leaders and consequently engage in little innovation.

The dynamic organizations are the pacesetters.

The managements of dynamic organizations help shape the future by continually monitoring the internal and external environment for new ideas and developments. They are the pacesetters in bridging the gap between the present and the future. About the time their conterparts catch up they are once again opening new frontiers. Dynamic managements continually add to their resources and look for every opportunity to assume a position of leadership.

Although there are many factors that distinguish a dynamic management and organization from the other two just described, one of the most critical is the amount of planning involvement.

IMPORTANCE OF PLANNING

From the standpoint of individual managers, the importance of planning can be illustrated by asking two basic questions.

1. Do they run the job or does the job run them? Are they always fighting fires and meeting emergencies? Are they continually "under the gun" on schedules? Is it a hectic job?

2. Do they get the results they want? Does the department operate at close to maximum productivity, or is its output just average?

Planning can help significantly in being able to answer these questions positively. It enables the manager to run the job and contributes toward achieving maximum results. Planning makes things happen that otherwise might not occur. It substitutes thinking for worry.

From the standpoint of the total organization, the importance of planning can be illustrated by comparing a historical or fiscal approach to planning with a modern-day performance or motivational approach.[2] (See Figure 3.1) In the historical or fiscal approach, planning is usually an exercise in assembling numbers. Someone adds up projected income, subtracts projected costs and concludes what next year's profits should be. This is merely a projection of what the organization believes will happen in the future based on what has happened in the past, and it is replete with all kinds of hopes. The key point is that it does

---

[2]Dale D. McConkey, "The Position and Function of Budgets in an MBO System," *The Business Quarterly*, Spring 1974, p. 48.

FIGURE 3-1

Fiscal Versus Motivational Approach to Planning

Fiscal Approach To Planning	*Motivational Approach To Planning*
• Exercise in assembling numbers.	• Historical performance is used only as a test of reasonableness.
• Projected income less projected costs determines what next period's profits should be.	• First determination is what should be achieved based on careful analysis of internal and external factors.
• What someone believes might happen based on the past.	• Plans are laid and strategies developed to achieve those results.
• It is replete with hopes and dreams and does not say what could happen if resources were mobilized.	• All efforts and resources are mobilized for accomplishments of goals.

not say what could or should happen if all resources were effectively mobilized.

When the performance or motivational approach to planning is used, historical performance is only a test of reasonableness. The first determination is what the organization *should* earn or achieve. Then plans are developed to accomplish those results and efforts are organized to meet the objective. In his book, *Planning Next Year's Profits*, McConkey cites the following example to illustrate the importance of planning.

> *A major U.S. food producer had for many years been subject to the vagaries of deriving about 80 percent of its income from one product. It wanted to reach the point at which 50 percent of its earnings would come from the major product and 50 percent from other sources. A fiscal approach, relying heavily on financial projections, indicated that in five years the income derivation would reflect an increase from other sources so that the earnings mix would then be 70 percent from the major product and 30 percent from other sources.*
>
> *Applying the motivational approach, the company established a concrete overall objective of changing its earnings mix to 50 percent and 50 percent within a five-year period. Once having established this as its objective, it went through the laborious process of laying plans to reach the objective. In developing these plans, the company first determined that the projected growth of its present products, at the end of five years, would result in having the income from the major product exceed the income from other sources by $8 million. Thus, the plans had to include provision for increasing the income from other sources by $8 million in five years. After carefully examining all alternative methods of earning this amount, the company's plans were structured to attain its goal primarily from new products and acquisitions. It then went about organizing efforts—additional management talent and additional sources of capital—to realize the objective. In the end, it met the objective in less than the allowed five-year period, much to the initial surprise of the fiscal advocates within the company.*[3]

---

[3] Dale D. McConkey, "Planning Next Year's Profits," *American Management Association*, 1968, pp. 14–15.

WHAT PLANNING IS NOT

First, planning is not budgeting, at least in the historical sense that budgets have often been used. Often, a budget is just a financial statement of what someone says is going to happen in a future period and later it becomes a historical record of what did happen. A budget is only one part of a well-constructed plan and even then it must be used as a living control and feedback mechanism to be of real value. If simply filed away only to be resurrected after the period in question is over, the budget is of limited value. The purpose of budgeting is to establish a financial statement target and to monitor progress toward that target.

A budget is only one part of a well-constructed plan.

Strategic planning is completely different. It extends beyond decisions involving how to reach a certain financial target to include decisions relating to the question of how to change operations to make the organization healthier. Before an attractive financial result can be achieved, many operating matters must dealth with which constitute the essence of planning. It is not just the end result measured in financial terms that is of concern but rather planning what needs to be done to cause the end result to happen in the first place.

Second, planning is not merely making projections. These are just estimates of the future. Projections indicate what may or may not happen but lack the means for insuring they will ever come true. In addition, projections often deal with only internal factors. Planning involves identifying the key factors, both external and internal, that affect the long term success of the organization and dealing with these to insure maximum results.

Planning goes beyond simply making projections. It identifies key factors that influence results.

Third, a plan is not static and must remain flexible to meeting changing conditions in the environment. If the objective is not being met, we do not automatically lower it to accommodate the present achievement level, but rather provisions in the plan change to make up deficiencies. This does not imply that goals are never reassessed because of environmental and other changes; indeed the evaluation must be a continuous process. The point is that we should lower goals only if it is indicated after thoroughly analyzing the situation and being convinced that an adjustment in plans will not, in fact, result in achievement. Figure 3-2 summarizes the things planning is not.

FIGURE 3-2

What Planning Is Not

Planning Is Not:

- Just budgeting — planning is concerned with operations and how to make the organization healthier.
- Projections — planning identifies and concentrates on key factors that affect the organizations success.
- Static — a plan must remain flexible and change if the conditions warrant it.

THE FOUR PHASES OF THE PLANNING FUNCTION

Peter Drucker defines long-range planning as "the continuous process of making present entrepreneurial (risk-taking) decisions systematically and with the best possible knowledge of their futurity and organizing systematically the efforts needed to carry out these decisions against the expectations through organized systematic feedback."[4] Planning then can be thought of as a system that begins with missions and objectives, develops strategies and policies, plans, and procedures, and provides for feedback of information in order to adapt to a changing situation.

The planning function can be divided into four phases. Each phase is in *itself* a system which, when combined with the other three, forms the planning function. These phases are as follows.

Phase I   Establishing the mission and objectives of the organization.
Phase II Formulating strategies and policies to carry out the objectives.
Phase III Developing intermediate and short-range plans.
Phase IV Stating detailed procedures for implementing each plan.

Each phase must be completed and interrelated for efficiency in planning. The development of all the departmental plans, which make up the total plan, will guide the organization toward its desired goals.

PHASE I: ESTABLISHING THE MISSION AND OBJECTIVES OF THE ORGANIZATION

Establishing the organization's mission and objectives is the first phase of planning.

A statement of purpose or mission broadly defines the thrust of the organization. In a general sense it sets forth what business the organization is in, what kind of organization it is, and the vision top management has for the organization's future. Figure 3-3 is a rather extensive statement for Hewlett-Packard's purpose or mission.

Two examples of shorter and more concise statements of company mission appear below.

- DuPont is a multinational, high technology company which manufactures and markets products that are predominantly chemically related, servicing a diversified group of markets where proprietory technology provides the competing edge.

---

[4]Peter Drucker, "Long-Range Planning," *Management Science*, Volume V, April 1959, pp. 238–239.

FIGURE 3-3

Hewlett-Packard's Corporate Purpose or Mission[5]

Profit. To achieve sufficient profit to finance our company growth and to provide the resources we need to achieve our other corporate objectives.

Customers. To provide products and services of the greatest possible value to our customers, thereby gaining and holding their respect and loyalty.

Field of interest. To enter new fields only when the ideas we have, together with our technical, manufacturing and marketing skills, assure that we can make a needed and profitable contribution to the field.

Growth. To let our growth be limited only by our profits and our ability to develop and produce technical products that satisfy real customer needs.

People. To help our own people share in the company's success, which they make possible: to provide job security based on their performance, to recognize their individual achievements, and to help them gain a sense of satisfaction and accomplishment from their work.

Management. To foster initiative and creativity by allowing the individual great freedom of action in attaining well-defined objectives.

Citizenship. To honor our obligations to society by being an economic, intellectual and social asset to each nation and each community in which we operate.

- The basic mission of Central Soya is to be a leading factor in producing and merchandising products for the worldwide agribusiness and food industry.[6]

The organization's mission statement should be meaningful and provide guidelines to its general direction.

It is important to note that some type of balance in terms of the comprehensiveness of such statements is in order. If they become too lengthy their meaning and significance is likely to be lost while if too brief they will lack any real meaning and fail to provide the organization with any guidelines to their general direction. The Hewlett-Packard statement of mission meets the guidelines of an effective one more so than the other two examples given. This is true because it refers to the organization's mission in several key areas.

Statements of objectives are more precise and include specific targets to be achieved.

Mission and Objectives—A Clarification. Statements of organizational objectives are much more precise and usually include quantitative targets to be achieved within some time frame. Figure 3-4 represents an example of specific goals as opposed to more general purpose or mission statements. The distinction being made is important because it is the achievement of specific objectives that serve as a basis for both intermediate and short-range plans. Mission statements serve to provide management with some general guides as to the areas where specific objectives need to be set and as a basis for deciding whether a given

[5]Y.K. Shetty, "New Look at Corporate Goals," *California Management Review*, Winter 1979, Vol. XXII, No. 2, p. 71.
[6]Ibid., p. 72.

FIGURE 3-4

Robertshaw Controls Company Corporate Goals 1977[7]

1. Minimize historical trends in sales and profits.
   (Objective: 10 percent profit before tax is necessary to assure adequate stockholder return and reinvestment in corporate growth.)
2. Increase Robertshaw's sales and profits in the international market.
   (Objective: 10 percent minimum annual profit growth assures compounding profitability and established positive trend line.)
3. Increase utilization of stockholders' equity through return on assets and return on investment justification.
   (Objective: 10–15 percent annual sales growth is required to double the sales of the corporation every five to eight years.)
4. Review all product lines and products that cannot justify continuance based on ROA.
   (Objective: Within the broad parameters of sensors and associated controls, Robertshaw can develop adequate diversification and maximize inhouse abilities and expertise.)
5. Establish corporate and divisional financial standards.
   (Objective: To evaluate and justify investments in new or old areas of opportunity to verify the potential for the corporation to achieve an industry position of no less than third.)
6. Develop improved consumer awareness and recognition of Robertshaw.
   (Objective: The criteria for growth must include favorable corporate identity at the consumer and investor levels.)

course of action falls within the spectrum of the organization's perceived scope of operation in a more general sense.

Before examining the objective setting process it is advantageous to develop an appreciation for some of the advantages of objectives from the standpoint of organization as a whole and the people in it and also take note of some important observations about objectives.

Objectives and Organizational Effectiveness[8]

Corporate goals are often considered the starting point of effective management. They are the foundation of strategies, plans, priorities, and resource allocations, the focal point for managerial action. The formulation and achievement of realistic goals is the essence of good management. It would seem that well-defined goals should be a first concern of every company.[9]

Research on objective setting has uncovered the following benefits.

---
[7]Ibid., p. 72.
[8]S. J. Carroll, and H. L. Tosi, *Management by Objectives: Application and Research*, New York, Macmillan, 1973.
[9]Y. K. Shetty, "New Look at Corporate Goals," *California Management Review,* Winter 1979, Volume XXII, No. 2, p. 73.

1. *A higher degree of purpose.* Objectives give the organization more specific direction. There is less tendency to operate on a day-to-day or week-to-week basis and otherwise drift aimlessly.
2. *A higher degree of manager motivation.* As with the organization as a whole, objectives also channel the efforts and energy of the individual manager. As she begins to experience the successes associated with the achievement of objectives, continued motivation becomes a self-generating process.
3. *More self-direction and control on the part of subordinates.* When subordinates are aware of the actual results they are expected to achieve and receive continuous feedback concerning where they stand in relation to those results, they are in a position to direct and control their own performances. This allows the manager to spend more of her time in overall planning and coordination of the total work effort.
4. *More demanding organizational tone.* Objectives tend to create a more demanding and accomplishment-oriented tone throughout the entire organization. This is because everyone in the organization is striving toward some commonly agreed-on goals. The emphasis is on achievement and accomplishment of specifics as opposed to merely operating on a short-term basis.
5. *Better communication and cooperation among managers.* A final advantage relates to the improvement in coordination of effort between various managers within the organization. To the extent and degree that the objectives of each unit or department in the organization relate to and are part of a total scheme, and also to the degree that the concept of coordination of effort to achieve total results is stressed, there tends to be a greater degree of cooperation among managers.

Impact of Objectives on Units or Departments in the Organization. In addition to the positive influence of objectives on the operation of the total organization, there are also some departmental related advantages to objective setting. First, when a manager sets departmental objectives, she is taking a step toward making things happen that might otherwise not occur. For the same reason that a navigator on an airplane must develop a flight plan to help guarantee a safe and on-schedule arrival at the destination, a manager must set objectives if she expects the department to accomplish its mission.

Second, objectives focus attention on results. They direct the stream of total effort toward achievement of specific goals and restrict random activity and ad hoc decisions. Without objectives, there is likely to be a tendency for the total operation to lack direction.

Third, objectives encourage efficient and economic operations. Cost are minimized because of the emphasis on consistency. Joint effort is substituted for uncoordinated piecemeal activity, an even flow of work replaces an uneven flow, and deliberate decisions take precedence over snap judgments.

Finally, objectives facilitate control and serve as a yardstick against which to measure accomplishment. The purpose of control is to insure that events conform to plans, and to make things happen that might otherwise not occur. Clearly

Objectives focus attention on results, encourage efficient operations, and facilitate control.

defined objectives aid in keeping the department or project "on track" by providing definite direction on a continuous basis.

The full effect of planning based on objectives may be summarized in the following manner.

1. A way of coordinating and giving direction to department activity.
2. A way of planning, organizing, and controlling work for an individual manager in her own department or functional area.
3. A system for insuring continued analysis, improvement, and growth.
4. A basis for coaching and developing people and recognizing individual achievements.

Objectives and Individual Motivation. The tie between the concept of objectives and individual motivation is a strong and basic one. Without clear objectives people often find themselves on the defensive.

> Objectives provide people with a sense of direction and give constructive purpose to work.

On the other hand, when clear objectives are established, people have a constructive purpose in their work. As a result of this, personal morale will be high. Reasonable and clear objectives and high motivation go hand in hand. Clear objectives give purpose, meaning, vitality, and direction to the work that people do. They contribute significantly to mental and emotional involvement and foster the type of personal commitment desirable for each person.

Some Observations about Objectives. The objectives of the organization must form a *hierarchy*. Those at lower levels that relate to a product, territory, or particular function must tie into the broader goals developed at the top of the organization. To illustrate, the total organization starts with an overall return on investment objective. Territory or product divisions then develop return on investment objectives for their particular areas. These are followed by determining objectives in marketing (such as gaining a certain share of the total market) and in research and development (product improvement and new products). Eventually the first-line supervisor ends up with objectives of so many units per man-hour, material costs, quality standards, and so on. Similarly, individual salesmen would end up with multiple objectives in their respective territories (total volume, product mix, new customers).

> Objectives set at the top become the basis for those at lower levels.

Thus, the objectives setting process is pyramidal in nature, with each level deriving and tying in its objectives with those set at succeeding levels.

> Objectives must be interconnected and mutually supportive.

Objectives must also form a *network*. They must be interconnected and mutually supportive, and cannot exist in isolation. For example, suppose that one unit of the company has objectives that will increase costs, at the same time that an overall austerity program is in effect. Obviously such a conflicting situation will not work, because these objectives are not mutually supportive. Or sales may want large stocks of all goods on hand so they can guarantee quick deliveries, but this will increase inventory and warehousing costs, and may place heavy burdens on production. The joint effect of pyramidal objectives that are tied together has been described by one writer as the *cascading approach* to goal setting.[10]

---

[10]Anthony P. Raia, *Managing by Objectives*, Glenview, Ill., Scott Foresman and Co., 1974, pp. 29–31.

MANAGERIAL PLANNING AND STRATEGY 63

Timing of completion is also important. Consider the introduction of a new product, in which the whole project is jeopardized by failure to meet a schedule on any subobjective in such areas as research and development, manufacturing, packaging, advertising, and engineering. An analogy to this is the type of precise timing required in completing individual assignments by every member of an offensive unit in football to execute a successful play.

Multiplicity refers to the idea that objectives must be set across a wide range of areas.

The concept of *multiplicity* is also a key factor in objective setting. As indicated in Figure 3-5, objectives must be set in all areas of importance to the survival, growth, and profitability of the organization. Figure 3-5 represents the response to a questionnaire survey sent to 193 companies in *Business Week's* list of largest industrial and nonindustrial firms, of the 193 firms 82 responded. The average number of goals listed by firms was five to six. Too many goals disperse attention from crucial areas critical to survival while too few may lead to neglect of important but perhaps not so obvious areas.

In establishing objectives organizations must be realistic.

Finally, organizations, like individuals, face *constraints* when deciding on objectives. Some of the constraints that might inhibit the adoption of what otherwise would be very progressive objectives include financial factors, legal considerations, limited resources, government regulations, public attitudes, and others. The organization must often settle for objectives that are perhaps less challenging but at the same time attainable. These same observations concerning

FIGURE 3-5

Range of Corporate Goals[11]
(N = 82)

Category[b]	Number	Percent[a]
Profitability	73	89
Growth	67	82
Market share	54	66
Social responsibility	53	65
Employee welfare	51	62
Product quality and service	49	60
Research and development	44	54
Diversification	42	51
Efficiency	41	50
Financial stability	40	49
Resource conservation	32	39
Management development	29	35
Multinational enterprise	24	29
Consolidation	14	17
Miscellaneous other goals	15	18

[a]Adds to more than 100 percent because most companies have more than one goal.
[b]The firms surveyed were from four groups: chemicals and drugs, packaging materials, electronics, and electrical and food processing.

---

[11]Ibid., p. 73.

hierarchy, network, multiplicity, and constraints would, of course, apply to any type of organization.

Establishing Objectives in a Business Organization. The eventual objectives of the organization are a function of a number of variables some of the more common of which are discussed as follows.

1. *Profits* are widely recognized as a major requirement for corporate existence. Profit goals are usually the most explicitly stated goals of an enterprise. They not only make other goals possible but provide an evaluating and decision-making criterion.

   Profits form many of the standards by which managers and employees are measured. Division managers of many firms are paid, promoted, or fired according to the rate of return earned on their investments. Boards of directors and presidents have been "proxied" out of office by stockholders dissatisfied over low profits. Many employee wage plans are directly related to the amount their production has contributed toward company profit.

   As a decision-making factor, profit is one variable in determining the selection among alternative investments. Although there are many qualitative factors involved, those projects with the highest net present value are often the ones selected for development.

2. The second input consideration is *social responsibility,* defined as an organization's obligations toward society. These obligations can be very complex and are continually being debated today. They include community service, educational and philanthropic grants and environmental control. Chester I. Barnard, in discussing authority, said there was a "zone of indifference" beyond which the individual would no longer accept direction from above.[12] Similarly, there is a "zone of indifference" on the part of stockholders and the general public toward organizations. Just as the individual is no longer accepting complete rule from superiors, the general public is no longer tolerant of socially unresponsive organizations. The zones of indifference of both the individual and the public have narrowed considerably in the past decade.

   It is top management's responsibility to perpetually review its objectives. Today's increased demand for social consciousness and social involvement is causing many stockholders to voice their opinions about how a firm should be run instead of merely selling one's stock in a corporation when it does not measure up. Top management is discovering that the demands of public and employees must be given more consideration.

3. *Personal objectives* influence decision making. Constituent democracy is being emphasized, stressing the objectives of stockholders, employees, and managerial personnel. These individuals have a major stake in the successful

---

[12]Chester I. Bernard, *The Functions of the Executive*, Cambridge, Mass., Harvard University Press, 1938, p. 167.

operation of the firm, their interests should therefore be considered in determining objectives. The personal goals of the above groups often differ and at times may conflict with one another. Of course each group would desire to receive the maximum amount of renumeration possible and have a significant voice in policy setting.

Within each group, the goals differ. Stockholder's interests range from high dividends to high stock appreciation through profit retentions. Young employees desire high salaries while older employees may place more emphasis on fringe benefits. Young managers may want an aggressive firm, and older managers are sometimes more cautious in accepting new ideas and strategies.

Thus the objectives of the firm and the individuals, while not in complete conflict, are not usually in complete harmony. Only with full recognition of these personal goals, plus a conscious effort to integrate them with the enterprise goals, can we hope to achieve both. One set of goals cannot be achieved without the other.

4. *Federal, state, and local governments* all have a major impact on objectives. Their influence is felt in such areas as minimum wages, working hours, safety regulations, pricing policies, antitrust regulations, collective bargaining, taxes, and accounting procedures. The list is long and significant.

5. *Industry and internal factors* must also be considered when determining objectives. A key initial question is, "What business are we in?" Is it glass bottles or containers, railroads or transportation, movies or entertainment, steel or structural materials? The question becomes particularly important when we consider that the world out there keeps changing so fast, and this makes it very difficult for an organization to dwell on the past, take the present for granted, and remain viable. Many of the products we consume, such as synthetic fabrics orginated in unrelated industries. An organization that is not alert and fails to adapt to changing conditions can very quickly find itself in serious trouble. Another valuable question for management is "Are we in a declining industry, an expanding industry, or one in a stationary state?"

Profits, social responsibility, personal objectives, governments and industry factors all affect objectives.

From an internal standpoint, the firm must also consider such factors as return on investment, cash flow, share of market, product mix, costs of manufacturing the product or providing a service, capabilities of human assets, technology, and new product development.

There are many other variables that management considers in determining its objectives. We have presented a few of the most important ones to illustrate how they influence management's thinking in deciding on objectives. Of course, management is unable to simultaneously satisfy every variable. At times, some variables will be emphasized more than others, and it remains top management's responsibility to assess changing conditions and make adjustments in its goals when necessary.

Establishing Objectives for a Church and Volunteer Service Organization.
Just as a business organization must consider a variety of variables in establishing its overall direction as well as its more specific objectives, so must a church

undertake a similar type of situational analysis in order to perform its mission (which will vary by church) and remain a viable force. Some of the variables that will influence the eventual objectives of a church are shown in Figure 3-6.

Considering these and others, the objectives of churches may vary as they relate to extensiveness of the youth program, support of world missions, community outreach activities, evangelism programs, expansion of facilities, and providing faith enrichment materials.

Similarly, a volunteer service organization such as a Lions Club or woman's community assistance group would need to consider several variables in order to establish viable objectives for the organization. Some possible areas include size and degree of involvement of members, fixed ongoing financial support commitments, revenue derived from present projects, community needs, support activities of other service groups, member talent inventory, national organization requirements for projects receiving local affiliate support, members' time commitments, and member preferences for the type of project support. Guided by the preceding examples, the variables needed for developing objectives for any type of organization can be delineated.

There is no set process to follow by which management feeds these variables into a machine and receives as output the organization's stated objectives. Instead all these variables must be analyzed in deciding on the objectives.

PHASE II: FORMULATING STRATEGIES AND POLICIES TO CARRY OUT THE OBJECTIVES

Formulating organization strategy and policy is the second step in the planning process.

Strategy involves a decision on how to use available resources to accomplish objectives.

Choosing a Strategy. Strategy involves a decision as to how available resources will be used to achieve objectives. Developing a strategy requires an analysis of the strengths and weaknesses of the organization, with an eye toward capitalizing

FIGURE 3-6

Variables to Establishing Objectives for a Church

Membership
  (a) Number of communication members
  (b) Composition of membership and families by age
  (c) Stability of residence
  (d) Economic background

Finances
  (a) Fixed support pledges
  (b) Trend of contributions
  (c) Fixed congregational obligations
  (d) Discretionary funds

Human Resources
  (a) Talent, skill, and ability survey of members
  (b) Extent of previous time commitment and involvement

on the former, while making allowance for the latter. The choice of a strategy can mean the difference between failure and success, or between mediocre results and maximum results.

Even the scientific approach to selecting a strategy does not guarantee results. In the 1950s the Ford Motor Company decided to market a middle-priced car called the Edsel. This decision was based on projected trends and consumer tastes made in an extremely scientific fashion. But due to a decline in the middle-priced automobile market during the years in which the Edsel was introduced, Ford lost over $200 million before withdrawing the car. Later, using the same basic approach, Ford launched the Mustang, with far different results. Scientific forecasting does not insure success, but it does help identify some of the factors that may become critical ingredients in the strategy mix.

Strategy in one area must be carefully matched with strategy in another. In the 1950s, Elgin Watch experienced falling sales and decided to diversify. Their strengths included precision and quality, so they chose to enter the market for high-precision industrial instruments and electronics. They had overlooked their greatest asset, a direct marketing organization going into every jewelry and department store. At the same time, they had underestimated their inexperience in marketing instruments and electronics in a growing but unfamiliar field. Diversification was sound, but product strategy was not. While all this was occurring, U.S. Time Corporation was experiencing a huge success in the watch business. They did it with a new product and marketing strategy—a throwaway Timex watch.

A more recent example of a company's long-term strategy comes from Sony Corporation. What their long-range plan for the 1980s and 1990s boils down to is balancing revenue among three sources: consumer electronics, nonconsumer electronics, and a variety of other businesses. Consumer electronics is still their main business but faced with severe competition they want to put some of their eggs in other baskets to improve the long-term outlook. Sony's expansion and diversification program is being funded by significant increases in their capital investment budget. In 1981 that increase was 40 percent more than in the previous year and totaled $332 million. One of their recent joint ventures involved Prudential Insurance Co. The Sony Prudential Life Insurance Co. was formed with each partner committed to invest $10 million. With the need to overcome certain cultural factors, it may take fifteen to twenty years for the venture to start paying off but it is believed that eventually it will give Sony a strong financial arm.

One of Sony's earlier investments involved getting into the office equipment field. Up to ten years ago Sony had nothing to do with the office but now claims the number three position with a 20 percent market share. They hope to increase that even more with several new products that are being introduced. Sony believes that as a company grows its planning horizons for product development and capital investment should be extended further into the future.[13]

The importance of strategy and the impact it can have on the total thrust and

---

[13]"Sony: A Diversification Plan Tuned to the People Factor," *Business Week*, February 9, 1981, pp. 88–90.

Many times long range strategy requires a break from what has been done in the past.

operation of an organization is illustrated by the following description regarding the change in direction General Electric is taking during the 1980s:

> *Radical change at old-line companies usually flows from disaster. But the radical changes rumbling along the halls at General Electric Co. these days are coming at a time of the company's greatest financial strength. The company is embarked on a strategy for the 1980s that calls for nothing less than a technical renaissance in its old operations and for new businesses that are to grow from anticipated break-throughs in electronics, genetics, and industrial engineering.*
>
> *There is strong reason for the change from a strategy that emphasizes financial performance to one that homes in on technology. The good earnings of the past few years conceal some developing problems. GE's cost-conscious management has wrung quick profits from some of its businesses and has not made major investments in technology and product quality. And although GE is a big user of electronic components, the company has had no manufacturing role in the high-technology businesses that appear to be the growth areas of the 1980s, such as semiconductors, microprocessors, and information processing equipment. To catch up, the company may now be forced to use more of its hard-won money than might have been necessary if it had kept abreast of the technology.*
>
> *Now, GE is throwing its vast resources behind a technology drive to bring it up to speed as rapidly as possible. Its $235 million acquisition of Intersil Inc., a producer of metal oxide semiconductors, and its potential acquisition of Calma Co., a company at the leading edge of computer-aided design and manufacturing technology, are the latest manifestations of that drive. A further indication is GE's sharply increased investment in research and development over the past few years.*
>
> *But the most significant sign of change in a company that is known for its sophisticated financial planning comes in the selection of John F. Welch Jr., 45, as GE's new chairman and chief executive officer. A chemical engineer by training, Welch has earned his credits not from the kind of legal, marketing, or financial coups that have brought success for the company's CEOs for the past 30 years but from his success in marrying technology and markets. Welch's appointment clearly signals the company's new focus—one that views both its existing businesses and future through a technological lens.*[14]

Strategic planning often goes in cycles.

Strategic Business Planning—A Current Perspective. During the 1960s strategic business planning for many organizations meant investment planning. Conglomerates attempted to buy profits by acquiring other companies with little regard to how well they would complement the existing businesses in the conglomerates stable of subsidiaries. One organization acquired more than 350 diverse companies in one year. Today, like many others who based corporate strategy on investment rather than operating considerations, that conglomerate is paying in terms of lagging profits, negative growth, and a drop in the market value of its securities. Investment planning as a substitute for corporate planning was destined to fail. The situation is explained by Peter Drucker as follows:

---

[14]"General Electric: The Financial Wizards Switch Back to Technology," *Business Week*, March 16, 1981.

MANAGERIAL PLANNING AND STRATEGY 69

> *Asset management as it relates to non-financial businesses is a function and not the definition of the business . . . the asset managers who acquired operating businesses [in the 1960s] performed a useful function when they closed down or sold off parts that were tying down large chunks of assets without producing returns. But once they had done this, they did not know how to manage a business—and the boom of asset management ended in predictable failure.*[15]

In the 1970s growth strategies began to change. The initial search focused on growth opportunities within the firm. This is an approach that Cohen and Cyert recommend as being more ideal.[16] The internal search might include reviews of the firm's entire marketing strategy and of innovative possibilities for research and development. Another possibility is the entire cost structure of the firm. If management is convinced that growth and profit goals cannot be achieved by internal means, then it can begin to look externally. The external emphasis should focus on acquisitions that result in economics of scale such as better utilization of existing personnel and facilities by producing or distributing a newly acquired product that utilizes present marketing capabilities. Another possibility is a complementary new product whose sale will also boost sales of firms present products.

Drucker makes a distinction between investment planning and corporate planning.

During the 1970s many firms have exhausted internal growth opportunities and are once again looking outward for growth possibilities. This is resulting in a new wave of mergers and acquisitions in the 1980s. But the lessons learned from conglomerate mergers of the 1960s that were often unsuccessful have not been lost. *Business Week* commented on this as follows:

> *The acquiring companies have been much more careful than their counterparts in the 1960s about analyzing merger candidates and assessing their potential fit. . . . The current trend is grounded in a lot more thoughtful, rational analysis . . . most recent big mergers have had sensible, often traditional purposes to them . . . such mergers as International Nickel with ESB (batteries) and H. J. Heinz with Hubinger (corn sweeteners) are classic examples of integration.*[17]

Thus, the emphasis today for most firms is on finding compatibility in business missions and achieving integrations as growth takes place. This is the strategy that proved as successful for many firms in earlier years and is being followed at this time by others.

Policies. A number of policies may be developed in order to carry out any one objective. Policies are more detailed than objectives and provide a framework for the development of plans.

Nicolaidis has defined *policy* as follows.

---

[15] Peter F. Drucker, *Management: Tasks, Responsibilities, Practices*, New York, Harper & Row, 1974, p. 682.

[16] "Strategic Business Planning: Yesterday, Today, and Tomorrow," *Business Week*, October 1979, p. 46.

[17] "The Great Takeover Binge," *Business Week*, November 14, 1977, p. 179.

Policy is a rule for action, manifesting or clarifying specific organization goals, objectives, values, or ideals and often prescribing the obligatory or most desirable ways and means for their accomplishment. Such a rule for action established for the purpose of planning, guiding, or directing organizational activities, including decision making, intends to provide relative stability, consistency, uniformity, and continuity in the operation of the organization.[18]

Policies are guides to administrative action and decision making.

Policies can be considered as general guides for administrative action. They set the boundaries within which managers can act. Figure 3-7 gives the Chase Manhattan Bank's thoughts regarding the usefulness of properly stated policies.[19]

The stated policies of an organization are developed at two levels of management and are explained as follows.

1. The primary stated policies are those developed by top management to carry out the objectives of the firm. These are most clearly stated and communicated of all policies. They can originate from the board of directors, the executive president's office, or the upper management group. These top management policies are broad in nature, usually leaving to lower management the task of developing operational policies and procedures. In our example of a community service organization, statements by national headquarters with whom the local is affiliated may have certain policy guidelines regarding the types of local service projects that will be approved. The church may also have certain policy guidelines regarding who should and should not be served communion.

FIGURE 3-7

Advantages of a Sound Policy

It secures consistency of action throughout the undertaking.
It acts as a basis for future action and decision.
It insures coordination of plans.
It requires control of performance in terms of the corresponding plan.
It provides a means by which authority can be delegated, thus contributing directly to one of the most important principles of organization.
It preserves the morale of employees when they know the declared policy of the undertaking, particularly if the policy is ethically sound and strictly followed.
It stimulates the staff to greater efforts and sustains loyalty in difficult times, with beneficial effect upon labor turnover.
It maintains sound relations with customers and agents.
It enhances prestige and reputation in the eyes of the public.

Source: M. Valliant Higginson, *Management Policies I,* American Management Association, AMA Research Study 76, 1966, p. 10.

---

[18]Ralph C. Davis, *The Fundamentals of Top Management*, New York, Harper and Brothers Publishers, 1951, p. 173.
[19]M. Valliant Higginson, *Management Policies I*, American Management Association, AMA Research Study 76, 1966, p. 10.

2. Policies also arise from less structured areas of the organization. In day-to-day operations, administrators may be confronted with situations requiring decisions on matters with no previous policy. Their analysis of the situation and their decisions may become future policy. But the formation of policy in this manner indicates little foresight on the part of management. Such policies must be clarified or else confusion due to lack of coordination will result.
3. The other major source is that of externally imposed policy. The government, unions, professional associations, and past practices impose certain policies on the organization. With respect to the latter (past practices), any consistent pattern of decisions or practices, implies a policy even if it is not formally stated.

These three areas—top management, middle management, and externally imposed considerations—provide the variables that management must consider in developing effective policies.

Formulating Policies to Carry Out Objectives. Each area needing policies should be specified, and pertinent information should be gathered. This information comes from stated objectives, past practices, government requirements, and internal and external environmental factors. Once the information has been assembled, top management, should work on drafting the policy statements. Figure 3-8 lists the guidelines for policy development.[21]

To be effective, policies must be communicated and not filed away in the written policy manual, never to be seen again. In communicating policies, the written statement seems to be the most efficient. In written form, policies can be referred to when situations call for action. If a particular policy is new or complex, it is easier to analyze in written form.

Oral communication can also be used in releasing policies. This form of

FIGURE 3-8

Guidelines for Preparing Statements of Policy[20]

1. Briefly define the subject matter so that there may be a common understanding of what the policy covers. This is particularly necessary when technical or other terminology can have different meanings.
2. State the overall policy clearly and concisely.
3. Establish the areas of authority, including levels of approval.
4. Include brief references to supporting policies if necessary.
5. Confine procedures to the practical minimum. An absolute minimum for company policies can be a reference to the executive whom the president holds responsible for administering or coordinating the policy, and reference to coverage in any supporting manuals such as the insurance manual, the accounting manual, employee relations manual, etc.

---

[20]Reprinted by permission of the publisher from M. Valliant Higginson, *Management Policies I*, American Management Association, AMA Research Study 76, 1966, p. 63.

communication is best used when introducing and explaining new policies, and should be supplemented at a later time in written form.

Formulating policies is a continuing process. Changes in technologies, government requirements, union demands, customer wants, and top management require constant policy review and appraisal. Management must continually analyze these changes in adjusting its policies.

Examples of Organizational Policies. In a typical business organization policies will exist in the following areas: administration, finance, employee relations, marketing, distribution, purchasing, production, engineering, and research. Policies are developed in each of these areas to give management consistent guidance in decision making. Figure 3-9 gives a few examples of company policies.

> *Policy formulation is a continuous and ever-changing process that requires constant review.*

FIGURE 3-9

Examples of Corporate Policies[23]

Marketing

1. To price each item with full awareness of that item's competition.
2. To place marketing emphasis on company brands and, most especially, company premium quality brands.
3. To develop a sound scientific research program in order to minimize unit costs and increase market effectiveness.

Corporate Growth

1. To grow in a carefully selected combination of directions which give balance to the total company operation.

Personnel

1. To delegate authority and accountability commensurate with responsibility, and to recognize that the three are inseparable. (See Chapter 4, Organization through Departmentation.)
2. To handle all company-employee relationships with understanding, honesty, and courtesy, recognizing the employee's individuality and dignity.

Finance

1. To extend credit, after satisfactory investigation, in line with sound credit principles.
2. To continually evaluate our risk exposures, controls, and ability to absorb losses; and in light of this evaluation, to assume risk or purchase insurance accordingly.

Production

1. To plan production to meet approved quantity and quality goals at the lowest possible cost.

   To provide prompt shipping service at the lowest possible cost consistent with high-quality packaging and distributor requirements.

Reprinted by permission of the publisher from M. Valliant Higginson, *Management Policies I*, American Management Association, AMA Research Study 76, 1966, pp. 80–82.

---

[23] Higginson, pp. 80–82.

Consider also the following policy of a local church regarding communion and of an education institution regarding patents.

Church. Communion Policy: This congregation of Evangelical Christians practices close, but not closed, communion. We believe, in accordance with God's Word, that the Lord's Supper is to be administered to only baptized and instructed Christians. If you are not a member or a past guest, please announce your wish to commune to the Pastor personally.[21]

Patent Policy. POLICY. All rights to and interests in discoveries or inventions, including patents thereon, which result from research or investigation conducted in any experimental station, bureau, laboratory, or research facility of the University or the Office of Research Administration (ORA) or from research or investigation of any member of the faculty, staff or student body, either in the course of employment by the University, or substantially through the use of facilities or funds provided by or through the University shall be the property of the University; and all rights therein shall be assigned as the President directs. The income from an invention or discovery may be shared with the inventor at the discretion of the President. He shall determine what interest, if any, an inventor shall be allowed in income from an invention or discovery and shall direct the manner in which the University will proceed with the development of the invention and direct the use to which any income of the University shall be applied. The President may seek the advice in these matters of the University Patent Committee.[22]

The policy formation phase of planning is represented in the Summary Chart located at the end of the chapter.

PHASE III: DEVELOPING INTERMEDIATE AND SHORT-RANGE PLANS

Plans are the extension of objectives through the incorporation of company policies. Intermediate and short-range plans will be developed where accomplishment of results is necessary. Although top management is involved in developing these plans, the middle management group is primarily responsible for their implementation.

Most managements prepare three types of plans. They vary in time, scope, and detail.

1. Strategic plans determine both the major objectives of an organization and the policies and strategies to achieve those objectives. Strategic plans are long run and give general guidance to the organization. The subject matter covered includes profits, pricing, capital expenditures, production, marketing, personnel, and others. For other types of organizations the terminology would change but all key areas would be covered. These high-level plans may not be in written form, but may merely exist in the thinking of corporate officers. This method, of course, is not recommended.

---

[21]From a church bulletin of Trinity Lutheran Church, Norman, Okla. April 11, 1981.
[22]From the faculty handbook of the University of Oklahoma, Norman, Okla., January, 1974.

2. Intermediate-range plans are detailed plans for carrying out and coordinating the functions of a firm. These plans usually cover a three- to five-year period and are mainly concerned with implementing the strategic plans. For example, the strategic plan may call for a certain growth rate in the organization, and the intermediate plan will provide the means, through acquisition, merger, and new product development, to fulfill this requirement.
3. Short-range plans are one-year plans for carrying on the actual work. They are very detailed and include some of the following: inventory replenishment, working schedules, advertising budgets, dispatching rules, salespeople's quotas, etc.

In developing plans to accomplish objectives, the manager must continually analyze (1) the organization's mission, (2) the objectives and policies, (3) external economic conditions, and (4) the outlook for the organization and its overall present position. Each of these factors is constantly shifting, causing the previous planning to become partially or wholly inadequate.

The changing external environment reveals the importance of population growth, the changing patterns of distribution, increasing education and skill levels, the rapid growth rate of technology and new production methods, and the growing role of the federal government.

The external environment, the industry outlook, and the firm's position in the industry all need to be examined.

The industry outlook determines the individual firm's future existence. A declining industry will not continue supporting healthy firms. The nature of an industry's product or service can greatly affect its demand and thus the company's plans. A demand for a product or service is influenced by the number of uses it has, its durability, the number of substitutes it has, and the type of customers who seek to use it.

The cost side of the industry should also be analyzed. Labor and material costs, taxes, and capacity of the industry will, of course, have a major influence on the profitability of the firm. The analysis of the industry outlook will indicate the environment in which a company must conduct its operations.

The final information needed to develop plans and forecasts is the firm's position within the industry and its ability to capitalize on future developments. Key factors to consider would be the reputation of the company and its products, the ratio of company sales to total industry sales, the efficiency of the equipment and plant, and the ability of management.

Developing Plans. Providing detailed answers to each of these questions is only a start. There are several other key considerations in developing plans. The first is planning premises based on the assumptions we make about the future. Following World War II, Montgomery Ward assumed we would experience a recession, as we had after previous wars, and restricted investment and expansion. Sears, on the other hand, launched a large expansion and gained considerable competitive advantage. Similarly in 1957, RCA correctly anticipated a continuation of the Cold War, and the resultant defense spending, thus gaining similar competitive advantages.

Planning premises can have a profound impact on eventual organizational success.

Timing and coordination of plans are also important. Timing means that all the things the plan calls for happen when they are supposed to happen. Coordination means that all of the units in the organization that have a role in the plan are working together, much as a football team must do in making a play work, or a company of actors must to insure a successful performance.

PHASE IV: STATING DETAILED PROCEDURES FOR IMPLEMENTING EACH PLAN

Developing procedures is the last step in planning. Procedures are the sequence of steps and rules that should be followed in implementing the plans developed in Phase III. Procedure development must not be separated from development of plans and should be done concurrently.

Procedures are the sequence of steps that will be followed in implementing the plan.

Each plan will have a different set of procedures for its implementation. For example, a production policy may call for a high-quality product. One of the plans a manager could develop would be a statistical quality control plan. This plan would include sampling, inspection, and running statistical inspecting techniques on incoming raw material, in-process production, and final finished goods. The statistical technique may have the following procedure.

1. Select a random sample of fifty items of each incoming lot.
2. Inspect each item and replace each defective item with a good item.
3. If the number of defects found exceeds three, subject lot to 100 percent inspection and replace each defective item.
4. If the number of defectives found is less than three, accept the lot and calculate average outgoing quality limit.

Every other area within the firm will have similar sequences of procedures for carrying out their plans. The procedure related to the University patent policy cited earlier is as follows.

When a discovery or invention which might be patentable is made by a University employee or by a University student using University facilities the discoverer or inventor shall submit a disclosure of the discovery or invention (hereinafter called simply "invention") to the President. The disclosure should be written and should include a statement describing the circumstances under which the invention was made and who participated in the research and a statement about its commercial possibilities and may include a statement by the inventor regarding his desire to either patent or dedicate the invention to the public.

The President will ordinarily refer the matter to the Patent Advisory Committee for its recommendation as to disposition.

The Committee shall commence study and deliberation as soon as possible after written disclosure is received. The Committee shall include in its recommendation:

(a) A statement as to whether or not to:

  (1) Make application for patent,
  (2) Dedicate the invention to the public, or
  (3) Relinquish all rights herein to the inventor,

(b) A statement regarding the manner in which the University should proceed with the application for patent and its development and licensing if appropriate,

(c) A statement setting forth an equitable division of income between the University and the inventor, and may include

(d) A statement setting forth any particularly appropriate use for the income retained by the University.[24]

SOME POSITIVE PAYOFFS OF LONG-RANGE PLANNING

The need for organizations and individuals to systematically plan for the future has been touted over and over again both in the literature as well as in seminars of all types which are conducted for purposes of management development. The fact remains, however, that research has shown that many managers and organizations do relatively little planning and generally do not engage in a great amount of reflective thinking. In light of this it would seem appropriate to supplement our earlier discussion of the advantages of planning by highlighting some additional payoffs to planning while at the same time reemphasizing some of the key points discussed as they relate to the planning process.

The fact that organizations exist in a dynamic, complex, and ever-changing environment is not a well-kept secret. Both the pace and magnitude of change have accelerated significantly in recent years. From the standpoint of the external environment the organization is affected by changes in the following four major areas.

1. Technology—new equipment, new processes, technology transfer, and information processing.
2. Social changes—demographic trends including age distribution, geographic movement, education, income; cultural changes that influence effective approaches to managing people as well as consumer taste and preferences.
3. Political development—the actions of special interest groups as well as federal, state, and local legislation and trends.
4. Economic changes—inflation, investor attitudes, cost trends—pricing requirements, imposed restrictions.

With respect to the internal factors that are critical to the organizations success it is just as important to have a good "fix" on where we stand. Whether the operation be international, national or local in scope, having an awareness of what is transpiring around us can increase our ability to not only adopt to change but also prevent being caught short by unanticipated developments. In the past the game of catch up undoubtedly worked more effectively than it will in the future and therefore the premium on adaptability and flexibility is becoming increasingly important.

The process of planning is a mechanism that forces the organization to ask important questions in areas that affect survival and get answers to these ques-

---

[24]From the *University of Oklahoma Faculty Handbook*, Norman, Okla., Section 3.15, January 1974.

tions. The end result is a management that is better educated and better informed about their own state of health and that of competitors, of the industry, and the environment in general. This should result in not only sounder long-range decisions but also decisions that are more current. Purposeful direction, increased stability, ability to survive "surprises" and the wherewithal to maintain a position of leadership are benefits that accrue to an educated management.

Perhaps most important is that planning can allow us to invent our own future. It facilitates letting the organization initiate action to make happen what it wants to happen as opposed to sitting back and waiting for events to determine its eventual course. Planning is the most important tool an organization has available in this respect. For the organization willing to devote the time, effort, and commitment involved in doing effective planning, the results can be most advantageous in insuring that the future can in fact be shaped albeit not guaranteed. This is infinitely a better position to be in than that of continual uncertainty about what tomorrow or next month or next year will bring.

KEY ELEMENTS AND BENEFITS OF SUCCESSFUL PLANNING

To have a totally successful planning effort for the organization, certain key elements must be present. First, there must be top management commitment to the planning effort. Unless they are behind it, the concentration of effort needed to develop forward-looking plans will not be forthcoming.

There must be an assignment of time. It is very easy for managers at all levels to become so wrapped up in day-to-day details and problems that planning takes a back seat.

Third, planning requires organization, beginning with a timetable scheduling the arrival of information and data needed for decision making. Next, everyone must clearly understand his or her role and responsibilities in the total planning effort. There must also be integration with other management systems: the system approach outlined in this chapter presumes such integration.

Fourth, planning must focus on action.[25] To assure this, it is important that individuals ultimately responsible for carrying out the plan at each level in the organization be involved in its formulation. Effective planning is a team effort, and this means participation

To have a successful planning effort requires commitment from top management, an assignment of time, organization, and a focus on action and achievement.

AN INTEGRATIVE VIEW OF PLANNING

Management must consider each phase of planning as influencing every other phase. The following points make up the frame for planning.

1. The four phases include establishing the mission and objectives, policy for-

---

[25]Paul J. Stonich, "Formal Planning Pitfalls and How to Avoid Them," *Management Review*, June 1975, p. 33.

mation and strategy, plan development, and statement of procedures for implementing plans. Each phase involves several variables, a managerial decision-making process, and an appropriate output.

2. Top management has full responsibility for the entire plan, but successively lower levels of management are delegated the authority for developing and implementing each phase.
3. The development of mission objectives is the most important and, at the same time, the most abstract of these four phases. But objectives have the greatest impact on the firm. The other phases become more and more detailed.
4. Every phase is influenced by every other phase, and feedback from each phase allows management to adjust continually to changing conditions. Planning is therefore a continuous process.
5. This framework can also represent a division's or department's approach to developing its plans. Combining such plans results in a "hierarchy of plans" representing the entire organization's plan.

This chapter has presented a conceptual model of business planning. A conceptual model is a framework for implementing an idea. The operational model may vary for individual firms, but the underlying framework used by most firms is similar to the one presented here.

EXAMPLE OF CORPORATE PLANNING

Figure 3-10 illustrates, in flowchart form, Allstate Insurance's major steps in corporate planning and its decision-making process. The six major steps are represented vertically, in the left column, and the decision-making process horizontally. Starting with Step 1 and following the arrows reveals the decision process for each step.

Comprehensive corporate planning, such as that suggested in this chapter, is desirable because it examines the future in a manner that allows erasures and corrections—on paper! Projected systematic paper plans prompt the manager to consider more alternatives than he or she would otherwise consider. Of course, continuous systematic planning may produce an Edsel once—but probably not twice. Most importantly, formal management techniques allow one to learn from successes as well as mistakes. Since a manager knows exactly what strategy was utilized, he or she can reproduce success as well as detect unsuccessful planning patterns which must be avoided. This is much like the process of carefully recording evaluation and windage while firing tracer bullets, in order to home in on target—after having projected the most likely location of the target. Or, as expressed by Steiner in quoting Piet Hein:

The road to wisdom? Well, it's plain and simple to express:
>*Err*
>*and err*
>*and err again*
>*but less*

MANAGERIAL PLANNING AND STRATEGY 79

FIGURE 3-10

Major Steps in Corporate Planning at Allstate Insurance

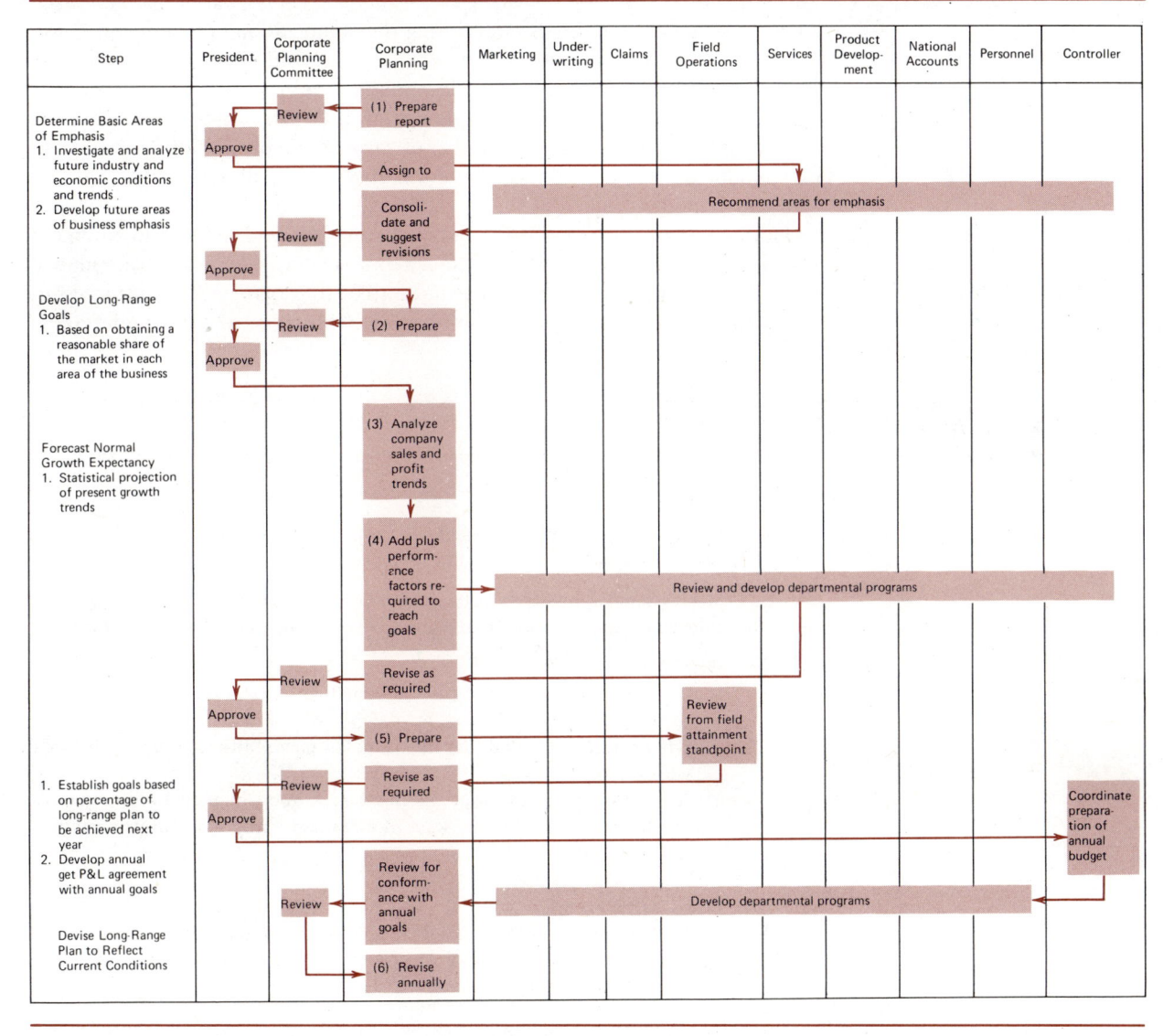

Step	President	Corporate Planning Committee	Corporate Planning	Marketing	Underwriting	Claims	Field Operations	Services	Product Development	National Accounts	Personnel	Controller
Determine Basic Areas of Emphasis 1. Investigate and analyze future industry and economic conditions and trends 2. Develop future areas of business emphasis	Approve	Review	(1) Prepare report Assign to Consolidate and suggest revisions				Recommend areas for emphasis					
	Approve	Review										
Develop Long-Range Goals 1. Based on obtaining a reasonable share of the market in each area of the business	Approve	Review	(2) Prepare									
Forecast Normal Growth Expectancy 1. Statistical projection of present growth trends			(3) Analyze company sales and profit trends (4) Add plus performance factors required to reach goals				Review and develop departmental programs					
	Approve	Review	Revise as required (5) Prepare					Review from field attainment standpoint				
1. Establish goals based on percentage of long-range plan to be achieved next year 2. Develop annual get P&L agreement with annual goals	Approve	Review	Revise as required									Coordinate preparation of annual budget
Devise Long-Range Plan to Reflect Current Conditions		Review	Review for conformance with annual goals (6) Revise annually				Develop departmental programs					

Source: George A. Steiner, *Managerial Long-Range Planning,* New York, McGraw-Hill, 1963.

and less
and less.[26]

---

[26]Piet, Hein, "The Road to Wisdon," *Life,* October 14, 1966. Quoted in George Steiner's *Top Management Planning,* New York, Macmillan, 1969.

SUMMARY

The first phase of planning is establishing the organization's mission and objectives. The statement of mission defines the thrust and direction in which the organization is going in broad terms. It represents the vision top management has for the future and what kind of organization it is. Objectives are much more precise and are influenced by a number of variables involving both internal and external factors. Objectives must be set in all areas critical to the organization's well-being and survival.

The second phase is the formulation of strategies and policies to carry out objectives. Strategy represents a decision about how to utilize available resources to accomplish objectives. In formulating strategy the organization must assess its strengths and weaknesses, opportunities, and threats as well as undertake a

SUMMARY CHART

I. Introduction to Planning
   A. Fiscal approach—relies on what has happened in the past to project the future. Does not say what could or should happen.
   B. Motivational approach—historical performance is only a test of what is reasonable. First determination is what should happen and plans are laid to achieve that.
   C. What Planning Is Not
      1. Not budgeting—planning is concerned with operations and how to make the organization healthier.
      2. Not projections—planning identifies key factors affecting success and deals with these.
      3. Not static—planning must be flexible. A good plan includes objectives, means for reaching them, ways of measuring progress, and provisions for adjustments.

II. Four Phases of Planning
   A. Establishing the mission and objectives of the organization—missions and general statements of purpose while objecties are more specific and lead to accomplishment of the mission.
   B. Formulating strategies and policies—strategy involves a decision on how to use available resources to accomplish objectives.
   C. Developing plans—organizations have three types of plans that vary in time, scope, and detail. They are strategic plans that set forth major objecties and strategies, intermediate plans of the various major functions of the firm (three to five years long) and short range plans of one year in length.
   D. Establishing procedures for implementing plans—procedures are the detailed steps or actions that must be carried out in implementing plans.

comprehensive analysis of the internal and external environment. Policies further refine the organization's chosen strategies. Policies provide guides to administrative decision making and need to be established in all key areas relating to the organization's daily operation.

The third phase of planning concerns the development of intermediate and short-range plans to implement strategies. In developing plans some of the key issues involved include planning premises that are assumptions we make about the future, timing of completion or implementation of those plans, and coordination of plans relating to various segments of the operation.

The final phase of planning is a statement of detailed procedures for implementing each plan. These procedures constitute the "how to" of carrying out plans.

DISCUSSION QUESTIONS

1. Distinguish between the historical or fiscal approach and a motivational approach to planning. Discuss precisely what planning is not.
2. Identify, discuss, and explain several advantages of planning as they relate to the total organization, a department or unit thereof, and individual motivation.
3. What is involved in the statement of mission for an organization? Choose an organization or unit thereof with which you are familiar and write a single or multipurpose statement of mission for it.
4. Briefly describe what you think are the most important variables in determining a firm's objectives. Why have you chosen each? Using an organization other than a business as an example, list some of the variables which would be important to consider in setting objectives. Suggested organizations might be a college or university, fraternity, sorority, or service group.
5. Explain the concepts of hierarchy, network, and multiplicity of objectives. Why is each important? How do constraints enter into the objective determining process?
6. What is meant by strategy? From the text or your outside reading cite one example of a strategy being followed currently by a business organization. Give an example of a strategy from your own personal experience that either worked or did not in pursuit of a particular objective. Why did it work or not work?
7. Define policy and describe how policy is related to objectives. Identify five areas where policies are needed for any type of organization, and explain why each is important. Give an example for each area.
8. What guidelines should be followed if policies are to be effective, and what are some of the advantages of having policies? Explain.
9. Briefly describe the three types of plans, and identify the three key considerations in developing plans. Tell why each is important.

10. In your own words, describe procedures. What purpose do procedures play in the planning process?
11. What are some of the key elements of successful planning? Why is each important? What benefits accrue from planning?

APPLICATION EXERCISES AND CASES

PLANNING FOR HOME IMPROVEMENTS

In early November, Jim Smith, an engineer with a local electronics firm, was faced with the task of doing some personal planning. Jim and his wife had been living in a modest, two-bedroom home for the past five years and were now considering the sale of that home and the purchase of a home that was larger and more in line with their recently improved economic situation. While Jim realized that they would not be moving to a new home until the end of the following summer, he felt there were a number of things that he needed to plan for.

When Jim and his wife had bought their present home, they had planned that they would make several improvements to the home in order to increase its value before selling it. However, because of Jim's busy schedule, they had only made improvements in the bedrooms and had not done much with the kitchen, living room, and dining room areas. Jim wanted to make a number of decorating improvements in these areas, but rather than doing it himself would prefer to hire a carpenter, a painter, and a floor specialist to help him with it.

Since he was uncertain as to how fast the house would sell, he also thought it would be important to have the work done by late spring, so that the house could be put on the market three to four months ahead of their anticipated moving date.

When considering the many things that would have to be done in the next few months, Jim had made a list of some of those that he felt were most important. This list included the following:

(a) Determine how much to spend on improvements.
(b) Define the tasks to be performed.
(c) Make arrangements for the performance of each task.
(d) Establish a timetable for all of the various activities.
(e) Specify performance standards in order to monitor progress.
(f) Coordinate the various activities.

Assignment

Assume that you are Jim Smith and that you have determined the overall cost and schedule of the completed improvements. Using the following form, go through the four phases of the planning function to develop a set of objectives, policies, plans, and procedures that you think are advisable for this situation.

Phase 1 Establishing Objectives. (List all of the objectives that you think are pertinent to this situation, and put an asterisk by the three or four that you think are most important. Two are given.)

- Have all work completed by June 1st.
- Limit the costs of all of the improvements to $3500.

Phase 2 Formulating Policies to Carry Out Objectives. (Develop a set of policies that will add detail to the objectives and serve as guidelines to administrative action.)

Phase 3 Developing Intermediate and Short-Range Plans to Implement Policies. (Define the three or four subplans that are to be adopted in order to reach the objectives that you indicated were most important in this situation.)

Phase 4 Stating Detailed Procedures for Implementing Each Plan. (Define those procedures that will provide for the implementation of each plan and handle such tasks as measuring performance, controlling and coordinating timing, and procuring needed capabilities and resources.)

PITT FOUNDRY[27]

Pitt Foundry had grown in a few years to the point where it employed more than twenty persons. The operation was a "one-man show" with Mr. Pitt, the owner still making all the decisions. Recently Mr. Pitt became ill with an ulcer after working eighty to ninety hours per week for several months. He recognized that he was overworked, but said there was no one to help him.

"My problem is," said Mr. Pitt, "that no one else knows what to do. If I let one of my men make a decision, it usually turns out wrong."

When asked about the company's future, Mr. Pitt said: "I don't have time to worry about that. I have enough trouble solving my real problems."

Questions

1. Do you agree with Mr. Pitt that only his present problems are real? Why?
2. Would managerial planning improve the operation of Pitt Foundry? What advantages would they gain?
3. Provide Mr. Pitt with an outline of what steps are involved in planning with a brief explanation of the key points or observations relating to each step.

---

[27]Herbert G. Hicks, *The Management of Organizations: A Systems and Human Resources Approach*, 2nd ed., McGraw-Hill Book Co., New York, 1972, p. 255.

CHAPTER 4
MANAGERIAL PROBLEM ANALYSIS AND DECISION MAKING

THE DECISION–MAKING SYSTEM
DECISION MAKING–FOUR ESSENTIAL PHASES
PROBLEM ANALYSIS–A SYSTEMATIC APPROACH
DEVELOPING ALTERNATIVE SOLUTIONS
ANALYSING ALTERNATIVE SOLUTIONS
IMPLEMENTING A DECISION–A PLAN FOR ACTION
PARTICIPATION IN DECISION MAKING
GROUP DECISION MAKING
GROUP DECISION–MAKING TECHNIQUES
BARRIERS TO EFFECTIVE DECISION MAKING
APPLICATION EXCERCISES AND CASES
INDUSTRIAL SCALE COMPANY
FOSTER CHEMICAL, INC.

CHALLENGES IN DECISION MAKING

The huge power failure that plunged into darkness the whole of Northeastern North America from the St. Lawrence to Washington in November 1965 was, according to first explanations, a truly exceptional situation. So was the thalidomide tragedy that led to the birth of so many deformed babies in the early 1960s. The probability of either of these events occurring, we were told, was 1 in 10 million or 1 in 100 million, and concatenations of these events were as unlikely ever to recur again as it is unlikely, for instance, for the chair on which I sit to disintegrate into its constituent atoms.

Truly unique events are rare, however. Whenever one appears, the decision maker has to ask: Is this a true exception or only the first manifestation of other things to come?

We know now that both the northeastern power failure and the thalidomide tragedy were only the first occurrences of what, under conditions of modern power technology or of modern pharmacology, are likely to become fairly frequent occurrences unless solutions are found.[1]

---

[1] Peter F. Drucker, "The Effective Decision," *Harvard Business Review*, Vol. 45, No. 1, January/February 1967, p. 93.

In this chapter we deal with a managerial approach to problem analysis and decision making. We are concerned with developing a general framework that when applied, can lead to decisions that solve the problems they were designed to solve and accomplish objectives. Because our concern at this time is with a general framework we are reserving our discussion of quantitative techniques that can be used to solve a variety of types of problems for later.

A manager is continually called on to make decisions that not only affect the eventual success of the organization but that may affect its survival in a continually changing and many times hostile world. Thus, decision making is an important factor in the success or failure of a manager. Peter Drucker emphasizes this in his classical book, *The Effective Executive*.

> *Effective executives, finally, make effective decisions. They know that this is above all, a matter of system—of the right steps in the right sequence.*[2]

Another reason for stressing the strategic role of decision-making skill lies in the changing environment in which today's manager manages. The era of results-oriented management, automation, electronic data processing and rapid technological and social change is here to stay. It calls for today's managers to put

---

[2] Peter F. Drucker, *The Effective Executive*, New York, Harper & Row, 1967, p. 24

Effective decision making is the result of a systematic process that when applied increases the probability that desired results will be achieved.

their decision making on a rational basis. No matter what functions they perform or activities in which they engage, the end result—the payoff—is based on the decisions that are made.

For these reasons managers need to find an approach to decision making that can significantly sharpen their own ability. The approach that will be developed is designed to foster both analytical thinking and an objective approach to problem solving. The need for a systematic approach to problem analysis and decision making is highlighted by the following observation.

The effective decision . . . results from a systematic process, with clearly defined elements, that is handled in a distinct sequence of steps.[3]

THE DECISION—MAKING SYSTEM

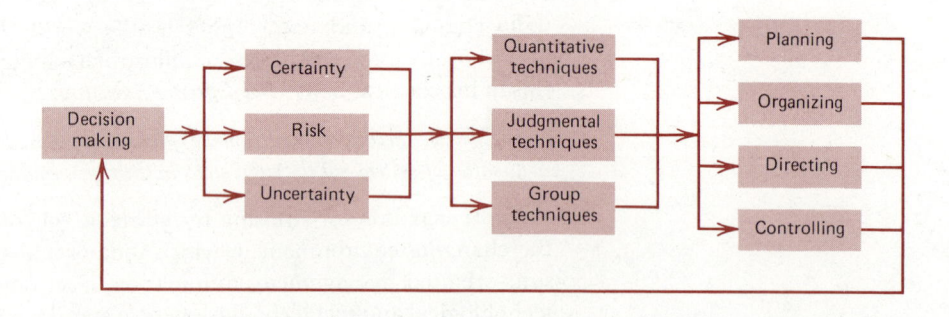

Decision making and its relationships to the four functions of management are depicted in Figure 4-1.

Note that decision making is divided into three possible states: certainty, risk, and uncertainty. In a situation of *certainty*, the manager is fully aware of the consequences of alternative decisions and the eventual outcome of each is highly predictable. Under *risk* the alternatives are recognized but the selection is more complex because the consequences of each alternative are not as clear. But the probability of certain outcomes is predictable. In the state of *uncertainty*, probabilities cannot be attached to outcomes and very little is known about the decision environment.

Decisions can be classified under three states: certainty, risk, and uncertainty.

The three techniques of decision making are the *quantitative*, *judgmental*, and *group techniques*. As noted previously, in Chapter 18, Quantitative Decision Making and Operations Research, we discuss normative decision models that use

FIGURE 4-1

The Decision-Making System

[3]Peter F. Drucker, "The Effective Decision," *Harvard Business Review*, Vol. 45, No. 1, January–February 1967, p. 92.

quantitative techniques in an attempt to find perfectly optimum solutions.[4] Figure 2-1 summarized some of these techniques and the types of problems they apply to.

The approach to decision making used in this chapter has been termed by one writer a behavioral decision model.[5] In dealing with judgmental or behavioral decisions one seldom has either the time or the information needed to consider all possible solutions. We settle for "satisficing," a word coined by Herbert Simon to represent the search for acceptable solutions that will accomplish our objectives when time and costs do not allow further efforts.[6]

Intuition often plays a significant role in all phases of the decision-making process. Intuition is that "feel" which a manager has toward something, based on her experiences or familiarity with a particular set of circumstances of a situation. The role of intuition in decision making should not be under emphasized. In practical reality, it plays a large role, as indeed it should and must. But at the same time, decision-making skills can be sharpened and better-quality decisions made when intuition is accompanied by a systematic approach.

Although decision-making often requires pooled judgment, the process is first analyzed as if decision making were an individual process. Then, in the latter part of the chapter, the concept of participation in decision making as well as various methods of combining judgments in the group decision process is considered.

Finally, Figure 4-1 illustrates how decision making relates to and is closely intertwined with each of the four management functions.

To illustrate this close relationship, in the planning function discussed in detail in Chapter 3, Managerial Planning and Strategy, decisions must be made concerning what variables to consider and how much weight each should carry when formulating the organization's objectives. Specific objectives covering all phases of the operation must be decided on. Policies must be formulated and decisions made regarding them. The strategies designed to achieve objectives involve decision making. Finally, the development of specific plans and the guidelines for implementing them require a systematic approach to problem analysis and decision making.

> Decision making relates very closely to all of the management functions.

Similarly, decision making permeates the activity of organization. What should be the basis for departmentation? At what point is it desirable and economically sound to create another level in the organization? When and where should horizontal growth be initiated? What should be the nature of various authority relationships? How can line-staff friction be minimized? What is the most desirable span of control? All these and many more are key issues that must be addressed and eventually decided on by management.

---

[4]Paul C. Nutt, "Models for Decision Making in Organizations and Some Contextual Variables Which Stipulate Optimal Use," *The Academy of Management Review*, Vol. 1, No. 2, April 1976, pp. 86–87.
[5]Ibid.
[6]Herbert A. Simon, "A Behavioral Model of Rational Choice" in M. Alexis and C. Wilson, eds., *Organizational Decision Making*, Englewood Cliffs, N.J., Prentice-Hall, 1967.

DECISION MAKING—FOUR ESSENTIAL PHASES

These steps involved in the decision-making process can be simply stated. The principal problem usually lies in the actual implementation of these steps. They are too often either forgotten completely or poorly executed. The four essential steps are as follows.[7]

1. Analyze the problem.
2. Develop alternative solutions.
3. Analyze alternatives.
4. Implement the course of action to be followed.

We will systematically explore the full ramifications of each step, by discussing its basic elements and developing a realistic approach to this important activity.

In order to illustrate the operational dynamics of the framework for managerial decision making that is being presented, we follow our discussion of each of the four major phases with an analysis using the concepts involved to the following case study "Your Leadman Ed." In addition to reviewing the case at this time you may find it advantageous to reread it after having studied each of the four phases as they are covered in the succeeding pages.

Case Problem (Your Leadman, Ed)

You are a day-shift foreman on a three-shift operation. You have twenty-seven men reporting to three leadmen under you. (A leadman is somewhat like a crew chief. They are not classified as supervisors but have quasi-"on the job" supervisory responsibilities. The position of leadman is usually a stepping stone to becoming supervisor.) Two of your leadmen are really good at their jobs. They are both thirty and with a little more experience either could be considered for a foreman opening when it comes up. They have been with the company for about five years each, and each has been a leadman for two years. Your third leadman is your oldest hand in point of service. He has fifteen years with the company and six years in your department. He has been a leadman for the last four years. Let's call him Ed.

Ed is one of the nicest guys you'd ever meet. He is sincerely accommodating to people both inside and outside the department. He's as loyal as they come. He served on the board of directors on the credit union after being a member of its loan committee.

Because he is such a nice guy he has made a lot of friends in the company, both inside the department and in neighboring departments. Ed wants to be a foreman in the worst way, but he never says so. He doesn't do the kinds of things people think of as "bucking for the job." But *you* know that he would only make a mediocre foreman even with a strong general foreman behind him—because you've gradually learned this the hard way.

---

[7] For a classic treatment of decision making and problem solving see Charles H. Kepner and Benjamin B. Tregoe, *The Rational Manager*, 2nd ed., New York, McGraw-Hill Book Co., 1976.

You are the person who recommended Ed for the leadman's job—and out of department seniority at that. Ed's problem, you've finally discovered is that he leans heavily on his "way with people" and his good nature. And what hurts is that you know that he really is *sincere* in his service mindedness. His big problem is that he really isn't very bright. His wheels just don't turn fast enough; he can't figure things out very fast. And he is especially poor—and slow—with paperwork reports.

He has trouble with complicated schedules—not big troubles—but trouble enough to take up twice as much of your time as either of your other leadmen and he really does need the help. Because you are naturally loyal to your people, your have never seriously complained to your supervisor about Ed. Perhaps also because you originally recommended him when you were a fairly green foreman yourself.

The maintenance department needs a night shift supervisor and claims none of their employees has had enough experience on the different jobs. Ed worked in both maintenance and one other production department before transferring into your department. Turnover has been fairly high in maintenance and they have been moving toward man-specialization. Anyway, they have asked for Ed. They have gone through the superintendent and you know that he will expect a release and transfer with no problems.

You hesitate to open up because you are sure they will think you are trying to hang onto a good man. (Everybody except you, the other leadmen, and a few of Ed's employees are fooled by Ed's sincere attitude, willingness to work any job, any hours.) You're not even sure they wouldn't accuse you of holding him back because he is such a good employee.

Define your problem and solve it.

PROBLEM ANALYSIS—A SYSTEMATIC APPROACH

If the doctor diagnoses appendicitis and the problem is ulceration, the treatment will inevitably fail. So it is in organizations. If the manager fails to identify the real problem correctly, one of two things happens when the decision is implemented: either the solution fails completely, or it puts out the fire only temporarily.

Unless the real problem is identified the eventual decision will fail completely or put out the fire only temporarily.

Complete problem analysis can be broken down into four steps, which can provide the manager with a practical, systematic first step to problem solving. This approach to problem analysis must be systematized, at least in the initial stages of use, if it is to be helpful to the individual manager. The four steps involved are (1) stating what is wrong or identifying the situation needing improvement, (2) gathering facts, (3) setting forth the requirements of a satisfactory solution stated as objectives and (4) determining the restrictions or limits on a solution.

Statement of What is Wrong or Situation that has Arisen. The first component in problem analysis involves stating specifically what is wrong, the situation where improvement is needed, or the area where results should be better. Often it is a situation that is quite obvious. For example, machine number 256 is producing defective parts, Jim Smith has an excessive number of absences, or department 40E is not meeting its budget. Such incidents come to the attention of the manager rather automatically. These are basic deviations from well-

Some situations needing improvement come to the attention of the manager rather automatically.

defined standards and usually receive prime consideration. For this reason, they present little difficulty in this part of problem analysis.

Note that many managers never get beyond handling these basic deviations in their decision-making activity. In other words, they make decisions but they do not solve problems. They put out fires but only temporarily. Viewed another way, the manager who is continually concentrating just on basic deviations or meeting crisis is dealing with effect rather than with causal problems. The same or similar types of crisis situations will continue to reappear. It is not until he identifies the real problem that action can be taken to permanently eliminate the appearance of its effects. Consider the following example.

> *A product control and engineering group will typically handle many hundreds of problems in the course of a month. Yet, whenever these are analyzed, the great majority prove to be just symptoms—and manifestations—of underlying basic situations. The individual process control engineer or production engineer who works in one part of the plant usually cannot see this. He might have a few problems each month with the couplings in the pipes that carry steam or hot liquids, and that's all.*
>
> *Only when the total workload of the group over several months is analyzed does the generic problem appear. Then it is seen that temperatures or pressures have become too great for the existing equipment and that the couplings holding various lines together need to be redesigned for greater loads. Until this analysis is done, process control will spend a tremendous amount of time fixing leaks without ever getting control of the situation.*[8]

Decision making should focus on identifying real or causal problems as opposed to dealing with individual crisis that occur over again.

The real challenge comes in the more nebulous situations. The manager just feels that results could be better or that something might be wrong. For example, the output of machine 319 is adequate but not as high as it could be; the employees in a given department are meeting the standards but there seems to be a degree of negativism present; department 11B seems to be always "under the gun" in keeping up with its schedule; or a given employee is doing his job but not performing to his full capability. Unlike the earlier examples, these situations are not fires, but only sparks. They are *symptoms* of larger problems. Too often they are overlooked completely, or perhaps just ignored until they become basic deviations.

Also of importance are those instances where a number of things seem to be wrong, which on the surface appear unrelated. For example, schedules are not being met, raw materials or component parts are not available when needed, supervisors constantly have to adjust to meet emergencies, people are overworked, and the job is generally one of constant pressures. All of these situations not only need improvement, but also reflect a much more complex difficulty, such as the lack of an effective system of work planning and control.

As long as the manager continues to attend to the individual circumstances and difficulties as they arise on a day-to-day basis, no permanent relief will be found. It is not until she reviews the total operation, and identifies the *real* problem (in this case, the lack of an effective planning and control program) that some permanent solution can be found. The distinction between situations

---
[8]Drucker, op. cit., pp. 92–98.

needing improvement and real problems will become more obvious after the third component is studied.

Application to Case: Your Leadman Ed. Situation that has arisen: The request by maintenance department to release Ed for the night shift supervisor's job.

Getting the Facts. The second essential component in problem analysis is getting the facts. This is the key to making the transition from the first component to the highly important third component. In a given situation some of the facts that are needed to make a decision are both obvious and easy to obtain while others may be hard to obtain. Of particular importance in fact gathering is a questioning attitude. What exactly are the complete facts surrounding the situation?

It is not enough to say that machine number 256 is producing defective parts, or that department 40E is not meeting its budget. These statements must now be sharpened considerably. What specifically is defective about the parts? It is that the holes are being drilled off center, or that they are not being reamed properly? Are the parts bad regardless of machine speed, or just when it is stepped up beyond a certain point? Where is it happening? Are the defective parts being produced on all shifts or just one particular shift? Is the same operator on the machine all the time?

In what account classification is the major trouble with the budget located? When is the particular situation occurring? Do the budget discrepancies happen all the time or just during rush periods or when certain types of work are being performed? Are other departments within the plant, or the same department in other plants, experiencing difficulty with the same phase of the budget?

Thus, this phase attempts to distinguish or identify the *key factors* surrounding the situation described in component 1. This fact-gathering process should enable the manager to crystallize his or her statement of the situation considerably.

Application to Case: Your Leadman Ed. Some facts surrounding the situation: Ed has experience in maintenance; turnover has been high in maintenance and the superintendent expects the release; you feel Ed is not too bright, has problems with paperwork and schedules, takes more of your time to supervise than others; you recommended Ed for his present leadman's job; you have never complained about Ed's work; you have always readily stepped in to help Ed (implied); Ed wants the job; Ed is loyal and works well with people outside his own department. (You would need to assess and evaluate all of this information in making your eventual decision from among the alternatives that are available.)

Requirements of a Satisfactory Solution, Stated as Objectives. The third component in the problem-analysis step of decision making is stating the requirements of a satisfactory solution as objectives. Its rationale has three dimensions. First, it insures that the remainder of the process has direction. The end purpose of any decision should be to accomplish certain results. If the manager does not first specify what results he is after, any decision is likely to be somewhat haphazard. The objectives the decision must accomplish establish certain boundary conditions.

Second, this statement of objectives serves as a focal point for getting additional facts. A close look at the desired results will suggest those areas where additional fact gathering is needed. Very often the requirements of a satisfactory solution will be derived from the statements of situations needing improvement; that is, the eventual decision will be that these situations should be removed as areas of difficulty.

Finally, this component insures objectivity in the development and analysis of alternatives. It insures that alternative solutions will not be developed for the wrong problem! To illustrate:

> *"Can our needs be satisfied," Alfred P. Sloan, Jr. presumably asked himself when he took command of General Motors in 1922, "by removing the autonomy of our division heads?" His answer was clearly in the negative. The boundary conditions of his problem demanded strength and responsibility in the chief operating positions. This was needed as much as unity and control at the center. Everyone before Sloan had seen the problem as one of personalities—to be solved through a struggle for power from which one man would emerge victorious. The boundary conditions, Sloan realized, demanded a solution to a constitutional problem—to be solved through a new structure: decentralization which balanced local autonomy of operations with central control of direction and policy.*[9]

Application to Case: Your Leadman Ed. Requirements of a satisfactory solution: to fill the maintenance foreman job with someone who has technical capability in terms of knowledge of maintenance, who can handle the administrative aspects of the job, who can work with people and positively contribute to reducing turnover. An additional requirement might include meeting any moral obligations which are felt to exist as they relate to Ed himself.

Restrictions or Limits on a Solution. Finally, problem analysis requires that any restrictions or limits to what otherwise might be an acceptable solution must be considered. Examples of some typical restrictions include cost, personnel, and facts that cannot be changed. It does little good to extensively probe and mentally debate solutions which, although good, cannot be implemented. This is not meant to imply that new ideas and new approaches for doing things should be rejected without first carefully weighing and analyzing them. If critical limitations are set forth initially, however, the decision-making process can be simplified and speeded.

Setting forth the restrictions or limits to a satisfactory solution enables us to speed up and simplify the remainder of the decision process.

Application to Case: Your Leadman Ed. Restrictions of limits on a solution: this step might involve some judgments as to the priority that should be attached to the various requirements for a satisfactory solution. A possibility might include designating each requirement on a must versus desirable basis. In a

---

[9]Ibid., p. 92.

different situation these could be cost restrictions, policies or union contractual limitations.

DEVELOPING ALTERNATIVE SOLUTIONS

Once a problem has been clearly defined, the decision maker develops and analyzes the desirability of various alternative courses of action. There are usually several different approaches which can be taken to overcome a given difficulty, with each having its own set of advantages and disadvantages.

The quality of the eventual decision depends to a large extent on whether there are good alternatives from which to choose. Only if a number of alternatives are considered can there be assurance that the decision made will be a good one.

Having a number of good alternatives from which to choose has a positive impact on eventual decision quality.

When faced with the need to develop alternative solutions to problems, managers have two directions in which to turn: to their own experience and to the experience and practices of the other managers.

The most logical and undoubtedly the most widely used approach to solving problems is to draw on one's own experience. This method is adequate in the majority of cases. Faced with a given situation, the manager compares it with similar occurrences which he may have experienced and successfully solved. Noting the circumstances that are peculiar to the present case, he can then follow a course of action similar to the previous one, with perhaps a few adjustments. Of course, the more experience he has had the better off he is in two respects. First, he can rely on experience to solve a bigger variety of problems, and second, this experience will suggest more possible alternatives, both those likely to work and those not so likely to work.

Past experience is the most logical initial direction in which to turn when developing alternatives.

But today's world is a world of change. Today's manager is continually called upon to solve problems and face challenges that go beyond what has already been experienced. The decisions that solved yesterday's problems are not always adequate for those of today. New and fresh approaches are needed. For these reasons it often becomes both desirable and necessary for the decision makers to look beyond their own experience when developing alternatives, and see how others are handling problems and what ideas they might have. Supplementing our own experiences in this way can contribute significantly to both the number and quality of alternatives developed.

Utilizing the experiences and ideas of others leads to the development of quality alternatives.

In the latter part of this chapter we explore participation as well as some group decision-making techniques that are useful in generating creative alternatives.

Application to Case: Your Leadman Ed. Some possible alternative courses of action might be as follows:

1. Refuse to release Ed saying you cannot afford to lose him.
2. Grant the release and say nothing regarding your reservations about Ed's capability.
3. Grant the release and make known your reservations about Ed.
4. Go to the superintendent and outline the situation as you see it asking the superintendent's advice.

ANALYZING ALTERNATIVE SOLUTIONS

The analysis of alternative solutions involves (1) compiling the advantages and disadvantages of each possible course of action and then (2) examining each one to see how effectively it will accomplish the objectives or requirements of a satisfactory solution, which were stated in the problem-analysis step. The alternatives analysis may necessitate gathering and interpreting extensive cost data as well as the use of various statistical techniques. The more comprehensive the problem, the more difficult the analysis becomes. Quantitative approaches discussed in Chapter 18 lend themselves to solving a wide variety of problems.

SETTING FORTH ADVANTAGES AND DISADVANTAGES

In considering the advantages and disadvantages that apply to each alternative, the decision maker will do well to go back and review thoroughly each component in the problem-analysis phase: specific attention should be given to the following considerations.

1. Will the alternative eliminate reoccurrence of the situation(s) originally identified as needing improvements?
2. Will the alternative meet the requirements of a satisfactory solution, stated as objectives?
3. Does the alternative meet any restrictions or limits that have been set forth?
4. What other specific benefits apply to the alternative?

Perhaps the most difficult step in analyzing alternatives is the identification of the disadvantages or consequences of each alternative. This is particularly true in cases where, either consciously or unconsciously, a favorable mental set toward a particular course of action has already been formed.

The consideration of disadvantages is extremely important. Many otherwise good decisions fail in the implementation stage simply because potential difficulties and shortcomings were not spotted and provisions were not made in advance for dealing with them.

By setting forth potential disadvantages to a decision, we may also uncover some problems that could inhibit effective implementation.

Application to Case: Your Leadman Ed. For each of the four alternatives cited in Phase II you might want to set forth at least two advantages and disadvantages and evaluate how important each is. This process will provide practice in applying the system. It should be apparent that there is some additional information that would be needed before choosing a course of action. Some unanswered questions include the following. (1) How much paperwork and scheduling if any does the night maintenance foreman's job require? (2) Is it possible Ed's training in these areas has been insufficient? (3) Is it possible that paperwork is the part of the job Ed doesn't like and since you have always stepped in for him, he has had no reason to show any initiative? (4) If his strengths in working with people are deemed a key factor in reducing turnover and if paperwork and schedules are in fact an important part of the job and Ed is truly not too bright in this regard, is there a way to cover the paperwork aspects of the job and still use his other strengths? Until we know the answers to some of these questions it would be impossible to make a quality decision. In any case it should be apparent that the decision-making process is not as simple and automatic as may appear on the surface. You might mentally compare your reactions to the case after initially reading it to those you have now after having followed this more systematic analysis. If yours is a typical situation your perceptions will have changed significantly.

IMPLEMENTING A DECISION—A PLAN FOR ACTION

Every decision requires a well-conceived plan for implementing it.

To make a good decision is one thing but to transform that decision into a plan of action or an effective approach to solving a problem is quite another. Every decision requires a well-conceived plan for implementing it.

The three essential steps involved in effective implementation are as follows.

1. A questioning attitude concerning every detail of the decision and the development of necessary procedures.
2. A plan for communicating the decision to those involved and affected by it.
3. A method for allowing participation in the dicision making process.

The first step deals with the technical aspects of decision implementation, while the last two concern themselves with what might be termed the human aspects.

Up to this point the problem area(s) where improvement is needed have been concisely presented, the objectives or goals to be reached have been explicitly set forth, and a proposed course of action has been decided on. The procedures that are now developed for making the decision operative form the core of a plan for action, and are indeed as strategic as the decision itself. These procedures specify in precise detail the steps or actions that must be performed, the sequence in which these actions must be carried out, the specific duties and responsibilities of the various individuals involved, and provisions for follow-up and control. The decision maker must consider and list what must be done, when or in what order these things must be accomplished, who should do them, how they can be most effectively completed, and why they are necessary. The thoroughness of this questioning process can be assured to the extent that the decision maker also asks what difficulties may be encountered or what could go wrong. Provision should be made for handling these difficulties when and if they do appear. Attempting to pinpoint the potential problems of implementing a decision *before* they appear can save considerable trouble later.

The procedures developed for implementation set forth what must be done, the sequence in which these things need to be accomplished, individual action responsibilities and provisions for follow-up.

A story that has become a legend among operations researchers illustrates the importance of the question, "Who has to know?"

A major manufacturer of industrial equipment decided several years ago to discontinue one of its models that had for years been standard equipment on a line of machine tools, many of which were still in use. It was, therefore, decided to sell the model to present owners of the old equipment for another three years as a replacement, and then to stop making and selling it. Orders for this particular model had been going down for a good many years. But they shot up immediately as customers reordered against the day when the model would no longer be available. No one had, however, asked, "Who needs to know of this decision?"

Consequently, nobody informed the purchasing clerk who was in charge of buying the parts from which the model itself was being assembled. His instructions were to buy parts in a given ratio to current sales—and the instructions remained unchanged.

Thus, when the time came to discontinue further production of the model, the company had in its warehouse enough parts for another 8 to 10 years of production, parts that had to be written off at a considerable loss.[10]

COMMUNICATING A DECISION

In the last analysis it is people who determine whether a decision is effectively implemented. Every decision and every plan for action must also have a plan for communicating it to those directly involved as well as those indirectly affected.

Thus, to insure effective implementation the decision maker must ask several questions.

What Should Be Communicated?   Much of the difficulty in obtaining cooperation for implementing decisions stems from individuals' lack of understanding as to how the decision will affect them. With a little effort, most of employees' vital questions can be answered before they are asked; such questions as: What is the reason for the action called for by the decision? Whom will it affect and how? What are the benefits that are expected to result from the standpoint of the individual, the department, and the company? What adjustments will be required in terms of how the work will be done? What specifically is each individual's role in implementing the decision? What results are expected from her? When does the action called for by the decision go into effect? Communicating answers to these questions can head off many of the difficulties that otherwise might be encountered.

Anything that directly or indirectly affects the people needs to be communicated.

When Should It Be Communicated?   Communication is most effective when it precedes action and events. When thus presented it can help to accomplish a very important function. It helps to insure that events conform to plans; that the things that are supposed to happen actually do happen in the way they should happen and when they should happen. Advance communication also helps insure that the manager is not always fighting fires or correcting things that went wrong.

Communication is most effective when it precedes action and events.

To Whom and How Should We Communicate?   Anyone who is directly involved in the implementation of a decision should receive communication concerning it. Only by doing this can there be a reasonable degree of assurance that the decision will be accepted and will have the necessary support.

How to communicate depends on the type and nature of information to be given. The more comprehensive it is, the more need there is for using multiple

---
[10]Ibid.

methods such as oral, written, individual communications, and meetings. These methods are covered in detail in Chapter 8, Organizational and Interpersonal Communications.

Application to Case: Your Leadman Ed.   Depending on the additional information gathered and the eventual decision made, a plan of action for implementation would be developed. You could conceivably include additional training for Ed in his areas of weakness, some type of probationary period that might be involved with the new job, a detailed orientation program spanning a six-month period and similar ingredients.

PARTICIPATION IN DECISION MAKING

Participative management may be defined as getting things done through other people by creating a situation in which they develop mental and emotional involvement that encourages them to contribute to goals and share the responsibility in them.[11] Advocates of participative management stress the human element of this definition.

Participative management involves not just worker behavior but also a situation. The appropriate degree of participation is dependent not only on the interpersonal relationships existing in the organization but also on the situation in which the organization is operating.[12]

Anyone directly or indirectly affected by a decision needs to be given consideration when communicating.

One of the main problems confronting the modern manager is how she can be "democratic" in her dealings with her subordinates and at the same time maintain the necessary authority and control within the organization for which she is responsible.

The effective use of participation requires that the process be effectively managed. This in turn involves determining what degree of participation is appropriate in a given situation. In any case, the motivating force for using it should be related to improving decision quality and gaining needed acceptance of decisions as opposed to using it as a "gimmick" to make people feel important.

One of the problems facing the manager is that of being democratic while at the same time maintaining control.

Specifically, participation should be used because employee contributions are truly valued. The fact that it can also lead to increased job satisfaction is an extra advantage.

DETERMINING THE PROPER DEGREE OF PARTICIPATION

The degree and the type of participation that are appropriate depend on any number of considerations. These include the nature of the problem, past managerial practice, the experience of subordinates, the manager's own skill and attitudes, and the time available.

---

[11] Keith Davis, "Management By Participation," *Management Review*, XLVI, February 1957, p. 69.
[12] Joel M. Rosenfield and Matthew J. Smith, "Participative Management: An Overview," *Personnel Journal*, XLVI, February 1967, p. 101.

FIGURE 4-2

Types of Management Decision Styles

AI	You solve the problem or make the decision yourself, using information available to you at that time.
AII	You obtain the necessary information from your subordinate(s), then decide on the solution to the problem yourself. You may or may not tell your subordinates what the problem is in getting the information from them. The role played by your subordinates in making the decision is clearly one of providing the necessary information to you, rather than generating or evaluating alternative solutions.
CI	You share the problem with relevant subordinates individually, getting their ideas and suggestions without bringing them together as a group. Then you make the decision that may or may not reflect your subordinates' influence.
CII	You share the problem with your subordinates as a group, collectively obtaining their ideas and suggestions. Then you make the decision that may or may not reflect your subordinates' influence.
GII	You share the problem with your subordinates as a group. Together you generate and evaluate alternatives and attempt to reach agreement (consensus) on a solution. Your role is much like that of chairman. You do not try to influence the group to adopt "your" solution, and you are willing to accept and implement any solution that has the support of the entire group.

Source: Victor H. Vroom, "A New Look at Managerial Decision Making," *Organizational Dynamics,* Vol. 1, No. 4, Spring 1973, p. 67. Reproduced with permission.

Figure 4-2 presents five alternative decision styles developed by Vroom and Yetton as they relate to varying amounts of participation. AI and AII are considered autocratic styles because they involve no or limited participation. CI and CII extend the degree of participation by subordinates, but the manager retains control over the final decision. They are democratic styles. GII represents maximum participation and the eventual decision is made by the group.

Based on these varying degrees of subordinate involvement, Vroom and Yetton established some problem attributes to aid in choosing a decision style appropriate to the situation. Figure 4-3 depicts these attributes. Attribute A relates to the importance of decision quality, while B and C are moderating variables to insure decision quality. Attribute D relates to the acceptance criteria and E, F, and G are supplementary conditions that can influence acceptance. Using this framework or model the manager can more systematically determine what degree of participation is most appropriate in a given situation while taking into consideration decision quality and acceptance, which researchers agree, are the two most significant dimensions of good decisions.

Consistent with research findings, a set of rules for choosing among alternative decision-making styles was developed. Figure 4-4 presents these rules. These rules were designed to protect decision quality and acceptance. Rules 1, 2, and 3 are designed to protect decision quality; rules 4, 5, 6, and 7 to protect acceptance.

> The two primary factors that determine the appropriate degree of participation are importance of decision quality and acceptance.

FIGURE 4-3

Problem Attributes

	Problem Attributes	*Diagnostic Questions*
A.	The importance of the quality of the decision.	Is there a quality requirement such that one solution is likely to be more rational than another?
B.	The extent to which the leader possesses sufficient information/expertise to make a high-quality decision by himself.	Do I have sufficient information to make a high-quality decision?
C.	The extent to which the problem is structured.	Is the problem structured?
D.	The extent to which acceptance or commitment on the part of subordinates is critical to the effective implementation of the decision.	Is acceptance of decision by subordinates critical to effective implementation?
E.	The prior probability that the leader's autocratic decision will receive acceptance by subordinates.	If you were to make the decision by yourself, is it reasonably certain that it would be accepted by your subordinates?
F.	The extent to which subordinates are motivated to attain the organizational goals as represented in the objectives explicit in the statement of the problem.	Do subordinates share the organizational goals to be obtained in solving this problem?
G.	The extent to which subordinates are likely to be in conflict over preferred solutions.	Is conflict among subordinates likely in preferred solutions?

Source: Victor H. Vroom, "A New Look at Managerial Decision Making," *Organizational Dynamics,* Vol. 1, No. 4, Spring 1973, p. 67. Reproduced with permission.

FIGURE 4-4

Decision Rules

1. *The Information Rule*—If the quality of the decision is important and if the leader does not possess enough information or expertise to solve the problem by himself, AI is eliminated from the feasible set. (Its use risks a low-quality decision.)

2. *The Goal Congruence Rule*—If the quality of the decision is important and if the subordinates do not share the organizational goals to be obtained in solving the problem, GII is eliminated from the feasible set. (Alternatives that eliminate the leader's final control over the decision reached may jeopardize the quality of the decision.)

3. *The Unstructured Problem Rule*—In cases where the quality of the decision is important, if the leader lacks the necessary information or expertise to solve the problem by himself, and if the problem is unstructured, the method used must provide not only for him to

collect the information but to do so in an efficient and effective manner. Under these conditions, AI, AII, and CI are eliminated from the feasible set. (They do not provide for a means to collect the necessary information, and permit those with the necessary information to interact.)

4. *The Acceptance Rule*—If the acceptance of the decision by subordinates is critical to effective implementation, and, if it is not certain that an autocratic decision made by the leader would receive that acceptance, AI and AII are eliminated from the feasible set. (Neither provides an opportunity for subordinates to participate in the decision and both risk the necessary acceptance.)

5. *The Conflict Rule*—If the acceptance of the decison is critical, and an autocratic decision is not certain to be accepted, and subordinates are likely to be in conflict or disagreement over the appropriate solution, AI, AII, and CI are eliminated from the feasible set. (The method used in solving the problem should enable those in disagreement to resolve their differences with full knowledge of the problem. Accordingly, under these conditions, AI, AII, and CI, which involve no interaction or only "one-on-one" relationships and therefore provide no opportunity for those in conflict to resolve their differences, are eliminated from the feasible set. Their use runs the risk of leaving some of the subordinates with less than the necessary commitment to the final decision.)

6. *The Fairness Rule*—If the quality of decision is unimportant and if acceptance is critical and not certain to result from an autocratic decision, AI, AII, CI, and CII are eliminated from the feasible set. (The method used should maximize the probability of acceptance, as this is the only relevant consideration in determining the effectiveness of the decision. Under these circumstances, AI, AII, CI, and CII, are eliminated from the feasible set. To use them is to run the risk of getting less than the needed acceptance of the decision.)

7. *The Acceptance Priority Rule*—If acceptance is critical, not assured by an autocratic decision, and if subordinates can be trusted, AI, AII, CI, and CII are eliminated from the feasible set. (Methods that provide equal partnership in the decision-making process can provide greater acceptance without risking decision quality. Use of any method other than GII results in an unnecessary risk that the decision will not be fully accepted or receive the necessary commitment on the part of subordinates.)

Source: Victor H. Vroom, "A New Look at Management Decision Making," *Organizational Dynamics,* Vol. 1, No. 4, Spring 1973, p. 67. Reproduced with permission.

GROUP DECISION MAKING

Consensus or group decision making is receiving increased attention in both the literature and in management practice circles. Previously we have alluded to the advantages in the total process.

The initial point of departure for our discussion is some of the characteristics of *groupthink*, which Victor Janis has studied extensively.[13] The value of recognizing these characteristics from the standpoint of the group leader is that when and if they do appear she can take the necessary steps to insure that objectivity prevails and the range of benefits from using groups can be realized.

---

[13]Based on the film "Groupthink," CMR/McGraw-Hill Films, produced by Steve Katten, 1973.

Groups may develop an illusion of invulnerability.

The first groupthink characteristic Janis points up is the tendency for the group to develop an *illusion of invulnerability*. Such would be the case in the instance of a company that has very firmly established itself in the marketing of a particular good or service. Within this company a group may be called together to analyze and discuss the potential impact of some new-to-the market, "upstart" organization trying to get a hold with the same or a similar product or service. This new organization has caused enough waves to at least get the attention of someone in the established firm. In the course of group interaction, an aura of invulnerability may develop as the group dismisses the new organization as a fly-by-night outfit that has been lucky so far and will soon fail in its efforts. An attitude of "they can't touch us" develops, and all kinds of rationalizations are heard, which inhibit an objective view of reality. *Rationalization* is another characteristic of groupthink Janis identifies.

Stereotyping involves putting other people or groups in a fixed mold based on certain assumed characteristics.

Closely related to these two is *stereotyping*. A production group may be meeting to solve scheduling problems. Someone suggests that perhaps with some input and possibly help from sales the areas of concern could be ironed out. The comment is made that "Sales people are all alike; they cause problems—don't help solve them." Heads nod in approval of this stereotyped characterization, and the potential for mutual cooperation is lost.

Three additional possible phenomena of groupthink situations are *direct pressures* exerted by some members on others, *self-censorship*, and the *illusion of unanimity*. The three are closely related. To illustrate their operation, one or two members of the group may verbally attack a third member, who is trying to give the group some input that is not supportive of the decision direction that appears to be developing. Through this pressure they are able to force the third person to either stop engaging in the discussion or to use a degree of self-censorship.

Some group members may exert pressure on other members to comply with what appears to be a developing group consensus.

This case is similar to the situation in which subordinates communicate what they think the boss wants to hear. The preceding scenario also illustrates how the illusion of unanimity can result from consensus decision making. Although there was potential disagreement, there now appears to be unanimity, because those ideas and opinions contrary to what the whole group seems to favor have been suppressed.

The negative influence of these oppressive groupthink characteristics is apparent. The important point again is that the leader be aware of them, and if they appear in a group setting the necessary actions should be taken to insure effective decisions.

Janis also lists the following six poor decision-making practices of groups that get caught up in groupthink.[14]

1. The group limits its discussions to a few alternative courses of action (often only two) without an initial survey of all the alternatives that might be worthy of consideration.
2. The group fails to reexamine the course of action initially preferred by the

---

[14] David W. Johnson and Frank P. Johnson, *Joining Together*, Englewood Cliffs, N.J., Prentice-Hall, 1975, p. 272.

majority after they learn of risks and drawbacks they had not considered originally.

3. The members spend little or no time discussing whether there are covert gains they may have overlooked, or ways in which to reduce the seemingly prohibitive costs of rejected alternatives.
4. The group makes little or no attempt to get information from experts within their own organization, members who might be able to supply more precise estimates of potential losses and gains.
5. Members show positive interest in facts and opinions that support their preferred policy.
6. Members spend little time considering how their chosen policy might be hindered by bureaucratic inertia, sabotaged by political opponents, or temporarily derailed by common accidents. They fail to work out contingency or alternative plans to cope with foreseeable setbacks that could endanger the overall success of their decision.

GROUP DECISION-MAKING TECHNIQUES

Groups provide several advantages in the decision-making process. First, technical knowledge and expertise may be brought to bear on the decision. Furthermore, different backgrounds and perspectives allow the group to do a more rigorous job of sifting ideas. Finally, staffing a decision group with those who will implement a decision promotes identification with goals.

Several processes have been developed to make groups more effective at generating usable ideas.

BRAINSTORMING

When a problem is relatively simple and specific, but requires an original solutions, brainstorming may provide the answer. The guidelines for this group procedure are as follows.[15]

1. Rule out criticism of ideas until later.
2. Welcome freewheeling and encourage wild ideas.
3. Encourage quantity. Strive for a large number of contributions.
4. Seek combinations of similar ideas and improvements.

This technique usually produces from 50 to 150 ideas and can be an enjoyable exercise for a group. Unfortunately it has many weaknesses. Usually no more than 8 or 10 contributions will be useful, while much time is expended on unusable ideas.

---

[15]William H. Newman, Charles E. Summer, and E. Kirby Warren, *The Process of Management Practice*, Englewood, Cliffs, N.J., Prentice-Hall, 1970, pp. 280–281.

NOMINAL GROUP TECHNIQUES (NGT)[16]

This is a structured group decision-making process that is normally used in program administration decision-making and planning, when a large number of individuals need to have inputs into a decision. Usually twenty or more people are involved, seated at individual tables of five or six each. The NGT technique proceeds according to the following format.

The nominal group technique is used when the decision process is complex and a pooling of individual judgments is needed.

1. Ideas are generated silently in writing.
2. Round-robin feedback is provided from group member to group member to record each idea in a terse phrase on a flip chart.
3. Discussion is conducted for each recorded idea for clarification and evaluation.
4. An individual rating is held on priority of ideas in order to mathematically derive a rank ordering or rating.

The NGT is an appropriate group process to use when the decision-making process is complex and calls for the pooling or aggregation of individual judgments. It does not provide quick information exchange and is not the appropriate technique for negotiations or bargaining, nor is it appropriate as policy setting in a representative body.

NGT is more appropriate for the diagnosis and analysis stages. NGT has other serious limitations. It requires approximately ninety minutes per session, extensive facilities for groups, and is limited to one problem per session.[17]

THE DELPHI TECHNIQUE[18]

Like NGT the Delphi Technique (DT) is a means for aggregating the judgments of knowledgeable individuals in order to improve the quality of decision-making. It differs from NGT in that it allows participants to respond by mail, thus remaining anonymous. It is administered through a series of questionnaires, the first of which asks individuals to respond to a broad question. For example, one study called on a panel of retailing executives to predict the future trends in retailing that would be brought about by thirty-one well-established trends in society.[19] Subsequent questionnaires are built on summary responses to the first questionnaire. The process stops when consensus has been approached by the participants.

The Delphi Technique allows for pooling of judgments when those involved are not in close physical proximity.

Like NGT, Delphi can be used to help identify problems and problem solutions. Delphi has most frequently been used for pooled judgment in technical

---

[16] Andre L. Delbecq, Andrew H. VandeVen, and David H. Gustofson, *Group Techniques for Program Planning*, Glenview, Ill., Scott Foresman and Co., 1975, pp. 14–82.
[17] Ibid., p. 81
[18] George Huler and A. L. Delbecq, "*Guidelines for Combining the Judgments of Individual Group Members* in Decision Conferences," *Academy of Management Journal*, Vol. 15, No. 2, June 1972, pp. 83–107.
[19] Subhash D. Jain, "Predicting Impact of Change, using Delphi Technique," September-October 1974 p.29.

forecasting and for forecasting trend development in society. It is particularly useful in clarifying positions in preconference training.

A most recent use of the Delphi technique has been in multinational corporate management. Corporations such as Weyerhaeuser, General Mills, and others use this technique to rank all of the diverse variables that affect political risk in international investment. By so doing they are able to classify countries in which they have an interest on a high-, moderate-, or low-risk basis.[20]

Delphi should not be used when time is limited since the minimum required time is usually forty-five days. It is also limited to use with groups that read well and explain themselves well in written communication. It also requires high participant motivation since a leader is not present to prompt response.

BARRIERS TO EFFECTIVE DECISION MAKING

Before leaving the matter of decision making it is desirable to point out some of the barriers to an effective approach. First, there is the tendency to become preoccupied with the immediate crisis.

Some barriers to effective decision making include preoccupation with immediate crisis, lack of careful investigation, and the desire for immediate action.

Another important barrier can be one person in a group who will not allow careful investigation.

Also, there is the time barrier. Thorough, analytical thinking takes time and it is also hard work. Ironically, however, if more time were spent making quality decisions it is possible that less time would be spent fighting the crises that arise every day.

Finally, there is the attitude that the area in question is someone else's responsibility. Although the corrective action needed may lie in someone else's territory, the manager should do her own analysis of difficulties and fact gathering.

SUMMARY

This chapter deals with a systematic approach to problem analysis and decision making. Managerial problem analysis and decision making can be divided into four steps: problem analysis, developing alternatives, analyzing alternatives, and decision implementation. A systematic approach to the problem analysis phase has four distinct components. The first involves the initial statement of what is wrong, the situation that needs improvement, or the area where results might be better. Once this initial statement has been presented, the decision maker must gather the facts, investigate possible causes and identify the real problem. Next the requirements of a satisfactory solution, as objectives, are established; and finally any restrictions or limits on a solution are specified.

---

[20] R. J. Rummel and David A. Heenan, "How Multi-Nationals Analyze Political Risk," *Harvard Business Review*, January-February 1978, p. 70.

SUMMARY CHART

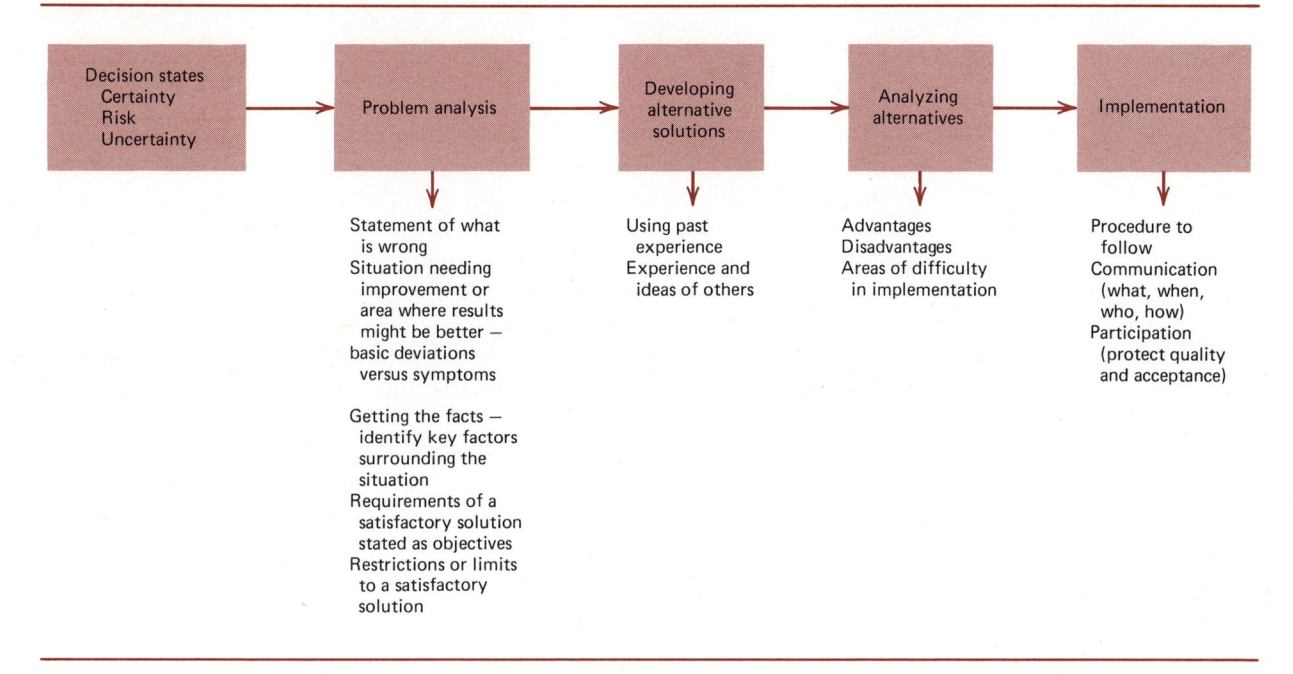

```
[Decision states      [Problem analysis] → [Developing      → [Analyzing    → [Implementation]
 Certainty                                   alternative       alternatives]
 Risk                                        solutions]
 Uncertainty] →
```

Problem analysis:
Statement of what is wrong
Situation needing improvement or area where results might be better — basic deviations versus symptoms

Getting the facts — identify key factors surrounding the situation
Requirements of a satisfactory solution stated as objectives
Restrictions or limits to a satisfactory solution

Developing alternative solutions:
Using past experience
Experience and ideas of others

Analyzing alternatives:
Advantages
Disadvantages
Areas of difficulty in implementation

Implementation:
Procedure to follow
Communication (what, when, who, how)
Participation (protect quality and acceptance)

In the second step of decision making (developing alternatives) the manager has two directions in which he can turn. He can rely on his own experience, and utilize the experience of others. Although one's own experience is valuable and also the most logical direction in which to turn in developing alternative solutions to problems, it should be noted that in today's changing world, it usually is not adequate by itself. Ideally, the decision maker will also draw on the experience of others to develop alternatives.

Analyzing alternatives involves considering both the advantages and disadvantages of each alternative, as they relate to accomplishing the objectives of the decision which were outlined in step one. Examining the potential disadvantages is particularly important since they may reveal problems that could occur in the implementation step. In that way provision can be made beforehand for overcoming these problems if and when they do appear.

The final step of decision making, implementation, involves developing a plan of action, communicating the decision, and participation. In developing a plan of action, the questions of alternative selection, sequencing, and implementation must be answered. The decision must also be communicated to those affected, and people should be given the opportunity to participate in various phases or steps in the total decision-making process. The two latter procedures determine the degree to which the people who must implement the decision will be committed to having it carried out successfully.

Participation in decision-making is useful because it utilizes the potential of subordinates. It is a vehicle for improving the quality of decisions as well as increasing the acceptance level on the part of those who must carry them out. These two factors (quality and acceptance) along with certain moderating variables will determine which of several possible degrees of participation is appropriate.

Before utilizing participation it will benefit the manager to become familiar with its advantages, potential disadvantages and where groups are involved some of the characteristics of groupthink which can inhibit effective group action.

Various group decision-making techniques have been devised for allowing more than one person to have inputs in the decision process. Brainstorming is useful in generating creative ideas. The Nominal Group Technique is the device for arriving at consensus when allowing large numbers of people to participate in decision making. The Delphi Technique is a means of aggregating the judgments of knowledgeable individuals in order to improve the quality of decision making.

DISCUSSION QUESTIONS

1. How is decision making related to planning and organizing?
2. Distinguish between decision making under risk, certainty, and uncertainty.
3. Discuss the four essential steps of the decision-making process in terms of what each involves and its key considerations.
4. What are the key questions a manager should ask when she attempts to identify the real problem in a situation?
5. When considering the advantages and disadvantages which apply to alternatives, what are the three questions a manager should ask in evaluating these alternatives?
6. Enumerate the steps involved in the effective implementation of a decision.
7. What is the importance of communication and participation in the decision-making process? Discuss the advantages and disadvantages of participation.
8. Set forth the range of possibilities a manager has in terms of choosing the proper degree of participation. How does the need for a quality decision and the need for acceptance influence the choice of decision style?
9. Cite at least three decision rules as they relate to decision quality and acceptance and explain how they operate.
10. What are the barriers to effective decision making?
11. What group decision-making styles would you use for planning (a) an office Christmas party, (b) a difficult technical problem in the computer system, (c) the administration of a new wage and salary plan, (d) a twenty-year

company forecast for new products? Why? What are the advantages of using participation?

Discuss and illustrate each of the characteristics of groupthink.

APPLICATION EXERCISES AND CASES

INDUSTRIAL SCALE COMPANY [21]

For years the Industrial Scale Company has been the leading manufacturer of automatic scales used in grain elevators. The product is so well accepted that probably 90 percent of the elevators in the United States are equipped with Industrial scales.

In recent years, Industrial has sold about 400 units of this type of scale annually. This is stable, attractive business, which accounts for about 15 percent of the company's total volume. The price per unit is $1500; but in view of general increases in steel prices and wages, this may go up 5 percent during the coming year. The product is sturdy and often lasts over twenty-five years, so most current sales are for elevator expansion, new elevators, or major remodeling jobs. The installation of a new scale, therefore, is only part of a larger project, and the project is typically in the hands of a contractor rather than of the elevator staff itself.

During the last five years a new competitor, Wilson, Inc., has sprung up. Wilson simply copied, in all essentials, the Industrial scale (patents have long since expired). Although the Wilson product does not have a recently improved gate and catch, its performance is clearly as dependable as thousands of Industrial scales now in use.

Wilson, Inc., is a small firm owned by a man with several other interests. Only a few employees and a small plant are needed to assemble purchased parts and make shipments. Sales promotion is almost all handled by direct mail to contractors who work on grain elevators, although the company puts an occasional advertisement in trade papers. The price of Wilson scales is essentially the same as comparable Industrial equipment, but Wilson gets its business by offering contractors a 20 percent discount whereas Industrial gives only 10 percent. Thus, if a contractor installs a Wilson scale rather than an Industrial scale, he may make $150 more profit. With its low overhead and investment, Wilson probably makes a good profit margin even with the larger discount.

The sales manager of Industrial is seriously disturbed about Wilson competition. He dislikes losing sales now and doesn't want Wilson to get a firm foothold in the industry. No figures are available, but he believes that Wilson's sales are growing and are "about three scales per week." He says contractors complain that they "like Industrial equipment but simply can't live on a 10 percent

---

[21] William H. Newman and Charles E. Summer, Jr., *The Process of Management: Concepts, Behavior, and Practice*, Englewood Cliffs, N.J., Prentice-Hall, 1961, pp. 346–347.

margin." This complaint is difficult to evaluate since contractors get less than 10 percent discount on some materials they use and more on others; moreover, they normally quote to their elevator customers either a total price for the job or a fee for their services, and these quotations can be adjusted for the discounts they receive on the materials required for each specific job.

The sales manager asks, "How about getting our costs down?" He knows the answer because he had heard it before: Industrial's sales organization, engineering staff, repair service organization, quality control, and related activities all cost money and must be covered by sales income. The controller's investigation of the economics of grain elevator scales shows that 40 percent of the total cost is fixed overhead, whereas the balance is variable (it fluctuates with volume). Total costs might be cut 3 percent by stripping the scale to match Wilson's design and with some engineering effort another 2 percent could probably be saved in processing and materials. On the other hand, a new streamlined model—the present scale with a new look—would probably cost 8 percent more than at present.

Industrial has a national sales organization that promotes all its products. The salesmen call on the larger contractors but do not attempt to reach the thousands of elevator operators in the country. Some advertising is placed in trade papers. Both salesmen and ads stress the following advantages of using Industrial scales: (a) proven quality; (b) dependable source of replacement parts; (c) national coverage of experienced servicemen; (d) improved gate and catch.

The Industrial Scale Company is in sound financial condition with no long-term debts. From its early start with grain scales it has developed much more elaborate equipment that it sells directly to large rubber companies, chemical firms, food processors, and many other users. This expansion has been financed by retained earnings. The company does not have excess cash and relies on commercial bank loans for increasing working capital. Profits after taxes are 3 to 5 percent of net sales.

Using the systematic approach to managerial problem analysis and decision making outlined in this chapter analyze the foregoing case.

FOSTER CHEMICAL, INC.[22]

Foster Chemical, Inc., had a problem of quality control in one of its manufacturing departments. The product produced in this department required an extremely complex process.

At a supervisor's meeting Mr. Knowles, the plant manager, said: "We must lick this quality control problem. Jim (a chemical engineer), I want you to study this problem and give me a recommendation next Monday."

Jim replied: "Perhaps the men in the department could give me some ideas if I talk to them."

---

[22]Herbert G. Hicks, *The Management of Organizations: A Systems and Human Resources Approach*, 2nd ed., New York, McGraw-Hill Book Co., 1972, p. 210.

"No, Jim, that won't be necessary. Those men just work; they don't think. They wouldn't be able to give you any ideas."

Questions
1. Do you agree with Mr. Knowles that the men in the department could not help in solving the problem? Why?
2. What effect will Mr. Knowles's attitude likely have on solving the problem?
3. Assuming you did decide to involve the men, how would you approach it? Utilize some of the material dealing with participation and group decision making in answering this.

CHAPTER 5

ORGANIZATION THROUGH DEPARTMENTATION

ELEMENTS AND FUNCTIONS OF ORGANIZATION

THE DEVELOPMENT OF AN ORGANIZATION

VERTICAL ORGANIZATION GROWTH

SCALAR CHAIN OF COMMAND

THE LINE ORGANIZATION STRUCTURE

THE GROWTH OF STAFF IN THE ORGANIZATION STRUCTURE

TYPES OF STAFF AUTHORITY

PERSONAL STAFF

SPECIALIST STAFF

DIVIDING WORK AND GROUPING JOBS

FUNCTIONAL DEPARTMENTATION

PRODUCT DEPARTMENTATION

CUSTOMER OR CLIENT DEPARTMENTATION

GEOGRAPHICAL DEPARTMENTATION

RESPONSIBILITY, ACCOUNTABILITY, AND AUTHORITY

THE STEPS IN ORGANIZING

LIMITATIONS TO THE STRUCTURAL STUDY OF ORGANIZATIONS

APPLICATION EXERCISES AND CASES

FORMING A NEW COMPANY

DOUGLAS FOWLER'S DILEMMA

MASTERING DIVERSITY AT GE[1]

As it moves vigorously through this centennial year into its second century of operation, General Electric Co. is performing at least four difficult management tasks at once, and doing each of them exceedingly well. Under the leadership of 61-year-old Chairman Reginald H. Jones, chief executive since 1972, the sprawling giant is managing diversity, managing growth, managing change, and managing people.

This year, as well, GE began to reap the first fruits of a major organizational restructuring completed at the end of 1977.

The restructuring process began in 1970. First of all, the number of company operating units was trimmed from around 200 to 43, each of which became a so-called strategic business unit. One unit might consist of a single department or several; the essential thing was that the components of each faced common market challenges, which lent themselves to common planning strategies.

To free top management from having to grapple with the mountains of detail pouring in from operating units around the world, the company set up a new layer of management just below the top. It divided its business into six sectors—consumer products and services, industrial products and components, power systems, technical systems and materials, international, and the recently acquired mining company Utah International, Inc.—and appointed an executive to head each sector, except Utah, which continues under its former president.

The sector executives have taken over much of the decision-making responsibility from Jones and his ten-man corporate policy board and also help to coordinate strategic planning. According to Jones: "In the year the sector executives have been in place, the load at the top has been reduced. And all sorts of new synergies in operations have been achieved—in advertising, in marketing and in the form of joint ventures between mining and manufacturing units."

---

[1]"The Five Best-Managed Companies: Mastering Diversity at GE," *Dun's Review*, Vol. 112, No. 6, December 1978, p. 30.

Organization involves the integration and coordination of all resources to accomplish objectives.

Having determined a particular course of action, designed to solve a problem or to meet an objective, the manager must organize so that the people who are to do the work may execute their tasks with maximum efficiency and effectiveness. Organizing sets the stage on which activity takes place. It involves the integration and coordination of all necessary resources (both human and technical) to accomplish desired objectives. The emphasis in organizing is on creating a structure that will result in maximum efficiency and effectiveness. In this chapter and Chapter 6, The Organization in Operation, we develop a basis for understanding the organizing function. Chapter 7, Organizational Dynamics, and Chapter 12, Contingency Approaches to Organizations, expand this material by examining some of the more intricate considerations involved.

ELEMENTS AND FUNCTIONS OF ORGANIZATION

The work to be done is the first and basic element of organization.

The whole purpose of organizing is to accomplish some objective, which in turn requires that certain specific *work* is done. Of necessity, these activities must receive primary consideration when organizing. *Work* is considered the first basic organizational element; but by itself it is not a sufficient basis for building an organization structure.

Because it is people who do the work, they also must receive consideration when designing an organization.

The *people* who will do this work constitute the second basic organizational element. The work to be done must be considered in relation to the skills and abilities of the people who must perform these activities. Thus, the work must be grouped and organized into units, each unit containing a series of activities that one person can accomplish. One of the purposes of organizing is to determine the proper relationship between the work to be done and the people who will do the work.

The work environment includes all the physical factors necessary to the performance of work.

The third element for consideration in organizing is the *work environment,* which refers not only to the specific location in which the work will be done but also all the physical factors necessary to the performance of this work by the people involved. The work environment includes machines, materials, tools, space, lighting, heating, automobiles, sale of materials, and report forms—everything necessary to implement the work. Just as people constitute the *animate* element in organizing, the work environment includes all the *inanimate elements.* The environment in which the people are to work is just as important an element in organizing as the first two—people and work.

Communication linkages are the final elements of organization.

The fourth element in organization design is the one that breathes life into it—the *communications linkages.* Chester I. Barnard defined organization in a vibrant manner, "as a system of conscious coordinated activities and forces of two or more persons."[2] To Barnard an organization was much like a magnetic field. But just as magnets and electricity do not constitute the entire electromagnetic field, buildings and the people in them do not constitute the whole organization—an organization includes the *feelings* of customers, clients, and employees.[3] Communication is the element that links these components together.

The organization process follows a sequence and the manager must achieve a balance among the four basic elements.

When organizing, the manager must consider these elements in the order in which they are named. First, he must determine the basic work activities involved in the plan. They must be clearly defined and broken down until it is possible to regroup them into jobs. Then the people and the jobs must be matched on a unit-for-unit basis. Next, the organizer must establish the proper relationship between the people who are to accomplish the work and the environment in which they must work. As we can see, the organizing process follows a specific sequence. The manager's objective is to achieve a balance among these

---

[2]Chester I. Barnard, *The Functions of the Executive*, Cambridge, Mass., Harvard University Press, 1947, p. 73.
[3]For an excellent review of Barnard, see James A. Gazell, "Authority Flow Theory and the Impact of Chester Barnard," *California Management Review*, Vol. XIII, No. 1, Spring 1970, pp. 68–74.

four basic elements, which will result in the best possible performance of the plan. Meeting this requirement is facilitated when effective communication linkages between all the components are provided for.

Finally, one should consider the fact that effective organization requires fine tuning to develop an organic synergy. This requirement is described vividly by one of the most distinguished of management consultants, Lt. Col. L. F. Urwick of Australia.

The reason why men organize is always the same: to insure that individual efforts are directed towards a common purpose and that they support each other. The latter is largely a question of timing, the timing of individual efforts. Every form of human collaboration, from two persons to 200 million, is like an orchestra. It only works really well if the individual players "keep time," so that their efforts support each other and are in accord with "the score." If a single player (instrumentalist) fails to "keep time," the whole effect may be ruined. That is why orchestras have "conductors" and business undertakings have managers.[4]

LINE FUNCTIONS

Consider the situation of a person who intends to start a small business. Whether she is making a product or performing a service, there are three basic functions that she must perform.

1. Something of value in the form of a utility must be produced. In a manufacturing concern a product will be fabricated or assembled; in a retail store, the means for sale of goods will be created; in an airline, a time and place utility will be created through the procurement and maintenance of airplanes and of facilities that will make air traffic possible; in an integrated petroleum company, oil must be extracted and refined. Every organization, profit or nonprofit, must perform this basic function of creating a utility. This value constitutes its primary reason for existence.

2. Next, this good or service of value that has been created must be distributed to users. The first function has only served to create a value that is potentially useful to people. The organization must make this good or service available to the consumers. In a manufacturing or processing concern, this function is sales; in a retail store, it is usually called merchandising. In our example of a retail store, the first function made possible the merchandising function by creating a place in which goods could be made available to customers when they wanted them. In all cases, this function is concerned with the exchange of a created value for some other value, usually money.

3. Finally, both of these first two basic activities must be financed. The capital necessary to create some good or service and to distribute it must be acquired and maintained if the organization is to survive. Financing includes not only

---

[4] L. F. Urwick, "The Word Organization," *The Academy of Management Review*, Vol. 1, January 1976, p. 90.

the gathering together of capital to create the organization, but also includes all the accounting and record-keeping activities necessary to the maintenance of capital.

Because these three functions *must* be performed regardless of the type of organization we are considering, they are known as *line* functions. No organization will be found that in some way does not perform these functions.

All other activities associated with organizations are auxiliary or supportive in nature, and are classified as *staff* functions. They result from the growth of the organization beyond the three basic line functions. For example, the personnel function is a necessary and strategic one, but only arises when managers of line functions can no longer handle all the details of personnel management. Consequently, a specialist is brought into the organization to relieve them of certain activities as well as to offer expertise. The same can be said of purchasing, production planning, and many other areas. The concepts of line and staff will be more fully developed later in the chapter. Figure 5-1 depicts the basic functions of a business organization, and also illustrates the points regarding organization charts that follow.

Line functions are basic to the organization's existence.

THE ORGANIZATION CHART

Earlier in this chapter, we quoted L. F. Urwick's analogy of conductors in orchestras as compared with managers in organizations. There is a major flaw in this analogy that Colonel Urwick points out, as follows.

> But in an orchestra all the players can see and hear the conductor. In a business undertaking they cannot. The conductor (Chief Executive) may live in an office ten thousand miles away. Concerted action (after all a musical performance is called "a concert") then depends upon communication. That is what organization is about. A so-called "Organization Chart" is a wiring diagram. It defines who should tell whom about what and, if anybody doesn't know, whom he/she should ask. Without orderly communication any effort at human cooperation tends to become a "disorderly house."[5]

The organization chart is like a wiring diagram.

FIGURE 5-1

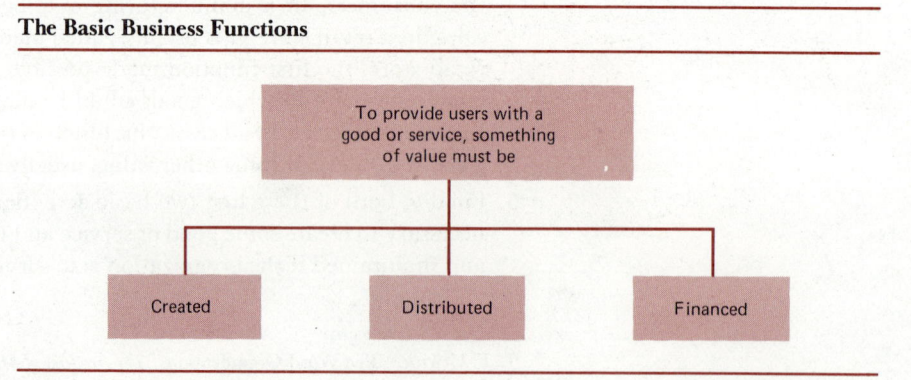

The Basic Business Functions

```
         To provide users with a
         good or service, something
         of value must be
         ┌──────────┼──────────┐
      Created    Distributed   Financed
```

[5]Ibid.

Organization charts come in various sizes, colors, and even textures. Most are black and white, printed on paper. Some are affixed to office walls and made of materials that are easily changed. Some charts are highly detailed; some are very sketchy. Some are stamped confidential and locked in the desks of a chosen few; others are broadly distributed and easily available.[6] Even the most current chart is to a degree somewhat inadequate as a diagram of the organization and as an explanation of how the organization works. Nevertheless, such charts are the best diagrammatic tools we have for communicating organizational relationships.

The organization charts of most organizations show the following two things.

1. Division of work into components. These components may be divisions or departments, or they may be individuals. Boxes on the conventional chart represent these units of work.
2. Who is (supposed to be) whose superior. The solid lines on the chart show this superior-subordinate relationship, with its implied flow of delegated responsibility, authority, and attendant accountability.

Implicit in these two points are three additional things the chart is designed to show.

3. Nature of the work performed by the component. Depending on the descriptive title placed in the box, what this shows may be specific (facilities engineering), speculative (planning), or spurious (special projects).
4. Grouping of components on a functional, regional, or product basis. This is also conveyed to some extent by the labels in the boxes.
5. Levels of management in terms of successive layers of superiors and subordinates. All persons or units that report to the same person are on one level. The fact that they may be charted on different horizontal planes does not, of course, change the level.

Organization charts are used throughout this chapter to illustrate principles and problems within organizations. As we have seen, Figure 5-1 depicts the primary functions of a manufacturing organization in chart form.

THE DEVELOPMENT OF AN ORGANIZATION

The development of an organization usually occurs in stages.

To illustrate the manner in which the three basic functions increase in scope and complexity as an organization grows, consider the case of a person who has just gone into business manufacturing a revolutionary new card table in his basement. The table is lightweight, the legs pop into place at the touch of a button, and another button releases them for easy folding. He supplies his own capital to begin the business, and in its first stages he performs all three basic functions. He purchases materials and produces the tables in his basement; he sells them on a

---

[6]This section draws heavily from Harold Stielglitz, "What's Not on the Organization Chart," *The Conference Board Record*, November 1964.

door-to-door basis; and he supplies his own capital and keeps his own financial records.

The demand for the product soon exceeds his capacity for production, and although he puts in longer and longer hours in the basement manufacturing the tables, the backlog of orders grows daily. Selling activities are quite limited, since word-of-mouth advertising alone is bringing in more orders than he can handle. The family helps with the production and delivery of the tables, but it soon becomes apparent that major adjustments are needed to relieve the situation.

The proper answer to this problem is of course to secure help. The owner-manager needs to hire personnel who can help with one of the three basic activities so that the total work load of the business can be handled.

As the volume of work increases, additional people must be added to the organization.

Let us assume that the owner-manager wishes to retain control over finance. Also, since orders for the table are coming in without expending much sales effort, he decides that the logical area in which to get help is that of production. Accordingly, he hires several people to help him produce the tables. Now his organization has developed to the point shown in Figure 5-2.

The owner continues to directly supervise all three basic functions, but hires workers to do the physical production. The owner's activities in this area are thus limited to supervision.

As demand for the product and the resultant workload continue to increase, the process of splitting up the three basic functions continues.

Over a period of time, more and more production workers are added. In addition, the owner finds that he must devote more time to selling his tables as well as to the financial aspects of the business. Once again he finds himself overburdened with work and in need of help. This time he decides to hire a production foreman to supervise that function as well as some sales people. The expanded organization is shown in Figure 5-3.

Eventually, some supervisory responsibilities must be delegated to other managers.

At this point the owner is still handling all financial matters and directly supervising the sales people, but he has relinquished the direct supervision of production to someone else.

FIGURE 5-2

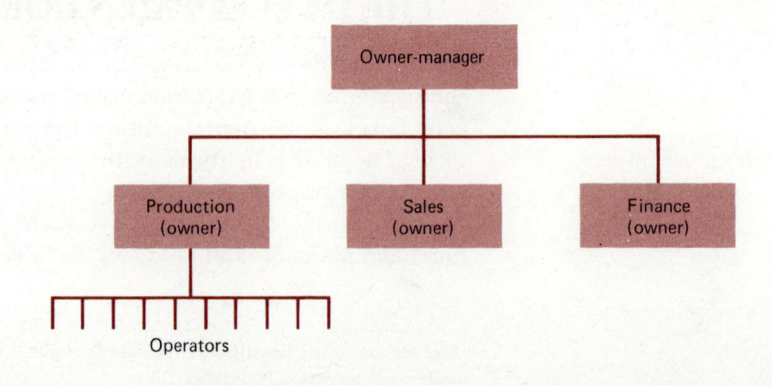

An Organization Begins to Develop

ORGANIZATION THROUGH DEPARTMENTATION

FIGURE 5-3

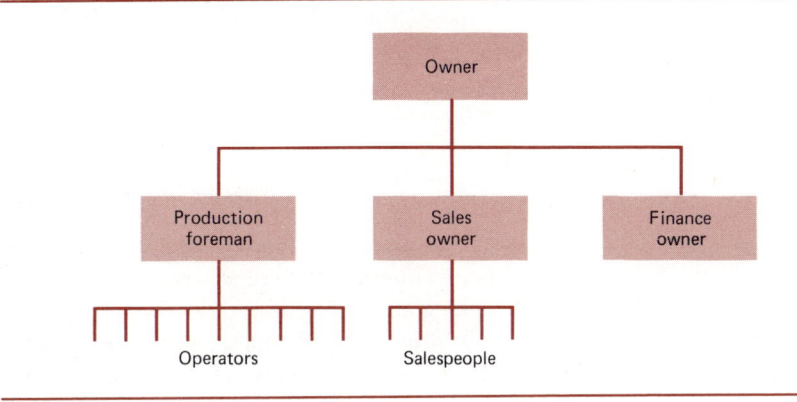

The Expanded Organization

```
                      Owner
         ┌──────────────┼──────────────┐
    Production        Sales         Finance
     foreman          owner          owner
    ┌┬┬┬┬┬┐         ┌┬┬┬┬┬┐
     Operators       Salespeople
```

VERTICAL ORGANIZATION GROWTH

The growth of the organization, shown in Figures 5-1, 5-2, and 5-3, in these first stages is vertical. That is, our card table manufacturing organization is getting taller. This is a result of the increased volume and necessary expansion of the basic line functions. The organization grows downward as activities are split off following the three basic lines, and this vertical growth will continue as long as the workload increases.

Since the organization has grown considerably past the one-person stage, and since the three basic activities have been first split off by themselves and then broken down further, with the addition of another level to the organizational structure, it becomes important for management to determine the way in which the work to be done might be grouped into jobs. That is, it has now become necessary to define the work that must be performed and then to arrange that work into units that one person can perform.

In the production division, the various operations necessary to manufacture the table could be arranged on the basis of the manufacture or assembly of component parts. They might also be arranged on the basis of the production methods involved or the type of machines or the materials used in the production process. They might even be grouped on the basis of their location.

SCALAR CHAIN OF COMMAND

A second phenomenon is that a scalar chain of command or a hierarchy of formal relationships is being established. Vertical growth results in a series of superior-subordinate relationships, where one delegates to another, forming a line from top to bottom. The line of authority so formed has the following three important advantages.

1. It is clearly understood.
2. The members know from whom they receive orders and to whom they report.

Vertical organization growth is represented by an expansion of the line functions.

Scalar chain of command refers to the hierarchy of formal relationships that results as delegation of authority takes place.

3. Decision making is expedited, since each member has complete authority in their area and need only consult with their superior when necessary.

In addition to establishing these superior-subordinate authority relationships, the scalar chain defines the lines of formal communication and decision making, indicates who is accountable to whom, and defines each person's work responsibilities.

THE LINE ORGANIZATION STRUCTURE

When only line authority is employed the organization structure is line, a type used primarily in small enterprises. Its principal advantages are quick decision making and clear-cut authority relationships.

Its principal disadvantages include the fact that managers are overloaded with duties, specialization is not practiced, managers with comprehensive knowledge in all areas are difficult to find, and insufficient time is given to planning, research, and control. To overcome these disadvantages, several kinds of staff authority are employed. Therefore let us examine the reasons for horizontal organization growth and the resultant line-staff organization structure.

THE GROWTH OF STAFF IN THE ORGANIZATION STRUCTURE

When line managers become overburdened it is necessary to relieve them of certain activities and responsibilities.

Staff is introduced into the organization structure when the line managers need to be relieved of certain activities and responsibilities that are overburdening them. In contemporary organizations the staff plays a very important role in (1) gathering and analyzing information for top-level decision making, (2) offering counsel and formulating policies that serve as a basis for the overall direction the organization will take, and, perhaps most importantly, (3) furnishing expertise in such areas as personnel management, organization and management development, marketing research, and numerous other areas critical to success.

At one time staff were considered auxiliary in nature, or perhaps even second-class citizens of the organization. But in today's world, staff positions are not only an integral part of any effectively functioning organization, but they are critical to the ability of the line to function properly.

HORIZONTAL GROWTH

As the organization continues to expand, the workload at the upper levels becomes greater. The managers at the heads of the three basic lines find it necessary to plit off more and more activities, and delegate more and more responsibility downward. Because the number of different work activities one person can attend to is limited, it soon becomes necessary for the people at the next lower level to also begin to delegate their work downward. As the activities

ORGANIZATION THROUGH DEPARTMENTATION 119

that are performed become more and more complex, the organization tends to grow downward at a rapid rate and the complexity of the activities being carried on at each level increases greatly.

In the production division, when the stage of having a production manager and several producing departments is reached, it is found that department foremen must perform many different kinds of activities. It is also found that these activities are the same for each foreman. Each one must obtain materials and supplies, plan and schedule work, train and place personnel, and keep records.

One of the first of these common activities to be noticed by management in the card table company was the increasing burden of paperwork. Manufacturing records, personnel records, sales records, order processing ledgers, journals, correspondence, and all the essential paraphernalia of modern business increased by leaps and bounds. Duplication or work was occurring in each of the three basic functions. Record-keeping files, and correspondence constitute a large portion of the owner's and foreman's work, and it was soon apparent that something must be done to relieve the line managers of this clerical work.

Since clerical work can be better performed by a specialist, the solution to the problem would be to hire someone proficient at office work. This specialist would fill a newly created staff position and serve each part of the organization. This could only be done if (1) all the office work that was being done by the line managers equaled a full-time job: and (2) if the performance of this work in one place by a specialist resulted in a greater economy of operation for the entire organization. The major objective of hiring a specialist is to aid the linemanagers by giving them more time for the primary work activities. In this case, an office manager would probably be hired who would constitute the beginning of an office staff to serve the organization. The organizational position of this new activity is shown in Figure 5-4.

This structure preserves the three basic lines of organization, production, sales, and finance, and attaches the specialist, office staff, who will serve all three lines at the point where they join. The organization has expanded, but the expansion has taken on an entirely different character from that in the first stages of growth. Up to this point the growth of the company was only vertical, following the three basic organizational lines downward. Now, rather than let the line continue to grow only downward, necessitating the addition of the same kind of specialists in each segment with consequent duplication and overlapping of work, the organization is allowed to grow horizontally.

The personnel function found in modern business enterprises evolved in a manner similar to the office specialty just described. An organization must hire, place, and maintain personnel for each of the three basic activities of production, distribution, and finance. With only vertical growth in organizational structure, this personnel function would have to be handled in each of the three primary chains of command. Of course this kind of growth can quickly lead to duplication of effort, to overlapping of responsibilities, and to unnecessary, wasteful competition within the organization for personnel. Before this situation can develop to the point where it causes inefficiency, it should be taken out of the three basic

Horizontal growth occurs with the addition of staff departments to the organization.

Allowing the organization to grow horizontally by the addition of staff prevents the need to add the same kind of specialists in each unit.

FIGURE 5-4

Organizational Position of Office Staff

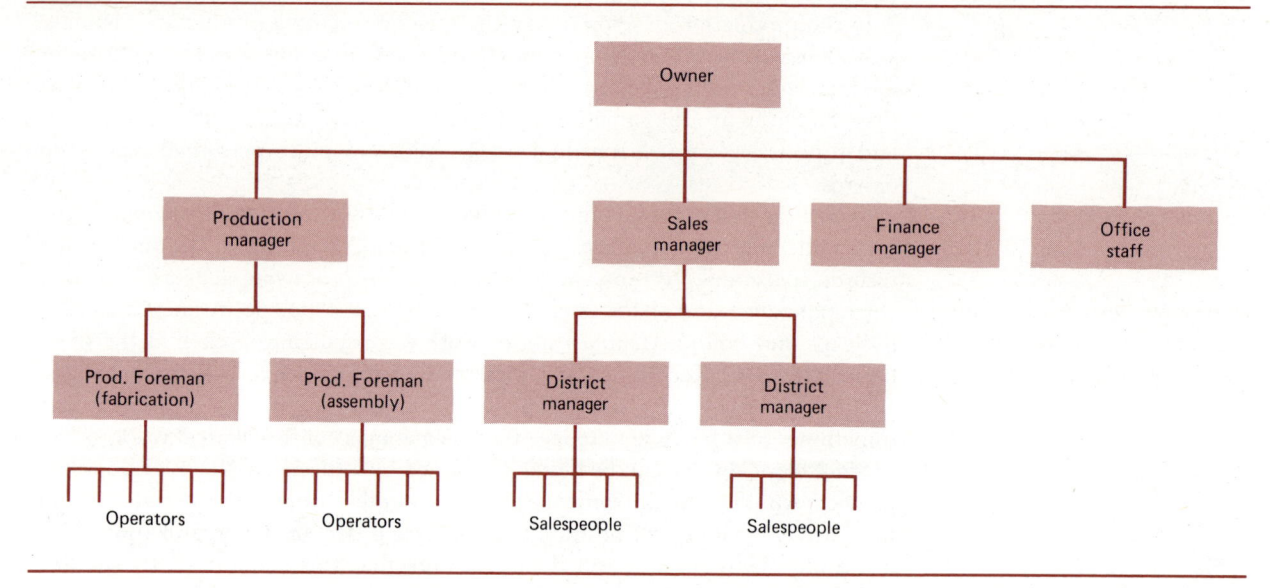

```
                                 Owner
        ┌───────────────────┬─────────────┬──────────────┐
   Production             Sales         Finance        Office
    manager              manager        manager         staff
   ┌────┴─────┐         ┌────┴─────┐
 Prod. Foreman  Prod. Foreman   District    District
 (fabrication)  (assembly)      manager     manager
      │             │              │           │
  Operators     Operators     Salespeople  Salespeople
```

lines and centralized in a single personnel function to service the rest of the organization. As with the office work example, economy of effort can be achieved and the line manager can be relieved of certain personnel-related responsibilities.

TYPES OF STAFF AUTHORITY

Up to this point our definitions of line and staff were primarily in terms of the activities or types of work that each unit performs. We said that production, marketing, and finance are the line activities in the organization, and all others are staff operations. But in modern organizations, line and staff must also be studied as authority relationships. In fact, much of the misunderstanding that develops in organizations is a result of management's failure to specify what type of authority staff people have in a given situation.

There are two broad categories of staff. The first is the *personal staff,* which includes the "assistant to" and the general staff. The second is the *specialist staff,* which consists of the advisory, service, control, and functional groups.

PERSONAL STAFF

The Assistant to. Figure 5-5 illustrates the position of the *assistant to* in the organization structure. Typically, this individual will have no major supervisory responsibilities but will have a limited set of duties assigned, to extend the manager's capacity for work.

FIGURE 5-5

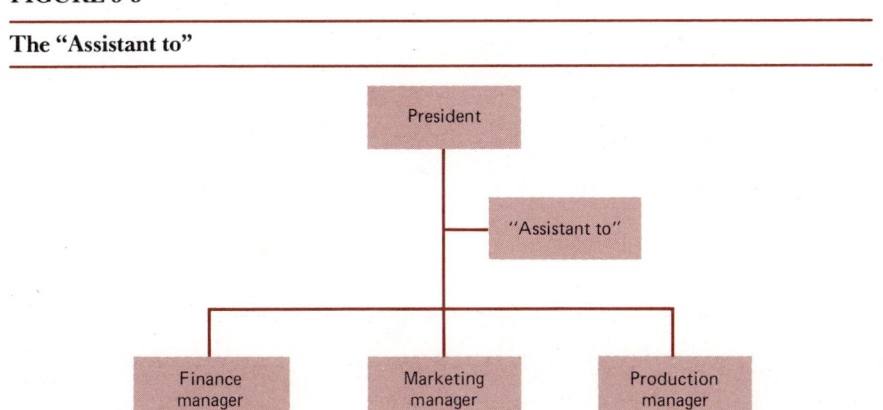

The "Assistant to"

```
                    President
                       |
                       |—— "Assistant to"
                       |
         ┌─────────────┼─────────────┐
      Finance       Marketing     Production
      manager        manager       manager
```

The purpose of the position of *assistant to* is to increase the effectiveness and efficiency of the manager by assuming certain routine managerial duties. Such work will include collecting and making preliminary evaluation of data needed for decision making, consolidating the information in various types of reports so it can be more easily assimilated and interpreted, processing certain types of documents for distribution to others in the organization, acting as a stand-in for the manager at meetings or functions, interpreting plans or budgets to others, and otherwise serving as an adjunct to the manager.

In some situations managers may actually give their assistant to the authority to act as an agent. This means that the assistant too can issue instructions in the superior's name as well as make decisions that affect the organization and other employees.

Staff members who occupy the positions of assistant to should be made clearly aware of both the extent and the limits of their influence, as should everyone in the organization who will come in contact with them.

General Staff. The place of the general staff in the organization structure[7] is depicted in Figure 5-6. The general staff is composed of all the chief administrators in the organization. Its typical purpose will be to bring together into one group all necessary expertise and input needed to make sound plans and decisions for the organization. The president is the ultimate decision maker, but he/she does so only after consulting with, and receiving input from key people. The role of the general staff is perhaps best illustrated by the military. During World War II, General Eisenhower was ultimately responsible for the conduct of the war in his sphere of operation, but major tactical decisions were made only after the key subordinate officers had the opportunity to contribute their particular knowledge and insight. In business, the general staff would typically be

The purpose of the assistant to, is to extend the managers capacity for work.

The general staff is composed of chief administrators who pool their expertise and counsel the chief executive.

---
[7]For a classical discussion of this principle and other staff relationships, see James D. Mooney, *The Principles of Organization*, New York: Harper and Brothers Publishers, 1947.

FIGURE 5-6

General Staff

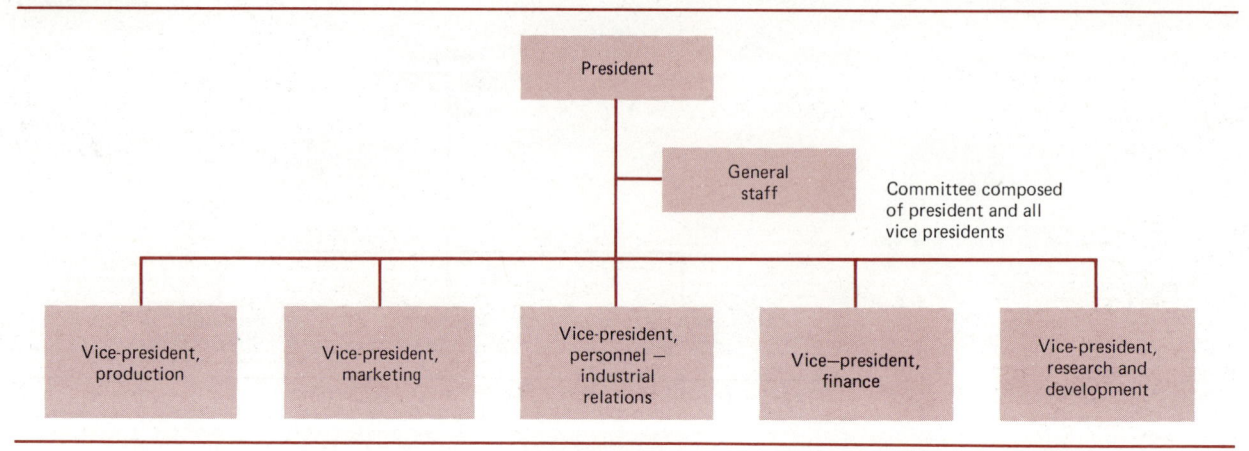

```
                    President
                       |
                       |——— General staff ——— Committee composed
                       |                       of president and all
                       |                       vice presidents
    _____|_____
    |         |            |          |          |
Vice-     Vice-      Vice-        Vice-      Vice-
president, president, president,   president, president,
production marketing personnel—    finance    research and
                    industrial                development
                    relations
```

involved in decisions dealing with such things as capital expenditures, plant location, new product introduction, profit planning, and organizational development. The theory behind general staff is essentially one of a coordinated group acting through the chief to insure maximum results.

SPECIALIST STAFF

There are four basic types of specialist staff.

Advisory Staff. The advisory staff counsels line managers. Either by request or on their own initiative, they will study problems, offer advice, and prepare plans. The work and thoughts of the staff person who is acting in an advisory capacity may be accepted, rejected, or modified by the managers in the organization. An example will illustrate this advisory function.

Assume there is a vacancy in one of the departments of the organization. The personnel department will normally recruit applicants for the job and screen two or three people who seem qualified to fill it. These two or three seemingly qualified people are referred to the departmental manager to be interviewed. Before making a decision, the manager would probably ask the personnel officer which applicant was considered the best. At this point, all the personnel officer can do is to advise as to which candidate seemed to be the best qualified. The manager is free to choose one of the others if he or she so desires and is not bound to follow advisory staff opinion.

Thus, when the staff is acting in an advisory capacity, they are using influence rather than line authority. Their proficiency in selling their ideas and backing up their opinions with logical thought will probably determine the extent to which their advice and suggestions are followed.

The advisory staff act in a specialized counseling nature to the line manager.

Service Staff. The service staff performs activities formerly done in the various line departments. The need for a service staff may arise because of duplication of effort and certain inefficiencies at several points in the organization. Service staff departments are formed when a concentration of facilities will provide more economical performance and better control. Once the specific activities have been removed from the line, they must be performed entirely by the service staff, to prevent continued duplication of effort. Thus, the service staff is not on a take-it or leave-it basis. If the job is going to get done, the line must rely on the staff to do it.

The service staff consists of activities that have been taken from the line to prevent duplication of resources.

A maintenance department in a manufacturing organization is a good example. When the organization was small, each production department had its own people who did the maintenance work, under the direct supervision of the departmental supervisor. As expansion took place, it became increasingly difficult to find enough people with the diverse knowledge necessary to handle all phases of maintenance. The number of people needed for maintenance increased as the number of departments increased, and a considerable dollar investment in special tools and equipment was required. Supervisors became overburdened as they attempted to oversee both production and maintenance. Then top management decided to establish a service staff, a central maintenance department, to provide maintenance for the entire production operation. The line manager is now dependent on the staff maintenance department to perform all maintenance work.

Control Staff. The control staff has direct or indirect control over other units in the organization. In the case of direct control, they may be serving as agents of the line manager. The quality control department is in a line relationship to the production manager but not to the various production departments, such as fabricating and assembly. The production manager may, however, give quality control direct authority to shut down the assembly line if a quality problem occurs.

The case of indirect control is illustrated when the staff can require procedural compliance, submission of certain reports, or must be consulted on policy interpretation. For example, departmental foremen may be required to contact the industrial relations department before formally answering any employee grievance. Implied in this requirement is the idea that Industrial Relations will give the foreman an answer to the grievance/that he can transmit to th employee as the organization's official response. In these and other ways, the line managers are subjected to some restrictions by staff in the operation of their departments.

Functional Staff. Functional staff authority exists when one manager has direct authority over a certain phase of another manager's operation, and exercises this authority along lines other than those established by the formal organization structure. More precisely, the staff manager is given limited line authority. To illustrate this point, assume an employee in a department is responsible for submitting a daily or weekly cost report on the department's activities. Although technically the formal structure dictates that this individual is responsible only to

The functional staff has direct authority over some phase of the line managers operation.

his departmental supervisor, someone from the cost accounting department may be given functional authority to see that the report is properly completed. If a problem arises, the cost expert may go directly to the responsible person, by passing the immediate supervisor in the process. Obviously, this type of staff authority should be restricted to exceptional situations; if carried too far, and if too extensive, it could destroy the line manager's effectiveness.

A vivid example of overuse of functional staff can be found in the writings of Frederick W. Taylor. Combining his bias for separating management and operating work with the advantages of specialization, Taylor proposed "functional foremanship" at the first level of supervision. He identified four distinct foremanship subfunctions that he believed should be performed in the office, and four that should be performed in the shop.[8] Figure 5-7 demonstrates the arrangement that he suggested. Note the eight supervisors to which each worker reported.

It should be noted that some staff may have combinations of these types of authority, depending on the particular situation. To the extent that this is true, more than a normal amount of confusion and/or conflict can result. This indicates that the type of staff authority in existence must be carefully defined and understood by all involved.

FIGURE 5-7

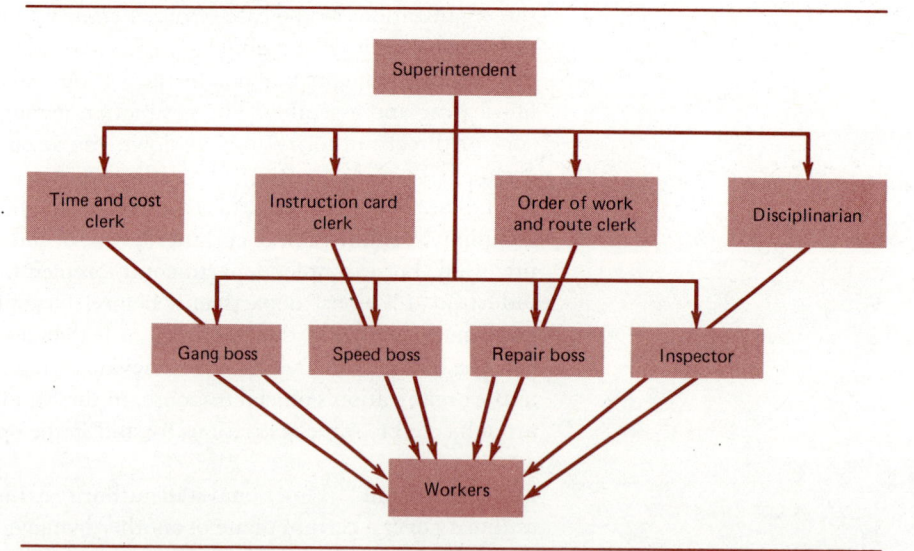

Taylor's Functional Organization

```
                          Superintendent
           ┌──────────────┬──┴──┬──────────────┐
           ▼              ▼     ▼              ▼
    Time and cost   Instruction card   Order of work    Disciplinarian
        clerk            clerk         and route clerk
           │              │              │              │
           ▼              ▼              ▼              ▼
       Gang boss     Speed boss      Repair boss     Inspector
           └──────────────┴──┬───────────┴──────────────┘
                             ▼
                          Workers
```

Source: W. Warren Haynes and Joseph L. Massie, *Management: Analysis. Concepts and Cases,* Englewood Cliffs, N.J., Prentice-Hall, Inc., 1961 p. 35.

---

[8]Frederick W. Taylor, *Scientific Management,* New York, Harper & Row, 1947 pp. 100–122.

DIVIDING WORK AND GROUPING JOBS

The process of grouping activities so that they can be easily coordinated is referred to as departmentation. The simplest method of organizing is by *number*, that is by grouping persons in hundreds or thousands as if they were perfectly interchangeable. This is the procedure recommended by Jethro, the father-in-law of Moses, when Moses found himself overburdened with decision making.[9]

> *What you are doing is not good. You and the people with you will wear yourselves out, for the thing is too heavy for you; you are not able to perform it alone . . . Moreover choose able men from all the people, such as fear God, men who are trustworthy and who hate a bribe; and place such men over the people as rulers of thousands, of hundreds, of fifties, and of tens. And let them judge the people at all times; every great matter they shall bring to you, but any small matter they shall decide themselves.*

Today most organizations follow patterns of departmentation that could be characterized as either functional, product, customer, or geographical. Consider Figure 5-8 as these means of departmentation are discussed.[10]

FUNCTIONAL DEPARTMENTATION

Departmentation by function is the most common form of grouping work.

The grouping of activities by function is based on the nature of the work to be performed. In Figure 5-8 the primary functions of a business manufacturing a product are depicted by Level A of the chart, marketing, manufacturing, and finance. Notice that the marketing department is also organized by function at Level B. Function is the most common form of departmentation for several reasons. First, it allows the grouping of specialists in a field, facilitating management control of that function. Furthermore, group cohesiveness and similarity of goals within the department are promoted by grouping persons with similar training and background. Moreover, the equipment and resources needed for a certain operation can all be in one location. Grouping by function also avoids duplication of skills. Establishing a personnel department, as demonstrated in Level A of Figure 5-8, allows for the specialization of skills in one place rather than having the managers of marketing, manufacturing, and finance all performing this function.

But functional departmentation possesses disadvantages as well. Specialists grouped together often develop narrow tunnel vision and may lose track of the overall goals of the organization. Furthermore, their strong allegiance to a profession, specialized vocabulary, and physical proximity may cause them to avoid interaction and communication with other groups.

When departments are organized into specialized functions we say that they are *differentiated*. But all of the parts of the organization must be coordinated in

---

[9]Exod. 18:17-22.
[10]For a complete discussion of formal organization, see Herbert G. Hicks and C. Ray Gullett, *Organizations: Theory and Behavior*, New York, McGraw-Hill Book Co., 1975.

FIGURE 5-8

Four Levels of Departmentation

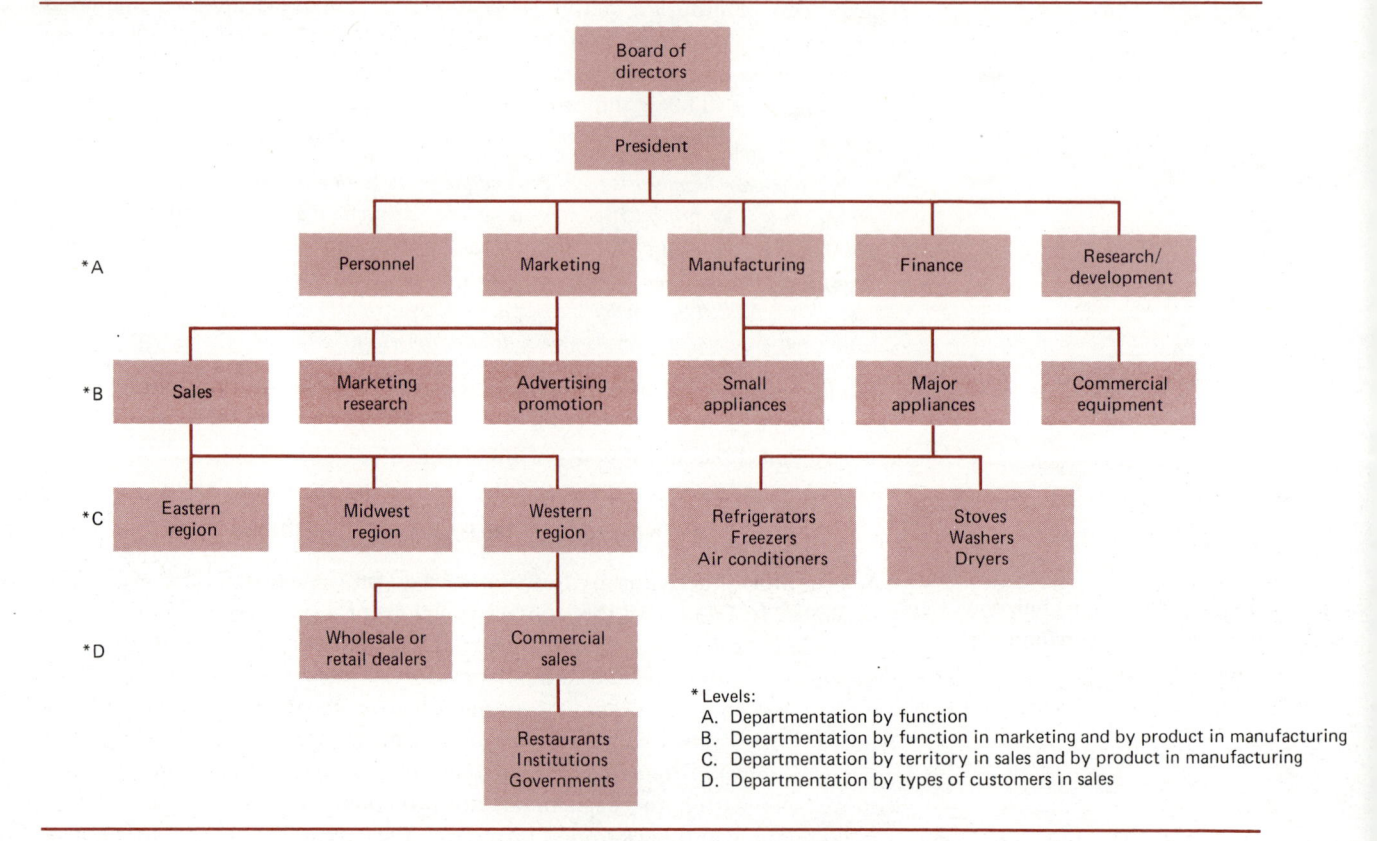

```
                        Board of
                        directors
                           |
                        President
       _____|_____
      |           |           |              |              |
*A  Personnel  Marketing  Manufacturing   Finance     Research/
                                                      development
       _____|_____     _____|_____
      |           |           |   |        |         |
*B  Sales    Marketing   Advertising  Small    Major      Commercial
             research    promotion    appliances appliances equipment
    ___|_____                 ____|____
   |        |           |               |         |
*C Eastern  Midwest   Western      Refrigerators  Stoves
   region   region    region       Freezers       Washers
                                   Air conditioners  Dryers
              _____|_____
             |                   |
*D       Wholesale or        Commercial
         retail dealers       sales
                                |
                            Restaurants
                            Institutions
                            Governments
```

*Levels:
A. Departmentation by function
B. Departmentation by function in marketing and by product in manufacturing
C. Departmentation by territory in sales and by product in manufacturing
D. Departmentation by types of customers in sales

order to accomplish the goals for which it was designed. When specialized functions are coordinated or brought back together we say that they are *integrated*. Functional departments tend to differentiate well, but often have difficulty with integration.

A final disadvantage of functional departmentation is the limiting effect it has on the development of personnel. Persons who have risen through several levels of organization within one function department may be poorly equipped to assume overall management responsibilities.[11]

PRODUCT DEPARTMENTATION

Product departmentation helps insure the full development of each individual product line.

In General Motors, the Buick, Cadillac, and Chevrolet divisions are examples of product departmentation. They are strongly interested in the full development of product lines and the development of specialized knowledge by engineering and

---
[11]Joseph A. Litterer, *The Analysis of Organizations*, New York, Wiley, 1973, p. 376.

FIGURE 5-9

Product Organization

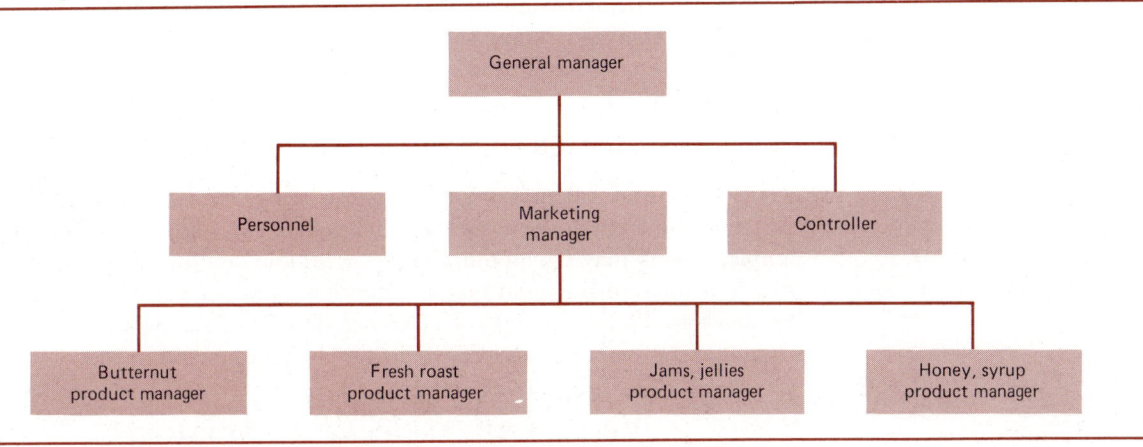

```
                        General manager
                              |
        ┌─────────────────────┼─────────────────────┐
     Personnel           Marketing              Controller
                          manager
                              |
        ┌──────────────┬──────┴───────┬──────────────┐
    Butternut       Fresh roast    Jams, jellies   Honey, syrup
product manager  product manager  product manager product manager
```

sales people on a product basis. Level B of Figure 5-8 illustrates a manufacturing department organized by product. Figure 5-9 depicts the organization of a food processor organized by product within the marketing division.

The following paragraph, taken from a case analysis of one company, explains the rationale for this organization.

> *Originally, at United Brands, as in most companies, each function—production, research, marketing, and financial services—played a specialized role in the total operation of the company. The general manager of a division coordinated the work of the functions in implementing the corporate strategy. However, as the number of products each division produced and sold increased the product manager type of organization was United Brands' response to this complexity in coordinating the functional departments in the development, production, and marketing of a large number of products.*[12]

The specialized functions of marketing, production, and finance can still be found in this structure, but the focus of company efforts is on the product lines. The main advantage of this form of organization is the focus of accountability on the development and sale of superior products. It has arisen in response to an economy so sophisticated that it will no longer beat a path to the door of anyone developing a superior physical product. Products, promotion, and distribution must be fine tuned. Although sticky engineering problems still confront these companies, a technical difficulty can usually be overcome. But this is not true of problems of competition and customer allegiance, which need strong product orientation.

Product departmentation also provides superior opportunities to train top

---

[12]Paul R. Lawrence, Louis B. Barnes, and Jay W. Lorsch (eds.), *Organizational Behavior and Administration: Cases and Readings* (Homewood, Ill.: Richard D. Irwin, Inc., 1976), p. 243.

128 CLASSICAL MANAGEMENT CONCEPTS

executives. Since product departments often operate with many of the functional specialties of total companies, opportunities to break up the tunnel vision of the specialists are provided. But a product approach to organization does have some problems. Competition among the different product managers for the resources often creates a considerable amount of conflict.

CUSTOMER OR CLIENT DEPARTMENTATION

Customer departmentation insures that the needs of a particular client group will be met.

Level D of Figure 5-8 depicts organization by customer, the type of departmentation used in order to give special attention to the customer or client. For example, a bank may have both a commercial loan and personal loan department. A manufacturing plant may have both an industrial and a governmental sales division. The advantage of customer departmentation is that it makes certain that the special needs of a particular client group will be met.

GEOGRAPHICAL DEPARTMENTATION

When an organization extends its operations over a large geographical area, it may be desirable to departmentalize by geography or territory, such as demonstrated by Level C of Figure 5-8. Sales organizations are often divided into geographical areas to facilitate coordination by regional managers as well as to take advantage of knowledge of local conditions. National manufacturers with heavy or cumbersome products must often locate plants in different geographical areas to avoid prohibitive transportation costs for supplies and products. The steel companies are prime examples of manufacturers with limited ability to ship long distances, because the shipping costs of a ton of steel can quickly match manufacturing costs.

Organizations extended over a large area often departmentalize geographically.

Figure 5-10 is an example of a geographical organization design coupled with a product organization within divisions, as suggested by Hicks and Gullett.

Other Types of Departmentation. Organizations may also be divided in numerous other ways. For example, departments can be organized on the basis of time, the day shift or the night shift; work position, machinist 1 or machinist No. 2; or to facilitate control and autonomy, such as the plant safety and security department or the audit department of a bank. There are other types of organization patterns, such as the matrix organization, and project organization, which meet the needs of certain specialized situations. Because a full understanding of their functioning is dependent on some additional background they are discussed in Chapter 12, Contingency Approaches to Organizations.

RESPONSIBILITY, ACCOUNTABILITY, AND AUTHORITY

The process of organizing must be accomplished in order to assign the appropriate responsibility, accountability, and authority to the people in the organization.

FIGURE 5-10

Geographical Organization Design

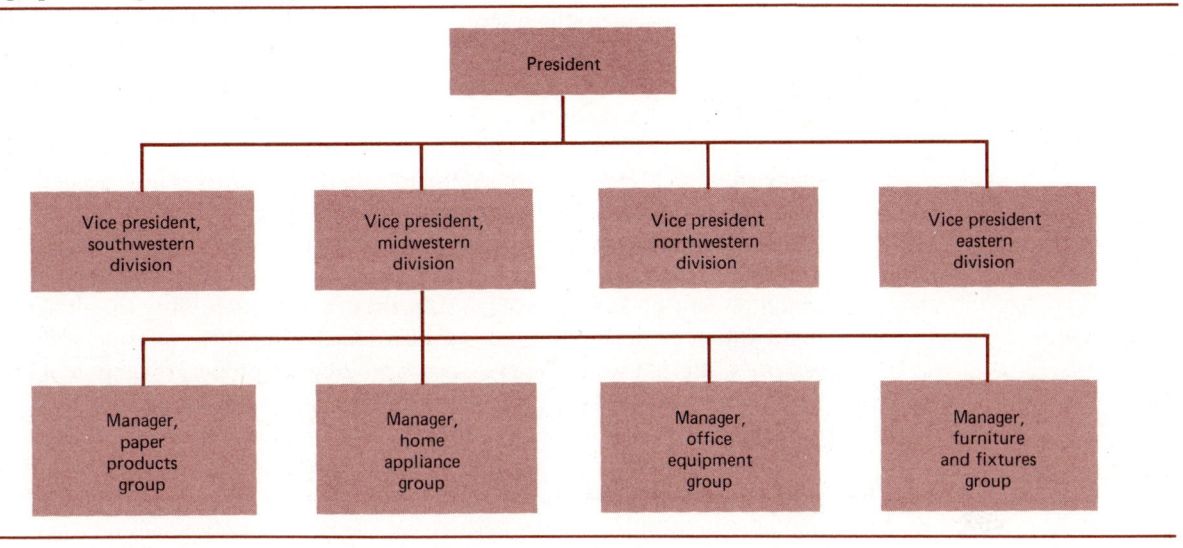

```
                              President
                                 │
        ┌────────────────┬───────┴────────┬────────────────┐
  Vice president,   Vice president,   Vice president   Vice president
  southwestern      midwestern        northwestern     eastern
  division          division          division         division
                        │
        ┌───────────────┼────────────────┬────────────────┐
    Manager,         Manager,         Manager,         Manager,
    paper            home             office           furniture
    products         appliance        equipment        and fixtures
    group            group            group            group
```

Source: Herbert C. Hicks and C. Ray Gullett, *Organizations: Theory and Behavior,* New York, McGraw-Hill Book Co., 1975 p. 77.

Responsibility is the obligation to perform a series of tasks that have been assigned. It flows downward.

Responsibility is the obligation to secure desired results—an obligation that people assume when they accept any task or combination of tasks that constitute a job. Responsibility is usually specified when a group of clearly defined duties is assigned to a person.

But responsibility has two phases. The first is the *obligation to perform to the best of one's ability those tasks that are accepted as an assignment.* The second phase is the *obligation to account to a higher authority for the degree of success achieved in the completion of those assignments.* The person to whom a series of tasks is assigned must be made aware of these two phases. More is involved than the performance of those tasks: the worker is also going to be held accountable for the results achieved. Thus, *accountability* flows upward in an organization, while *responsibility* is assigned downward.

Responsibility and authority must be coequal if people are to be held accountable for results in a given area of activity.

If people are to be held accountable for the results they achieve in the performance of tasks, they must have the right to make decisions within the limits of assigned responsibility. The right of decision is a necessary adjunct to accepting responsibility. Without this right they cannot be held accountable for the performance of specific tasks. This implies then that a release of *authority* must accompany release of responsibility from one level of an organization to another. Formal authority is the power to issue valid instructions which others are expected to follow. Power and authority relationships will be discussed in more detail in Chapter 6. For present purposes it is sufficient to recognize that responsibility and authority in any organization must be coequal if the individual is to be held accountable. *Accountability for results cannot be expected to flow upward unless commensurate authority and responsibility have first flowed downward.* It should also be noted that when a manager delegates responsibility and grants authority to a subordinate the resulting eventual accountability to someone higher in the organization is shared.

In a case where the authority released is less than the scope of subordinate responsibility assigned, the responsibility will tend to shrink until it is within the limits of the delegated authority. If the authority is not sufficient to enable one to carry out a given responsibility, accountability can be expected only within the limits of the authority. If the reverse were true, that is, if the authority delegated had been greater than the responsibilities assigned, the tendency would be for the responsibilities to broaden to correspond with the authority. The right of decision making will always determine the extent of responsibility.

If the organization structure had to grow downward only along the three primary vertical chains of command, the flow of authority and responsibility would present no special problems. In that case, responsibility for all activities could always be definitely fixed, even with increasing differentiation of the basic activities. All that would be necessary would be the proper delegation of authority commensurate with these responsibilities, and with all persons then being accountable upward for results. It has been seen, however, that with increasing organization growth, it becomes necessary to relieve these primary lines of authority and responsibility of certain special duties. Thus, a horizontal delegation of responsibility and authority from the basic lines becomes necessary. The staff specialists must derive their authority and the assigned responsibility from the primary chains of command, but they cannot exercise authority along these lines. They can exercise authority only within their own organizational units. The only exception to this occurs when a staff unit is given functional authority.

THE STEPS IN ORGANIZING

On the basis of the preceding discussion of the process of organizing, the following steps summarize this process.

1. *Organization should be based on the objectives in view.* The first consideration when organizing to accomplish work is a clear statement of the objectives that the work should achieve. This is necessary in order that the work to be done may be properly defined. Sound organizational structure rests basically on a logical definition of necessary work.

2. *The work to be done should be separated into its component activities.* This second step involves the differentiation of the basic work activities into the component activities necessary for successful performance. It was seen that any organization performs the three basic activities—the creation of a utility, distribution, and financing of some good or service. Next these basic work activities must be differentiated downward. This splitting up of necessary functions should be progressive by levels, until they can be grouped into full-time jobs. At the same time, provision must also be made for special staff activities common to several line functions, which are split off horizontally. This centralization of staff specialties in secondary chains of command is done whenever it becomes necessary to relieve the line of some of its work activities.

ORGANIZATION THROUGH DEPARTMENTATION   **131**

3. *Build the organizational structure on work to be performed, people who must do the work, and environment.* Once all the necessary activities have been logically defined and broken down, it is possible to group the work to be done into work units, which constitute jobs that can be performed by people. The activities as defined in step 2 do not bear any necessary relationship to the people who must do the work. One can begin talking about assigning tasks to people only after the tasks themselves have been defined. This third step is concerned with building up practical work units that can be assigned to people.

Attention must also be paid to the basis used for grouping work. The managers should understand that their first consideration is whether the work is similar; and the second consideration is whether the work is complementary. That is, work groups should be involved in activities that are basically similar. But if the grouping of similar work does not result in full-time jobs, it then becomes necessary to group work that is complementary; that is, the work that precedes or follows must be included. With these two considerations in mind, the manager may use one or a combination of the following primary bases for organizing: physical location (geographic), product, customer, and other types of departmentation. These constitute the most generally useful bases for building work structure.

4. *Managers should thoroughly understand the responsibility-accountability-authority* relationship. The flow of authority and responsibility downward and of accountability upward should be definitely established and communicated to all people in the organization. All personnel in the organization must be made aware of their position and of their relationship to others in the structure. A clear-cut definition of this basic relationship to others is essential if cooperation and coordination of all activities are to result. Too often in organizations people are left in the dark as to their exact status. In many cases a lack of definition of authority and responsibility leads to friction in the carrying out of the organization's business. These difficulties can be avoided only if each individual understands his or her relative position.

These basic steps in organizing have been considered primarily in relation to the work of an entire organization. But it should be apparent that these steps are applicable to any part of an organization as well. Managers at every level must organize to accomplish their work. In doing so they must follow this basic process. While the nature of the basic work functions may change from one type of organization to another, the process remains the same.

> While the nature of various types of organizations may vary considerably, the process of organizing remains essentially the same.

One sound and basic principle appears most important when organizing. This is called the *principle of functionalization.* It says that *any organization should be built around the work to be performed, and not around individuals or groups of individuals.* This applies not only to the organization as a whole but also to any part of it. If this principle is not followed, then the permanence and stability of the organization become dependent solely on people; and it is a fact, although a seldom admitted one, that people do not last forever. Moreover, you cannot upgrade people successfully if you have to train them in the image of their predecessors. No two persons are identical in skills and abilities. But if the work has been properly and clearly defined, then people with adequate capabilities will be found and trained to do that work satisfactorily. It is apparent that the rational allocation of work is the basis for organizing.

LIMITATIONS TO THE STRUCTURAL STUDY OF ORGANIZATIONS

In this chapter, we have looked at formal organizations, primarily from a *structural* viewpoint. Our tools of analysis were organizational principles and the formal organization chart. Although we will continue to use the chart to examine organizations, our next chapters begin to examine the more subtle interactive relationships in organizations. The following limitations to organization charts will serve as a prelude to the new concepts to come.

Although the organization chart is a valuable tool it has limitations.

WHAT THE CHART DOES NOT SHOW[13]

The first thing the chart does not show is the *degree of authority and responsibility* of the various people. It is true that the chart does depict superior-subordinate relationships and the attendant process of delegation of authority and influence between two people who appear on the same plan of the chart. For example, a given chart may show the manufacturing manager and the personnel manager both reporting to the president; this would imply that both (with respect to their functional areas) have equal authority and influence within the organization. In actual practice the personnel manager may have only very minimal influence. She may only rarely be consulted for decision-making purposes, may not be given much insight concerning day-to-day operations, and her responsibilities may be limited to the paperwork aspects of employee relations. Taken a step further, it may be that there are people at the second level of management in the production phase of the operation who have more influence and authority than the personnel manager. These phenomena are, of course, not apparent from viewing the chart.

Because two people appear on the same level of the chart does not mean they necessarily have the same degree of influence.

Suppose that suddenly the firm is faced with a concentrated unionization drive. The firm would probably turn to the personnel manager for help, and her stature in the organization would be substantially enhanced as her role takes on increased significance. If the union is defeated in its attempt at organizing the work force, the personnel manager's newfound stature may be permanent. This is because of the respect she has gained due to her successful efforts. Even if the union succeeds, her role in day-to-day operations may take on increased significance because of the need to negotiate a labor contract, train production supervisors in dealing with union stewards, administer the contract on a day-to-day basis, settle grievances, and the many facets of operating with a union. The preceding example thus illustrates that the organization chart does not show the degree of authority, responsibility, and influence of people within the organization.

---

[13]Stieglitz, ibid.

ORGANIZATION THROUGH DEPARTMENTATION   133

The organization chart does not show the type of authority staff may possess in a given situation.

A second thing that the organization chart does not show is the true *distinction between line and staff*. Though both are authority relationships, staff authority may range all the way from advisory and counseling to functional. Chapter 6, The Organization in Operation, fully explores staff authority. Since the organization chart does not typically indicate what type of authority the staff has in various areas, the viewer is left in the dark as to how the organization really operates.

Third, the chart does not show all the *lines of communication*. It does indicate a few of the major channels of contact, but if the organization uses only these, nothing will get done. In an organization, no one unit or individual operates in isolation from all the others. All are linked by an intricate network of communication. Proper organization performance relies *both* on this network and on each unit and individual within it. To chart the total communication network is impossible.

If all communication were to follow the formal lines suggested by the organization chart very little would get done.

Finally, the chart of the formal organization structure does not show the *informal organization*. The latter encompasses all of the informal relationships, communication channels, and influences or power centers that develop over time as people interact with one another. The informal organization is an extension of the formal and arises to facilitate the accomplishment of the task. According to some, the informal organization gets work done in spite of the formal structure. The manager who knows the informal structure and how to use it has a distinct advantage because many times he can cut through the red tape and get much faster results.

VALUE OF THE CHART

The essential value of the chart seems to lie in the fact that it does strip the organization down to its skeletal framework. In so doing, the chart serves the useful purposes of being both a tool of organizational analysis and a means of communication. But as a complete picture of the organization, it is recognized as being inadequate.

SUMMARY

In the process of organization, three elements must be given consideration: the work to be done, the people who are to do the work, and the work site and communication linkages. Since the purpose of organizing is to accomplish some objective, work must receive the primary emphasis, but at the same time, a balance among all three must be struck.

In addition to the elements of organizing, there are three basic functions that an organization must perform to continue in existence. It must create a utility (production), there must be a means of distribution (marketing), and it must be financed (finance). These are known as line functions because they are keys to continued survival. As an organization grows and develops, these line functions expand downward (vertically), forming a scalar chain of command from top to

134 CLASSICAL MANAGEMENT CONCEPTS

SUMMARY CHART

I. Elements and Functions of Organization

   A. Elements
      1. Work
      2. People
      3. Work Place
      4. Communication linkages

   B. Functions
      1. Create a utility
      2. Distribution
      3. Finance

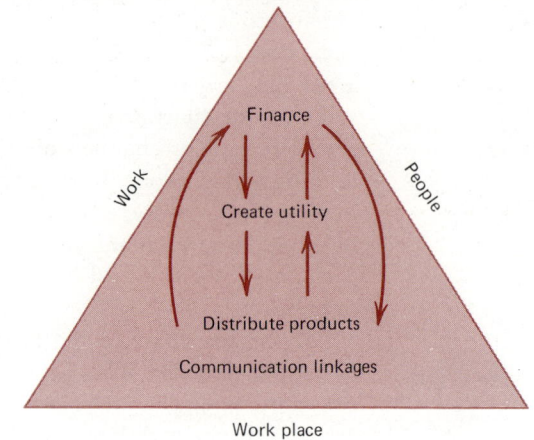

II. Line Functions—Vertical Growth

   A. Development of Scalar Chain of Command

   B. Departmentation
      1. Function
      2. Product
      3. Geographic
      4. Customer

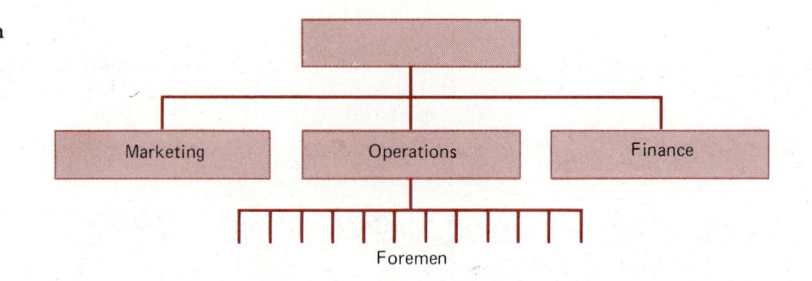

III. Staff—Horizontal Growth

   A. Personal Staff
      1. "Assistant to"
      2. General staff

   B. Specialist Staff
      1. Advisory
      2. Service
      3. Control
      4. Functional

IV. Responsibility—Accountability—Authority

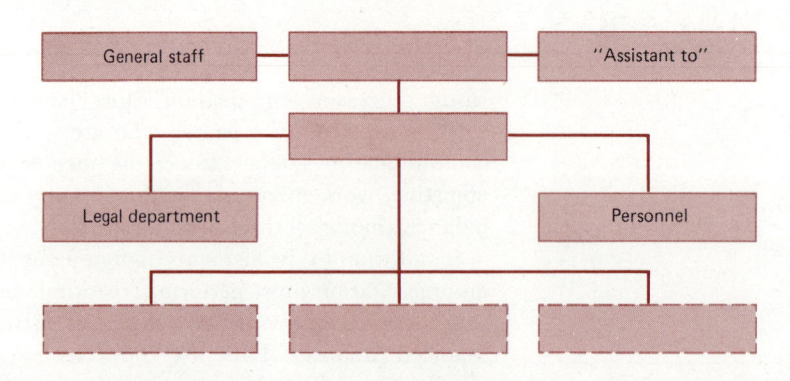

bottom. This scalar chain of command or hierarchy of formal relationships specifies the line of authority and responsibility as well as the lines of communications and decision making. As long as expansion occurs only in terms of these three basic functions, it is a line organization structure.

As the organization continues to grow, it eventually becomes necessary to introduce into it people who have other areas of specialty such as personnel management or production control. These specialists are necessary for many reasons, two of which are to relieve line managers of detail and to introduce expertise. As specialists in various areas are added, the structure begins to experience horizontal organization growth; and the resultant structure is one of line and staff.

Staff authority may range all the way from being advisory in nature to the functional staff that has limited direct authority over some phase of another manager's operation. Other types of staff include the service staff, control staff, assistant to, and general staff.

The most common pattern of organization is to divide the work on a functional basis but one often finds organization based on other considerations such as product, customer, or by geographical location.

The responsibility of organization results in the distribution of responsibility, accountability, and authority among the people in the organization. Responsibility is usually specified by a group of clearly defined duties that the person is expected to accomplish. Accountability is the obligation on the part of the person to account to a higher authority for the degree of success achieved in performing the assigned task. Therefore, accountability flows upward.

Authority is the right to issue valid instructions that others must follow. Every release of responsibility must be accompanied by a release of enough authority to make decisions within the limits of the assigned responsibility. In other words, if accountability is expected, authority and responsibility must be equal.

Since organizations are usually represented by an organization chart it is also important to note what the chart does and does not show. The typical chart will show the viewer how the work is divided into components, how the components are grouped, and levels of management in terms of successive layers. It will not show the degree of authority and responsibility of various people, types of staff authority, the status or importance of various individuals, lines of communication, quality of interpersonal relationships, or the informal organization.

DISCUSSION QUESTIONS

1. What are some of the important issues which organizers must deal with? Briefly discuss the elements of organization and the basic functions of any organization.
2. Discuss vertical organization growth. Be sure to cover the following areas.
   (a) To what does it refer?
   (b) Fully present all aspects of the scalar chain concept.

(c) What are some of the advantages and disadvantages of a strictly line organization?

3. What do we mean by horizontal organization growth? Why does it occur? What are some of the reasons for introducing staff into the organization structure?

4. Be able to identify the two major categories of staff authority and the subcategories within each. Demonstrate your understanding of each type of staff authority by explaining it and giving an example.

5. What are some disadvantages of the functional approach to organization? Discuss two other bases on which departmentation may be based.

6. We usually get our picture of the organization from the organization chart. Discuss what the chart does and does not show.

7. Discuss the relationship between the concepts of responsibility, accountability, and authority.

APPLICATION EXERCISES AND CASES

FORMING A NEW COMPANY[14]

Bob Smith and Elton Jones had been friends for many years. One day, as they were fishing, Bob said, "Say, Elton, why don't we set up an organization to manufacture that special fishing lure you designed? It catches more fish than anything else we've ever used."

"That sounds like a good idea, Bob, but we would have to get some help. I don't know anything about accounting or selling. I just know how to make things."

"Yeah," said Bob, "and all I can do is engineering. But I still think we ought to look into it."

Questions

1. In what ways would an organization enlarge the abilities of Bob and Elton?
2. Would the organization be a formal or informal one? Explain.
3. In their conversation how did Bob and Elton recognize the principle of specialization? In addition to accounting and selling what other talents do you think they need to bring into the organization?
4. Assume the company Bob and Elton formed grew in the following stages:
   (a) Sales of $20,000 employing 6 people.
   (b) Sales of $50,000 employing 20 people.
   (c) A company with 500 employees and seven major product lines.

---

[14]Herbert G. Hicks, *The Management of Organizations: A Systems and Human Resources Approach*, 2nd ed., New York, McGraw-Hill Book Co., 1972, p.19.

For each of the three cases draw an organization chart and explain how it would function. Be sure to bring into your discussion the role of staff in the organization structure.

DOUGLAS FOWLER'S DILEMMA[15]

Douglas Fowler, sales manager of the Denver region, considered the performance of Robert Allen, one of his salesmen, to be unsatisfactory. On five separate occasions Mr. Fowler had talked with Mr. Allen about his problems, suggesting ways that Mr. Allen might improve his sales. During the last conference Mr. Fowler said, "Bob, I'm going to have to let you go if your sales are not up to quota this month."

Mr. Allen failed to meet his quota, and Mr. Fowler wrote him a letter informing him of his dismissal. Three days later Mr. Fowler received a call from Mr. Jones, general sales manager, "Doug, I want you to put Bob Allen back on the payroll immediately. You know he's the old man's nephew."

"O.K.," sighed Mr. Fowler, "I'll see that it's done."

Questions
1. What are the authority-responsibility-accountability problems in this case?
2. What effect will this situation have on the organization?

---
[15] Ibid., p. 276.

CHAPTER 6
THE ORGANIZATION IN OPERATION— SOME CRITICAL ISSUES

MANAGERIAL DELEGATION IN PERSPECTIVE
A POSITIVE MANAGEMENT PHILOSOPHY— KEY TO EFFECTIVE DELEGATION
ADVANTAGES OF DELEGATION
AUTHORITY AND POWER
ALTERNATIVE VIEWS OF AUTHORITY
POWER VERSUS AUTHORITY
BASES OF POWER
FLOW OF AUTHORITY
THE EFFECTIVE USE OF POWER AND AUTHORITY
THE TRUE MEANING OF MANAGERIAL DELEGATION
ASSIGNING RESPONSIBILITY
GRANTING AUTHORITY
CREATING ACCOUNTABILITY
WHAT DELEGATION IS NOT
SPAN OF CONTROL
REASONS FOR A WIDE SPAN OF CONTROL
EFFECT OF SPAN OF CONTROL ON COMMUNICATIONS AND DECISION MAKING
FACTORS AFFECTING THE SIZE OF SPAN OF CONTROL
HOW LARGE SHOULD THE SPAN OF CONTROL BE?
REVIEW OF ORGANIZATION STRUCTURE
APPLICATION EXERCISES AND CASES
IMPORTANCE OF MANAGEMENT PHILOSOPHY
CENTRAL HIGH SCHOOL

DELEGATING FOR MAXIMUM RESULTS

On the theory that the real management experts are top managers themselves, Fortune asked the chief executives of the Fortune 500 companies to name the best CEO on the list. The first choice of the 164 who responded was Reginald Jones, 63, chief executive of General Electric from 1972 until he retired on April 1, 1981. John Swearingen, 62, of Standard Oil of Indiana took second place and Henry Singleton, 64, of Teledyne and Charles Knight, 45, of Emerson Electric tied for third.

Speaking out on matters of concern to business is practically the only job Jones doesn't delegate. He has insisted that the actual running of GE be shared with people down the line who head GE's forty-three autonomous "strategic business units"—a term GE coined. "The leader of a company has to develop entrepreneurial spirit through the organization," Jones says. Developing that spirit at GE means giving young managers freedom to operate within a few policy guidelines.

John Swearingen, who has been chief executive at Indiana Standard since 1960, also loves to delegate authority, right down to the geologist in the field. "It's important for people to be able to spend a certain amount of money on their own, and be answerable for it after the fact," he says.

Teledyne's founder, Henry Singleton, says that early on he gave his division heads autonomy out of necessity: he didn't know much about how they ran their businesses. People would ask me if I got the jitters because I didn't know what the units were doing," Singleton recalls. "I always figured I'd get more jitters if I did know."[1]

---

[1] Ann M. Morrison, "C.E.O.s—Pick the Best C.E.O.s," *Fortune*, May 4, 1981, pp. 133–134.

Having developed a formal organization structure designed to achieve our objectives, it now becomes necessary to provide for the effective functioning of that organization. In this chapter we begin, in a preliminary way, to consider the integration of people into the structure we have established. Specifically, attention is focused on these areas that are critical to the successful operation of the enterprise. In the order examined they include managerial delegation, concepts of authority, and span of control. Chapter 7, Organizational Dynamics, and Parts Three and Four build on the concepts presented here.

MANAGERIAL DELEGATION IN PERSPECTIVE

It was 5:30 Friday afternoon and Vic Mack, manager of engineering, had just finished packing his briefcase in preparation to go home. As he was about to leave the office, Sharon Lanson, the personnel manager, popped her head in the door to wish Vic a pleasant weekend. Somewhat sarcastically, Vic replied, "With all the work I have to do, I'll be lucky if I get a chance to sleep." As the conversation

Although delegation is one of the most talked techniques of effective management it is one of the least practiced.

continued, Vic complained that there just didn't seem to be enough hours in the day to get everything done. He talked about the constant pressure of the job, how hard it was to find good people, and how no one seemed to want to assume any responsibility. When Sharon subtly suggested that maybe some of Vic's problems could be solved by adequate delegation, he countered with comments like, "Subordinates lack experience. It takes more time to explain than to do the job myself, and experimentation and mistakes can be too costly. I can get quicker action myself; most of my people are specialists and don't have the overall knowledge many decisions require." He repeated the thought that most people are not willing to accept responsibility anyway.

Historically, delegation has been labeled as potentially one of the most effective techniques of management. Writers have referred to delegation as a key factor that will cause people to become excited about work, grow in their jobs, assume more responsibility, and manage their assignments more skillfully. Delegation makes it possible to achieve maximum results through people. Yet the problems faced by Vic Mack and his comments about delegation and people in general are not unusual. That old saying, "Easier said than done," about many management techniques, certainly applies to delegation.

A POSITIVE MANAGEMENT PHILOSOPHY— KEY TO EFFECTIVE DELEGATION

Delegation begins with the manager's philosophy about people and how they react to work.

Effective delegation begins with the manager's philosophy about people and their reaction to work. If managers have a negative philosophy about people and their willingness to assume responsibility, they are less likely to practice true managerial delegation. Their management style will tend instead to reflect all of the following factors.

1. Very close control over people and the work they do.
2. Overinvolvement in day-to-day details.
3. One-person decision making.
4. Reliance on authority, power, pressure, and discipline to get results through people.

On the other hand, the manager whose general philosophy about people is positive will tend to adopt an approach to management that achieves the following.

1. Creates a climate where people are mentally and emotionally, rather than just physically, involved in their jobs.
2. Gains the commitment of people by involving them in decision making and planning.
3. Concentrates managerial efforts on overall goals and objectives and how to achieve them, rather than on performing all the day-to-day details.
4. Helps other people achieve results through effective communication with them.

Thus, a positive philosophy toward people and their reaction to work serves as a springboard for a positive approach to management, of which delegation is such an important part. Managers who are willing to remain open-minded are much more willing to use delegation as a way of motivating people, of making sure they grow and develop on the job, and of utilizing people to their maximum potential.

At this point it should be noted that delegation is undoubtedly given more lip service than actual use. There are two aspects to this phenomenon. First, most managers will quite readily endorse delegation as one of the most important leadership techniques available, and yet not actually put it into practice. Second, managers have a tendency to overestimate the amount of delegation they use when compared to their subordinates' perceptions of that use.[2]

The following discussion of four important reasons for delegating is designed to create an understanding of and appreciation for the importance of this dimension of managing people.

ADVANTAGES OF DELEGATION

CONTRIBUTES TO SUBORDINATES' GROWTH AND DEVELOPMENT

Two often-quoted and widely agreed on statements are that "people learn by doing" and "experience is the best teacher." Delegation is a key factor in making these statements operating principles rather than just cliches. This increased responsibility may take the form of adding more tasks, upgrading the work in terms of degree of difficulty, giving increased authority, requiring greater accountability, or allowing independent decision making. Clearly, the manager must share responsibility with the people under him if they are to grow in ability.

The important relationship between delegation and subordinate growth and development was brought out in a study conducted several years ago by Professor Norman Allhiser. When a group of over 1000 managers was questioned as to what they considered the most effective approach to develop subordinates, 8 out of 10 managers felt delegation was a prime developer of men.

There is a close relationship between the practice of managerial delegation and the growth and development of subordinates.

The managers were convinced of the importance of providing opportunities to learn by doing on the job. To accentuate the benefits of this principle, work must be deliberately designed to provide more and better opportunities to learn by doing as the individual grows on the job.

Deliberate planning effort should be made to feed the subordinate increased responsibility as rapidly as he is able to assimilate the assigned duties and tasks. The challenge to the manager is to consciously plan new learning and encourage additional stretching. Considerable thinking must be exercised in determining the following factors:

---

[2]Roger M. Atherton and Burt K. Scanlan, "Actual vs. Preferred Leadership Practices," *Atlanta Economic Review*, March–April 1977, pp. 46–50.

1. What opportunities exist for learning by doing?
2. Which responsibilities should be shared?
3. How should the increased responsibility be implemented?
4. With whom? Which subordinate?
5. When would such added responsibility be appropriate?

> *Depending upon the organization requirements and individual situations with the scope of the job, the manager must deliberately seek to provide more opportunities for planning, organizing, leading, coordinating, and controlling on a graduated basis for all subordinates with demonstrated potential.*[3]

MAXIMUM UTILIZATION OF SUBORDINATES' SKILLS AND ABILITIES

A second advantage of delegation is that it insures the maximum utilization of the skills and abilities of subordinates. In addition to not fully utilizing employee skills and abilities, the manager who never delegates or delegates only to a small degree, never discovers the true capabilities of those people when they are challenged. Not only does delegation enable us to make maximum use of employee skills and abilities, but it is also the only way we have to initially determine the extent of those qualities.

Without delegation we fail to fully utilize the skills and abilities people have.

Organizations today are concerned about finding people who are qualified to do the increasingly complex work that must be done. Investigations have revealed that in many cases there is a considerable amount of talent that is not being used. In the Allhiser study, the managers were asked to characterize their most ineffective boss; that is, the one who contributed the least to their growth and development. Such comments as, "He made all the decisions," "He controlled and watched over all details of the work," "He restricted responsibility to only minor matters or performing physical tasks," "He checked everything," were frequent. All such remarks in one way or another reflect a failure either to delegate or to delegate properly.

DELEGATION AND MOTIVATION

Over the past few years, organizations have become increasingly aware of the impact that nonfinancial incentives can have on motivation. More specifically, we have learned that if people are to be motivated beyond a neutral point there must be a leadership climate that gets people mentally and emotionally involved in their jobs. Although many leadership techniques go into creating this type of total job climate, delegation is without question one of the most strategic. The manager who delegates work and responsibility is building a climate which contains challenging and rewarding job opportunities. She is, in essence, offering incentives for work by providing employees with a opportunity for full and

The relationship between delegation and motivation is a close one.

---

[3] Norman C. Allhiser, "Development of Subordinates in Purchasing Management," *Journal of Purchasing*, May 1966, p. 1.

meaningful involvement in their work. This usually creates employee commitment and a sincere desire to achieve.

FREEDOM OF THE MANAGER TO MANAGE

When a person moves into a position of supervising the work of others, his job changes. His prime responsibility is to "get things done through people." This means that he must define jobs in terms of results to be achieved, work with people in determining how to obtain the best results, help people identify and overcome problems that hinder accomplishment, counsel, coach, give assistance as needed, and, finally, give people that opportunity to perform the job. There is a limit to what one person alone can accomplish, yet without delegation, the entire operation is limited to that extent. Thus, delegation is one of the main tools that managers can use to enable them to spend their time managing rather than doing.

AUTHORITY AND POWER

ALTERNATIVE VIEWS OF AUTHORITY

Delegation means entrusting part of the work of operations or management to others. When managers delegate, they normally assign operating duties, grant authority, and create an obligation simultaneously.[4] Usually delegation of authority occurs jointly with the process of departmentation. In Chapter 5 when our hypothetical owner organized a production department (Figure 5-3), he automatically delegated to someone else the authority to supervise the operators. This raises two questions: "Of what does authority consist?" "What is the nature of delegated authority?"

Delegation involves assign responsibility, granting authority and creating accountability.

Various writers have viewed authority in very different ways. Alvin Brown, former president of Johns-Manville Company, held the view that authority is *power to command*. "In this sense . . . authority is the exact reciprocal of responsibility. It cannot be less in extent since responsibility without authority would be empty duty."[5]

While agreeing with the necessity for some bond of reciprocity between authority and responsibility, Chester I. Barnard, former president of New Jersey Bell Telephone Company, did not see authority as being so absolute.

> *Authority is the character of a communication (order) in a formal organization by virtue of which it is accepted by a contributor to or "member" of the organization as governing the action he contributes . . . Therefore under this definition the decision as to*

---

[4]William H. Newman, Charles E. Summer, and E. Kirby Warren, *The Process of Management*, Englewood Cliffs, N.J., Prentice-Hall Book, 1972.
[5]Alvin Brown, *Organization of Industry*, Englewood Cliffs, N.J., Prentice-Hall, 1947, p. 61.

144 CLASSICAL MANAGEMENT CONCEPTS

whether an order has authority or not lies with the persons to whom it is addressed, and does not reside in "persons of authority" or those who issue orders.[6]

Barnard formulated an acceptance theory of authority.

From this definition, Barnard has acquired the title of the father of the "acceptance theory of authority." Later in his book, he softened his statements with a number of important qualifications. Nevertheless, he was one of the first to point out the ultimate ability of a subordinate to refuse an order—albeit with extreme penalties at times.

Mary Parker Follett takes an even more idealistic view of authority in what she calls "the law of the situation," as follows.

Mary Parker Follett proposed a "law of situation" concept of authority.

The head of the sales department does not give orders to the head of the production department, or vice versa. Each studies the market and the final decision is made as the market demands. This is, ideally, what should take place between foreman and rank and file, between any head and his subordinates. One person should not give orders to another person, but both should agree to take their orders from the situation.[7]

These views on authority might be placed along a continuum and illustrated as in Figure 6-1.

Examining views which have been held by prominent writers and practitioners should help to emphasize the complexity of the delegation process.

POWER VERSUS AUTHORITY

Our discussion in Chapter 5 on departmentation indicated that organizations rely on some type of hierarchy of authority in order to accomplish work and achieve their objectives. The assumption is that when individuals join an organization, they agree to accept and abide by the authority structure of that organization. Within certain limits, they subordinate their own right of decision and action by agreeing to follow the decisions and directions of superiors.

There is a very distinct difference between power and authority. Power implies

FIGURE 6-1

Views on Authority

Power to command	Law of situation	Acceptance
Alvin Brown	Mary Parker Follett	Chester I. Barnard

Authoritarian ←――――――――――――→ Democratic

---

[6]Chester I. Barnard, *The Functions of the Executive*, Cambridge, Mass., Harvard University Press, 1962, p. 163.
[7]Henry C. Metcalf and L. Urwich, *Dynamic Administration—The Collected Papers of Mary Parker Follett*, New York, Harper and Brothers Publishers, 1940, p. 59.

that either the organization or the individual has the ability to coerce someone into doing something she does not want to do. This is illustrated most dramatically in a situation where one person can coerce another because of an advantage in sheer physical strength. In an organization, the exercise of power can be attempted by manipulating rewards or applying sanctions against people. The important point is that an organization cannot function at a maximum level of efficiency by relying on pure power alone. At best, it will result in antagonistic cooperation and minimum levels of performance. More likely results will be subtle sabotage, or open rebellion, or exodus on the part of those people who cannot be coerced.

Thus authority can be defined as *legitimate power*.[8] When defined in this way, the authority to which we are referring is formal authority. It is formal because the organization has conferred it on the individual by virtue of his occupying a particular position in the hierarchial structure. Presumably, whoever occupied that same position would automatically be accorded the same degree of authority. Thus, formal authority attaches to a position rather than to an individual. Justin G. Longenecker has emphasized the nature of this type of authority by calling it institutionalized power.[9]

> Formal authority is conferred by the organization to a position.

In contrast to power, authority implies a degree of consent on the part of the persons being governed. In a sense, the subordinates grant to their superior the right to make decisions that affect them (recall Barnard's acceptance theory). The process of people consenting to be governed, or being positively influenced by decisions made by others which affect them or their behavior, is referred to as *legitimacy*. Power becomes legitimate only when those who are affected by it consent to it.

> The process of people consenting to be governed by the decisions of others that affect their behavior is known as legitimacy.

In our present society, the use of pure power to accomplish results is limited in its effectiveness because most people are not completely dependent on one job, with one organization, in one department of that organization for their livelihood. They have employment alternatives available and will exercise these alternatives if necessary. To the degree that some do not have alternate sources of employment available, or do not choose to exercise them, the result of reliance on pure authority is minimal acceptable cooperation and performance.

Douglas McGregor graphs such a situation, as shown in Figure 6-2.

The more dependent the individual is, the more effective formal authority of power can be in getting the job done (this assumes, of course, that the holder of power can apply sanctions). As people become more independent, the effectiveness of sheer power goes downhill quite rapidly. According to McGregor, most people are only partially dependent on their job situations. Therefore, normal authority is usually only partially effective.

---

[8] Herbert G. Hicks and C. Ray Gullett, *Organizations: Theory and Behavior*, New York, McGraw-Hill Book Co., 1975, p. 230.
[9] Justin G. Longenecker, *Principles of Management and Organizational Behavior*, Columbus, Ohio, Charles E. Merrill Publishing Co., 1969, p. 397.

FIGURE 6-2

Effectiveness of Authoroity

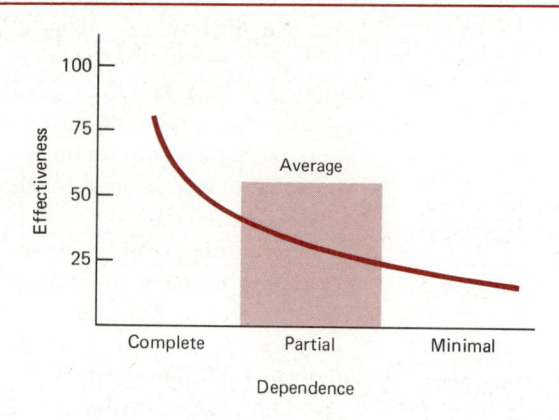

BASES OF POWER

The concepts of power, acceptance, and legitimate authority based on consent can be summarized and clarified by reviewing five bases of power as listed by French and Raven.[10]

1. Coercive power is based on the superior's ability to apply sanctions, either in the form of direct punishment, such as temporary suspension, or discharge.
2. Reward power is based on the superior's ability to grant or withhold rewards, such as a promotion or wage increase.
3. Legitimate power refers to the power a person has because of his or her position in the organization. The further up one is in the hierarchy, the more legitimate power they have.
4. Expert power is that which accrues to an individual because of certain special knowledge or skill they possess. People will follow their lead because they have confidence in the fact the "expert" knows what he or she is doing or saying.
5. Referent power is based on the follower's admiration of and identification with the leader. As noted earlier, the leader has a certain charisma that attracts people and causes them to be willing to follow.

The first three bases relate to organizational factors or position power, while the last two relate to personal factors or personal power. A logical question to ask is, which is best for a leader to have — position or personal power? The answer is obviously both, but that is not always possible. If given a choice between the two, most people would pick personal power because it seems to have a better ring to it.

The various basis for power may relate to organizational factors or personal factors.

---

[10]John R. P. French and Bertram Raven, "The Bases of Social Power" in Dorwin Cartwright and A. F. Zander, (eds.), *Group Dynamics*, 2nd ed., Row Peterson and Co., 1960, pp. 607–623.

THE ORGANIZATION IN OPERATION—SOME CRITICAL ISSUES 147

From a practical standpoint, however, it is important to note that personal power is more volatile and subject to change. It can be withdrawn very quickly. Position power is more stable, because the employees must be willing to take certain not-always-known chances if they choose to go against it. A manager must sometimes be willing to forgo short-term popularity by using position power in order to insure longer term results as well as subordinates' growth and development.

THE FLOW OF AUTHORITY

Barnard proposed that in actuality authority flowed from the bottom to the top of the organization.

Chester I. Barnard was quoted earlier as being an advocate of the acceptance theory of authority, the belief that authority flowed from the bottom to the top of the organization rather than from the top down. Figure 6-3 contrasts these two possibilities.

In spite of his view that authority flows upward in organizations, Barnard still believed that significant abiding cooperation could be maintained between

FIGURE 6-3

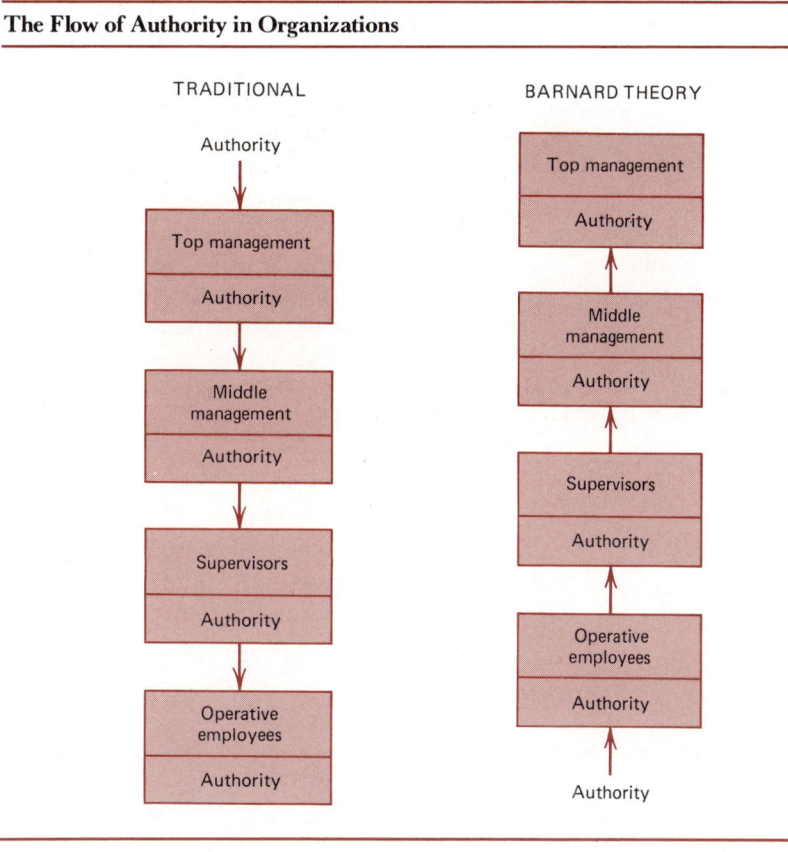

The Flow of Authority in Organizations

TRADITIONAL

Authority → Top management → Authority → Middle management → Authority → Supervisors → Authority → Operative employees → Authority

BARNARD THEORY

Top management ← Authority ← Middle management ← Authority ← Supervisors ← Authority ← Operative employees ← Authority ← Authority

superiors and subordinates. This seemed true to him for the following three reasons.[11]

1. Most of the time superiors deliberately issue orders that comply with subordinate expectations–that is, they (a) are understood, (b) are consistent with organizational goals, (c) are consistent with employee goals, and (d) are capable of being complied with physically and mentally.
2. There exists for each employee a "zone of indifference" within which she accepts orders without question.
3. Fellow employees bring pressure on others to comply with legitimate authority.

One writer, in reviewing the thoughts of Barnard, has concluded that his theory brought significant changes to management's beliefs about the flow of authority.[12] Where once management theorists and practitioners looked at authority relationships as rather simply determined, they are now viewed as complex relationships. More attention is given to the human relations area and its effect on authority. Superiors have begun to realize that their own actions may increase or decrease their authority, power, and influence over subordinates.

Many have begun to label downward flow as *authority* and the upward flow as *influence*, which is determined by the personal skills of the manager.

THE EFFECTIVE USE OF POWER AND AUTHORITY

Managers are dependent on others in the organization to accomplish job related objectives.

The fact that managers are dependent on superiors, peers, and subordinates to accomplish job related objectives is a reality of managerial life. These are the vulnerable areas of the job, areas where lack of cooperation from others can negate achievement. Managerial dependencies, whether they be in the form of the need for interdepartmental cooperation, information that others have that the manager does not possess, or numerous other forms of needed support, result in a situation where managers must be able to positively influence those on whom they are dependent. Dependencies tend to increase at higher levels in the organization hierarchy and also with the number of people who report directly or indirectly to the manager. Dependencies also vary considerably as a function of organization size, environment, goals, technology, formal structure, and the reward system.[13] The greater the number and extent of dependencies, the more managerial time and energy that must be put into authority and power oriented behavior that facilitates rather than hinders the accomplishment of objectives. As a result, effective managers, even when they must use less participative and

---

[11] Barnard, ibid., pp. 167–169.
[12] James A. Gazell, "Authority-Flow Theory and the Impact of Chester Barnard," *California Management Review*, 1970, Vol. XII, No. 1, pp. 73–74.
[13] John P. Kotter, "Power, Success, and Organizational Effectiveness," *Organizational Dynamics*, Winter 1978, pp. 26–40.

more authoritative approaches, typically avoid being coercive, arbitrary, and self-serving because of the short- and long-range negative impact of these actions.

The issue at hand is not whether the use of power and authority is necessary to perform the managerial job but rather how it is used or, more specifically, using it in a way that will have overall favorable effects. The successful use of power and authority requires (1) sensitivity to what people perceive as legitimate behavior in acquiring and using power, (2) a good understanding of the various types of power and authority and methods of influencing others, (3) the development of skill in using various types of power and authority, (4) the use of influencing methods that are in tune with the situation, (5) tempering the use of power with maturity and self-control, and (6) the recognition that the use of power and authority is legitimate and necessary.

POWER, AUTHORITY, AND PARTICIPATION

In Chapter 4, Managerial Problem Analysis and Decision Making, the concept of participation in decision making was introduced. The key to the successful use of both power and participation is knowing when and how to use them effectively. It may well be that the opposite of participation is nonparticipation, varying with the manager's assessment of the situation and willingness to share decision making with subordinates. Similarly, the opposite of the use of personal power may be using authority in such a way that it gains the acceptance of those being managed and consequently their motivation and commitment. A manager who uses authority effectively will show a concern for group goals, finding goals that will move people because they can relate to them, helping the group formulate goals as opposed to dictating them, and giving people a feeling of confidence and strength that they can accomplish the goals. This is what David McClelland has termed socialized power.[14]

Figure 6-4 portrays a scale ranging from boss-centered, nonparticipation, and nonshared decision making on the left to employee-centered, participation, and shared decision making on the right. At each end and in the center of the scale are listed various approaches to using authority which the manager might take. As we move from left to right on the scale, higher degrees of participation are involved because there is (1) more two-way communication, (2) more information passed back and forth, (3) more opportunity for subordinates to have an influence, (4) a less aggressive posture taken by the manager, and (5) a higher degree of recognition of the potential for people to make positive and meaningful contributions.

The "soft" approaches on the right end of the scale will usually yield more favorable long-term results for two reasons. First, they contribute to the process of authority by gaining the consent of the people subject to it. Second, for the reasons cited above they serve to unleash the potential of people to make positive

---

[14]David C. McClelland, "The Two Faces of Power," *Journal of International Affairs*, 1970, Vol. 24, No. 1, pp. 29–47.

Power and authority must be used in a way that promotes rather than hinders cooperation from people.

A manager who uses authority effectively will show a concern for group goals, and finding goals with which people can identify.

As a generalization, the soft approaches contribute to the process of authority being legitimatized.

FIGURE 6-4

Alternative Uses of Authority[15]

Boss-Centered *Nonparticipative* *Nonshared decision*	*Employee-Centered* *Participative* *Shared decision*
1. Coercive—threat of punishment.	1. Personal disclosure-admitting need for help to gain support.
2. Reward—promise of rewards.	2. Finding common ground—discovering areas of agreement so cooperation will be forthcoming.
3. Formal—that which is conferred by the organization and attached to a position-tion.	3. Recognizing others by listening and understanding their position and needs.
	4. Cooperative problem solving—working together to solve problem for mutual benefit.
Hard Approaches	Soft Approaches

contributions. Since these are more likely to result in mental and emotional involvement, both motivation and commitment is heightened.

At different times and in different circumstances it is necessary to use alternative approaches to authority in order to accomplish the objectives at hand. As a generalization, the "hard" approaches that appear on the left of Figure 6-4 may be effective in the short run, but in the long run achieve less than a full measure of success. The earlier discussion concerning the effectiveness of purely formal authority helps explain why this is true.

A very important word of caution is in order. We do not mean to imply that the hard approaches are "off limits" and should be avoided. This is far from the case. Situations will arise where they are not only a feasible alternative, but in fact may be the most appropriate course of action available. The important point of emphasis is that just as the degree and form of participation used must fit the situation, the personnel involved, and the managers own personality must also be

---

[15]Figure 6-4 was developed from material contained in the film "Effective Uses of Power and Authority," CRM McGraw-Hill Films.

flexible to insure maximum results. For the operating manager the key ingredient is having a knowledge of the alternative available, developing skill in utilizing the various approaches, and being able to assess when they are most appropriate. Like other management techniques, the human element that surrounds the actual application is critical.

THE TRUE MEANING OF MANAGERIAL DELEGATION

Whenever managers delegate, they do three things: assign responsibility, grant authority, and create accountability for results. Each of these phases of delegation will be discussed in sequence.

ASSIGNING RESPONSIBILITY

The assignment of responsibility must include the results to be achieved.

The assignment of responsibility is the phase of delegation that traditionally has received the greatest emphasis. Most managers give their people a clear indication of the duties or tasks they are to perform. Similarly, most employees could give a quite adequate description of their jobs from a physical or "operations" standpoint. In assigning responsibility, however, the manager must go beyond the typical job description that outlines what work the person should undertake or what activities they are to perform. This is only half of what assigning responsibility is all about. The other half—the important half—is to specify what results are expected after the person has performed the work. It is in this latter area that management has most often been remiss.

In defining the expected results, one must ask the question, "For what do we pay people?" "Do we pay for working some number of hours, during which time employees are expected to perform certain tasks, or are we trying to achieve certain specified results through the performance of these tasks?" The latter is much more logical. Accordingly, Hank Jones' job amounts to more than running a drill press or assembling component parts; instead, he is responsible for producing a given quantity of parts, for meeting certain quality requirements, for informing the supervisor when materials needed are in low supply, and so on.

Similarly, the job of the production control manager goes beyond the designing and day-to-day administration of a production control program. The stated responsibility should also include minimizing lost time due to shortages of parts manufactured in the plant; establishing the most economical work flow and equipment utilization; and scheduling work so that manufacturing occurs in the most economic lot sizes.

The assigned responsibility of the quality control manager, in terms of results to be achieved, might include such things as analyzing the quality of production, isolating the causes of problems, suggesting remedial action, and recommending quality specifications.

Delegation requires a clear understanding and agreement between a manager and each subordinate about the following.

1. The activities or tasks they are responsible for performing.
2. The areas of the job in which they are responsible or accountable for achieving results.
3. The specific results for which they are accountable in each area.
4. The way performance will be measured in each area of accountability.

Of course, delegation doesn't relieve the manager of responsibility: it is always shared.

GRANTING AUTHORITY

A manager cannot grant authority without at the same time incurring some personal managerial and leadership obligations. The process of granting authority can be divided into two phases: a preliminary planning phase and a continuing support phase. Assuming understanding and agreement have been reached concerning the results expected, the planning phase of granting authority involves the following steps.

1. Having the subordinates present ideas and plans as to how the desired results can best be achieved.
2. By raising questions, suggesting possible alternatives, and opening discussion to help them explore all aspects of the situation.
3. Helping the subordinates identify potential problems and develop solutions to overcome them.
4. Obtaining mutual agreement on the proposed course of action to be followed.

The continuing support phase of granting authority can be summed up as follows.

> *The manager has responsibility downward, to his subordinate managers. He has first to make sure they know and understand what is demanded of them. He has to help them set their own objectives. Then he has to help them reach these objectives. He is, therefore, responsible for their getting the tools, the staff, the information they need. He has to help them with advice and counsel. He has, if need be, to teach them to do better.*[16]

The granting of authority is a blending of two factors: a subordinate's skills, abilities, knowledge, and potential to contribute and a manager's guidance, counsel, and help. The latter aspect is encompassed in the following thought.

> *The manager is responsible for helping the assistant to discover how he can perform his own objectives more effectively and how to make the best use of his potentialities to carry out his, the subordinate's, assigned responsibilities.*[17]

---

[16]Peter F. Drucker, *The Practice of Management*, New York, Harper and Brothers Publishers, 1954, p. 143.
[17]Nathaniel Cantor, *The Learning Process for Managers*, New York, Harper Brothers Publishers, 1958.

CREATING ACCOUNTABILITY

Accountability on the part of the person receiving the delegated responsibility is the end production of delegation. Without this accountability, there is no true delegation. Provided that the ingredients of effective delegation discussed in the preceding section are present, the recipient of the delegated responsibility and authority must be held accountable for the results (good or bad) of his activities.

Accountability flows upward. It is the obligation that the receiver accepts.

In theory, the subordinate's acceptance of accountability should be a semiautomatic process which logically flows from, and is a part of, the total delegation process. But in practice, this acceptance is not always present. Subordinates may quite actively resist being held accountable for results. When this situation is present, there are two possible explanations. First, we can assume that the individuals themselves are negative. In this case, the answer is to replace them, threaten punishment, withhold rewards, or exert constant pressure through close control and exercise of authority. Second, we should investigate the possibility that motivational factors are either only partially present or missing completely in the work climate. The latter represents a much more constructive approach.

WHAT DELEGATION IS NOT

In the process of describing delegation, we have indirectly alluded to several things it is not. In order to both reemphasize what has been discussed as well as to remove some common misconceptions about delegation, it will help to briefly examine what is *not* part of delegation. At the same time we point out many of the reasons why attempts at delegation may fail.

Delegation does not mean giving someone a job to do without any kind of guidance.

First, delegation is not *abdication*. It is not simply a matter of giving someone a job to do and telling her to go ahead and do it. When this approach is taken, the results the manager wants or expects are seldom achieved. Ineffective delegation also occurs when only routine or meaningless activities are delegated. To be effective, the responsibilities must be meaningful to subordinates. They must know why the results are important, what their contribution means in terms of its impact, and then receive feedback on successful completion.

Second, delegation is not *abandonment*. When managers delegate, they may very often set forth certain perimeters or limits within which the employee is expected to operate. These perimeters take the form of limiting the type or magnitude of decisions a subordinate can make without first clearing them. The perimeters may also take the form of operating within the limits of certain policies and procedures. It is important to point out, however, that if *every* decision must be cleared, there is no delegation because there is no opportunity to perform.

When delegating the manager needs to establish certain perimeters within which the subordinate can act and make decisions.

Third, delegation does not mean that the manager *loses control*. Whenever a major delegation occurs, it is assumed that various checkpoints in the operation will be established. When and where these checkpoints occur will be based on the manager's knowledge and experience. In any operation or project there are usually certain critical stages. If results are on target at each of these stages we can be reasonably sure that the final results will meet the goal. By identifying these critical points and arranging for a review, managers can effectively maintain control of the project.

Finally, delegation does not mean *avoiding decisions*. The manager who delegates still makes decisions. The important point is that she can concentrate on those decisions and issues of most importance and allow subordinates to make those which are best made at the point of direct contact.

SPAN OF CONTROL

The span of control refers to the number of subordinates that a manager supervises. Span of control is an important consideration in the operation of the organization because of its effects on the total organization structure, the levels of morale and motivation of the employees, and on communication and decision making within the organization. A narrow or small span of control means that managers have few people who report to them. A broad or large span of control indicates that each manager directly supervises many subordinates. Figure 6-5 depicts these concepts.

V. A. Graicunas, a classical management theorist, provided an interesting analysis of the problems of wide spans of control.[18] Graicunas points out that we are all limited in the number of items to which we can attend at a time. For example, only in rare cases can a person memorize groups of figures of more than six digits. In a similar manner, managers are limited in terms of the number of subordinate relationships for which they can maintain responsibility.

Graicunas argued that span of control was further limited by the group relationships and cross-relationships among subordinates.

> *Thus, if Tom supervises two person, Dick and Harry, he can speak to each of them individually or he can speak to them as a pair. The behavior of Dick in the presence of Harry or of Harry in the presence of Dick will vary from their behavior when with Tom alone. Further, what Dick thinks of Harry and what Harry thinks of Dick constitute two cross-relationships which Tom must keep in mind in arranging any work over which they must collaborate in his absence.*[19]

Graicunas concluded his studies with a formula that gives the number of total relationships possible for any number of subordinates: For twelve subordinates, a total of 4,161 total relationships would have to be understood and managed. Most writers think that Graicunas overemphasized the complexity of relationships a bit.

Graicunas argued that a manager's span of control needed to be limited because of the complexity of human relationships.

REASONS FOR A WIDE SPAN OF CONTROL

As can be seen from Figure 6-5, a narrow span of control leads to a tall organization structure; that is, a structure that has numerous layers of supervision and

---

[18]V. A. Graicunas, "Relationship in Organization" in Luther Gulick and L. Urwich (eds.), *Papers on the Science of Administration,* New York, Augustus M. Kelley, 1969, pp. 183–187.
[19]Graicunas, ibid., p. 184.

FIGURE 6-5

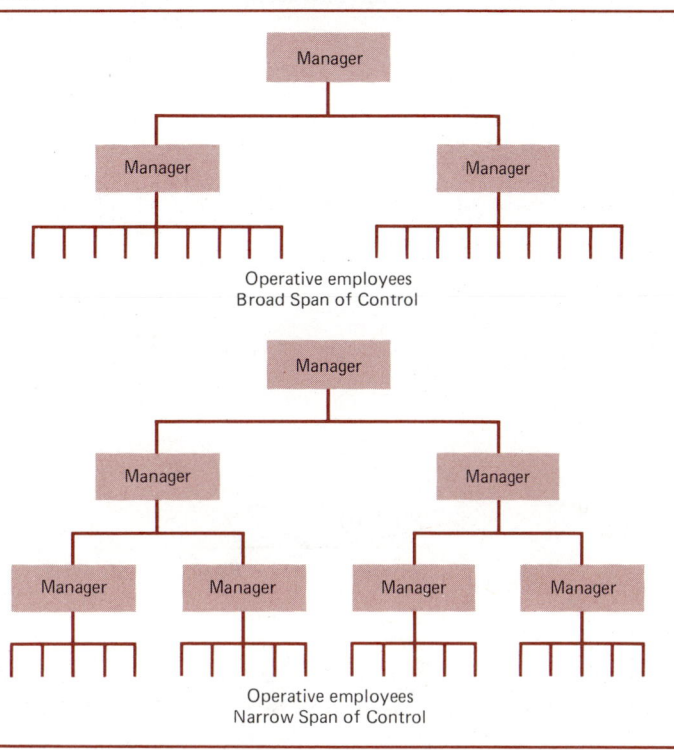

Span of Control

Operative employees
Broad Span of Control

Operative employees
Narrow Span of Control

A narrow span of control leads to a tall organization structure.

management associated with it. The chief characteristic of this tall structure is that it contains a considerable amount of administrative overhead in the form of salaries that must be paid to the managers at the various levels. As long as the organization is operating in a climate where the availability of profits or budget money presents no problem, everything can go along smoothly. (But it should be noted that these managers' salaries are causing a drain on the financial resources of the organization). If, however, the organization suffers financial losses, problem set in. Either it will be impossible to support this extensive administrative structure, or else it will continue to be supported, but only at the expense of sacrificing other, perhaps very strategic, areas.

A classical study of the effect of the number of organizational levels on business efficiency was conducted several years ago at Sears, Roebuck, and Company.[20] Two groups of stores were analyzed, both of which were located in the same town, employing approximately the same number of persons. In Group A, the manager had organized utilizing an assistant manager in a staff capacity and approximately thirty merchandise managers in charge of store departments (see Figure 6-6).

---

[20]J. C. Worthy, "Organization Structure and Employee Morale," *American Sociological Review*, April 1950, Vol. 15, pp. 169–179.

156 CLASSICAL MANAGEMENT CONCEPTS

FIGURE 6-6

Group A (Wide Span of Control)

Level 1 — Store manager — Flat structure

Assistant store manager

Level 2 — 30 Merchandise managers

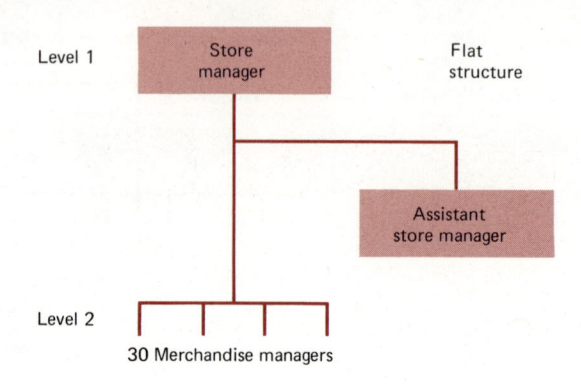

FIGURE 6-7

Group B (Narrow Span of Control)

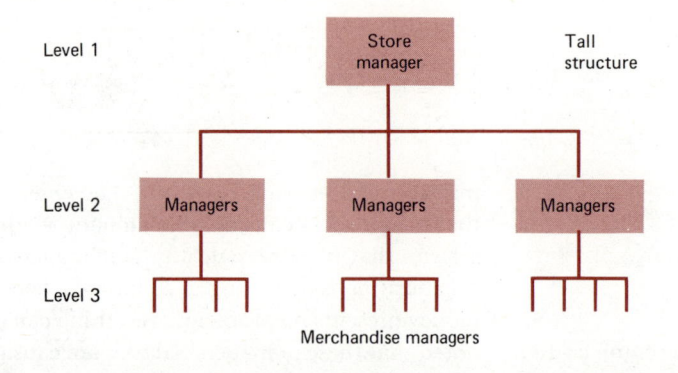

Level 1 — Store manager — Tall structure

Level 2 — Managers | Managers | Managers

Level 3 — Merchandise managers

In Group B, an extra level of management was utilized between store managers and department heads (see Figure 6-7).

An analysis of sales volume, profits, morale, and other success criteria all indicated that the two-level structure was superior on all counts to the traditional Group B type organization. Of particular note was the fact that merchandise managers in Store A seemed to be developing into better managers than in Store B. The principal conclusion drawn from the study was that store managers who had a large number of subordinates reporting to them were forced to delegate authority, which in turn required that merchandise managers learn to make their own decisions in most matters. Communications were expedited and morale was heightened because the second level of communications filtering was removed.

Wide spans of control reduce the number of layers in the organization, lead to forced delegation, and facilitate communication.

The studies of span of control conducted at Sears found that wide spans of control led to better overall favorable results.

The Store A manager, knowing that he had to delegate considerable amounts of authority was more careful in selecting, supervising, and training his merchandise managers. He also made better use of control methods.

From the Sears study and others, managers are learning that span of control greatly affects leadership style. When span is limited, the manager is likely to become involved in the small details of the operation. A limited span leads to close supervision of subordinates, restricting their range of freedom in performing work. Eventually the manager is so heavily involved that her people find themselves performing piecemeal activities without having a meaningful understanding of long-run plans and goals.

In contrast, by expanding a manager's span of control, she is forced to allow her people more freedom in action. In addition, she must delegate authority and responsibility. It is generally accepted that these factors can all be instrumental in creating a motivational climate.

EFFECT OF SPAN OF CONTROL ON COMMUNICATION AND DECISION MAKING

As noted previously, a broad span of control reduced the number of layers in the organization. This facilitated both upward and downward communications since messages traveled through fewer layers and were therefore more direct. Another advantage of communications in the two-level organization was that they were likely to be face to face rather than written, thus increasing understanding.

Where the span of control is broad, it is more likely that decision making will be delegated further down the line. This happens because the managers cannot handle everything without either being overburdened or letting many things go undone. Like the delegation of authority and responsibility, the delegation of decision making often has a very positive effect on the motivation of subordinates.

FACTORS AFFECTING THE SIZE OF SPAN OF CONTROL

Up to this point, it has seemed evident that a broad span of control is always desirable. But the decision as to size of span of control must be made not only on the basis of the issues discussed above, but also on the basis of some other very practical considerations. First, the nature of the work should be considered in determining the size of the span.

Generally speaking, the more routine, repetitive, and less specialized the work being performed, the greater can be the number of subordinates for which the manager is responsible. The reason for this is that there is less need for the manager to work and interact directly with subordinates to get the job done. Provided that the people have been adequately trained, they can perform the simplified work with a minimum of supervision.

But if the work is more technical and less structured, there will be a need for considerably more interaction and teamwork not only between the manager and his people as individuals, but between all the members of the work group. Thus, the span of control must be smaller. If it is enlarged too much, the work will not be properly done because coordination of effort will not be possible.

Second, the size of a manager's span of control must be decided according to the training and experience of subordinates. If subordinates are well qualified to perform their jobs, there is less need for supervision. Assuming they know what is expected, receive periodic feedback on their performance, and have the necessary help and support, subordinates can control their own performance and function independently. In this case, rather than exercising direct supervision over the work itself, the manager's job centers both on coordinating the work of individuals to insure a team effort and on the overall planning of departmental activity. When these conditions exist, the span of control can be enlarged.

On the other hand, if subordinates have only limited training or the work is very technical or specialized, closer supervision is required, and the manager's span of control must necessarily be limited. If it is not, the job will simply not get done because the manager's efforts will be spread too thin. Because of inadequate supervision, the manager will have to spend considerable time meeting crises that develop.

A third determinant of the size of the span concerns the manager himself. Like people in general, managers differ in their individual capacities, energy levels, and capacities for work. They also differ in that some may pour all their efforts into the job, while others may have personal outside interests that occupy some of their attention. What may be the proper span of control for one manager may be inappropriate for another. Some consideration must, therefore, be given to the individual who occupies the job in question. Of course this is not to suggest that the organization can go overboard in tailoring the spans of control to fit every individual.

The proper span of control will be influenced by the nature of the work, capabilities of subordinates, and the manager's own capacity for work.

HOW LARGE SHOULD THE SPAN OF CONTROL BE?

The Sears Roebuck study cited earlier probably suggested that a wide span of control is preferable to a narrow one. But as we have seen in the preceding paragraphs, this is too broad a generalization.

Porter and Lawler Study. Porter and Lawler conducted a study among over 1900 managers, designed to measure their reaction to tall (narrow span) and flat (wide span) organization structures.[21] Among the conclusions drawn from the Porter and Lawler research were the following.

1. In larger firms employing over 5000 people there was more satisfaction reported by managers in tall structures, particularly with respect to security and social aspects of the job.

---

[21] L. W. Porter and E. E. Lawler, "The Effects on Tall versus Flat Organization Structures on Managerial Job Satisfaction," Summer 1964, *Personnel Psychology,* Vol. 17, pp. 135–148.

2. In firms employing less than 5000 people there was more satisfaction reported by managers in flat structures particularly with respect to things such as challenge, sense of achievement, and responsibility.

These findings suggest that the size of the organization must be taken into consideration when deciding on the size of span of control.

Woodward Study. Another of the extensive studies in this area was conducted by Joan Woodward.[22] It included 100 firms in southern England. They were broken down according to the type of manufacturing technology in use. The three categories used were as follows.

1. Job order—each unit made to customer specifications.
2. Mass production—an assembly line type operation with continuous flow, standardized parts and specialized machinery.
3. Continuous long runs of a standardized product.

The patterns of span of control for each firm were compared with various success measures such as profit figures. The findings revealed that successful firms in the job order and continuous long-run technologies tended to have wider spans of control, with corresponding greater degrees of delegation and individual freedom. Successful firms in the mass production classification were found to have narrow spans and adhered more to classical concepts, such as specialization of labor.

The findings suggest that although there is no one ideal approach to determining the proper size for span of control, certain technologies do suggest a certain structure.

REVIEW OF ORGANIZATION STRUCTURE

There are certain principles that can help insure that organization structure will facilitate achievement.

A principle is a statement formulated as a guide to action. Principles are not designed to be irrevocable laws but rules of conduct that help us cope with life's situations. While no two organizations are exactly alike, certain fundamental characteristics and principles are common to all. We will next review some of these basic principles that, when adhered to, can help insure organizational effectiveness.

PRINCIPLES OF ORGANIZATION

The following listing of principles of organization presents some of the most important factors that management must consider when structuring the organization.

---

[22] Joan Woodward, *Industrial Organization: Theory and Practice*, London, Oxford University Press, 1965, pp. 52–62.

Statement of Objectives. The prerequisite to establishing any organization or to embarking on any activity is a clear, complete statement of the desired objectives. Only after this can the organization be projected and built in such a way that it will advance the attainment of those objectives with the least amount of effort and cost. Objectives also give the organization a sense of long-range direction and continuing purpose. Without specific objectives there is a decided possibility that the organization will drift and fail to respond adequately to its environment. The process of deciding on objectives starts at the top and moves down through the entire organization structure.

Nonconflicting Objectives. Organizations are a complex of departments and units. If the long-range objectives are to be achieved, the departmental objectives must be derived from those of the overall organization. Moreover, each department's own set of objectives must complement, supplement, support, and otherwise blend with those of the other departments.

Coordination. The principle of coordination states that the organization framework must provide for the integration and blending of both human and technical resources to accomplish the specified tasks. Coordination results when (1) the established systems and procedures facilitate the accomplishment of results, and (2) when each unit in the organization thoroughly understands and cooperates with the role and function of every other unit. Coordination also concerns the establishment of effective lines of communication as well as the creation of an organization-wide team climate. All of these issues are discussed in succeeding chapters.

Parity of Authority, Responsibility, and Accountability. When an individual is held responsible for accomplishing something, she must also be given the authority necessary to perform. If the assigned responsibility is greater than the authority that is granted, then responsibility will tend to shrink within the limits of the authority. If the opposite is true (i.e., more authority is granted than is needed to meet a given responsibility), then there will be a tendency for responsibility to expand. In any case, accountability can only be expected within the limits of the authority extended.

Unity of Command. The unity of command concept refers to the idea that each subordinate should be accountable and answerable to only one superior. The New Testament statement, "No man can serve two masters," illustrates this point. If the subordinate is receiving directions from more than one superior, sooner or later he will become confused. This is particularly true when the two sets of directions are not the same. The subordinates will not know which way to turn, and as a result there will be uncertain action.

Delegation. An organization begins when one person cannot do a job alone. Thus, other people are employed and some type of organizational structure appears. If the people who are brought in are to make a meaningful contribution and be productive, then true managerial delegation must take place. Delegation is the process by which a manager assigns responsibility, grants authority, and creates accountability. Without delegation the managers will defeat their purpose of bringing others into the organization: they will end up doing everything themselves.

ORGANIZATIONAL REALITY

In our earlier discussion of span of control it was emphasized that there is no absolute rule for determining exactly how big a given manager's span of control should be. Many variables must be taken into consideration when making such a decision. Similarly, it was noted that the organization chart does not represent an exact replica of the real organization. It is useful, however, as a road map and a tool for organizational analysis.

Classical principles of management serve as guidelines and ideals to strive for.

The six principles of management previously cited present the manager with some fundamental guidelines that are valuable first, when designing the organization structure, and later, when analyzing how effectively it is functioning on a day-to-day basis. For example, the principle of unity of command was discussed. In real life, there are many situations where a person may have more than one superior; this in itself is not necessarily bad. The important thing is that management must make sure no one is put in the position of receiving conflicting instructions from the two superiors. The principle of parity of authority, responsibility, and accountability was also cited. In practice, managers are often held accountable for things over which they do not have complete control. To do otherwise would result in many serious gaps in responsibility as far as total performance is concerned. Numerous other examples of discrepancies between management theory and reality could be cited. However, the classical principles of management can serve both as valuable guidelines and as ideals to strive for.

SUMMARY

The process of delegation is greatly influenced by the manager's philosophy about people and their reaction to work. The manager with a positive philosophy is much more likely to practice true managerial delegation than a manager with a negative philosophy. When delegation is practiced, it contributes to subordinate growth improves their motivation, and frees the manager to manage.

It is important to distinguish between authority (legitimate power) and illegitimate power in the delegation process. Because the manager is dependent on others in the organization for cooperation, information, and in other ways, power and authority must be used effectively if results are to be accomplished and

SUMMARY CHART

1. Management philosophy influences delegation.
2. The delegation process includes: assigning responsibility, granting authority, and creating accountability.
3. Delegation of authority to positions leads to formal legitimate power based on sanctions and rewards.
4. Influence leads to informal authority and power, based on personal disclosure, recognizing others and cooperative problem solving.
5. Delegation can create a narrow span of control or wide span of control.
6. Research suggests that wider spans of control tend to develop subordinates and improve morale.
7. The appropriate span of control depends on the work, subordinates, and the size of the organization.

motivation and commitment forthcoming. As a generalization, collaborative approaches to using authority will contribute to the process of authority being accepted.

The process of delegation has three major phases. The first is the assignment-of-responsibility phase. When assigning responsibility, the manager must be sure to go beyond the assignment of tasks or physical activities, and also specify the results to be achieved. The second phase of delegation is that of granting authority. This involves a preliminary planning step where the manager and subordinate jointly come to some agreement as to how to go about achieving the desired results; and a continuing support step where the manager gives assistance and help if it is needed. Creating accountability is the final phase of delegation. Accountability is not something that a subordinate can accept or reject at his own discretion. Every act of delegation must simultaneously be accompanied by accountability for results. Accountability refers to the obligation one has to answer for the results he achieves or does not achieve, as the case may be.

In addition to what delegation is, there are also several things that it is not. Delegation is not abdication or abandonment; it does not mean that a manager loses control or that she avoids decisions. Although there are many excuses given by managers for not delegating, they are seldom rational ones. Conversely, the reasons subordinates do not always accept delegation, fear and indifference, are usually traceable to improper methods of delegation in the past.

Span of control refers to the number of subordinates that managers have reporting to them. There is no set formula for determining exactly how large or how small a manager's span should be. It depends on the nature of work, the competence of subordinates, and other factors. The importance of the size of span of control lies in the effect that it has on the organization structure, the morale and motivation of people, communication, and decision making.

DISCUSSION QUESTIONS

1. Discuss the importance of a positive management philosophy as it relates to delegation. What are some of the advantages to delegation and why is each significant?
2. What is the difference between power and authority? Contrast the two. Discuss the different bases for authority. As a manager in a business, would you rather have more position power or more personal power? Why? As a coach or student club president? Why?
3. Discuss the concept of managerial dependency. Distinguish between the "hard" and "soft" approaches to using authority and explain why in the long run the soft approaches yield more favorable results.
4. Fully discuss each of the three major phases of the delegation process. Be sure to detail the important subelements of each phase and why they are important to the total process.
5. Discuss the relationship between the degree of delegation from a superior to a subordinate and the degree to which the supervisor loses control of the subordinate's actions. Can a supervisor delegate, and at the same time retain the same degree of control? In detail, discuss some of the ways in which a manager can delegate authority and still maintain necessary control that does not give the subordinate a feeling of being watched.
6. Tell which of the three theories of authority seems most realistic: Brown's power to command, Follett's law of the situation, or Barnard's acceptance theory. Discuss.
7. Discuss fully the concept of span of control. Be sure to include in your answer the answers to the following questions.
   (a) To what does the concept refer?
   (b) What is the relationship between the size of span and administrative overhead, motivation, and communication?
   (c) What factors determine the size of span, and how do they operate?

APPLICATION EXERCISES AND CASES

IMPORTANCE OF MANAGEMENT PHILOSOPHY

Steve Relbin, vice president of purchasing, was engaged in a rather lengthy conference with Roger Gilbert, a buyer who was new to the company. Mr. Relbin's comments could be summarized as follows.

Frankly, Roger, I'm a bit disappointed in your performance since you came to this company a year ago. Sure, you somehow manage to get the job done and all that, but what bothers me are two things. First of all, you are a very indecisive supervisor. A manager is supposed to make decisions, but you have your subordinates making certain contracts, visiting with the suppliers in the field, and other things. I could go on all day describing the things you let them do. But let's take Jim Davis as an example. He worked for me before I was promoted to this position, and in those two years, I couldn't trust him to do anything by himself. Now you have him doing things which I did when I was in your position. Sure, I know he hasn't made any mistakes so far, but what's going to happen when he does? I'll tell you one thing, it's you who is going to get the blame, and not him. Finally, I noticed that you put in only eight hours a day here, and sometimes even less than that when the weather is nice. Most of us here put in twelve to fourteen hours a day, and often more than that. A manager is supposed to devote more time on the job than anyone else. All of us here burn the midnight oil, yet you think that you are too good for this.

When Roger asked if he was performing his job satisfactorily, Mr. Relbin replied that as far as the technical part was concerned, he was satisfactory. But he did not see how anyone who let subordinates make major decisions and devoted as little time to the job as Roger did could ever perform his job satisfactorily.

Questions

1. Using the concepts in this chapter, discuss Mr. Relbin's criticism of Roger. Would you want a man like Roger working for your organization? Explain why or why not.
2. Discuss the process of delegation as Roger Gilbert was apparently using it. Point out the key elements of each phase of delegation that are necessary to insure that delegation is effective.

CENTRAL HIGH SCHOOL[23]

Carl Estes was appointed principal of Central High School shortly after the death of Mr. Beane, who had been principal at the school for twenty-three years.

During his first week at Central Mr. Estes prepared a list of seventeen major changes that he thought ought to be made. At his first faculty meeting Mr. Estes said: "We must make these changes immediately so that Central will get out of the dark ages." Mr. Estes pushed so hard for his changes that he received some rather violent reactions from his faculty.

Three weeks after Mr. Estes's appointment, Mrs. Cox, faculty representative, presented a petition signed by all members of the Central faculty to Mr. Farrow, the superintendent. The petition sought the immediate dismissal of Mr. Estes. After considering the petition, Mr. Farrow replaced Mr. Estes with Mr. Henry.

---

[23]Herbert G. Hicks, *The Management of Organizations: A Systems and Human Resources Approach*, 2nd ed., New York, McGraw-Hill Book Co., 1972, p. 276.

Mr. Henry's policy was to go slow on changes. However, three years after his appointment Mr. Henry successfully implemented the majority of the changes originally suggested by Mr. Estes.

Questions

1. Discuss and analyze Mr. Estes's use of authority drawing on the chapter material.
2. Why was Mr. Henry successful when Mr. Estes had not been?
3. What possible differences were there in the uses of authority?

CHAPTER 7
ORGANIZATIONAL DYNAMICS

SCIENTIFIC MANAGEMENT AND HUMAN RELATIONS
PRINCIPLES OF MANAGEMENT
LIFE CYCLE OF AN ORGANIZATION
BUREAUCRACY
ADVANTAGE OF A BUREAUCRACY
DISADVANTAGES OF A BUREAUCRACY
A BALANCE BETWEEN BUREAUCRACY AND ENTERPRISE
DECENTRALIZATION AND THE PROFIT CENTER CONCEPT
THE PROFIT CENTER CONCEPT
REASONS BEHIND DECISIONS TO DECENTRALIZE
FACTORS THAT ENCOURAGE DECENTRALIZATION
ADVANTAGES OF DECENTRALIZATION
DISADVANTAGES OF DECENTRALIZATION
TRENDS IN DECENTRALIZATION
MANAGEMENT BY OBJECTIVES
APPLICATION EXERCISES AND CASES
RESEARCH COORDINATION IN THE PHARMACEUTICAL INDUSTRY
NAYLOR CORPORATION

ESTABLISHED FIRM REORGANIZES TO REMAIN DYNAMIC

"It is a staid old company that got more and more staid while the rest of the world was passing it by," says one security analyst.[1]

"It is a very strong company, and I believe it will have even more market clout in the future," says another.

The company evoking such a diversity of opinion among analysts is none other than Sears Roebuck and Co., the world's biggest retailer. And it is no wonder they disagree. Of late, the Sears Tower in Chicago has been emitting a barrage of signals that would confuse even the most experienced Sears watcher.

During its ninety-two-year history, Sears has been a pacesetter in the retail industry and a financial innovator in the business world. But in the last decade, its leaders made serious blunders, not only in merchandising strategy but in the overall management of the company. As a result, Sears' pretax profit margins slipped badly—from a high of 11.1 percent in 1969 to 7.4 percent in 1977.

To reverse this precipitous state of affairs, Edward R. Telling, who replaced Arthur M. Wood as chairman and chief executive officer in February 1978, lost no time unleashing the most comprehensive reorganization in Sears' history. Among other things, it calls for establishment of a new distribution network, drastic reductions in merchandising staff, a massive cutback in the number of suppliers, and less spending on advertising and promotion.

In line with these changes, Sears also announced that it would be relocating its women's fashions buying operation from New York to Chicago.

The drastic changes now planned for Sears are an attempt to overcome two fundamental problems. The first is the basic merchandising problem and second how top management can more efficiently control and monitor the far-flung network of an $18 billion sales giant. "The phenomenon of size makes these changes essential," comments Joseph T. Moran Jr., who takes over as Sears senior executive vice president of merchandising this month. "The management of size is probably the single largest managerial problem that faces most American business."

For the first time in years, management is attempting to gain control over the layers and layers of bureaucracy that have grown up in an empire of almost 900 retail stores, 12,000 suppliers and 400,000 employees.

---

[1] "Can Sears Come Back?", *Dun's Review*, February 1979, pp. 68–70.

Classical writers sought an almost mechanical approach to building organizational structures.

In Parts One and Two we presented much of the literature that describes classical organization theory. The writers built on the scientific management and human relations concepts. But the classical writers went further to investigate the principles of planning, organizing, and controlling in large organizations. They viewed these functions primarily from a structured approach. Early organizations had typically been operated by personal leadership with very few rules or

168 CLASSICAL MANAGEMENT CONCEPTS

policies. As they began to grow in size, theorists and practitioners alike began looking for rules and principles that could be applied to large organizations on a universal basis to offer order and stability to its functioning. They sought almost a mechanical approach to building organizations.

SCIENTIFIC MANAGEMENT AND HUMAN RELATIONS

The management theorists of the scientific management era were continually looking for the one best way to do things. They were seeking efficiency through routinization, standardization of work methods, training programs, and economic incentives. Specialization and standardization are important in obtaining efficiency. But the path to optimal management appears to rest with answers to the question, "How can we standardize the work of an institution and still make sure that individuals as well as programs will remain personable, spontaneous, and enterprising?"

A justifiable complaint against scientific management in its original form was that it should expand to include elements that would humanize it. Frederick Taylor, the father of scientific management, knew this. He realized that cooperation is basic to efficiency, but he also recognized that too little was really known about human relations at that time for it to make a valid contribution to scientific management.[2] Since the early 1900s, human relations has received emphasis in administration, and a good fusion with scientific management is already taking place.

To operate effectively large organizations need to blend the concepts of scientific management and human relations.

If it can be assumed (1) that scientific management must be combined with human relations to form a balance, (2) that standardization must not be carried to the point of overlooking individual differences and discouraging initiative, and (3) that even the one best method is constantly subject to change and improvement, then scientific management is an indispensable tool of administration, not only in matters of technology and efficiency, but also in the matter of human relations. Enlightened management has found that system is essential to efficiency, but it must be combined with the complementary human factors.

PRINCIPLES OF MANAGEMENT

Whereas scientific management contributors focused on shop management and efficiency in operations, the classical management contributors were intent on developing the principles by which large organizations should be managed. The most systematic and provocative statement of such principles must still be attributed to an early writer, Henri Fayol.[3] Fayol's original work, *Administration*

The most comprehensive statement of classical management principles was formulated by Henri Fayol.

---
[2]Harold J. Leavitt, "Unhuman Organizations," *Harvard Business Review*, 40, 1962, pp. 92–94.
[3]Henri Fayol, *General and Industrial Administration*, London, Sir Issac Pitman and Sons, Ltd., 1947, pp. 19–20.

FIGURE 7-1

Henri Fayol's General Principles of Management

1. Division of work
2. Authority
3. Discipline
4. Unity of command
5. Unity of direction
6. Subordination of individual interests to the general interests
7. Remuneration
8. Centralization
9. Scalar chain (line of authority)
10. Order
11. Equity
12. Stability of tenure of personnel
13. Initiative
14. Esprit de corps

Source: Henri Fayol, *General and Industrial Administration,* London, Sir Issac Pitman and Sons, Ltd., 1947, pp. 19–20.

industrielle et generale, was published in 1916. In Figure 7-1, his fourteen principles of management are summarized. Most of them are still applicable to some degree today. However, we will also note many ideas that bring some of Fayol's principles into question as we study Part Three, Organizational Behavior and Design, and Part Four, The Management of Human Resources.

Division of work is simply a statement of the advantages of specialization. The principle of authority suggests the right to give orders and the power to exact obedience. Note, however, that Fayol in this early period anticipated modern management writers by distinguishing between official authority conferred by the job and personal authority deriving from the manager's own abilities. The principle of discipline is restated by Fayol as consisting of the following elements:[4]

1. good superiors at all levels;
2. agreements as clear and fair as possible;
3. sanctions (penalties), judiciously applied.

To Fayol, unity of command and direction meant that there should be one head and one plan for a group of activities having the same objective. Regarding subordination of individual interest, Fayol said: "This principle calls to mind the fact that in a business, the interest of one employee or group of employees should not prevail over that of the concern."[5]

His principle on remuneration of personnel is broken down into a discussion dealing with fairness and with the motivating power of different pay plans. Fayol

---
[4]Ibid., p. 24.
[5]Ibid., p. 26.

concludes all of his principles with an admonition for balance. This is particularly true of his discussion on centralization, where he suggests "finding the measure (of centralization and decentralization) which will give the best overall yield."[6]

One of Fayol's many farsighted discussions comes in his statement of the scalar chain principle. He at first seems to suggest an unbroken chain of authority from the top to the lowest rung of the organization. But he quickly adds thoughts about the delay required in order to get messages up and down the organization. It was at this point that he suggested the occasional use of horizontal communications by means of what he called the "gangplank."[7] See Figure 7-2.

This is one of the earliest explicit statements about the need to loosen organization structure and promote freer communications. Note that the scalar principle calls for the employees, represented by F and P to communicate only by going through A. The gangplank, or *Fayol Bridge* as it has become known, allows swift horizontal communications unfiltered by other levels of the organization.

The principle of order is summarized by Fayol as "a place for everyone and everyone in his place."[8] During the period in which Fayol wrote, labor unions were weak or nonexistent. Civil service legislation had not been implemented. Often employees were treated arbitrarily and in such cases, they had no recourse. Therefore, his statement of the equity principle was very reasonable during his time, but sounds paternalistic today. "For the personnel to be encouraged to carry out its duties with all the devotion and loyalty of which it is capable, it must be treated with kindliness, and equity results from the combination of kindliness and justice."[9]

> Fayol developed the scalar chain of command concept.

FIGURE 7-2

Fayol's Gangplank

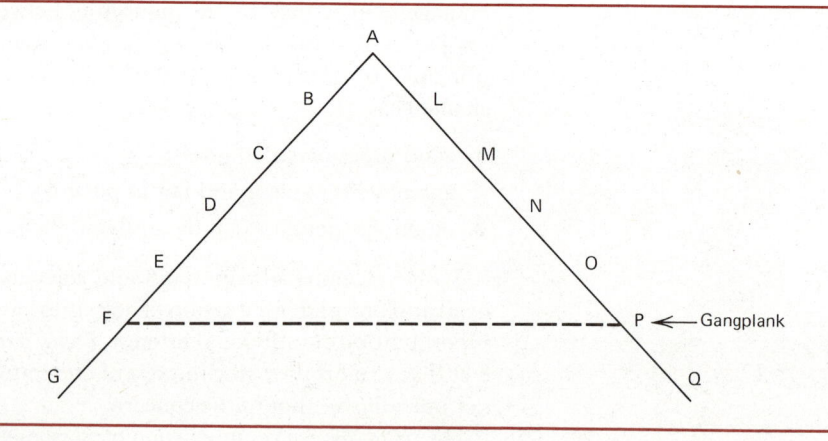

[6]Ibid., p. 33–34.
[7]Ibid., p. 34.
[8]Ibid., p. 36.
[9]Ibid., p. 38.

Fayol was very concerned about tenure of personnel. Citing the complexities of business and the long period required to learn the ropes, he concluded that the "mediocre manager who stays is infinitely preferable to outstanding managers who merely come and go."[10] This principle would provide considerable controversy in management circles today. Fayol's statement about the need for initiative is a forerunner of modern thoughts on job enrichment and job enlargement (see Chapter 10, Job Design). He began by stating that the opportunity to establish a plan and carry it through to success is one of the most powerful stimulants of human endeavor. He then says that "the manager must be able to sacrifice some personal vanity in order to grant this sort of satisfaction to his subordinates."[11]

Perhaps the most farsighted principle advocated by Fayol is his last one, esprit de corps. In order to obtain this level of relationships, he suggests that managers not violate the principle of "unity of command." Furthermore, he warns against creating jealousies and the overuse of written communications. These, he says, often bring differences in understanding that verbal communications would clear up. This process of formulating principles and guidelines was extended by other authoritative writers such as James Mooney and Alvin Brown.[12]

Fayol had an insight into the need for an organization to have an effective working managerial team.

LIFE CYCLE OF AN ORGANIZATION

Organizations are much like people in that they tend to follow a fairly predictable life cycle, as depicted in Figure 7-3. In Stage I, the organization is new, headed up by a small nucleus of key people who are highly enthused about the product, service or purpose of the organization. These key people have a lot of personal drive and are successful in instilling a sense of excitement in others. They recruit people who are achievement oriented and who are looking for a new challenge. Many times, these people come from organizations that have reached the plateau of Stage III or are in its downturn phase. Having become disenchanted or frustrated with their present situations, they seek new horizons and opportunities where they can channel their energies and exercise their talents.

Organizations tend to follow a cycle in their growth and development.

Stage I is also characterized by relatively rough organization. If there is an organization chart and job descriptions, they tend to be somewhat sketchy. What needs to get done somehow gets done. It is a climate that plays on the strengths of the various individuals, with each one left relatively free to make maximum contributions in their areas of expertise. The organizational climate of Stage I includes such factors as personal relationships, flexibility, a certain informality, face-to-face communication, and the absence of constraints to individual achievement.

Stage I is characterized by things as personal relationships.

---

[10] Ibid., p.39.
[11] Ibid., p. 40.
[12] James D. Mooney, *The Principles of Organization*, rev. ed., New York, Harper and Brothers Publishers, 1947 and Alvin Brown, *Organization of Industry*, Englewood Cliffs, N.J., Prentice-Hall Book Company, 1974.

FIGURE 7-3

Life Cycle of an Organization

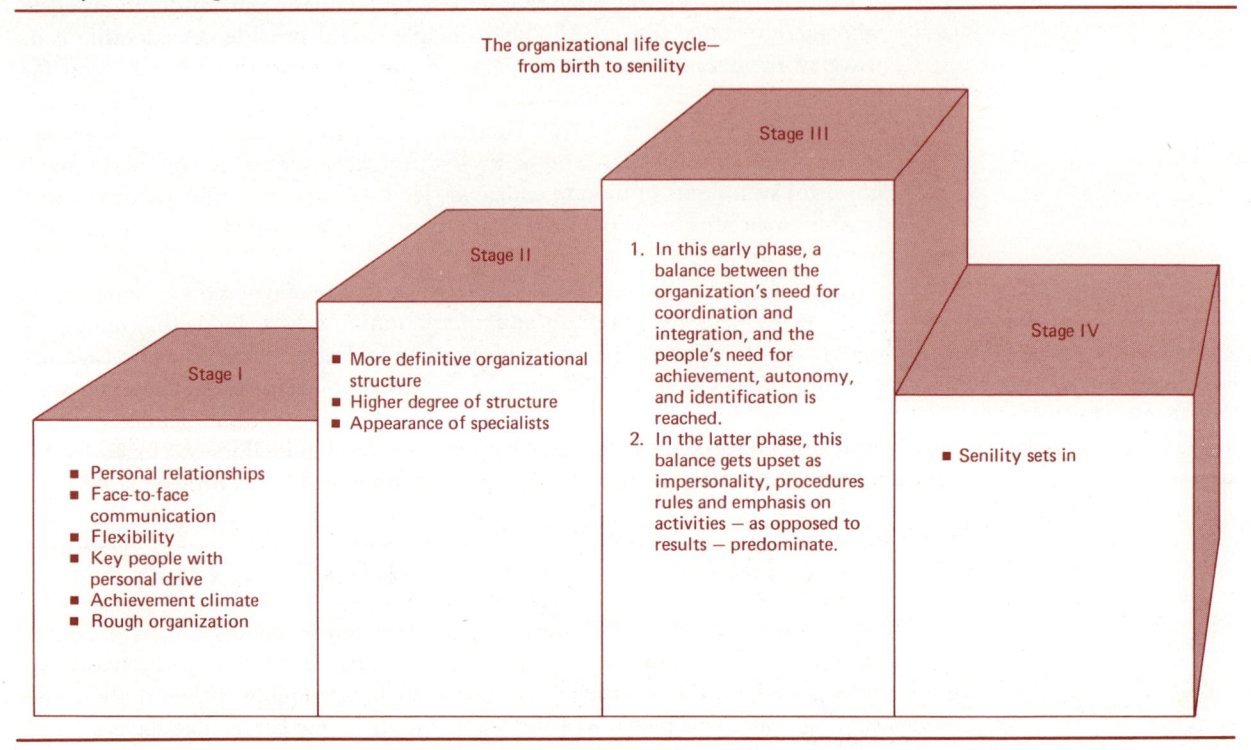

The organizational life cycle—from birth to senility

Stage I
- Personal relationships
- Face-to-face communication
- Flexibility
- Key people with personal drive
- Achievement climate
- Rough organization

Stage II
- More definitive organizational structure
- Higher degree of structure
- Appearance of specialists

Stage III
1. In this early phase, a balance between the organization's need for coordination and integration, and the people's need for achievement, autonomy, and identification is reached.
2. In the latter phase, this balance gets upset as impersonality, procedures rules and emphasis on activities — as opposed to results — predominate.

Stage IV
- Senility sets in

In Stage II more formality develops.

In the early phases of Stage III there is a balance between the needs of the organization and the people.

With the passage of time and increase in size, Stage II begins. By necessity, a need for more formality arises. The organization chart becomes more definitive and job descriptions more precise. People grow more effective in performing certain individual responsibilities, and specialists appear on the scene. By the latter phases of Stage II, there are more formal policies governing decisions, and the climate is characterized by a higher degree of structure. This structure is introduced in an attempt to facilitate coordination and prevent chaos, confusion, and uncontrolled individualism.

Stage III becomes critical in maintaining organizational vitality. In Stage II and the early phase of Stage III, the organization has achieved a balance between the need of the organization for coordination, integration, uniformity, consistency and formality in decision processes, and the need of the people for growth and development, a sense of achievement, autonomy in performing their jobs, and identification with the broader organization.

It is in the latter phase of Stage III that the balance between the organization and the people can topple as the former begins to dominate the latter, illustrated by the following specific points.

1. Relationships between people become increasingly impersonal.
2. Rules, regulations, and procedures become ends in themselves, as opposed to means to an end.
3. Written communication replaces much of the face-to-face contact.
4. Flexibility is lost because of red tape.
5. An orientation toward activities instead of results predominates and becomes the criteria for making decisions and evaluating performance.
6. Units within the organization become entities in themselves as they pursue sometimes unidentified missions unrelated to the whole.
7. The top levels in the hierarchy become less and less visible to lower levels.
8. A lot of politicking takes place.

As this process continues, the organization eventually moves into Stage IV, which is senility.

When viewing the organizational life cycle, two very logical questions come to mind.

1. If an organization is in the downturn phase of Stage III or in Stage IV, how can it get out?
2. How can the organization keep on the upswing phase of Stage III in the first place?

The answer to both these questions lies in the following actions.

1. Developing a sensitivity to the kinds of leadership practices and organizational climate factors that cause ill health.
2. Formally or informally assessing the degree to which these causal factors may be present in the organization.
3. Where necessary, taking some corrective actions.

Two additional observations are in order. First, an organization can remain in the latter phases of Stage III, and even Stage IV, for a long period time without going completely under. How long will be determined by the extent of its financial resources, the kind of competitive environment that exists and many other factors.

Second, maintaining an effective and dynamic organization requires commitment from the top levels of management. Without this support, any action taken at lower levels will meet with only minimal success. It is those people at the top who are in a position to exert the strongest influence and trigger a progressive and positive ripple effect throughout the entire structure.

The causes of organizational malaise are many. Among them are included overly authoritative supervision, a perceived inequitable reward system, lack of clearly defined objectives that furnish the organization with a central thrust, negatively structured and administered control systems, and numerous others. Some aspects of the foregoing received attention in previous chapters and others will be explored later in the text. For the present we will concentrate on the concepts of bureaucracy and enterprise and some approaches that have been used to blend the advantages of each in attempts to foster organizational vitality.[13]

The organizational style spawned by traditional management writers can best be described as bureaucracy. While many persons use this term loosely to mean governmental red tape, a bureaucracy is the pyramidal form of organization resulting from Fayol's principles of management discussed in the preceding section.

BUREAUCRACY

Most persons today associate the term bureaucracy with governmental organizations. For example, the head of the Treasury Department is called a "bureaucrat," while the treasurer of U.S. Steel is an "administrator." The truth of the matter is, however, that all large-scale, complex organizations, both private and public, can be described as bureaucracies.[14]

The term bureaucracy can be used to describe any large-scale and complex organization.

Following are some of the common characteristics of this form of organization.[15]

> A clear-cut division of labor among the members of the organization, in such a way that a high degree of specialization is possible.
>
> The organizational positions arranged in a hierarchical authority structure. (usually a pyramid-shaped organization structure results)
>
> A system of formal rules and regulations that govern all administrative decisions and actions.
>
> Organizational members assume an impersonal attitude in their contacts with clients and other officials.
>
> Advancement of the organizational members is based on a combination of both their technical qualifications and seniority.

Thus, the bureaucratic organization exhibits a highly formalized structure and operation. Although some of the above characteristics may exist in a non-bureaucratic organization, it is reasonable to assume that if *all* are present to a high degree, a bureaucratic organization exists.

Several factors contribute to the development of the bureaucratic characteristics listed above. Included are environmental volatility, complexity, technology, strategy, size, and time, etc. We will discuss the latter two as illustrative.

Size definitely affects the role patterns of the organization's members. The management of a large organization is unable to directly supervise and implement its policies and must delegate this work to others with specialized

---

[13] John A. Drexler and Edward E. Lawler, "Entrepreneurship in the Large Corporation: Is it Possible?" *Management Review*, February 1981, pp. 8–11.
[14] Richard W. Scott and Peter M. Blau, *Formal Organization*, San Francisco, Chandler Publishing Company, 1962, p. 32.
[15] Ibid., p. 32–33.

Two of the main factors that contribute to bureaucracy are organizational size and the passage of time.

abilities, whose roles have become differentiated.[16] In addition, verbal exchanges are replaced by written messages, which result in standardized formats, routine procedures, and organizational structuring so that individual responsibility and accountability can be precisely pinpointed.

The second factor is *time*. It takes the passage of time to firmly root the characteristics of a bureaucracy so that participants can become experts in their functional specialties. It takes the passage of time to destroy the informal behavior patterns and to substitute the standard operating procedures and bureaucratic orientation that will eventually evolve in the minds of operating personnel.[17]

The type of organization that existed prior to the establishment of bureaucracy might be best described as "enterprise." The chief differences in bureaucracy and enterprise structure can be found in the way each style is coupled together. The primary coupling device in any organization must always be the means of tying together goals at the top of the organization to goals and decisions at the lower level of the organization. The means for accomplishing goals at the top often become subgoals for decisions further down in the organization. Carried through several stages, this allows one to establish a means-end chain for an organization as depicted in Figure 7-4. Note how goals at one stage in the organization become subgoals at lower levels.

Prior to the development of the bureaucratic organization, entrepreneurs operated without such formally defined goals, policies, and procedures as were described in Chapter 3. The typical response to organizational development was simply to "hire" good people and put them to work."[18] Persons who were trusted might be assigned to widely different responsibilities without regard to special training, background, etc. According to one writer:[19]

FIGURE 7-4

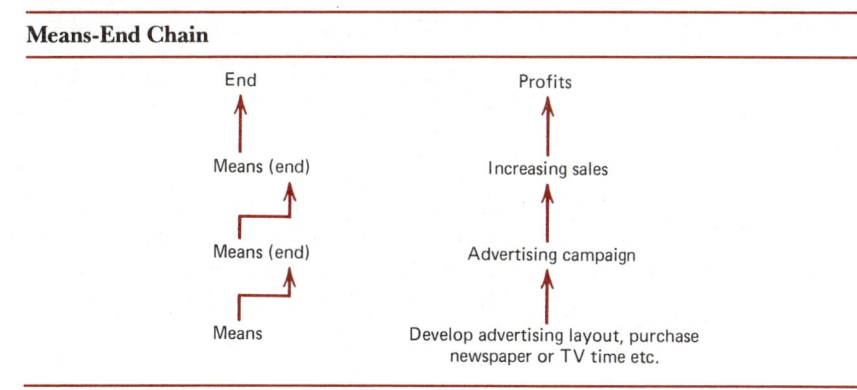

Means-End Chain

```
End                          Profits
 ↑                             ↑
Means (end)              Increasing sales
 ↑                             ↑
Means (end)            Advertising campaign
 ↑                             ↑
Means              Develop advertising layout, purchase
                      newspaper or TV time etc.
```

---

[16] Daniel Katz and Robert L. Kahn, *The Social Psychology of Organizations*, New York, Wiley, 1966, pp. 49–50.
[17] Ibid., p. 48.
[18] Joseph A. Litterer, *The Analysis of Organizations*, 2nd ed., New York, Wiley, 1973, p. 326.
[19] Ibid., p. 326.

FIGURE 7-5

Characteristics of Enterprises and Bureaucracy

ENTERPRISE (Personalized)	BUREAUCRACY (Institutionalized)
Means-end chain individually determined	Means-end chain established by central authority
Personnel selected on basis of personal preference	Personnel selected on basis of competence
Personnel must be told overall objectives and ends	Personnel must be told means only
Personnel must develop own methods and programs	Personnel are trained in existing programs
Personnel highly motivated through work incentives	Motivation often minimal acceptable level
Organization highly innovative, adaptable to change	Organization orderly, slow to change, technically competent
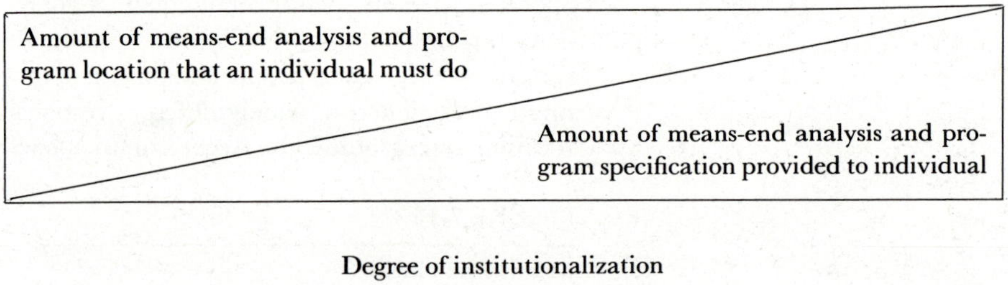 Amount of means-end analysis and program location that an individual must do	Amount of means-end analysis and program specification provided to individual

Degree of institutionalization

Source: Adapted from Joseph A. Litterer, *The Analysis of Organization*, 2nd ed., New York, Wiley, 1973, p. 328.

Such an arrangement is often expedient, but it raises several fundamental problems, among them, that the means-end analysis and often the programs developed to accomplish the objectives exist primarily in the mind of the subordinate assigned the job. If he were to die, or for some reason leave, another person undertaking the task would have to develop all the steps for himself.

As opposed to bureaucracy, an organization characterized by enterprise is more personalized in nature.

Figure 7-5 outlines the chief differences in the bureaucratic and the enterprise (personalized) type organization. We call the process of establishing standard roles, duties, and behavior *institutionalization*. As one moves toward the bureaucratic organization, a higher degree of institutionalization is found.

ADVANTAGES OF A BUREAUCRACY

Basically, bureaucracy is an administrative device that may be employed to accomplish an effective means-end relationship. The advantage of the administrative device is the simplification of complex tasks. A complex problem can be subdivided into simple problems through specialization. The second advantage follows from the first; functional specialization allows experts to focus their knowledge on narrow segments of a total problem and respond with precision, speed, and maximum efficiency.[20] The third major advantage (theoretically, at least) is that a bureaucracy encourages an increase in objective, impersonal decision making at the subunit level.[21]

The simplification of complex tasks and functional specialization are two potential advantages of the bureaucratic form.

DISADVANTAGES OF A BUREAUCRACY[22]

One of the major problems of a bureaucracy is in the area of administrative control. Often it is quite difficult to communicate to the individual the organization's demands and expectations through the hierarchical structure. Thus, there is a tendency to try to eliminate individual behavior that is contrary to the responses desired by the organization.[23] Theoretically this can be done by narrowing the discretionary range of alternate courses of action. But, in practice, this is difficult to do because the organization cannot anticipate all the possible alternatives, especially at management levels. A second way to eliminate undesirable individual behavior is to assume the subordinate will always gage her decisions and actions in terms of the best interests of the organization. This can only be done if (1) the individual clearly understands what is expected of her, (2) she is very much aware of the resources that can be used to reward approved behavior, and (3) she is convinced that the disadvantages of deviating outweigh any advantage that might be incurred.

Administrative control can become a problem in bureaucracies.

A second problem for a large, complex bureaucratic structure is the difficulty of stating clear and precise organizational goals. For the most part, goals of bureaucratic organizations are quite ambiguous in content. Subunits translate the general goals to their specialized interests and situations. But in the process of translation, the organization can lose a certain degree of control over its component subunits.[24]

Getting clear and concise goals and achieving adequate communications are also problems.

---

[20]Robert K. Merton, "Bureaucratic Structure and Personality," *Social Forces*, 18, Wilmington, University of North Carolina Press, 1940, pp. 560–562.
[21]Ibid.
[22]For a discussion of increasing organization effectiveness by blending the elements of structure, strategy, systems, style, skill, staff and superordinated goals see "Look Who's Covered in Red Tape," *Fortune*, May 1981, pp. 357–362.
[23]Warren G. Bennis, "Organizational Developments and the Fate of Bureaucracy," invited address delivered before the Division of Industrial and Business Psychology, American Psychology Association on September 5, 1964.
[24]N. Eisenstadt, "Bureaucracy, Bureaucratization, and Debureaucratization," *Administrative Science Quarterly*, 4, December 1959, pp. 303–306.

A third major problem that exists in a bureaucratic organization is the inability to obtain adequate information for making effective decisions. In this age of advanced technical complexity, top-level policy makers have to rely increasingly on the information supplied by their subordinates. This involves information abstraction, since an administrative subordinate acts as a data filter for his immediate supervisor, who in turn also serves as a filter for his superior. Vital information is often lost or information is condensed to the point at which its true value is distorted. Keeping the information channels open to the top of the organization is a fundamental problem facing every complex structure, and certainly must be considerd as a major problem of bureaucratic organization.

Bureaucratic specialization tends to encourage conflict between staff specialists and line personnel. The specialist tends to monopolize information, resulting in some instances in a reverse dependency of the superior-subordinate relationship. Specialization also creates a problem by limiting the feeling of responsibility of managers whose contributions are too narrow to be measured in traditional output terms. Moreover, experts often develop the inflated concept that their judgment cannot be challenged.

The problems of morale resulting from bureaucracy can also be serious. The creation of narrow specialized jobs often results in both executives and employees becoming restless and dissatisfied on the job. Employees are conditioned by rules and regulations to stereotype their relations with the customer, and "personal attention" is usually lacking.

These excesses of bureaucracy usually result from an overemphasis on impersonality, status, conformity, and routine that have been prescribed in formal rules and regulations.[26]

A BALANCE BETWEEN BUREAUCRACY AND ENTERPRISE

Bureaucracy and enterprise can complement one another.

Bureaucracy is formal and orderly, and its strength is authority through technological competence. Enterprise is personal and spontaneous, and its strength lies in innovation and adaptation to change. The weaknesses of bureaucracy are self-centeredness, the tendency to avoid personal responsibility, and a quest for power. The weaknesses of enterprise are confusion, lack of completion of projects, and a disregard for a systematic approach to problem solving. But *bureaucracy and enterprise can complement each other.*

Both bureaucracy and enterprise contain a large element of logic because both are concerned with the achievement of a goal. They are alike also in being essentially neutral concepts, neither good nor bad in the customary moral sense. Both are inherent in all administration and *it is the balance between them* that determines the vitality or the lethargy with which organizations operate. Undue

---

[25]Merton, ibid.
[26]Ibid.

emphasis on order encourages efficiency to the point of stagnation, and undue emphasis on flexibility sacrifices the efficiency of a smooth operation. So, while bureaucracy needs the counterbalancing factors of enterprise to control its excesses, enterprise in turn needs the counterbalancing factors of bureaucracy to keep it from running uncontrolled.

Many of the early writers in management recognized the need for maintaining the spirit of enterprise—the adaptability, incentives, and crisp communications—while bringing about orderly day-to-day operations. But it was not until the 1940s that entire systems of management were developed to return some of the advantages of enterprise to the bureaucratic organization. We will introduce three such systems in this section: decentralization, the profit center concept, and management-by-objectives.[27]

DECENTRALIZATION AND THE PROFIT CENTER CONCEPT

The term decentralization has been used in many ways. A firm that has several manufacturing plants located throughout the country would be described as having a decentralized manufacturing system. Similarly, a firm with warehousing facilities located in all its key marketing centers would have a decentralized distribution system. Both of these are examples of *physical* decentralization. However, when we refer to decentralization in this chapter, we will be referring to the *degree to which the decision-making function is decentralized* or dispersed throughout the organization.

Decentralization is one method of balancing bureaucracy and enterprise.

Decentralization can be defined as "an increasing by the superior of the subordinate's authority to make decisions at any given level in the organization."[28]

Decentralization implies both the selective spreading and the concentration of authority, at the same time. As companies become more decentralized, certain other decisions must by necessity remain at the top. In discussing decentralization at Massey-Ferguson Limited, John G. Staiger made the following observation.[29]

> *The principle upon which decentralization is carried out is most often thus: authority to take initiative or initiate action should be delegated as close to the scene of action as possible. But decentralization is not merely a matter of delegation on paper. In our own organization manual we state:*

---

[27]For a discussion of increasing organization effectiveness by blending the elements of structure, strategy, systems, style, skill, staff and superordinate goals see Robert H. Waterman, Jr., Thomas J. Peters, and Julien R. Phillips, "Structure Is Not Organization," *Business Horizons*, June 1980, Vol. 23, No. 3, pp. 14–26.

[28]Albert K. Wickesberg, *Management Organization*, New York, Appleton-Century-Crofts, Inc. 1966, p. 60.

[29]John G. Staiger, "What Cannot be Decentralized," *Management Record*, 25, 1, January 1963, pp. 19–21.

Delegation of authority must be real. It includes not only what a superior says to his subordinates, but also the way in which he acts. An important ingredient in delegation is the willingness to permit the subordinate to make a reasonable number of mistakes. The question in delegation is: When does delegation and permission to make mistakes become softness? Within the broader content of company management, decentralization poses the question: When does top management give up effective control of the business?

The extent to which decentralization can be implemented depends on the answers to the following questions.

1. Is the subordinate competent to make the required decisions? As pointed out previously, some latitude to make mistakes must be allowed subordinates in order to develop their decision-making ability.
2. Does the subordinate have adequate information to make the decision? Decision making should not be pushed below the point at which all information bearing on the decision is available.
3. How great is the scope of the impact of the decision? If a decision affects more than one unit of the enterprise, the authority to make the decision must rest with the manager accountable for the several units affected by the decision.

THE PROFIT CENTER CONCEPT

The profit center concept is an approach which has developed as an outgrowth of decentralization. The basic idea behind the profit center concept is simple enough to understand. The organization is broken down into manageable units called *profit centers*. Each profit center is treated as an independent organization, and is operated by a management team whose responsibility is that of earning a satisfactory return on the investment at its disposal. The management of each profit center is given considerable latitude in making operating decisions; because they are held responsible for the effect of their decision on profits, these managers are presumably motivated to make decisions that will result in maximum profits.

As might be expected, the creation of separate profit centers is usually characteristic of large-scale enterprises with multiple product lines. The product organization described in Chapter 5 has grown in favor because of the profit center concept. Based on similarity of products and customers who purchase these products, a number of different divisions are also usually established. Each of these divisions then functions as a profit center, as described previously.

Because profit centers are simply a variation of the decentralized concept, the reasons for one generally apply to the other.

> Profit centers are usually found in large organizations with multiple product lines.

REASONS BEHIND DECISIONS TO DECENTRALIZE

Decentralization and the profit center concept can perhaps be better understood by examining some of the reasons for their development. The post-World War II experiences of the General Electric Company illustrate some of these reasons. In

1939, the company's sales volume was $342 million a year. By 1943, under the pressure of war production, sales had risen fourfold to a level of $1,370 million. Furthermore, forecasts indicated that postwar growth would be even more phenomenal. It was obvious to management that a company with such growth potential would require a different management approach than that used at the time. Ralph J. Cordiner, chief executive Officer and chairman of the board of General Electric, summarized the company's position as follows:[30]

Unless we could put the responsibility and authority for decision making close in each case to the scene of the problem, where complete understanding and prompt action are possible, the company would not be able to compete with the hundreds of nimble competitors who were, as they say, able to turn on a dime.

More specifically, the company perceived the need for the following elements.[31]

1. Better planning.
2. Greater flexibility.
3. Faster and more informed decisions.
4. The development of capable leaders.
5. More friendly and cooperative relationships between managers and other employees.
6. The need to stay ahead of competition in serving customers.
7. The need to make the work of managers at all echelons of the organization more manageable.

GE believed that these needs could not be met within the framework of the centralized structure that existed at the time. Decentralization was the solution ultimately chosen.

FACTORS THAT ENCOURAGE DECENTRALIZATION

Whether authority will be decentralized frequently depends on the way the business has been built. Those businesses that expand from within show a marked tendency to keep authority centralized, as do those that expand under the direction of the owner-founder. On the other hand, companies which grow by merger tend to remain decentralized.[32]

Before a merger, officers in each company make all their own decisions, and even though they give up some power when their company merges with another one, they still tend to keep a great deal of power.

---

[30]From Ralph J. Cordiner, "Decentralization at General Electric," *New Frontiers for Professional Managers*, New York, McGraw-Hill Book Co., 1956, pp. 40–79. Copyright 1956 by McGraw-Hill Book Co. Reprinted in Harold Koontz and Cyril O'Donnel (eds.), *Management, A Book of Readings*, New York, McGraw-Hill Book Co., 1964. Used with permission of McGraw-Hill Book Co.
[31]Ibid.
[32]Harold Koontz and Cyril O'Donnel, *Principles of Management*, New York, McGraw-Hill Book Company, 1968, p. 321.

Decentralization is encouraged by the need to develop managerial talent.

Another factor that encourages decentralization is geographic dispersion, which is a result of the growth in size of the organization. As the number of customers grows and spreads throughout a region or nation, facilities must often be expanded to serve these customers satisfactorily. More authority is often given to the local managers so that they may better cope with the immediate situation.

The larger the organization becomes, the more likely it is that diverse activities may be undertaken. As the corporation begins to handle widely different product lines and undertakes different production technologies associated with these different lines, more autonomy will probably be granted.

Finally, broadening and perfecting the younger executive's decision-making ability can come only through the opportunity to exercise this skill. Many larger firms whose size makes decentralization a necessity continue to push decision making down into the organization for the purpose of developing managerial talent.[33]

ADVANTAGES OF DECENTRALIZATION

Decentralization has resulted in many advantages, generally divisible into five areas: (1) a reduced burden on top management, (2) decision making brought closer to the action, (3) improved accountability, (4) better individual motivation, and (5) the advantages of profit centers. The advantages are discussed in sequence in the following paragraphs.

One advantage of decentralization is that it greatly reduces the burden on top management. Since divisions are judged largely on their profit-and-loss statements, it is not necessary for top management to supervise the divisions closely. This freedom from direct day-to-day supervision enables top management to concentrate its attention on the organization's overall objectives and long-range planning.

Second, decentralization brings the decision-making process closer to the scene of the action. Decisions can be made more quickly because communication problems are minimized.[34]

The third advantage that decentralization provides is that it helps in fixing accountability and encourages competition. Profit reporting by divisions provides a yardstick to compare the performance of one management or manager against another. Because the manager is being measured by the amount of profit growth she can produce, her efforts are kept in line with the primary corporate objectives.[35]

Fourth, through decentralization, the corporation is able to instill a positive motivating force.[36] In a very large corporation, long chains of command result in

---
[33]Albert K. Wickesberg, *Management Organization*, New York, Appleton-Century-Crofts, Inc. 1966, p. 61.
[34]Ibid., p. 61.
[35]Donald O. Harper, "Project Management as a Control and Planning Tool in the Decentralized Company," *Management Accounting*, L, November 1968, p. 29.
[36]Theodore Haimann and William Scott, *Management in the Modern Organization*, Dallas, Houghton Mifflin, Inc., 1970, p. 266.

an impersonal organization structure. Decentralization of decision making provides shorter chains of command and encourages a feeling of individuality.[37] Employees can see the results of their own actions and decisions more readily and, therefore, take a greater interest in and greater responsibility for results.[38]

A final advantage of decentralized management relates to the profit center principle. In theory, the company gets the best of both worlds. When divided into relatively small operational units, a large organization gains all the advantages of being small: flexibility, close control, and ability to make quick decisions. At the same time, central staff control of the individual profit center allows the company to retain the many obvious advantages of size.

DISADVANTAGES OF DECENTRALIZATION

In the last section, some of the principle advantages of decentralization were discussed. There are also a number of disadvantages that may result from decentralization.

Decentralized divisions can become so independent that they may actually begin to work against the best interest of the total organization. This occurs when the managers become more division or department conscious and less company conscious. Only if organization identification is quite strong can this conflict between divisions be avoided, or at least kept under control.[39]

Decentralization can result in divisions that become too independent.

The second disadvantage is an economic one. The advantages gained from decentralization must be weighed against the costs incurred. One of the costs that is easily measurable is the permanent extra cost that results from the necessity of a large staff of specialists. Since many of the staff functions at headquarters of the corporation have to be duplicated in the divisions (at least under profit decentralization), the result is an increase in cost.[40]

Some disadvantages of decentralization are unique to the profit center variation. Perhaps the greatest danger is the sacrifice of overall organization objectives in the pursuit of short-range profitability. With constant pressure from top management to increase profits year after year, the division head must continually prove himself, thus leaving him little time to devote to anything other than his immediate performance. With only a year in which to maneuver, division heads are forced to move fast to produce the results that have been targeted. Naturally, the managers protect themselves as best they can, often by sacrificing long-run goals for short-term results.

TRENDS IN DECENTRALIZATION

Since the early 1960s, the trend toward decentralization seems to have slackened for several possible reasons. It appears that many organizations carried decen-

---

[37] Harper, ibid.
[38] Raymond A. Ehrle, "Management Decentralization: Antidote to Bureaucratic Ills," *Personnel Journal*, LXI, May 1970, p. 397.
[39] Mayer N. Zald, "Decentralization-Myth vs. Reality," *Personnel*, XLI, July 1964, p. 26.
[40] Ibid., pp. 23–24.

tralization too far, losing needed control that caused problems during recent recessions. Furthermore, the recent advances in communication and transportation technology—especially computerization—has allowed top management to operate with information once available only to lower levels.[41] This will be discussed more fully in Chapter 8, Organizational and Interpersonal Communications.

MANAGEMENT BY OBJECTIVES

A recent approach to management that includes a healthy blending of bureaucracy and enterprise is management by objectives (MBO). This approach was suggested in 1954 by Peter Drucker in his book, *The Practice of Management*. At that time, he pointed out the advantage of managing by *objectives* rather than by *drives*.[42] Another early contributor to the field was Douglas McGregor, who argued that many performance appraisal systems failed because they seemed to measure the wrong things. He suggested that appraisal would be more acceptable if superiors and subordinates jointly established goals on which subordinates would be evaluated.[43]

George Odiorne defines MBO:[44]

as a process whereby the superior and subordinate managers of an organization jointly identify its common goals, define each individual's major areas of responsibility in terms of the results expected of him, and use these measures as guides for operating the unit and assessing the contribution of each of its members.

Carroll and Tosi list the following elements as being necessary for an effective MBO program.[45]

1. Effective goal setting by top levels of the managerial hierarchy.
2. Organizational commitment to the approach.
3. Mutual goal setting.
4. Frequent performance review.
5. Some degree of freedom in developing means for the achievement of goals.

Harold Koontz, a prominent writer and consultant from the University of California, considers MBO to be "one of the most influential hallmarks of modern management." Furthermore, he thinks that it is "potentially the most powerful tool of management that has so far been put into practice."[46]

> MBO is an approach to management that emphasizes the existence of specific agreed-on objectives at all levels of organization.

---

[41]"Moving Decisions Down to Where the Action Is," *Business Week*, December 6, 1969, p. 138.
[42]Peter Drucker, *The Practice of Management*, New York, Harper & Row, 1954.
[43]Douglas McGregor, *The Human Side of Enterprise*, New York, McGraw-Hill Book Co., 1960.
[44]George S. Odiorne, *Management by Objectives*, New York, Pitman Publishing Company, 1965, pp. 55–56.
[45]Stephen J. Carroll, Jr., and Henry L. Tosi, Jr. *Management by Objectives, Applications and Research*, New York, Macmillan, 1973.
[46]Harold Koontz, "Making MBO Effective," *California Management Review*, Vol. 20, No. 1, Fall 1977, p. 50.

There are several ways in which MBO attempts to combine the advantages of both bureaucracy and enterprise. First, since mutual goal setting is emphasized, some goals are established by top management to filter down through the organization, while subgoals (means) are determined at each step in the process. Mutual goal setting conferences insure that lower-level employees understand goals as well as means.

In MBO, ample opportunity is available for lower-level managers to develop their own methods. In fact, part of the goals and objective setting process requires that each manager request the resources and support needed to accomplish her own goals. This could include a request for training or for support in program development.

Research in MBO programs has indicated that motivation is strengthened when goals are mutually determined and when they are communicated clearly.[47] On the other hand, MBO has not increased the adaptability of organizations during periods of rapid change but seems to work best in organizations that are rather stable.[48] While MBO has not changed selection procedures, it has caused a higher priority to be placed on performance rather than personal preference in appraisal and promotion procedures.

Objectives, particularly when people participate in setting them, can have a favorable effect on motivation.

In summary, adoption of MBO as a management system has tended to allow systematic goal setting and problem solving while maintaining frequent interaction between levels of management. Whether this interaction has become more interpersonal and informal depends to a great extent on the philosophy of management and the organizational climate in existence when MBO is implemented.[49] Chapter 22, MBO—An Integrative System of Management, explores this concept in considerable detail.

Bass explains the backward metamorphosis from bureaucracy to enterprise with the following statements.[50]

It may be that such emphasis on the attainment of objectives rather than on obedience to prescribed procedures make visible and discernible the difference in esteem of individuals (their value as persons regardless of the positions they occupy).... Indeed such attention to objectives makes it possible for the formal organization not to stand in the way of effective cooperation between individuals regardless of the position they occupy. Thus, while lines of authority may be set up, sufficient flexibility is maintained in the horizontal flow of necessary information.

If MBO is carried out well, officials attached to the organization will develop loyalty and energy because, to a large extent, they are their own bosses. Top management will be more free to reflect, to plan ahead, to look for evidence of decay, and to stimulate enterprise, all of which is not very feasible when administrators are burdened with the details of direction and control.[51]

---

[47]Ibid., pp. 3-16.
[48]Martin J. Gannon and Frank T. Payne, "Source of Referral, Job Orientation, and Employee Effectiveness," *Academy of Management Proceedings*, Minneapolis, Minn., 1972, pp. 39-42.
[49]Robert W. Hollmann, "Supportive Organization Climate and Managerial Assessment of MBO Effectiveness," *Academy of Management Journal*, Volume 19, No. 4, 1976, pp. 560-576.
[50]Bernard M. Bass, *Organizational Psychology*, Boston, Allyn and Bacon, Inc., 1965, p. 254.
[51]Ibid.

186 CLASSICAL MANAGEMENT CONCEPTS

SUMMARY

Organizations go through a life cycle, and one of the challenges facing management is to maintain the vitality of the organization as it grows and develops with the passage of time. In this chapter, we considered two ways to classify organizations, in a discussion of bureaucracy and enterprise. Both bureaucracy and enterprise have their distinguishing characteristics as well as their advantages and disadvantages.

Bureaucracy developed because of the need for an orderly, technically competent system of organization. The scientific management and classical man-

SUMMARY CHART

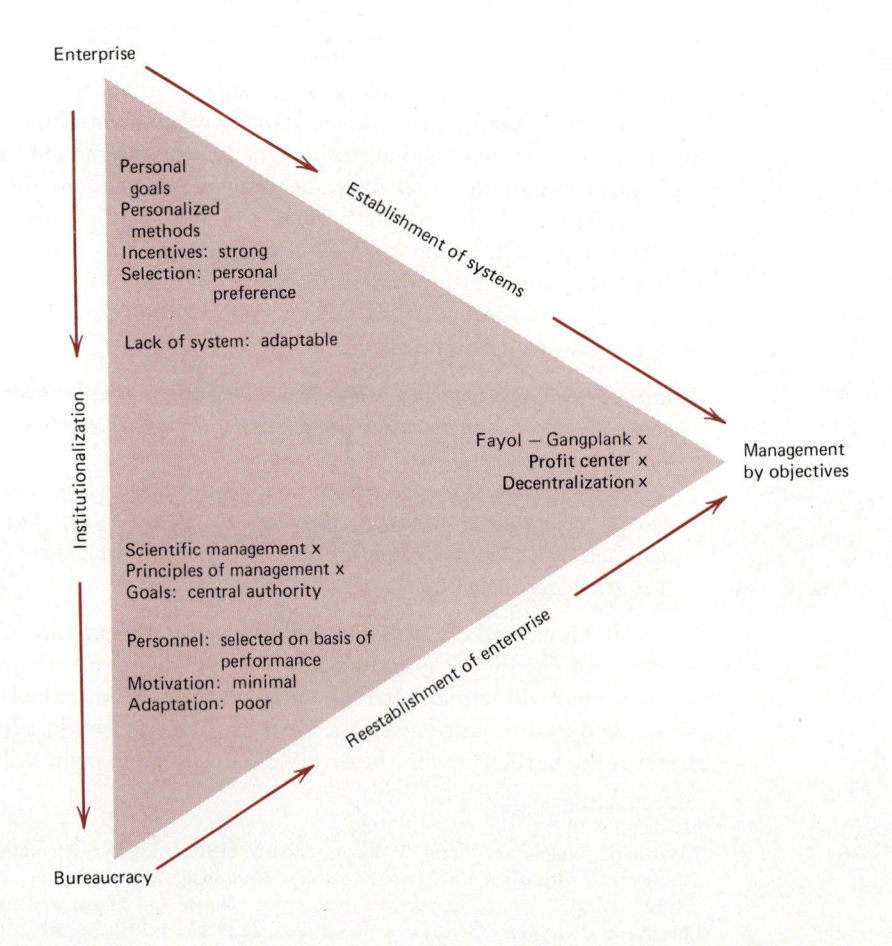

Enterprise

Personal goals
Personalized methods
Incentives: strong
Selection: personal preference

Lack of system: adaptable

Institutionalization

Establishment of systems

Fayol — Gangplank x
Profit center x
Decentralization x

Management by objectives

Scientific management x
Principles of management x
Goals: central authority

Personnel: selected on basis of performance
Motivation: minimal
Adaptation: poor

Reestablishment of enterprise

Bureaucracy

agement writers favored this type of organization. However, as organizations became more and more institutionalized, many disadvantages appeared. The system of organization became slow and cumbersome. It had difficulty adapting to change. Communications were stifled. The motivation of employees was often minimal.

Several modifications in organizational arrangements developed over the years in order to reestablish the spirit of enterprise in organizations. Decentralization, which disperses decision making throughout the lower levels of the organization, seemed to improve bureaucracy. In large corporate organizations, the profit center concept often grew out of decentralization attempts. This profit center plan involves dividing an organization into divisions, each of which is responsible for profit and loss, just like the overall company. In recent years the trend toward decentralization seems to have slowed because of both computerization and a depressed economy that required stricter control of operations.

A recent approach to enterprise type management is called management by objectives (MBO). It includes mutual goal setting by superiors and subordinates frequent performance reviews, and some degree of freedom for subordinates in developing the means of achieving these goals. Whether MBO will provide the final solution to a proper blending of bureaucracy and enterprise remains to be seen.

DISCUSSION QUESTIONS

1. Identify and explain at least six of Fayol's principles of management.
2. Diagram the life cycle of an organization and describe each one of the stages in its development.
3. Briefly describe the characteristics of enterprise, and contrast these characteristics with those of bureaucracy. What are the advantages and disadvantages of bureaucracy?
4. In what way is decentralization related to decision making? Cite several reasons that encourage decentralization and factors that govern how much decentralization can occur.
5. Briefly describe the profit center principle. How does it assist the company that is decentralizing?
6. What are the advantages of decentralization as described by the author of this text and by Peter F. Drucker? What are the five basic disadvantages that may result from decentralization?
7. What are the various business trends that are affecting the amount of decentralization?
8. In your own words define management by objectives. What are the five elements of an effective MBO program?
9. If you were president of a firm, what indications would you use to determine whether your organization was too centralized? What specific steps would you

take to decentralize the organization? What criterion would you use to determine whether the decentralization had been carried out far enough, or perhaps too far?

APPLICATION EXERCISES AND CASES

RESEARCH COORDINATION IN THE PHARMACEUTICAL INDUSTRY[52]

One of the country's, and the world's, largest pharmaceutical companies has major research laboratories in five countries: The United States, Great Britain, Ireland, France, and Japan. The laboratory in the United States goes back to the 1920s. The one in Great Britain grew out of the work in World War II, when the company was among the pioneers in large-scale production of penicillin. The fundamental knowledge about antibiotics was then still primarily in Great Britain so that the necessary massive scientific and technical effort had to be based there. The Irish laboratory was a by-product of the decision to take advantage of exceedingly favorable Irish tax laws when locating a major new plant—a plant meant to produce intermediates primarily for the European market. Since the techniques used in the plant were mostly new, there was a need for a substantial group of technical and scientific plant-chemists, as well as plant-engineers. This made it logical for the Irish government to suggest that the company build a full-scale research lab, if only to hold well-grained Irish scientists in Ireland rather than have them emigrate to the United Kingdom, the United States, and Canada, and logical that the company pick up the suggestion. France was chosen for a laboratory in veterinary products, an old French specialty and one in which French government and French universities gladly cooperate with industry. Also, the French scientists the company wanted for the work were rather cool to the idea of moving to the United States and positively icy about the alternative suggestions: to move to the British midlands and to exchange the climate and scenery of the Loire for the fogs of Manchester. Japan first came with a joint venture. But when the American company bought out the Japanese partner in 1968, as the Japanese business grew so fast and so successfully that the Japanese could no longer finance it, it had to take over a large, flourishing, and completely Japanese lab. At first only one man understood enough English to participate intelligently in the company's annual worldwide research conference. But that did not stop the Japanese from doing first-rate work in tropical medicine in which none of the company's other labs had much competence or strength.

However, *all* five labs complained that there wasn't any coordination between them, that there was constant duplication of effort, and worse still, that important and promising work wasn't being done at all because each lab thought the

---

[52] Peter F. Drucker, *Management Cases*, New York, Harper's College Press, 1977, pp. 159–161.

other one was doing it, and that no one in any of the five labs really knew where to go in the other four to find help, to get advice and to talk over matters of common interest.

This was the situation when a new companywide research vice-president took over. Or, rather, Dr. Rodney VanDelden—Dutch born, American educated, chief biochemist in the British lab until he moved to America around 1968 to finish a research job on central nervous system drugs the American group had botched—was really the FIRST companywide research chief ever. His predecessor had still been Research Director in the United States, the first among five equals, and expected only to "coordinate." VanDelden was expected to *manage*, and had, as visible sign of his new authority, control of the budgets of all research labs whereas formerly each country had set and managed the research budget for its own research efforts.

Questions
1. What problems can VanDelden anticipate?
2. What patterns of organization and coordination are available to him?
3. What kind of structure and method of operation would you choose? Justify your answer.

NAYLOR CORPORATION[53]

The consumer products division of the Naylor Corporation consisted of the marketing, production, research, accounting, and personnel departments. Each department had a full-time secretary.

Because of the seasonal demand for some of its products, the work of the secretaries in the consumer products division was often unbalanced. Usually when one department was temporarily overloaded, secretaries in other departments had free time available.

Each time the secretary of a department became overloaded, her departmental manager vigorously requested funds for additional secretarial work from Mr. Parks, the division manager. The reply Mr. Parks gave was to call the department heads into a meeting and request that those with extra secretarial time available should assist the overloaded departments. All department heads claimed that their secretaries were already overworked but that they would see what they could do.

After each of these meetings the department heads reluctantly shared a minimum amount of secretarial work. However, in every case the practice was discontinued within two weeks after the meeting called by Mr. Parks. Both the department heads and the secretaries resented the practice.

In each yearly budget every department continued to press for additional secretarial funds although it was apparent that the overall work load of the division did not justify additional funds.

---
[53]Herbert G. Hicks, *The Management of Organizations: A Systems and Human Resources Approach*, 2nd ed., New York, McGraw-Hill Book Co., 1972, p. 442.

Questions

1. Why were the department heads and their secretaries reluctant to share the available time?
2. What bureaucratic game is being played by the department heads and their secretaries? What is Mr. Parks's part in the game?
3. What recommendations do you have for Mr. Parks? For the department heads?

PART TWO
CASES

THE STELLAR STEEL PRODUCTS COMPANY[54]
A Plan to Provide Staff Assistance for Manufacturing

The Stellar Steel Products Company manufactures and sells processing equipment for the canning and dairy industries. Originally, the product line consisted of a few standard items for the two principal industrial groups. Subsequently, special equipment was designed and made for customers, and modifications of the standard equipment were frequently made to comply with customer specifications. The company began operations about ten years ago with a few key people and several good equipment designs. The excellence of engineering design and quality of production quickly established the company.

Since the start of the company, the more important problems were discussed and solutions decided upon through somewhat informal meetings of the key executives. At such a meeting nine months ago, the group decided that some staff assistance be provided for the factory manager. In this decision he fully concurred. Accordingly, a purchasing agent and a production-control supervisor were employed (see Figure 1). These two individuals gave some relief to the factory manager, but nevertheless conditions did not improve as much as anticipated.

The factory manager was still overburdened. Furthermore, finding it difficult to delegate responsibilities and authority, he continued to pass on virtually all manufacturing matters. For example, he continued to approve all purchase orders, regardless of the monetary commitment involved. Together with each of the foremen, he would determine daily the orders that were to be processed, even though such schedules might be contrary to the overall production program worked out by the production control supervisor. Recently, the president suggested a new organization structure, shown in Figure 2. Primarily, the concept behind the proposed Manufacturing Committee was to break down the one-person control situation in the factory. The president also recognized that additional staff assistance was a further prerequisite to correcting the conditions in the plant.

Questions

1. What advantages do you see in the president's reorganization plan? What are its major weaknesses?

---

[54] From Paul E. Holden, Frank K. Shallenberger, and Walter A. Diehm, *Industrial Management,* 2nd ed., Englewood Cliffs, N.J., Prentice-Hall, *Selected Case Problems in* 162, pp. 346–344.

192 CLASSICAL MANAGEMENT CONCEPTS

FIGURE 1

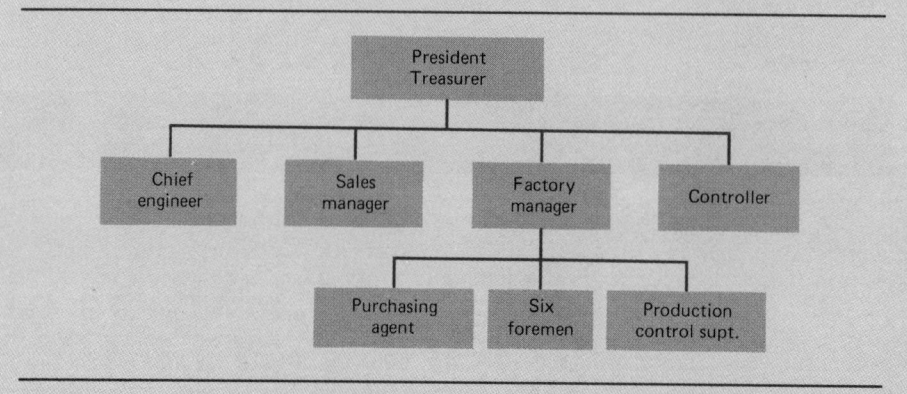

```
                    President
                    Treasurer
    ┌───────────────┬────┴──────┬──────────────┐
  Chief          Sales       Factory       Controller
  engineer       manager     manager
                   ┌───────────┼────────────┐
               Purchasing    Six         Production
               agent         foremen     control supt.
```

FIGURE 2

```
                    President
                    Treasurer
       ┌───────────────┼───────────────┐
   Sales manager   Manufacturing    Controller
                   committee
                   ─────────────
                   President, chairman
                   Factory manager
                   Chief engineer
                   Purchasing agent
                   Production control, supt.
                   Methods engineer
       ┌──────┬────────┬────┴─────┬─────────┬──────────┐
    Chief  Purchasing Factory  Production Methods  Personnel
    engineer agent    manager  control    engineer manager
                         │     supt.
                       Shop
                       foremen
```

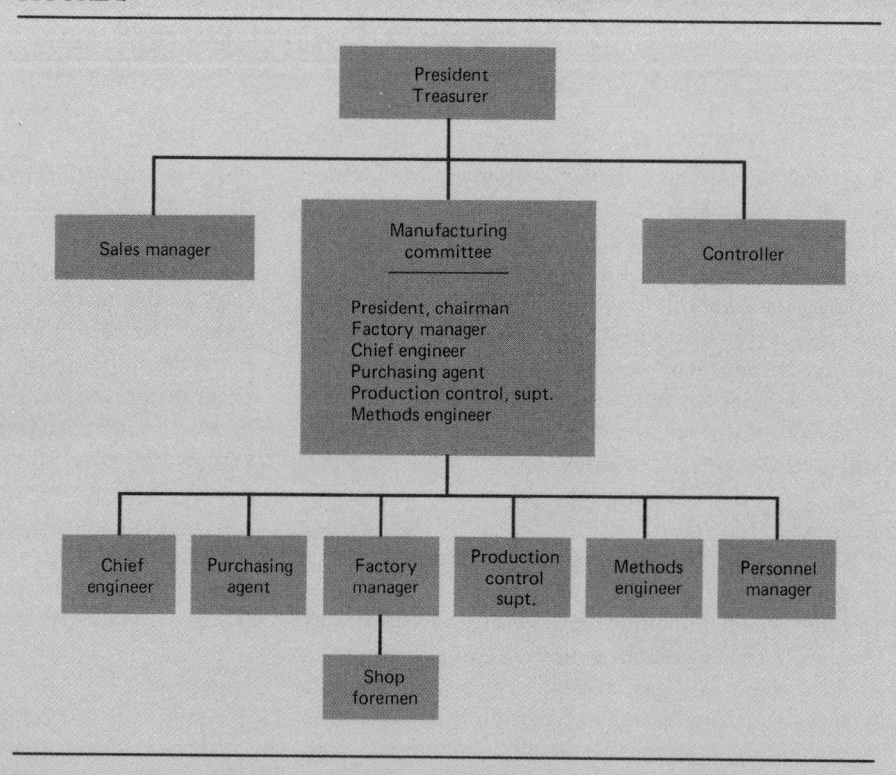

Prepare what you believe would be a more effective organization structure for the company.

(a) Draw an organization chart and explain its major features and reporting relationships.

(b) What are the advantages of your suggested plan?

(c) Give some examples of the type of authority various staff managers would have in selected situations.

THE HARDER COMPANY[55]
Development of a Safety Program

Mr. Roland Harder, president and principal owner of the Harder Manufacturing Company, was deep in thought over a recent comment by a close friend. The friend had said, "You know, Rolly, considering the size of your company, you owe it to your workers to think about having a top-flight safety engineer. We have hired a man in this position recently, and have experienced a significant drop in accidents."

Mr. Harder was the first to admit that he had devoted too little attention to safety, but he wasn't sure what a safety engineer could accomplish beyond that already being done by the Workers' Safety Committee and the plant engineer.

The Harder Company manufactured a broad line of machine parts for the automobile industry and employed nearly 2000 people. As a result of this surging growth Mr. Harder was not able to devote as much of his time as he would have liked to all phases of the business. He was convinced, however, that he had been able to surround himself with capable executive talent in key company positions.

Mr. Harder continued to think about the safety question, he recalled a speech he had heard some six months earlier. The speech had been given by John Greene, general manager of the Swallow Company. Among other subjects, Mr. Greene had praised the safety work done at this plant. Mr. Harder, his mind on retooling and preparing for orders that arose from the automakers' style changes, had accepted this information as interesting, but as yet had done nothing about it.

Now that the subject of safety had come up again, Mr. Harder called Mr. Greene to see what more he could learn about safety activities. During the course of the conversation he learned that the assistant safety engineer of the Swallow Company, Mr. Jack Stanton, was interested in changing jobs. Apparently the company's safety engineer was quite young, and Mr. Stanton was somewhat stymied as far as advancement was concerned. Mr. Greene added that, although he would hate to lose Mr. Stanton, he did not feel he could stand in the way of his applying for a position with more potential. Mr. Harder arranged through Mr. Greene to meet Mr. Stanton.

THE INTERVIEW

When Jack Stanton arrived at the Harder Company plant, he was first taken on a tour of the facilities. During the tour, he noted several things that seemed to be indicative of the company's safety program.

In one instance, he noticed a large machine that was not operating. Upon questioning his guide, he found that a new employee had failed to follow instructions for operating the machine. The worker had been told to use wedges to secure the pieces he was working on, but since these wedges slowed down his pace, he attempted to get by without them. This shortcut worked for a while, but eventually resulted in extensive damage to the machine. The worker himself was not hurt, but the machine was shut down for several weeks for repair.

In one of the machine shops, Stanton observed another machine under repair, a large rotating surface grinder that had a magnetized table for holding a casting in place. The operator made the mistake of pushing the button that rotated the table before he pushed the button that magnetized the table.

The result was that the casting was totally ruined and an expensive grinding wheel was damaged. Again, the worker had not been injured. Following a brief inspection, Stanton found that a simple relay could be installed that would prevent the table from rotating until the magnetizing button had been pushed.

Stanton also noticed that many workers doing grinding and chipping work were not fitted with the

---

[55] Paul E. Holden, Frank K. Shallenberger, and Walter A. Diehm, *Management*, 2nd ed., Englewood Cliffs, N.J., Prentice Hall, 1962, pp. *Selected Case Problems in Industrial* 238–242.

proper type of eye protection. When he asked who fitted the workers with goggles and shields, he was told that all protection devices were stored in the tool crib, and it was up to the worker to choose what he needed.

It was obvious that the company had been growing rapidly, and that the plant engineer had not been able to devote much time to safety. Apparently he had done little more than appoint a safety committee and make monthly accident reports. General conditions in the plant indicated to Stanton that foremen and supervisors were not safety conscious. Among the conditions that he noted were the following:

1. A ladder was left unattended in an aisle; workers passing the location had to ease between the ladder and the operating machines.
2. The floor around one machine was covered with oil; the operator explained that the supply room was out of nonslip preparation for absorbing spilled oil.
3. Several wrenches and other tools were observed resting on operating machines.
4. The seat of a chair used by one worker had broken and a slat of wood was laid across the frame as a substitute.
5. An air hose had been left stretched across a heavily used passageway.
6. Several drums of highly concentrated cleaning fluid were left uncovered in a corner of the building.

Stanton learned that the Harder Company had an accident frequency rating of 29.7 and an accident severity rating of 3100. The respective rates for the Swallow Company were 8 and 150, and the rates considered good for the industry were 10 and 500.

In talking to other management people Stanton gained the following impression of each man.

Roland Harder, president, had a friendly, warm personality, was quite proud of his company, and seemed concerned with management-worker relations. Although he was relatively uninformed about safety, he was much interested in improving conditions in the Harder Company plant and receptive to Stanton's ideas.

Clint Steele, plant manager, intent on getting out production was apparently quite strict, but fair, in his dealings with people. He was obviously skeptical of the value of a safety program, and uninterested in generalities. Extremely interested in how much a safety program could save in dollars, he wanted specific facts on how safety could help cut costs and increase production efficiency. Stanton thought that if Steele were completely sold on a program he would back it completely.

Joe Mullen, plant engineer, seemed to be fairly easygoing and not particularly opinionated. He had handled safety in the past, but only to the extent of supervising mechanical and physical aspects. Mullen thought that safety was more of a human problem, than one of making safety guards, and so forth. He seemed a little concerned about the additional workload for his department that might be generated by a full-time safety engineer.

Jake Welsh, production engineering manager, seemed very touchy about any interference with his department's normal activities. Welsh, quite outspoken, commented to the effect that all safety people want to do is to put guards on this or that and hamper the worker so that he can't get out production.

Questions

Plan the safety program you would propose. Be sure to consider the following points.

1. Set forth a statement of the general mission for a safety program at Harder Company.
2. Identify at least three specific objectives for such a program.
3. Give two examples of policies you would recommend.
4. Formulate a step-by-step plan you would follow in implementing your safety program.

Note. A knowledge of safety management is not required to accomplish the above. For each of the questions refer back to the chapter to refresh your understanding of the concepts involved. A minimum safety program would include safety consciousness throughout the entire organization, widespread participation, physical safeguards, continual accident analysis, and policies and procedures.

PART THREE
ORGANIZATIONAL BEHAVIOR AND DESIGN

CHAPTER 8
ORGANIZATIONAL AND INTERPERSONAL COMMUNICATIONS

CHAPTER 9
HUMAN MOTIVATION

CHAPTER 10
JOB DESIGN—CREATING MORE MEANINGFUL WORK

CHAPTER 11
ROLE AND FUNCTION OF THE GROUP IN ORGANIZATIONS

CHAPTER 12
CONTINGENCY APPROACHES TO ORGANIZATIONS

KENTOWN CORPORATION

THE CREATIVE ORGANIZATION—A JAPANESE EXPERIMENT

As we progressed through our study of organizations in Part Two, we focused on developing a structure geared to accomplish the work to be done to dealing with numerous technical considerations. Emphasis on people as they influence organizational effectiveness occurred primarily in the latter part of Chapter 7, blending elements of bureaucracy and enterprise.

In Part Three and Part Four we emphasize the body of management thought known as organizational behavior. Part Three develops an understanding of human behavior in general and, in a more specific sense, the behavioral dynamics of people as they interact within an organizational setting.

Chapter 8 is devoted to the very important area of organizational and interpersonal communications. Following a discussion of the major problems in organizational communications, a model of the communications process is presented. Using this as a base, the dynamics of interpersonal communications is fully developed and guidelines for effective communications are discussed.

Chapter 9 explores the process of motivation. We will be examining several theories of motivation as an explanation of human behavior; the relationship between incentives offered by the organization and individual motivation; the role of money as a motivator; and the interrelation between internal achievement motivation and external incentives.

Chapter 10 delves into the area of job design. It summarizes the historical approach to designing jobs, the advantages expected, and the results in terms of the effect on human resources. The concepts of job enlargement and enrichment are explored in detail and the contingency nature of job design is examined. The final portion of the chapter relates job design to motivation and leadership.

The subject of concern in Chapter 11 is the behavior of groups in organizations. Following a definition of both formal and informal groups and a discussion of how they develop, the criteria for evaluating effective and ineffective groups is presented. The internal dynamics of groups are investigated, as well as how management can use this knowledge of work group behavior.

Chapter 12 examines some of the newer approaches to organization. A contingency approach to organizing is suggested, which presumes that no single type of organization will satisfy every task.

As a result of studying Chapters 8 through 12 you should have a rather thorough understanding of and appreciation for the operational aspects of human behavior in organizations.

CHAPTER 8
ORGANIZATION AND INTERPERSONAL COMMUNICATIONS

THE COMMUNICATION PROBLEM IN PERSPECTIVE

IMPORTANCE OF TOP-LEVEL COMMITMENT

COMMUNICATION DEFINED AND AN OVERVIEW OF THE MANAGER'S COMMUNICATION ENVIRONMENT

INFORMATION SIDE OF THE COMMUNICATION PROCESS

INTERPERSONAL BEHAVIOR AND COMMUNICATION

ESTABLISHING A MANAGEMENT APPROACH

THE IMPORTANCE OF LISTENING

BARRIERS TO CREATING UNDERSTANDING AND HOW TO OVERCOME THEM

ORGANIZATIONAL PROBLEMS IN ESTABLISHING EFFECTIVE COMMUNICATION

APPLICATION EXERCISES AND CASES

C.I.T. FINANCIAL CORPORATION

ADLESON SALES

LEGENDS OF BUSINESS[1]

Those old company stories never die. They live to motivate managers, and they inspire employee loyalty and trust much better than a dry recital of corporate statistics.

When Henry Wells and William G. Fargo opened a general freight-forwarding agency in San Francisco during the Gold Rush days of 1852, the two enterprising expressmen had no idea that they were about to create a corporate legend in their own time. Dealing in "the purchase and sale of gold dust, bullion and specie, also packages, parcels and freight of all descriptions," Wells Fargo has since conjured up images of what a company history calls "stage-coaches plying Western trails, of treasure boxes laden with gold, of gallantry, gumption and dering-do."

Thus, when Wells Fargo, now a leading California bank, marked its 125th anniversary in 1977, employees proudly sported buttons proclaiming, "I have a legend to live up to."

Alan L. Wilkins, professor of organizational behavior at Utah's Brigham Young University, has made a study of corporate legends and maintains that telling stories about the company's past is "one of the most effective ways to motivate managers and inspire employee loyalty and trust." As an example, he cites the case of a big California vintner that divided its work force into three groups, and gave each a different presentation supporting the company's claim that its wines are superior to other American brands. Later, in a test evaluating belief in the claim, the group that had been told a story about the winery's legendary founder scored highest.

Another corporate legend that registers well with employees, according to Wilkins, is the so-called, "Nine-Day Fortnight" at Hewlett-Packard Corp. In 1970, when the electronics industry was straining under cutbacks and layoffs, the company kept everybody on the payroll by having the corporate staff take a 10 percent pay cut and receive an extra day off every other week. By propagating the Nine-Day Fortnight legend, Hewlett-Packard has successfully imbued its workers in the belief that "the company takes care of its own," says Wilkins, and that "this is a good place to work."

---
[1] Robert Levy, "Legends of Business," *Dun's Review*, June 1980, Vol. 115, No. 6, pp. 92–98.

Communications plays a major role in how effectively people work together.

Communications play a major role in determining how effectively people work together and coordinate their efforts to achieve objectives. Management's awareness of the importance of communications is evidenced by the fact that since the mid-1950s, American business and industry has been spending billions of dollars annually on improving communication with employees. With this great expenditure, it would seem that all of the communication problems that exist would have been solved long ago. Most managers agree, however, that communication continues to be a major problem.

---
*The authors gratefully acknowledge the assistance of Dr. Elmore Alexander, Associate Professor of Management, Memphis State University, who helped to revise this chapter.

THE COMMUNICATION PROBLEM IN PERSPECTIVE[2]

Inadequate communications fall mainly into two types. The first type results from poor or insufficient instructions from the manager to the subordinate concerning the work to be performed. Failure to communicate properly the job requirements and task assignments can result in misunderstandings, and lead to the job being performed incorrectly or incompletely, with a resultant monetary loss to the organization. The importance of giving clear and precise instructions cannot be overemphasized.

The manager who asked the new secretary to "burn a copy of this report" and found his only copy of his hard work in ashes understands this point quite well. Next time, she will state carefully, "Please reproduce a copy of this on our office copier."

The second inadequacy is the failure to communicate to employees general information that may bear no direct relationship to the actual work which they perform. This may result in the damaging and lowering of morale, not only of a few individuals, but also of the entire organization. It is important, therefore, that an organization be aware of the benefits that can be derived from communicating information that the employees wish to know, but do not necessarily have to know to do their jobs. It is not hard to imagine a significant difference between the impact of hearing about your company's new acquisition from the chairman of the board over a closed circuit TV hookup as opposed to hearing about it over dinner from your spouse via the neighborhood "busybody."

Management should realize that employees want to be well informed about the affairs of the organization, and, since they do have a stake in the success of the organization, they also want to be well informed about matters which affect them on their jobs. Information of this nature is being constantly generated and, if properly communicated, enables the employees to feel that they are integral parts of the organization; that is, that they are working *with* it, not just *for* it.

Employees want to be well informed about the affairs of the organization since they have a large stake in it.

IMPORTANCE OF TOP-LEVEL COMMITMENT

A climate for effective communication must be initiated and actively participated in by top management. Most frequently communication is man made: the communication patterns in a given department, group, or unit reflect the communication behavior of the person in charge. For example, if the superior in charge is silent and uncommunicative, his subordinates are likely to be the same; if he takes a negative attitude toward the communication program, his subor-

Communications in a department reflect the behavior of the person in charge.

---

[2]The material in this section draws heavily from the following source: Lynn A. Townsend, "A Corporate President's View of the Internal Communications Function," *Journal of Communication*, December 1965. In 1965, Mr. Townsend, president of Chrysler Corporation, was awarded the "Communicator of the Year" award for his firm's program. C. J. Dover headed the team that developed the communications program at Chrysler.

dinates will likely reflect his negativism. Therefore, the communication behavior prevailing at the top level will be reflected throughout the organization.

Due to the complexity of most organizational structures, it is a mistake to assume that oral communication in its original form from either top or bottom will filter through the many layers. Managers must not view the information they receive as their possession, to be passed on as they see fit. They must cooperate actively with the total communication effort and be aware of their individual responsibility in the flow of information. Individual managers must be denied the privilege of deciding whether communication is desirable or not, and must recognize that it is part of their duties to communicate regularly and effectively with both superiors and subordinates.

It is the manager's duty to communicate regularly and effectively with superiors and subordinates.

Perhaps the greatest difficulty and most common deficiency in communication is in the area of the upward flow of information. Employee suggestions and opinions should be regarded as an important organizational asset that can contribute to increased production and organizational efficiency. Opportunities for employees to communicate can be provided by supervisors when they interact and listen to their employees in the work environment. Many managers tend to underestimate employee willingness and desire to help the organization operate better, and also to underrate the power of good communication to turn this latent desire into constructive action.

The following factors will provide a solid foundation for building a results-producing communication program within the organization.

1. Internal communication must be recognized as an essential tool of good management.
2. Employees must be well informed concerning their mutual interest in organizational success.
3. Individual managers must actively support the organization's communication effort.
4. Substantial emphasis must be placed on communication planning and measurement.
5. Top management must establish a good communication climate.
6. A long-term investment in professional talent and communication programming must be made. By this we mean utilizing the services of people who are trained in designing and administering effective communication programs.
7. Management must recognize the responsibility to listen as well as to speak.
8. Managers must recognize both that employees desire to help their company and that the power of communication can tap this potential.

The purpose of the material that follows is to explore the key elements of the communication process as it affects and is influenced by the individual manager. The overall objective is to develop an awareness of the need to communicate and an appreciation of why managers do not always communicate effectively. More specifically, the following topics will be discussed.

1. The definition of communication and an overview of the effective communication process.

2. The manager's communication environment.
3. The information side of the communication process.
4. A communication transaction.
5. Barriers to creating understanding and how to overcome them.

COMMUNICATION DEFINED AND AN OVERVIEW OF THE MANAGER'S COMMUNICATION ENVIRONMENT

Communication is the process of passing information and understanding from one person to another.

Communication can be simply defined as the process of passing information and understanding from one person to another.[3] There are several important considerations involved in this rather simple definition.

First, there must be a receiver if communication is going to occur. The receiver side is too often forgotten completely or taken for granted. Communicators may assume that having sent the message, the process has been consummated; however this is seldom true. The sender of a communication must consider the receiver both when structuring the message.

Second, this definition stresses the importance of the creation of understanding. Communication is not an end in itself. Its purpose is to elicit a positive action or response on the part of the receiver, and this requires understanding. Communication is the means by which a manager interacts with people in a leadership capacity. If she can effectively communicate with them, she can also motivate them. Understanding also involves an attitude of wanting to respond positively. Effective communication will result only with the careful attention of both parties to the total communication process.

Third, communication is a dynamic as opposed to a static process. It is impossible to understand a communication by taking a "snapshot" of a communication situation. Neither a single word nor a single sentence has complete meaning in and of itself. It is only when one considers the entire process of activities and messages that communication becomes understandable. This is analogous to what one sees from a movie or videotape as opposed to a single picture. Imagine how confusing just one or two sentences from a discussion between two managers would be if that were the only thing that you knew about the interaction. Communication can only be understood as a process.

THE MANAGER'S COMMUNICATION ENVIRONMENT

Every manager lives in what can be described as a two-way, tridimensional communication environment. It is tridimensional in the sense that regardless of where he stands in the management hierarchy, he becomes involved in communication with respect to his superior, the people he directly supervises, and other departments with which he must interrelate in order to accomplish results. These other departments include both line and staff. It is a two-way process in

---
[3] Keith Davis, *Human Behavior at Work*, New York, McGraw-Hill Book Co., 1972, p. 379.

FIGURE 8-1

Communication as a Two-Way Tridimensional Process

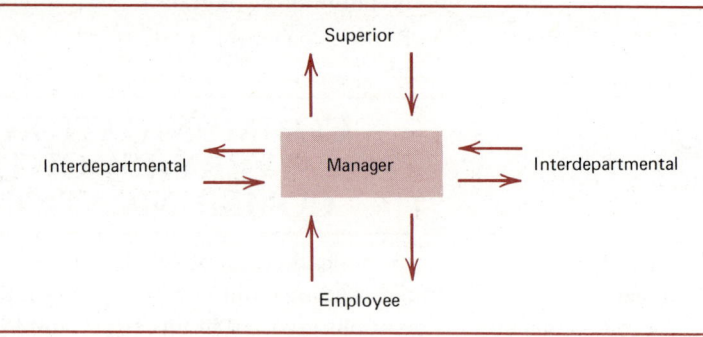

[Diagram: Manager at center with bidirectional arrows connecting to Superior (above), Employee (below), and Interdepartmental (left and right)]

that the manager must be concerned with both the downward and the upward flow of information. These relationships are depicted in Figure 8-1.

When identifying communication problems, the manager must look at himself as well as elsewhere. Figure 8-1 very effectively illustrates that managers stand at the crossroads of effective communication, and they must each take the initiative if communication is going to occur. If information he desires from his superior is not forthcoming, he must take the initiative in requesting it. If feedback from his employees is not forthcoming, certain positive actions can elicit it. The manager can foster improvement in interdepartmental communication when it is not satisfactory. Only when each and every manager accepts responsibility for the process of effective communication, with this affirmative attitude, can improvement be made.

INFORMATION SIDE OF THE COMMUNICATION PROCESS

The entire process of communication involves five steps and three major elements as shown in Figure 8-2. The first two steps, conceiving of a message or idea and converting it into words or numbers, is controlled by the sender. The accuracy of these steps is crucial and depends primarily on the ability of the sender to empathize with the receiver during the encoding stage. The message must be the correct one, but, most importantly, it must be coded in unmistakeable terms. S.I. Hayakawa succinctly stated this thought in saying, "the meaning of words is *not* in the words, it is in us."[4] Finally, by using nondirective interviews one can continually "feel the pulse" of the receiver and modify communication to fit his personality state.

The meaning of words is in those who hear and interpret them.

We have several choices when dealing with communication channels, the third step in the process. For policies, rules, and procedures, the formal organizational

---
[4]S. I. Hayakawa, *Language in Thought and Action*, New York, Harcourt Brace and World, Inc., 1949, p. 292.

FIGURE 8-2

Development of Communications

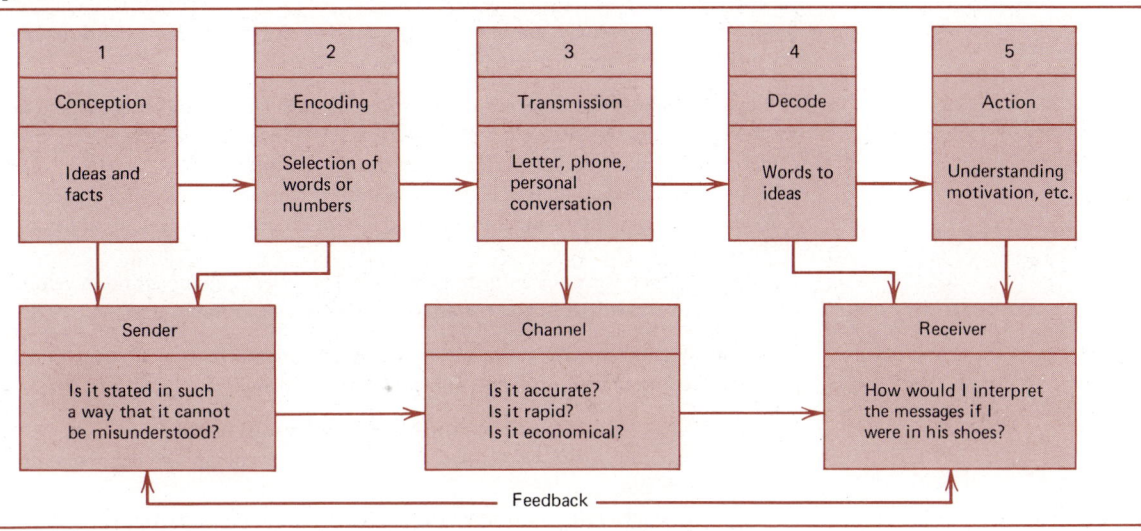

1 Conception	2 Encoding	3 Transmission	4 Decode	5 Action
Ideas and facts	Selection of words or numbers	Letter, phone, personal conversation	Words to ideas	Understanding motivation, etc.

Sender: Is it stated in such a way that it cannot be misunderstood?

Channel: Is it accurate? Is it rapid? Is it economical?

Receiver: How would I interpret the messages if I were in his shoes?

Feedback

---

channels will most likely be used. Other situations may dictate the use of informal channels, such as the informal group or the grapevine.[5] Furthermore, the effective communication should consider the effect of group norms on messages transmitted. Will the group be receptive to the new policy on days off? Will resistance develop to the new promotion policy?

When considering the choice of communication channel, one should keep in mind the well-documented fact that the use of multiple communication channels improves the effectiveness of the communication.[6] A recent study,[7] indicates that it is also improved by the use of audiovisual communication techniques such as slide presentations. The implication here is simple—the more often a message is repeated and the greater the number of places in which it is presented the more likely it is that the message will be understood and remembered.

When viewing the decoding and action steps, an accurate picture of the receiver should be established in the communicator's mind. How will he or she interpret this word or these numbers? Does my choice of words mean the same thing to the receiver as it does to me?

Figure 8-3 summarizes the information side of the communication process as it relates to superiors and subordinates. Figure 8-4 summarizes some of the things

The use of multiple communication channels improves the effectiveness of the communication.

---

[5] Arlyn J. Melcher and Ronald Bellor, "Toward a Theory of Organization Communication," *Academy of Management Journal*, Vol. 10, No. 1, March, 1967, pp. 39–52.

[6] D. T. Dahle, "An Objective and Comparative Study of Five Methods of Transmitting Information to Business and Industry Employees," *Speech Monographs*, 21, 1954, pp. 21–23 and D. A. Level, "Communication Effectiveness: Method and Situation," *The Journal of Business Communication*, Vol. 10, 1972, pp. 19–25.

[7] R. W. Driver, "The Relative Efficacy of Different Methods for Communicating Benefits: A Quasi-Experiment in a Field Setting," *Academy of Management Proceedings*, 1979, pp. 336–340.

FIGURE 8-3

Information Side of the Communication Process

Types of information the manager should communicate to employees and that she wants her superior to communicate to her (*downward communication*)

1. Key areas where she is accountable for results, and what specific results she should be achieving in each area.
2. Periodic feedback on her performance, in a quantitative sense.
3. Information relating to overall departmental performance and achievements.
4. Where the department fits into the total operation; and where each job fits and why it is important.
5. Information concerning both short-term and long-term changes and developments as they relate to and affect the employee both now and in the future.

Types of information the manager should communicate to her superior and that she wants her people to communicate to her (*upward communication*)

1. Problems involved in accomplishing the desired results in her job.
2. Her feelings and attitudes toward the company in general, the department, and her own supervision.
3. Ideas and suggestions to improve the overall operation or a particular job or process.
4. Advance information concerning her progress on the job as it relates to a schedule or specific standards.

---

each manager should be communicating to other departments and they, in turn, should communicate to him.

In examining Figure 8-3, it will be noted that there is a definite overlap in the various lists. This phenomenon brings out two important ideas as they relate to the process of communication.

First, effective communication is an interdependent process. A manager cannot fully meet her communication responsibility unless someone else meets hers. For example, one type of information the manager should be communicating to her subordinates is what the department should be achieving in certain key areas of accountability, such as quality and quantity. Unless the manager's superior gives her this information, she obviously cannot pass it on to her people. Therefore, the interdependent nature of communication creates a situation where all personnel in the organization must be conscious of the need to communicate and also must have a clear understanding of what they should be communicating.

The second important idea that Figure 8-3 illustrates is that effective communication is a continuous chain: that any break in the chain can have far-reaching consequences. It takes an overall, concerted effort and dedication on the part of everyone involved to insure that the process is completed and effective.

Regarding Figure 8-4, accomplishment of optimal results in organizations usually rests on a certain amount of interunit cooperation and integration of effort. For this to occur, communication between units must take place. The types of information listed illustrate the kinds of things that will enable units to work together on a more positive basis.

INTERPERSONAL BEHAVIOR AND COMMUNICATION

Oliver Wendell Holmes once described a conversation between John and Henry in which six "persons" took part: John, as John knew himself; John, as he was known to Henry; the "true" John, as he was known only to God; and the equivalent trio of Henrys.

Unless one sees himself realistically, he will not develop maturity.

Although these characters seemed to be nominal (to exist in name only), they play an important role in the development of personality. As has been pointed out by numerous sociologists a person cannot come to a mature perception of himself without interacting with other people. Schein captures the importance of self-insight when he describes it as a *competence*—the ability to see oneself accurately and to evaluate oneself fairly. He suggests that through feedback from others and systematic self-study we can improve this ability. Furthermore it is by increasing self-insight that we lay the foundation for *self-acceptance*, an important foundation for interpersonal competence.[8] Unless one sees himself realistically, he is not likely to develop the maturity required of a manager in modern sophisticated organizations.

THE SELF

Numerous classifications of personality structure have been developed over the years in order to explain different types of self-perception. Probably none of these have had more prominence than the ideas of Eric Berne. Berne, building on the studies of Sigmund Freud, popularized the parts of the personality by captioning them the Parent, Adult, and Child.[9]

According to Berne, these are not concepts describing different facets, but are

FIGURE 8-4

Interdepartmental Communication

Types of information managers want communicated to them and they should communicate to other managers.

1. Areas of difficulty which, as they see it, are hindering interdepartmental cooperation and effectiveness.
2. Specific data on the status of production in their department that might later affect other departments.
3. Ideas and suggestions on how departments might work together to solve common problems.
4. Advance notice of a potential development, which will have repercussions in other areas later.

---

[8] Edgar H. Schein, "SMT Forum: Improving Face-to-Face Relationships," *Sloan Management Review*, Winter 1981, p. 44.
[9] Eric Berne, *Games People Play*, University Plains, Grove Press, Inc., 1964, pp. 23–29.

actually parts of our personalities that exist at various times in our daily behavior. Each of these personalities is brought out by a mental playback of our recorded past, that recalls events involving real people, real times, actual places, previous decisions, and even feelings.

There are three parts of the personality: the Parent, Adult, and the Child.

THE THREE PERSONALITY STATES

The Parent is the taught personality state.

The parent is the *taught* personality state. It is primarily a collection of recordings of instructions from the child's parents, but it also includes other authority figures such as teachers, grandparents, law enforcement authorities, and others.

While the Parent side of the personality is recording external events, internal events are being recorded simultaneously by the Child. Just as the Parent was described as the *taught* personality, the Child can be defined as the *felt* personality. The Child ego state is important because it is the source of creativity and innovation. In addition, it is Thomas Harris's opinion that the Child seldom approves of himself. Most of his admonitions and communications are corrective ones. Therefore, most children develop what is known as a *Not OK Self.* When an employee procrastinates in completing a job or experiences undue anxiety about an upcoming performance review, he can be said to be operating in a Child ego state.[10]

The Child is the felt personality.

The Adult is the thought personality state.

The Adult is the *thought* concept of life, but is more like a data processing computer, rather than the playback tape recorder of the Parent and Child. First the Adult gathers information from all three major sources, the Parent, the Child, and his own experiences. Then it processes these data, and usually makes correct decisions. This is the decision-making process described in Chapter 4. Although not perfect, the Adult's decisions are based on facts and objectivity and are usually more accurate than those made by the Child or Parent alone. Figure 8-5 is a representation of the processing taking place inside the Adult personality. Note that it is not necessary for the Adult to discard the preliminary information, or to completely withdraw from emotional expression. But it is important that the childhood feeling and parental information be updated with *data processing* and *probability-estimating* to make sure they are appropriate.

ESTABLISHING A MANAGEMENT APPROACH

A manager's approach to leadership will be built on one of the combinations of emphasis on Parent, Adult, and Child. These various combinations have been used to describe four life positions found to exist among people in our society: (1) I'm Not OK—You're OK; (2) I'm Not OK—You're Not OK; (3) I'm OK—You're Not OK; and (4) I'm OK—You're OK.

There are four life positions based on how one views herself as well as other people.

An essential part of reaching maturity is learning to evaluate other people's appraisals of us. During early childhood, we are reprimanded by others for our

---

[10]William D. Cushnie, "A Manager's Introduction to Transactional Analysis," *Advanced Management Journal*, Vol. 40, No. 4, Autumn 1975, p. 40.

FIGURE 8-5

Adult Data Processing

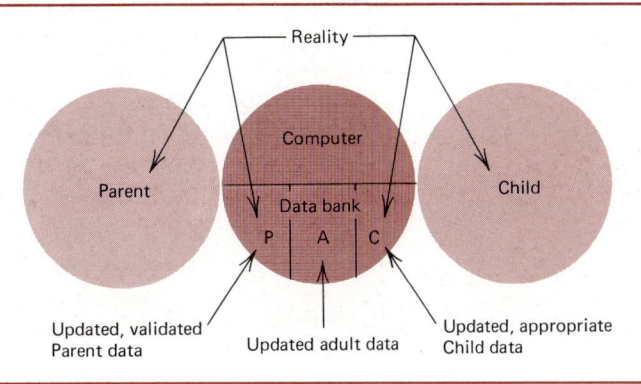

mistakes. These reprimands are called negative *strokes*, in the language of transactional analysis. Negative strokes often cause a person to develop the life position of I'm Not OK—You're OK.

An early childhood in which little or no stroking or compassionate behavior exists creates an I'm Not OK—You're Not OK position. Such a person tends to stop using the Adult altogether. In extreme cases, withdrawal may take the form of neurosis or psychosis.

A life position of I'm OK—You're Not OK grows out of a situation in which a Child is brutalized to the point where he or she decides other people are Not OK, but they themselves are OK. It is not surprising that this position is often known as the criminal position. Persons who are abused throughout the early part of their childhood often come to the point of uncertainty, frustration, and an inordinate fear of failure. A life position that views others as being Not OK will demonstrate little faith and confidence in the ability of subordinates to change and to improve. Such a manager may be suspicious, and manage with a "look over the shoulder." The third life position, if it should lead to constructive rather than destructive occupations, will often produce managers who try to acquire an inordinate number of *strokes* or *"yes* men." Few lasting relationships will be built, and subordinate loyalty will probably not be forthcoming.

The I'm OK—You're OK life position will allow one to begin from a positive attitude. It is a position which promotes faith in others, and inspires them to do their best. Most importantly, managers operating from this position believe that people and organizations can be changed. Their optimism and enthusiasm can keep projects rolling. They *know* they can make things happen.

> The I'm OK You're OK life position enables one to approach leadership with a positive attitude.

A COMMUNICATION TRANSACTION

We behave at various times as if one of these parts is in control of our personality. It is important to understand how one's personality state affects the way that one communicates. It is equally important to understand how, by the way in which

208 ORGANIZATIONAL BEHAVIOR AND DESIGN

We need to understand how our personality state affects the way we communicate.

one communicates, one person tends to activate or turn on the Parent, Adult, or Child of another person.

When we communicate with another person in verbal or nonverbal ways, we are engaging in a transaction: the analysis and development of such interactions is known as *Transactional Analysis* (TA). The process of communication in TA is diagrammed by two interacting sets of circles representing the states of Parent, Adult, and Child. (See Figure 8-6).

Steps in the transaction are shown by drawing arrows from one circle to another. Consider the following example of a superior-subordinate interaction.

Subordinate: *"Can you really believe what the corporate office wants us to do this time. The questions for this report are ridiculous. It's just like always; they want answers to questions that can't be answered."*

Superior: *"I know what you mean. I encounter the same problems in the reports that they want from me. It's really frustrating."*

In this interaction both the subordinate and the superior are responding in the Child personality state. Figure 8-7 provides a diagrammatic representation of this transaction. This is a complementary transation, meaning that the two communication lines do not cross. Thus, this type of transaction may continue indefinitely. Unfortunately, it is not a productive kind of transaction for the organization. Organizations cannot operate effectively with its members communicating in the Child state.

A typical response to the subordinate's complaint other than the one that was illustrated by the preceding interaction would be for the superior to say something like: "What do you mean their questions are ridiculous?!! Your job isn't to evaluate the questions, it's just to answer them." This would turn the transaction into a Parent- Child interaction (see Figure 8-8). Again, this is a complimentary but an undesirable transaction. It is undesirable because it encourages the subordinate to remain in the Child state.

What would be desirable, in this case, would be to shift the interaction into the

FIGURE 8-6

The Personality States

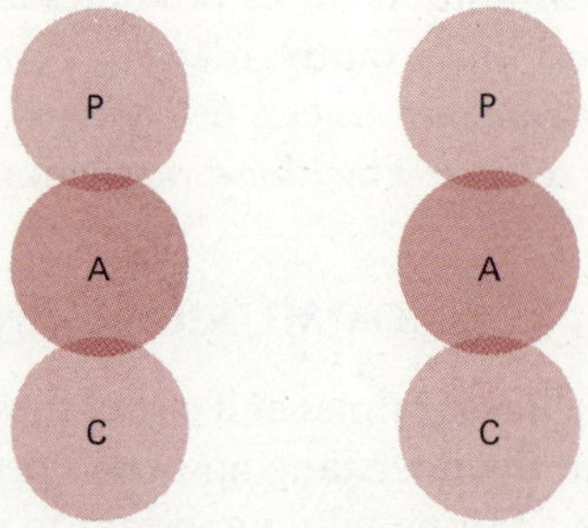

FIGURE 8-7

Complementary Transaction

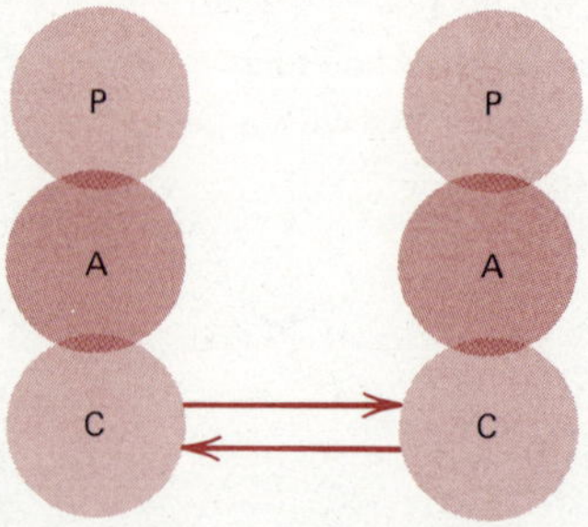

FIGURE 8-8

Data Processing in Transactions

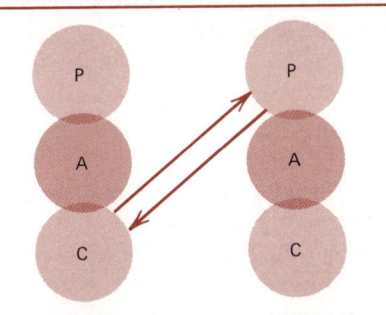

FIGURE 8-9

The Child Response

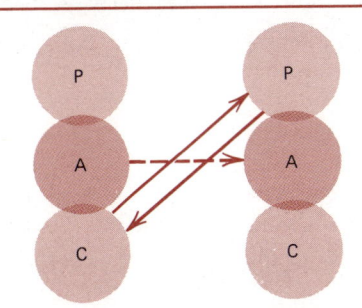

Adult-Adult state. The superior might do this by responding to the subordinate's statement by asking: "What are the particular problems that you're having with the questions?" This question is an Adult-Adult one and results in a crossed transaction as illustrated by Figure 8-9. This crossed interaction will cause conflict to arise for the subordinate. The subordinate may respond by reiterating his or her Child-Adult statement. In such a case, the superior should continue to make Adult-Adult responses. If the crossed transaction is maintained, the subordinate will have to change his or her response to yield a complementary Adult-Adult transaction.

While imagination and creativity reside with the Child state, the ability to change behavior is formed in the Adult state. The Adult state evaluates facts, processes data, and operates without undue emotion. It is this type of communication that we usually want to encourage within organizations. Of course, all three personality states are important in communication. An effective manager will be alert to the expected response in any interaction and will use additional effort in cases of necessarily crossed transactions.

This completed transaction would now appear as shown in Figure 8-10.

Notice that it is not the physical crossing of lines, but the expectations of the receiver, which effect success or failure in a transaction. Transactions between people can be classified as (1) complementary, (2) crossed, or (3) ulterior.[11]

A complementary transaction occurs when a message elicits the predicted response from the ego state of another person. It is expected and follows the natural order of human relationships. For example, suppose a supervisor tells a subordinate: (1) "We need to be in Kansas City one half day before our training session begins." If the subordinate replies, (2) "Okay, I'll make plans to leave a bit early," we have a complementary transaction. But suppose instead the subordinate replies, (3) "Why must I always miss the club tennis tournaments?" We would then have a crossed transaction. A crossed transaction occurs when an unexpected response is made to the stimulus, activating an inappropriate ego

To be effective, Parent-Child and Child-Child transactions must be shifted to the Adult-Adult state.

The Adult state evaluates facts, processes data, and operates without undue emotion.

A complementary transaction occurs when a message elicits the predicted response from the receiver.

---

[11]Muriel James and Dorothy Jongeward, *Born to Win: Transactional Analysis with Gestalt Experiments*, Reading, Mass., Addison-Wesley Publishing Company, 1971, p. 24.

Crossed transactions result from an unexpected response. They cause the conversation to veer from its normal path.

state. Crossed transactions cause the conversation to veer from its normal productive path and are a frequent source of difficulty in organizations. But, as noted earlier, they can also be used to move the conversation from a Child or Parent state to the Adult state.

Ulterior transactions are more complex than crossed transactions because they always involve more than two ego states. Ulterior messages are disguised—usually under a socially acceptable transaction. See Figure 8-11. For example, suppose an employee comes to work and boasts, (1) "Boy, I really blew it last night and drank myself under the table. What a head I've got today." (2) On the surface this person is giving factual information, but at the ulterior level, (3) his Child ego state is looking for the Parent of the other to smile indulgently and thus condone his excessive drinking.

Ulterior transactions are disguised usually under a socially acceptable transaction.

The five important communication principles that can be derived from Transaction Analysis are as follows.

1. The primary determinant of the response we receive in transactions is the personality state from which we communicate.
2. Most communications in industry need to be Adult-Adult transactions. This requires extensive use of data-processing and information sharing, as opposed to dealing in emotions and attitudes.
3. Communicators should watch for crossed transactions since these are likely to cause more difficulty than others. Ulterior transactions should also be avoided. See Figure 8-12.
4. Skillful use of facts, information, and courtsey can often turn Child-Parent or Parent-Child transactions into Adult-Adult transactions. Tactful use of this approach can reduce the frequency of ulterior transactions.
5. While imagination and creativity reside with the Child state, the ability to change behavior is formed in the Adult state. The Adult state evaluates facts, processes data, and operates without undue emotion. Of course, all three personality states are important in communication. An effective manager will be alert to the expected response in any communication and will use additional effort in cases of necessarily crossed transactions.

FIGURE 8-10

Adult to Adult

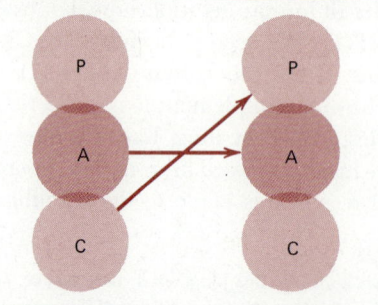

FIGURE 8-11

Crossed and Ulterior Transactions

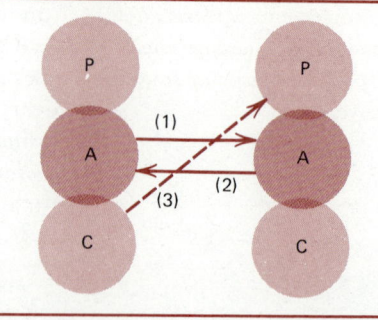

FIGURE 8-12

Ulterior Transaction

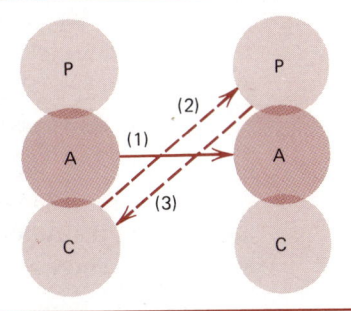

THE IMPORTANCE OF LISTENING

Effective communication requires listening with the desire to understand.

Two-way communication requires listening with the desire to understand rather than listening to replies only. It requires a willingness to change or to be changed and, in short, an openness is needed to hear not only what others have to say, but also to give their ideas a chance to become operative.

In any situation, the manager will do well if she first determines her communication objective and then proceeds on that basis. If the objective is, in fact, to persuade someone to a particular position, then the communication climate should recognize this. Explain the situation, present the reasons, get reaction—but do not try to disguise the purposes.

The importance of good listening on the job to effective performance cannot be emphasized too much. Ralph Nichols[12] estimates that managers devote at least 40 percent of their workdays to listening. Unfortunately, he goes further to suggest that most of these managers are only listening at 25 percent efficiency! Obviously, there is much need for improvement in this key area of communication.

Managers devote 40 percent of their workdays listening—but only at a 25 percent efficiency rate.

One of the most effective approaches to listening is called *nondirective interviewing*. The procedure follows.[13]

Take time to listen. Listening helps the talker "clear his mind" and may prevent an emotional outburst.

Be attentive. Try to put yourself in the talker's position. Let him finish his thoughts.

Employ verbal reactions to encourage the conversation. As long as the talker proceeds, acknowledge what he says occasionally with "Hmmm," "Uh-huh," "Oh," or "I see." If he pauses, remain silent and show attentiveness until he proceeds again. If he becomes irrational, restate what he has just said. An

---
[12] Ralph G. Nichols, "Listening is a 10-Part-Skill," *Nation's Business*, Vol. 45, July 1957, p. 56.
[13] Ibid.

example of a restatement might be, "You really think that your crew is restricting output?"
4. Be cautious about probing for additional facts. Nondirective interviewing solves problems in the "listening" state, not in the finding of "villains."
5. Avoid evaluating what has been said. Try not to moralize or give advice.
6. Never lose faith in the ability of the talker to solve his own problems. As the talker speaks, you will witness him working things out for himself. In a sense, he is really talking to himself much of the time.

The alert reader is aware that listening is one of the most effective ways of hooking into the Adult state. Coming on as the Parent or moralizing tends to elicit defensiveness, and often activates the Child or Parent in the talker.

BARRIERS TO CREATING UNDERSTANDING AND HOW TO OVERCOME THEM

The barriers to creating understanding and thereby obtaining cooperation and enthusiasm from people can be classified into two categories. The first barriers are technical, relating to the organizational framework in which communication occurs. The second type of barriers are those that are human in nature.

TECHNICAL BARRIERS

The first of the technical barriers is the *bypassing or omitting someone from the communication chain*. Whether these two things occur singularly or in conjunction with one another, they have the effect of undermining the person involved, thereby creating a problem of morale, hard feelings, and eventually an uncooperative "I don't care" attitude.

The second barrier is *incomplete communication*. This is created by the sender if he oversimplifies or lacks explicitness in his communication. In either case, the receiver must interpret the message. If the message is incorrectly interpreted and the intended results are not achieved, the receiver is usually blamed, thus creating a breach between two people who must cooperate to produce good results.

A third barrier revolves around *poor personal relationships*. Lack of respect or personal conflict between persons in an organization may produce ineffective communications. Many organizations who spent considerable sums of money on communications training for all their personnel may still find they have a higher-than-normal amount of communications problems, due to conflict between people or departments.

Another technical barrier is *spontaneous or spur-of-the-moment communication*. Communication is most effective when it precedes action or events. Late communication is usually accompanied by, and occurs in conjunction with, someone applying pressure to achieve results. Full cooperation is seldom gained in these situations.

Finally, communication can be incomplete in the sense that the "why" is

Technical barriers to communication include bypassing, incomplete communications, poor personal relationships, spur of the moment, and incomplete communications.

Communicating the "why" increases the performance level of workers.

omitted. Most people are willingly cooperate and help when they know why something is important or why a particular action is needed. Communicating the "why" shows respect for the individual and indicates that his help is valued and appreciated. Recent research indicates that managers who emphasize communicating the "why" increase the performance level of their workers.[14]

HUMAN BARRIERS

The first important human barrier to effective communication is *failure to see the need*. The first step toward overcoming this barrier is a realization and crystallization of what information we should be communicating. The second step to overcoming the failure to see the need is developing empathy, the ability to put ourselves in the other man's shoes. Once the manager develops sensitivity as to how he feels when someone does not communicate with him, he is more likely to do a better job of communicating with others.

Human barriers to communication involve a failure to see the need, semantics, failure to listen, self-intent, and inadequate planning for communications.

A second human barrier is embodied within the concept of *semantics*, the meaning of words. This barrier can become operative in a number of different ways: using specific words with which the receiver is not familiar; using words that have a variety of meanings and assuming they are interpreted the way they are meant; talking over the head of the receiver in general; or making a message unduly complicated and long. In illustrating, the industrial engineer who talks to the line supervisor about therbligs or economic lot sizes may meet with no response. Similarly, the line supervisor who tries to train a new worker using unfamiliar terminology or shop jargon may find that he can not "get through." Talking over peoples' heads usually results in creating a negative impression and consequently receiving negative results.

A third human barrier involves the *failure to listen*. The importance of listening has been discussed in depth in an earlier portion of this chapter. Failure to listen has many dimensions and may manifest its affect in various ways. Listening may be complicated by the fact that our capacity to listen in terms of words per minute is far greater than the average speaking rate, thus leaving a gap of available time for woolgathering, or for planning a reply instead of listening for comprehension.

Related to listening is the barrier of *self-interest* or *preoccupation with one's own situation*. To communicate effectively, therefore, requires the sender to be sensitive to the state of mind of her receiver, to be able to sense whether or not she is tuned in.

Another human barrier is inadequate planning in terms of the what, when, how, who, and why of communications. Before any communication commences, the following five questions should be asked, and answered.

1. What is the specific idea or message I want to get across? (Simply stated.)

2. When is the best time to do it? (Timing is important.)

---

[14]R. C. Huseman et al., "Development of a Conceptual Framework for Analyzing the Communication-Performance Relationships," *Academy of Management Proceedings,* 1980, p. 181.

3. How can it best be accomplished? (The media is strategic. Verbally, in writing, a meeting, individually?)
4. To whom should it be communicated?
5. Why is it necessary?

Effective communication does not occur by accident. Like anything else, it requires some advance planning, and the time spent in planning is usually more than compensated for in long-term results. Similarly, most communication failure can be traced to one or more failures in the planning stages.

ORGANIZATIONAL PROBLEMS IN ESTABLISHING EFFECTIVE COMMUNICATION

The purpose of this section is to touch very briefly on some additional barriers and potential problems to effective communication which were not mentioned previously. They arise both as a result of the organizational structure and in the types of people in the organization.

PROBLEM CREATED BY THE ORGANIZATION STRUCTURE

Individuals viewing the formal structure of an organization in chart form get an impression of the relative power of various positions. This impression carries over into their function within the organization. As a result, communication barriers may be presented by the following perceptions of organization structure and the individual's role or place within that structure.

1. *Positional and Authority Difference Barriers.* Persons in higher positions may fear a loss of power or status if they engage in open communication with subordinates. Communication is the thing that binds people together and brings them closer. The manager who feels that this closeness will threaten him because he will not command the same degree of respect from his people may naturally be hesitant to communicate too much. On the other hand, subordinates sometimes hesitate to send any but the most favorable communications upward because of a fear of the consequences of making the superior unhappy.

2. *Interdepartmental Competition.* This category includes such situations as line-staff relationship problems and mutual secrecy between departments striving for high output recognition. The persons involved in both these cases fail to communicate because they fear that to do so will give advantage to the other department and lower their own standing in the eyes of superiors. This is a great barrier to horizontal communication in the organization.

3. *Hiding Behind the Organization Chart.* In this case, the individual draws a wall around his block on the chart and makes a conscious effort to remain behind it. The reasons may be fear of incompetence or of having others infringe upon his area of responsibility. He refuses to entertain ideas about topics not spelled

out in his position description, and will not allow others to cross into his territory.

4. *Physical Layout of the Organizational Facilities.* This problem is related to the status problem mentioned earlier. Organizations require that people on the same level be located or housed in the same type of facilities and in close proximity. The result is that many times the manager finds himself physically isolated from those with whom he should be communicating most, and must conduct most of his daily business with subordinates who are as much as half a mile away. Thus, face-to-face relationships are replaced by telephones and written memos, and the result is inadequate communication. Furthermore, the very layout of a manager's office can affect communication. Offices arranged to highlight status, for example, tend to cause others to view the individual as being closed to their involvement.[15]

PEOPLE PROBLEMS IN COMMUNICATION

The communication problems presented by people in organizations result both from their perception of the role expected of them by the organization and their own individual attitudes.

One of the greatest hindrances to effective organizational communication is the individual who communicates more effectively toward his own ends than toward anyone else's. This paradox in communication effectiveness is the "empire builder." He utilizes interpersonal communication and persuasion to enhance his own image. He is a manipulator of communication.

Related to this is the individual who selectively pries into areas that do not directly concern him. An aspect of this additional problem is circulating rumors, spreading incomplete information, and voicing opinions on affairs beyond the scope of one's knowledge . . . in other words, overcommunication.

On the other end of the spectrum is the person who is reluctant to communicate at all, mainly because no one has informed him that the organization depends on his communicative efforts.

In between these two extremes lie various degrees of communication problems. An awareness of these existing problems and a conscious and continual effort to eliminate them are necessary for an organization to build a successful communication program.

A grapevine usually transmits information accurately but often begins with inaccurate information.

The Grapevine. These people aspects of communication within the organization can be organized into the concept of the informal organization. The communication that goes on in this organization is typically referred to as the "corporate grapevine." Contrary to popular knowledge, the grapevine does not distort information as it disseminates it. The information transmitted by the

---
[15]J. C. McElroy and P. C. Morrow, "Object Language as Nonverbal Communication: The Role of Interior Office Design in Impression Management," *Academy of Management Proceedings,* 1981, p. 205.

grapevine is usually transmitted with a fair degree of accuracy. When the grapevine is passing inaccurate information, it is because the individuals started with inaccurate information.

The effective manager learns to manage grapevine communication within his or her unit. The best way to do this is to make accurate information available so that inaccurate information will not be developed and transmitted. With accurate information available from the manager, the grapevine does not need to create information on its own. Furthermore, this task is not an overwhelming one for the manager. Usually, only one or two individuals within a unit are responsible for passing on grapevine information. By keeping those individuals informed, the manager can more effectively manage the grapevine.[16]

The effective manager learns to feed accurate information to the grapevine.

SUMMARY

In this chapter, we have pointed out the importance of both organizational and interpersonal communications. An effective communication program must exist if the objective of employee loyalty and identification is to be achieved. Commitment at the top management levels is essential.

Communication is defined as passing information and understanding from one person to another. This definition stresses the importance of the fact that more is involved in communication than just a sender dispensing information. There must be understanding on the part of a receiver. Every manager lives in a two-way, tridimensional communication environment. It is two-way in the sense that there are certain key types of information that he must communicate to his people; and other information that she in turn wants them to communicate to her. It is tridimensional because she must communicate with her own superior, her subordinates, and managers of other departments.

The steps in organizational and interpersonal communication are complementary. As shown in the summary chart, management first needs to determine what needs to be communicated. Trust and top-level commitment must be established. Next the three dimensions of communication upward, downward, and horizontal must be considered. Management must determine when to use formal channels such as the chain of command and where to use the informal group as channels of communication.

In order to develop the proper empathy with the receiver, management must be aware of which personality exists—Parent, Adult, or Child. Special counseling and problem solving will often require nondirective interviewing.

The wise manager will listen carefully, while remaining alert to technical, organizational, and human barriers to the communication process. She will also watch out for empire builders who monitor communications for their own personal aggrandizement. Finally, she will learn to effectively manage information in the grapevine.

---

[16]Keith Davis, "The Care and Cultivation of the Corporate Grapevine," *Dun's Review*, July 1973.

SUMMARY CHART

COMMUNICATIONS

1. Determine what needs to be communicated.
   (a) Top management goals
   (b) Interest of employees
   (c) How organization is progressing
   (d) Prospects for future

2. Establish trust and top-level commitment.

3. Consider the three dimensions of communication—upward, downward, and horizontal.

4. Choose the correct channel.
   (a) Written versus spoken
   (b) Informal versus formal

5. Consider the personality state of sender and receiver: Parent, Adult, Child.

6. Use nondirective interviewing to discover problems.

7. Remember to listen.

8. Watch for problems.
   (a) Technical barriers
   (b) Organizational barriers
   (c) Interpersonal barriers

DISCUSSION QUESTIONS

1. From a broad perspective, discuss the problem of communication as it relates to organizations. Include in detail some of the inadequacies of communication, the types of information the organization needs to communicate, and the importance of top-level commitment.

2. Define communication and discuss the implications of your definitions. Discuss the communication environment of the manger as both a two-way and a tridimensional process.

3. Discuss the information side of the communications process, being sure to point out (a) some examples of the types of information a manager should communicate to his people and (b) the type he wants his superiors to communicate to him. Also point out (c) some of the things a manager should be communicating to his superior and (d) the things he wants his people communicating to him.

4. Identify and describe each of the technical and human barriers to communication. What suggestions would you make for overcoming each barrier?
5. What factors in the organization structure create problems in communication? Discuss each.
6. Think of the last conversation in which you engaged. Were you operating in the Adult, Parent, or Child state?
7. Using Transactional Analysis, diagram a recent conversation with a supervisor or professor. How would you have communicated more effectively? Discuss.
8. Cite the steps in nondirective interviewing. Try this process out on a friend who has a problem. Does it work?
9. How can the grapevine be useful to management? Explain.

APPLICATION EXERCISES AND CASES

C.I.T. FINANCIAL CORPORATION: MERGER AND MORALE

At the start of 1971, C.I.T. Financial Corporation, the nation's largest independent financing corporation, announced a sweeping change: it would bring together its four consumer-financing subsidiaries—with several thousand employees in hundreds of locations—under a single name.

The Problem
Each of the four companies—Universal C.I.T. Credit Corporation, Universal C.I.T. Finance Corporation-Laurentide, Time Finance Company, and Home Finance Service—had its own president and executive staff, personnel, advertising, accounting, and supervisory functions. The companies were headquartered in New York City, Louisville, New Orleans, and San Francisco. In some areas, offices of these companies competed with each other.

The Strategy
Such a broad move had a great potential for producing morale problems. Such problems could be met by telling employees how the merger could benefit them—telling them about the increased efficiency the improved customer that would result. The decision was made to communicate the reasons for the merger, the procedure to be followed, and the timetable. In addition, major emphasis would be given to the exciting prospects of working for one large company with facilities stretching from the Hawaiian Islands across the United States to Puerto Rico.

The massive reorganization was placed in the hands of the parent-company executive in charge of consumer financing. He met with chief executive officers of each company to explain the plan and schedule. In turn, each held meetings with his own home office and field level management staffs.

Implementation

Employees of the four companies first learned officially of the consolidation through a personal letter from the parent company consumer-finance vice president. This was followed up by letters from each subsidiary company president.

Meanwhile, the parent company's communication services manager worked closely with those handling the merger and reorganization to tell the story in greater depth to employees. The company publication, *Citations*, distributed to all employees of consumer finance, business finance, leasing and insurance companies, and to executives of C.I.T.'s banking and manufacturing companies, was chosen as the chief medium to do the job.

Meeting at regular intervals with those directing the merger, the communication services manager worked out a timetable for feature stories that would supplement intra-company meetings and mailings.

Citations kicked off its program in the March–April, 1971 issue. The front cover carried the words "New Name over America," with pictures of the executive directing the merger, C.I.T. Financial Corporation's president, and a brand new sign featuring the company's new name, C.I.T. Financial Services. The lead story was an in-depth interview with the executives involved in the merger. This article covered the reasons for the name change, the choice of name, the scope of the task ahead, a timetable, and advertising and promotion planning. In addition, the interview stressed how each employee could help to promote the new identity.

In its next issue, *Citations* featured an article called "The Face-lifting Gets Underway." This detailed the big job of telling the public about the change through advertising, promotion, a new marketing symbol, and a new color scheme. Emphasis was given to pictures showing new signs going up.

Early in 1972, an article entitled "The Future Is Now" brought everyone up to date on the progress of the consolidation. The article described the completely restructured organization and pointed out the broadened opportunities for each employee.

While these stories provided in-depth coverage and sought to create and maintain excitement about the formation of a company with over 750 offices across the country, all executive staffs continued to communicate at the local level. Meetings detailed what was going on and the timetable for the next steps. Personal letters were also sent on a regular basis to each employee.

Question
1. How would you evaluate the procedures used by this company in light of the principles outlined in this chapter?

ADLESON SALES

Dave Jameson, sales manager for Adleson Manufacturing Company, was visiting with Ted, a salesman who had been with the company for two years.

Dave: Ted, sales have dropped in your territory by over 15 percent. Do you have any ideas as to why this happened?

Ted: Well, the sales have dropped in most of the territories. Jim Davis, who handles the usually active Chicago north side told me that his sales have dropped over 20 percent. Everyone seems to think that our regular customers are switching to Brownsen Company products because their prices are lower and also their quality is . . .

Dave: Listen, Ted, you know as well as I do that the reason for the low sales volume is because you're not getting around to our present customers as well as trying to make new contacts. When I first started here fifteen years ago, I used to see at least twenty people in one day.

Ted: But I have been contacting more customers and potential customers than I have in previous months, but still . . . .

Dave: Look, Ted, I really don't want to hear any more of your excuses. That's all you people seem to be able to do well these days. Just get with it and get to those customers. I expect to see a big improvement in sales next month. Do you think you can do it?

Ted: Yes, sir.

Questions

1. Discuss the type of communication that has taken place. In doing so utilize the chapter material to analyze the transactions.
2. What barriers to communication are applicable here?

CHAPTER 9
HUMAN MOTIVATION

CONTENT THEORIES
MASLOW'S NEED HIERARCHY
E.R.G. THEORY
PROCESS THEORIES
VROOM'S THEORY OF MOTIVIATION
EQUITY THEORY
ACHIEVEMENT MOTIVATION
HERZBERG'S DUAL FACTOR THEORY
THE PORTER AND LAWLER MOTIVATION MODEL
SYSTEMATIC APPROACHES TO INCENTIVE APPLICATION
REINFORCEMENT THEORY
GOAL SETTING AND MANAGEMENT EXPECTATIONS
NATURE OF SUPERVISION AND MOTIVATION
SOME CONCLUDING NOTES ON MOTIVATION
APPLICATION EXERCISES AND CASES
ANALYZING MOTIVATIONAL PATTERNS
DR. HOLT'S DILEMMA

WORKING SMARTER[1]

It's at least possible, over the long haul, that there's a new day for American industry in general. A powerful movement is under way to reexamine and, as necessary, break with old managerial assumptions and formulas. Today's executives are confronting the knowledge that the business system they mastered is no longer the world-beater it used to be. They are considering options that are more flexible and participative than the rigid hierarchies they grew up in. These alternative organizations take a long-run view of corporate self-interest, and are guided by a sense of common purpose that motivates all who work within them.

By whatever name, and on whatever scale, this kind of effort is most broadly described as the process of expanding the responsibility and influence of rank-and-file employees. It assumes that people want to work together in common purpose, and it challenges the sharp distinction, inherent in classical Western industrial organization, between the actual work of producing goods or services and the planning and coordination of that work.

Most of these undertakings have been called quality-of-worklife programs. They are applicable not only in the factory but also to office and service workers in banks, insurance companies, government bureaucracies, and even the military. Although the concept is only now emerging as a practical managerial concern, it is likely to become a full-blown management discipline.

What is perhaps the best definition of quality of worklife yet comes from Charles Bisanz, a consultant to the Northwestern Bell Co.: "It is not a solution devised by management so much as it is a decision by management to share responsibility with employees in devising solutions."

A major survey of U.S. workers' attitudes toward productivity conducted by Gallup for the U.S. Chamber of Commerce in 1979 found "the overwhelming majority believe that if they are more involved in making decisions that affect their job, they would work harder and do better." A more recent international survey on productivity developed by Louis Harris and sociologist Amitai Etzioni and released in April 1981 echoed the point in some of its findings, and produced a striking complementary message about the kind of human resources that lie untapped.

---

[1] Charles G. Burck, "Working Smarter," *Fortune*, June 15, 1981, Vol. 103, No. 12, pp. 68–73.

One of the best, although not most sophisticated, definitions of motivation ever given is that it is the ability to get a person to do what you want her to do, when you want it done, in a way you want it done, *because she wants to do it*. Our discussion will concentrate on the latter part of this definition. Why should people want to cooperate and work toward the goals of the organization? What motivates people?

In answer to this question, psychologists tell us that people behave in certain ways and pursue particular courses of action in order to satisfy their needs.

> Motivation is the results of people doing things because they want to do them.

Because behavior is directed toward need satisfaction, it is of strategic importance to know what people desire from a job if we are to motivate them. In terms of a motivation equation,[2] the process appears as follows.

$$\text{Motivation} = f(\text{need; incentive; ability})$$

On the right side of the equation are those things that people want or need, or the drives that cause and explain behavior. Added to this is the incentive. If the proper incentives are provided, incentives that hold the potential for satisfaction of needs, we get the desired type of behavior. Viewed another way, if the organization can build a climate that offers people an opportunity to satisfy their needs, a positive motivational response will be elicited. The ability portion of the equation recognizes that, regardless of the level of motivation, a certain amount of ability to do the job must also be present. The relationship of ability to job performance will be discussed fully in Chapter 10, Job Design.

> Organizations need to build climates that offer people an opportunity to satisfy their needs.

Thus, these two initial considerations, knowledge of people's needs and of incentives, are of importance for management. The big challenge for a manager is to know and understand people as individuals. Motivation is a personal thing. Because of their differing needs, the incentives that appeal to and work with one employee may be less than fully successful with another. It is valuable to be generally knowledgeable about needs, but even more important to know each employee in terms of those things that he personally wants most. Only when we have this type of insight are we in a position to successfully motivate people.

Management can contribute in a number of ways to the incentive side of the equation. If, due to an overall favorable organizational climate, job design, or individual approach to leadership, incentives are built in which offer employees an opportunity to satisfy their needs, we may expect higher performance levels from them.

In this chapter we will examine human needs and several behavioral models that depict them. In the following chapters we discuss the importance of various organizational and situational settings on incentives.

> Content theories focus on internal needs, process theories on processes, and strategies of behavior.

Motivational theory has developed around two main approaches—content theories and process theories. *Content theories* focus on internal needs that energize and sustain behavior. Alderfer describes them as ". . . primary needs or innate tendencies which individuals possess, though it is not always clear whether these are necessarily biological or physiologically rooted."[3] *Process theories* deal with the thought processes and strategies that cause individuals to choose a particular pattern of behavior. The content theories to be discussed include Maslow's Need Hierarchy and E.R.G. Theory. In dealing with the process, we initially consider Vroom's expectancy theory and equity theory. In addition, the chapter discusses McClelland's concept of achievement motivation, Herzberg's Dual Factor Theory, Porter and Lawler's Theory, and systematic approaches to incentive applications.

---

[2]For a more detailed discussion of motivation Equation, see Abraham Korman, *The Pyschology of Motivation*, Englewood Cliffs, N.J., Prentice Hall, 1974.
[3]Clayton P. Alderfer, *Existence, Relatedness, and Growth*, New York, The Free Press, 1972, p. 7.

CONTENT THEORIES

MASLOW'S NEED HIERARCHY

The psychologist usually begins talking about needs in terms of some type of hierarchy or priority. Although both the number of steps or levels in the hierarchy and the descriptive terminology may vary among authors, the following framework, developed by Abraham Maslow, and depicted in Figure 9-1, is representative.[4]

Maslow arranged needs in a hierarchy.

Physiological Needs. The needs of the body for shelter, food, and water are physiological in nature. They are part of a human's strong drive toward self-preservation.

FIGURE 9-1

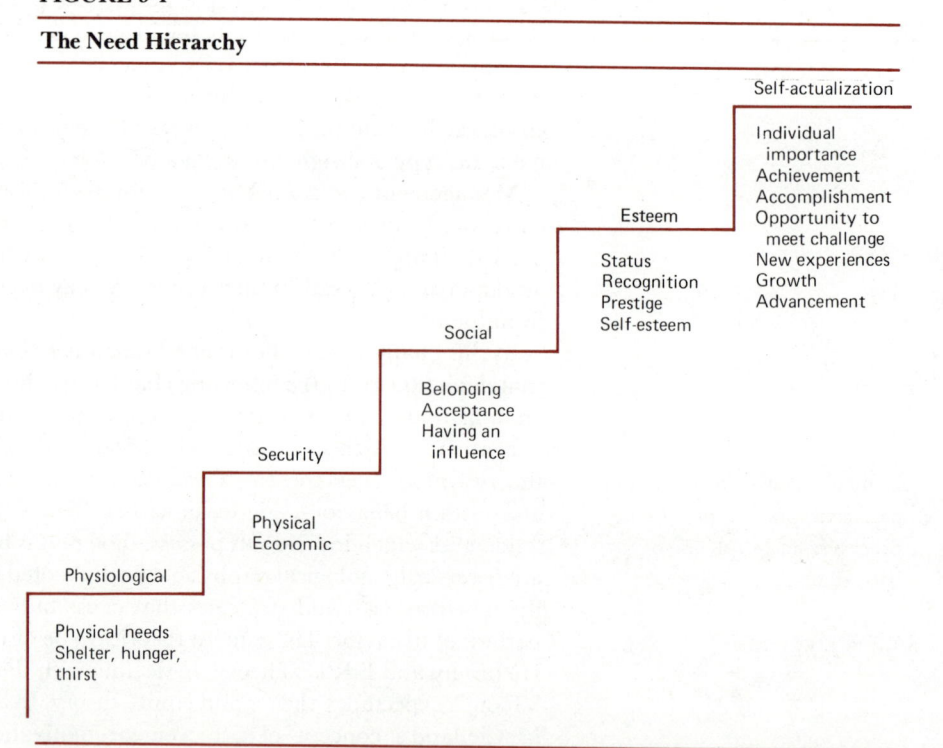

The Need Hierarchy

```
                                                            Self-actualization
                                                            
                                                            Individual
                                                              importance
                                                            Achievement
                                                            Accomplishment
                                            Esteem          Opportunity to
                                                              meet challenge
                                            Status          New experiences
                                            Recognition     Growth
                                            Prestige        Advancement
                              Social        Self-esteem
                              
                              Belonging
                              Acceptance
                              Having an
                  Security    influence
                  
                  Physical
                  Economic
    Physiological
    
    Physical needs
    Shelter, hunger,
    thirst
```

Source: Adapted from Abraham Maslow, *Motivation and Personality*, 2nd ed., New York, Harper and Row, 1970.

[4]The five-step hierarchy outlined here follows the general approach developed by Maslow in his work concerning a theory of motivation. See Abraham Maslow, *Motivation and Personality*, 2nd ed., New York, Harper & Row, 1970, pp. 35–58.

Security Needs. The two types of security needs are physical and economic, the latter of which concerns us here. People have a basic need to meet their own expectations of an acceptable living standard. Once people reach this economic level, they want the assurance they will remain there. Without sufficient security needs fulfillment, anxiety about loss of income due to old age, employment cessation, or other reasons will begin.

Social Needs. People need to feel they belong and that they are an accepted and important part of the group. Also, they want to be able to have an influence on and within the group.

Esteem Needs. Human egos normally want such things as status, recognition, and prestige. People need to feel that they are important, that what they are doing means something, and that they are making a contribution. These types of things reflect a desire for self-esteem.

Self-actualization often comes from striving for, rather than attainment of goals.

Self-Actualization. The apex in the need hierarchy is the need for self-actualization. People must be allowed to try for a better life. They have a need to feel that they are making progress toward reaching their full potential; that they are doing what they are suited for in terms of their skill and ability, and the type and level of job in which they are employed. Such factors as a feeling of job importance, accomplishment, individual importance and achievement, responsibility, advancement, challenging work, and growth opportunity are included here. In Maslow's earlier work, he termed this last need self-fulfillment, but later changed it to self-actualization.[5] Self-actualization seems more appropriate because the greatest fulfillment for persons operating high on the need hierarchy appears to come from the *striving for* instead of the *attainment of* goals.

Significance of the Need Hierarchy. Several very important points must be stressed about the need hierarchy. First, these needs operate in an ascending order of importance. The most strategic motivators of on-the-job behavior are the physiological and security needs. For discussion purposes it is convenient to combine these into a category called "economic needs," and recognize they can be largely satisfied through wages.

Needs operate in an ascending order of importance.

Not until these economic needs become reasonably well satisfied do any of the higher level needs take on a great deal of significance as motivators. To illustrate, if a person's general wage level is so low that he is having trouble buying food for the family, he probably will not respond very well to incentives designed to satisfy the social, esteem, or self-actualization needs. We must first reasonably satisfy the economic needs through an adequate and relatively secure wage before efforts in other directions will bear fruit.

A second important point is that people want most what they do not have. Once a need is reasonably well satisfied, it starts to decrease in importance as a

---

[5] Abraham H. Maslow, *Eupsychian Management: A Journal*, Homewood, Ill., Irwin Dorsey, 1965.

strong motivator of behavior relative to other needs. By reasonably well satisfied we mean 70, 80, or 85 percent. A need is seldom completely satisfied and never completely ceases to be a motivator. For example, once people feel that the wages they are receiving are reasonable and equitable and they feel secure about continuing to receive them, further attempts to motivate them to high levels of performance on the basis of wages alone will meet with minimal success. At that point employees are more apt to respond to incentives that offer them the opportunity to satisfy their social, esteem, and self-actualization needs. According to Maslow's theory a satisfied need is not a motivator of behavior.

Maslow said that a satisfied need is not a motivator of behavior.

Since no two people are alike, needs vary in type and intensity from individual to individual. For one person, the economic and social needs may be readily satisfied, while the need for recognition, prestige, and status may be almost insatiable. For another, the overwhelming driving force, at least for the present, may be the economic needs and, consequently, the desire for more money. In a third case, the need to belong to and be an accepted and integral part of a group may prevail. The very difficult task faced by the manager who wants to motivate subordinates is to apply her general knowledge about needs in order to discover the specific needs an individual workers may have.

Needs vary in type and intensity.

The social, self-esteem, and, in some cases, the self-actualization needs are not always outwardly and directly expressed. It is not quite acceptable to ask for a feeling of belonging and a sense of importance. The typical answer to the question, "What motivates you?" is money. The manager, however, must be sensitive to indirect cues that indicate employees are seeking other types of satisfaction.

Some needs are not outwardly expressed.

A final factor that complicates the motivation process revolves around the fact that people may behave in different ways to satisfy a given need. We mentioned earlier that all of us want recognition and a certain amount of individual attention. One person (probably with above-average ability) gets this recognition and attention through positive behavior, by producing top quality and quantity work, developing positive attitudes toward the job, and being willing to put forth additional effort in an emergency. Another employee may seek recognition by marginal work and continually causing problems, much like the child who gains an inordinate amount of attention through misbehavior.

Behavior of people may vary in order to satisfy a given need.

Support for the Need Hierarchy. Maslow's hierarchy of needs is quoted rather extensively. It does indeed provide a good starting point for gaining initial insight into the process of motivation. Research dealing with the theory is rather sparse, however. This is undoubtedly because it is a difficult theory to research. Maslow himself expressed reservations concerning its widespread applicability and made a bid for more extensive research in a variety of settings.

Generally, researchers have tried to obtain statistical validity to Maslow's need hierarchy through a complex approach known as factor analysis. Using a group of accountants and engineers as their sample, Mitchell and Moudgill found good statistical evidence that Maslow's categories do in fact exist. But their research supports a stronger distinction between lower-order and higher-order needs than

Research support regarding Maslow's theory has not been extensive.

it does a five-way classification. According to the researchers, the two are not mutually exclusive.[6]

E.R.G. THEORY

> E.R.G. Theory includes three categories of needs: existence, relatedness, and growth needs.

E.R.G. Theory is the result of an attempt by Clayton Alderfer to stem some of the omissions in Maslow's Need Hierarchy and to develop a theory consistent with the view that operates according to the logic of an open-system and to bridge "... the gap between those views of man which tend to view him primarily in reactive, tension-producing ways and those orientations which tend to focus on his proactive, stimulus-seeking qualities."[7] It includes three categories implied by the initials: *existence* needs, *relatedness* needs, and *growth* needs.

Existence Needs. This category includes all of the various physiological and safety-material categories described in Maslow's first two categories. Being tangible, existence needs can be divided among people in such a way that competition for them often forms a zero-score game.[8] In other words, if one person wins the other must lose.

Relatedness Needs. These needs operate only through relationships with others, such as family members, work peers, and friends and associates. In contrast to existence needs, their satisfaction depends on sharing, mutual understanding, and interactive influence.[9]

Growth Needs. These needs are the result of active involvement of persons in their various environmental settings, such as home, job, and recreational activities. Satisfaction of growth needs comes through a person's encountering problems in these settings that call upon their full capacities and that may involve the development of additional capacities—thus, the idea of growth.[10]

E.R.G. Theory assumes that these three broad categories are inherent in all living persons, although they differ in strength for each person. Alderfer's summary of the way in which the three categories operate is enlightening:

> Each of the three needs in E.R.G. theory is defined in terms of a target toward which efforts at gratification are aimed.

> *Each of the three basic* needs *in E.R.G. theory was defined in terms of a target toward which efforts at gratification were aimed and in terms of a process through which, and only through which, satisfaction could be obtained. For existence needs, the targets were material substances, and the process was simply getting enough. When the substances are scarce, the process quickly becomes a "win-lose," and one person's gain is correlated with another's loss. For relatedness needs, the targets were significant others (persons or groups), and the process was mutual sharing of thoughts and feelings. For growth needs,*

---

[6]Vance F. Mitchell and Pravin Moudgill, "Measurement of Maslow's Need Hierarchy," *Organizational Behavior and Human Performance*, Vol. 16, 1976, pp. 334–349.
[7]Alderfer, *Existence, Relatedness, and Growth*, p. 9.
[8]Ibid.
[9]Ibid., p. 10
[10]Ibid., p. 13.

the targets were environmental settings, and there were joint processes of a person becoming more differentiated and integrated as a human being.[11]

E.R.G. Theory posits several major propositions which can be summarized as follows:

P1. The less existence needs are satisfied, the more they will be desired.

P2. The less relatedness needs are satisfied, the more existence needs will be desired.

P3. The more existence needs are satisfied, the more relatedness needs will be desired.

P4. The less relatedness needs are satisfied, the more they will be desired.

P5. The less growth needs are satisfied, the more relatedness needs will be desired.

P6. The more relatedness needs are satisfied, the more growth needs will be desired.

P7. The more growth needs are satisfied, the more they will be desired.[12]

According to its author, E.R.G. Theory differs from Maslow's Theory in four ways. The first difference involves the differing interpretations of similar need categories and is explained best by referring to Figure 9-2.

Note that only those safety needs pertaining to physiological existence are included by Alderfer under the existence category. For example, a physical threat to a person would be included in Alderfer first category, but a psychological threat would be considered more akin to love and therefore relatedness needs. In a similar sense, Alderfer places esteem from others in the relatedness category since to Maslow it stems from the regard a person receives from others and is therefore closely allied to the broad category of relatedness. Alderfer also points out that the self-actualization category under Maslow's need hierarchy takes on the unnecessary connotation of self-indulgence. By recognizing the role that environmental settings play in stimulating and supporting growth, Alderfer avoids any such problem.

Second, E.R.G. Theory does not presume a strictly ordered hierarchy. Maslow argues that "man lives by bread alone when he has no bread," but Alderfer would say that he is still motivated somewhat by relationships with family and other primary groups. Furthermore, E.R.G. Propositions 3 and 6 suggest that Alderfer's need categories have an upward orientation, but ". . . they do not require lower level gratification as an additional condition as Maslow's theory does."[13]

A third difference between the two sets of categories concerns Maslow's argument that needs tend to cease motivating one as soon as they are gratified. Alderfer posits that the need hierarchy operates in reverse when an upper-level need is frustrated, causing the next lower level to be activated. For example,

> E.R.G. Theory does not presume a strictly ordered hierarchy.

---

[11]Ibid., p. 24
[12]Ibid., p. 28
[13]Ibid., p. 24

FIGURE 9-2

Comparisons of Masloe and E.R.G. Concepts

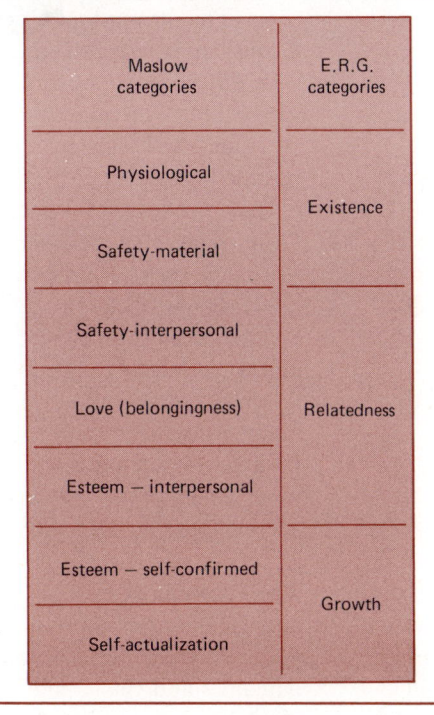

Maslow categories	E.R.G. categories
Physiological	Existence
Safety-material	
Safety-interpersonal	Relatedness
Love (belongingness)	
Esteem — interpersonal	
Esteem — self-confirmed	Growth
Self-actualization	

Source: Clayton P. Alderfer, *Existence, Relatedness, and Growth,* New York: The Free Press, 1972, p. 25.

persons thwarted in romance or friendship often overeat as a substitute for relatedness.

Finally, "E.R.G. Theory attempts to deal not only with how satisfaction affects desire but also with how chronic desire affects satisfaction by using the same set of concepts."[14]

PROCESS THEORIES

VROOM'S THEORY OF MOTIVATION

Vroom has outlined a conceptual model of motivation that includes many of the concepts discussed earlier in this chapter.[15] The three dimensions to his model can be expressed by the following formula:

$$\text{Force (of motivation)} = \Sigma \text{ valence} \times \text{expectancy}$$

---

[14] Ibid., p. 28
[15] Victor H. Vroom, *Work and Motivation,* New York, Wiley, 1964.

Valence refers to the preference a person has for a particular outcome.

Valence. Valence refers to the orientation of a person to a particular outcome. Outcomes that a person has available may be positively valent or negatively valent, according to whether the person prefers attaining that particular outcome. This strength of a person's desire for an outcome is dependent not on its intrinsic property, but on the anticipated satisfaction or dissatisfaction associated with other outcomes to which it is expected to lead. For example, a person's valence for overtime work is dependent not on the actual attraction of the overtime itself, but on the satisfaction anticipated from promotion or extra income.

Expectancy refers to the likelihood that a particular act will be followed by a particular outcome.

Expectancy. In all outcomes that a person seeks, there is a degree of risk. If a person chooses a training program or a self-development opportunity, which he anticipates will lead to a job promotion, there is a risk that the promotion will not be forthcoming. In these cases, the behavior of the person making the choice is affected not only by his preferences among outcomes, but also by the degree to which he believes these outcomes to be probable. "An expectancy is defined as a momentary belief concerning the likelihood that a particular act will be followed by a particular outcome."[16] If all operatives who enter a foreman's training program are promoted, an employee might develop a strong expectancy that the act (engaging in that program) will lead to the outcome (promotion to foreman).

Motivation in Vroom's theory depends on ones preference for an outcome and the degree of confidence that effort will lead to achieving it.

The Concept of Force. The directional concept that describes how valences and expectancies combine in determining choice is known in Vroom's model as *force*. Vroom defines force as a algebraic sum of the products of the valences of all outcomes and the strength of expectancies that the act will be followed by the attainment of these outcomes.

It should be noted that the concept of force as it is explained by Vroom is synonymous with the word *motivation* as it is used by most persons. His formula can be illustrated by Figure 9-3.

There is one other dimension to Vroom's model that is quite important to understanding his theory of motivation. Vroom captions this dimension the *situation variables*, and says they affect the valence of possible outcomes and consist of such things as the knowledge about previous outcomes and acts, their frequency of occurrence, and their desirability.

FIGURE 9-3

Vroom's Motivational Equation

Force	=	Σ	*Valence*	×	*Expectancy*
Motivation to enter training program for foreman	=	Σ	Preference for training	×	Confidence training will lead to promotion

---
[16]Ibid., p. 17.

HUMAN MOTIVATION

Vroom's theory has not been extensively researched. It is difficult for many to understand, and presents several problems, such as assigning values to the various segments.

EQUITY THEORY

The idea of equity, particularly as it relates to wages, is not new. In the mid-1920s Whiting Williams, an executive, quit his job to pursue the question, "What's on worker's minds?" In his book, *Mainsprings of Men*, he set forth an equity theory of wages.[17] Williams said that it was not the absolute level of pay a person received that was so important but what he received relative to what others were receiving. He also stressed that it was the worker's point of view that was the key, not what someone else might think.

In the 1960s scholars began to formulate the basis for modern equity theory. Although there are some differences among proponents of this theory, most recognize that there are three components to what is referred to as the exchange process. Inputs are what the individual gives or invests in the employment relationship. Effort, education, experience, and training are examples of inputs. The second component in the exchange process is the outcomes or things received as a result of inputs. Pay, status, recognition, growth opportunities, promotion, and increased opportunities to participate represent possible outputs. The third and a very important part of the exchange process is the reference person or group that is used in evaluating the equity of one's own exchange relationship.

> Perceived inequity exists when a person feels that what they receive is out of line.

Perceived inequity exists when the ratio of a person's inputs to outputs departs significantly from that which they perceive to exist for the reference person or group. When a person is subject to perceived or real inequity they may engage in one of several types of behavior. First, they may alter their inputs. An example of this would be to put forth less effort on the job. This is likely to occur when they feel they are achieving more than others who expend less effort but the outcomes in terms of pay for example do not reflect this.

> When inequity is perceived a person may alter their inputs.

Second, perceived inequity may be met by an attempt to alter outcomes or balance them with one's expectations by exerting pressure. Threatening to leave would illustrate this and indeed has been used effectively by many people in numerous situations. It is not a recommended course of action however unless one is indeed prepared to leave and has other desirable employment alternatives available.

A third possibility is to exert pressure on the reference person to alter their behavior. This could take the form of exerting social pressure to get others to conform to group norms in terms of certain "acceptable" levels of performance. This type of action does not of course alter a person's own outcomes but does "bring others in line" so to speak. Finally, inequity may trigger a decision to leave the organization. This will usually occur only when the unfavorable inequity is very great and persists over time. Some additional observations pertinent to equity theory include the following:

---

[17] Whiting Williams, *Mainsprings of Men*, New York, Charles Scribner's Sons, 1925.

1. Both inputs and outputs may have varying utility or value to the parties involved. For example, an employee may feel tenure and experience is deserving of more emphasis in determining rewards (output) than the employing organization attaches to them. If this situation exists perceived inequity on the employee's part is bound to occur.
2. People's threshold for the amount of perceived inequity they can be comfortable with before undertaking some type of action to change the situation will vary.
3. In cases where people are being overrewarded, research shows the overreward is usually considered as good fortune and does not trigger increased outputs. Therefore, it is not motivational. Only when the overreward is very large will it trigger improved performance.
4. To reemphasize the foregoing, it is not the absolute amount of various forms of output that is the key issue but rather how those outputs compare to those received by others. The individual's perception of the situation is what matters. If the perceptions are not accurate in light of reality, the manager must work at changing them through effective communications.
5. As managers, unfortunately we may not always be aware of perceived inequity and thus may experience unfavorable behavioral consequences on the part of those involved. This suggests that we need to be in close touch with how people perceive and react to various elements in the work environment.

Thus far equity theory has focused primarily on pay, and needs to be extended to include other rewards that are important to employees. Research on equity theory is just beginning and its conclusions are incomplete. One study concluded it was most powerful in predicting satisfaction.[18] However, since the reciprocal relationship between satisfaction and productivity has not been firmly established, caution is in order. The latter does not necessarily follow from the former.

ACHIEVEMENT MOTIVATION

David McClelland of Harvard University and his associates have been studying and doing research in the area of motivation for over twenty years. He has identified three motives that all people have:[19]

Power motive—having an impact on others, directing their efforts and exercising influence.

Affiliation motive—establishing and maintaining friendly relations with people.

Achievement motive—doing something better and more efficiently and achieving results.

---

[18] Stuart M. Klein, "Pay Factors as Predictors of Satisfaction: A Comparison of Reinforcement, Equity, and Expectancy," *Academy of Management Journal*, Vol. 16, No. 4, December, 1973, pp. 398–410. See also L. L. Cummings and Randall B. Dunham, *Introduction to Organizational Behavior*, Homewood, Ill., Richard D. Irwin, Inc., 1980, pp. 142–144.

[19] David C. McClelland, "That Urge to Achieve," *Behavioral Concepts in Management*, 2nd ed., David Hampton, ed., Belmont, Ca., Dickenson Publishing Company, Inc., 1972, p. 78.

The following discussion concentrates primarily on achievement motivation (usually denoted as N(ACH)) but we will also relate it to the power and affiliation motives as well as discuss some of the dynamics of N(ACH). All three of the motives are present in people to some degree. One of the three will usually predominate however.[20] Persons high on N(ACH) tend to:

People high in achievement desire challenging but achievable goals.

1. Seek challenging but realistic and achievable goals. If goals are not set they will tend to set their own. Once the chance of reaching a goal approaches the 50 percent level achievers will start to lost interest and as this percent increases there will be a greater tendency and desire to move on to other things.
2. Develop plans to help them attain goals.
3. Seek concrete and measurable feedback of the results of their efforts. Achievers want both positive and negative feedback. The former serves to provide a sense of accomplishment and self-gratification while the latter (negative feedback) lets them know where they stand so they can make the adjustments needed to realize success.
4. Will take calculated risks but want reasonable control over eventual results. A situation where success is influenced by too many external factors not within the achievers control will not be appealing.
5. Seek and assume high degrees of personal responsibility.
6. Seek out opportunities where their desire to achieve will not be thwarted.

Dynamics of Achievement Motivation. McClelland emphasizes that environmental factors greatly influence achievement motivation. Of great importance for the manager to recognize, is that motivation is a combination between what people bring to the job plus the conditioning they receive. Specifically in this regard (1) subordinates hear and adopt their manager's motivational message (e.g., enthusiasm can be contagious as can apathy); (2) managers, to a degree, create subordinates in their own image and that image differs as a function of the manager's level of achievement; (3) level and quality of motivation of subordinates may say more about the manager than about the subordinates themselves. Regarding this latter point, research has shown that managers can have a significant impact on the N(ACH) level of their subordinates via the kind of leadership climate they provide. We discuss the elements of a favorable climate more extensively in Chapter 13.

At this time the following will serve to illustrate what is being suggested.

Robert A. Stringer, Jr., building on the research of McClelland and others, has proposed eight propositions that will produce management control processes that reinforce and reward high achievement-oriented behavior. These propositions will be useful to us in relating motivational theory to a healthy organization climate later in this text.[21]

---

[20] David C. McClelland, *The Achieving Society*, Princeton, N.J., D. Van Nostrand Company, Inc., 1961.
[21] Robert A. Stringer, Jr., "Achievement Motivation and Management Control," *Behavioral Concepts in Management*, 2nd ed., David Hampton, ed., Belmont Ca., Dickenson Publishing Company, Inc., 1972, p. 89.

Proposition 1: Achievement motivation will tend to be aroused if the goals of the responsibility center are made explicit.

Proposition 2: Achievement motivation will tend to be aroused if goals represent a moderate degree of risk for the individuals involved.

Proposition 3: A higher level of achievement motivation will tend to be aroused if provision is made in the management control process for adjusting specific goals when the chances of goal-accomplishment change significantly (from the 50-50 level).

Proposition 4: Achievement motivation will tend to be aroused if managers are evaluated in terms of their goal-setting behaviors.

Proposition 5: Achievement motivation will tend to be aroused if individuals are given feedback of the progress they are making toward their goals.

Proposition 6: Achievement motivation will be aroused if there is a climate that emphasizes individual responsibility.

Proposition 7: Achievement motivation will be aroused if the rewards and punishments formally provided for as part of the management control system are perceived as consistent with achievement goals.

Proposition 8: Achievement motivation will tend to be increased when there is a climate of mutual support and encouragement.

Managerial Implications of Achievement Motivation. Research on achievement motivation has yielded several findings that are of significance to organizations and individual managers interested in utilizing the maximum potential represented by their human resources while at the same time providing employees with meaningful work experience. Some of these findings are summarized below.

The achievement motive in people can be developed.

People can be trained in achievement and the climate for achievement is more important than the N(ACH) motive itself; or put another way the achievement motive can be developed. To illustrate this, McClelland and his associates have taken ghetto children, trained them to be achievers and when returned to the ghetto they revert to their former status. When, however, the parents of these same children have been trained to provide a climate that nurtures achievement and both groups return to the ghetto setting the children continue to be achievers.

High achievers do not necessarily make the best managers and in fact may be very uncomfortable in the managerial role. There is a significant difference between achieving oneself and inspiring others to achieve. The latter takes a different set of skills, abilities, and values. Among other things it requires a person who can draw satisfaction for what others accomplish, not just what they accomplish.

Good managers tend to be higher in power motivation than in achievement. The type of power referred to however is not personal of coercive power that denotes a desire to dominate people and use them as pawns for one's own personal aggrandizement. Rather it is a socialized kind of power. This is represented by the leader who:

HUMAN MOTIVATION

Good managers tend to be higher in the power motive than in achievement.

1. Shows a concern for group goals.
2. Finds goals that people can and will identify with and become enthused about.
3. Helps people formulate goals as opposed to dictating them.
4. Gives people a feeling of confidence and strength to work hard for goals and the feeling they can be achieved.[22]

People high in affiliation tend to make poor managers.

An even more important comparison is how the N(ACH) motive compares to the affiliation motive. People high in affiliation relative to achievement tend to make poor managers. Their subordinates or those they lead often feel little personal responsibility and accountability and these is a lack of any sense of urgency to accomplish results.

Finally, good managers have been found to use a coaching style of leadership. Chapter 15 explores the area of Human Resource Development and Quality of Work Life. For present purposes an effective coach is one who is interested in bringing out the best that each employee can give and contributing to the employees' growth and development.

Being part of a high achieving group can raise individual standards.

Group Effects on Achievement Motivation. Recent research indicates that membership in informal groups may affect achievement motivation.[23] In some cases, belonging to high achievement groups may tend to raise individual standards. In cases where group norms are below individual standards, the group may reduce the effects of achievement on the individual. As we will learn from Chapter 11, Role and Function of the Group in Organizations, we can seldom view people in the work situation as operating apart from their informal group.

HERZBERG'S DUAL FACTOR THEORY

Organizations, as well as individual managers, were at one time preoccupied with the idea that the only incentive that could be provided to motivate people was money. The first significant breakthrough in dispelling this philosophy was made by Frederick Herzberg.[24]

Herzberg maintains that the factors associated with dissatisfaction are not the same as those that lead to satisfaction.

Herzberg began his inquiry by conducting in-depth interview studies of more than 200 engineers and accountants representing Pittsburgh industry. His interviews probed sequences of events in the work lives of the respondents to determine the factors that were involved in their feeling both exceptionally happy and, conversely, exceptionally unhappy, with their jobs. He concluded that the factors involved in producing job satisfaction were not the same factors as those that led to job dissatisfaction. Figure 9-4 lists, on the left side, the items

---

[22]David C. McClelland, "The Two faces of Power," *Journal of International Affairs*, Vol. 24, No. 1, 1970, p. 29
[23]Manuel London and Greg R. Oldham, "A Comparison of Group and Individual Incentive Plan," *Academy of Management Journal*, Vol. 20, No. 1, March 1977.
[24]Frederick Herzberg, "The Motivation-Hygiene Concept and Problems of Manpower," *Personnel Administration*, January-February 1964, pp. 3–7.

FIGURE 9-4

Dissatisfiers and Satisfiers on the Job

Dissatisfiers (Hygiene)	*Satisfiers (Motivators)*
Company policy and administration	Achievement
Supervision—Technical	Recognition
Salary	Work itself
Interpersonal relations—supervision	Responsibility
Working conditions	Advancement

Source: Adapted from Frederick Herzberg, et al., *The Motivation to Work,* New York, Wiley, Sons, 1959.

that were most often mentioned in the interviews when dissatisfaction occurred. When the respondents experienced satisfaction, factors such as those on the right were usually present.[25]

Summarized as follows are some of the more important concepts developed by Herzberg.

1. There are two distinctive dimensions to the motivational problem. On one end of the continuum are those factors that can either cause or prevent dissatisfaction. Herzberg calls these "hygiene factors." They are usually known as "extrinsic" factors related to the environment in which one works. On the other end of the continuum are motivational factors that, if present, can actually lead to positive attitudes and motivation. These are known as intrinsic factors (i.e., those related to the nature of the job itself). But if these are not present, no positive attitudes result.

2. The hygiene factors (those that can either cause or prevent dissatisfaction) include such things as wages, fringe benefits, physical working conditions, and overall company policy and administration. When these things are adequately taken care of, dissatisfaction will disappear, but no positive attitudes and motivation result. Thus, the hygiene factors are preventive. They can prevent dissatisfaction but do not act as personal incentives which motivate people to high levels of productivity. As Herzberg points out, people can be brought only to a neutral point on the basis of hygiene factors.

3. The motivational factors (those that lead to the development of positive attitudes and motivation, and act as individual incentives) include such things as recognition, feelings of accomplishment and achievement, opportunity for advancement and potential for personal growth, responsibility, a sense of job and individual importance, new experiences, and challenging work. As Herzberg notes, these are things that surround the job. While the hygiene factors satisfy the physiological and security needs, the motivational factors are concerned with esteem and self-actualization needs.

Herzberg summarizes the situation:

> *Because the factors on the left serve primarily as preventives, that is to prevent job dissatisfaction, and because they also deal with the environment, I have named these*

---
[25]Ibid.

factors the "hygiene" factors in a poor analogy with the way the term is used in preventive medicine. The factors on the right I call the "motivators" because other results indicate that they are necessary for improvement which in substance amounts to coming up to a fair day's work.[26]

According to Herzberg, the organization or individual managers who have traditionally approached the subject of motivation from a solely "hygienic" perspective have been seriously handicapping themselves in several ways. Assuming they have correctly applied the hygiene factors, all they have succeeded in doing in most cases is preventing dissatisfaction. Second, no positive motivation has resulted beyond perhaps the neutral level. Third, it should be recognized that to some degree all managers are limited in their control over wages (one of the most important of all the hygiene factors). Generally speaking, the lower the management level, the less the control. All organizations have policies concerning salary review dates, wage and salary structures, and a limit of some sort with respect to the general level of wages paid. Therefore, not only does Herzberg question the effectiveness of money as a motivator, but he questions the extent to which any individual manager has control over it. Of course, managers cannot motivate people with incentives over which they have no control.

In addition, Maslow estimated that for the average person, the physiological needs are 85 percent satisfied, the security needs 70 percent satisfied, the social needs 50 percent satisfied, the psychological needs 40 percent satisfied and the self-fulfillment needs 10 percent satisfied. If one assumes that these estimates concerning the degree to which the various needs are satisfied for the average person are representative, the greatest potential for motivation quite obviously lies in providing incentives that satisfy the social, esteem, and self-fulfillment needs.

The theory does not suggest that the economic needs and the hygiene factors are not important. They are very important and cannot be overlooked. The important point is that the lack of hygiene factors can cause dissatisfaction, but they do not get at the root of job satisfaction and motivation as far as the individual is concerned. The latter is a separate dimension and depends on a totally different set of needs and factors. Herzberg's satisfaction continuum can be observed in Figure 9-5.

Herzberg implies that to a certain degree weaknesses on the hygiene side can be offset by positive factors on the motivational side. The opposite, however, does not hold true. Many organizations that pride themselves on their wage and fringe

> Herzberg does not suggest that the hygiene factors can be neglected but only that they hold minimum motivation potential.

FIGURE 9-5

The Relationship of Hygiene and Motivational Factors

	Hygiene	*Motivational*
If not present	JOB DISSATISFACTION	NO JOB SATISFACTION
If present	NO JOB DISSATISFACTION	JOB SATISFACTION

---

[26]Ibid., p. 5.

benefit programs as well as general working conditions have found that these things alone have not furnished the answer to maximum cooperation and productivity from employees. While it is true they may help to attract good people initially, they are likely to be taken for granted after a relatively short time and only a neutral point of motivation reached. Motivation beyond a neutral point requires that attention be given to self-esteem and self-actualization needs.[27]

An extension of Herzberg's work was undertaken by Myers at Texas Instruments Company. His study included salaried as well as hourly employees, and managers as well as nonmanagers. Using essentially the Herzberg research approach, he came to the same general conclusions with regard to specific motivational factors as they relate to various classifications of employees. In addition, Myers states his belief that managers on all levels have two responsibilities: (1) to provide for satisfaction of the economic needs or potential dissatisfiers, and (2) to provide conditions for motivation.[28]

MOTIVATION-HYGIENE THEORY—A CRITIQUE

Herzberg's motivation-hygiene theory has received a great deal of attention both in management thought literature and in management development training. Some studies, such as the one cited earlier by Myers, have substantiated his findings among varying groups of employees. Others however, have found the theory to be an oversimplification. In addition, there have been serious questions with respect to his methodology. A number of his critics seem to be "wrestling with semantics," and a few seem to be attacking him in areas that indicate they misunderstand his theory. As one reviewer suggests, some critics are not as interested in adding knowledge to the field as they are in "being the gun that gunned down the biggest gun in the west."[29]

Research on Herzberg's theory would seem to indicate that it is somewhat of an oversimplication.

However, note that in one recent study equal levels of job involvement existed among managers who expressed primary concern for hygiene factors as those who were primarily concerned with motivational factors.[30] Thus, in opposition to Herzberg's suggestions, motivation was not necessarily linked solely to the presence of those factors he labeled as motivational.

These findings support those of Fein, who contends that only 8 to 12 percent of the work force respond to what Herzberg labels as motivators and a study by Reif with similar findings that employees are not primarily concerned with higher-order needs.[31]

---

[27]Frederick Herzberg, *Work and the Nature of Man*, Cleveland, World Publishing Co., 1966.
[28]M. Scott Myers, "Who Are Your Motivated Workers?" *Harvard Business Review*, January-February, 1964, pp. 73–38.
[29]Valerie M. Bockman, "The Herzberg Controversy," *Personnel Psychology*, 1971, Vol. 24, p. 186.
[30]Gerald J. Gorn and Rabindra N. Kanungo, "Job Involvement and Motivation: Are Intrinsically Motivated Managers More Job Involved?" *Organizational Behavior and Human Performance*, Vol. 26, 1980, pp. 265–277.
[31]Mitchell Fein, "Job Enrichment: A Reevaluation," *Sloan Management Review*, Winter 1974, p. 87. William E. Reif, "Intrinsic Versus Extrinsic Rewards: Resolving the Controversy," *Human Resource Management*, Summer 1975, p. 2.

In total, evidence based on research as well as the practical experiences of managers, would suggest that the Herzberg theory contains some potentially useful ideas in understanding the motivation process but should not be accepted as a definitive explanation of motivation in the world of work.[32] Two areas where the theory seems deficient pertain to the role of money in motivation and the role of supervision. The former is discussed next and the latter at a later point in the chapter.

MONEY AND MOTIVATION IN PERSPECTIVE

Before leaving the Herzberg theory of motivation, some additional observations on the role of wages in the motivational process might be helpful. As Herzberg has observed, wages are the most important hygiene factor, and, if people are not paid more in the future than they are presently receiving, they will become dissatisfied. Similarly, he notes that even if they receive an increase, the favorable effect will only be temporary and they will soon again become dissatisfied.

Under certain conditions wages can have motivational value.

These observations certainly have validity, but it should be noted that under certain conditions wages can have a degree of motivational value.[32] The first requirement of a motivational wages system is that it must pay people on the basis of the results they achieve on a job, instead of the mere physical routine performance of a series of activities. Unfortunately, in many cases we have not held people accountable for results after giving them predetermined challenging objectives, and thus have permitted less than maximum performance. This problem has been compounded as we continued to pay higher and higher wages, thereby training people to expect wage increases even for mediocre effort and average performance.

A second requirement for a motivation-oriented wage system is that it must adequately distinguish dollarwise between the different levels of efficiency for people performing essentially the same job. Here again, most wage plans have not done this in practice, although they were designed to originally.

The problem lies in the administration of plans. To illustrate the above observation, N. B. Winstanley, Compensation Research Manager for Xerox Corporation, recently conducted a survey of over 100 personnel professionals and executives to determine the extent to which they felt merit salary increases are related to the quality of job performance.[33] Sixty percent of the 120 respondents believed there is little or no relationship between size of merit increases and performance in a majority of industrial companies across the United States. These results reflect serious doubts about how effectively merit pay is administered in most companies.

Winstanley also asked many of the professionals and executives about conditions in their own companies, in other words, to what extent does the system in your own company truly reward quality job performance. A typical response was a grin and silence. This same type of conclusion was reported by William Evans

---

[32] Saul W. Gellerman, "Motivating Men with Money," *Fortune*, Vol. LXXVII, No. 3, March 1968.
[33] N. B. Winstanley, "A Personnel Perspective on Pay-for-Performance", *Personnel Journal*, November 1979, p. 758.

in his extensive research on compensation. He noted in an overwhelming majority of the companies, job performance is not the primary determinant of wage and salary progression for nonsupervisory employees.[34]

In addition to the above discussion other points are worthy of note.

1. Nonmotivational wage payment systems can cause dissatisfaction among the better performers, because they are not being rewarded equitably for their achievements in relation to others.
2. Good performers may become discouraged with the system, and lower their levels of commitment to excellence.
3. Average performers can be encouraged to remain average and to do less than their best, because the system fosters it.

Two additional requirements of a motivation-stimulating wage system are (1) that the increases awarded must be given voluntarily, and (2) must be large enough to have a favorable effect on the individual's standard of living. Regarding the first factor, increases that are paid because of threats by the employee to leave will have no positive effects. For the second requirement, if an individual receives a 6 percent wage increase and the rate of inflation is running at 10 percent, he can hardly be expected to react enthusiastically to this good fortune.

> If wages are to have motivational value increases must be given voluntarily.

Management should remember that both the incentive being offered and the kind of behavior needed to achieve it *must* be viewed from the employee's frame of reference. For example, when the organization offers a wage increase based on achieving a given level of performance, the employee will be motivated only if the following conditions are present.

1. Superior performance does actually result in some type of *extraordinary* financial reward. The fact that the organization advertises that this relationship exists is of no consequence. If, rightly or wrongly, employees have come to feel there is no relationship, or only a small one, between superior work and superior wages, they will not be motivated to do their best.
2. The size of the potential increase must be perceived as being worth the extra effort required to earn it. If employees are accustomed to receiving a 4 to 5 percent increase as a matter of course, and a mere 6 to 8 percent increase is offered as an incentive, they may not feel motivated to work for the higher rate.
3. The employee must be interested in making more money in the first place.

The preceding discussion should illustrate the very complicated and frustrating relationship between the wage issue and motivation. The members of an organization always want more money, regardless of the wage system in existence. From the standpoint of the organization's management, it is frustrating because resources are always limited. Perhaps the most important point that can be made about this subject is that the system must be equitable in the eyes of the employees.

---

[34]William A. Evans, "Pay for Performance: Fact or Fable?" *Personnel Journal,* September 1970.

THE PORTER AND LAWLER MOTIVATION MODEL

The conventional perception of job satisfaction defines it as "the total feeling an individual has about his job." From the Hawthorne studies of the 1930s (Chapter 2), the prevailing view of the satisfaction-performance relationship was that satisfaction leads to performance. One of the first studies to contradict this relationship was reported in the *Psychological Bulletin* in 1955, in which it was reported that there was little evidence of any simple or appreciable relationship between persons' attitudes and the effectiveness of their performance.[35]

Porter and Lawler point out that job satisfaction and job performance are caused by quite different things. "Job satisfaction is closely affected by the assortment of rewards that people derive from their jobs and level of performance is closely affected by the basis of attainment of rewards. Individuals are satisfied with their jobs to the extent to which their jobs provide them with what they desire, and they perform effectively in them to the extent that effective performance leads to the attainment of what they desire."[36]

> Research indicates that there is no consistent correlation between job satisfaction and job performance.

This observation is supported by a great deal of other research in the area of job satisfaction that indicates no *consistent* correlation between job satisfaction and job performance. The conditions that determine each are different. It is possible to have high satisfaction and high performance or high satisfaction and low performance. Conversely, there may be low satisfaction and low performance or low satisfaction and high performance. However, all studies have found other measures of job behavior, such as turnover and absenteeism, to be associated with satisfaction: that is, high satisfaction is associated positively with low turnover and low absenteeism of employees.

According to one group of researchers, it is wiser to think of job satisfaction as *resulting* from high performance than as being the *cause* of good or bad performance. Since satisfaction is a result of need fulfillment, the job itself may constitute one of the greatest sources of satisfaction. The model presented in Figure 9-6 illustrates this thought.

Note that the first two blocks to the left in the model depict the conditions described by Vroom—attractiveness of outcome and likelihood that effort leads to reward. These determine the strength of effort. This effort is moderated by an individual's abilities and his or her interpretation of the kind of effort that the job calls for. All of these factors lead to and affect "performance." Performance in turn can lead to both intrinsic and extrinsic rewards.

> Intrinsic rewards are the result of things done by us.

At this point, we need to distinguish between *intrinsic* and *extrinsic* rewards. Intrinsic rewards are a result of things done by us, such as the sense of accomplishment felt when we overcome difficulties and carry through a difficult task successfully. Performing the task administers the reward. Other rewards are

---

[35]Charles W. Greene, "The Satisfaction Performance Controversy," *Business Horizons*, October 1972, pp. 31–34. For an extensive treatment of this subject, see Edwin A. Locke, "The Nature and Causes of Job Satisfaction," *Handbook of Industrial and Organizational Psychology*, Marvin D. Dunnette, ed., 1976, Rand McNally College Publishing Co., pp. 1297–1349.
[36]Ibid.

FIGURE 9-6

Porter and Lawler's Motivation Model

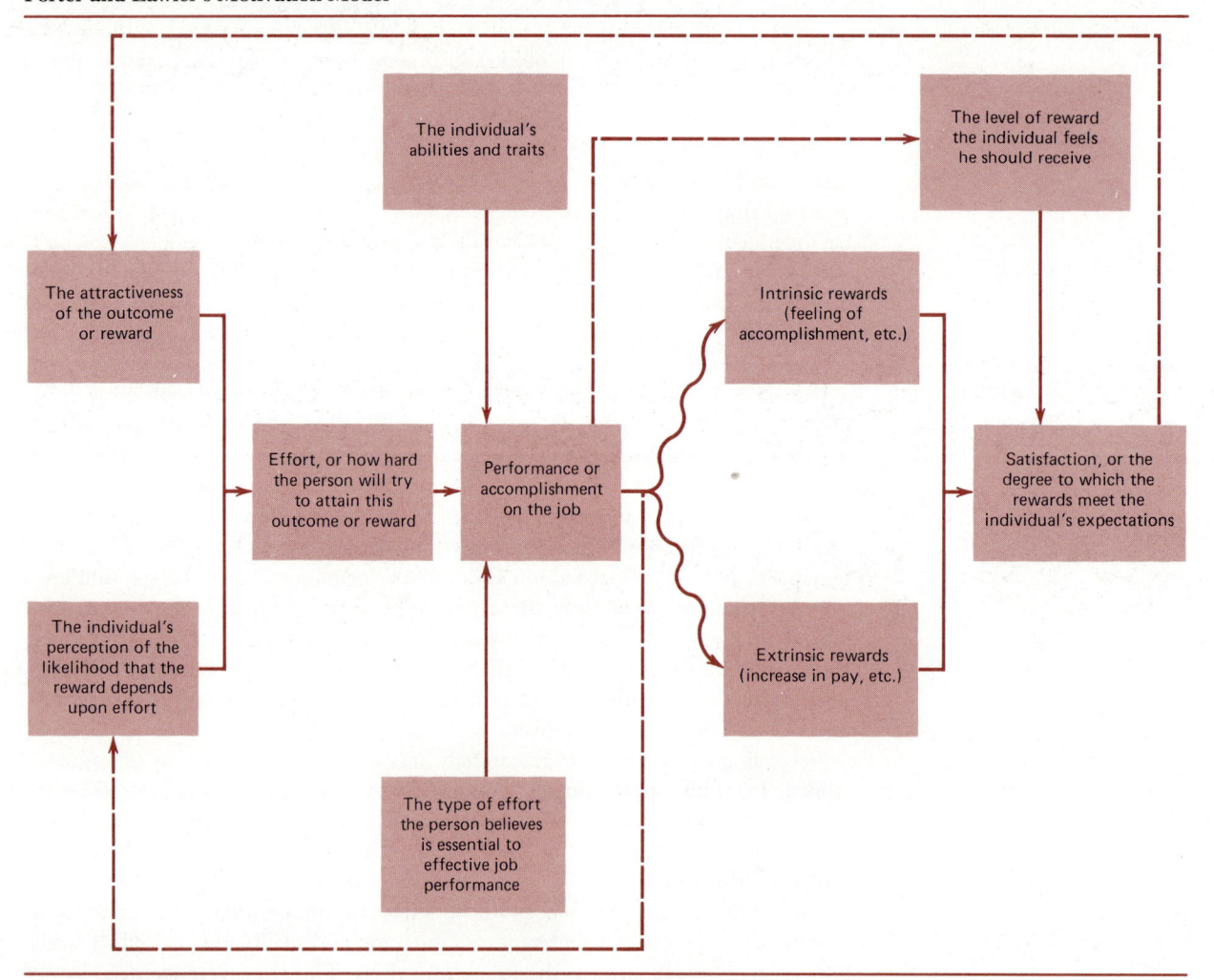

[Diagram: Porter and Lawler's Motivation Model, showing boxes connected by arrows:
- The attractiveness of the outcome or reward
- The individual's perception of the likelihood that the reward depends upon effort
- Effort, or how hard the person will try to attain this outcome or reward
- The individual's abilities and traits
- The type of effort the person believes is essential to effective job performance
- Performance or accomplishment on the job
- Intrinsic rewards (feeling of accomplishment, etc.)
- Extrinsic rewards (increase in pay, etc.)
- The level of reward the individual feels he should receive
- Satisfaction, or the degree to which the rewards meet the individual's expectations]

Source: Adapted from Lyman W. Porter and Edward E. Lawler, III, *Managerial Attitudes and Performance*, Homewood, Ill. Richard D. Irwin, 1968, p. 165.

extrinsic, "provided by people other than ourselves—such as when the boss gives us a promotion, or when the organization awards us a year-end bonus."[37]

The differences in this model and some of the other theories presented in this chapter are noticeable. First and most important, performance on the job

---

[37]Lyman W. Porter and Edward E. Lawler, III "What Job Attitudes Tell About Motivation," *Harvard Business Review*, January-February, 1968, p. 120.

precedes satisfaction (although ultimate satisfaction feeds back and affects future decisions). This much of the model is consistent with Herzberg's theory that satisfaction must come from the work itself. However, in the Porter-Lawler model, extrinsic rewards such as pay can lead to satisfaction. Herzberg would say they can only prevent dissatisfaction.

It is not always possible or practical to increase the total satisfaction of employees. Usually, however, the strength of the relationship between satisfaction and productivity can be increased. This can be done by following these steps.

1. Examine employee attitudes regarding what people want from their jobs.
2. Investigate the strength of their effort-reward expectancies.
3. Realign job tasks so that superior performance on the job will lead to satisfaction (as defined in Step 1). This will lead to intrinsic satisfaction.
4. Realign effort-reward expectancies so that employees will perceive a high probability that increased effort will lead to the rewards they desire.[38]

The next section of this chapter will explore several possibilities for doing these things.

SYSTEMATIC APPROACHES TO INCENTIVE APPLICATION

REINFORCEMENT THEORY

Reinforcement theory is based on the research of B. F. Skinner who concluded that a person's behavior or motivation is a function of the consequences of that behavior. When desired behavior is positively reinforced it tends to be repeated and if it is not reinforced it is less likely to continue to occur. Reinforcement theory has led to an approach to management known as behavior modification or as practitioners more commonly refer to it or performance feedback and positive reinforcement.[39]

An understanding of the principles of performance feedback and positive reinforcement systems enables the manager to avoid several frequent mistakes in motivating employees. Some of these mistakes have been summarized as follows:

In many instances employees are given rewards that are not conditional or contingent on behavior the manager wishes to promote. Even when they are, long delays often intervene

When a desired behavior is reinforced positively it is likely to reoccur.

---

[38] Richard A. Guzzo, "Types of Rewards, Cognitions, and Work Motivation," *Academy of Management Review*, 1979, Vol. 4, No. 1, pp. 75–86.
[39] W. Clay Hamner and Ellen P. Hamner, "Behavior Modification on the Bottom Line," *Organizational Dynamics*, Sperry, 1976, p. 4

Reinforcement should be as immediate as possible.

between the occurrence of the desired behavior and its intended consequences. Special privileges, activities, and rewards are often furnished according to length of service rather than performance requirements. In many cases, positive reinforcers are inadvertently made contingent upon the wrong kind of behavior. In short, intuition provides a poor guide to motivation.[40]

Behavior modification assumes that behavior can be engineered or altered by manipulating reward structures for various forms of behavior. The process of influencing behavior through managing reward structures is called shaping. It requires that we are able to break down a total job into smaller steps and set up a systematic way of providing a reinforcement for a success within each of those steps. An important underlying assumption is that people like to succeed and success is in and of itself reinforcing. Some possibilities for positive reinforcement include more control by the employee in performing the job (this may take the form of determining work methods and pace), more responsibility (quality control checks performed by the individual versus an outsider) participation (in determining outputs goals or methods), opportunities to learn new skills, money or recognition. Some important managerial implications in using this approach include the following:

Reinforcement theory assumes people like to succeed.

1. Inform people of desired behaviors that will be rewarded and those that will not.
2. Provide continuous feedback on the nature and quality of work including errors.
3. Provide help and support to the individual when performance improvement is needed.
4. Reward good performance equal to behavior. Do not reward all people the same when there are differences in performance levels.[41]

In addition to the above, reinforcement should be specific particularly in the case of recognition. Do not say you did a good job. What was good about it? People must not only be reinforced but they must know what they are doing that is commendable. It is not a series of "atta boys." Also, reinforcement should always be an if-then proposition. If you mow the lawn then you will get ice cream. The reinforcer should always follow not precede the desired behavior.

The process of behavior modification (performance feedback-positive reinforcement) is unique in three ways. It calls for a maximum use of positive rewards and minimum use of punishment. Note that the latter has its appropriate place and may be necessary to stop undesired behavior. Second, by analyzing the work situation and focusing on desired behavior and behavior change, it avoids the need to probe attitudes and continuously deal with the negative only. Finally, it is results oriented.[42]

---

[40]Ibid., p. 6.
[41]From H. L. Tosi and W. C. Hamner, eds., *Organizational Behavior and Management: A Contingency Approach*, Chicago, St. Clair Press, 1974.
[42]Ibid.

GOAL SETTING AND MANAGEMENT EXPECTATIONS

Establishing goals and objectives in the work environment accomplishes three major things as they relate to motivation. First, they serve to guide and direct behavior. Without goals attention and effort is more likely to be random and any form of accomplishment may lack meaning. Second, goals provide a mechanism whereby the efforts of people are coordinated toward goal attainment with an emphasis on where the organization wants to go in the future versus where it has been in the past. Finally, the establishment of goals generally suggests management confidence in people's ability to achieve those goals. This expression of confidence is important because we know, based on research, that managers of high-achieving employees tend to have much higher performance expectations than do managers of average- and low-achieving employees. Specifically, the power of positive expectations cannot be overlooked in relation to subsequent levels of motivation.

Managers of high-achieving employees tend to have higher performance expectations.

Based on a review of twenty-seven published and unpublished reports of field research Latham and Yukl conclude that there is strong support for the contention that goal setting represents an effective means for enhancing employee performance[43] In addition, research has established the following regarding the presence of goals:

Research indicates that goal setting is an effective means of enhancing employee performance.

1. Performance tends to improve more when specific versus more generalized goals are established.
2. Participation in the goal-setting process results in higher levels of achievement than when it is not present.
3. Goals that are challenging in terms of requiring the individual to "stretch" result in higher levels of accomplishment than do easy goals. The latter tend not to result in better performance.
4. Performance is most favorably affected when the manager is present to encourage goal acceptance and accomplishment.

NATURE OF SUPERVISION AND MOTIVATION

Herzberg identifies supervision as a hygiene factor and therefore not related to satisfaction or motivation. His conclusion on this point is questionable. To the extent that the manager has control over the hygiene factors (it should be noted that many times her control, as in the cases of wage rates or organization policy, is highly limited) her job is to maintain or administer these factors on an equitable basis. In other words, she can make sure that people are treated equitably in relation to others and can attempt to clarify situations where they may perceive equity does not exist.

With regard to the factors Herzberg associates with satisfaction and motiva-

---

[43] Gary P. Latham and Gary A. Yukl, "A Review of Research on the Application of Goal Setting in Organizations," *Academy of Management Journal*, December 1975, pp. 824–845.

tion, there is a lot the manager can do by using a professional approach to leadership that will bring out the highest potential in people. Conversely, the absence of certain leadership practices may suppress that same motivation potential.

A more extensive discussion of the specific leadership practices that form the cornerstone of modern professional management and contribute to a climate that fosters motivation will be provided in Chapter 14 that deals with Leadership Styles. Some of the elements of effective leadership that are pertinent and will be discussed include:

1. Explicit goals.
2. A climate where accountability is emphasized.
3. High performance expectations.
4. Identify reward paths.
5. Rewards that are consistent with achievement.
6. Supportive relationships.
7. Creation of a team climate.
8. Participation.

SOME CONCLUDING NOTES ON MOTIVATION

Before concluding our discussion of motivation, it might be well to review some observations made earlier in the chapter as well as cite some additional significant points.

1. Each person has different needs, based on age, education, environment, background, and personality. The manager must, therefore, get to know people and what is important to them individually, in order to provide a climate conducive to triggering the motivation potential in people.

2. Many needs can be satisfied on the job, and employees will not be satisfied unless their job-oriented needs are met. Motivation depends on matching those things that are important to the employee with what the total job climate has to offer.

3. When people's need satisfactions are frustrated, several possible behavior patterns may emerge. One may be to attack, which may be either verbal against the organization and/or supervisor, or, in some cases, even physical. Attack on a less obvious scale would be represented by deliberate although, many times, subtle quality defects, machine breakdowns, and similar phenomena.

Another very common behavior response to frustration is retreat. By this we mean that employees withdraw their commitment. They remain physically on the job, but mentally and emotionally they are absent.

4. All behavior is caused and the causes can be analyzed, understood, and affected by the empathetic manager. Put another way, people try to behave in ways that will satisfy their needs. We sometimes say that people are irrational or

unreasonable in their behavior. What is rational to one person, however, may seem completely irrational to another. We think people are rational when they agree with us; when they behave the way we think they should, and have the attitudes we think they should have. When we say people are unreasonable in their behavior, perhaps what we are really saying is that we are unable to see the reason for the behavior.

5. Finally, different attitudes, interests, and values affect the needs of individuals. These factors in turn are influenced by the cultural setting in which one is raised. One of McClelland's interesting findings has been that people can be taught achievement values. Research has also shown variations in motivation patterns based on both age, and urban–rural background differences. Young workers, for example, show a preference for individual incentives, seek to satisfy higher-order needs (self-actualization), and are quicker to express dissatisfaction. Older workers respond more positively to group incentives, express more satisfaction, and place more emphasis on social needs.

The material in this chapter should point up the fact that although a great deal of research has been conducted in the area of motivation theory, much more needs to be done. There is no one theory that gives us all the answers. We should perhaps not be as concerned with disproving various theories as we are with shedding new light on them and building up our total knowledge. There appear to be no formula-type answers on how to motivate people.

SUMMARY

The behavior of people is goal directed, in the sense that it attempts to satisfy certain needs. Abraham Maslow arranged needs in a five-step hierarchy, ranging from physiological needs to the self-actualization needs. According to Maslow's theory, people first attempt to satisfy lower-level needs and not until these are reasonably well taken care of do they direct their behavior toward satisfying the higher-level needs. Alderfer has refined this theory and added several concepts to it. In their attempts to motivate employees, organizations have traditionally centered their effort on appealing primarily to the physiological and security needs. These efforts have fallen short of their goals, because they ignore other values for which people. If the opportunity to satisfy needs other than economic ones is not present on the job, a good share of the employee's effort, ingenuity, and creativity will be directed toward off-the-job activities to satisfy her remaining needs.

Building on Maslow's original theory, Herzberg formulated a motivational-hygiene theory. According to this theory, the factors that lead to job satisfaction and motivation are distinctly different from those that cause dissatisfaction. Herzberg labeled the factors associated with dissatisfaction as hygiene factors. They included such things as pay, fringe benefits, working conditions, and company policy. He maintained that the absence of the factors would lead to dissatisfaction, but their presence would only serve to bring an individual to a

SUMMARY CHART

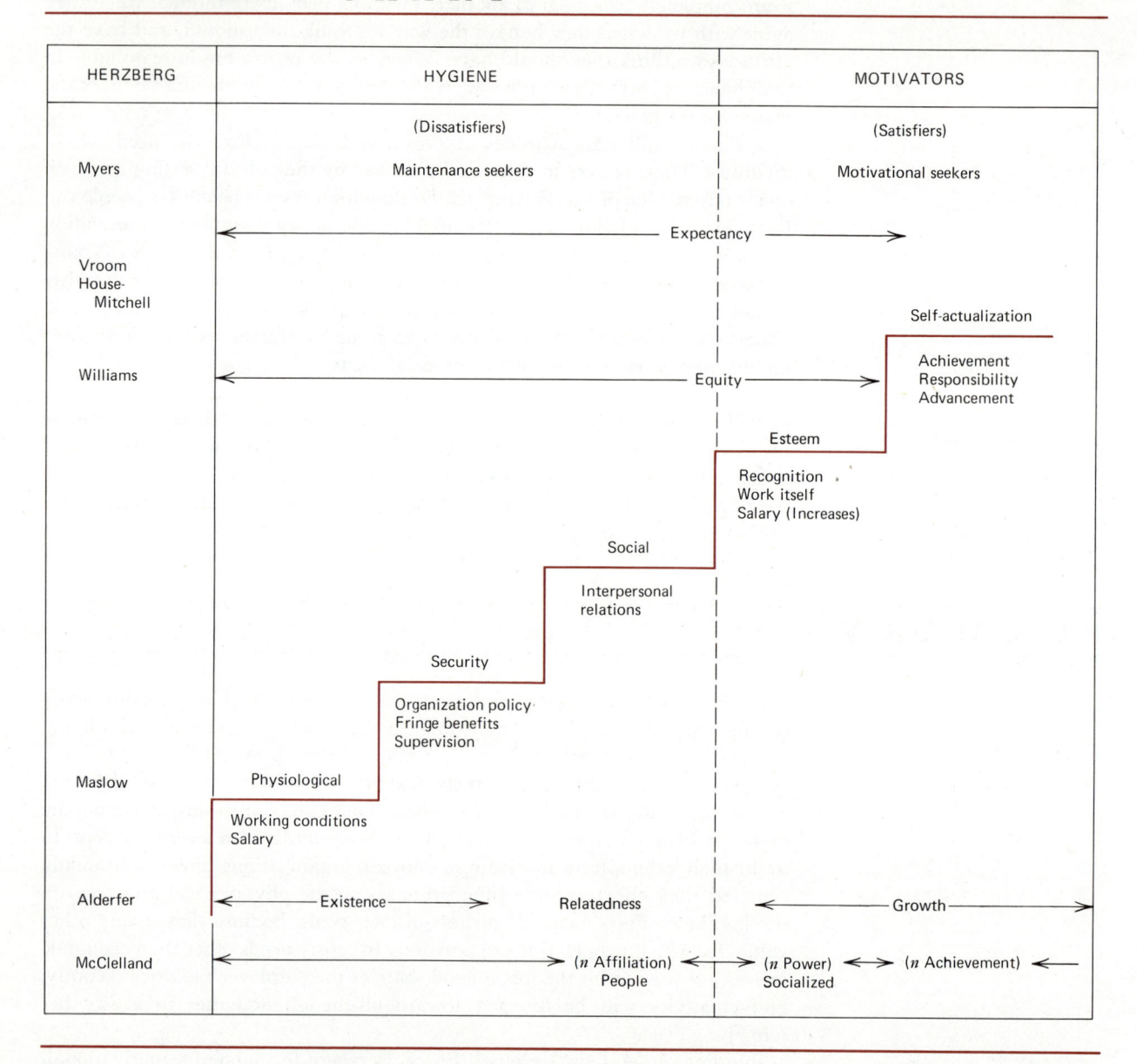

HERZBERG	HYGIENE	MOTIVATORS
	(Dissatisfiers)	(Satisfiers)
Myers	Maintenance seekers	Motivational seekers
Vroom House-Mitchell	←――――――― Expectancy ―――――――→	
Williams	←――――――― Equity ―――――――→	Self-actualization Achievement Responsibility Advancement
		Esteem Recognition Work itself Salary (Increases)
	Social Interpersonal relations	
	Security Organization policy Fringe benefits Supervision	
Maslow	Physiological Working conditions Salary	
Alderfer	←― Existence ―→ Relatedness	←――― Growth ―――→
McClelland	←――――― (n Affiliation) ←→ People	(n Power) ←→ (n Achievement) ← Socialized

neutral point. In order to motivate people, Herzberg felt that the job climate must offer the employee an opportunity to satisfy his higher-level psychological and self-actualization needs. Vroom's model of motivation maintains that the force of motivation is dependent on the valence or value an individual places on a particular outcome and the expectancy that a given act or pattern of behavior will lead to the desired outcome.

Another concept about motivation we discussed in this chapter is the Porter-Lawler model and path-goal relationships. According to this theory, if an employee is going to be motivated, she must, first, value the incentive being offered; and second, believe that good performance will in fact be rewarded by her achieving that incentive. If either of these conditions is not present, no motivation will result.

Equity theory suggests that, rather than the absolute level of wages, it is their relative level as perceived by the employee that is important. Relative value refers to what an individual receives in relation to what others receive and also in relation to the effort expended on the job.

While some persons tend to possess a greater amount of built-in achievement motivation [N(ACH)], the climate that exists will also greatly affect overall motivation. It is possible to structure a climate that fosters or triggers the achievement motivation potential in people.

DISCUSSION QUESTIONS

1. Compare Maslow's and Herzberg's theories of motivation. Which of Maslow's needs corresponds to Herzberg's motivators? Are Herzberg's and Maslow's theories consistent with each other? Explain why or why not.
2. Cite some specific examples (perhaps from your own experiences) where pay, supervision, and job environment might be good, but yet the job posed few motivators. Could people who work in these types of jobs be kept from being dissatisfied? Are there many jobs that have few motivators? What are your suggestions for (a) putting motivators in these job situations, and (b) eliminating these types of jobs if motivators cannot be put in them?
3. Laura received a pay raise of 10 percent of her hourly rate. What conditions must be necessary in order for this pay increase to have a positive effect on her motivation to work?
4. Cite and elaborate on at least five of the significant observations about the operation of the need hierarchy that were discussed. Be complete in your elaboration, and include a comment concerning why you chose each of the particular observations.
5. List five things or acts for which you have a positive valence. Now list to the right of each the probability that the acts will lead to a desirable outcome. Weight your valences on a scale of one to five. Multiple weight times probability for each act. Which item has the greatest force for you?
6. Discuss the basic ideas behind the concept of achievement motivation. What conditions will tend to arouse the achievement motive in people? Describe the characteristics of a person with a high need for achievement.
7. Explain the basic idea behind both the equity and expectancy theories.

APPLICATION EXERCISES AND CASES

ANALYZING MOTIVATIONAL PATTERNS

Mrs. Ellen Johnson has a routine repetitive job. She works in a garment factory where she sits over a Singer sewing machine from 8 A.M. until 4 P.M., and by the end of a week she has guided 1500 linings into 1500 coats.

How does Mrs. Johnson feel about her job? She likes it. Mrs. Johnson has been with her present employer since the death of her husband twenty-nine years ago. Her day begins at 6:40 A.M. when she leaves her home in Brooklyn. Two subway trains and fifty minutes later, she changes into a work smock in a makeshift dressing room.

She can do any job on the assembly-line in the garment factory where she works. Most of the time, by her own preference, she sews linings into coats. She moves with astonishing speed and deftness and her productivity rate is far above the engineered standard for the job. After over a quarter of a century of practice, she can carry on a lively conversation with co-workers and still keep the coats flowing through her sewing machine with faultless precision.

Mrs. Johnson earns about $200 a week. She has more than made her peace with the job. "I wouldn't recommend it to someone with an education," she says, "but for someone like me, it's good. You learn to take it in stride. You make up your mind it's your livelihood and then you don't get bored."

Mrs. Johnson cannot imagine any other way of spending a day. To her, going to the garment factory is almost an involuntary function of the body and mind. It is, she says, "like everything else—you gotta eat, you gotta sleep, you gotta work." Indeed, to her, the rundown garment factory is almost like a home. "I'd come in here with a fever," she says. "Even if there's a blizzard, I come."

Mrs. Johnson is fiercely proud of her good record as a worker and is scornful of younger workers who are not willing to devote as much to the job as she is. "They want easy jobs, like office jobs. I like this place here, but I do sweat for a dollar. We know what a dollar is worth here."

One of the women Mrs. Johnson is scornful of is Mrs. Janet Henson. Mrs. Henson works in the same garment factory as Mrs. Johnson. Most of the time her job consists of cutting loose threads off finished coats and packing the coats in boxes. She is twenty years old and a high school graduate. Mrs. Henson failed to find an office job when she graduated from high school two years ago. As she says, "This was the cleanest factory job I could find at the time."

Although she used to try hard, Mrs. Henson has never mastered her job and her performance is constantly below standard. She seems to lack the finger dexterity and hand speed required to do her job.

How does she feel about her job? "I dread coming to work. The pay is too low and the boredom is driving me crazy. I am starting to have nightmares about it. If I could get a better job, I would take it in a minute. My biggest fear is that I am trapped in this job and that I will never be able to get an office job."

Mrs. Henson may not find an office job, but there is a good chance she will be leaving her present one before long. Her supervisor, Miss Abelson, has just about given up on her. According to Miss Abelson, "Janet is a nice girl, but she just doesn't fit here. She doesn't seem to be able to learn the job and she is more interested in her appearance than in the work. I just cannot tolerate this any longer. I am afraid I am going to have to let her go."

Questions

1. Using Maslow's principles, concepts, and operational dynamics of the motivational theories, Herzberg and McClelland analyze and explain the differences in orientation between Mrs. Johnson and Mrs. Henson. Cover one theorist at a time comparing and contrasting the two women. Be specific.
2. What factors (comment on each) might help explain why the women have different orientations?

DR. HOLT'S DILEMMA[44]

After studying the personnel and work situation in an industrial plant, Dr. Holt, a management consultant, concluded that additional motivation of workers was needed. In his week at the plant, Dr. Holt had found that working conditions were good, employment was steady throughout the year, and the average pay was well above the community average.

Recommend a motivational program for the plant.

Dr. Holt has another week available to spend at this plant. What additional work would you suggest he do? Why?

---

[44]Herbert G. Hicks, *The Management of Organizations: A Systems and Human Resouces Approach*, 2nd ed., McGraw-Hill Book Co., New York, 1972, p. 292.

CHAPTER 10
JOB DESIGN—CREATING MORE MEANINGFUL WORK

HISTORICAL APPROACH TO DESIGNING JOBS
JOB DESIGN AND MOTIVATION
FIRST AID ATTEMPTS AT JOB REDESIGN
EFFECTIVE JOB ENLARGEMENT
JOB ENRICHMENT
EXPERIMENTS IN JOB ENRICHMENT
WORK MODULES
JOB NESTING
WORK TEAMS AND QUALITY OF WORK LIFE
RESEARCH ON JOB ENLARGEMENT AND JOB ENRICHMENT
A CONTINGENCY APPROACH TO JOB DESIGN
ECONOMICS IN JOB DESIGN
PERSONALITY AND JOB DESIGN
RESEARCH RELATING TO JOB DESIGN
APPLICATION EXERCISES AND CASES
IMPLEMENTING CONCEPTS IN JOB DESIGN
TURNING PEOPLE ON

WHY VOLVO ABOLISHED THE ASSEMBLY LINE

Peter G. Gyllenhammar, president of Volvo, frets when someone describes his company's self-managing work teams as just "experiments" in worker participation and job enrichment. The Swedish executive regards the Kalmar plant and other new Volvo plants, where group work has replaced the traditional moving assembly line, as unshakable commitments to his humanist thesis that "work must be adapted to people, not people to machines."

Gyllenhammar bristles even more when critics categorize Volvo's innovations in human relations and in technical support systems as "PR gimmicks," as something that works "fine with a small manufacturer but not on a large scale," or as a management technique specific to the Swedish political system and socioeconomic climate.

Such critics seem to be behind in their facts. In the first place, Gyllenhammar pointed out in a recent interview, Volvo goes far beyond the small-company category. With 65,000 employees, it's the largest employer in Sweden, on *Fortune*'s international 500 list, it ranked 61st in 1976, up from 80th in 1975. And citing Volvo's record as a profitable enterprise in a competitive capitalistic society. Gyllenhammar pooh-poohed the thought that in reorganizing work to create more meaningful jobs and to involve workers in decision-making processes, "we have taken a philanthropic approach and are willing to give up important objectives, such as increased productivity, in order to attain some sort of naive happiness."

The corporation's objective, Gyllenhammar said, must be to handle its resources in the public interest so "we get economic growth and utilize our growth in the interest of society." And that's why Volvo must be "interested in profit and must generate cash flow and productivity," he explained. "Whatever we do has to be in line with these overriding goals."

The record shows that the new work organization formats at the Kalmar plant—in operation since 1974—and elsewhere in the Volvo production complex are as productive as the traditional ones, such as the one at Torslanda, the automotive manufacturer's main assembly plant, an 8000-worker production center whose assembly line stretches almost a mile from end to end.

"That's a very important comparison," Gyllenhammar says. "You can't sweep our program aside as some sort of philanthropic experiment that we tried when the going was good."[1]

---

[1] John M. Roach, "Why Volvo Abolished the Assembly Line," *Management Review*, September 1977, pp. 43–49.

In Chapter 9, Human Motivation, we learned that high levels of productivity are most often achieved when the work that people do has meaning and significance. If employees are to be motivated, they must be challenged and offered opportunities for achievement, new experiences, and growth. With these general thoughts in mind, we will now explore the area of job design.

HISTORICAL APPROACHES TO DESIGNING JOBS

The basic elements typically considered in designing jobs are work processes in relation to output requirements, existing machines or equipment, the physical layout, and time requirements. Historically, our approaches to designing individual jobs have emphasized maximum degrees of specialization with each person doing only a small segment of the total task, rather rigid training of people in terms of specifying the "how to" in completing assigned tasks, and the establishment of control systems designed to monitor performance. The preciseness with which the design of jobs has often been approached is illustrated in Figure 10-1.

The design of jobs has often utilized a very mechanical procedure.

This figure depicts an operation chart that analyzes the motions of the right and left hands by such movements as those captioned "reach," "grasp," or "transport." Sometimes symbols are added, usually with large circles to indicate manipulative activity, small circles to indicate reaches and transports of material, and a simple connective line to indicate the idle hand."[2] Industrial engineers have used the operation or process chart, motion picture cameras, and time studies to develop general principles of time and motion.

There are two important phases in time and motion studies. The first is the research phase, which involves finding the best method for performance of the task. A good worker's performance is observed, completion time is recorded, efficiency is indicated, and a time standard constructed. The standard established (second phase) may be used either as a basis for a piece rate or to furnish data that is used in estimating costs of a particular job. It is also used for scheduling machine production time.

The scientific approach to designing jobs is illustrated in the use of time and motion study.

To better comprehend the concept of time and motion study, it is essential to understand its goals. They are as follows.

1. Redesigning a job in order to make the movements simpler and quicker.
2. Developing more efficient patterns of movement for workers, so that they can do the job faster and with less fatigue.
3. Setting standards for given jobs to be used as a basis for determining pay scales and criteria for the evaluation of the worker.
4. Developing a complete job description to aid in the process of recruiting and selecting new workers, and orienting and training them.[3]

In the quest for even more productivity, management turned to mass production technology. The principles of this technology consist of five concepts: (1) standardization, (2) interchangeability of labor, (3) orderly movement of the product through the plant in a series of planned operations at specific work

---

[2] Elwood S. Buffa, *Production Management*, New York, Wiley, 1975, p. 331.
[3] Edgar H. Schein, *Organizational Psychology*, Englewood Cliffs, N.J., Prentice-Hall, Inc., 1970, p. 26

FIGURE 10-1

An Operation Chart

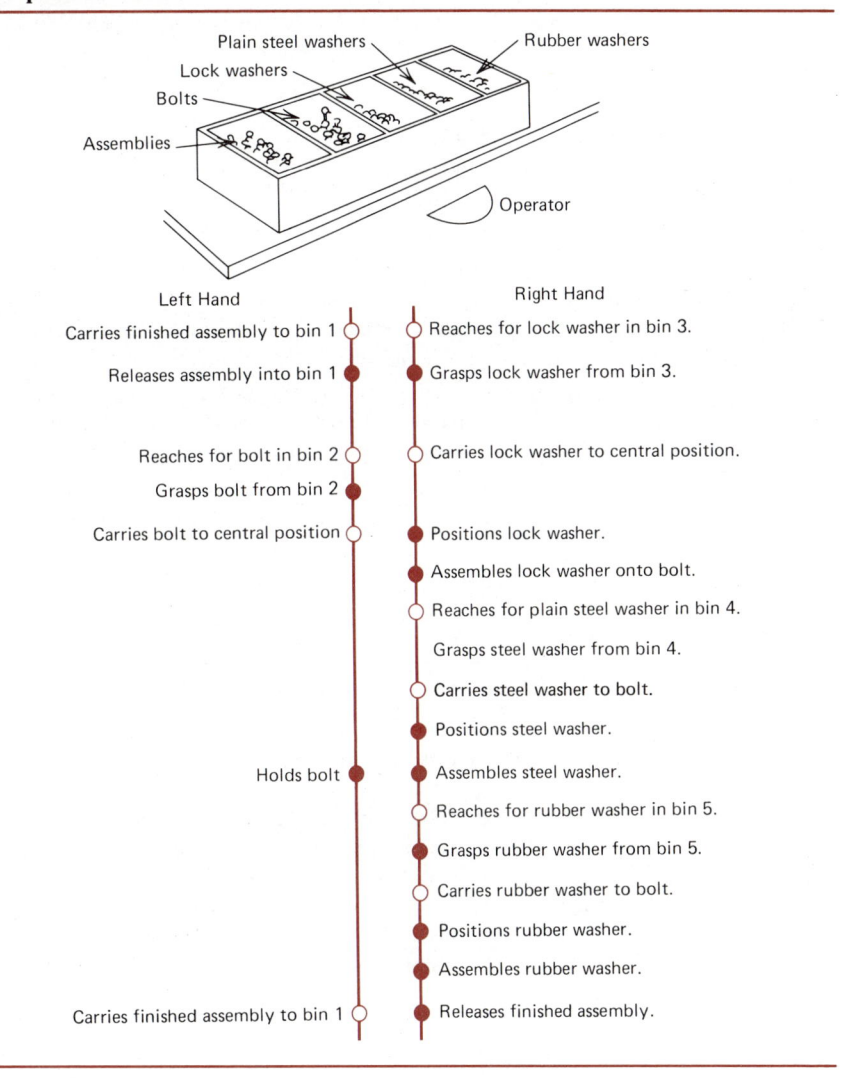

Left Hand	Right Hand
Carries finished assembly to bin 1	Reaches for lock washer in bin 3.
Releases assembly into bin 1	Grasps lock washer from bin 3.
Reaches for bolt in bin 2	Carries lock washer to central position.
Grasps bolt from bin 2	
Carries bolt to central position	Positions lock washer.
	Assembles lock washer onto bolt.
	Reaches for plain steel washer in bin 4.
	Grasps steel washer from bin 4.
	Carries steel washer to bolt.
	Positions steel washer.
Holds bolt	Assembles steel washer.
	Reaches for rubber washer in bin 5.
	Grasps rubber washer from bin 5.
	Carries rubber washer to bolt.
	Positions rubber washer.
	Assembles rubber washer.
Carries finished assembly to bin 1	Releases finished assembly.

Source: Elwood S. Buffa, *Basic Production Management,* New York, Wiley 1975, . 348

stations, (4) mechanical delivery of parts to work stations and removal of assemblies, and (5) breakdown of operations into simple, continuous motions.[4]

It was believed that mass production technology, combined with a time and motion study approach to simplifying individual jobs, would lead to higher

---

[4]Louise E. Davis, "Job Design and Productivity: A New Approach," *Personnel,* Vol. 33, March 1957, p. 42.

productivity, increased quantity, reduction in costs, and better quality of workmanship.

ANTICIPATED ADVANTAGES AND ACTUAL RESULTS OF THE HISTORICAL APPROACH TO JOB DESIGN

Figure 10-2 summarizes the anticipated advantages and actual results of the approach to designing jobs outlined previously. As indicated by the items listed as anticipated advantages, management was oriented toward the desire to gain maximum productivity and keep control of the total production process. In earlier years many organizations did realize these advantages. Developments during the 1960s and 1970s however have served to focus attention on the negative effects of the historical approaches to job design. These negative effects are manifested primarily in the areas of worker motivation and apathy.

The primary reason is that economic and social conditions of today are substantially different from those of the past. The educational level of employees is much higher. They have learned to expect more from a job and have become increasingly vocal about deficiencies in the work climate. People are also generally more mobile and have more employment alternatives available. In the

During the 1960s and 1970s, the negative effects of the mechanical approach to job design has been brought into focus.

FIGURE 10-2

Anticipated Advantages and Actual Results of the Historical Approach to Job Design

Anticipated Advantages	*Actual Results*
1. Jobs can be learned quickly, thus little training is required.	1. Savings in training cost fail to materialize because of excessively high turnover.
2. Jobs can be filled with unskilled people—presumably an inexpensive, readily available commodity.	2. High rates of absenteeism require that extra workers must be available on a standby basis. This increases labor costs.
3. Because of low skill required and ease of training, workers are interchangeable.	3. Because assembly line work is so dissatisfying in nature, a high wage must be paid just to get people to accept jobs on the line.
4. Because of mechanization, workers do not become physically tired.	4. Substantial quality problems occur because of a lack of commitment on the part of workers.
5. Standardization permits ease of quality control. Also, the chance of mistakes is minimized.	5. Because of turnover, costs of recruiting and selection of workers are also increased.
6. Mechanization makes production predictable.	6. Problems of supervision develop as the gap between labor and management broadens.
7. Management has control over workers and to a degree can supervise by observation.	

cases where they cannot afford to leave the job because of lack of options, or because pay and benefits are too good to forsake, adaptation takes various forms. One sociologist took a job on a General Motors assembly line to report as objectively as possible what actually occurs on the line. First, he described a difficult job that he had to learn of assembling a stabilizer bar on the chassis as it passed along the line.

> *To do the stabilizer bar job, I had to build two pieces of stock for each car, take one of three possible stabilizer bar models, move to the line as the chassis came by upside down, place the bar on it so it would not slip, put down one of the pieces of stock, and, finally, install the other piece on the chassis to secure the bar.*
>
> *Each piece of stock was composed of a bolt approximately eight inches long on which I had to place, in order, a metal ring much like a washer, two rubber bushings that had to face each other, another ring, a bar to keep the sections separate, a third ring, two more rubber bushings facing each other, one more metal ring, and, finally, a nut to keep the whole assembly together. To install the piece of stock, I had to disassemble it so that only one rubber bushing and one metal ring remained on the bolt.*
>
> *While holding the rest of the pieces, I'd insert the bolt through a hole in the chassis, replace the parts on the bolt, insert the bolt through a hole in the stabilizer bar, and finger-tighten the nut. Unless I did it right, my carefully constructed piece of stock would come apart and fall on the floor, and I'd have to start over. By the time I'd finish, I could see the next chassis arriving, so I'd go back again to the bench and start the whole process again.*
>
> *The entire process—build stock, select bar, install bar—was supposed to be completed in 75 to 80 seconds. Because it was impossible to do the job in the time allotted, I would often arrive early and build up a backlog of stock in case I got behind, which I did regularly. If there was any stock left at the end of a shift, I'd hide it to use the next day. (The job was so hard that workers from one shift would not leave their extra stock for workers on the next shift. It was every man for himself.)*[5]

But John found the hardest job, for him, to be very different. (He was able to rotate more frequently due to a prior agreement with management.)

> *My most boring, monotonous, and, therefore, hard job was as a driver in the repair section. In this job, along with two others, I was expected to ferry cars from one section of the repair floor to another. Although three of us were assigned to the task, most of the time two were sufficient; we were only needed if a car had to be moved. We worked out a schedule so that two of us were available at any one time, with the third hiding out of sight, reading a newspaper, napping, or eating lunch.*
>
> *If you subtract the relief time given to each worker during a normal eight-hour day (a total of 46 minutes according to the union contract), as well as the other official and unofficial time off from my paid eight hours, I actually worked a total of about two and one-half hours. Most workers I talked to wanted this type of job and looked forward to the time when their seniority would give them access to such position.*[6]

---

[5] John F. Runcie, "By Days I Make the Cars," *Harvard Business Review*. May-June 1980, p. 106.
[6] Ibid., p. 108.

How do workers adapt to such boredom? Runcie gives a vivid account from his first-hand experiences:

> Workers generally adapt to boredom and monotony in one of two ways: remain in the plant and find a way to get along or take off. Absenteeism is an extremely big problem. As one utilityman said, "People take time off because they're bored. They get tired of the same old routine." During hunting season, for example, so many take off that other workers are often asked to "work a double," that is, to work two shifts back to back. Even during the rest of the year, on rainy mornings the line could not start due to the shortage of workers. Often we would stand around waiting for the company to find people to fill the holes in the line.[7]

Workers adapt to boredom in the plant in unique ways.

Workers find many individual ways to combat the boredom and monotony of the job. Some daydream, some talk and gossip, some find inventive ways to combat the monotony. Runcie found himself in need of the same diversions as the permanent work force even though he was only there for a few months.

> Other means for decreasing the boredom and monotony are trading jobs (where two people agree to trade jobs for some specified period of time); doubling or tripling up (where one worker does the work of two or three workers for some period of time, after which he or she rests and another person does the jobs for a while); alternating jobs (where two people agree that one will do both jobs on cars no. 1, 3, 5, and 7 and the other will cover for cars no. 2, 4, 6, and 8); and working up the line (where workers work as fast as possible to get ahead and actually work "up the line: from their assigned work stations); or, as mentioned earlier, letting work fall far behind so that extraordinary effort is required to catch up.
>
> Not all the techniques the workers use to decrease the boredom and monotony are quite so benign, of course. Workers often block out monotony and boredom with alcohol or drugs. When I asked one young worker why he used drugs, particularly marijuana (which tends to be the drug of choice in the plant), he answered, "If I smoke (marijuana) I can stare at a spot on the floor all day long and not get bored."[8]

JOB DESIGN IN BROAD PERSPECTIVE

Up to this point we have been referring primarily to factory or manufacturing type jobs in discussing job design. It should be noted that as we discuss the area of job design in general and job enrichment in particular we are referring to more than just the application of these terms to typical factory-type jobs. Instead, we are referring to whole breadth and scope of routine and semiautomatic clerical jobs, as well as such areas as technicians, engineers, accountants, secretaries, and even supervisors. To illustrate, the accountant who after receiving a college degree and completing a training program involving a variety of experiences, is then placed in a job that requires compiling the same cost reports, using the same data, week after week is in the same position as the assembly line worker. Engineers forced into a high degree of specialization within their broader

---
[7] Ibid.
[8] Ibid., p. 109

capabilities are similarly stifled. The secretary who is unaware of background information surrounding much of what he or she does, and is sometimes treated as the butler of the executive suite, finds the job lacking in meaning. The technician whose potential for growth is not used becomes discouraged. Supervisors who find themselves the proverbial "person in the middle" because they are not communicated with, lack any real authority, and are held responsible for things over which they have no control, feel completely frustrated.

Lack of meaningful work is a widespread problem.

All of the preceding examples illustrate a lack of meaningful work, which is just as draining on the individual from a physical and psychological standpoint as is tightening the same ten bolts day after day on an assembly line. From the standpoint of the organization, the negative implications are even greater because the potential of some very high-priced human assets are not being realized. This is not to imply that one type of work is not important relative to another, but the higher up the job hierarchy one goes the greater is the potential loss due to wasted talent and uncommitted people. Our emphasis is that we should be wary of linking the issue of ill-defined jobs and efforts at job enrichment with only a few restricted types of situations. It is a very broad-based problem that cuts across the whole spectrum of job levels and some of the most serious problems organizations face in terms of the negative reactions to historical job design approaches occur other than in factory-type situations. The question surrounding job design is essentially as follows.

Does the job via its design and structure control a person and fit them into a routine, standard and controlled pattern of behavior, or does the individual via their motivation control the end product of their effort.[9]

JOB DESIGN AND MOTIVATION

Hackman and Oldham[10] developed a model relating how job characteristics affect satisfaction, motivation, and productivity. They postulate that there are three psychological states that impact on job satisfaction and motivation.

1. Experienced meaningfulness—work must be seen as important, valuable, and worthwhile.
2. Experienced responsibility—the person must feel responsible and accountable for the results of the work performed.
3. Knowledge of results—feedback must be received on a fairly regular basis concerning how effectively the job is performed.

The more these three conditions are present the better people will feel about what they do and the more satisfaction and motivation that will result. They then identify five job dimensions or characteristics that contribute to people experiencing these three psychological states.

Skill variety, task identity and task significance can lead to increased meaningfulness.

Meaningful work is experienced when the following elements are present.

[9]Edward E. Lawler, "Motivation and the Design of Jobs," *ASTME Vectors* August 1968, p. 14.
[10]J. R. Hackman and G. R. Oldham, "Motivation Through the Design of Work: Test of a Theory," *Organizational Behavior and Human Performance*, Vol. 16, 1976, pp. 250–279.

Skill variety—the job requires a variety of different activities requiring the use of a number of different skills and talents that the individual possesses and values.

Task identity—the job requires the completion of a whole and identifiable piece of work (i.e., doing a job from beginning to end with a visible outcome).

Task significance—the degree to which the task has an impact on the lives or work of others in the immediate organization or external environment.

Personal responsibility for work outcomes is fostered when there is autonomy built into the job. Autonomy refers to the extent to which the job allows freedom, independence, and discretion in scheduling the work and determining procedures.

Knowledge of results requires feedback in a direct, clear and timely manner. Based on the need to experience these three psychological states and the five job dimensions a set of principles for creating more meaningful work can be formulated. These principles relate back to the required job dimensions.

Principle	*Job Dimension*
Combining tasks	Skill variety
Forming natural or complete units of work	Task identity
Establishing a client relationship—to whom does the completed work go and why it is important	Task significance
Control over work methods and pace	Autonomy
Opening feedback channels	Feedback

Lawler has divided the solutions to job design into two groups. The first group he calls first aid approaches to redesigning jobs. In this group, he includes such things as more time off the job, job rotation, and some forms of horizontal job enlargement.[11] Herzberg delineates four first-aid forms of job enlargement. They include challenging the employee, removing more difficult parts of the job, job rotation, and assigning the worker more tasks.[12] Each of the foregoing items will be briefly discussed in the remainder of this section. The second solution to job design is designated by Lawler as being the major surgery approach. This involves the concept of job enrichment, to be discussed in the concluding part of this chapter.

FIRST AID ATTEMPTS AT JOB REDESIGN

Giving Time Off the Job. The possibilities here range all the way from longer coffee breaks, a reduced work week and sabbaticals or extended vacations.[12a] According to Lawler, this would seem to be a defeatist approach, since it assumes

Time off the job would seem to be a defeatist approach to job redesign.

---
[11]Lyman W. Porter and Edward E. Lawler, III, "What Job Attitudes Tell About Motivation," *Harvard Business Review*, January-Febrary 1968, p. 120.
[12]Frederick Herzberg, "One More Time: How Do You Motivate Employees?" *Harvard Business Review*, January-February 1968.
[12a]Porter and Lawler, "Job Attitudes," p. 18.

that a tight job structure must exist and that work is inherently unpleasant. He also states that the result of this approach is destined to produce a subculture of alienated workers who must necessarily look to off-the-job activities for all of their satisfactions. Commenting on the same point, Herzberg states:

> *This represents a marvelous way of motivating people to work—getting them off the job! We have reduced (formally or informally) the time spent on the job over the last 50 or 60 years until we are finally on the way to the 6½-day weekend. Any interesting variant of this approach is the development of off-hour recreational programs. The philosophy here seems to be that those who play together, work together. The fact is that motivated people seek more hours of work, not fewer.*[13]

If Herzberg is correct, that motivated people seek more work not less the following excerpt from *American Business* is a poor commentary on American work force motivation.

Americans Work the World's Shortest Week

Geneva, Switzerland—American workers have the shortest work week in the world, the International Labor Organization claims in a new report.

Taking all economic sectors together, except for farming, the United States work week averages 35.6 hours, the study reveals.

In most countries around the world, however, the U.N. agency says even the 40-hour week "is still as elusive as ever."

South Koreans work the most, with a 50.5 hour average work week, notes the ILO.

Among Western industrialized nations, Switzerland with 44.5 hours has the highest average.

However, the Swiss rejected a motion to limit working hours to 40 per week in a recent national referendum, says the ILO.

Aside from the U.S., only three nations have average working weeks of less than 40 hours. According to the ILO study, Sweden ranks second with 35.7, Belgium is third with 35.8, and New Zealand is fourth with an average of 37.6 hours each week.

Other hourly averages, 41.2 in France, 41.9 in West Germany, 40.7 in Japan, and 44 in Britain for men, 37.4 for women.

Communist countries supplied statistics only for the manufacturing sector. Average weekly working hours are 43.5 in Czechoslovakia and 40.6 in the Soviet Union.[14]

Americans enjoy one of the shortest work weeks among any country in the world.

As usually applied, challenging the employee represents a rather superficial approach.

Challenging the Employee. This represents one of the more superficial, and as usually applied, naive attempts at job enlargement. According to this approach, if a secretary types fifty letters a day, one should challenge him to do seventy-five. If the worker assembles twenty subassemblies a day, she should be challenged to see if she can do twenty-six. The very logical response of the worker to these challenges is "Why should I?" This type of response should be easy to understand

---

[13] Herzberg, "How Do You Motivate Employees?", p. 55.
[14] *American Business*, May 1981.

since all the challenge really amounts to is asking the person to do more of something she does not to do in the first place.

Removing More Difficult Parts of the Job. The theory here is that if we take away the more difficult parts of the job, the employee can accomplish more of what is left. The thinking represented here is obviously backward, since removing the more difficult tasks amounts to nothing more than simplifying and making a job even more meaningless than it was in the first place. Perhaps Herzberg overstates the case a bit when he states, "This traditional industrial engineering approach amounts to subtraction in the hope of accomplishing addition."[15] Certainly the automobile assembly line workers discussed earlier wanted simpler and easier jobs, but it could be argued that none of the assembly line jobs offered hope of being intrinsically satisfying.

Job Rotation. This attempt at job improvement involves moving the employee from job to job. This movement may occur every few hours or two or three times a week. Research has shown that job rotation is somewhat effective in offsetting monotony and boredom, and workers generally prefer it to performing one and only one assignment. You will recall that the automobile assembly line workers used this technique to escape boredom and fatigue—even when not condoned by management. It is still an incomplete solution to the problem, however. This is especially true if jobs people are rotated to are machine paced, simplified ones that give the individuals no control over what they do or how they do it.

Assigning More Tasks. Under this approach, instead of doing just one thing over and over again, the employee is given several tasks to accomplish, all of which are usually simplified and unrelated. Although this can relieve some of the physical monotony, the problem lies in the fact that the new tasks that are assigned are often no more meaningful than the old.

EFFECTIVE JOB ENLARGEMENT

Job enlargement is an approach to job design in which the job is extended in complexity horizontally. It involves making a job structurally larger by any one of five approaches which we will discuss: variety, meaningful work modules, performance feedback, ability utilization, and worker-paced control.[16]

Task Variety. A fragmented job such as the wiring of an endless number of solder joints or placing tin lids on strawberry cans can lead to boredom. Increasing task variety, such as soldering plus applying a cover using an electronic unit, or activating the machine that fills the can with strawberries prior to placing the lids on, can reduce monotony a bit.

Meaningful Work Modules. If a job can be enlarged to the point where a worker completes the job and feels a sense of satisfaction, motivation will be

---

[15] Herzberg, "How Do You Motivate Employees," p. 59.
[16] Kae H. Chung and Monica F. Ross, "Differences in Motivational Properties Between Job Enlargement and Job Enrichment," *Academy of Management Review*, Vol. 2, No. 1, January 1977, pp. 115–116.

increased even more. For example, one firm was having trouble keeping keypunch operators on the job. Absenteeism and tardiness was rampant and morale was low. The job consisted of a liaison person giving each operator several hundred cards each day, some of which came from marketing, some from operations, and some from accounting. When the cards were punched, the liaison person collected the cards and returned them to the appropriate departments.

Meaningful work modules can be provided by giving a person a complete unit of work.

This job was enlarged by simply removing the liaison person and having each keypunch operator do the work for a separate department. This helped the keypunch operator establish identity with meaningful work, such as "the work of the marketing department." If the keypunch operator completed the assigned work early, she received recognition from the marketing department; "We have a good key punch operator." If she made errors, she had to face the department for whom the errors were made. Morale improved greatly and tenure on the job increased.[17]

Performance Feedback. A worker accomplishing a fractional job with short performance cycles repeats the same set of motions aimlessly. Occasionally performance feedback can be arranged without changing the physical product appreciably. For example, note the performance feedback elements of the keypunch experiment, cited as follows:

It occurs to me that this is truly a transactional episode; we enriched the interchange between employee and "customer," an internal one. The interchange existed before, but only in stunted form. There were transactions previously between clerk and supervisor, or clerk and clerk. They occurred over coffee, but they were about dates, clothing, etc. These are not potentially rich as work motivators. Turnover dropped appreciably, as you have probably guessed, and so did absenteeism. It is one matter to be feeling poorly on a day when your own payroll is due to go out, and quite another matter to feel poorly on a day when you are merely one of 14 girls who get that same payroll out.[18]

Often a job will have to be enlarged physically so that there is a work cycle of greater than thirty minutes on each product.

Ability Utilization. People derive satisfaction from jobs that permit utilization of skills and abilities. Enlarged jobs usually require more mental and physical abilities.

When the worker controls the pace of work, autonomy is increased.

Worker-Paced Control. Job enlargement that moves a worker from a machine-paced production line to a worker-paced production line usually results in greater motivation. Sometimes compromises can be made. For example, in one conveyor-paced job where workers spray-paint dolls hanging on a movable line, the workers asked for and obtained an electronic control that could change the

---

[17]Robert N. Ford, "The Obstinate Employee," *Public Opinion Quarterly*, Vol. 33, No. 3, Fall 1969, pp. 301–310. Reprinted in David R. Hampton's *Behavioral Concepts in Management*, 2nd ed., Belmont, Cal., Dickenson Publishing Co., 1972, pp. 64–77.
[18]Ibid., p. 306.

pace of the conveyor. Since several workers spray painted simultaneously, the entire group had to agree on the speed at which they would operate the line during the various periods of the day. The average speed of the line turned out to be greater under group control than under management's former control.

JOB ENRICHMENT

Job enrichment is a concept that encompasses vertical job loading. Many experts think it holds the key to creating meaningful work that can satisfy the employees' full range of needs on the job. The difference between job enlargement and job enrichment and between horizontal and vertical job loading is illustrated by Figure 10-3, which summarizes some principles of vertical job loading and the motivators involved with each principle. The key factor of the points listed in Figure 10-3 is that instead of simply giving the workers more tasks, they are allowed to perform managerial functions previously restricted to supervisory personnel. The worker is granted additional authority and allowed to maintain some control over the job.

Job enrichment allows the worker to perform some of the managerial functions of the job.

In Figure 10-3 items 3, 6, and 7 could be properly considered extensions of job enlargement. The Department of Health, Education and Welfare's report on *Work in America* advocated that a work system should include both horizontal and vertical job loadings if it is to have a strong impact on employee satisfaction and job performance.[19]

EXPERIMENTS IN JOB ENRICHMENT

The distinction between horizontal and vertical job loading is illustrated by an experiments conducted by Frederick Herzberg among a group of stockholder correspondents employed by a very large corporation.[20] Herzberg noted the following:

Vertical job loading includes adding additional elements to a job.

> Seemingly, the task required of these carefully selected and highly trained correspondents was quite complex and challenging. But, almost all indexes of performance and job attitudes were low, and exit interviewing confirmed that the challenge of the job existed merely as words.[21]

Figure 10-4 summarizes the types of change that were made in the job. The changes listed on the left represent horizontal or job enlargement suggestions, which were eventually rejected. The ones on the right are vertical or job enrichment suggestions, which were the changes actually introduced over a period of months. The numbers to the right of the vertical suggestions represent the corresponding motivators involved, as listed in Figure 10-3.

The following comments represent the major results and findings.

---

[19]Department of Health, Education, and Welfare, *Work in America*, Cambridge, Mass., MIT Press, 1973.
[20]Ibid., p. 59.
[21]Ibid., p. 59.

FIGURE 10-3

Principles of Vertical Job Loading

Principle	Motivators Involved
1. Removing some controls while retaining accountability	1. Responsibility and personal achievement
2. Increasing the accountability of individuals for own work	2. Responsibility and recognition
3. Giving a person a complete natural unit of work (module, division, area, and so on)	3. Responsibility, achievement, and recognition.
4. Granting additional authority to an employee in his activity; job freedom	4. Responsibility, achievement, and recognition
5. Making periodic reports directly available to the worker himself rather than to the supervisor	5. Internal recognition
6. Introducing new and more difficult tasks not previously handled	6. Growth and learning
7. Assigning individuals specific or specialized tasks, enabling them to become experts	7. Responsibility, growth, and advancement

Source: Frederick Herzberg. "One More Time: How Do You Motivate Employees?", *Harvard Business Review*, January–February 1968.

1. At the end of six months, the groups where the new job design changes had been introduced were outperforming their counterparts by a considerable amount.
2. Marked increases in liking for their jobs were exhibited.
3. Absenteeism was lower among those whose jobs had been enriched.
4. There were improvements in quality of letters, accuracy of information, and speed of response to stockholders' inquiries.
5. Sharp increases in positive job attitudes were noted.

Since this earlier experiment, numerous job enrichment experiments similar to the one described by Herzberg have been conducted—some successfully and some with mixed results.

WORK MODULES

In a study at AT&T in 1968, job enrichment was implemented by allowing clerks compiling telephone directories to do their own error checks, thereby reducing the number of steps in assembly from twenty-one to fourteen. Next, selected employees were allowed to "own" their own books by electing to do all fourteen steps with no verification of their work. Improvements in the reduction of employee turnover and other success factors led AT&T to many other experiments with job enrichment that provided employees "ownership" in a complete job or what AT&T defines as a *work module*. This is defined by the company

A work module is a slice of work that gives an employee ownership in the job.

FIGURE 10-4

Enlargement Versus Enrichment of Correspondents' Tasks

Horizontal Loading Suggestions (Rejected)	*Vertical Loading Suggestions (Adopted)*	*Principle*
Firm quotas could be set for letters to be answered each day, using a rate which would be hard to reach.	Subject matter experts were appointed within each unit for other members of the unit to consult with before seeking supervisory help. (The supervisor had been answering all specialized and difficult questions.)	7
The women could type the letters themselves, as well as compose them, or take on any other clerical functions.	Correspondents signed their own names on letters. (The supervisor had been signing all letters.)	2
All difficult or complex inquiries could be channeled to a few women so that the remainder could achieve high rates of output. These jobs could be exchanged from time to time.	The work of the more experienced correspondents was proofread less frequently by supervisors and was done at the correspondents' desks, dropping verification from 100 percent to 10 percent. (Previously, all correspondents' letters had been checked by the supervisor.)	1
The women could be rotated through units handling different customers, and could then be sent back to their own units.	Production was discussed, but only in terms such as "a full day's work is expected." As time went on, this was no longer mentioned. (Before, the group had been constantly reminded of the number of letters that needed to be answered.)	4
	Outgoing mail went directly to the mailroom without going over supervisors' desks. (The letters had always been routed through the supervisors.)	1
	Correspondents were encouraged to answer letters in a more personalized way. (Reliance on the form-letter approach had been standard practice.)	3
	Each correspondent was held personally responsible for the quality and accuracy of letters. (This responsibility had been the province of the supervisor and the verifier.)	2, 5

Source: Frederick Herzberg, "One More Time: How Do You Motivate Employees?" *Harvard Business Review*, January–February 1968.

as a "slice of work that gives an employee a thing of his own."[22] Job enrichment at AT&T has progressed in well-defined steps, including (1) physically defining a worker's module, (2) giving up control of the module as the employee progresses in ability, and (3) providing feedback regarding success and failure, often through self-monitoring of data.[23]

JOB NESTING

Job nesting is bringing together several interdependent jobs.

From job modules, AT&T moved to a more complex enrichment of several interdependent jobs by a concept that they call *job nesting*. Robert Ford describes the concept of explaining how a group of supervisors and their service represen-

---
[22]Robert N. Ford, "Job Enrichment Lessons From AT&T," *Harvard Business Review*, January–February 1973.
[23]Ibid., pp. 96–99.

tatives at Southwestern Bell moved their service quality and productivity from near the bottom to near the top among all districts in the St. Louis area. Before the project described below began, their office was laid out as it appears in Figure 10-5.

Figure 10-5 shows their desks in the standard, in-line arrangement fronted by the desks of their supervisors, who exercised close control of the employees.

As part of the total job enrichment effort, each service rep group was given a geographical locality of their own, with a set of customers to take care of, rather than just "the next customer who calls in" from anywhere in the district. Some service reps—most of them more experienced—were detached to form a unit handling only the businesses in the district.

Then the service representatives and their business office supervisors (BOS) were moved to form a "wagon train" layout. . . . They were gathered into a more-or-less circular shape and were no longer directly facing the desks of the business office supervisors and unit managers. (The office of the district manager was further removed too.)

FIGURE 10-5

Ferguson District Service Representatives' Office Layout Before Job Enrichment

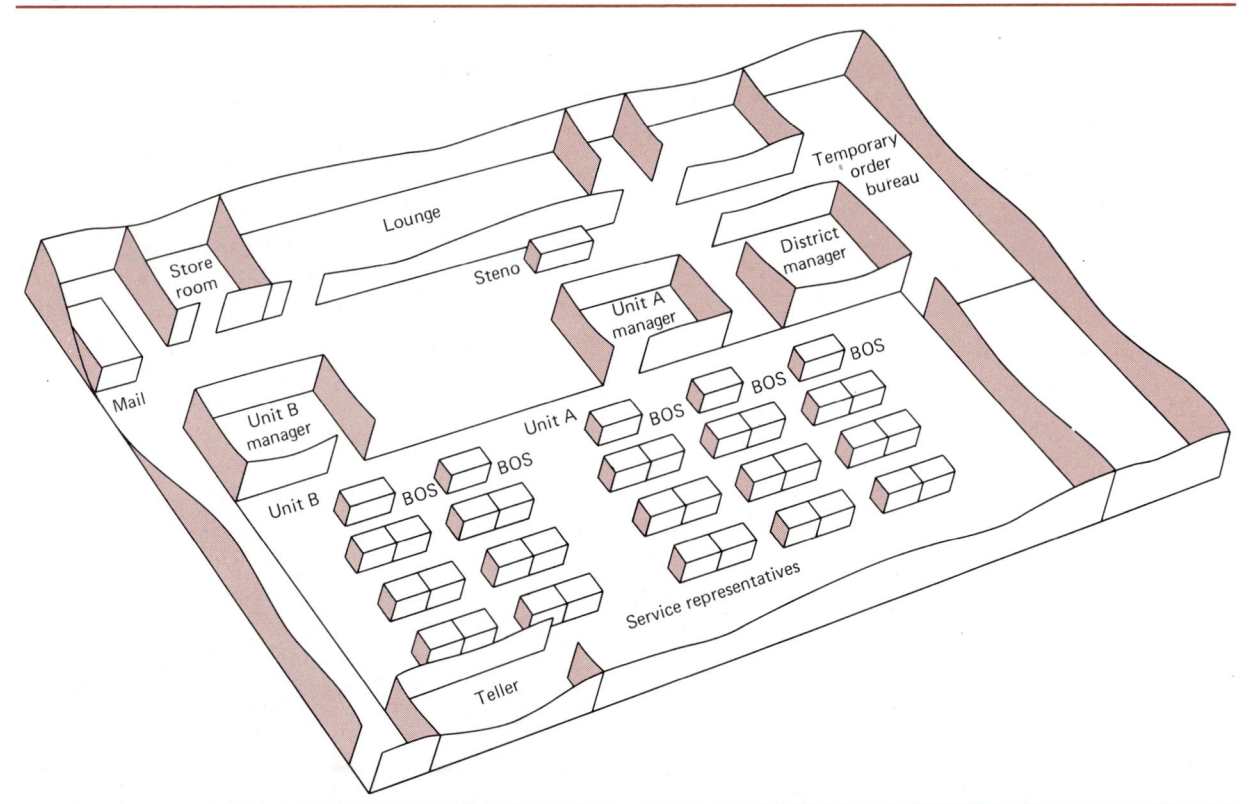

Source: Robert N. Ford, "Job Enrichment Lessons from AT&T," *Harvard Business Review*, January–February 1973, p. 102.

Now all was going well with the service representatives' job, but another function in the room was in trouble. This was the entry-level job of service order typist. These typists transmit the orders to the telephone installers and the billing and other departments. They and the service order interviewers—a higher-classification job—had been located previously in a separate room that was sound-proofed and air-conditioned because the TWX machines they used were noisy and hot. When its equipment was converted to the silent, computer-operated cathode ray tubes (CRTs), the unit was moved to a corner of the service reps' room.

But six of the eight typists quit in a matter of months after the move. Meanwhile, the percentage of service orders typed "on time" fell below 50 percent, then below 40 percent.

The reasons given by the six typists who quit were varied, but all appeared to be rationalizations. . . . As the arrangement existed, any service order typist could be called on to type an order for any service representative. On its face, this seems logical; but we have learned that an employee who belongs to everybody belongs to nobody.

An instantly acceptable idea was broached: assign certain typists to each service rep team serving a locality. "And while we're at it," someone said, "why not move the CRTs right into the group? Let's have a wagon train with the women and kids in the middle." This was done (over the protest of the budget control officer, I should add).

The new layout appears in Figure 10-6. Three persons are located in the station in the middle of each unit. The distinction between service order typist and service order reviewer has been abolished, with the former upgraded to the scale of the latter. . . .

Before the changes were started, processing a service request involved ten steps—and sometimes as many persons—not counting implementation of the order in the Plant Department. Now the procedure is thought of in terms of people, and only three touch a service order on its way through the office.[24]

Ford gives strong evidence that the new arrangement has worked well. Before moving into the wagon train, the typists were issuing only 27 percent of the orders on time. In thirty days this improved to 90 percent and in one particular month even reached 100 percent. Such results could not be attributed to a lighter work load, since the amount of work processed increased by 21 percent after "nesting."

WORK TEAMS AND QUALITY OF WORK LIFE

Since the AT&T experiments job enrichment has been expanded in many cases to encourage work teams as opposed to individual efforts—even in jobs previously performed by assembly lines. Some of these, such as the one at the Bolivar, Tennessee, plant producing hi-fidelity speakers, have actually started with union and management teams working on hygiene factors, and progressed to "core" groups in all departments (a foreman, shop steward, and employee) continually working on job improvement projects that include almost any aspect of work life quality.[25] Another company producing optical equipment has moved toward independent teams operating in each unit of the plant. Each team is so structured

Job redesign experiments are now being extended to look at the total quality of work life.

---

[24]Ibid., p. 103
[25]Sidney Harmon, "The Transforming Influence of a Work-Quality Program," *S.A.M. Advanced Management Journal*, Vol. 41, No. 1, Winter 1976, pp. 4–12.

FIGURE 10-6

Office Layout after Service Order Typists were "Nested"

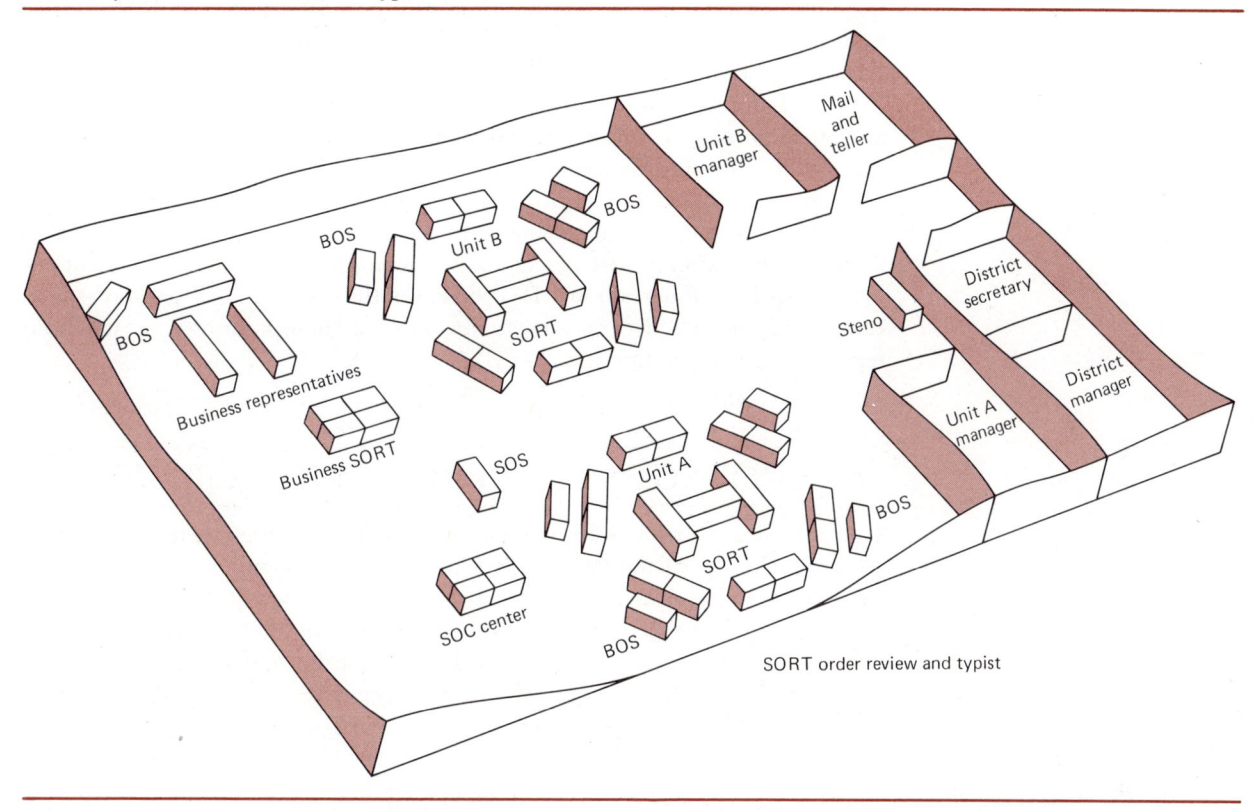

Source: Robert N. Ford, "Job Enrichment Lessons from AT&T," *Harvard Business Review,* January–February 1973, p. 103.

that they have become business groups, producing a product, receiving feedback and servicing its customers. Significant productivity and moral improvements are cited from a study of the operation.[26] Enrichment projects that encompass total organizational changes will be discussed in Chapter 16, Organizational Development.

RESEARCH ON JOB ENLARGEMENT AND JOB ENRICHMENT

Research regarding the success of both enlargement and enrichment programs is ambiguous. In both cases, many studies have indicated an improvement in morale and job satisfaction as well as factors such as quality and quantity of output and reduced absenteeism and turnover. However, this tends to be true

---

[26]M. Scott Fisher, "Work Teams: A Case Study," *Personnel Journal,* Vol. 60, No. 1, January 1981, pp. 42–45.

only if current work environment satisfies basic physiological and security needs, including reasonable pay. This may be another justification for total "quality of work life" redesign projects rather than simply redesigning jobs. Performance improvements have usually only resulted when quality rather than quantity is used as a performance indicator.[27]

While failures of job enlargement and enrichment reported in the literature are few in number, they are notable, such as in the tax return auditing department of the Internal Revenue Service.[28] Automobile assembly lines have had very mixed results and most projects have had trouble meeting quantity standards equal to the traditional line.[29] Roseman, using a sample of 102 Illinois firms, found that only 14.1 percent of the respondents used formal job enrichment procedures. Interestingly, 43.3 percent of the responding firms reported job enrichment failures. He questions why more of these failures have not been reported in the literature.[30]

A CONTINGENCY APPROACH TO JOB DESIGN

Current research on job redesign is indicating that Herzberg's theories about how motivators and hygiene factors affect performance are subject to considerable qualification. For example, it now appears that a given job factor can cause satisfaction for one person and dissatisfaction for another. The importance of intrinsic and extrinsic factors (what Herzberg calls motivation and hygiene factors) is not clear. Herzberg has also probably overly simplified the relationship between motivation and satisfaction.[31] The contingency approach to job design corrects for this oversimplification by suggesting that many things have to be considered before designing or redesigning a job. First, job design, to be successful, must consider two major factors, which include economics, or the least-cost combination of people and resources, and the personality of the workers. Not all economies rest with rigidly designed jobs. Buffa emphasizes the point with these statements.

Contingency job redesign looks at the costs of a potential change as well as the personality of the workers.

> *Man's greatest potential is not in the repetitive mechanical activities, et al., but rather*

---

[27]Wm. E. Gallagher, Jr., and Hillel J. Einhorn, "Motivation Theory and Job Design," *Journal of Business*, July 1976, pp. 358–373.
[28]Ibid., p. 127
[29]See, for example, Charles E. Summer, "SAAB Automobile Engine Assembly Department" in David R. Hampton, Charles E. Summer, and Ross A. Webber, *Organizational Behavior and the Practice of Management*, Glenview, Ill., Scott Foresman and Co., 1978, pp. 447–451, and Wm. E. Fulmer, "General Motors Corporation—Detroit Plant," Harvard Intercollegiate Case Clearing House, President and Fellows of Harvard College, 1975.
[30]Tillman H. Roseman, "A Study of Job Enrichment," *Industrial Management*, May-June 1980.
[31]For an extensive review of over 50 Herzberg related studies between 1960 and 1970, see Valerie M. Bockman, "The Herzberg Controversy," *Personnel Psychology*, 1971, Vol. 24, pp. 155–189. For a summary of recent research see Gene Milbourn, "A Primer on Implementing Job Redesign," *Supervisory Management*, January 1981, pp. 27–37, and "Research Spotlight," *Management Review*, July 1980, pp. 57–58.

in situations requiring improvisation, reasoning and judgment. From a human point of view, we have been misusing man's capabilities. In the current era of highly organized and expensive labor, it is becoming obvious that we may also be misusing man's capabilities from an economic point of view.[32]

But many job design programs do cost money. Volvo found that a new work system would cost 10 percent more than a comparable conventional auto plant. Workers and supervisors need to be retrained to adjust to new work systems. Many companies experience drops in productivity during the initial stage of new work system implementation. Finally, under job enlargement workers perform more complicated jobs and may demand higher wages.[33]

ECONOMICS IN JOB DESIGN

In searching for jobs that lend themselves most economically to job enrichment, the concept of the *automation continuum* as developed by Lawler is useful. Porter and Lawler's automation continuum is depicted in Figure 10-7.

With respect to this continuum Porter and Lawler write as follows.

At one end of the continuum is unit production performed by individual craftsmen. At the other end is the completely automated production facility, where the worker controls vast amounts of automated equipment. By virtue of its position in the continuum, the assembly line is neither fish nor fowl—neither highly automated nor highly individualized. Research suggests that unit production is quite satisfying, involving, and

FIGURE 10-7

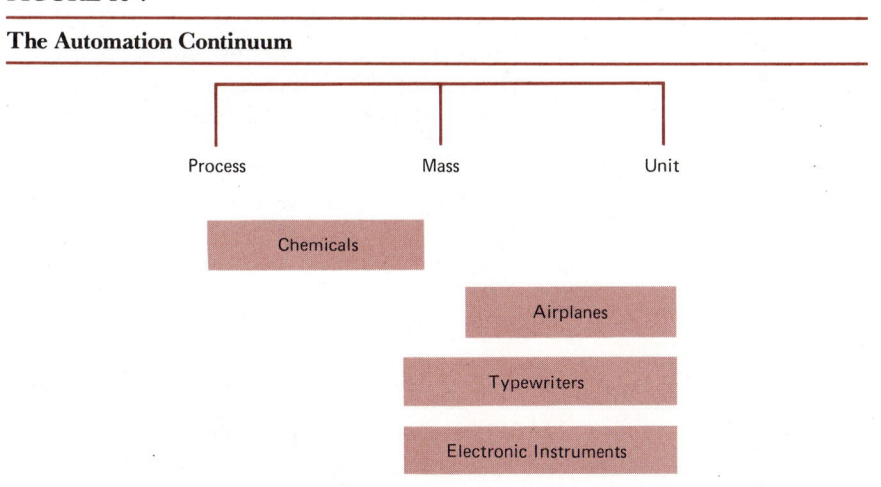

The Automation Continuum

Source: Lyman W. Porter and Edward E. Lawler, III, "What Job Attitudes Tell About Motivation," *Harvard Business Review,* January-February 1968. p. 19.

---

[32]Buffa, *Production Management,* p. 334.
[33]Chung and Ross, "Differences in Motivational Properties."

motivating to the worker. It provides him with responsibility for production of an entire product—it enables him to take justifiable pride in his work.[34]

The automation continuum suggests that we either move toward unit production or automate the process.

Research also suggests that jobs in automated plants can be satisfying and involving because high skill levels are required. Moreover, the workers—even at the lower skill levels—feel that they are controlling the production process. In contrast, assembly line workers feel that the production process controls them. Thus, despite their basic differences, jobs at both ends of the automation continuum fit the needs of the workers in that they provide opportunities for their satisfaction. Porter and Lawler's recommendation was as follows.

The graphic portrayal of the automation continuum presents a recommendation for a change in strategy. Essentially, it suggests that jobs be moved away from the center of the continuum toward either end, a process that would often involve reversal of the historic movement from unit production toward mass production. The kinds of changes that any organization could make would, of course, be dictated by its products. In the case of automobile manufacture, a move toward greater automation is suggested. In the manufacture of electronic instruments, however, it would make good sense in many instances to move from mass production to unit production.[35]

PERSONALITY AND JOB DESIGN

Not all employees desire more meaningful work. For example, the union at the Lordstown, Ohio, General Motors Plant asked for a simplification of some jobs for the workers. GM had enlarged the jobs to alleviate the boredom of workers endlessly doing one simple repetitive job.[36] Several researchers have found that because of values learned in the socialization process in the family and community, some workers seem to be satisfied with relatively uncomplicated jobs, while others are unhappy unless their jobs are more complex and more challenging.[37] For this reason, the following personality variables should be examined both prior to designing jobs and to selecting persons for jobs.

1. Attitude toward authority.
2. Attitude toward working alone or in groups.
3. Tolerance for uncertainty.

Researchers are now experimenting with questionnaires to determine which persons react positively to job enrichment projects.

RESEARCH RELATING TO JOB DESIGN

William Reif and Robert Moncza have summarized the findings of research that relates to the conditions that would seem to favor attempts at job enrichment and

---

[34] Lyman W. Porter and Edward E. Lawler, III, "What Job Attitudes Tell About Motivation," *Harvard Business Review*, January-February 1968, p. 120.
[35] Ibid., p. 19.
[36] Ibid., p. 20.
[37] Ibid.

those conditions that are unfavorable. Figure 10-8 contains the results of their efforts. From this material and our previous discussion, it is apparent that the potential success of job redesign is contingent on a number of considerations.

Generally speaking, members of organizations doing relatively uncertain tasks tend to prefer working alone, independent of authority relationships.[38]

---

[38]Ibid., p. 72.

FIGURE 10-8

An Organizational Audit Format for Job Enrichment

	Most Favorable Conditions for Implementation	*Least Favorable Conditions for Implementation*
I. Job Design		
1. Variety	Little variety exists because of the way jobs are presently structured, but there is potential for variety.	The work environment is such that little potential for increasing variety exists (e.g., a toll booth attendant on a highway).
2. Autonomy	Inputs to the job and methods of doing the job (procedures, sequence, pace, etc.) do not have to be totally dictated to the worker by the production/operation system.	The production/operation system defines work flow, methods, pace, and sequence and changes cannot be made easily.
3. Interaction	The opportunity exists for people to work together as a team—that is, the job naturally requires the coordination of tasks or activities among several workers.	The job can be performed best by an individual working alone.
4. Knowledge and skill	The job can be made more challenging by adding additional or more complex tasks, and workers are capable of meeting more demanding job requirements.	It would be inefficient to incorporate new tasks into the existing job structure, and/or increasing worker proficiency would be difficult to achieve
5. Responsibility	It is feasible to reduce reliance on the "only one way to do the job" approach to performing work and making work-related decisions.	It would be economically or technically unrealistic to allow variability in the way job situations are handled.
6. Task identity	The job can be redesigned so that the worker can see the value of his work in terms of its contribution to the total work effort.	An increase in the scope of the job would reduce the likelihood that the individual could successfully complete his task efficiently.
7. Feedback	It would not be difficult to redesign the control system to provide feedback on the job.	Information cannot be readily provided workers because of cost and data-collection problems.
8. Pay	The wage payment plan is not based solely on output.	Workers are paid under a straight piecework wage plan.
9. Working conditions	Working conditions, along with other hygiene factors, are perceived as satisfactory by most workers.	Working conditions are considered to be unsatisfactory by most workers.
10. Cycle time	Short, with potential for expansion.	Longer cycle times would interfere with other, interrelated work activities.

FIGURE 10-8 (continued)

An Organizational Audit Format for Job Enrichment

	Most Favorable Conditions for Implementation	*Least Favorable Conditions for Implementation*
II. Psychosocial environment		
1. Personality 2. Work attitudes, values, skills	Workers are self-confident and achievement oriented and positively oriented toward the work ethic. Primarily concerned with fulfilling higher-level needs.	Workers lack self-confidence and have low achievement drives; do not readily identify with the work ethic and fear change; primarily concerned with fulfilling lower-level needs.
3. Work group characteristics	Workers are capable and motivated to develop talents to fullest. Younger, more highly educated.	Workers have little interest in developing new knowledge and skills or lack capacity to do so; little education, unsatisfying work experiences.
III. Technology		
1. Dominance	Workers, not technology, are primarily responsible for output and quality levels.	Emphasis on equipment, machines, and systems in job design; technology primarily dictates the quantity and quality of work.
2. Cost	Low dollar investment in technology.	High dollar investment in technology.
3. State of technology	Technology is available to improve the quality of working life. A high state of technology exists.	Technology is not capable of dealing with problems of worker dissatisfaction.
IV. Management		
1. Management philosophy	Concerned with the utilization of human resources to the mutual benefit of the individual and the organization.	Primarily concerned with production; view job enrichment only as a means of increasing output.
2. Attitude toward change	Positive.	Negative.
3. Leadership style	Democratic, employee centered.	Authoritarian, task-centered.
4. Superior-subordinate relationships	Built on Theory Y set of assumptions about work behavior.	Built on Theory X set of assumptions about work behavior.
5. Union-management relationships	Open, supportive.	Closed, antagonistic.

Source: Adapted from William Reif and Robert Monezka, "Job Redesign: A Contingency Approach to Implementation," *Personnel,* May–June 1974, AMACOM.

SUMMARY

The Summary Chart contains a capsule of the discussion on this chapter. The way in which jobs are designed and work is structured has a significant effect on employees' level of motivation and productivity. The historical approach that has been taken to designing jobs was primarily mechanistic, based mostly on principles and concepts of industrial engineering. The result has been that jobs, in many cases, have been reduced to their least common denominator, in that

SUMMARY CHART

Stages in Job Design

I. Industrial Engineering
    (a) Specialization
    (b) Simplification
    (c) Standardization
    (d) Interchangeable labor
   Results: Productivity increases per worker
           Worker dissatisfaction
           Employee turnover
           Productivity decreases (in some cases)

II. First Aid Measures
    (a) More time off
    (b) Job rotation
    (c) Remove difficult parts of job
    (d) Assign more tasks
   Results: Alienated workers
           Rotation sometimes helpful

III. Job Enlargement
    (a) Vary task
    (b) Provide meaningful work modules
    (c) Provide performance feedback
    (d) Utilize more abilities
    (e) Allow worker-paced control
   Results: Improved satisfaction and productivity for nonprofessionals on some jobs
           Higher level needs still unsatisfied
           Production costs may increase

IV. Job Enrichment
    (a) Share managerial work with employee
    (b) Enlarge job vertically
    (c) Grant additional authority
    (d) Allow some employee control of the work
   Results: Improved satisfaction and job performance for certain personalities
           Some employees reject

V. Contingency Job Design
    (a) Economics
        Automate jobs that must be machine-paced
        Enlarge jobs that must be worker-paced
    (b) Personality
        Match task difficulty with individual readiness of employee
    (c) Organizational factors

they are highly specialized and require only a minimum degree of skill. It should be emphasized that this highly structured approach to designing work is true not only of manufacturing jobs but also of clerical, semiprofessional, and professional work.

Because of social and economic changes over the past forty years, as well as increased expectations on the part of employees, several disadvantages have resulted from this historical approach to job design. These disadvantages cause boredom, apathy, turnover, absenteeism, low quality, and other disutilities.

To solve these and similar problems, organizations have undertaken several approaches to redesigning jobs. Some have been successful while others have not. When not, it has been due to the fact that either the approach itself was unsound or the way it was implemented left something to be desired. Some of the early approaches which were tried included time off the job, challenging employees, removing the more difficult parts of the job, assigning more tasks, and job rotation.

Job enlargement can be effective for certain employees when jobs can be redesigned to form meaningful work cycles, include performance feedback and strong utilization of the employees' abilities. This usually requires that jobs be worker paced rather than machine paced.

More recently, the concept of job enrichment has come into focus. Job enrichment represents a vertical approach to job design. It is vertical in that it involves expanding the scope of the job in any one of several ways. These may include giving the employee some control of the work, increasing accountability, expanding the scope of the job, and granting additional authority. Job enrichment is more effective when coupled with job enlargement.

As job design specialists have become more experienced, they have discovered that it is not practical economically to enlarge or enrich all jobs. This has led to a contingency approach to job design. Jobs that lie on the automation continuum in the direction of unit production, which lend themselves to worker pacing, have been found more suitable for enlargement. Those that fall into the process category should be more fully automated. Furthermore, certain persons have indicated more or less ability to adapt to job enlargement and job enrichment. It is important to match the task difficulty of a job with the individual readiness of the worker to accept more responsibility instead of simply presuming that any increase in job complexity will improve satisfaction for any worker.

DISCUSSION QUESTIONS

1. What are some of the goals of time and motion study and the five basic principles of mass production? What negative effects often result from mass production? What did these concepts often backfire on management?
2. What were the anticipated advantages of the historical approach to job design? What were the actual results? Why weren't the anticipated advantages realized?

3. Summarize the major determinants of job satisfaction and what each involves. What are the components of the work role most conducive to job satisfaction?
4. What is the relationship between job satisfaction and job performance? What are the determinants of job performance?
5. Why have the concepts of time off the job and job enlargement failed to be effective in job design? Give some examples of various forms of job enlargement.
6. What is meant by the term "meaningful work" as defined in this chapter? Summarize the five effective approaches to job enlargement.
7. What is the basic difference between job enlargement and job enrichment? Set forth the principles of job enrichment.
8. Explain the concept of the automation continuum. Of what importance is it?
9. Cite the elements in the contingency model of job design. How can this model be used to improve jobs?

APPLICATION EXERCISES AND CASES

IMPLEMENTING CONCEPTS IN JOB DESIGN

Assume you are a manager in an organization that among others has the following departments.

Hot Plate Department and Glass Shop

In this hot plate department, employees assemble a number of different models of hot plates. In the glass shop, employees use lathes to form tubing and other shapes for electrodes. Both departments have been organized into the normal assembly line operation.

Materials Control

This department has responsibility for the functions of purchasing, inventory control, plant scheduling, and expediting with various people specializing in each area.

Accounting

This department has two primary responsibilities. One is to keep on a continuous and current basis a variety of accounting and financial records. The other is to prepare various reports for use by management. These reports may be required on a daily, weekly, or monthly basis. All the employees have formal education in accounting and each has been assigned to work in a limited number of specialized areas. Systems and procedures are well defined.

The foregoing three situations differ in that each involves a different type of employee. In the first case the workers are unskilled or at the most semiskilled.

The second situation involves white collar employees who might be perceived as semiprofessional. In the third instance we have people who have professional training in accounting.

The situations are similar in that in each case the traditional or historical approach to designing jobs, discussed early in the chapter, has been followed. More specifically, the jobs of the employees are highly specialized in the sense that they are involved in only a small segment of the total task.

The entire organization has been experiencing a number of problems, including absenteeism, turnover, and less than desired levels of productivity. In addition, there are other indications that a degree of negativism is present. Your assignment has been to study the situation, and having done so you conclude that many of the problems revolve around the way the various jobs are designed. You are in the process of preparing a report to top management. For that purpose consider and respond to the following questions.

Questions

1. In terms of the way jobs are presently structured, explain why the apparent apathy among employees exists.
2. Enumerate the conditions that should exist if a job is to provide intrinsic motivational value to its holder.
3. For each of the three situations outlined, make some very specific recommendations as to how these jobs could be improved. In addition to being creative in your thinking, try also to be practical. Because of the limited information you have to work with you will necessarily have to make some assumptions. Include these assumptions.

TURNING PEOPLE ON[39]

Since 1970, Texas Instruments has been focusing its attention on maximizing the effectiveness of its employees. The name given to this program is "People and Asset Effectiveness," and the results thus far has been very gratifying. *Business Week* reports:

Net sales per employee rose from $14,600 in 1970 to $18,500 in 1972, while after-tax profits went from $510 to $870. Return on assets per person shot up from 5.6% to 10.1% over the three years.

The People and Asset Effectiveness program was devised to force TI planners to think hard about employees right down to the woman on the assembly line—and about their ability and willingness to produce.

And TI management expects the program to keep paying off. By the late 1970's, sales billed per person are expected to rise from this year's $18,500 to $30,000. Similarly, the goal for profits produced by each employee is $1,500 to $1,800 by that time, compared to last year's $870. That level of after-tax profits would result in a return on assets of 10%

---

[39]Richard M. Hodgetts, *Management, Theory, Process and Practice,* Philadelphia, W. B. Saunders Co., 1975, pp. 497–498.

to 12%. Now, the strategy is to move "diagonally," increasing assets and productivity, toward the 1980s and TI's stated goal of $3-billion in annual sales.

What leads to such results? Frederick C. Ochsner, vice president and director of corporate personnel, says that it is a host of things acting synergistically, including attitudes, team improvement programs, an open-door management policy and a nonstructured pecking order.

Ochsner is unwilling to say which of the programs has contributed most to TI's productivity gains. The key, he says, is flexibility. Some programs work well with one manager or supervisor or group of workers, some work well with others.

What makes it work, says Ochsner, is simple. "There are two things in life that people want," he explains. "They want to achieve and they want to be loved. And if you provide an atmosphere where these things can occur with a minimum amount of structure in the work flow, you are going to get what you want."

Questions

1. People are an organization's most valuable asset. Explain this statement.
2. What does Mr. Ochsner mean by "if you provide an atmosphere where these things can occur with a minimum amount of structure in the work flow, you are going to get what you want"?
3. What concepts and techniques described in this chapter do you think TI might be using? Explain.

CHAPTER 11
ROLE AND FUNCTION OF THE GROUP IN ORGANIZATIONS

A SMALL GROUP DEFINED
TYPES OF GROUPS
FORMAL GROUPS
INFORMAL GROUPS
FACTORS IN GROUP FORMATION
GROUP COHESIVENESS
CONDITIONS INFLUENCING GROUP COHESIVENESS
NORMS
A MODEL OF INTRAGROUP BEHAVIOR
BACKGROUND FACTORS
REQUIRED AND GIVEN BEHAVIOR
ORGANIZING BACKGROUND FACTORS AND REQUIRED GROUP BEHAVIOR
EMERGENT BEHAVIOR
EXAMPLES OF EMERGING BEHAVIOR
CONSEQUENCES
INTERGROUP BEHAVIOR
CLIQUES
INTERGROUP COMPETITION
MANAGING INTERGROUP CONFLICT
MANAGERIAL IMPLICATIONS OF GROUP BEHAVIOR
APPLICATION EXERCISES AND CASES
THE PLATING ROOM GROUP
RIVER GLEN MANUFACTURING PLANT

STENO POOL'S MEMBERS, BURIED BY PAPER FLOOD, YEARN FOR OTHER THINGS[1]

Working 9 to 5; what a way to make a living.
Barely getting by; it's all taking and no giving.
They just use your mind, and they never give you credit;
It's enough to drive you crazy if you let it.
                              9 to 5 *by Dolly Parton*

It's only midmorning, but the fancy electric typewriters and other machines are already pounding with the sound and rhythm of muffled jackhammers. Another boss in a vest enters the room, clips a blue work order to the six-page penciled memo he is carrying and—without a word or an expression—piles it on to the stack of paper on a supervisor's desk.

The man in the vest doesn't mean much to Teresita Clamucha, Jean Hill, or Mimi Tong, one of whom will soon be typing his memo. He is just another contributor to the paper flood that constitutes daily life in the government-affairs stenography pool of Chevron USA Inc.'s public-affairs department.

Life in the pool—seven hours of typing and filing, broken up by occasional dictation duties—is clean, safe and fairly well paid. It is also dull, according to stenographer Jean Hill. "If I could possibly earn my living any other way, I'd do it," she says. "Sheer necessity and lack of education, that's why I'm here."

The pool is crowded and stuffy; rows of file cabinets eat up one-third of the space, and two fans with aqua blades push the stale air around. There aren't any windows; a mural with a forest scene provides the only "view."

Each member of this Chevron pool harbors some fantasy about working elsewhere. On most corporate ladders, the steno pool remains only a rung or two above the bottom. Few aspire to it, and it still is almost exclusively the province of women. They are as likely to be former teachers as they are to have barely finished high school. Some hope the pool will be the first step toward becoming an executive's personal secretary—as in the movies—but many more regard it simply as a steady paycheck. The most common gripe is that management doesn't appreciate the work and rarely says thank you.

Although much of this complaint is as old as the typewriter itself, the recent advent of sophisticated word-processing technology has wrought considerable change—and some new dissatisfaction—among the five million people in this country who, according to the Labor Department, earn their livings as typists, stenographers, and secretaries.

Steno work isn't restricted any longer to taking letters in shorthand and typing them. Word processors capable of almost instantly turning out hundreds of error-free "original" letters have transformed some stenographers, at the pool here and at other offices, into computer operators, too. And the processors have almost precluded the luxurious old concept of providing every manager with his own secretary.

Many managers hail the increased productivity made possible by this new technology. But some workers think their jobs have been made even more impersonal than they were before. They feel they are beginning to take on the traits of the machines they operate.

"We can't really spend any creative energy at our work; I guess you'd say we're kind of like cogs in a machine," says Miss Tong, a senior clerk-typist. "The best we can do is work quickly and not make mistakes," Miss Clamucha, who is classified as a management stenographer, adds: "They (the managers) do all the thinking around here; we just do the punching."

---

[1] Kathryn Christensen, "Life on the Job—Steno Pool's Members, Buried by Paper Flood, Yearn for Other Things," *Wall Street Journal*, May 6, 1981, p. 24.

Part of the dissatisfaction in the steno pool described above stems from the nature of the work itself. But much of it derives from the nature of a stenographic pool—a lack of interdependence among the work group, and a lack of belonging to a definite unit.

Why does one study groups like the steno pool described above? One answer is that both formal and informal groups exist in any organization and are essential to an organization's performance. There is ample evidence that groups have a major impact on their members, on other groups, and on the host organization.

Both formal and informal groups in any organization are essential.

An organization divides its ultimate task into subtasks that are assigned to various subunits, and the subdividing continues until the divisions of work can be achieved individually. The division of labor is what basically breaks an organization into groups. Thus the organization generates the formation of its various functional task groups.[2]

If one wishes to better understand an entire organization and how it operates, one needs to understand groups and how they operate. We need answers to questions such as these. When and under what conditions do groups form? What is a group? What conditions are necessary for their growth and effective functioning? What functions do groups fulfill for the organization and for their members? How does one manage and influence groups?

The study of small groups is an important area of study in sociology and social psychology.[3] The small group is an essential mechanism of socialization and a primary source of social order. Little doubt remains that a small group provides the major source of the values and attitudes people have and provides an important source of pressures to conform to social values and attitudes. The small group serves as an important mediating function between the individual and the larger society.[4]

A SMALL GROUP DEFINED

It is easy to appreciate the importance of the study of small groups, but it is a little more difficult to define exactly what a small group is. Although composed of people, a group is certainly more than a collection of people. On a bus or in a waiting room, we are part of a cluster of people, yet we cannot claim to be part of a group.

A group is any number of people who interact with one another, are psychologically aware of one another and perceive themselves as a group.

Since we are examining behavior in organizations and because this involves psychological questions, an appropriate definition would include psychological terms. A group is any number of people who (1) interact with one another, (2) are psychologically aware of one another, and (3) perceive themselves to be a group.[5]

This definition should be further expanded to contain certain qualifications

---

[2]Edgar H. Schein, *Organizational Psychology*, Englewood Cliffs, N.J.: Prentice-Hall, Inc., 1980, p. 146.
[3]Over 1,300 articles and books have been referenced on the subject, most of which have been published since 1950. See A. Paul Hare, *Handbook of Small Group Research*, New York: The Press of Glencoe, 1962.
[4]Leonard Broom and Philip Selznick, *Sociology*, New York: Harper & Row Publishers, 1963, p. 135.
[5]Schein, *Organizational Psychology*, p. 145.

ROLE AND FUNCTION OF THE GROUP IN ORGANIZATIONS 283

outlined by Clovis Sheperd.[6] One qualification is that the small group is a kind of social phenomenon which is more enduring and tighter than a social relationship, but is looser or less organized than a formal organization. Another qualification is that small groups of two or more persons possess characteristics due to their size which are sharply modified or tend to disappear in groups of four or more.[7] A third qualification is that as a small group increases in size, it reaches some upper limit where the group seems to become altered so that its members establish formal rules and regulations and the group becomes more like a formal organization than a small group.

The fourth qualification is that a small group possesses some general characteristics.[8] The members share one or more goals or objectives. They develop norms or informal rules and standards that mold and guide the behavior of group members. When a group exists for an extended period of time, structure develops that has individual members more or less permanently filling different roles. These members develop attractions for other group members, the group itself, and things it stands for.

Small group members share goals, develop norms, fill certain specific roles.

TYPES OF GROUPS

Having defined groups and qualified the definition, we now look to different types or kinds of groups. These include both formal and informal groups.

FORMAL GROUPS

Formal groups are created and maintained to fulfill specific needs or to perform tasks which are related to the total organizational mission. Formal groups can be either permanent or temporary according to the organizational need for the group. A permanent formal group is a body such as the board of directors, accounting division, or other work units within the organization. Temporary formal groups are committees or task forces who are used to perform a particular job or function, but who are dissolved when that function or need no longer exists. A budget committee for a Christmas party is an example. Temporary formal groups may continue over an indefinite period of time since the temporary nature of the group is dictated by the purpose which the organization assigns to the group,[9] rather than a specific time period.

Formal groups may be permanent or temporary.

INFORMAL GROUPS

Schein contends that informal groups result from the nature of man; that is, man seeks fulfillment of some needs through a variety of relationships with other members of the organization. If the environment permits, these informal rela-

Informal groups result from people seeking fulfillment of needs.

---

[6]Clovis R. Sheperd, *Small Groups,* San Francisco, Chandler, 1964, pp. 3–5.
[7]Robert F. Bales and Edgar F. Borgatta, "Size of a Group as a Factor in the Interaction Profile," *Small Groups in Social Interaction*, New York, Knopf, 1955, p. 396.
[8]A. Paul Hare, *Handbook of Small Group Research*, New York, The Free Press of Glencoe, 1962, p. 10.
[9]Schein, *Organizational Psychology*, p. 146.

tionships will develop into formal groups. If the organization wants to prevent the formation of these groups, it can do so by manipulation of the workers' environment.[10]

FACTORS IN GROUP FORMATION

People form groups or join existing groups for various reasons. These reasons can be divided into two areas: social elements, which are the satisfactions a person hopes to realize from group membership; and task objectives, which a person wants accomplished, but are difficult or impossible to accomplish outside of team activity.[11]

A person may be attracted to a group by the social element or the personal attractiveness of its members. When the members of a group have qualities that a person deems attractive, he will lean toward membership in that group. This situation is most predominant in friendship cliques. On an organizational level, a person may prefer to work for a company because he has friends there or because the people are pleasant.

Another social element that affects group membership is the activity of the group. People join bridge clubs, sports teams, and church choirs because they enjoy the activity. The attractiveness of persons in the group may or may not be a strong factor in determining group membership.

A second category of elements in group membership involves the goals or means to achieve goals. Sometimes people join groups because the goal of the group is one that they personally would like to see achieved. Examples of groups of this nature are charitable organizations and political parties.

In the course of accomplishing their group goal, the members of the group receive personal satisfaction or advancement. Sometimes the goal of the group is not important to the member, but the fact that he is a part of an advancing group is very important to him. A member of a sports team wants to be known as a member of a winning team. Likewise, a member of a rapidly advancing company enjoys the publicity that the company brings.

A person may join a group because it is a means by which he may achieve his personal goals. Although the group may not achieve its goal, this provision for achieving personal goals is attactive to him. A student may want to be president of the student senate, a personal goal, but needs the group to achieve this goal.

Finally, a person may join a group for the status he will gain from it. This element is similar to the social elements, but differs in that the status he obtains occurs outside the group. A freshman may join Alpha fraternity over Beta fraternity because Alpha has a better reputation or higher status on the campus.

The term "intragroup behavior" refers to behavior within the small informal or formal group. In this section, we will discuss some of the characteristics of this behavior.

Intragroup behavior refers to behavior within the group.

---
[10]Ibid., pp. 82–83.
[11]D. Cartwright and A. Zander, *Group Dynamics*, New York: Evanston, Row, and Peterson, 1953, pp. 73–91.

GROUP COHESIVENESS

A cohesive group is one in which all members work together for common goals.

One of the major perplexities confronting those who want to understand groups and to work with them effectively is how to explain the great differences in "groupness" that distinguish one group from another. What do we mean when we speak of the cohesiveness of a group? A number of meanings quickly come to mind. We think, for example, of a group that has a strong feeling of "we-ness," meaning that the members are more likely to talk in terms of "we" than "I." We think, too, of a group where everyone is friendly or where loyalty to fellow members is high. A cohesive group might be characterized as one in which the members all work together for a common goal, or one where everyone is ready to take responsibility for group chores. The willingness to endure pain or frustration for the group is yet another possible indication of its cohesiveness. Finally, we may consider a cohesive group as one which its members will defend against external criticism or attack.

CONDITIONS INFLUENCING GROUP COHESIVENESS

Dependency. The more dependent a person is on the group, the greater the attractiveness that group will have to the individual. The greater the dependence of the members of the group as a whole, the greater the cohesiveness the group will have.[12] This situation is illustrated in Figure 11-1.

FIGURE 11-1

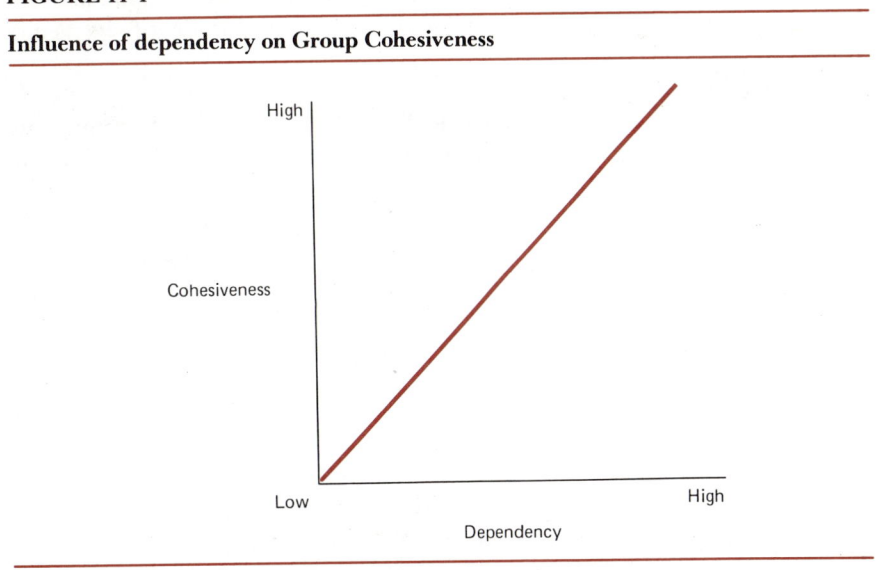

Influence of dependency on Group Cohesiveness

[Graph: Cohesiveness (vertical axis, Low to High) vs Dependency (horizontal axis, Low to High), showing a linear positive relationship]

---

[12] Joseph A. Litterer, *The Analysis of Organizations,* New York, Wiley, 1973, pp. 219–220.

Size. Size has an inverse relationship to group cohesiveness.[13] The earlier definition of a group reinforces this point. Cohesiveness increases in part through interaction among group members. The larger a group becomes, the less opportunity exists for interaction among the members. In this situation, we have the large groups splitting into subgroups.

Homogeneity and Stable Membership. Groups whose members have different interests and backgrounds are often less effective in promoting their interests. When, for example, people with sharp differences in rates of pay and job duties work near each other, the resulting group is seldom cohesive. The group may often be characterized by conflicting cliques which hinder common action. Stable membership also contributes to higher cohesion. In time, the members come to know each other, they learn the values and expectations of the group, and they learn how to behave.

Communication. To be a group, people must be able to talk with one another. Only in this way can their similarities and common interests be developed, their values and standards established, and joint action initiated. Groups in which the members can communicate easily with one another are more likely to be cohesive.

Isolation. Physical isolation from other groups tends to build cohesiveness. Miners have demonstrated, in many lengthy strikes, that isolated workers will stick together more stubbornly than workers who are socially integrated with the rest of the community. Physical boundaries around a group may be essential for cohesion. If a group cannot identify its members and clearly differentiate itself, cohesion will be low.

Outside Pressure. Members of groups tend to come together under stress. Continuous outside pressure from management may produce high cohesion. Personal differences are minimized when threatened by a common danger, such as a tough supervisor. This closeness may remain after the threat is gone. Perceived unfair management policy toward personnel may well encourage the formation of strong informal groups as a protective and retaliatory device. The relationships within the groups must exist for a period of time to give the members a chance to know one another and develop common understandings of values and goals.

Competition. Two classes of competition have a very vital effect on group cohesion: competition between members of the same group (intragroup) and competition between groups as wholes (intergroup). Competition between members of the same group is usually destructive to group cohesiveness. Studies made in this area have indicated that when competition between members of the

---

[13]Ibid., p. 220.

same group occurs, hostility and bitter feelings may leave the group totally ineffective.[14]

Competition between groups usually has a positive influence on group cohesion. Success resulting from intergroup competition increases cohesion even further. However, losers in intergroup competition usually experience tensions and disruptive forces that upset internal relationships. If the group continues after defeat, a stabilization will occur and the degree of cohesion will return to near the former level.[15]

Goals. Cohesiveness declines as members or subgroups within the group tend to use different methods to accomplish the same goal. Differences regarding the goal or goals of the group can have an adverse effect on cohesiveness. Differences of this nature, however, are not as disruptive as differences about methods to achieve a single recognized goal.

Status. Generally, group cohesiveness increases as the status of the group is recognized as being higher.[16] (See Figure 11-2.)

The straight line may not always hold and does not mean that all low-status groups have low cohesion or that all high-status groups have high cohesion. When low-status group members see no possibility of bettering themselves, many times they tend to "make the best of it."

FIGURE 11-2

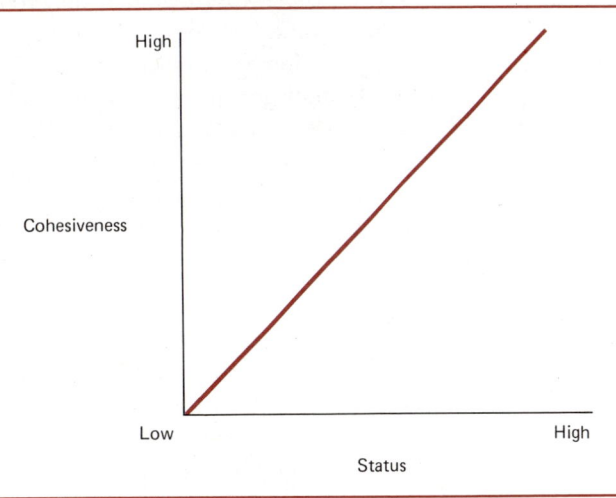

Cohesiveness Increases as Status Increases

---

[14]Litterer Cities the research of Chris Argyris, *The Impact of Budgets on People*, New York, The Controllers Institute, 1952.
[15]Robert R. Blake and Jane S. Mouton, "Reactions to Intergroup Competition under Win-Lose Conditions," *Management Science*, VII, July 1961, p. 420.
[16]Litterer, *Analysis of Organizations*, pp. 224–225.

NORMS

Norms are rules of behavior or proper ways of acting that are accepted as legitimate by the group.

Group members tend to form and conform to norms. "Norms are rules of behavior or proper ways of acting, which have been accepted as legitimate by members of a group."[17] Once a group sets its goals, the norms define the kind of behavior that is necessary for, or consistent with, the realization of these goals. Norms will develop in those areas where it is necessary to influence the behavior of one another and this condition will occur particularly where members are interdependent.[18]

Groups very often use pressure to make their members conform. Two functions are served by the uniformity in behavior resulting from such pressure. The first function is to help the group accomplish its goals. If the methods are seen as assuring progress toward a goal, then members view these procedures as the proper way to behave.

The second function of norms is to help the group maintain itself as a unit. Requirements that members regularly attend meetings or wholeheartedly support the party platform are examples. These serve to assure that the group will continue to exist as an entity. Also, pressures against behavior that may bring disrepute to the group, or divide the group and thus threaten its existence, or make members uncomfortable and ready to resign also serve to ensure group survival.

A MODEL OF INTRAGROUP BEHAVIOR

Emergent behavior is that which is in addition to or different from that required to perform the job.

When people work together, they soon develop ways of thinking and behaving that are different from, or in addition to, behavior which is required to perform the job. Homans has captioned this behavior as "emergent" behavior.[19] The astute manager quickly realizes that this emergent behavior may assist in the more effective performance of the task or may hinder the task performance, depending on the nature of the group. We will examine how emergent behavior arises within the organization. The elements of work group behavior are depicted in Figure 11-3.

BACKGROUND FACTORS

Background factors give rise to three types of required behavior as depicted in Figure 11-3. Notice in column 1 that such factors as job design, management practices, policies, and economic and social environments are specified for the worker. These factors give rise to several types of behavior as indicated in columns 2 and 3.

---

[17] Hare, *Small Group Research*, p. 24.
[18] Litterer, *Analysis of Organizations*, p. 245.
[19] Paul R. Lawrence and John A. Seiler, "A Conceptual Scheme for Describing Work Group Behavior," *Organizational Behavior and Administration*, Homewood, Ill.: Richard D. Irwin and the Dorsey Press, 1965, p. 154.

FIGURE 11-3

Work Group Behavior—Relations Between Elements of External and Internal Systems

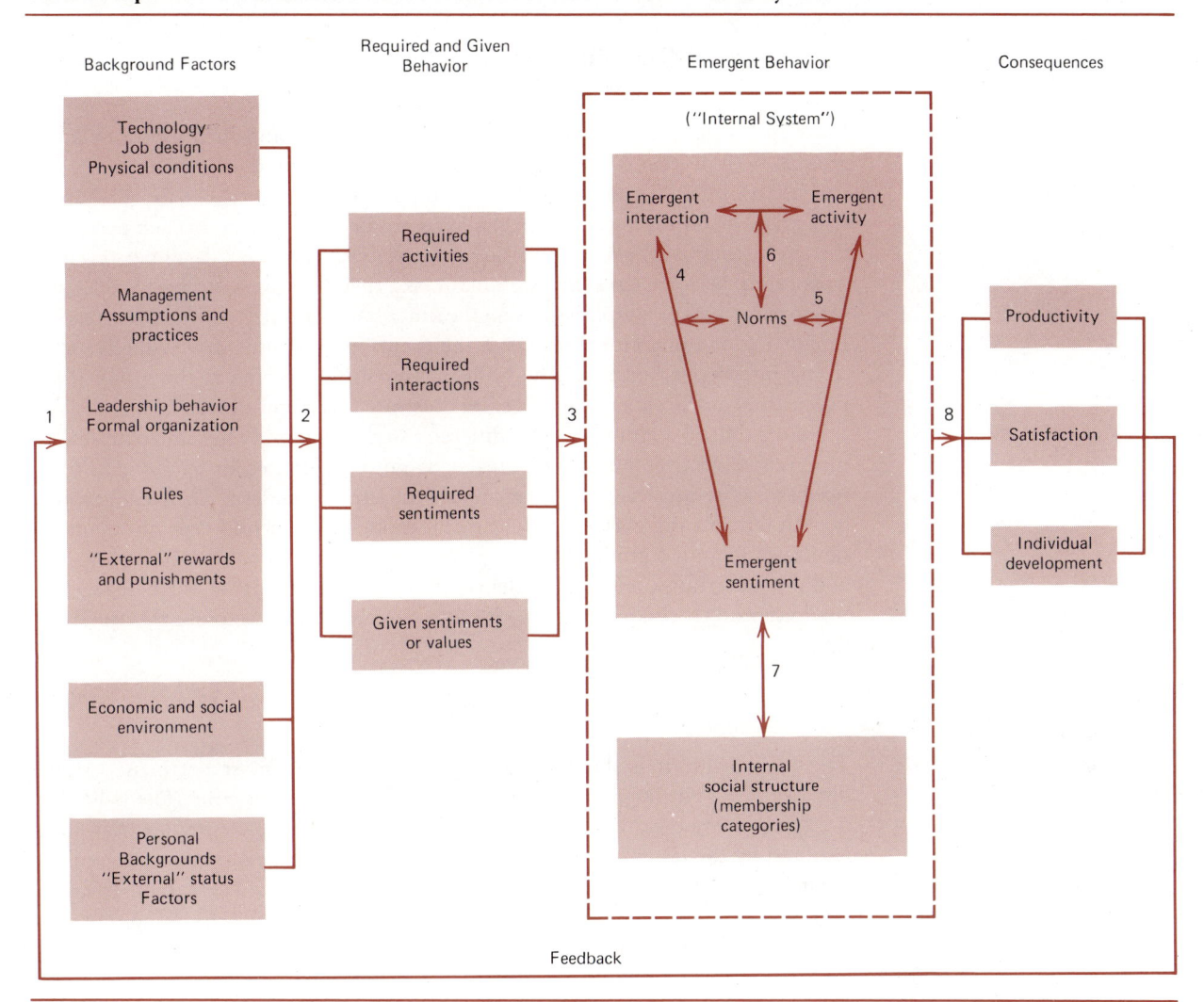

Source: Paul R. Lawrence and John A. Seiler et al., *Organizational Behavior and Administration,* Homewood, Ill., Richard D. Irwin and the Dorsey Press, 1965, p. 158.

REQUIRED AND GIVEN BEHAVIOR

Required behavior includes *activities*, or what a person is required to do on the job. It also includes *interaction*, a communication or contract between two persons required by the job, and, finally, it includes *sentiments*, a belief or feeling that an employee must have in order to be willing to perform the assigned task.

As shown in column 2, Figure 11-3, given sentiments and values are brought with the employees to the group from their lives outside.[20]

ORGANIZING BACKGROUND FACTORS AND REQUIRED GROUP BEHAVIOR

Most large organizations organize their tasks into jobs and their jobs into work groups. This is part of the integration process required of differentiated or specialized organizations. Usually individuals are assigned to jobs in which they specialize. A central question for management becomes, "Should each person in the work group perform a *similar* task or a *complementary* task?" If all persons in a work group perform the same or similar tasks, their jobs are interchangeable and supervision may be simplified. If, on the other hand, groups of several persons do supporting or complementary tasks, the group may become more cohesive and strong interdependence may be built in. Integration occurs at the group level rather than at the supervisory level, as illustrated by Figure 11-4.

Notice that in Figure 11-4 the differentiated group with specialized roles, of machinists, electricians, and pipefitters, is not coordinated or *integrated* until it reaches the second level of management—the superintendent. The stenographic pool in our introductory example fits this model. The second type of organization, the integrated group with complementary roles, is often used for task teams and project groups, and a high degree of integration occurs at the first level of supervision. Which kind of group is more effective? Let us explore this question next.

EMERGENT BEHAVIOR

The third column in Figure 11-4 represents the one most pertinent to our discussion. It is a diagrammatic presentation of an *informal group*. The behavior here simply emerges. The behavior in this group is far more complex than that required by the organization, but in many ways, it parallels the formal requirements. There are activities, interactions, and sentiments—all emergent. In addition, you will notice the term *norms*, discussed previously. A work group norm is an emergent idea or belief about what the sentiments, activities, or interactions in a particular group should be.[21] Finally, the bottom block depicts an internal social structure.

> Emergent behavior includes activities, interactions and sentiments.

The social structure of an informal work group will usually include *regular members, leaders,* and *deviants*. A regular member conforms to the work group on formal norms in a reasonable fashion. He or she does not overproduce, "squeal" on members who violate minor policies, or shirk the duty to perform what the group considers to be a fair day's work. The work group informal leader satisfies the members' leadership needs, especially for safety and security from what they view as arbitrary decisions of management. Deviants are persons who violate

---
[20]Ibid., p. 156.
[21]Ibid., p. 157.

FIGURE 11-4

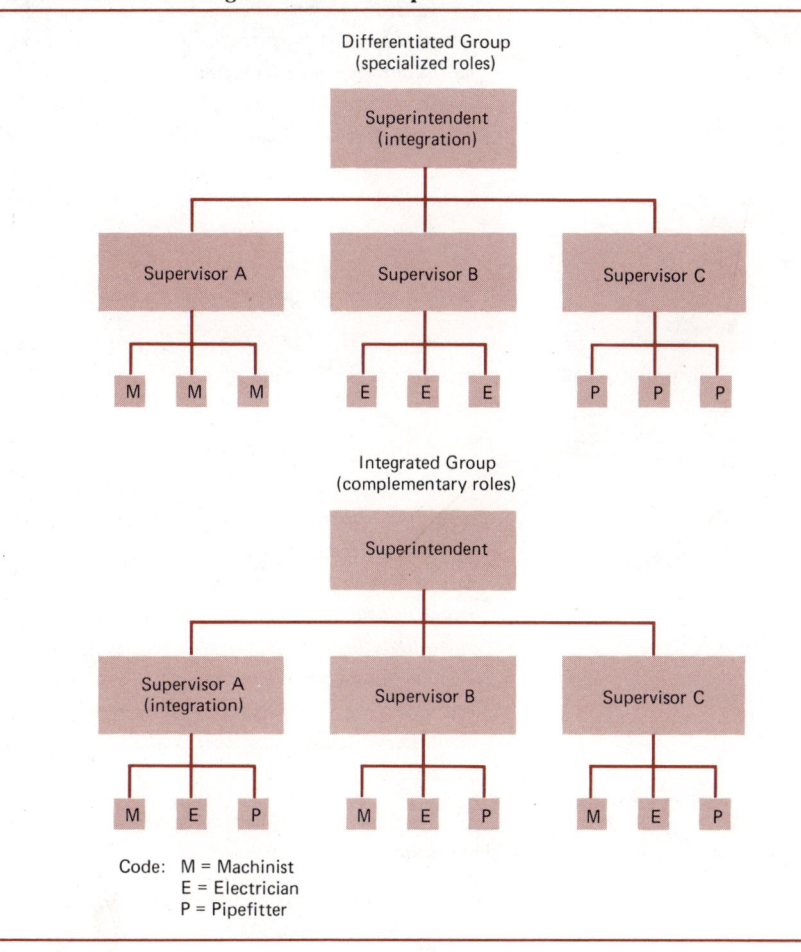

Differentiated and Integrated Work Groups

Differentiated Group
(specialized roles)

Superintendent (integration)
├── Supervisor A — M M M
├── Supervisor B — E E E
└── Supervisor C — P P P

Integrated Group
(complementary roles)

Superintendent
├── Supervisor A (integration) — M E P
├── Supervisor B — M E P
└── Supervisor C — M E P

Code: M = Machinist
E = Electrician
P = Pipefitter

---

group norms consistently, but who manage to remain on the fringe of the group. Persons who are not accepted by the group as regular members are called "isolates."

EXAMPLES OF EMERGING BEHAVIOR

Some of the best examples available in the literature of emerging behavior and group formation come from an early study performed at the Hawthorne Works of the Western Electric Company in Chicago, between 1927 and 1932. Two of the most notable experiments dealt with a group of five girls assembling electrical relays and a group of men working on a large bank wiring assembly. One writer describes the emerging behavior from the relay assembly group as follows.

Another factor in what occurred can only be spoken of as the social development of the group itself. When the girls went for the first time to be given a physical examination by the company doctor, someone suggested as a joke that ice cream and cake ought to be served. The company provided them at the next examination, and the custom was kept up for the duration of the experiment.... Often one of the girls would have some good reason for feeling tired. Then the others would "carry" her. That is, they would agree to work especially fast to make up for the low output expected from her.... The girls made friends in the test room and went together socially after hours. One of the interesting facts which has appeared from Whitehead's analysis of the output records is that there were times when variations in the output rates of two friends were correlated to a high degree.... Also, these correlations were destroyed by such apparently trivial events as a change in the order in which the girls sat at the workbench.[22]

Norms and sentiments may be supportive or nonsupportive of company goals.

In this particular work group, norms developed in a manner supportive of company goals. Notice also the emergent social group leader and membership factors.

Finally, the group developed leadership and common purpose. The leader, self-appointed, was an ambitious young Italian girl who entered the test room as a replacement after two of the original members had left. She saw in the experiment a chance for personal distinction and advancement. The common purpose was an increase in the output rate. The girls had been told in the beginning and repeatedly thereafter that they were to work without straining, without trying to make a race of the test, and all the evidence shows that they kept this rule. In fact, they felt that they were working under less pressure than in the regular department. Nevertheless, they knew that the output record was considered the most important of the records of the experiment and was always closely scrutinized. Before long they had committed themselves to a continuous increase in production.[23]

In the bank wiring group, a well-defined, shared, common body of sentiments developed.

A person should not turn out too much work. If he did, he was a "rate-buster." The theory was that if an excessive amount of work was turned out, the management would lower the piecework rate so that the employees would be in the position of doing more work for approximately the same pay. On the other hand, a person should not turn out too little work. If he did, he was a "chiseler"; that is, he was getting paid for work he did not do. A person should say nothing which would injure a fellow member of the group. If he did, he was a "squealer." Finally, no member of the group should act officiously.[24]

The group will use various forms of pressure to bring members in line.

Interestingly enough, the norms in the bank wiring group encompassed both low and high performance in spite of a group bonus system. Both slow and fast workers were pressured to "come into line." Deviants were punished by various means including a system called "binging."

---

[22]Ibid., p. 172–173.
[23]Ibid., p. 173.
[24]Ibid., pp. 178–179.

Binging consisted of hitting him a stiff blow on the upper arm. The person who was struck usually took the blow without protest and did not strike back. Obviously, the virtue of binging as a punishment did not lie in the physical hurt given to the worker but in the mental hurt that came from knowing that the group disapproved of what he had done. Other practices which naturally served the same end were sarcasm and the use of invectives. If a person turned out too much work, he was called names, such as "Speed King" or "The Slave." [25]

The importance of the informal or emerging work group (in addition to, or in support of, the formal work group) can be best explained in terms of Maslow's need hierarchy and Herzberg's motivation hygiene concept. If workers are operating at the dominant need level of safety—security from management, and outside groups—much of their energy and imagination will be diverted from the work situation. Furthermore, social needs are largely satisfied through face-to-face informal group activities such as the cake incident in the relay assembly group. If any degree of esteem or self-actualization needs are to become active, safety and social needs must first be satisfied. The informal group is the source of much of this satisfaction.

Consider also the kinds of needs categorized as hygiene (company policy, rules, leadership behavior, interpersonal relationships). Many of the hygiene needs are provided within the context of the formal organization. Conversely, if they are not provided, if company policies are unrealistic, if leadership behavior is unfair, or if management attempts to separate groups, group norms will often form in opposition to management and the task. Therefore, in order to allow hygiene levels of satisfaction and to afford the possibility of motivators to occur, the normal, informal group emergence must not be thwarted. Or, in extreme cases, when informal work group norms are unacceptable and the group must be dissolved, management should exercise extreme care.

If company policies and leadership are unfair, group norms will form in opposition to management.

CONSEQUENCES

In column 4 of Figure 11-3 labeled consequences, the results of formal and informal group interaction are depicted—productivity, satisfaction, and individual development. As we noted earlier in the text, these three consequences are strongly interrelated. Sometimes productivity on the job leads to satisfaction. Satisfaction has been shown to lead to greater productivity at times. Usually both productive work output and a reasonable level of satisfaction is required to prompt individual development. Individual development will be discussed further in Chapter 15, Human Resource Development. The important points to understand from the model are these:

1. Background factors and required behavior always lead to emergent behavior.
2. The quality and quantity of these consequences is directly dependent on how closely emergent behavior conforms to and reinforces required behavior.

---

[25] Ibid., p. 179.

3. Only in rare circumstances can formal organizational procedures and required behavior be converted into productivity, satisfaction, and individual development without working through the formal organization.

Two illustrations might help clarify this point. The U.S. postal system has many formal rules and policies that route delivery workers are supposedly required to follow. None of these men and women are required to perform their work satisfactorily while following all of these rules to the letter. Complete conformity is so ridiculous that postal employees have chosen to follow rules perfectly only when they wish to "strike" in opposition to federal law against "strikes." In such cases the "strike" is called a "work by the rules strike." The deliverers leave in the morning, park on the opposite side of the street from their postal box (a rule), unlock their trucks, get their bags out, lock the trucks back (a rule), go across the street, unlock the boxes, take out the mail, lock the boxes back, go back across the street, unlock the trucks, put the mail in, lock their trucks back, etc. Thus by following rules perfectly the deliverers come in late from their daily activities with only half the mail delivered, and free from any possible prosecution. Similarly, when New York City police officers wish to register a grievance about pay and working conditions, they simply ticket every car in New York City that they see in violation of the law. New York traffic and activities come to a screeching halt. Again it is made clear that perfectly formal ways of working without emergent behavior are not satisfactory.

Informal work methods and behavior are often more efficient than the formal.

INTERGROUP BEHAVIOR

Intergroup behavior includes that between several groups, and both departmental and interdepartmental behavior. Several types of informal groups or cliques may be formed when the organization does not actively try to limit them and when the work environment permits them. A clique is a group of persons who hold different positions throughout the organization and exchange rumors and information. A clique might consist of the presidential secretary, an engineer who is a friend of his, and a key punch operator in computer services. To label these cliques, Dalton relies on the basis of the clique's relationship to the formal organizational chart and the services they provide to members.[26]

CLIQUES

Cliques can be divided into classes of vertical cliques and horizontal cliques. Vertical cliques usually occur in a single department, with a tie between the top officer and some of her subordinates. It is vertical in the sense that it is an up-and-down alliance between formal unequals. The top officer will aid and protect her subordinates. She does this by concealing or minimizing their errors. She humanizes the impersonal situations and the demands she must make. The

Cliques are informal groups that form with members from different organizational levels.

---
[26]Melville Dalton, *Men Who Manage*, New York, Wiley, 1959, pp. 57–65.

subordinates reciprocate by advising her of threats to her position and informing her of current work situations. They may confer on ways of dealing with troublemakers outside the clique and may discuss interdepartmental maneuvers. When urgency demands action and the leader is absent, lower members of the clique confer and make decisions with the welfare of the superior in mind.

The horizontal clique is characterized by cutting across and including employees of various departments. It is usually created by a crisis condition such as the threat of reorganization or the introduction of new disliked controls. Often a clique will be the action of a cross-departmental drive to effect changes rather than resist them and to redefine or possibly shift responsibility. The goals may be to get increased operating allowances, bring on reorganization, or win favored consideraton over other units in the organization.[27]

INTERGROUP COMPETITION

As groups become more committed to their own goals and norms, they are likely to become competitive with one another and seek to undermine their rival's activities, thereby becoming a hindrance to the organization as a whole.

The consequences of intergroup conflict were first studied systematically by Sherif. He organized a boy's camp in such a way that two groups would form and would become competitive. He then studied the effects of the competition between the groups.[28] The effects can be described in terms of the following categories.[29]

1. What happens within each group.
   (a) Each group becomes more tightly knit and elicits greater loyalty.
   (b) Group climate changes to a work and task orientation and away from the informal.
   (c) Leadership patterns move toward being more autocratic; the group becomes more tolerant of autocratic leadership.
   (d) Each of the groups becomes more highly organized and structured.
   (e) In order to show a unified front, each group demands more loyalty and conformity from its members.

2. What happens between competing groups.
   (a) Each group views the other as an enemy.
   (b) Each group begins to experience distortions of perception by tending to perceive only the best parts of itself while overlooking its weaknesses.
   (c) Perceptual distortions cause hostility toward the other group to increase while interaction and communication with the other group decrease.
   (d) If groups are forced to interact, they listen only for that which supports their own position and stereotype.

---

[27]Ibid., pp. 61–62.
[28]M. Sherif, O. J. Harvey, B. J. White, W. R. Hood, and Carolyn Sherif, *Intergroup Conflict and Cooperation: The Robber's Cave Experiment*, Norman, Okla., University Book Exchange, 1961.
[29]Edgar H. Schein, *Organizational Psychology*, Englewood Cliffs, N.J.: Prentice-Hall, Inc., 1980, p. 173.

Intergroup competition can have favorable effects within groups.

Thus, we see that intergroup competition can have some very favorable effects as far as the functioning of each individual group is concerned. The introduction of competition tends to solidify each group and to make it more effective and highly motivated in task accomplishment. However, the same conditions that result in bettering intragroup performance may have the opposite effect as far as intergroup cooperation is concerned.

Although the gains of intergroup competition may under some conditions outweigh the negative consequences, the opposite is usually true, and management generally looks for ways of reducing intergroup tension. The conflict of goals and the breakdown in cooperation between departments and individuals are the fundamental problems of intergroup competition. The following discussion will suggest ways to resolve intergroup conflict.

MANAGING INTERGROUP CONFLICT

The reasons for group conflict are similar to those of individual conflicts: the opponents have different value systems and interpret facts differently because of different education and background. One of the major viewpoints that tends to create conflict among groups is the feeling "that other persons' or groups' control over certain resources will be detrimental to their own interests."[30] In one situation extreme conflict leading to a union grievance developed because an engineering group began instilling electrical conduit for a new laboratory test cell. Maintenance considered the work their domain and resented having to do piecemeal tasks while engineering chose the more interesting aspects of the work.

There are numerous strategies for dealing with intergroup conflict.

Figure 11-5 presents a summary of seven strategies for resolving intergroup conflict. These will be discussed briefly as follows.[31]

1. *Physical Separation*. Occasionally two departments or work groups cannot be trusted to interact. Physically separating them will prevent more damage, provided that cooperation between the competing groups is not necessary to get the job done. Salespeople specializing in different product lines in different geographical areas might be an example of such a group.

2. *Limited Interaction*. In cases similar to number 1, where strong cooperation is not required, interaction might be reduced to the few cases where superordinate goals exist. For example, conflicting accounting departments and marketing departments in a university college of business might be limited to infrequent meetings to discuss the common body of courses required of all majors.

3. *Using Integrators*. When this strategy is chosen, the integrator and liaison person must be seen by both groups as possessing high legitimate status, and high expertise; and must be personally attractive to both conflicting groups.

---

[30]Eric H. Neilsen, "Understanding and Managing Intergroup Conflict" in Paul R. Lawrence, Louis B. Barnes, and Jay Lorsch, *Organizational Behavior and Administration*, Homewood, Ill., Richard D. Irwin, 1976, pp. 291–296.
[31]Ibid., p. 301.

FIGURE 11-5

Strategies for Resolving Intergroup Conflict

Behavioral Solution						Attitudinal Change Solution
1	2	3	4	5	6	7

1. Separate the groups physically, reducing conflict by reducing the opportunity to interact.
2. Allow interaction on issues where superordinate goals prevail and decision-making rules have been agreed to beforehand.
3. Keep groups separated but use as integrators individuals who are seen by both groups as justifying high status for the job, possessing personal attributes consistent with both groups' ideals, and having the expertise necessary for understanding each group's problems.
4. Hold direct negotiations between representatives from each group on all conflictual issues, in the presence of individuals who are seen as neutral to the conflict and who have personal attributes and expertise valued by both groups.
5. Hold direct negotiations between representatives from each group without third-party consultants present.
6. Exchange some group personnel for varying periods of time, so that contrasting perceptions and the rationales for them are clarified through day-to-day interaction and increased familiarity with the other group's activities, and then attempt direct negotiations after returning members have reported to their groups.
7. Require intense interaction between the conflicting groups under conditions where each group's failure to cooperate is more costly to itself than continuing to fight, regardless of how the other group behaves.

Source: Eric H. Neilsen, "Understanding and Managing Intergroup Conflict," in Paul R. Lawrence, Louis B. Barnes, and Jay Lorsch, *Organizational Behavior and Administration*, Homewood, Ill., Richard D. irwin, 1976, p. 296.

For example, in a conflict situation between a sales department and an engineering department regarding the design of products, it would be helpful to secure a highly competent engineer who had been successful as a salesperson.

4. *Third-Party Consultants*. As we move toward solutions to the right of the scale in Figure 11-5 the solutions became less oriented toward constraining conflicting parties and more oriented toward changing attitudes. This suggests direct negotiations between representatives of the disputing parties in the presence of a third-party consultant who is respected by both parties.

5. *Negotiations Without Consultants*. This is a high-risk solution since there is no one to keep tempers under control. If the reward for resolving conflict is great enough, however, attitudinal change may be better accomplished when parties work things out for themselves. Usually representatives of each group are chosen to do the negotiating.

6. *Exchanging Members*. Representatives of the groups who negotiate are likely to be viewed as traitors once they go back to their groups. Their groups, who have not taken part in the negotiations, have not been subjected to the stress

of having come to an agreement. Exchanged individuals return to their groups without having worked under the strain of having to negotiate. Therefore, they are better able to communicate the viewpoints of the other side. For instance, numerous firms in industries that require close coordination between production and applied research departments require newcomers in each department to work for a time in the other one to gain a greater familiarity with the problems faced by the latter members.[32]

7. *Multilevel Interaction.* Firms may take the opposite position from physical separation and encourage intense interaction among many or all of the members of opposing groups. These approaches ideally force an open confrontation of differences, followed by basic attitudinal changes. In less effective situations, the competing groups may make peace but retain negative attitudes toward each other. At worst, some of the leaders of one or more groups may choose to leave the organization.

MANAGERIAL IMPLICATIONS OF GROUP BEHAVIOR

It is important for management to examine group norms and characteristics before taking action with individuals. For example, high group cohesiveness promotes strong group control over the level of individual production in a plant or office. As noted in the bank wiring group, very little variation in production will be tolerated among strong group members.

If management and labor have a similar goal, there is little problem. But, for example, if management wants high production in order to cut costs and labor wants low production in order to protect jobs, and group cohesion is high, then there is little possibility of any member of the group approaching the norms of management. If there is little or no group cohesion, some members of the group will probably approach management's standards. Yet when the group is clearly in error, a single individual can seldom hold out against group judgment.

A successful management is one that can develop environments in which groups will develop around norms supportive of or complementary to management goals. Hygiene factors should be provided and motivators should be built into jobs when possible. Communications of management should be frequent and complete enough to prevent worker preoccupation with rumors. Finally, a climate of trust must be established between management and employees.

Today many companies are attempting to organize operations people into interdependent *work teams* in order to provide social satisfaction through the formal organization. Of course they are also trying to create a formal environment (the work team) that can in many cases serve as the "informal work" group that we have been describing under emerging behavior. Some of these work teams are extensions of job enrichment programs—such as a highly successful one

A successful management is one that can develop groups around norms complementary to management goals.

[32]Ibid., p. 301.

in an optical laboratory[33] discussed in chapter 10. Some are formed as quality and productivity improvement teams that meet only periodically. These will be discussed in a later chapter.

Regardless of the stance the informal groups within your organization take, there are three cautions every manager should keep in mind.

1. Efforts to get rid of an informal group can cause trouble. If the group is benign, it probably isn't interfering with your "control" of the operation. Being a "buster" when there is little justification creates unnecessary friction.

2. On the other hand, if the group is strong and protective, it is probably too tough to crack. Any attempt to do so can provoke an outright confrontation. Even if a manager forces the members to be less vocal, resistance will remain. And, pushed underground, it will be harder to deal with.

3. Don't try to gain entry into an informal group. Managers may feel that by cozying up to the group, they will gain its members as allies. But it usually isn't possible to join it or to coopt it. And if the group consists of only some of the members of your operation—as is likely—how will the excluded subordinates feel about the membership of their boss? How comfortable will they be if their manager is "in" and they are "out"?[34]

Schein suggests reducing organizational conflict by rewarding groups which interact and aid one another.

Management's strategy toward intergroup conflict should include preventive measures to reduce it before it can start. Schein lists four steps the organizational planner should follow in creating and handling his different functional groups.[35] The first step is putting more emphasis on total organizational effectiveness and the role of departments in contributing to it. Departments should be measured and rewarded on the basis of their contribution to the total effort rather than their individual effectiveness. High interaction and frequent communication should be stimulated between groups to work on problems of intergroup coordination and help. Second, organizational rewards should be given partially on the basis of aid which groups given to each other. The third step is the frequent rotation of members among groups or departments to stimulate a high degree of mutual understanding and empathy for another's problems. Finally, win-lose situations should be avoided. This can be achieved by preventing groups from competing for the same organizational reward. Emphasis should be placed on pooling of resources to maximize organizational effectiveness and sharing of rewards equally with all the groups of the departments.

It is important to recognize that the preventive strategy does not imply absence of disagreement and artificial "sweetness and light" within or between groups. Conflict and disagreement at the level of the group or organizational tasks is not only desirable, but essential for the achievement of the best solutions to problems. What is harmful is interpersonal or intergroup conflict in which the task is not as important as gaining advantage over the other person or group.

---

[33]Bernard Berelson and Gary Steiner, *Human Behavior*, New York, Harcourt, Brace, and World, 1964.
[34]"The Organization Within the Organization," *Research Institute Personal Report for the Executive*, February 10, 1981, p. 2.
[35]Ibid., p. 179.

It can be assumed that the great interest in the study of group dynamics will continue. A democratic society derives its strength from the effective functioning of the multitude of groups that it contains. Its most valuable resources are the groups of people found in its homes, communities, schools, churches, business concerns, union halls, and various branches of government. Now, more than ever before, it is recognized that these units must perform their functions well if the larger system is to work successfully.

SUMMARY

A group is defined as any number of people who interact with one another, who are psychologically aware of one another, and who perceive themselves as a unit. Some of the key elements of a group are that they share one or more goals, they develop norms and a group structure where different members fill certain roles, and where attractions for other members or the group itself exist.

Groups may be informal. A formal group is created by the organization and may be either permanent or temporary in nature. Informal groups are those that arise spontaneously. Vertical informal groups, cliques, occur within a single department or unit, and represent up and down alliance between formal unequals. In a vertical clique, the manager often aids and protects her subordinates and in return they protect her interests.

Informal horizontal groups cut across departmental lines and include managers of different departments. A horizontal aggressive clique forms in order to

SUMMARY CHART

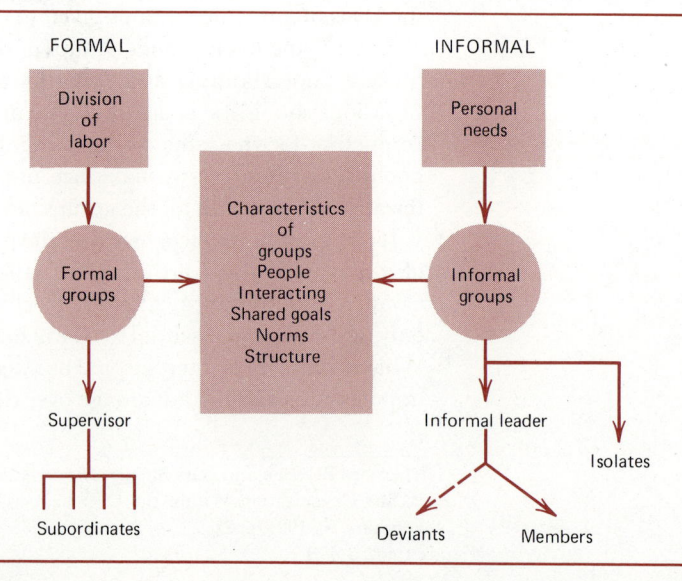

effect some type of change, while a defensive clique may form to prevent a change from being enacted. People join groups either because of social reasons or because it is the only way to accomplish a task. Informal groups almost always emerge in organizations. They are usually necessary for productive effort.

Two important aspects of the study of groups are group cohesion and group competition. The more cohesive a group is, the stronger it will be. There are many factors that affect cohesion such as size, homogeneity, stability of membership, and others. Generally speaking, intragroup competition tends to destroy cohesion while intergroup competition tends to build cohesion.

DISCUSSION QUESTIONS

1. Briefly describe the elements which are basic to small groups.
2. What are the basic reasons why people form groups? Give an example of a group that is attractive to a person for the following reasons.
   (a) Activities of the group.
   (b) Personal attractiveness of the group members.
   (c) Means to achieve goals.
   (d) Achieving status.
   (e) Give an example of a group that would provide all of the above.
3. What are the conditions influencing group cohesiveness? Give an example of a group which is cohesive due to any three of these conditions.
4. What factors or forces will result in a decrease in group cohesiveness?
5. Which of the following is characteristic of a cohesive work group? Explain your answer.
   (a) Highly variable productivity.
   (b) Stable productivity.
   (c) High productivity.
6. Why does intragroup competition tend to decrease group cohesiveness? Why does intergroup competition tend to increase group cohesiveness? What factors are involved in each of the above two types of competition?

APPLICATION EXERCISES AND CASES

THE PLATING ROOM GROUP[36]

The following incident describes a group of men working in an electroplating department of a plant.

The Sarto group invariably ate lunch together on the fire escape near Aisle 1.

---

[36]Paul R. Lawrence, Louis B. Barnes, and Jay W. Lorsch, *Organizational Behavior and Administration*, Homewood, Ill., Richard D. Irwin, Inc., 1976, excerpts from The Slade Company Case, p. 134.

On those Saturdays and Sundays when overtime work was required, the Sarto group operated as a team, regardless of weekday work assignments, to get overtime work complete as quickly as possible. Off the job, Sarto group members often joined in parties or weekend trips. Sarto's summer camp was a frequent rendezvous.

Sarto's group was also the most cohesive one in the department in terms of its organized punch-in and punch-out system. Since the men were regularly scheduled to work from 7:00 A.M. to 7:00 P.M. weekdays, and since all supervision was removed at 5:00 P.M., it was possible almost every day to finish a "day's work" by 5:30 and leave the plant. What is more, if one man were to stay until 7:00 P.M., he could punch the time cards of a number of men and help them gain free time without pay loss. (This system operated on weekends, also, at which times members of supervision were present, if at all, only for short periods.) In Sarto's group the duty of staying late rotated, so that no man did so more than once a week. In addition, the group members would punch a man in in the morning if he were unavoidably delayed. However, such a practice never occurred without prior notice from the man who expected to be late and never if the tardiness was expected to last beyond 8:00 A.M., the start of the day for the foreman.

Sarto explained the logic behind the system:

You know that our hourly pay rate is quite low, compared to other companies. What makes this the best place to work is the feeling of security you get. No one ever gets laid off in this department. With all the hours in the week, all the company ever has to do is shorten the work week when orders fall off. We have to tighten our belts, but we can all get along. When things are going well, as they are now, the company is only interested in getting out the work. It doesn't help to get it out faster than it's really needed—so we go home a little early whenever we can. Of course, some guys abuse this sort of thing—like Herman—but others work even harder, and it averages out.

Whenever an extra order has to be pushed through, naturally I work until 7:00. So do a lot of the others. I believe that if I stay until my work is caught up and my equipment is in good shape, that's all the company wants of me. They leave us alone and expect us to produce—and we do.

Questions
1. Fully discuss and critique the Sarto group using the model discussed in this chapter.
2. How would you react to this group as a manager? What changes would you suggest?

RIVER GLEN MANUFACTURING PLANT[37]

Note the following example, written by a manager, about the relationship between a worker group and a management group.

---
[37] Alvar Elbing, *Behavioral Decisions in Organizations*, 2nd ed., Glenview, Ill., Scott Foresman and Co., 1978, pp. 301–305.

I was transferred [to general manufacturing] from River Glen, South Carolina, where Modern Chemical has a new fiber plant. The River Glen plant was built in 1965. The entire plant, including the shop, is air conditioned, and incorporates the latest in "daylight" lighting. The grounds are beautifully landscaped. River Glen has no union, and in general the employees seem enthusiastic about making fiber. They are paid a straight day rate. Measured against standard motion-time study (MTS) data, the plant averages 85 to 90 percent productivity.

The general manufacturing plant was a shock to me. Although the hourly workers are generally paid more than those in River Glen, their productivity is only 40 to 45 percent of MTS. The shop starts at 7 A.M. but there is seldom a machine operating at 8 A.M. when the office force arrives. The machines start around 8:30 and shut down at 11 to 11:30 A.M. for an unofficial two-hour lunch. During this morning work period there is a 40-minute coffee break. The afternoon period of actual production work is from 1 to 3 P.M.

I work in manufacturing engineering and have developed some communication with the shop. One day I needed a small pad milled and a hole drilled and tapped in a brass fitting for my boat. It fit in my pocket, and since it was a five-minute job I took it to a machinist to be done.

He said he needed a shop order for two hours in order to do it and it would require a sketch by a union draftsman. When I told him it was for my boat, he said, "O.K." and did the operations in less than five minutes. He said he would be glad to do any personal work I brought in, since he was bored at not being able to work very much during the day. I never had another occasion to use him for personal work, but I get engineering jobs done "free" by telling him they are for my boat.

Questions

1. Explain the behavior taking place in the River Glen plant.
2. What do you think of the managerial approach to getting your engineering work performed?

CHAPTER 12
CONTINGENCY APPROACHES TO ORGANIZATION

PATTERNS OF ORGANIZING
MECHANISTIC PATTERNS
ORGANIC PATTERNS
CHOOSING THE APPROPRIATE ORGANIZATIONAL FORM
ORGANIZATION STRUCTURE
TECHNOLOGY AND STRUCTURE
ENVIRONMENT AND STRUCTURE
THE FUNCTIONAL ORGANIZATION
DESIGN PRINCIPLES
DESIGN LOGIC
ORGANIZATIONAL ADAPTATIONS
PROJECT ORGANIZATIONS
MATRIX ORGANIZATIONS

APPLICATION EXERCISES AND CASES
FREE-FORM CHAOS
THE OFFICE OF THE PRESIDENT

THE GENERAL MILLS BRAND OF MANAGERS[1]

When General Mills completed a ten-story tower at its suburban Minneapolis headquarters last summer, the company discovered that not all the telephones could be installed at once. "Hook up the product managers first," a senior executive ordered. "The business can't run without them."

Though none of these product managers is over 35, the concept of having one person watch over one brand has been around since Procter & Gamble first assigned a man to manage Camay soap in 1927. Today product managers, also called brand managers, exist in a variety of multiproduct companies. In single-product companies, the chief executive is the brand manager—or should be.

"I want to run my own show"

The role of the brand manager differs from company to company: like a sales executive in some, an advertising manager in others. At General Mills he or she acts as a business manager, collecting all the internal and external information that might affect the brand, setting goals for it and plotting strategies and tactics to achieve them.

The brand managers in Minneapolis's Golden Valley like to think they are running their own not-so-little businesses. They are, in the sense that they are responsibile for their brands; but in fact they aren't, because they have very little real authority and virtually no financial risk. Still, General Mills product managers feel just about as entrepreneurial as a young executive could in an established, hierarchical organization with sales of $4.2 billion a year. Of course, their common ultimate goal is to be at the top of that—or some other—hierarchy. As one product manager expresses it: "I want.to run my own show, with the only other people in the organization being below me."

At General Mills, that dream has plenty to nourish it. Last week, for the first time in its history, the company appointed three executives, all of whom came up through the product-management system, to its top posts. H. Brewster Atwater Jr., 49, president, will succeed Chairman E. Robert Kinnery, 63, as chief executive in April. F. Caleb Blodgett, 53, and Donald F Swanson, 53, have been named vice chairmen. As product manager of Betty Crocker Instant mashed Potatoes in the early 1960's, Bruce Atwater helped take that product right out of the market, and bring in a technologically superior one—Potato Buds. General Mills' market share went from 8 percent to 25 percent, its rank from third to first place in the spud stakes.

[1]Ann M. Morrison, "The General Mills Brand of Managers," *Fortune*, January 12, 1981, pp. 99–103.

How does one implement the principles of effective organizational behavior discussed in Part III? Combining the thoughts of the preceding five chapters, one anticipates that the ideally effective organization would include: managers who posses a positive self-concept; an organizational climate that is supportive of mature individuals; use of reasonable approaches to settling conflict; work groups that are cohesive; an effective communications network; and jobs that produce a sense of achievement and accomplishment.

Effective organizational arrangements often simply evolve.

Obviously, such an ideal organizational arrangement is difficult to implement. Moreover, one seldom begins an organization without remnants from the past. External requirements such as legal regulations and internal technological needs may dictate types of organizations that do not measure up to these requirements. Often rather than implementing a total design, unique effective organizational arrangements simply evolve, as did the product managers at General Mills.

PATTERNS OF ORGANIZING

When sufficient flexibility presents itself, such as in the establishment of new organizations or in major reorganizations, the following questions should be asked before organizing.

1. How uncertain is the task environment in which the organization operates?
2. In what ways should the organization be mechanistic and in what ways organic?
3. How should the subtasks be divided and how should the organization be differentiated? Should subsystems be organized according to the functions people perform, or by the products or services the organization provides, or should some other form, such as a matrix organization, be used?
4. What kind of people are (or can be recruited to become) members of the organization? Under what conditions do they work and learn best?
5. How are the activities to be coordinated and integrated? What mechanisms will be used, involving what costs?[2]

MECHANISTIC PATTERNS

The mechanistic organization reflects an emphasis on traditional hierarchies of authority.

The two approaches to organizing are the mechanistic pattern and the organic pattern. The *mechanistic pattern* is utilized by the bureaucratic organization described in Chapter 7, Organizational Dynamics. This is the traditional hierarchy of organization that works toward automated efficiency. Tasks are broken into small parts, which are joined together at the end of the work process. Decision making is centralized, with authority, influence, and information increasing by degrees as one moves up the organizational level. This type of organizational pattern may be likened to a machine. "People are conceived of as parts performing specific tasks. As employees leave, other parts can be slipped into their places."[3]

The mechanistic form is a useful form of organization. But it is inflexible and once goals, objectives, and procedures are established, it is difficult to change them. Often the morale and motivation of workers create a problem, since little feeling of accomplishment is felt in such an environment.

---

[2] Michael B. McCaskey, "An Introduction to Organizational Design," *California Management Review* Volume XVII, No. 2, Winter 1974, p. 14.
[3] Ibid.

ORGANIC PATTERNS

The *organically patterned* organization is built on the order of the human body, as was the enterprise organization in Chapter 7. It is much more complex and much more fluid in its operation. Tasks, procedures, objectives, and goals are more loosely stated and are continuously changing. Jobs in the organization are continuously redefined. Such an organization is able to react to the environment more rapidly than do the mechanistic patterns of organization.

Organic patterns should be used in situations where the task to be performed is uncertain and not well known enough to be programmed. It is flexible and responds quickly to unexpected opportunities. The major disadvantage of the organic form of organization is that it can be wasteful of resources. Duplication of efforts may occur because of lack of definition.

Organic organizations are more fluid than mechanistic ones.

CHOOSING THE APPROPRIATE ORGANIZATIONAL FORM

The above discussion suggests that the appropriate organization is *contingent* upon several factors. Two of the most important considerations are the *certainty* of the task to be performed and the *people* involved. Most organizations contain some organic units and some mechanistic units. Instead of observing entire organizations, we need to look at the subunits of large organizations and determine whether they should be more mechanistic or organic on a unit-by-unit basis.[4]

DIFFERENTIATION AND INTEGRATION

Two major characteristics of organization mentioned, but not yet studied are differentiation and integration. *Differentiation* is the degree to which various persons and different subgroups in an organization specialize in their tasks. By differentiating, an organization gains the advantages of economics of scale, and allows its people to become experts in highly specialized areas, such as industrial engineering, wage and salary administration, auditing, and other functions. An important question in organizing is, "How differentiated should the organization be?" Generally speaking, it has been found that the more modern industries such as aerospace, electronics, and other space age industries are more highly differentiated in order to allow a greater degree of specialization. Organizations that are relatively stable, such as well-established manufacturing organizations, often have uniform rules and procedures, vocabulary, and patterns of thinking that require less differentiation.

Differentiation is the degree to which various persons and subgroups specialize in their tasks.

Since all organizations are designed to produce an entire product or to arrive at a complete service previously performed by individuals, all the specialized tasks must eventually be coordinated. We call this reuniting of the organizational units or subdivisions within a unit *integration*. It follows that the more an orga-

The coordination of the differentiated units within an organization is called integration.

---
[4] Ibid., p. 15.

nization is differentiated, the more difficult is the task of integration. That is, if departments have similar goals, values, and vocabulary, it is easier for them to communicate and to reach an understanding of their total task. But when highly specialized groups, such as scientists, market research personnel, engineers, and others are trying to work together, the task of integration is much more difficult, since they are not as likely to understand the terminology, methodology, and value systems of the other groups. (See the discussion on conflict resolution in Chapter 11, Role and Function of the Group in Organizations.) The second question that must be asked of organizations then becomes "How can integration be successfully performed for an organization?"

ORGANIZATION STRUCTURE

Extensive research in organization design supports a *contingency* approach to organizing. That is, it has been learned that the proper form of organization is one that will effectively integrate the various differentiated units. Two characteristics of organizations that are important in determining the correct structure will now be discussed—technology and environment.

TECHNOLOGY AND STRUCTURE

Much of the research regarding the relationship between technology and organization has come from a study of 100 manufacturing firms in southern England.[5] Firms were categorized into job-order manufacturing, process or continuous flow manufacturing, and mass production. Job-order manufacturers produce units to customer specifications, and use nonrepetitive, nonstandardized processes for each operation. The sequencing of material through the plant varies from product to product, and general purpose equipment is used, requiring a great amount of skill on the part of workers. Some customized furniture manufacturers in the United States also operate as job lot shops.

In the process or continuous flow of manufacturing type plants, the product is standardized and moves in a predictable manner from operation to operation. A petroleum refinery is an example of process manufacturing.

Mass production manufacturing describes the reasonably standardized manufacturing process in the automobile or the appliance industries.

Woodward found that job lot firms producing to customer specifications had to be quick in adjusting to changes. Therefore, more flexible organization styles produced more effective organizations. In a similar manner, flexibility and adaptability are required for firms engaging in process manufacturing because of their emphasis on new products new chemicals, improved processes, etc., which can be manufactured with established facilities. In the mass production industries where firms are producing standardized products by routine operations, the

Woodward concluded that the success of a particular firm depends on the appropriateness of an organization's structure for a particular technology.

---

[5] Joan Woodward, *Industrial Organization Theory and Practice*, London, Oxford University Press, 1965.

bureaucratic organization described in Chapter 7, Organizational Dynamics, tends to be the most efficient.[6]

Woodward concluded that the success of a particular firm depends upon the appropriateness of an organization's structure for a particular technology. Other studies have suggested that the degree of change taking place in an organization may be as great or greater a determinant of required organization structure as technology.[7]

ENVIRONMENT AND STRUCTURE

The Woodward study established the relationship between organization structure and technology. Lawrence and Lorsch investigated the relationship between organization structure and the environment within which an organization operates.[8] Their study was also important because they investigated the differences in the environments of various departments within an organization rather than simply the overall organization environment. They examined marketing departments, production departments, and research departments in various industries by analyzing three dimensions: (1) the rate of change of conditions over time, (2) the certainty of information about conditions at any particular time, (3) the time span of feedback on the results of employee decisions.

Lawrence and Lorsch investigated the relationship between organization structure and the environment.

These writers examined these basic departments in six different organizations. They learned that departments with the more certain environments, such as production, utilized a more formal structure. "Compared with the other departments, the production units had more levels in the managerial hierarchy and a higher ratio of supervisors to subordinates, as well as more frequent and more specific reviews of both the department's and individual manager's performances."[9]

Production departments tended to have a more formal structure.

Interpersonal relationships also tended to differ among departments with differences in the certainty of their tasks. Sales departments were found to be the most relationship oriented, with production departments positioning themselves more toward a task orientation. "Since the production procedures and controls and the processing technology provided the necessary coordination within the department, production personnel generally did not see positive social relationships as essential."[10] Research personnel fell between the extremes of production and sales in their interpersonal orientation.

Sales departments were more relationship oriented.

The third dimension that varied among the departments with environmental differences was the time orientation. Production and sales departments learned

---

[6] James L. Gibson, John M. Ivanevich, and James H. Donnelly, Jr., *Organizations, Behavior Structure, and Processes*, Dallas, Texas, Business Publications, Inc., 1976, pp. 293–294.

[7] Jeffery D. Ford and John W. Slocum, Jr., "Size, Technology Environment, and the Structure of Organizations," *Academy of Management Review*, Vol. 2, No. 4, October 1977, pp. 562–564.

[8] Paul R. Lawrence and Jay W. Lorsch, "Differentiation and Integration in Complex Organizations," *Administration Science Quarterly*, June 1967, pp. 1–47.

[9] Paul R. Lawrence and Jay W. Lorsch, *Organization and Environment*, Homewood, Ill., Richard D. Irwin, Inc., 1969, pp. 31–32.

[10] Ibid., p. 34.

about their effects on profits almost immediately, while scientists in the laboratories often had to wait several years. For this reason it was not surprising to find that production and sales had a shorter time perspective than research.[11]

Some of the most important findings of the Lawrence and Lorsch study came from their examination of the concepts of differentiation and integration among the departments in different organizations. Their findings, along with those of several other researchers, can be summarized as follows.[12]

1. Differences in the ways subdepartments are organized within departments are due to differences in the environments to which the departments must adapt.
2. The more stable and certain the environment, the more bureaucratic should be the departmental organization.
3. A high degree of differentiation calls for a greater amount of intergration. That is, the more departments specialize, the more difficult it is to coordinate their work. The structured departments with low uncertainty and short time frames were most effective when they organized along the lines of the bureaucratic organization. But organizations with relatively diverse and uncertain environments tended to be more effective where they organized along flexible lines, with a stronger relationship orientation. In these cases, management must be more adept at coordinating by promoting communications and understanding through persons who serve as coordinating links in the organization.[13]
4. The relative effectiveness of a manufacturing organization is dependent upon the extent to which it achieves a required degree of differentiation. Given this optional degree of differentiation, departments must be integrated to the degree dictated by the total environment. It should be noted that Herbert and Matthews have found integration to be more important in the banking field than differentiation. Apparently, banks do not require as great an amount of specialization as do manufacturing firms, but find that coordination is of greater importance.[14] The research on the effects of size and structure is contradictory. But certainly increasing the size of an organization tends to create more differentiation and, hence, complicates the management task of integration.[15] For example, individuals on structured tasks prefer closer authority relationships and less uncertainty than individuals working on variable or more complicated tasks.[16]
5. There is no one best organizational structure. The appropriate structure

> The major finding of these studies was: there is no one best way to organize.

---

[11]Ibid., p. 35.
[12]Gibson, et al., *Organizations, Behavior Structure, and Processes*, pp. 298–299.
[13]McCaskey, *"Introduction to Organizational Design,"* pp. 17–18.
[14]Theordore T. Herbert and Ronald D. Matthews, "Is the Contingency Theory of Organization A Technology-Bound Conceptualization?" *Journal of Management*, Vol. 3, No 1., 1977, pp. 1–10.
[15]Daniel Robey, M. M. Bakr, and Thomas S. Miller, "Organizational Size and Management Autonomy: Some Structural Discontinuities," *Academy of Management Journal*, Vol. 20, No. 3, 1977, pp. 378–397.
[16]Ibid.

THE FUNCTIONAL ORGANIZATION

The functional organization was described and discussed in Chapter 5, Organization Through Departmentation. While it is still the most prevalent form of structure used in government and industry today, some significant changes are taking place. You will recall from our previous discussion that the functional organization is based on grouping by specialized skill, with similar skills grouped together by departments. Engineers report to an engineering department, accountants to the controller's areas, and production workers to the plant superintendent. Such an organization aids differentiation and makes supervision easier at the departmental level. "The assumption is that the common occupational background of the participants provides an effective bond that encourages cooperation within the group and makes the supervisor's direction more unified."[17]

The functional approach to organization aids differentiation but creates problems in integration.

But what about the process of integration? At the departmental level, coordination works well, but often parochial interests are promoted. Short-term departmental goals take precedence over total organizational goals and interdepartmental conflict is often excessive. Furthermore the functional organization with its bureaucratic tendencies is having difficulty adjusting to the rapidity of change in technology, shortened product life cycles, and accelerated sophistication and growth in organizations.

Accordingly, one writer has summarized the weaknesses of the functional organization around the following basic arguments.[18]

1. *Functional organizations tend to emphasize the separate functional elements at the expense of the whole organization.* Engineers with a functional department orientation often are more concerned about incorporating unique or interesting design features in a product than they are in the problems of producing the product. Marketing personnel give little attention to cash flow problems when requesting inventory levels. Lower and middle management, when organized functionally, think only of their own groups when making decisions, instead of seeking optimum decisions for overall organizational goals.

2. *Under functional departmentation, there is no group that effectively integrates the various functions of the organization.* Typically, this has been the general manager's responsibility. But since the general manager probably rose through one of the functional specialties, he frequently lacks the knowledge and objectivity to serve effectively as an integrating force.

3. *Functional organizations emphasize functional relationships on the vertical organizational*

---

[17] Howard M. Carlisle, "Are Functional Organizations Becoming Obsolete?" *Management Review*, January 1969, p. 2.
[18] Ibid., pp. 4–6.

hierarchy. Remember Fayol's gangplank? Unfortunately, it has not found its way into general usage. Middle managers need to provide integration between such functions as marketing, operations management, and finance, but their communications do not produce such integration. Their activities and relationships are primarily lateral, but they communicate primarily upward with superiors and downward with subordinates. Any lateral communications are usually incidental and often very formal.

4. *Functional organizations tend to be closed systems.* In the specialist or functional department, a common bond is formed around specialized knowledge and expertise—not around organizational objectives. The group lauds its own abilities and downgrades outsiders. Such a bond discourages the openness required to listen and understand other departmental viewpoints. It is a "We're OK—You're Not OK" position.

<small>The functional approach to organizing may not be flexible enough to insure continued vitality and adaptability.</small>

5. *Functional organizations develop a strong resistance to change.* Since conformity to traditional specialty education, vocabulary, and viewpoints are encouraged, there is little internal group reward for change. A person who takes on the generalist viewpoint, or interacts frequently with other specialty departments, is likely to find himself in the category of the isolate (see Chapter 11, Role and Function of the Group in Organizations).

As organizations grow in complexity and size, other forms of organizations must be developed in order to meet the many contingencies which may be faced.

DESIGN PRINCIPLES

The ultimate objective of any organizational structure is to facilitate the accomplishment of the objective at hand. If the structure fails to accomplish this, it is not a good one. Therefore, a contingency approach to organizational design seems the most appropriate one.

<small>The contingency approach to organization suggests that one should use the most appropriate design principles.</small>

The design principles incorporated by modern adaptive organizations can be divided into three types.[19] As was suggested earlier in this chapter, these design elements may be characteristic of the subunits of large organizations as well as being descriptive of the entire organizations themselves.

1. *Functional Organization.* While the functional organization is utilized by all bureaucratic forms, it is also found to varying degrees in newer organizational designs. As was suggested in Chapter 7, profit decentralization is one attempt to overcome the laggard nature of the bureaucratic organization. Subdivisions of process and service industries such as the chemical, petroleum, and banking corporations are able to use this approach by allocating cost and profit centers. When this design principle is used as the primary coordinating principle, we usually end up with some form of bureaucracy. Standardization of the work to be performed usually leads to what Mintzberg has called

---

[19] Peter F. Drucker, "New Templates for Today's Organizations," *Harvard Business Review*, January–February 1974, p. 49.

CONTINGENCY APPROACHES TO ORGANIZATIONS

machine bureaucracy. Standardization based on the skills of employees leads to what he called *professional bureaucracy.* Finally standardization based on outputs and performance of large subunits leads to what he terms a *divisionalized bureaucracy.*[20]

2. *Team Organization.* In team organization, a group is formed around a specific task or project rather than a specific skill or stage in a work process. The idea is to move toward a more organic or highly coordinated subunit in organization.

3. *System Organization.* This is an organization built around relationships rather than specialty or teams, but may include combinations of teams and profit centers. Often, it will include a number of interacting organizations operating rather informally. It is difficult to define except by example, as follows.

The prototype for this design was NASA's space program, in which a large number of autonomous units—large government bodies, individual research scientists, profit-seeking businesses, and large universities—worked together, organized, and informed by the needs of the situation rather than by logic, and held together by a common goal and a joint top management.[21]

DESIGN LOGIC

Each of the three organizational structures we have described includes a specific logic that makes that design applicable to a particular situation, as do the functional and decentralized structures discussed earlier. For example, both the functional organization and the team design principles "embody *work and task* and are thus an appropriate design to consider when faced with work or task-oriented management problems."[22]

> Both the functional and team design principles are appropriate when faced with work or task.

The last of the design principles discussed above, systems design, is geared to the logic of maintaining *relationships.* This structure is difficult to implement because relationships are more numerous and less clearly defined than either work, task, or results. According to Peter Drucker, there may yet be one logic or organizational design which has not been utilized, the logic of organizing around *decision.* "Decision is as much a dimension of management as work and task, results and performance, and relations. Yet, so far, we know of no decision-focused principle of organization structure, but should one ever be developed, it might have wide applicability."[23] His summary statement captures vividly the optimum desired in organization.

> The systems approach to organizing is heavily geared to relationships.

Ideally, an organization should be multiaxial, that is, structured around work and task, and results and performance, and relationships, and decisions. It would function as if it were a biological organism, like the human body with its skeleton and muscles, a number of nervous systems, and with circulatory, digestive, immunological, and respiratory

---

[20]Henry Mintzberg, "Organization Design; Fashion or Fit?" *Harvard Business Review*, January-February 1981, p. 104.
[21]Drucker, "New Templates for Today's Organizations."
[22]Mintzberg, "Organization Design," p. 104.
[23]Ibid., p. 50.

systems, all autonomous yet independent. But in social structures, we are still limited to designs that express only one primary dimension.[24]

For practicality in designing organization structures, we generally emphasize one design principle built around one logic in each subunit of the organization. That is, each department, division, or work group is usually organized around one of these design dimensions.

In order to meet certain unique requirements, several relatively new types of organization structures have emerged. These structures include various combinations of the design principles and logic discussed above. The first two, the *project and matrix* organizations, are built around the design logic of work or task, utilizing a team approach. The latter two, *the collegial and free form* organization, include the logic of systems or relationships in their organizational structure.

ORGANIZATIONAL ADAPTATIONS

PROJECT ORGANIZATIONS

The project system of organizing received its greatest impetus during the late fifties and early sixties in the aerospace industry. It represents an attempt to deal with two difficulties that conventional structures do not always cope with (1) the need for flexibility and (2) the problem of coordinating the flow of work between the vertical divisions of the organization. New tasks, such as building a factory, introducing a new product, or developing a weapons system, create a need for a temporary organization structure that will effectively and efficiently accomplish the mission at hand. These types of projects usually require contributions from several vertical functions such as finance, research and development, marketing, production, and others. Project organization provides a way of coordinating these diverse functions. When the project is completed, the project structure is discontinued.

The need for flexibility and strong coordination calls for a project organization form.

Although there are several alternative ways of framing a project organization, one of the more common ones is shown in Figure 12-1. The solid lines represent *primary* authority and the dotted lines *project* authority.[25] The solid lines also represent the temporary organization that is superimposed over the permanent and that will disappear when the project is completed. The project team is composed of the project manager and individuals with certain skills from the permanent organization who are needed for the completion of the project. The latter may be assigned on a full- or part-time basis to a particular project and may either remain in their regular work place or be transferred to another location. Several projects may be in operation at the same time.

The heads of the functional departments retain what is thought of as line

---

[24]Ibid.
[25]Allen R. Janager, "Anatomy of the Project Organization," *Business Management Record*, November 1963, p. 14.

FIGURE 12-1

Project Organization

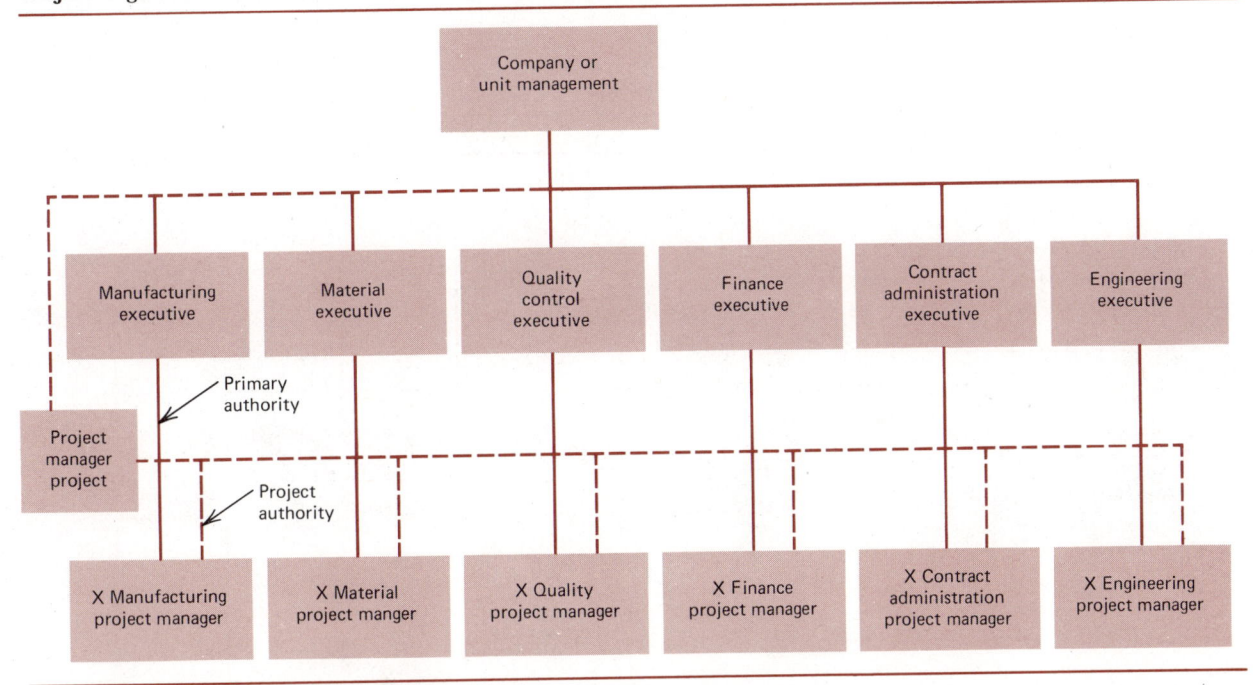

```
                          Company or
                         unit management
     ┌──────┬──────────┬──────┬──────┬──────────┬──────┐
Manufacturing  Material  Quality   Finance   Contract    Engineering
 executive    executive  control   executive administration executive
                        executive            executive
           ← Primary
             authority
Project
manager
project
           ← Project
             authority
X Manufacturing  X Material  X Quality  X Finance  X Contract      X Engineering
project manager  project      project    project    administration  project manager
                 manger       manager    manager    project manager
```

Source: Allen R. Janager, "Anatomy of the Project Organization," *Business Management,* November 1963, p. 13.

In the project organization the heads of functional departments retain line authority.

Project managers must be highly skilled in human relations.

authority while the project manager has the responsibility for defining the work of the project, setting schedules, and controlling the progress of the project. This manager does not typically have the authority to issue orders to functional people; therefore, she gets things done by consulting, moral persuasion, arguing, compromising, and by relying on special knowledge and competence. Conflicts that develop between the functional manager and the project manager must be settled by the individual to whom they both report. The project manager will, of course, try to prevent any such conflicts since the idea is to work toward *collaboration.*

The prevention and/or solution to potential personnel problems is critical to the successful functioning of the project organization. Obviously, the project managers must be highly skilled in human relations techniques (especially communications) if they are to gain the cooperation and commitment of the various functional specialists who have been assigned to or volunteered for the project in question.

The dotted lines in Figure 12-2 define the boundaries of a project group operating in a state far from its headquarters' office. The parent corporation is a large manufacturer of electrical equipment for industry, the armed services, and the consumer. The division to which this project group reports develops missile guidance equipment. The Florida Test Facility was organized to conduct per-

FIGURE 12-2

Partial Organization Chart—Missile Control Department

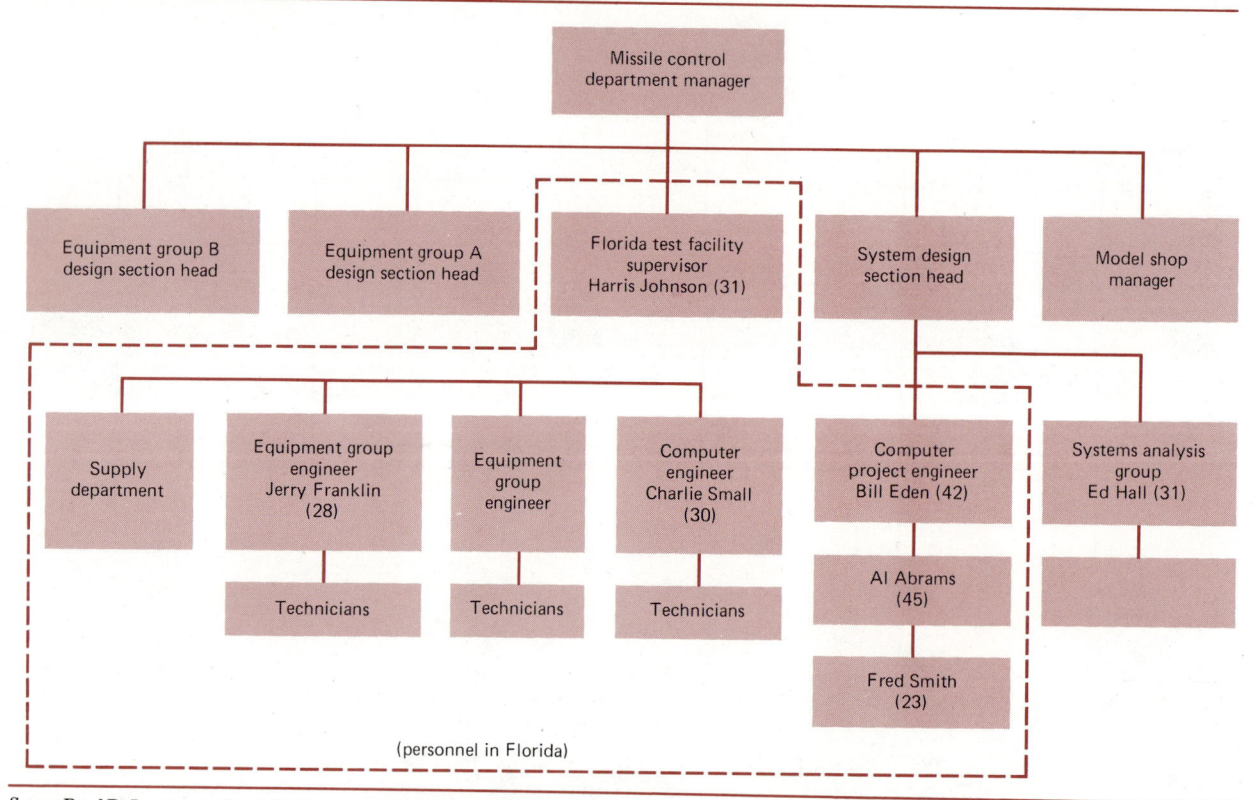

```
                          Missile control
                        department manager
    ┌──────────────┬──────────────┼──────────────┬──────────────┐
Equipment      Equipment      Florida test    System design    Model shop
group B        group A        facility        section head     manager
design         design         supervisor
section head   section head   Harris Johnson (31)
                                              │
    ┌──────────┬──────────┬──────────┐        ├──────────────┐
Supply     Equipment   Equipment  Computer  Computer      Systems analysis
department group       group      engineer  project       group
           engineer    engineer   Charlie   engineer      Ed Hall (31)
           Jerry                  Small     Bill Eden (42)
           Franklin               (30)
           (28)
               │          │          │          │
           Technicians Technicians Technicians  Al Abrams
                                                (45)
                                                 │
                                              Fred Smith
                                                (23)
```

(personnel in Florida)

Source: Paul R. Lawrence, Louis B. Barnes, and Jay W. Lorsch, *Organizational Behavior and Administration: Cases and Readings,* Homewood, Ill., Richard D. Irwin, 1976, p. 279.

formance tests on a missile guidance system designed and built by the company. The following quote from a report on the organization depicts its temporary nature and the character of its operations. Although on a military base, the test facility operated as an independent entity insofar as the direction of its activities were concerned, and it relied on military personnel and supply for support only.

> *Organizationally, the Sturbridge test facility supervisor reported directly to the manager of the missile control department at headquarters in Allentown, Pennsylvania. Johnson was placed in charge of the operation when it was first set up and took with him from Allentown several key people who would form the nucleus of the field organization. To these were added technicians and others from the local area in Florida.*[26]

Companies operating in manufacturing plants can also make good use of the project organization in order to respond to change that is rapidly occurring

---

[26] Paul R. Lawrence, Louis B. Barnes, and Jay W. Lorsch, *Organizational Behavior and Administration: Cases and Readings,* Homewood, Ill., Richard D. Irwin, 1976, pp. 279–280.

today. For example, General Motors began in the early 1970s to restructure its management to cope with accelerating change.

> From the standpoint of new-car development, its most important innovation was the project-center concept. This involves forming an engineering group to shepherd each new car through its development, bringing together experts in design, manufacturing, assembly, customer service, and marketing. The basic job of a project center is to eliminate redundant work by the different divisions and ensure that nothing falls between stools. The center strives to keep manufacturing costs down and, at the same time, helps the divisions strengthen their separate indentities.
>
> Without the project center, it is doubtful that G.M. could have developed the kind of X-car it did.[27]

Manning a project can present a problem. Some necessary personnel may not wish to leave the security of their home base, because they are unsure about their position and status upon returning to the functional unit. The importance and excitement of the project and recognition (sometimes tangible rewards) are relied on to encourage participation by individuals in a project.

A problem may arise when functional heads are reluctant to assign or relinquish their best people to various projects. Since the functional units remain accountable for their own results, it is a natural desire to keep the better qualified people working on functional area activities instead of on various special projects.

The chief problems of the project organization involve personnel.

A final issue relating to project management, and more specifically to a project organization, is the ability of the permanent organization to absorb or reabsorb project personnel. If, as has sometimes been the case, people with specialized talents are hired to work on one or more projects, there may be a problem in terms of what to do with them once the project is completed. Related to this is the question of who will take the place of someone in a functional speciality who is assigned to a given project. The situation becomes even more complicated when a number of people from a given area are away working on various projects. In order to survive, the functional unit must hire replacements. The result can be an almost permanent float of personnel from one project to another. Such a situation is satisfactory as long as business flourishes and projects continue to develop, but it is difficult to implement during business declines.

MATRIX ORGANIZATIONS

The matrix organization includes a permanent horizontal organization.

The matrix organization is similar to project organization in that it provides a vehicle for achieving teamwork between vertical functional divisions. It differs from the project organization in two respects: (1) the horizontal organization is permanent, and (2) the horizontal division head (frequently called the business manager or product manager) has line authority over his jurisdictional area. Figure 12-3 depicts the vertical and horizontal lines of authority from which the matrix organization derives its name. In the case of a business organization, the

---
[27]Charles G. Burck, "What's Good for the World Should be Good for G. M.," *Fortune*, May 7, 1979, p. 126.

FIGURE 12-3

Matrix Organization

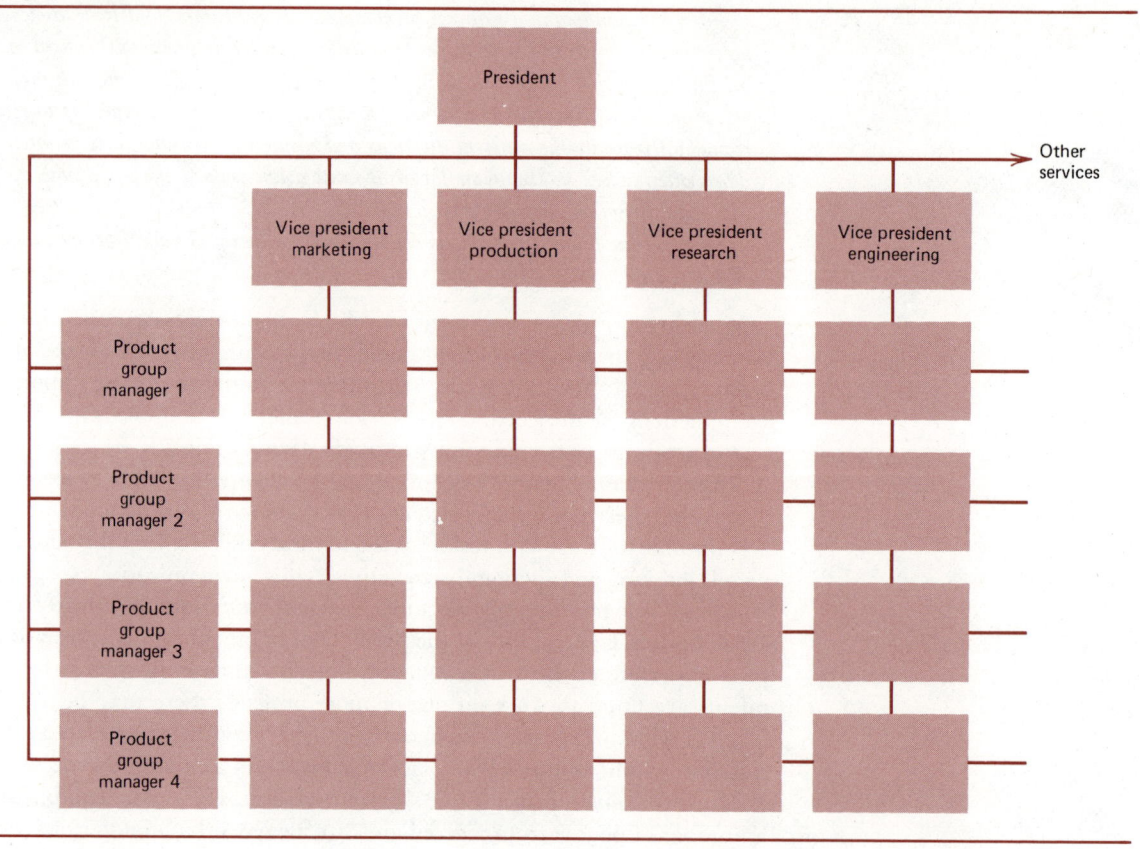

vertical functional divisions have certain tasks to perform for each of the product divisions. Closely related products are grouped together and placed under the jurisdiction of a group manager, who has the authority to see that the functional divisions perform their tasks for his product group in a timely and adequate fashion. The product groups are typically designated as profit centers, and the group manager is held responsible for meeting agreed-on goals. The product manager's job, or brand manager as they are called at General Mills, is considered an excellent middle management laundering job for top executive positions. Other companies that utilize similar key people are Proctor & Gamble and General Foods. At General Mills, product managers start out as marketing assistants after obtaining an M.B.A. degree and usually advance to product manager within three years. They may spend two years on one brand, such as a cereal, two years as manager on an entirely different product such as cake mix or snack food. At most of these companies a product manager is responsible for submitting an annual plan for her brands, based on research of the market and competition, including a total budget, sales forecast, and the creative advertising, pricing, and other marketing strategy necessary to complete it.[28]

Matrix organizations utilizing such functions as the product manager offer several advantages over the traditional or functional organization. First, an organization can maintain its functional expertise, for example, a strong engineering and manufacturing function, while focusing strongly on marketing efforts by product lines development or geographical coverage. This is true because each side of the matrix has quick access to the chief executive officer (CEO). (See Figure 12-3.) Second, the organization can decentralize decision making at the proper level when the appropriate decision can be made. Finally, the information received by the CEO is accurate because it comes through lower levels and is filtered and distributed less.[29]

The matrix organization maintains functional expertise while focusing strongly on the horizontal organization such as by product lines.

The authority of the product group manager will help greatly to achieve the desired teamwork and coordination of effort for a product line; however, the vertical and horizontal flows of authority make a person responsible to two bosses. Dow Corning, which instituted a matrix system in 1967, has attempted to alleviate their problem by making both the functional department head and the product or business manager jointly responsible for performance reviews of individuals, and by providing the business or product manager with a "board of directors" composed of representatives from each of the functional divisions. They rely both on establishing an atmosphere of trust and confidence and on convincing everyone of the worthiness of corporate goals and objectives.[30] This is an excellent example of an attempt to develop healthy life positions within a positive organizational climate, as described in Chapter 8, Organizational and Interpersonal Communications.

Matrix organizations are finding applications in public service and governmental organizations, such as health care facilities. Just as a product often needs a manager to coordinate efforts in the functional departments, so a client in a public health care unit may need one. Bureaucratic institutions usually treat client's problems as distinct and separate entities and process them accordingly. Consider the following hypothetical situation.

The client is an alcoholic. He has not worked for six months and has always had difficulty in holding a steady job. His family is currently on welfare, his wife is known to be psychologically disturbed, and his three children are very slow learners in school. One of the children has been arrested as a juvenile and is currently on probation.[31]

Under the functional or bureaucratic organization, the client would be processed by as many as six different social service agencies, with little if any coordinated effort in caring for him or his family. But a matrix organization

---

[28] Ann M. Morrison, "The General Mills Brand of Managers," *Fortune*, January 12, 1981, pp. 99–103.
[29] Harvey F. Kolodny, "Managing in a Matrix," *Business Horizons*, Vol. 24, No. 2, March/April 1981, p. 19.
[30] L. Gray, "Matrix Organizational Design as a Vehicle for Effective Delivery of Public Health Care and Social Services," *Management International Review*, Vol. 6, 1974, p. 77.
[31] Ibid., p. 78.

established to serve the client and coordinate services would look like the one depicted in Figure 12-4.

The lack of formal structure and the flexible nature of the matrix organization will tend to generate much more conflict than exists in the functional organization.

Although the trend in industry today is toward the matrix organization, recently a number of prominent firms have abandoned it, probably because of the complexity of human relations it required. Kolodny captures this complexity well in the following statement:

> *While the business or product manager has the responsibility for a task, more often than not he or she has less than the required authority to carry it out. Resources are incomplete and must be shared, borrowed, or bargained for. Amongst themselves, product managers compete for capital funds and budget allocations. Functional managers negotiate for preferred people, the best facilities, and the newest equipment. Where the product managers negotiated outcomes are unsatisfactory, they search outside the organization and its constituencies of outsiders (clients, suppliers); as a result, they transact heavily with that external world. The reality of their situations drives them into an extensive network of lateral communication—they have far more horizontal interactions than vertical contacts with their bosses. This is the way that matrix organization's capacity to process large amounts of information manifests itself.*[32]

COLLEGIAL AND FREE-FORM ORGANIZATIONS

Collegial and free form organizations are frequently classed together as a single type, but they are quite different.

The *collegial system*, the main features of which are borrowed from university administration, consists of operating a conventional organization structure in a particular way. It is not so much a difference of structure as it is a different way of managing. The main characteristics are: a loose structure in which the hierarchy is deemphasized; extreme delegation with plural decision centers; a deemphasis of status or titles; extremely free and frequent communications between all offices; a small or lean headquarters staff; and profit centers at low levels in the organization, with individuals held rigidly responsible for results. The theory is that the extra amount of real participation will capture the imagination and enthusiasm of all individuals, but especially the middle managers, who frequently feel left out.

The collegial organization, utilizes a loose structure, extreme delegation, and free and open communications.

The *free-form* organization is more of a prediction for the future by some behavioral scientists than a present reality. Objecting to the rigidities of the bureaucratic organizations, these individuals visualize the organization of the future as having a structure that will be in a continual state of flux. Much of the work of the organization will be accomplished by small ad hoc groups or task forces composed of a necessary mix of skills or knowledge to deal with a particular problem or function. When the work has been accomplished, the group will

---

[32] Kolodny, "Managing a Matrix," op. cit. See also Thomas J. Peters, "Beyond the Matrix Organization," *Business Horizons*, October, 1979, pp. 15–27.

FIGURE 12-4

Social Service and Public Health Matrix

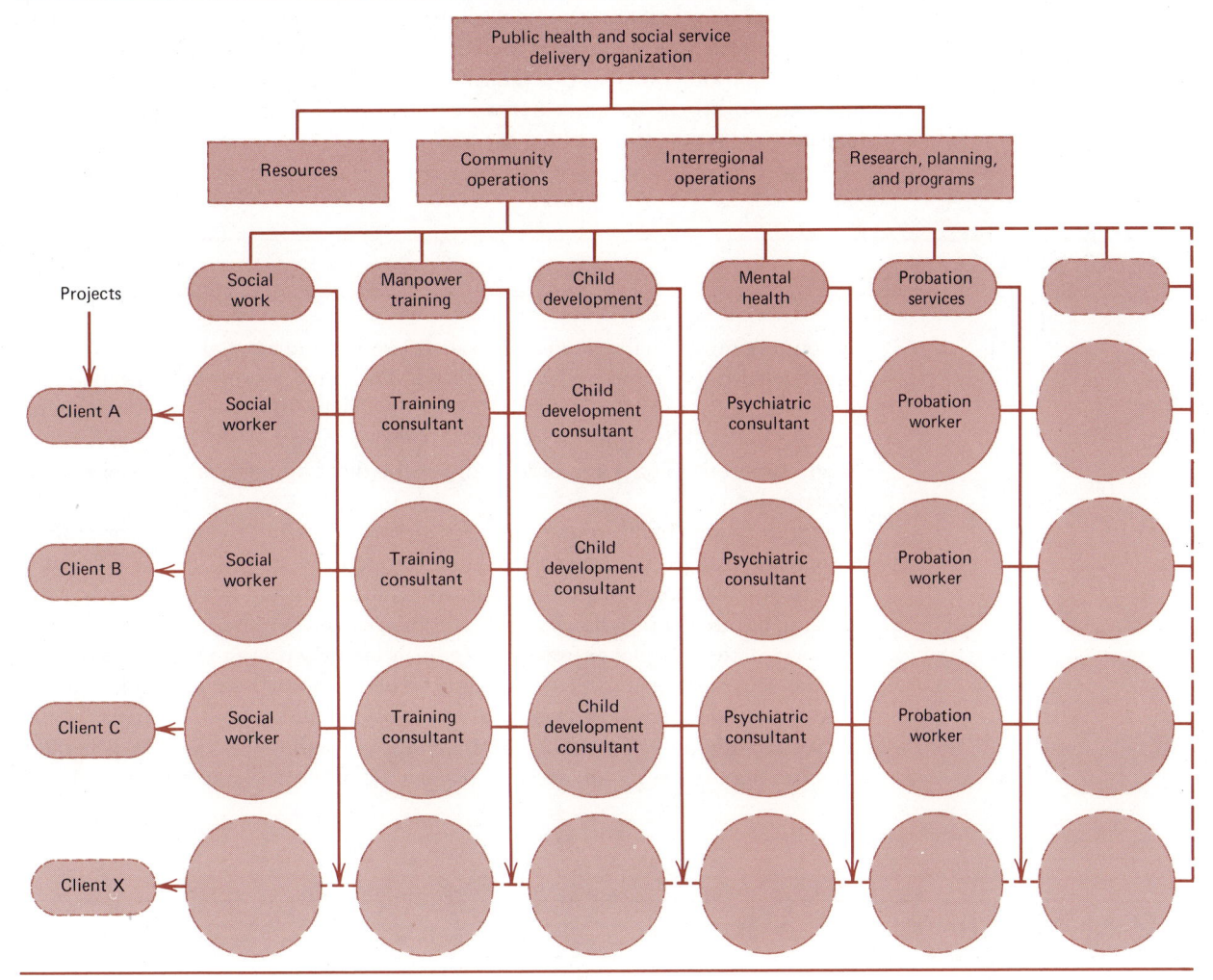

Source: J. L. Gray, "Matrix Organizational Design as a Vehicle for Effective Delivery of Public Health Care and Social Services," *Management International Review,* Vol. 6, 1974, p. 80.

dissolve, with the individuals moving on to different groups. This assumes—or requires—free movement of individuals within the organization. The presumptions are that the abilities of the individual will be utilized to the fullest possible degree and that the organization will become more and more responsive and innovative. Such a work environment would be challenging, exciting, and satisfying to the individual, according to these prognosticators. This organization may be built around relationships, often incorporates profit decentralization, and, in a few cases, could foreseeably be built around the design logic of decision.

In summary, there is no concept of organizational structure that is necessarily best for all situations. As pointed out originally, the structure and approach to management must fit the situation at hand.

The summary chart presents a continuum of organizational patterns showing the design principle and logic of each of the organizational structures. Across the bottom of the diagram is a scale indicating the mechanical-organic dimensions of these organizational structures. Some writers predict that the forms to the right may be used more extensively in the future.

SUMMARY

No one organizational structure will satisfy every organizing task. A contingency approach to organizing must be utilized. The more established, mechanistic organizations—especially corporations with stable product lines—will be able to operate successfully with the functional principle on a bureaucratic basis. Most large corporations have removed many of the disadvantages of bureaucracy by decentralizing.

Organizations built around the work or task often find the matrix or project organization to be more beneficial than a functional design. This is especially true in organizations or subunits of organizations requiring close teamwork of an organic nature. In rapidly changing environments where relationships are very important, the collegial or free form organization may prove to be more effective.

The new organization structures tend to be more adaptive to change than is true of the older ones. The price paid for flexibility and loose structure is that of increasing amounts of conflict and uncertainty. Dealing with conflict generally requires mature employees and effective conflct resolution methodology.

SUMMARY CHART

A Continuum of Organizational Patterns Arranged by Design Principle and Logic

Design principle	Functional		Team	System	
Organizational structures	Bureaucratic	Decentralized Profit decentralization	Matrix project	Collegial Free form	
Design logic	Work	Results	Work Results	Relationship	Decision

Mechanical   **Organic**

DISCUSSION QUESTIONS

1. To what do the concepts of differentiation and integration refer? Explain why differentiation is increasing in organizations. Why does this make integration more difficult?
2. Explain how technology and environment influence organization structure.
3. Why is the functional organization losing its attraction? Discuss its disadvantages.
4. Would you prefer to work in a project, a matrix organization or a decentralized functional organization? Discuss the advantages of each.
5. What type of organization would most likely be used for each of the following? Use your knowledge of design principles and design logic.
   (a.) The manufacturer of an automobile.
   (b.) A petroleum firm.
   (c.) A hospital.
   (d.) A research hospital.
   (e.) The organization that put a rocket on Mars.
   (f.) A management consulting firm dealing with new product development.
   (g.) A Democratic or Republican party organization.
6. Discuss the principle features and logic behind each of the following types of organization: project, matrix, collegial, and free form.

APPLICATION EXERCISES AND CASES

FREE-FORM CHAOS[33]

Chuck Garver, executive vice president of Babbs Manufacturing Company, was in the middle of his presentation, when Barry Sitig, head of manufacturing, entered the conference room. Barry took a chair at the back, hoping that he was not too late to catch the gist of what Chuck had to say. Chuck paused for a minute and then continued.

"Thus, if we were to sum up our operations, it would be accurate to say that we have a group of young, dynamic managers. In addition, we are competing in an industry that demands quick reaction time. If our competitors come out with a new product, we have to be able to respond with the counterproduct almost immediately. The company that can't adapt to, or move with, the market in this industry is through. This brings me to my main point. For the last ten years we have used a product form of departmentation. However, I think it's time we

---

[33]William F. Glueck and Lawrence R. Jauch, *The Managerial Experience: Cases, Exercises, and Readings,* Hinsdale, Ill., The Dryden Press, 1977.

started looking for a different structure. I think we should consider switching to a free-form organization. Xerox, American Standard, and IBM, among others, use this approach. The free-form structure has, generally, no more than a half dozen divisional units, and this would mean a reduction from our current number of nine. However, it offers many important contributions that are not available with our present structure. First, each unit is encouraged to plan its own operations by identifying, evaluating, and determining its own objectives. Central headquarters then analyzes this plan to see if it is in line with overall company plans. If it is not, it is revised in light of total enterprise commitments and objectives. In addition, all resources are controlled by the central management, which allocates them on the basis of priority. Thus, there is high decentralization of operations but effective centralized control. Top management is given an opportunity to utilize synergistic interconnections to improve overall corporate performance."

As Chuck continued with his report, elaborating upon the free-form organization, Barry felt he had heard enough. How, he wondered, can such an organization be of greater benefit than the present product organization structure? Furthermore, he asked himself, is a free-form organization really more flexible than the current structure, or is this nothing more than free-form chaos? To Barry, somehow, the proposed reorganization just did not seem to have much in the way of relative merits when compared to the present one.

Questions

1. Is Barry right in tuning out Chuck, or is he overlooking a chance to pick up some useful information?
2. What are the advantages of a "free-form" organization as opposed to the product form of structure now used?
3. Are there any undesirable features of the proposed structure?

THE OFFICE OF THE PRESIDENT[34]

Irving Bacon is the 55-year-old president of Electro Products Company, a firm manufacturing a broad line of small electrical appliances sold primarily for household use. During fiscal 1971, the company's sales volume amounted to approximately $75 million. Sales have increased each year, and the net earnings have been most satisfactory to management and the board of directors. The following officers report to Mr. Bacon: Mr. Powers, vice-president for production; Mr. Schiller, vice-president for marketing; Mr. Findley, vice-president for finance; the director of personnel relations; and the director of research and development.

Mr. Bacon, who has been president of the company for ten years, recently read in some business magazines that several large companies have abolished the president's position and have instituted an "office of the president" shared by

---

[34]Theo Haimann and William G. Scott, *Management in the Modern Organization*, 2nd ed., Boston, Houghton Mifflin Co., 1974, p. 251.

several—perhaps three—officers. Under this plan, each co-president has the authority to make any decision that is brought to the presidential office; each must support every decision made by his copresidents; and each must keep the others informed.

Mr. Bacon called a meeting with the five officers previously mentioned to discuss the feasibility of implementing this idea at Electro Products. He emphasized that his presidential task was becoming increasingly burdensome, especially since the company had entered international markets and was being pressured by new environmental factors and social responsibilities. He stated that he, of course, intended to remain as one of the three members of the president's office.

Questions
1. How would you respond to such a proposal? Explain your reaction.
2. Suggest one alternative form of organization Mr. Bacon might consider. Explain how it would operate and its potential advantages and disadvantages.

PART THREE

CASES

KENTOWN CORPORATION[35]

Leo Simpson received a lot of publicity concerning his management of Kentown Corporation's plant in Barnardsville, North Carolina. Simpon's management style ("I'm willing to try almost anything . . . as long as it pays off") helped boost Kentown from a bottom ranking in the Kenrose Corporation Division to number one in production in just a matter of months.

The small unincorporated town of Barnardsville (population 350) is located in the mountains of western North Carolina, about 15 miles from Asheville. When Simpson took over as plant manager, the Kentown plant was eleven years old. It was a combination of the old and the new. The administrative offices and factory outlet store were located in the old part of the plant, which was once a grammar school. The sewing machines and other equipment were located in the spacious, well-lighted, newer portion of the plant. Kentown was one of six plants in the Kenrose Division of Genesco Corporation. The plant manufactured women's ready-to-wear apparel, dresses, pantsuits, sportswear, and robes, part under its own label and part under contract work for other outlets.

In addition to Simpson, the plant staff included Mrs. Inez Payne, assistant manager; David McDonald, plant engineer; and a secretary/receptionist. The plant was organized into six or seven *Manufacturing Sections* (depending on products in process). Each section had twenty-eight to thirty-two operators who worked on sewing machines and related equipment. Each section was managed by a supervisor, who planned the work and followed its progress through the section. A service girl supplied operators with work materials.

After a manufacturing section finished a batch of garments, they were forwarded to the supervisor of the *Finishing Department*. The finishing department completed extra hemming, buttonholing, or special stitching. The work was then forwarded to the *Pressing Department*, where the materials were pressed, put on hangers, and prepared for shipping. Trucks picked up boxed materials each night and transported them to a central distributing facility.

Leo described his experience at Kentown:

I grew up with the business. My dad was in the textile business for 42 years, primarily at Beaver shirt division of Blue Bell, Inc. I worked there part time and summertime doing a little bit of everything. When I went to college, I changed from pre-med to business during the last semester of General college at the University of North Carolina. I graduated from the business school in 1960 with a triple major in Accounting, Industrial Management and Personnel Management. I went into the Army, finally retiring from the reserve in 1968 with the rank of First Lieutenant. I went to work for my Dad's firm and went into an industrial training program.

I left Blue Bell and went into an Industrial Engineering position in Simpson county, North Carolina at the age of 32 years. Within three months I was offered the plant manager's job with the same company. I stayed eight years with that company, got to be a general manager over three plants and a warehouse.

I had a friend who worked as personnel director for the Kenrose Company. He knew of a plant they were having a

---

[35] This case was prepared by Robert R. Bell of Tennessee Tech University. This case is designed to be used as the basis for classroom discussion rather than to illustrate either effective or ineffective administrative behavior.

hell of a time with. He thought I might be interested in trying to turn the plant around. He wanted me to know "You might only be there for six months if you can't get it turned around."

There was a Northeastern fellow running the Kenrose plant—he just couldn't relate to the local people somehow. I decided to try it, and we moved to Asheville, North Carolina, in 1970 and took over the plant. Kenrose had purchased the plant in 1967 or 1968. When they went in, the people just didn't want to work in a plant environment. Kenrose went to all types of expense to get people to work in the plant which fit into the foothills of the Smokies at the foot of Mt. Mitchell.

The plant had a work force of 150 people when I started. These people just didn't have factory work in their minds. They weren't industrialized; they didn't have many plants in the area. The people hunted a little, fished a little, and raised a little tobacco. They didn't have a lot of money, but they didn't need a lot. They were very clannish, close to Mamma and Daddy.

They really aren't backward people. I found out early that they were proud of themselves and of what they could do. If you told them you didn't like what they were doing, you just didn't see them at work the next day. I remember that right after I took over as plant manager, I had an interview with a little girl. She was making about 25 percent efficiency on her machine. I talked with her about her problems and tried to find out why she wasn't more productive. She didn't show up for work the next day. In fact, she didn't show up again. Some of the other girls on the line reported that her husband had said, "You don't need to work if he's going to talk to you like a dog." I even went out to visit that girl at her house, to try to talk her into coming back. She still wouldn't come back to work.

I learned that you had to use positive approaches rather than negative approaches. You also had to let them know where you were coming from. Within a couple of months, they had accepted me as a person. They knew I wasn't going to eat them up. I could critique them in a joking sort of way.

Over the years, I tried a lot of things to make mundane, repetitious jobs more interesting. For example, when we had problems with daily absenteeism in the plant, we came out with a catalog which had "same-cost" items in it. We distributed the catalogs throughout the plant, and told the girls we were going to have daily drawings. We put all the workers' names in a big barrel. Then sometime in the morning I'd get on the public address system and say, "Hold it everybody, time for another drawing." And I'd draw somebody's name. At the start of the program, I'd first draw somebody's name that I knew was absent that day. The girls knew I was playing a game, but they also knew that somebody who was at work would get their choice of something from that catalog. Near Thanksgiving we'd have drawings for turkeys.

The thing that has received the most publicity, though, is the music program we started at Kentown. I had learned about the psychology of background music during my studies at UNC, so we had installed a music system in the plant. We had been playing bland, soothing instrumental stuff, nothing to distract the workers. One day a few girls came to me and said, "Couldn't we hear Conway Twitty instead of this Muzak stuff?" I jokingly responded, "I can't afford to have you get any slower." One of the younger girls said, "Look, how about if we do better if we have country music? Would you install it then?" I said, "Yeah, I might give it a try." It was a union plant. Word got around through the union that "He'll play better music if we start doing better."

We decided to try it. Right away we saw an upsurge in production. Freddy Fender's "Easy Loving" was their favorite song. I acted like a cheerleader over the PA system in the plant, saying things like, "As long as you keep coming up, we'll keep playing the country." "If you do bad, we'll bring back the orchestras!" That's the way it kind of grew.

A little later we had a series of staff meetings, and we sort of "formally" decided to use the positive motivation approach in the plant. We had discussed that the women responded to what industrial psychologists would call "recognition for work well done." We felt that money alone would not motivate the women. But a combination of recognition, prizes, bigger paychecks, and commitment on their part should make higher productivity.

The plant staff felt that if we got the girls to say they would do something, they would usually follow through and do it, so we started with some individual recognition. We tried to develop things aimed at the individual. We had a Polaroid camera and we took pictures of the most productive workers. The first "prize" we gave was a rose we put on the machine of every girl who had the productivity goal we set for her.

We had an engineer and two time-study girls that really tried to keep this recognition thing going. It seemed to work well, and we decided to try to set unit type goals as well as individual type goals. We came up with a board—a big piece of plywood. On this board went unit names. Each of the unit names had the supervisor's name on it (Christine's Champs; Judy's Jets; Rita's Rebels). The board spelled out the goals the unit was shooting for and the previous day's average. The board had three lights on the top of it. Red lights on the board indicated that the section was not doing well. A green light indicated that the unit's production goal had been reached, and a gold light meant that the section was producing at a rate of over 100 percent.

The girls took real pride in their accomplishments. We went to K-Mart and got an agreement with them on some small appliances. We gave away percolators, frying pans, anything that the girls could take home with them and use and show our recognition for their work. We played that game as long as we could. When we failed to get too much more out of a particular game, we'd see that we needed to move to something else. After several months of the recognition program, we were at 75 to 80 percent efficiency and the company was really happy with us.

At the time, Kenrose's best plant was averaging 86 percent. I had to go to Roanoke every month for staff meetings of all plant managers. One day in a meeting with the girls, I said, "You girls would really make me happy if I could go to Roanoke and say, 'The black sheep is heading the list.'" One of the girls said, "The company used to talk about a big, nice picnic for us. Why don't you see if we can do it?" My response was that things like picnics come out of profits, and we were just getting to where we could think about profit. But I said, "If you hit 87 percent efficiency, we'll do it."

Well, the girls really got into the picnic idea. We set a date to do it sometime in June. We had them participate in every aspect of the planning. We had entertainment committees, a committee to judge the best cakes, and had everyone in the plant involved in some way. We had committees for children's games, committees to conduct plant tours, etc. We hit 87 percent several weeks before the picnic.

As it turned out, it really wasn't a plant picnic. It turned into a whole community affair. We had about 300 workers in the plant. I told them to invite whomever they wanted to invite to the picnic. Over 1000 people showed up.

It was unbelievable what they had lined up for the picnic—mostly for free. For example, we had a battle of the bands. We got several bands to come in to play during the day, and some of the girls had talked local merchants into donating prizes to give away to the best band. One band was from the local prison, and those prisoners won the battle of the bands. I remember I was sitting around a picnic table with Dave McDonald, the plant engineer and with several of the employees. The prison band was playing and the atmosphere was really getting good. One of the girls asked, "What do we have to do to get a steak dinner for everybody?" I replied, "When you hit 95 percent, we'll have us a steak dinner." Another girl, really turned on by the music, said, "If you'll get that band to play for us, we'll show you how to hit 95 percent."

I told them I didn't know about bringing a live band into the plant to play for them while they were sewing. I was afraid they might get so interested in the band that they wouldn't get their work out. I got to looking into it and called the prison to see if we could get the band. For some reason they wouldn't let the prisoners come to the plant to play. So I called local disc jockey, Quinton Ramsey. He knew of a band and I told him that we wanted him and the band to come into the plant and play for us all day long on a Friday.

On the first Friday the band was supposed to show up at 7:30. Nobody came. About 9:00, Quinton Ramsey showed up alone. He said there had been a problem and the band would be a few hours late. Since he was a disc jockey, he suggested that we play records while we waited for the band. But we didn't have a record player. So I sent David McDonald to my house to pick up my little girl's record player. When he got back, we put the speaker for the record player in front of the microphone for the public addrees system. That's how it all started. Once it got going, it was like a three-ring circus. We gave him production figures to "broadcast" every hour, and he gave out prizes every hour. He kept up a continual chatter when the music wasn't playing . . . just like a radio show. He'd take the microphone away from the speaker and say things like, "O. K., this is for Janet in Unit 5," or "this one's going out to the girls in Unit 6." He'd really get after them: "Unit 4, I've been giving out prizes to everybody but you. What's the matter with you people?" When the band finally did *arrive, it was sort of anticlimactic. But we had seen what Quinton Ramsey could do. The girls on the production lines loved it.*

From that point on, we did a disc jockey show every Friday for the next two and one-half years. Sometimes we'd have a "mystery man," sometimes a local TV personality, to do the show. Sometimes we'd have a battle of the DJs, divide the plant up and see who could get the most productivity.

We've gotten quite a bit of notoriety out of all of this. ABC News came down one week and messed up our production for two or three days. They interviewed everybody and filmed everybody in the plant. Eventually they put together about a seven-minute program for part of a news documentary.

The highest average plant productivity we've ever reached was 132 percent. The plant had held a 125 percent average for over two years. In order to keep it going, to help keep the glimmer, we have to keep adding little things to it. Mostly, though, it has been things that came from within the girls. They were so proud that they could perform. They really enjoy being the number one plant in the company . . . and they enjoy working at the plant. A typical comment might be, "Yeah, I work over there . . . we have a good time over there!"

These things have never been tried in any of our other plants. I think it's something that has to come from within. These are good people. I'm really wondering what I should do next.

Questions

1. Comment on Leo Simpson's communicative abilities. Does he understand the importance of listening? What hurdles did he have to overcome in the early days of his work with the Kentown plant?
2. At what level of Maslow's need hierarchy are the women in the Kentown plant presently working? At what level were they working when Leo took over the plant?
3. How would you best describe Leo's motivational techniques at Kentown? Have they changed over time? Explain.
4. Could any of the changes at Kentown be described as job enrichment? Job enlargement? Discuss.
5. Is the Kentown plant composed of more or less cohesive groups than before Leo began as manager? Why? What major conditions influencing groups have changed?

THE CREATIVE ORGANIZATION— A JAPANESE EXPERIMENT[36]

Starting virtually from scratch, Sony Corporation had grown into a company of 5000 employees within the short span of fifteen years when the author became manager of its Atsugi plant in 1961. A company almost always reaches a turning point after its rapid early development, because the very quality of vitality that enabled it to grow has a tendency to be weakened as increasingly larger numbers of people are employed. Those who joined during the start-up period were fighters, who staked their future on a company that might turn out to be a failure or a success, but those who come in after the company is solidly established are inclined to "ride" with it, counting on the stability it has achieved.

Moreover, as a rule when a firm grows in size, it increasingly demands a well-defined organization structure, but Sony has always been opposed to a rigid structure, preferring to be a stage on which people, uncoerced, could display their talents for creativity and independent activity. This freedom assured Sony

---

[36]From Shigeru Kobayashi, "The Creative Organization—A Japanese Experiment," *Personnel*, November-December 1970, reprinted by permission.

of its initial dynamism and flexibility; as it grew, though, it could no longer maintain control without any form of organization, and the result was the establishment of departments, sections, subsections, and what-not, all leading to smaller and smaller subdivisions and to a management hierarchy of department managers, section chiefs, subsection chiefs, and so on, with detailed rules and regulations for all jobs.

CHANGING THE POWER STRUCTURE

Here I shall describe, first, how we set about breaking down the concept of organization as a means of ensuring authority and power.

Our plant organization comprises the crew (at the lowest level), which has about six members; the group, which includes several crews; the section, which includes several groups; and the department, which includes several sections. The first difficulty arose in connection with the titles given to the individuals in charge of these various units. Department superior (*ka-choh* in Japanese), section superior (*kakari-choh*), group supervisor (*kumi-choh*), and crew supervisor (*han-choh*) all reminded both managers and workers of the old superior-subordinate relationship. We therefore decided to discontinue the use of the suffix *choh*, meaning superior, head, or chief. The department superior and section superior were to be called simply manager (*shunin*). We also decided to use the English words for titles—for instance, leader, in the case of the crew, and chief, in the case of the group. In addition, we encouraged people to address a man with a managerial position not as Mr. Department Manager, for example, but simply by his last name.

PARTICIPATIVE DECISION MAKING

The organization climate in which people must be accorded status because they are "somebody" and are expected to exercise the authority of their position to use people was gradually eliminated. But how are managers to do their jobs if they are not to use people to get the work out? I believe they should *assist* people to carry out the necessary tasks voluntarily. When managers use people to do their jobs, orders are called for, but when managers assume a role in which they assist people, they need only explain the general situation and the relevant policies. Then all they have to do is teach people how to act.

The worst kind of manager is the one who blames his people in case of fiasco, yet who wants to exercise his power and authority by taking credit for their success.

"THE RULE IS EVERYTHING"

Almost as damaging as the concept justifying managers' using their men is the one that makes manuals and rules all-important. In Japanese companies one often finds a kind of thinking that defines organizing as drawing up detailed charts, precise job descriptions, and careful statements of job authority. Employees who don't obey such rules and regulations to the letter are regarded as organization dropouts.

Nothing could be sillier. Rules and regulations are stipulated to aid efficient administration under a certain set of prevailing conditions. Even if we could arrive at perfect rules and regulations, some of them would almost immediately be made impractical by the inexorable change of circumstances.

DEFINING JOB DUTIES

Texas Instruments Incorporated maintains a highly commendable position on rules and regulations. On an annual basis, managers define their own duties to best serve the company's interest under the generally prevailing conditions. Therefore, their statements of job duties are not static but are reviewed, revised, and adjusted as the need arises, depending on the requirements of the company during a particular fiscal year. By coincidence, we at Sony follow exactly the same practice.

As was mentioned earlier, during the initial phase of management innovation in our plant, we decided that small-group organization was necessary to motivate people and ensure voluntary action on their part and to enable every member to strive for the achievement of common goals. We began by breaking down production functions on the basis of crews—teams made up of two to a maximum of twenty people. Those who work in the same process in the manufacture of transistors are grouped together, and we may have one, two, or even three crews, depending on the number of workers in a process.

SECRET OF SMALL-GROUP SUCCESS

What is the difference between such a team and the equivalent unit in the traditional organization? First, the leaders of our teams are not supervisors who get the work out by using subordinates. Most of the leaders in our plant are girls 18 to 19 years old; there is practically no age difference between leaders and operators, although we also have some older housewives in the ranks of both leaders and operators. Since our leaders are free of status-consciousness, they assume and resign leadership quite freely.

Until the crew system was established, the first-line supervisors—called group chiefs—had managed every process in the plant. Under the new setup, however, the crews were created within the old groupings and each was assigned to a single work process. Operators in each crew selected a leader from among themselves. The initial task of the crews was to record and control attendance after time clocks were taken out. With such an important control function delegated to the crews, the result was an immediate demonstration of teamwork. Autonomous checking and control over attendance led naturally to autonomy in production control at crew level.

Second, it should be kept in mind that a team is managed chiefly through meetings of its members. Herein lies the basic difference between the team and the traditional work group, in which superiors give instructions individually to their subordinates without holding any meetings.

Rensis Likert writes in his *New Patterns of Management* that management will make full use of the potential capabilities of its human resources only when each person in an organization is a member of one or more effectively functioning work groups that have a high degree of group loyalty, effective skills of interaction, and high performance goals.

All our experience testifies to the truth of what he says. The large, traditional organization fails to take advantage of the aggregate power of small groups that enables them to deliver superior performance, sometimes exceeding the most optimistic hopes.

LINKING OF TEAMS

It is our goal to reach the point where the full range of our activity is based on teamwork. Each team is necessarily small in size, whereas the plant is large, but we resolved this conflict with the establishment of a cell type of organization, linking small teams with each other, as in a living organism, to make up a single larger body. This structuring did not call for any changes in the way the plant was then organized—the various groupings could remain as they were, and so could the managers at the various levels. The only things that had to be changed were management style and management attitudes.

First, the monthly meeting—in which it is intended that every manager participate—clearly brought out the management style and attitudes of the plant manager, an opponent of power-consciousness. Gradually, then, the new climate came to be understood and percolated down through the entire plant with the help of talks, the way in which those talks were handled, and a succession of new policies implemented one by one. Everybody came to welcome the feeling that grew out of working in an atmosphere of mutual trust, as exemplified by the elimination of time clocks and the introduction of a cafeteria without attendants.

Then there was our practice of holding a meeting for the department managers every morning. Any matters pertaining to the plant as a whole were reported and discussed in this meeting and the resulting decisions were then implemented. The participants—the plant manager and the entire department manager group—formed a team in themselves. Thus, the top team was formed simultaneously with the teams at lower levels, and these teams at the top and bottom led to the formation of intermediary teams, like a chain reaction.

With the number of plant employees exceeding 3000, the number of departments standing at 20-odd, and our lines of business diversified, we seemed to have reached a stage where we could no longer manage and control our affairs unless we established divisions, but I was reluctant to increase the layers of management. We solved the problem by dividing the weekly morning meeting into four sessions; general meeting, meeting for general affairs, meeting for semiconductors, and meeting for calculators.

As a result of all this, from the plant manager down no one is involved in more than three layers of meetings. Communications have thereby been reduced proportionately, but the results show that the merits of the new arrangement far outweigh its drawbacks.

THE PAIR SYSTEM

To return to organization by teams, an important role in team development is played by our pair system, a combination of two workers whose relations on the job are like those of a man and his wife in the Japanese home. The fundamental difference between team formation (including the pair system) and the authoritarian, directive type of organization lies in the fact that the latter results in human relations based on the ruler-and-ruled dichotomy, whereas the former bases human relations on partnership. In this partnership one member, it is true, is the leader and the other is a follower, but this is not the relationship between the ruler and the ruled.

A pair must necessarily be composed of two individuals with different characteristics. Man and women, teacher and pupil, senior worker and junior worker, worker on the morning shift and worker on the afternoon shift, manager and secretary, scientist and technician, two professionals with different academic disciplines and skills, two men with different personalities—all lend themselves to pair formation. The requirements are that the two individuals be heterogeneous, that they be performing the same job to achieve an identical goal, and that they assume responsibility for their work.

COMMUNICATIONS SUPPORT

Most important to organization by team is reliable information, since the employees are not individually directed or commanded to perform tasks expected of them. Each team member does his own sizing up of a given situation, makes his decision, and takes action in accordance with the facts. Obviously, unless each member understands the information that comes to him from above, below, and around him, the sum total of the action will not be properly coordinated.

Communication that supports the team type of organization depends not only on providing access to information, but also on an atmosphere of mutual respect. No one will take communication seriously if it comes from a person whom he holds in contempt, and vice versa. Nor will communication serve to establish reliable information unless both parties are free from prejudice and favoritism.

At Sony we have formal reports presented at weekly meetings, monthly reports by all personnel above the level of leader, and published media, including a *Management Memo* and companywide magazines, *Sony News*, published monthly, and *Weekly Reports*. At our Atsugi plant we have *Atsugi Topics*, published every other day, and the monthly *Home News*, directed to employees' families. We also have many publications issued by dormitory residents and by members of various work stations.

However, much depends on the unrestricted flow of information. A case in point is the Sony "Dial 2000." Any Sony employee can dial this number directly and get or give information through the personnel who respond to his call. All are encouraged to "dial 2000" for these purposes:

■ To confirm the validity of rumors being circulated or of "tips" from other employees.

■ To get information on whom to approach about problems having to do with their jobs, to find out more on topics they are concerned about, or to get helpful ideas about certain problems.

■ To get information as to which groups or people within Sony are trying to do or are already doing things they are planning to do in their own jobs.

■ To find out who should receive information, proposals, or opinions that employees think will be helpful to Sony.

In simple terms, each person has access to a source where he can easily obtain the information he needs and discuss it with someone well informed. When it seems appropriate, he can even circumvent his immediate manager, but he has to exercise his judgment and plan a course of action on his own responsibility. And if he does act on the advice of his immediate manager, he cannot and should not be permitted to pass the buck to that manager in the event of failure.

It has become clear to us that organizations supported by free-flowing information and by responsible judgment and actions on the part of every one of their members are lively organizations, without any confusion or chaos to disturb their order. They represent genuinely creative organizations firmly based on effective communication and identification with the company through the self-realization it affords.

Questions

1. Utilizing the material in Chapter 8 analyze and describe the kind of communication environment Sony is attempting to create. Give attention to both interpersonal as well as organizational communication. What specific actions are they taking that lead to effective communications and explain the reasoning behind these actions? What barriers to effective communications are they attempting to avoid and how?
2. After reviewing Chapter 9, Human Motivation, describe in detail the kind of motivational climate Sony seems to be working toward. Specifically, what kind of needs of employees are they working to satisfy? How are they going about this (cite specific actions being taken)? What kind of assumptions regarding employee motivation are they making and do you agree with these assumptions? Discuss the difference between "using" workers and "assisting" them.
3. In Chapter 10 we discussed job design. Summarize the elements of the historical approaches to designing jobs that Sony seems to be trying to avoid or change. What advantages are they seeking to derive from their approach? Set forth the principles and concepts of job design that relate to these principles and concepts.
4. Refer back to the model of group behavior presented in Figure 11-3. Using this model as a basis for discussion, thoroughly analyze the Sony case as presented. In completing your analysis pay attention to not only the major segments of the model but the subelements of each major segment. What other aspects of the dynamics of group behavior are involved in this case?
5. Is Sony truly a creative organization? Why or why not? How do some of the concepts discussed in Chapter 12 apply to this case? Be specific.
6. Since this case was written by an employee with a very positive view of Sony, which elements of Sony do you think are believable and which may tend to be idealized?

PART FOUR
THE MANAGEMENT OF HUMAN RESOURCES

CHAPTER 13
DEVELOPING AN ORGANIZATIONAL AND LEADERSHIP PHILOSOPHY

CHAPTER 14
LEADERSHIP STYLES

CHAPTER 15
HUMAN RESOURCE DEVELOPMENT AND QUALITY OF WORK LIFE

CHAPTER 16
ORGANIZATIONAL DEVELOPMENT

SOUTH PACIFIC HOTEL
JOHN ANDERSON

In Part Three we examined the dynamics of human behavior in organizations. An understanding of those concepts is a prerequisite to the material in this part of the book, which concentrates on effective management of the human assets of the organization. Our overall objective for the next four chapters is to give the reader a comprehensive overview of the key elements of a results-oriented organizational climate.

Chapter 13 lays the groundwork for the remaining three chapters in the unit. It discusses the role and importance of a positive overall organization philosophy and climate as it relates to the human element, presents three alternative views of people and the approach to management they suggest, and establishes the importance of an individual manager's approach to leadership.

Leadership styles is the subject of Chapter 14. The fundamental aspects of several leadership models are explored with respect to construction, their underlying conceptual basis, their operational characteristics, and the impact that various styles of leadership have on motivation and overall organizational effectiveness.

Chapter 15 examines the process of human resource development and quality of work life. The emphasis is on the constructing of a good development plan through performance analysis, appraisal, and counseling.

The final chapter in part 16 investigates the process of changing people and organizations through organizational development techniques. The chapter presents several processes of organizational development.

CHAPTER 13
DEVELOPING AN ORGANIZATIONAL AND LEADERSHIP PHILOSOPHY

CONCEPTS ABOUT PEOPLE AND THE APPROACHES TO MANAGEMENT THEY SUGGEST
THE ECONOMIC PERSON
THE SOCIAL PERSON
THE SELF-FULFILLING PERSON
THE COMPLEX PERSON

ORGANIZATIONAL PHILOSOPHY— A CONCLUDING NOTE

HOW ORGANIZATIONS GET RESULTS THROUGH PEOPLE

THE WORK OF A LEADER
THE FIRST-LINE SUPERVISOR
MIDDLE MANAGEMENT
THE TOP EXECUTIVE

LEADERSHIP SKILLS

THE ACTIVITIES OF SUCCESSFUL LEADERS
MAINTAINING OBJECTIVITY
DELEGATING AUTHORITY AND USE OF PARTICIPATION
PROVIDING SECURITY FOR SUBORDINATES
PROVIDING A REWARD SYSTEM
DEALING WITH INTERPERSONAL CONFLICT
TYPES OF CONFLICT
RESOLVING CONFLICT IN COMPATIBLE SITUATIONS
RESOLVING CONFLICT IN NONCOMPATIBLE SITUATIONS

SOME GENERAL OBSERVATIONS CONCERNING LEADERSHIP

APPLICATION EXERCISES AND CASES
ONE OUT OF THREE
COMMUNICATION AT THE JAMES RIVER PLANT

TO CHECK ON RANKS, A FEW TOP OFFICIALS FAVOR SNEAK ATTACKS[1]

The lanky 63-year-old draws little attention most Sundays as he peddles around the city on a three-speed bicycle, wearing a meter-reader's cap.

But employees of Consolidated Edison Co. have learned that the utility's chairman, Charles Luce, can turn up almost anywhere on his regular thirty- to forty-mile bike trips to inspect work crews: peeking into open manholes in Brooklyn or slipping past security barricades in Queens. The employees "think the old man is kind of nutty, but friendly," Mr. Luce declares.

Sometimes, however, Mr. Luce's excursions aren't so convivial. One recent Sunday he discovered a Con Ed cable truck left running and unattended on Manhattan's Third Avenue. Mr. Luce climbed into the driver's seat and waited. When the driver returned, he got a lecture from the boss and later was suspended from work for a day. "I was obviously unhappy," Mr. Luce says.

Of the different ways captains of industry choose to review their corporate troops, the sneak attack favored by Mr. Luce is easily the most controversial. For some employes, it also can be the most costly.

Consider the New Jersey supermarket cashier a few years ago whose customer politely pointed out that she had forgotten to ring up a jar of jelly. "Just take it," the cashier said to the customer, who turned out to be the company's president. She was fired.

Unacceptable as the cashier's behavior might be, those who study management techniques think top executives who habitually make surprise tours often act just as capriciously. "The leader's job isn't to show authority when he visits the boondocks," says Eugene Jennings, a consultant and management professor at Michigan State University, "That's what he pays managers for. A knee-jerk reaction is typical of the chief executive who goes out and meets with the employees."

Mr. Luce doesn't see it that way. He says he never takes punitive action on the spot but waits until Monday to tell managers of any transgressions uncovered during his bike outings. Disciplinary decisions are left to the managers, he says. "It would be a great mistake for me to start issuing orders. It would undermine the foremen."

---

[1] Jeffrey H. Birnbaum, "To Check on Ranks, A Few Top Officials Favor Sneak Attacks," *Wall Street Journal*, June 25, 1981.

In this and the next three chapters we will concentrate on how to manage the human element in organizations, particularly the leadership function.

In managing people to obtain maximum results, there are three significant objectives, summarized as follows.

1. To improve the performance of employees on their present jobs.
2. To prepare employees to accept increasing responsibility in their present jobs.
3. To help employees grow and develop so that they may attain higher level jobs.

None of these will occur without sufficient *initiative and desire* on the part of employees. People must be motivated to want to grow and develop both in their present jobs and in the future.

Thus, the key to productivity is securing individual job performance and the key to securing job performance is eliciting motivation. This is the challenge that faces management—to motivate people toward maximum levels of productivity. These connecting links can be diagrammed as follows.

The key to productivity is securing individual job performance, which depends on eliciting motivation.

Maximum Productivity—depends on—Individual Job Performance—depends on—Individual Motivation

There are two ingredients of a proper motivational climate. First is the overall philosophy and image that the organization presents and which serves as a guideline for dealing with people. It consists of the underlying assumptions about people that form the basis for dealing with them. The second important aspect of generating proper motivational climate is the personal approach to leadership exhibited by the managers of the organization. In this chapter we explore some alternative concepts about people and the overall organizational philosophy and climate they suggest. Then we look at some of the important activities of leaders.

The two ingredients of a motivational climate are the philosophy of the organization and the manager's leadership.

CONCEPTS ABOUT PEOPLE AND THE APPROACHES TO MANAGEMENT THEY SUGGEST

Figure 13-1 depicts the assumptions, the approaches to management they suggest, and the results achieved by three alternative ways of viewing the basic nature of people. In examining Figure 13-1, it should be apparent to the reader that any one of the assumptions represent a restricted view of the situation, and therefore eventually falls short of producing a climate conducive to achieving maximum results through people.

THE ECONOMIC PERSON

This concept fails because it relies so heavily on the wage and related economic incentives. People do not live by bread alone. Although it is true that economic incentives can motivate performance up to a point, that point is usually far short of the maximum level possible. With money you can buy a person's time and you can also buy a certain amount of physical activity, but you cannot buy dedication, commitment, loyalty, respect, or the desire to excel. These must be earned by providing the opportunity for satisfying all the many other needs.

You cannot buy dedication, commitment, loyalty, respect, or the desire to excel.

THE SOCIAL PERSON

This concept is equally ineffective because it is superficial. The approach to management that it suggests is based too heavily on artificial niceties rather than concrete positive human relationships. In addition, research has pointed out that a happy, contented, and satisfied employee is not necessarily a productive one.

FIGURE 13-1

Concepts of People and the Approaches to Management They Suggest

	Economic Person	*Social Person*	*Self-fulfilling Person*	*Complex Person*
Assumptions about people	Primary motivation is money and long-range economic security. Continual promise of and possibility of successfully higher wage will motivate increased effort to earn that wage.	Positive social relations and interaction are a must. Within the work environment he seeks an affinity with fellow employees. Assuming this exists, he will respond with effort on the job.	People are self-fulfilling in that they seek achievement, accomplishment, and meaning in what they do. Said another way, a feeling of significance and importance.	People are complex and any single theory or set of assumptions about their natures will be deficient. We cannot compartmentalize people or fit everyone into a neat package.
Approach to management suggested	Reliance on economic factors to attract, keep, and motivate employees. These factors are primary. Either the promise of higher wages or the threat to withhold a potential increase can lead to motivation.	Creation of a climate where big, happy family atmosphere prevails. Manager goes out of his way to eliminate or forestall any type of interpersonal conflict. Heavy promotion and support for group atmosphere.	The premium here is on a flexible environment where the work climate permits the individual a certain degree of freedom. Fitting people to the right job is strategic.	Neither the organization nor the individual manager can rely on any single approach to management to insure a motivation-producing climate. A balanced approach is based on a comprehensive view of people.
Results	Although money is a strategic aspect of motivating job performance it only goes so far. Beyond that point there must be more to a job than a paycheck if high levels of commitment are to be achieved.	Contentedness or satisfaction and productivity do not necessarily go hand in hand. In fact, people can be so happy and contented that they do not want to do any work.	Implies a peculiar kind of motivation which all people do not respond to for one reason or another, for example, they may prefer to satisfy these needs in off-the-job activities.	A well-conceived balanced management climate which places overall emphasis on positive management practices will hold the best long-range potential for appealing to a majority of employees.

Source: Edgar H. Schein, *Organizational Psychology*, Englewood Cliffs, N.J., Prentice-Hall, 1970.

THE SELF-FULFILLING PERSON

The principles and concepts underlying the self-fulfilling person concept are more sound than the other two. But, it presupposes that the motivators being emphasized are powerful enough in all people to elicit the same response. This is an overgeneralization. The degree to which various factors act as motivators vary in type and intensity between people. Many people would prefer to satisfy their needs by off-the-job activities. They do not look to work itself as the be-all and end-all of their need satisfaction.

A second factor is the tendency to interpret self-fulfillment as meaning that everyone wants to rise to the pinnacle of his profession, that is, to continually climb the proverbial ladder of success. According to this line of reasoning, all salespeople eventually want to become the district or regional manager, all operative employees want to become supervisors, all engineers technical administrators, and so forth. Such does not appear to be the case.

Following this approach, organizations created a climate where a person must continue to be willing to move up to avoid having a stigma attached to him or her.

Properly interpreted, if self-fulfillment needs are to be used as motivators it means that people must have the opportunity to find their own niche, that is, to do that which they want and enjoy doing in a climate that is encouraging and conducive to growth and personal motivation.

THE COMPLEX PERSON

The complex person concept is essentially a combination of all of the others. It recognizes that any attempt at generalization usually falls short of the mark and leads to a management approach which, for one reason or another, is restricted in its effectiveness. The situation is adequately summed up by the following.

People are complex and no single set of assumptions about all people is sufficient base to build a leadership climate.

> *Not only is he complex within himself, being possessed of many needs and potentials, but he is also likely to differ from his neighbor in the patterns of his own complexity. It has always been difficult to generalize about man, and it is becoming more difficult as society and organizations within society are themselves becoming more complex and differentiated.*[2]

Beyond the overall organizational climate, there are also important implications for the individual manager. Schein has summarized this aspect as follows.

> *Perhaps the most important implication is that the successful manager must be a good diagnostician and must value a spirit of inquiry. If the abilities and motives of the people under him are so variable, he must have the sensitivity and diagnostic ability to be able to sense and appreciate the differences. Second, rather than regard the existence of differences as a painful truth to be wished away, he must also learn to value difference and to value the diagnostic process which reveals differences. Finally, he must have the personal flexibility and the range of skills necessary to vary his own behavior. If the needs and motives of his subordinates are different, they must be treated differently.*[3]

Because people are complex, an organization's approach to managing the human element must be flexible.

The premium, then, is on having a sensitivity to what motivates job performance in general; building an overall organizational climate conducive to motivation; having a keen insight into the individual in particular; and to the degree possible, tailoring a personal approach to leadership and job design to which the employee will respond with commitment. The latter phase must be

---

[2]Edgar H. Schein, *Organizational Psychology*, Englewood Cliffs, N.J., Prentice–Hall, 1980, p. 93.
[3]Ibid., p. 96

accomplished by the person's immediate superior; and is reflected in the kind of person-to-person, day-to-day relationship that exists between the two.

> *Human behavior is a complex result of our intentions, our perception of the immediate situation, and our assumptions or beliefs about the situation and the people in it. These assumptions are, in turn, based upon our past experience, cultural norms, and what others have taught us to expect. In order to understand how organizations function, it is necessary first to understand how the people in those organizations, especially the managers who make organizational decisions, policies, and rules, function. The kinds of assumptions managers make about human nature and motivation determine to a large extent organizational policies with regard to incentives, rewards, and other personnel matters.*
>
> *For example, if an entrepreneur strongly believes that one cannot trust people to work hard on their own, he or she will build an organization with tight controls to ensure that workers come to work on time and are closely supervised. Another entrepreneur in the same business may start with the assumption that people work because they get excited about a product and identify with it and will, therefore, demonstrate a management style that encourages feelings of participative ownership of and identification with the company. This entrepreneur may distribute stock, encourage worker autonomy, and rely mainly on self-discipline rather than close supervision. Both people are operating from assumptions that may be partly or totally wrong insofar as a given worker is concerned. Nevertheless, these initial assumptions strongly influence how we initially design our incentives, rewards, and controls.*[4]

> Our assumptions about people determine how we design our incentives, rewards, and controls.

ORGANIZATIONAL PHILOSOPHY— A CONCLUDING NOTE

Formal or informal, written or unwritten, an organizational philosophy does exist. If it is not written and formally subscribed to it is implied by actions on the part of individual managers. Also, sometimes what is said is in variance with what actually happens and how the human element is handled in the day-to-day situation.

Every organization can derive substantial benefit from sitting down and formulating a written statement of their underlying philosophy about people, communicating and discussing this philosophy with all managers at every level, and continually analyzing themselves in light of the degree to which they are actually operating and working with people based on the philosophy and its underlying assumptions. This approach is the only sure way to guarantee uniformity and consistency in practicing what is professed.

A second important observation is that the organizational philosophy (as stated or implied by action) influences that which the individual manager formulates. This in turn affects how the manager manages her people. Research shows that managers learn their jobs primarily by example and from above and,

---
[4]Ibid., pp. 50–51.

accordingly, the better the example the better the management down the line. Therefore, a total organizational philosophy which will lay the groundwork for positive approaches to managing people must come from the very top.

Often employees' perception of the organization's climate and philosophy differs from that intended by management. This may be because enough effort has not been expended in communicating the guiding philosophy throughout the organization. An organization can do a great deal toward building eventual favorable response by letting its guiding philosophy be known.

The organizational philosophy must be communicated throughout the entire organization.

Similarly, managers can enhance their own individual efforts by making known to subordinates how they perceive the leadership function and how they would like to interact with their people on a day-to-day basis; managers must outline what they feel are the ingredients that are essential for effective integrated team effort to produce results. Assuming that a manager's concept of the leadership job is based primarily on a *positive* foundation, she will have laid the groundwork for, and increased the probability of, gaining understanding and commitment from her people.

A second factor contributing to differences in perception may be a discrepancy between what is said or professed and what actually occurs in practice.

HOW ORGANIZATIONS GET RESULTS THROUGH PEOPLE

It is important at this point to tie together some of the principles studied in the early sections of this text and to preview some of the concepts that will be expanded in later chapters dealing with management by objectives.

Edgar H. Schein defines an organization as follows.

> *An organization is the planned coordination of the activities of a number of people for the achievement of some common, explicit purpose or goal, through division of labor and function, and through a hierarchy of authority and responsibility.*[5]

This concept of organization has several important implications. First, it implies that there is coordination of effort to reach common objectives. Modern organization structures are a complex of individual departmental units as well as functional areas such as production, sales, personnel, finance, engineering, research, etc. In actual practice, coordination between departments and functional areas may be difficult. Not only do individual units often fail to work together toward common goals but they develop competing or different objectives in regard to the total organization. We speak frequently of self-centered people, but departments or functional areas may also be self-centered. Only after the individual or functional area solves its problems does a broader perspective of the organization become apparent. In short, over a period of time, the unit itself may become the central and first concern and the welfare of the organization becomes

---

[5]Schein, *Organizational Psychology*, p. 15.

second. Organizations can learn from some of our successful coaches of athletic teams in this regard. Whenever you find a winning team you usually find a commitment on the part of everyone on the team.

Another factor of importance is the existence of organizational goals that are known to all. If goals are not defined well, there is little chance of success.

Schein's definition also refers to a hierarchy of authority and responsibility. If authority is to be effective it must have the consent of those who are being governed by it. This consent hinges on whether the organization is providing the employees with a climate in which they can satisfy their needs. If the organization or the individual manager fails to provide this climate and cannot, via wages, bribe the employees, they will either leave or perform at low levels of efficiency.

In summary, then, if an organization is to achieve maximum results through people, some of the basic requirements that must be met are as follows.

1. There must be some central overall goals or objectives toward which the organization is striving. Preferably these will be fairly specific and will change and be modified as conditions warrant.
2. These objectives must be communicated down the line, with the idea of gaining commitment and agreement as to their value, reasonableness, and feasibility.
3. Functional areas, departmental units, and individuals must also have specific goals to obtain. These must be derived from the central goals and their interrelationships must be perceived.
4. The interdependency of all subunits within the organization to accomplish results must be clearly established and a framework and climate for interunit cooperation must exist. Similarly the strategic role and contribution of the individual must be specifically pinpointed and recognized.

THE WORK OF A LEADER

These points are reviewed here so that the work of leaders may be fully understood in the following chapters. It is the leader who must implement the foregoing principles. Leaders at different levels of the organization hierarchy perform different functions. In this section, we will examine the roles of the first-line supervisor, the middle manager, and the top executive.

THE FIRST-LINE SUPERVISOR[6]

First-line supervisors[7] occupy an important position in organizations, being positioned only one step removed from the hourly workers. As such, they must

The supervisor is the most vital link between higher management and the hourly employee.

[6]This section draws heavily from William E. Fulmer, "A New Look at First-Line Supervisors: The Increasing Pressures of the Job," *Industrial Management*, October 1975, pp. 1–7.

serve as the connecting link between management and the work force. In this role, they are not only responsible for maintaining approved levels of quality and cost but they are also directly responsible for people and equipment under them.[7]

The first-level supervisor has been described as the "person-in-the-middle," meaning that, of all management roles, theirs is the most prone to conflicting pressures. These pressures also seem to be increasing in number.

The first-line supervisor has always suffered from the dual pressures of maximizing production and minimizing costs. An additional pressure associated with the job of the first-line supervisor is a personal one that results from making the transition from an operative employee to a supervisor. As this shift is made, the supervisor is cut off from the informal work group of which he or she was a part. The supervisor's new reference group is presumed to be management, but management often regards him or her as a glorified hourly worker.

By the 1920s, supervisors had lost much of their control of production schedules, rates of pay, hiring, promotion, demotion, discharge, and discipline of workers. Specialists took over the planning, the control of people, and operations, leaving supervisors with little more to do than administer the plans and programs developed by staff departments. Furthermore, first-line supervisors are often promoted to this relatively powerless position from hourly jobs without proper training. Therefore, it is not surprising that the role often turns out to be a very frustrating one.

The first-level supervisor is a person whose successful achievement depends on human relations skills and technical knowledge of the work that subordinates perform. These supervisors must show concern for employees and their welfare. But in order to be able to maintain employee respect and allegiance, they must have upward influence, which comes largely through proper attention to organizational goals. The more successful they are at achieving goals the more likely it is that they will be able to influence higher level decisions and policies.

MIDDLE MANAGEMENT

The middle manager can best be described by comparison with the first-level supervisor who, working under considerable time pressure, has frequent and direct contact with the workers. Their orientation is more often downward, whereas second-level managers spend more time with their superiors and usually have an upward orientation. Second-level managers usually require less technical expertise and more general knowledge of several departments than do first-level supervisors. Since they are more removed by technological, geographical, and time barriers from the work situation, they must rely on the formal authority of their position more than their personal and technical ability. This also requires them to communicate more often by means of formal communication, such as memoranda, letters, and the telephone. The primary function of middle management is *interpolation*, that is, of knowing how to get what from

Middle managers have more of an upward orientation than do supervisors.

[7]Ibid., p. 4

whom and to maintain the pipelines of their suborganization to other components of the organization.[8]

One study revealed four major classes of functions required of the middle manager: "(1) planning, (2) decision functions, (3) supervisory and human relations functions, and (4) communication functions."[9]

A review of management styles over the past forty years indicates that a definition of satisfactory middle-management behavior depends largely on how one defines the goals of the organization. When jobs were scarce in the 1920s and 1930s and industry was tuned largely to productivity, the typical manager "was characterized as the tough, hard-nosed, bull-of-the-woods, tobacco-chewing-type guy" who was probably as good at dealing with a hammer and pliers as with men.[10] With the coming of World War II, immigration, and a labor shortage, human relations style management began to flourish. When the overproduction and spiraling costs of the late 1940s and early 1950s hit business, a third style of middle management developed, defined by one writer as "management by pressure." Management goals became focused on short-term results. "Management development emphasized such things as budget controls, improving mechanized methods and redesigning of products with the idea of engineering costs out of the product."[11]

Since middle management was being evaluated almost entirely on immediate results, their decisions began to reflect short-run expediency at the expense of long-run goals. The result was that problem-solving decisions tended to create more problems than they solved. Consequently, top management again communicated a different set of goals and objectives, stressing that middle management would be evaluated on a balanced criterion of long- and short-run goals. One writer has captioned this new approach "management of situations."[12]

As suggested earlier, the middle manager's chief responsibility is to maintain an interpolation and communication system for the goals and policies formulated by top management. The middle manager must be acutely aware of the realities, conditions and trends of the firm and position, and must have enough knowledge of methods and techniques to convert goals and policies into methods for their accomplishment. Since the knowledge of methods and techniques was probably acquired on the way up the managerial hierarchy, the middle manager's chief concern is in establishing the proper communication networks through organizational design that will either let the goals and policies be adjusted to fit the people, or persuade them to accept the goals. Since their experiences have probably provided an adequate knowledge of both the work

---

[8] Stanley M. Nealey and Fred E. Fiedler, "Leadership Functions of Middle Managers," *Psychological Bulletin*, LXX, No. 5, 1968, pp. 319–332.
[9] Foundation for Research on Human Behavior, *Assessing Managerial Potential*. Report of a Seminar, Ann Arbor, Mich., and Gould House, Ardsley-on-Hudson, New York, 1957, pp. 6–9.
[10] Jerry T. Emrick, "Training and Development of Middle Managers," *Advanced Management Journal*, XXX, No. 4, October 1965, p. 52.
[11] Ibid., p. 54.
[12] Ibid.

situation and of human relations, a large portion of middle management's time is spent with superiors, trying to interpret and clarify the firm's objectives.

THE TOP EXECUTIVE

The next major distinction in the management hierarchy is between a middle manager and a top manager or executive. Although the lines are shaded, it seems that the chief characteristic of a top executive position is the responsibility for policy making in the organization.[13]

Chester I. Barnard in a classic book introduced what he considers to be "the essential executive functions" as follows.

> *They are, first, to provide the system of communication; second, to promote the securing of essential efforts; and third, to formulate and define purpose.*[14]

In a much later intensive study of managerial potential these points of emphasis came to the forefront in a similar fashion. First, the upper-level manager, much as a navigator, requires impressive judgmental and conceptual abilities. Second, the top person was shown as one who must have integrating abilities "to fit together bits of information from different sources. They must sense, or even impose, a pattern where none appears to be."[15] These types of skills enable the top executive to provide the innovative direction and leadership which every organization needs if it is to remain competitive. Finally, this research group found that top people must have many of the lower-level skills, if for no other reason than to reach upper-level management.

Top executives are responsible for conceptualizing long-range goals.

The higher one moves toward the top of an organization the easier it is to evaluate her effectiveness on the basis of the achievement of tangible organizational goals. Another way of viewing this would be to say that at the lower levels of an organization the goals and objectives become so splintered and so diverse that it is often difficult to trace the effects of an activity back to the key objectives of the overall organization. Not only is the performance of the top manager expected to be aligned closely with goal achievement, but the major knowledge requirement is that of goals, policies, and procedures, many of which she must establish. Thus top managers must be well endowed with judgment and conceptual abilities and be able to integrate the diverse activities of the organization. Their orientation is outward toward the customer, the public, and the stockholders.

The Educational Testing Service (ETS) at Princeton University performed an extensive survey of a wide variety of organizations to learn what criteria (reflecting organizational goals) are most often used in evaluating the effectiveness of executives. Their findings were in turn synthesized into a list of

---

[13] Nealey and Fiedler, "Leadership Functions of Middle Managers," p. 320.
[14] Chester I. Barnard, *The Functions of an Executive*, Cambridge, Mass., Harvard University Press, 1938, p. 217.
[15] Foundation for Research on Human Behavior, *Assessing Managerial Potential*, p. 4.

"Seven Expressions of Executive Effectiveness." These characteristics of successful executives are listed, with their clarifications summarized, as follows.

1. *Their organization produces profits.* But ETS emphasizes that profits can rarely stand alone as an indicator of success because of the lack of complete control of the organization by one executive and because of the possibility of sacrificing long-run profits for short-run profits through the inadequate maintenance of physical and human resources.
2. *They operate efficiently.* This measure would include the use of input-output analysis, cost-accounting procedures, budgets, and realistic goal setting, in such a way as to reduce costs to a minimum and maximize results.
3. *They maintain good relations with others in the organization.* This is a difficult area to appraise, but ETS is sure that it includes such things as "avoiding personal conflicts, observing customs and traditions, displaying loyalty to the organization, etc."
4. *They make realistic plans for the future.* The emphasis here is on the results achieved by each plan instituted by an executive. ETS makes the approach clear by stating that, "Even though success or failure may well have resulted from factors over which he had no control, his reputation depends on his batting average, and perhaps more on the strike-outs and home runs than on the number of base hits."
5. *They develop high morale.* ETS says that this factor is "frequently studied through morale surveys and indicators, such as employee turnover, absenteeism, labor grievances, extent of voluntary participation in benefit plans, etc."
6. *They develop the competence of their subordinates.* ETS notes that this is measured largely by the use of subjective ratings.
7. *They foster good public relations.* One chief way in which this can be accomplished is through active participation in civic affairs.[16]

LEADERSHIP SKILLS

As Figure 13-2 illustrates, human relations skills are important at every level, although they vary in nature and complexity. At the lower levels, the supervisor must deal primarily with interpersonal problems and informal work groups. The middle manager is more often concerned with interdepartmental conflict. Top management must be concerned with avoiding personal conflicts, observing customs and traditions and displaying loyalty to the organization.

Communication skills, important at every level, are particularly critical for the middle manager. Their primary job is to take the goals and objectives defined by top management and interpolate them into implementable plans for lower level management. The first-level supervisor must be skilled at interpersonal com-

Communication skills are important at every level.

---
[16]Ibid., pp. 6–7.

DEVELOPING AN ORGANIZATIONAL AND LEADERSHIP PHILOSOPHY 349

FIGURE 13-2

Leadership Skills Required of Managers at Different Organizational Levels

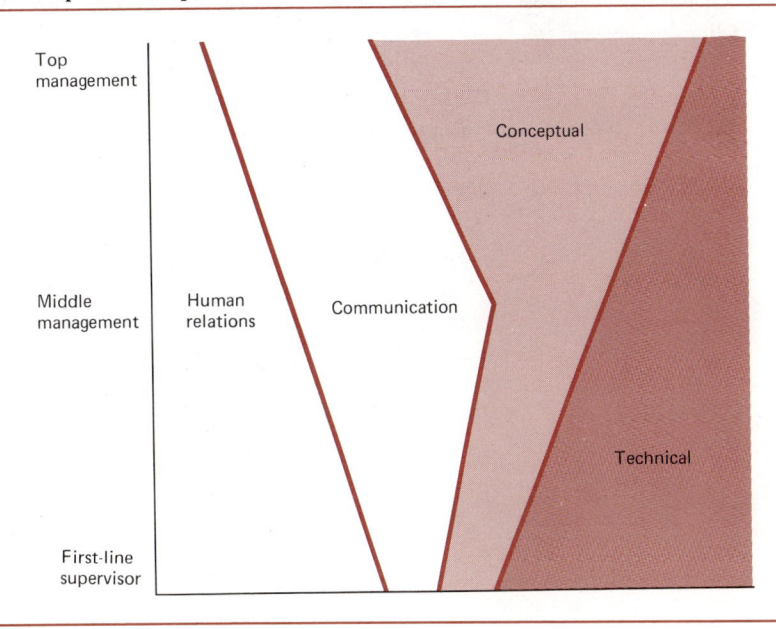

munications. Chapter 8, Organizational and Interpersonal Communications, discussed the communications process in modern organizations.

Conceptual skills include the ability to combine a large number of bits and pieces of information—often seemingly unrelated ones. This requires knowing operations of several departments and how they contribute to the overall goals and plans of the organization. The more rapidly first-line supervisors learn to apply this skill, the sooner they will be equipped to perform middle- and upper-level duties. The need for technical skill decreases as one moves up the hierarchy.

THE ACTIVITIES OF SUCCESSFUL LEADERS

As a result of our previous discussion, the activities engaged in by successful leaders at all organizational levels can now be summarized. Leaders must (1) maintain objectivity, (2) delegate authority and use of participation, (3) provide safety and security for their subordinates, (4) provide a system of rewards, and (5) deal with conflict and administer discipline.

MAINTAINING OBJECTIVITY

The first step in maintaining objectivity is to develop *self-awareness,* an understanding of why we behave as we do. Chapter 8, Organizational and Interpersonal Communications, and 9, Human Motivation, should assist in developing

350 THE MANAGEMENT OF HUMAN RESOURCES

To develop objectivity we must develop self-awareness and empathy.

self-awareness. Next, we must develop *empathy*. Empathy is the ability to look at things from another person's viewpoint.[17] It is the capacity to project one's self into another's position, to perceive how an employee feels about the job, the company, the boss, and to understand the values placed on the various need levels, such as physiological, social, and self-esteem goals. Empathetic leaders have the advantage of being able to project accurately the way in which subordinates will interpret their words and actions.[18]

DELEGATING AUTHORITY AND USE OF PARTICIPATION

Generally speaking, the research suggests a participative management style. But participation produces superior results only when the leader using it is relationship oriented, warm and supportive, and possesses trust in his or her subordinates.[19]

Several factors determine whether participation is in fact appropriate for a supervisor. First, time constraints are important. "In a crisis, you simply do not have time to run around consulting people." Obviously, building-burning crises, battlefield decisions and life-or-death surgical actions do not allow time for consultation.

> *However, managers often employ the "time won't permit" argument primarily to justify autocratic, and at least partially risk-free, behavior. If he succeeds, the credit is his, if he fails, he can defend his actions by pointing out that he had no time to explore alternatives.*[20]

Second, *technology* is a major factor in determining the flow and timing of decisions. Managers can often be heard repeating phrases like: "Look, I've got fifteen subordinates scattered over the building. What do you expect me to do—shut down the plant and call a meeting every time something happens?"[21] A good manager does not regularly "stop the presses" and call a conference. Instead, he or she agrees on advance objectives, schedules, and priorities. If these do not work, the subordinate should consult with him or her. Work planning and scheduling for this purpose are not performed just to sell the manager's views.[22]

The degree of participation used by management must depend on time and temperament of the leader.

Finally, the temperament of the leader is sometimes a barrier to the use of participation. Many employees have had the experience of being called to a meeting to share in making a decision only to learn that the mind of the boss had already been made up on the question.[23] Most executives in this situation are

---

[17]William H. Newman, Charles E. Summer and E. Kirby Warren, *The Process of Management*, Englewood Cliffs, N.J., Prentice Hall, 1972, pp. 494–496.
[18]Ibid., p. 494.
[19]Fred E. Fiedler and Martin M. Chemers, *Leadership and Effective Management*, Glenview, Ill.: Scott Foresman and Co., 1974, pp. 111–112.
[20]Raymond E. Miles and J.B. Ritchie, "Participative Management, Quality vs. Quantity," *California Management Review*, Vol. XIII, No. 4, 1971, pp. 48–56.
[21]Ibid.
[22]Ibid.
[23]Ibid.

probably saying to themselves, "I have this thing pretty well in mind, but I'd better call in the troops and do some explaining." Such executives may simply feel they are not the type that can run around asking subordinates how things are going.

In summarizing, it can be noted that it is the quality and substance of participation, not the frequency and gregarious nature of it, that determine its effectiveness.

PROVIDING SECURITY FOR SUBORDINATES

Leaders play a critical role in the life of subordinates by giving them the most important information from top management. The subordinate is vitally interested in the company's future plans, projected policy changes, pay raises, promotion possibilities, and numerous other tidbits of information. Without sufficient information, subordinates feel insecure and uncertain about their future.

Perhaps an even more important role of the leader is that of representing his people with upper level management. Research has indicated that being people oriented or production oriented does not fully explain the reason for the success of supervisors. It is only when their "upward influence" with top management is considered that a meaningful pattern unfolds. Supervisors with upward influence can get things done for their subordinates. How do they obtain upward influence? By getting things accomplished for the company.[24]

Supervisors with upward influence can get things done for their subordinates and for the company.

PROVIDING A REWARD SYSTEM

This subject has been touched on in Chapter 9, Human Motivation. Successful leaders are able to choose the proper reward to fit the occasion at hand. While first-level supervisors have little control over pay raises, they can show recognition for work well performed. In such a case, the timing of the recognition and the way in which it is given are important. But if a supervisor compliments heavily when persons are merely "doing their job," the value of his or her compliments depreciates rapidly. On-the-job rewards are usually more effective than "time off" and other off-the-job rewards.

The supervisor plays an important role in administering rewards, especially recognition.

Often the technical ability or special knowledge of a supervisor is great enough to warrant admiration by her subordinates. In such cases, it is easy for the supervisor to become an inspiration to her followers. As such, she performs the role of the initiator or catalyst simply by modeling correct behavior. It is for this reason that effective leaders have often been superior public accountants, battlefield soldiers, professional athletes, salespeople, and so on. This gives them credibility when they become controllers, military officers, coaches, or sales managers. Scott Myers of Texas Instruments has found that even where mo-

---

[24]M. Scott Myers, "Who Are Your Motivated Workers?", *Harvard Business Review*. Vol. 42, No. 1, January-February 1964, pp. 73–88.

tivators such as job advancement or pay raises are used, the leader's role in administering the reward is a factor critical to its success.[25]

DEALING WITH INTERPERSONAL CONFLICT

Whenever two or more persons work together, conflict is bound to arise occasionally. Leaders are expected to arbitrate conflict situations between individuals, groups, and departments under their supervision. Emotions are likely to run high between two secretaries when only one of them can receive a new self-correcting typewriter, or between sales representatives disputing their territorial boundaries.

TYPES OF CONFLICT

One writer has organized conflict into four groups:

1. A person or group desires to do two things which are liked equally well, but it is possible to do only one.
2. A person or group has the choice of doing two things, each of which is disliked equally.
3. A person or group has a choice of doing something that is liked, but runs the risk of punishment or loss.
4. A person or group has several choices of desirable things to do, but runs the risk of some loss or punishment.[26]

According to Argyris, conflict dealt with correctly is an experience of growth for the personality. The healthy personality is one that tends toward activity, reasonable independence, the capability of behaving in many different ways, deep-seated interests, long-time perspectives, and a reasonable awareness of self.[27] While this definition is pointed toward individuals, many of the same characteristics might equally apply to the healthy organization.

Conflict, dealt with correctly, is an experience leading to growth.

While it is true that conflict often produces frustration and discomfort, most executives agree that conflict also can have positive outcomes. One group of executives who were recently polled as to the outcome of conflicts in their respective companies mentioned the following positive and negative outcomes.[28]

1. Better ideas were produced.
2. People were forced to search for new approaches.
3. Long-standing problems surfaced and were dealt with.
4. People were forced to clarify their views.

---

[25]Ibid.
[26]Chris Argyris, *Personality and Organization: The Conflict Between System and the Individual*, New York, Harper and Row, 1957, p. 39.
[27]Ibid., p. 53.
[28]Warren H. Schmidt, "Conflict: A Powerful Process for (Good or Bad) Change," *Management Review*, December 1974, p. 5.

DEVELOPING AN ORGANIZATIONAL AND LEADERSHIP PHILOSOPHY 353

5. The tension stimulated interest and creativity.
6. People had a chance to test their capacities.

Negative outcomes of conflict were:

1. Some people felt defeated or demeaned.
2. Distance between people increased.
3. A climate of distrust and suspicion developed.
4. People and departments that needed to cooperate looked after only their own narrow interests.
5. Resistance—active or passive—developed where teamwork was needed.
6. Some people left because of the turmoil.

The typical manager spends about 20 percent of his or her time dealing with conflict.

"According to a recent survey of executives . . . the typical manager is likely to spend about twenty percent of his time dealing with some kind of conflict—either as a participant or as a third party helping others resolve their differences."[29]

What happens when persons engage in conflict? First, *frustration* occurs when a person or group feels blocked from satisfying a concern. Next *conceptualization* takes place when the person begins to answer the question, "What's the problem—what issues are at stake?" Third, *behavior* flows out of conceptualization and sets in motion a pattern of interaction between the parties involved. Finally, an *outcome* is reached when decisions or actions are taken, and the feelings of the parties involved are brought out into the open.

RESOLVING CONFLICT IN COMPATIBLE SITUATIONS

When two people or two groups are involved in a conflict situation, it is usually because they find themselves in one (or more) of the three areas of disagreement.[30]

1. Informational—The two parties have been exposed to different information, and thus have arrived at a different understanding of the issue and of what course of action makes the most sense.
2. Perceptual—Although the parties have been exposed to the same data, their experience causes them to interpret it in different ways. Perhaps their value systems are different.
3. Role—The situations or roles of people cause them to take different positions. They have been taught different methods of doing things.

By categorizing the reasons for their differences, persons can often come to an Adult view of conflict resolution. For example, instead of allowing Not OK feelings to enter into their communications, they may determine that they have simply been exposed to different data and may view their job as being that of mutual education rather than argument. If their backgrounds are very different,

---

[29]Ibid., p. 5.
[30]Ibid., p. 7.

354 THE MANAGEMENT OF HUMAN RESOURCES

as, for example, that of engineering versus personnel management, they may decide that each needs to spend some time reviewing the other's experiences and learning why the other approaches problems differently. Of course, managers operating in a Not OK state would have difficulty utilizing the adult data processing equipment they have at hand. When the parties recognize that the principal reasons for their different views grow out of their backgrounds and roles, they can often take a more objective approach by asking, "If I were in his place, what would I do? Would I be advocating the same view?" The task then becomes one of satisfying the question, "How can I help a person in that role to understand and appreciate my concern, and what does he need from me?"[31]

By looking objectively at the reasons for their differences, persons can often handle conflict in an adult manner.

RESOLVING CONFLICT IN NONCOMPATIBLE SITUATIONS

When the diagnosis of a disagreement is clear and there is misunderstanding, conflict resolution takes on a different turn. The two parties want things that are clearly incompatible. In such a situation, the parties can exhibit behavior that is assertive (trying to satisfy one's own interests), or cooperative (trying to accommodate the other party's interest), or some combination of these. Five conflict handling modes may be utilized in resolving these particular situations. Figure 13-3 diagrams these modes and behaviors.

Competing. When a person chooses this mode, he or she is going all out to win. It is important that the person making such a choice knows what he or she wants to achieve and estimates the consequences to the other party.

Accommodating. This means neglecting any concern for self in order that the other party may win. A person who chooses this mode desires to preserve personal relationships at the expense of winning a particular point.

Avoiding. This is a mode that makes sense when the timing for resolving the conflict is wrong or the issue is not really critical.

Compromising. A person using this approach is subscribing to the time-honored wisdom of settling for "half a loaf" when the possibility of losing the entire loaf looms too large.

Collaborating. This last mode is that of mutual problem solving. The parties first educate each other as to their goals and then work together to achieve the best solution for both. When this mode is chosen by managers or organizational role players, they often find some method of accomplishing even greater things for both parties. This is the search for a creative outcome—or what Mary Parker Follett has captioned the *integrative solution* to conflict. According to Follett, if we settle for compromise in strong conflict situations, the conflict will come up again

When two persons want things that are clearly incompatible, they should collaborate rather than compete.

---
[31]Ibid., p. 8.

FIGURE 13-3

Ways of Handling Conflict

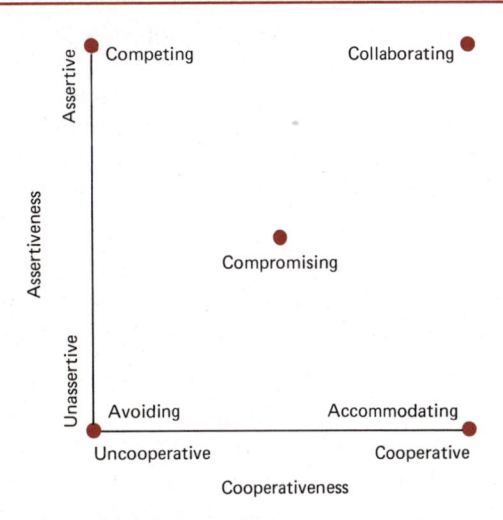

A 2D plot with Assertiveness on the vertical axis (Unassertive to Assertive) and Cooperativeness on the horizontal axis (Uncooperative to Cooperative). Five conflict-handling modes are plotted: Competing (assertive, uncooperative), Collaborating (assertive, cooperative), Compromising (middle), Avoiding (unassertive, uncooperative), Accommodating (unassertive, cooperative).

Source: Warren H. Schmidt, "Conflict: A Powerful Process for (Good or Bad) Change, "*Management Review*, December 1974, p. 9.

and again in some other form. Only collaboration or what she has called *integration* really stabilizes conflict. Collaboration requires an OK management working within a positive or OK organizational climate.

SOME GENERAL OBSERVATIONS CONCERNING LEADERSHIP

First it should be observed that *people are* already *motivated*. The important questions are: (1) How strong is the motivation? (2) In what direction is it working? If employees are consistently performing at a low level when they are capable of much more, it may be because the strength of their motivation is insufficient. Perhaps they are not gaining the satisfaction that they want from the job and this dampens their initiative. Managers should build into the job climate and their own approach to leadership those incentives that will trigger their latent potential.

Effective leadership is one of the most challenging and difficult tasks that a manager faces. It is the result of a comprehensive approach which emphasizes the development of a climate conducive to employment development and recognizes individual differences. Also, it is a task that demands continuous effort and conscientious application.

Employees must become mentally and emotionally involved in their jobs. This requires mutual agreement between the boss and the subordinate concerning the

People are already motivated but not always at the level nor in the direction desired.

design of work, its importance, the results or objectives to be accomplished, performance measurement, and progress on the job.

In any operation it is the manager who sets the pace which determines ultimate accomplishment of results.

Enthusiasm in an organization is very contagious. Once it spreads, it is difficult to stop. Managers can do much toward building a favorable climate for maximum results by establishing a good "mental set" themselves. If they are excited and interested, the chances are excellent that their subordinates will be enthusiastic toward their work.

Some time ago, the Champion Paper Company produced a film entitled "1104 Sutton Road," which contains the following two statements:

1. "To get more of what you want, you must produce more of what the other people want."
2. "We can't control what comes to us, but only what goes from us."

A manager cannot dictate the level of performance of others but he can change his own performance.

These statements are apropos to both individual job performance and managerial leadership. A manager cannot dictate the level of job performance he desires from employees, he can only determine how he treats them and the climate he assists in creating for them.

SUMMARY

Whether it is formal or informal, written or unwritten, every organization and every individual manager develops a philosophy for dealing with people. This philosophy is important because it determines how the human assets of the organization will be managed. If top management has the necessary commitment it is possible to develop a total organizational philosophy that will act as a base for positive approaches to management.

The organization's philosophy is primarily determined by the set of assumptions about humanity that is adopted. The economic person concept views people as being only in pursuit of money and security. It leads to an approach to management based solely on economic factors and usually fails because people look for more in a job than a paycheck.

The social person concept sees people as primarily seeking an affinity with fellow employees and looking for social interaction on the job. This assumption suggests that management create a happy family atmosphere and forestall any type of interpersonal conflict. The theory also usually fails because contentedness and productivity do not necessarily go hand in hand.

The self-fulfilling person concept views people as seeking challenges as well as opportunities for achievement and continued advancement. This suggests creating an environment that is flexible and that offers continued opportunity for new experiences and growth. The main weakness of this concept is that it implies that the same degree and type of motivation exists in all people.

SUMMARY CHART

I. Concepts About People and the Approaches to Management They Suggest

   A. The Economic Person
   B. The Social Person
   C. The Self-Fulfilling Person
   D. The Complex Person

II. Different Degrees of Skills are Important at Different Levels

Manager	Most Important Skill
A. First-line supervisor	Human relations and technical knowledge
B. Middle managers	Communications
C. Top management	Conceptual

III. Activities of Successful Leaders

   A. Maintaining Objectivity
   B. Delegating Authority for utilizing participation
   C. Providing Security for subordinates
   D. Providing a reward system
   E. Dealing with conflict

IV. General Observations Regarding Leadership

   A. Leadership is not an easy job
   B. Effective leadership should foster commitment through involvement
   C. The manager sets the pace
   D. Enthusiasm on the leader's part is a must

A complex person concept is needed which views people as being both complex and different from their neighbors. This means a management approach that adjusts somewhat to fit the individual.

In addition to the existing management philosophy, the organization must have coordination of effort to reach common objectives, organizational goals that are known to all, and a hierarchy of authority and responsibility. Of particular significance are the ideas of common goals and coordination of effort.

Leaders at different levels of organizations face different kinds of problems, and use different managerial skills. First-line supervisors, only one step removed from the hourly work force, must be skilled at dealing with people—human relations. Often they are also required to have a strong knowledge of the technical operations which their subordinates perform.

Middle managers serve as the interpolators of top management in communicating goals and objectives downward and sentiments and requests upward. They must be skilled in communicative abilities.

The top manager or executive is responsible for guiding the organization with policies and objectives. This role can be depicted as that of a navigator, requiring strong conceptual abilities. This skill allows the top executive to arrange bits and pieces of information from employees, customers and other sources into some kind of managerial pattern. At all levels it is important to realize that leadership is not an easy job. The leader must foster commitment through involvement. The process begins with the manager setting the pace by showing personal enthusiasm and sincerity in her approach to supervision.

DISCUSSION QUESTIONS

1. Briefly describe each of the assumptions behind the economic person, social person, self-fulfilling person, and complex person concepts. What are the approaches to management that each of these sets of assumptions suggests, and what are the results of each of these approaches?
2. Discuss the implications of the definition of organization given by Schein. What are the basic requirements that must be met if an organization is to achieve maximum results through people?
3. What are the most important skills possessed by successful first-line supervisors? Middle managers? Top managers? Discuss.
4. Why is a first-line supervisor often called "the man in the middle"?
5. Identify and discuss briefly each of the activities of successful leaders. Which of the activities of successful leaders would you enjoy most? Why? Least? Why?
6. Cite four general observations regarding leadership and why you feel each is significant.
7. Identify some of the potential positive and negative outcomes from conflict as well as types of conflict that can arise. Discuss the various alternative approaches that are available to solving conflict.

APPLICATION EXERCISES AND CASES

ONE OUT OF THREE[32]

A midwestern insurance company recently had an opening in one of its lower-middle management positions. After evaluating a number of possible candidates, the selection committee narrowed its list to three people.

---

[32]Richard M. Hodgetts, *Management, Theory, Process and Practice,* Philadelphia, W. B. Saunders, 1975, p. 125–126.

The first candidate was a newly hired management trainee who had only recently received a master's degree in business from a large eastern university. The man's major area of study at the undergraduate level had been general management, whereas at the postgraduate level he had a concentration in management theory and insurance. Although the company liked the individual's general management background and felt his insurance courses provided him with some of the technical training he would need in supervising company personnel, some of the committee members were afraid that the man's background was too general. "We need someone with a little more background and training in this business," said one of the members.

The second individual being considered for the position was a salesman who, for the past two years, had been the leading salesman in his regional office. He did not want to remain a salesman for the rest of his life, so when he learned that the company was looking for a lower level middle-manager, he immediately applied for the job. On the positive side, the committee liked his track record. "This man has illustrated that he can deliver in the field," said one member. "This has seasoned him for the management ranks. After all, isn't a manager a salesman selling management's point of view to the employees?" On the negative side, however, some of the committee members were afraid that the man might be too interested in personal selling and its behavioral aspects and fail to see "the complete picture." One of them put it this way, "There's more to managing than just getting along with people."

The third person being considered for the job worked in the firm's actuarial department. He did fine technical work, and one committee member who felt this man would be ideal for the job remarked, "The backbone of an insurance company is its actuarial department. This fellow knows the ins and outs of insurance. This technical competence will help him do a good job." There was, however, concern that the man might be too used to working with numbers and not accustomed to managing people. "Technical skill is important," said one member, "but it's no substitute for handling people."

After discussing the three individuals for the better part of an hour, the chairman called for action. "Gentlemen, we have to make a decision on this matter today. Now we have a fair idea of the strong and weak points of each candidate. What do you say we choose one of the three and then adjourn for lunch?" Every one agreed.

Questions

1. Discuss what you consider to be the significant aspects of the work of a leader for the vacant position and what are the important skills he or she should possess? Rank the latter in terms of importance and defend your ranking.
2. Similar to the above, what are the most important activities this leader will have to perform? Explain each.
3. Based on the above question which of the three would you choose? Why?

COMMUNICATION AT THE JAMES RIVER PLANT[33]

The James River Plant of the Harcog Manufacturing Company has been experiencing low productivity and high costs when compared to the company's other plants. William Holliday, the James River plant manager, believes that if costs are to be reduced and productivity increased, employees must be willing to put more effort into their work for the same amount of pay.

During a discussion with Holliday about his approach for improving productivity, union leaders at the plant realized that the manager considered his viewpoint to be very rational and logical. The union leaders pointed out to the plant manager that there had been a large number of employee grievances within the past three months. In addition, most had concerned contractual agreements covering overtime work and job descriptions that specified who was to perform certain jobs in the plant. Employee morale had grown progressively worse during this period; and, at the present time, there is a high degree of mistrust between the workers, the plant manager, and management in general.

The plant manager has analyzed the situation and feels that the problem of low productivity is caused by poor communication between the supervisors and the workers. If supervisors could properly explain management's position and the reason for seeking lower costs, he feels that productivity could be increased. Thus, as Holliday sees it, the solution is to inform the workers properly, regardless of the amount of information and data that will be required to do the job. Company newsletters and pay envelope stuffers have been the traditional communication links with employees. Holliday now proposes that the spouses of workers must be informed of the necessity for higher productivity. As a result communication will be improved and workers will be more rational toward management's viewpoint.

The plant manager also feels that communication by example is very useful. In fact, he is planning to cut top management salaries at the plant by an average of 12 percent and will slow down merit and annual pay increases throughout management ranks.

Questions

1. How would you characterize Holliday's assumptions about people? What alternative do you feel is more reasonable? What do you see as the plant's basic problem and how does an organization get results through people?
2. Would you suggest another approach to solving the plant's problem? Discuss the elements of your approach and how they relate to material in the chapter.

---

[33] Robert L. Trewatha and M. Gene Newport, *Management Functions and Behavior*, Dallas Texas, Business Publications, Inc., 1976, p. 492.

CHAPTER 14

LEADERSHIP STYLES

NORMATIVE THEORIES OF LEADERSHIP
BLAKE AND MOUTON—THE MANAGERIAL GRID
LIKERT'S FOUR SYSTEMS OF MANAGEMENT
PATH-GOAL THEORY
CONTINGENCY APPROACHES TO LEADERSHIP
FRED FIEDLER
HERSEY-BLANCHARD STUDIES
W.T. REDDIN—THE TRIDIMENSIONAL GRID
SUMMARY OF CONTINGENCY THEORY OF LEADERSHIP
APPLICATION EXERCISES AND CASES
IDENTIFYING LEADERSHIP STYLES
CAN ONE LEARN TO MANAGE SUBORDINATES?

CEO LEADERSHIP STYLES[1]

Irving Berlin Kahn, the once and future communications magnate, is tooling his red Jaguar down the street in Palm Beach, Florida, running a red light or two and talking business. "You should see the people we've hired away from Bell to work on our laser project," Kahn says in his raspy voice, waving his hands for emphasis. "This laser thing could be bigger than anything I've ever done."

. . . .

Kahn is a hands-on manager who knows everyone's name. He also wants everyone to know he's the boss. "I'm not very good in a democracy," he says. "I'm a totalitarian operator." Occasionally he abuses employees, using frightful language. But then he sends them gifts and tells them how wonderful they are. He also holds out the vision of the carrot—a piece of the profits.[2]

. . . .

Legend has it that the black brick, golden-crowned headquarters building of American Standard Inc. in midtown Manhattan was designed to suggest a coal fire. The architect may have had something there. For on the twenty-first floor of the 56-year-old neo-Gothic skyscraper, Chairman and President William R. Marquard has been quietly generating considerable heat at the old plumbing and heating company over the past decade. Indeed, Marquard has transformed the once-troubled company into a top performer, with a unique ability to generate red-hot earnings growth in the mature, mundane capital goods business.

As a manager, Marquard is known for his low-key businesslike style. A great believer in face-to-face discussions, he likes to "keep pretty good hands on people" by popping into their offices unannounced. "I'm a no-nonsense person," he says, puffing on his ever-present Jamaican cigar. "Our people know that once we set objectives, they have to perform. I do not suffer mediocrity."[3]

. . . .

As might be expected of an innovative, high-technology company, Raytheon has a number of "firsts" it can boast about. It produced the world's first electronic depth sounder and first guided missiles to intercept ballistic missiles and aircraft in flight. It bounced the first laser signal off the moon and was the first to apply microwave energy to the heating of food.

Tom Phillips, Chairman of Raytheon, on the other hand, is not one to take personal credit for such accomplishments, but instead emphasizes the team concept. The thirty-one-year company veteran is a self-effacing man who insists on giving credit for Raytheon's record to others. "Don't say our success is a one-man job," he insists. "We are a conservative New England company with a lot of high-caliber, dedicated people."[4]

---

[1] "The Five Best-Managed Companies," *Dun's Review*, December 1979, Vol. 114, No. 6, pp. 48–49.
[2] Allan Sloan, "At Sea With Irving Kahn," *Forbes*, November 24, 1980, Vol. 126, No. 11, pp. 62–67.
[3] "American Standard's Spectacular Comeback," *Dun's Review*, December 1979, Vol. 114, No. 6, pp. 40–41.
[4] "Raytheon: The Rewards of Engineering," *Dun's Review*, December 1979, Vol. 114, No. 6, pp. 59–60.

Notice the difference in the leadership styles of each of the chief executives described in these incidents. They obviously vary greatly. How does one describe a successful leader? What style of behavior is most typically effective in leadership situations? How should leaders behave? In this chapter we will examine the more prominent leadership theories. First we will discuss *normative* theories, ones that imply that there is one best style of leadership. Next we will discuss *contingency* theories of leadership, those that suggest that the appropriate style of leadership is contingent on the situation.

NORMATIVE THEORIES OF LEADERSHIP

BLAKE AND MOUTON—THE MANAGERIAL GRID

Blake and Mouton developed a framework for describing managerial styles which they call the *managerial grid*.[5] (See Figure 14-1.) The horizontal axis of the grid represents the manager's concern for production, while the vertical axis represents concern for people. Each axis is on a 1-to-9 scale indicating that a manager may have from a 1, or minimal degree of concern for either production or people, up to a 9, or maximum degree of concern.

On the grid are five basic styles located at each of the corner positions and at the midpoint. Each style is labeled with a descriptive name and numeral. The

The managerial grid represents the manager's concern for production on the horizontal axis and his concern for people on the vertical axis.

FIGURE 14-1

The Managerial Grid

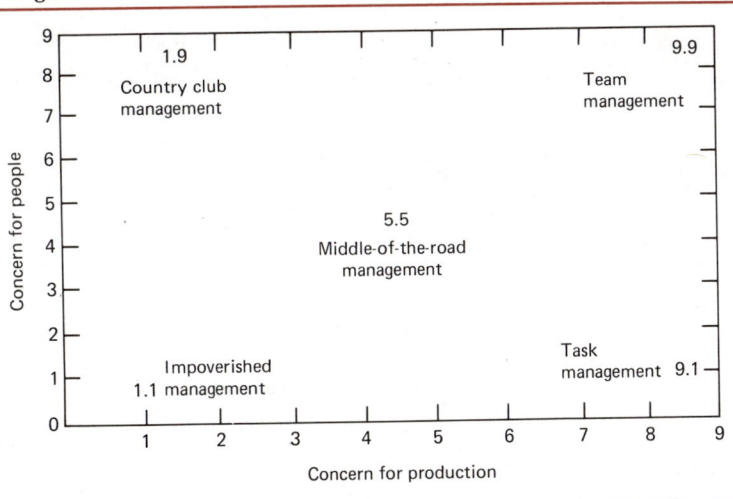

Source: Robert R. Blake and Jane Srygley Mouton, "The Developing Revolution in Management Practices," *Journal of the American society of Training directors,* Vol. 16, No. 7, 1962, pp. 29–52. Reproduced with permission.

first number in the numeral always denotes the degree of concern for production, while the second one indicates degree of concern for people. The grid has three principle values, as follows.

1. It can help managers identify their style.
2. It can help managers understand why they get certain reactions from subordinates.
3. It suggests alternative leadership styles that may be available for different situations.

Task Manager (9.1). The task manager has 9 degrees of concern for production and only 1 degree of concern for people. Managers who have a 9.1 style are primarily concerned with output and see their central responsibility as that of achieving production objectives. People are seen as tools of production, similar to machines. They are paid to do what they are told, when they are told, not to ask too many questions in between. To question their superiors is considered equal to insubordination. When interpersonal conflict arises, management handles it is through disciplinary action. Under the task management theory, if people do not comply after a certain amount of control has been applied, they should be replaced. With respect to certain selected areas the task manager feels as follows.

Decision making—Inner directed. Depends on own skills and beliefs in approaching problems and making decisions.

Conflict with subordinates—Suppresses by the use of authority.

Creativity—Ideas are the responsibility of the manager. Ideas of others are rejected. Creative ideas serve personal goals to succeed.

Promotion of creative effort—Competition among employees to develop new ideas by use of rewards and promotions.

Conflicts with superiors and peers—Takes a win-loss approach and fights to win his own points as long as possible.

Country Club Manager (1.9). In contrast to the task manager, the country club manager has only 1 degree of concern for production, but 9 degrees of concern for people. With this style the assumption is that if people are kept happy and harmony is maintained, a reasonable amount of productivity will be achieved. People are pretty much like cows and if you keep them contented they will produce. If human problems and conflicts arise they are glossed over or ignored, with the idea that time will take care of them. If the country club manager is asked the question, "What is your primary responsibility?", she would most likely answer, "To keep people happy." When employed to its extreme, the people who work for the 1.9 manager will usually sense an insincere quality in such human relations, because they are not related to the conditions of work and production. Thus, long-run meaningful human relations gains are not achieved in the organization. The following observations summarize the approach of the 1.9 country club manager.

LEADERSHIP STYLES 365

Decision making—Outer directed. Anxious to find solutions which reflect opinions of others so the solutions will be accepted.

Conflict with subordinates—Smooths over conflict and tries to release tension by appeals to the "goodness of man."

Creativity—Innovations usually are to make jobs easier and the workers more comfortable. Ideas usually further group morale rather than production goals.

Promotion of creative effort—Encourage innovations by accepting any and all ideas uncritically. Ideas which will generate conflicts are side-stepped.

Conflict with superiors and peers—Avoids conflict by conforming to the thinking of the boss or her peers. She seeks knowledge of the boss's position so that expression of this position will put her in the inner circle.

Impoverished Management (1.1). Managers at this position deemphasize concern for production, with just enough being done to get by. They also disregard the importance of human relationships. Impoverished managers are going nowhere and trying to take everybody with them. For all practical purposes they have retired, although they may be around for several more years. An impoverished management orientation can be found in circumstances where a person has been repeatedly passed over for promotion or feels he has otherwise been unjustly treated. Rather than looking for another job, such persons adjust to the work setting by giving minimal performance. If the organization had too many 1.1 managers it would disappear, as is apparent from the following observations.

> Impoverished managers are going nowhere and trying to take everyone with them.

Decision making—Problems are avoided or deferred to others for solutions.

Conflict with subordinates—Just does not get involved. Usually able to avoid completely issues which might give rise to conflict, by not discussing them with subordinates.

Creativity—Good ideas will sometimes "pop up" but ideas are usually not related to company goals or morale. Often connected with outside hobbies and the like.

Promotion of creative effort—Supervisory actions will not affect creativity. Ideas are not discussed on the job so conflicts are not likely.

Conflict with superiors and peers—Keeps his mouth shut and does not express any dissent.

Middle-of-the-Road Management (5.5). Push enough to get acceptable production but yield to the degree necessary to develop morale is the theory behind dampened pendulum or middle-of-the-road management. The 5.5 manager constantly shifts between emphasis and concern for production and people. It represents a live-and-let-live approach under which the real issue is muted. With a 5.5 approach, compromise is the name of the game. The 5.5 manager never does anything wrong, but never does anything dramatically right either. It is a safe position.

> The middle-of-the-road manager pushes enough to get acceptable production but yields to the degree necessary to develop morale.

All the approaches described so far see the matter of people and production as being in conflict with one another. They assume that you can have one but not the other, or you can have a little of one and a little of another, but you cannot have both together.

Team Management (9.9).   Team managers believe that people and production can be integrated. They believe that a situation can be created that allows people to satisfy their needs and objectives by working toward the objectives of the organization. They seek to integrate people around production. When a problem arises, managers will consult with their group, present the situation, encourage discussion, and get ideas and commitment. They will delegate results and give their people some freedom to operate. When problems of feelings and emotions arise in working relationships, the team manager will confront them directly and work through the differences, as indicated by the following observations.

Decision Making—Solutions are developed with aid of those who have relevant facts and knowledge to contribute.

Conflict with Subordinates—Confronts conflict directly. Feelings and facts are communicated so that there is a basis for understanding and working through the conflict.

Creativity—High degree of interplay of ideas and cross-stimulation. Experimentation is the rule rather than the exception. Innovations further the shared goals and solve important problems.

Promotion of Creative Effort—Feedback used as a basis for further development and thinking. Innovation encouraged by defining and communicating problems that are in need of solutions.

Conflict with Superiors and Peers—Confronts conflict directly and works it through at the time it arises. Those involved are brought together to work through differences.

SIGNIFICANT OBSERVATIONS ABOUT THE MANAGERIAL GRID

1. Although the four corners and the midpoint of the grid are emphasized, these extreme positions are rarely found in their pure form in the working situation. In other words, a manager would more likely have a style of 8.3 or 4.6 or similar moderate position.

2. In their research on the grid, Blake and Mouton have found that managers tend to have one dominant style that they use more often than they use any other. In addition, they have a backup style, which is adopted if the dominant style does not work in a particular situation. For example, a manager with a 9.1 orientation who finds that subordinates will not submit to his authority may have a 5.5 backup style. Similarly, 1.9 managers attempt to keep people happy and forestall interpersonal conflict; however, if this does not work, they may retreat and move in a 1.1 direction.

3. Another research finding is that the style that individual managers choose as being most descriptive of themselves (dominant style) is very often not the way

they really are. Rather, it reflects how they would like to be or how they would like to think their subordinates see them. A manager's second choice usually gives a better reflection of how he really manages.

4. The ingredients of each managerial style are found to some degree in every manager.
5. What a manager's style is will be influenced by any number of factors, including the superior, the kind of people supervised, the situation in which he finds himself, and his own personality. Obviously it is suggested that the closer a manager can come to a 9.9 style the better. But we *should also note that there is no one style that works best in all situations and with all people.*

In 1967, Blake and Mouton added a third dimension to their managerial grid. The third dimension represents the thickness or depth of a given style. It also ranges from 1 to 9. This third dimension deals with how long a managerial style is maintained in any given situation of interaction, particularly when the manager is under pressure from tension, frustration, or conflict. If, when threatened by conflict, managers change their style very readily, they have thin style. If, regardless of circumstances, they tend to maintain their style, it is a thick one. For example, if a manager's style is a 9.9 style, but he or she tends to turn away from it at the slightest hint of pressure, they would be a 9.9.1. If another 9.9 manager under the same pressure continues to resist changing style, it would be a 9.9.9.

The third dimension of Blake and Mouton's grid measures the depth of a manager's style—how long a style is maintained in a given situation.

LIKERT'S FOUR SYSTEMS OF MANAGEMENT

For more than twenty-five years, Rensis Likert has conducted leadership studies at the Institute for Social Research at the University of Michigan. This research has culminated in what Likert calls "four systems of management," which describe four general leadership styles. The key dimension of behavior differentiating the styles is the amount of *participation* the superior allows subordinates in the leadership process. The four systems form a continuum, with System 1 describing a style comparable to Blake's Task Manager (9.1) and System 4 closely aligned with the 9.9 Team Manager. Figure 14-2 summarizes each of Likert's four managerial systems along several dimensions of leadership.[5]

Likert also isolated three variables that were representative of his total concept of System 4, or *participative management*. These include the use by the manager of supportive relationships, the use of group decision making and group methods of supervision, and high performance goals.

Likert's System 4 variables include supportive relationships, group decision making, and high performance goals.

The first variable is exemplified by the following factors.

1. The degree to which the superior exhibits confidence and trust.
2. Interest in the subordinates' future.

---

[5]For a discussion of some specific leadership techniques that spur job performance see Burt K. Scanlan, "Managerial Leadership In Perspective: Getting Back to Basics," *Personnel Journal*, March 1979, Vol. 58, No. 3, p. 168.

FIGURE 14-2

Diagnose Your Management Style

		Authoritative Exploitive	Authoritative Benevolent	Consultative	Participative Group
Leadership	How much confidence is shown in subordinates?	None	Condescending	Substantial	Complete
	How free do they feel to talk to superiors about job?	Not at all	Not very	Rather free	Fully free
Motivation	Is predominant use made of (1) fear, (2) threats, (3) punishment, (4) rewards, (5) involvement	1,2,3, Occasionally 4	4, some 3	4, some 3 and 5	5, 4, based on group set goals
	Where is responsibility felt for achieving organization's goals?	Mostly at top	Top and middle	Fairly general	At all levels
Communication	How much communication is aimed at achieving organization's objectives?	Very little	Little	Quite a bit	A great deal
	What is the direction of information flow	Downward	Mostly downward	Down and up	Down, up and sideways
	How is downward communication accepted?	With suspicion	Possibly with suspicion	With caution	With an open mind
	How accurate is upward communication?	Often wrong	Censored for the boss	Limited accuracy	Accurate
	How well do superiors know problems faced by subordinates?	Know little	Some knowledge	Quite well	Very well

3. Understanding of, and desire to help overcome problems.
4. Training and helping the subordinate to find better ways of doing the work.
5. Giving help in solving problems, as opposed to always giving the answer.
6. Giving support by making available the required physical resources.
7. Communication of the information that the subordinates must know to do their jobs as well as those things they would like to know, to be able to identify more closely with the operation.
8. The degree to which the superior seeks out and attempts to use the subordinate's ideas and opinions.
9. Approachableness.
10. The extent to which credit and recognition for accomplishments is given.

The second variable, the use of group decision making and group methods of supervision, is somewhat self-explanatory, but should not be interpreted literally.

FIGURE 14-2 continued

Diagnose Your Management Style

		Authoritative Exploitive	Authoritative Benevolent	Consultative	Participative Group
Decisions	At what level are decisions formally made?	Mostly at top	Policy at top, some delegation	Broad policy at top, more delegation	Throughout well integrated
	What is the origin of technical & professional knowledge used in decision making?	Top management	Upper and middle	To a certain extent, throughout	To a great extent, throughout
	Are subordinates involved in decisions related to their work?	Not at all	Occasionally consulted	Generally consulted	Fully involved
	What does decision-making process contribute to motivation?	Nothing, often weakens it	Relatively little	Some contribution	Substantial contribution
Goals	How are organizational goals established?	Orders issued	Orders, some comment invited	After discussion, by orders	By group action (except in crises)
	How much covert resistance to goals is present?	Strong resistance	Moderate resistance	Some resistance at times	Little or none
Control	How concentrated are review and control functions?	Highly at top	Relatively highly at top	Moderate delegation to lower levels	Quite widely shared
	Is there an informal organization resisting the formal one?	Yes	Usually	Sometimes	No—same goals as formal
	What are cost, productivity, and other control data used for?	Policing, punishment	Reward and punishment	Reward some self-guidance	Self-guidance problem solving

Source: Adapted from Rensis Likert, *The Human Organization,* Englewood Cliffs, N.J., Prentice-Hall, 1967.

It does not mean that the group necessarily makes all decisions or that a nonaction committee-type approach is used. Instead, the main emphasis is on involving people in the decision-making process to the extent that their opinions are asked on what the problems are that hinder accomplishment; their ideas on alternative solutions to problems are cultivated; and their thoughts on practical methods of implementing management decisions are solicited. It should be remembered that the participative process can be applied on an individual as well as a group basis, and that participation is not synonymous with abdication.

The final variable, high performance goals, implies that the superior is maximum-result oriented. This also must be interpreted with some caution. It does not mean that people should take a back seat to production and that the latter should be achieved at all cost without regard to the people involved. By definition, participative management involves the integration of people around production. There must be a climate where psychological satisfaction is a potential reward and the achievement of this satisfaction is tied directly to accomplishment on the job.

> Likert contends that in the long run, his System 4, group participative style, will yield best results.

Having defined these three key variables, Likert proceeded to measure their relationship to productivity. Without going into the details of his research, there was strong evidence to suggest that the manager or organizations that exhibited a high degree of supportive relationships, utilized the principles of group decision making and supervision, and developed high performance aspirations also had much higher levels of achievement for both individuals and for the organization in the long run.

Likert also makes a distinction between what he calls *causal, intervening*, and *end result variables*. The causal variables refer to the characteristics of the four different management systems discussed above.

The end result variables refer to such tangible items as volume of sales and production, lower costs, higher quality, and so forth. Of key importance are the intervening variables. These include such things as loyalty, performance goals of subordinates, degree of conflict versus cooperation, willingness to assist and help peers, feelings of pressure, attitude toward the company, job, and superior, and finally, the level of motivation.

> Intervening variables such as turnover and absenteeism may deteriorate under an authoritarian leader.

Likert maintains that an authoritative approach may initially achieve improvements in the end result variables, but at the same time, the intervening variables will begin to disintegrate. Eventually, turnover, absenteeism, and a progressive deterioration in the end result variables themselves will occur. On the other hand he says that the participative group approach will lead to a gradual upgrading of the intervening variables and long-run permanent gains in the end result variables. The critical factor is, of course, time.

In summary then, according to Likert, participation is one of the very important ingredients in gaining employee commitment on an overall basis. This commitment in turn can lead to less need for the use of formal authority, power, discipline, threat, and pressure as a means of motivating job performance. Therefore, participation and its resultant commitment become a substitute for pure authority. Commitment may be much harder to achieve initially, but in the long run will usually prove much more effective.

The Linking Pin Concept. According to Likert, the effective manager must view himself as a member of two groups. In one, he is the superior and in the other, he is the subordinate. It is important that the manager be skilled in both leadership and membership functions.

> The "Linking Pin" concept means that the manager must view himself as a member of two groups.

By being an effective member of his superior's work groups, the manager is able to exert *upward influence*. The ability to exercise influence upward is essential if a manager is to perform his supervising functions successfully. The reason for this requirement is clear: by making use of influence with his superiors, the manager gains support for the goals and objectives of his subordinates.

Through this dual group membership, a manager is seen in the important role captioned by Likert as the "Linking Pin" Concept, as follows.

He serves as the main link between his department and the rest of the company. He is a communication link downward in serving as the channel for flow of information on goals and objectives, as the disseminator of policies and practices, and as the interpreter of change. He also serves as the chief channel for upward communication. Through him, the needs, goals, and feelings of his subordinates are transmitted to upper echelons.[6]

Figure 14-3 depicts this linking pin function. To change this membership in the two groups—her peers, together with her superiors, and the group that she leads—into something more than a hierarchial reporting system, the manager must have a positive *interaction-influence* principle working for her. The interaction-influence principle in essence says that the amount of influence that a manager exerts over her subordinates is determined by how much she allows herself to be influenced by them.[7] "The extent to which she considers their opinions in reaching a decision whose outcome has impact on the group, for example, determines the degree of commitment and involvement in carrying out that decision effectively."[8]

FIGURE 14-3

The Linking Pin Function

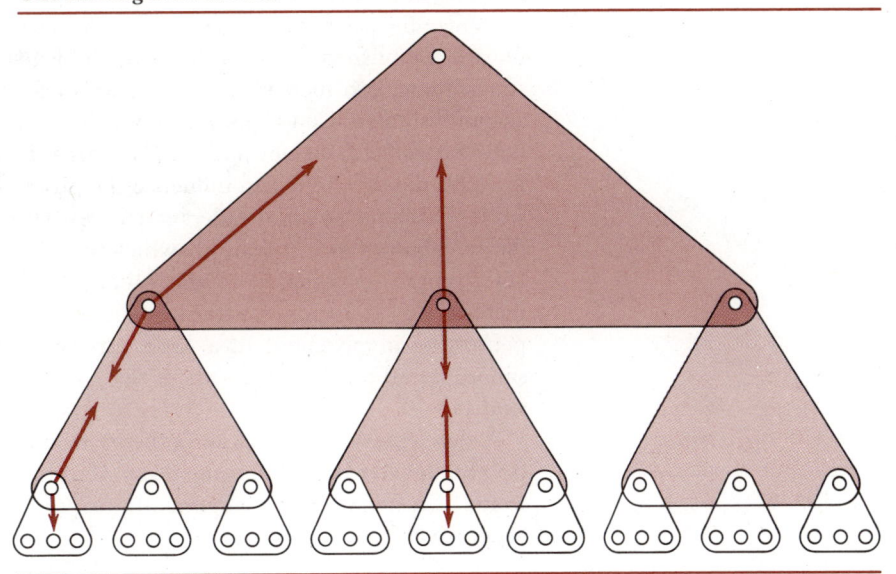

Source: Rensis Likert, *New Patterns of Management*, New York, McGraw-Hill Book Co., 1961, p. 105.

---

[6]Rensis Likert, *New Patterns of Management*, New York, McGraw-Hill Book Co., 1961, p. 114.
[7]Harold M. F. Rush, *Behavioral Science Concepts and Management Application.* The Conference Board Personnel Policy Study, No. 216, New York, 1969, p. 32.
[8]Ibid, p. 33.

The second major implication of the interaction-influence principle is a summation of the upward influence factor previously discussed. "If the manager is seen as having enough influence with his boss to affect the boss's decisions, he is perceived by his group as being able to gain more effective solutions to their problems and to look after their well-being; and they clothe him with more authority."[9]

PATH-GOAL THEORY

A path-goal theory[10] of leadership effectiveness has been presented by Robert J. House. This theory builds, according to Likert's theory, on Maslow's need hierarchy and includes our earlier thoughts about aligning the goals of employees with the goals of the organization. The theory states that employees form subjective probabilities regarding factors in their work. First, employees estimate the probability of that accomplish-work goal. Next, they estimate the probability of the accomplishment of attaining personal outcomes of value to them. For example, a salesperson may estimate the odds of selling 1000 units of office equipment during a year. Next, he estimates the probability of this leading to his transfer to a better sales territory.

The leader is seen as a vital force in aligning the goals of the organization with those of employee.

The leader in this situation is seen as the person who, at least in part, controls the rewards associated with work-goal accomplishment. First, he can choose to recognize the sales results as successful or unsuccessful, and help determine the reward established for such. Second, the leader, through interaction with the subordinate, can increase the assurance of forthcoming rewards for work-goal accomplishment. Consistency of action here will clarify the subordinates' linkage between work goal achievement and rewards. Third, through supportive behavior for subordinate efforts can influence the probability that the work will result in work-goal achievement. Leaders can increase the importance of goal achievement for the subordinate by the way in which they delegate and assign tasks. Finally, the net strength, or valence, of the subordinate's goal-directed behavior can be increased by reducing frustrating barriers, being supportive in times of stress, permitting involvement in a wide variety of tasks, and being considerate of subordinates' needs.[11] Elements of this theory have been supported by research studies.[12]

House's theory is closely aligned with a management-by-objectives approach to leadership.

A close observation of House's theory will lead one to the conclusion that it is closely aligned with a management-by-objectives approach to leadership. The key words are: path-goal alignment, superior-subordinate interaction, and supportiveness.

---

[9]Rensis Likert, *New Patterns of Management*, New York, McGraw-Hill Book Co., 1961, p. 105.
[10]Robert J. House, "A Path-Goal Theory of Leader Effectiveness," *Administrative Science Quarterly*, Vol. 16, 1971, pp. 321–338.
[11]Ibid., p. 323.
[12]Robert J. Justis, "Leadership Effectiveness: A Contingency Approach," *Academy of Management Journal*, 18, March 1975, pp. 160–167.

CONTINGENCY APPROACHES TO LEADERSHIP

The discussion of leadership that has been presented thus far has suggested that careful attention must be given to the expectations of employees and to the philosophy of leaders, as well as to establishing a balance of emphasis on people and on the task to be completed, the use of participation, and the supportive nature of supervision. Because of these factors, many leading observers have concluded that leadership effectiveness depends upon a multitude of factors rather than just one or two dimensions. These theories have been named *contingency* approaches to *leadership*, since success is presumed to be contingent on many factors, including the situation facing the leader.

FRED FIEDLER

Fiedler stresses the situational nature of successful leadership.

Fred Fiedler has suggested that one should take a contingency approach to leadership, based upon the situational factors of leader-member relations, task structure, and position power.[13] Fiedler measures *leader-member relationships* by asking members of various groups to indicate on a sociometric preference scale whether they accept or endorse their leader.

Task structure is measured by the degree to which the task is rigidly defined or left undefined. The more highly structured the task the greater the ability of the leader in obtaining compliance from subordinates. For example, employees on an automobile assembly line have very little opportunity to vary their work behavior compared to a maintenance crew in a large plant.

The third situational element in Fiedler's contingency theory is that of *position power*. The degree of position power is measured by having subordinates answer a check list of items regarding the things which a supervisor can and cannot do, such as rewarding, promoting, demoting, and evaluating subordinates. From these three dimensions, Fiedler has developed a situational favorableness dimension scale, which is shown in Figure 14-4. But Fiedler recognizes that other aspects of the situation such as motivation, intelligence, training, and experience of leaders and group members, as well as extraorganizational factors, such as the community's economic situation, may also need to be considered in determining leadership effectiveness.

Fiedler describes his contingency model of leadership effectiveness as one in which the performance of a group is contingent upon both the motivational system of the leader and the degree to which the leader has control and influence in a particular situation—the *"situational favorableness."*

A second major element of the contingency model is personality measure of the leader, which is determined by the so-called Least Preferred Coworker Score (LPC). This score is obtained by asking an individual to think of everybody with whom he has ever worked and to describe the person with whom he could work

---

[13]Fred E. Fiedler, *Leadership and Effective Management*, Glenview, Ill., Scott, Foresman and Co., 1974.

FIGURE 14-4

The Situational Favorableness Dimension Scale

	I	II	III	IV	V	VI	VII	VIII
Leader-member relations	\multicolumn{4}{Good}				Poor	
Task structure	High		Low		High		Low	
Position power	Strong	Weak	Strong	Weak	Strong	Weak	Strong	Weak
Most appropriate leadership style	T	T	T	R	R	R	R	T

Key: T = Task-oriented
R = Relationship-oriented

Source: adapted from Fred E Fiedler and Martin M. Chemers, *Leadership and Effective Management*, Glenview, Ill., Scott, Foresman and Co., p. 70.

The key variables are leader-member relations, task structure, and position power.

least well, his "least preferred co-worker." A low LPC score indicates the degree to which an individual is overly emotional in his reaction and tends to reject completely coworkers who have some negative attributes. The high LPC leader is one who evaluates good and bad points objectively and takes a more analytical point of view toward those with whom he prefers not to work. Note the similarity between the high LPC leader and the I'm OK-You're OK person described in Chapter 8, Organizational and Interpersonal Communications.[14]

In commenting on the Fiedler model described earlier, Hersey and Blanchard paraphrased it, as shown in Figure 14-4 in the following manner.

> *In this model, eight possible combinations of these three situational variables can occur. The most favorable situation for a leader to influence his group is one in which he is well liked by the members (good leader-member relations), has a powerful position (high position power), and is directing a well-defined job (high task structure): an example, a well-liked General making inspection in an army camp. On the other hand, the most unfavorable situation is one in which the leader is disliked, has little position power, and faces an unstructured task: an unpopular chairman of a voluntary hospital fund-raising committee.*[15]

Fiedler concludes that there is no such thing as an ideal leader for all situations.

The major conclusions from Fiedler's contingency model are as follows.

1. Persons who are unsuccessful in one leadership situation may be quite successful in another.

---

[14]Paul Hersey and Kenneth H. Blanchard, *Management of Organizational Behavior Utilizing Human Resources*, Englewood Cliffs, N.J., Prentice-Hall, Inc., 1972, pp. 80–81.

[15]A discussion of alternative approaches to providing a better fit between the organization and the individual is provided by Dennis R. Briscoe, "Organizational Design: Dealing with the Human Constraint," *California Management Review*, Fall 1980, Vol. 123, No. 1, pp. 71–80.

2. No one set of personality traits or leadership characteristics will determine an effective leader for every situation. Both the situation and the leader's personality must be evaluated in order to select a successful leader.
3. There is no such thing as an ideal leader. Task-motivated (low LPC) as well as relationship-motivated (high LPC) leaders excel in some situations and not in others.
4. The contingency model offers some guidelines to help management to predict the appropriate situation for a specific leadership style.
5. The contingency model suggests some possibilities for changing the behavior of leaders to fit situational requirements. In cases where this is not possible, perhaps the situation can be changed to fit the behavior of the existing leaders.[17]

HERSEY-BLANCHARD STUDIES

Hersey and Blanchard combined the Fiedler studies with previous studies at Ohio State University to construct a tridimensional leader effectiveness model.[17] Their first two dimensions consists of task behavior and relationship behavior. These dimensions are defined by Hersey and Blanchard as follows:

Hersey and Blanchard define leadership effectiveness as matching leadership style with a situation.

Task behavior—The extent to which leaders are likely to organize and define the role of the members of their group; to explain what activities each is to do and when, where, and how tasks are to be accomplished; characterized by endeavoring to establish well-defined patterns of organization, channels of communication, and ways of getting jobs accomplished.

Relationship behavior—The extent to which leaders are likely to maintain personal relationships between themselves and members of their group by opening up channels of communication, providing socioemotional support, "psychological strokes," and facilitating behaviors.[18]

Note in Figure 14-5 that their leadership styles are defined by four quadrants that depict various blends of task-relationship behavior. To these basic leadership styles Hersey and Blanchard then add the dimension of effectiveness. Leadership effectiveness is defined as the matching of the appropriate leadership style with the appropriate situation. The writers explain their modifications in the following manner.

While Fiedler's model is useful to a leader, he seems to be reverting to a single continuum of a leader behavior, suggesting that there are only two basic leader behavior styles, task oriented and relationships oriented. It is felt that most evidence indicates that leader behavior must be plotted on two separate axes rather than on a single continuum. Thus a

---

[16] Roger M. Stogdill and Alvin E. Coons, eds., *Leadership Behavior; Its Description and Measurement*, Research Monograph, No. 88, Ohio State University, 1957.
[17] The Ohio Studies are discussed in Roger M. Stodgill and Alvin E. Coons, eds., *Leadership Behavior; Its Description and Measurement*, Research Monograph, No. 88, Ohio State University, 1957.
[18] Paul Hersey and Kenneth H. Blanchard, *Management of Organizational Behavior*, 3rd ed., Englewood Cliffs, N.J., Prentice-Hall, 1977, pp. 103–104.

FIGURE 14-5

The Basic Leader Behavior Styles

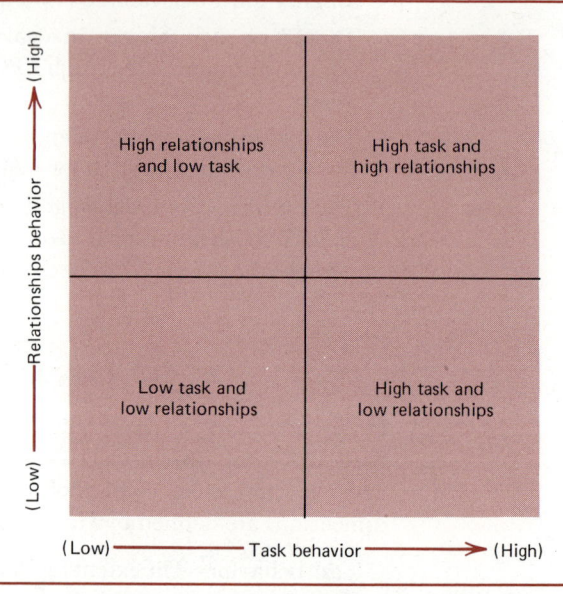

	(Low) Task behavior (High)
(High) Relationships behavior	High relationships and low task | High task and high relationships
(Low)	Low task and low relationships | High task and low relationships

Source: Hersey and Blanchard, *Management of Organizational Behavior Utilizing Human Resources.* Englewood Cliffs, N.J., Prentice-Hall, Inc., 1977, p. 103.

leader who had a high concern for tasks does not necessarily have a high or low concern for relationships. Any combination of the two dimensions may occur.[19]

Any leadership style can be judged effectively only according to how well it fits the situation at hand. Figure 14-6 indicates how such combinations are possible. In summarizing, these writers indicate the following three points.

1. Empirical studies tend to show that there is no normative (best) style of leadership: Successful leaders adapt their leader behavior to meet the needs of the group in the particular situation.
2. Effectiveness depends upon the leader, the follower(s), and other situational variables.
3. A person interested in increasing her own success as a leader must give serious thought to all behavioral and environmental considerations.

Situational Leadership Theory. There is yet one other dimension to the Hersey-Blanchard studies that is critical. It has been captioned the situational leadership theory and is depicted in Figure 14-7. Maturity is defined as the degree of achievement motivation, willingness and ability to take on responsibility, and the task-relevant education and experience of an individual or a group. This model suggests that leader behavior should check the maturity of the work group or

---
[19] Ibid., p. 102.

FIGURE 14-6

How the Basic Leader Behavior Styles May Be Seen by Others When They Are Effective or Ineffective

Basic Styles	Effective	Ineffective
High task and low relationship	Seen as having well-defined methods for accomplishing goals that are helpful to the followers.	Seen as imposing methods on others; sometimes seen as unpleasant, and interested only in short-run output.
High task and high relationship	Seen as satisfying the needs of the group for setting goals and organizing work, but also providing high levels of socioemotional support.	Seen as initiating more structure than is needed by the group and often appears not to be genuine in interpersonal relationships.
High relationship and low task	Seen as having implicit trust in people and as being primarily concerned with facilitating their goal accomplishment.	Seen as primarily interested in harmony; sometimes seen as unwilling to accomplish a task if it risks disrupting a relationship or losing "good person" image.
Low relationship and low task	Seen as appropriately delegating to subordinates decisions about how the work should be done and providing little socioemotional support where little is needed by the group.	Seen as providing little structure or socioemotional support when needed by members of the group.

Source: Paul Hersey and Kenneth H. Blanchard, *Management of Organizational Behavior Utilizing Human Resources*, Englewood Cliffs, N.J.: Prentice-Hall, 1977, p. 107.

The appropriate balance between task and relationship is dependent on the maturity level of the employees.

organization being dealt with, and apply the appropriate leadership style that fits that maturity level. Generally speaking, as one moves from less to more mature organizations and groups, leader behavior should move through the quadrants counterclockwise from (1) high task-low relationships behavior to (2) high task-high relationships, and (3) high relationships-low task to (4) low task-low relationships behavior.

Figure 14-7 depicts how maturity levels may be matched with various leadership styles. As pointed out by Hersey and Blanchard, higher standards of living, education, and sophistication of employees and society suggest changes in our viewpoints about basic management concepts. For example, concepts such as span of control and the direction and control functions of management may need to be evaluated. In the more sophisticated world of mature employees, a manager may

FIGURE 14-7

Designations for Styles of Leadership and Maturity Levels of Follower(s)

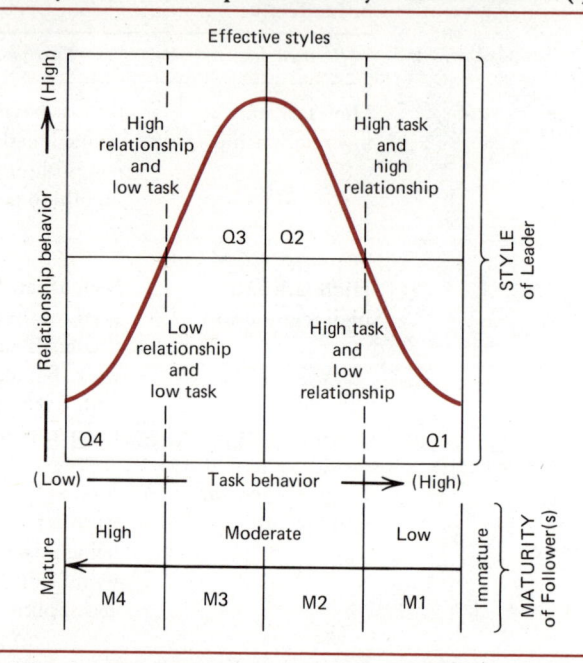

[Figure: A quadrant chart with Relationship behavior on the vertical axis (Low to High) and Task behavior on the horizontal axis (Low to High). Quadrants: Q1 (High task and low relationship), Q2 (High task and high relationship), Q3 (High relationship and low task), Q4 (Low relationship and low task). Below is a Maturity of Follower(s) scale: M4 High (Mature), M3 Moderate, M2 Moderate, M1 Low (Immature). A bell curve labeled "Effective styles" passes through the quadrants.]

Source: Hersey and Blanchard, *Management of Organizational Behavior Utilizing Human Resources,* Englewood Cliffs, N.J., Prentice-Hall, Inc., 1977, p. 167

Generally, employees exhibiting lower levels of maturity require more task emphasis.

need to spend more time in the long-range planning, interdepartmental coordination, and acquisition of resources. This would require that more time be spent with superiors and less time on organizing, directing, motivating, and controlling subordinates. An important conclusion from these models and the research conducted with their use is that a strictly functional or process view of management may need to give way to a more behavioral organic view of management. The functional approach to management becomes less relevant in a world in which employees are capable of operating on their own volition, given the proper organization climate.[20]

W.T. REDDIN—THE TRIDIMENSIONAL GRID[21]

Reddin conceptualized a tridimensional grid, borrowing some of the ideas from the management grid (see Figure 14-8). A central part of the three-dimensional

---

[20]The following article provides an insight into practices that which develop maturity and lead to employee self-control and commitment in Japan. See Ralph Townshend, "Why the Japanese Are So Successful," *AMA Forum,* October 1980, p. 29.

[21]This discussion of the tridimensional grid is based on material contained in the following sources: W. J. Reddin, *Managerial Effectiveness,* copyright 1970, McGraw-Hill Series in Management, and used with permission of McGraw-Hill Book Company. W. J. Reddin, "The 3-D Management Style Theory," *Training and Development Journal,* April, 1967.

FIGURE 14-8

The Integrated Tridimensional Grid

		Developer	Executive
Missionary	Compromiser		
		Bureaucrat	Benevolent autocrat
Deserter	Autocrat		

Relationship orientation (vertical axis) • Task orientation (horizontal axis) • Effectiveness (depth axis)

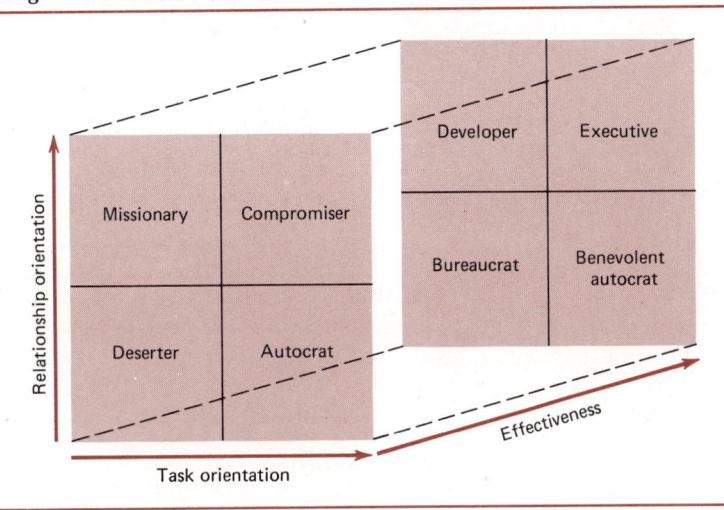

Source: W. J. Reddin, "The 3-D Management Style Theory," *Training and Development Journal,* April 1967.

theory is an eight-style model of management behavior. These eight styles form the eight possible combinations of task orientation, relationship orientation, and effectiveness. The main purpose of this concept is an attempt to show leaders that they can move from a plane of less to one of more effectiveness by changing their management styles.

Three-Dimensional Axes. Task orientation is defined as the extent to which a manager directs subordinates' efforts toward goal attainment. It is characterized by planning, organizing, and controlling.

Relationship orientation is defined as the extent to which a manager has personal job relationships. It is characterized by mutual trust, respect for subordinates' ideas, and consideration for employee feelings.

Effectiveness is defined as the extent to which a manager achieves the output requirements of his position. Either a degree of task orientation (TO), relationship orientation (RO), or a combination of both is used by leaders in managing. Reddin says managers sometimes emphasize one element and sometimes the other, since these two elements of behavior can be used in large or small amounts. As shown in Figure 14-9 when both TO and RO behaviors are high, Reddin calls the resulting style integrated. When TO is high and RO is low, the style is dedicated. When RO is high and TO is low, the style is related, and the use of each element to a small degree is the separated style.

These four styles represent four basic types of behavior. Any of the styles could be effective in some situations and not in others. Each one of the four basic styles has a less effective equivalent and a more effective equivalent. (See Figure 14-10). When one of the basic styles (e.g., integrated) is used inappropriately, a less

Reddin's model depicts a plane of more effective and less effective leadership styles.

FIGURE 14-9

Task and Relationship Orientations

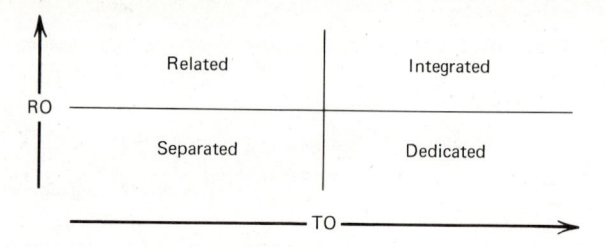

	Related	Integrated
RO	Separated	Dedicated

TO →

Source: William J. Reddin, *Managerial Effectives,* copyrighted 1970 by McGraw-Hill Book Co., p. 12. Used with permission of McGraw-Hill Book Co.

FIGURE 14-10

Managerial Style

Basic Style	Less Effective Managerial Style	More Effective Managerial Style
Integrated	Compromiser	Executive
Dedicated	Autocrat	Benevolent Autocrat
Related	Missionary	Developer
Separated	Deserter	Bureaucrat

Source: William J. Reddin, *Managerial Effectiveness,* copyrighted 1970 by McGraw-Hill Book Company. Used with permission of McGraw-Hill Book Company.

effective style (compromise) results. When it is used appropriately, a more effective style (executive) results.

Arranging the more and less effective leadership styles around the four basic styles, Reddin brings the third dimension of effectiveness into play. The manager's effectiveness cannot be measured just by the extent he achieves production requirements. She must be flexible in selecting styles and must strive for the most effective styles and therefore higher output. This flexibility is not used to keep the peace or to lower pressure, but to maintain an appropriate style under stressful situations.

The Four Basic Styles. The four basic styles with their more and less effective equivalents are (1) integrated (compromiser, executive), (2) dedicated (autocrat, benevolent autocrat), (3) related (missionary, developer), and (4) separated (deserter, bureaucrat).

Integrated Manager. The integrated manager gets people involved with the organization. There is free two-way communication with others and strong identification and emphasis on teamwork. The more effective style (executive) has

> The tridimensional grid shows managers how they can move from a less effective to more effective plane by remaining flexible.

a high task and high relationship orientation in a situation where such behavior is appropriate. They are good motivators who set high standards, treat people as individuals, and prefer team management. The less effective style in this plan (compromiser) uses a high task and relationship orientation in a situation that may not require a high concentration in either. They are poor decision makers and allow various pressures in the situation to influence them too much.

Dedicated Manager. These managers are domineering, interested only in production, and do not identify with subordinates. They cannot work without power. They do not communicate to subordinates any more than is absolutely necessary for production, and use punishment to correct deviations. The most effective style (benevolent autocrat) results in a directive manager who knows what he or she wants and can often get it without creating resentment. The less effective autocrat is concerned with only the immediate job and has no concern for others.

Related Manager. Related managers accept others as they find them, know employees, do not worry about time, see the organization as a social system, like to work with others, and obtain cooperation of others by setting a good example. Stressful situations tend to make them depressed. Subordinates characteristically suffer from lack of direction. The more effective style (developer) tends to display implicit trust in people. The less effective style (missionary) shows only interest in harmony.

Separated Manager. The separated manager is concerned with correcting deviations. He writes rules and policies and strictly enforces them. Other than routine work is avoided, and employees do not feel their achievements are recognized. The more effective style (bureaucrat) is characterized by belief in rules for their own sake. The less effective style (deserter) is uninvolved and passive.

Style Flex Concepts. The three-dimensional theory recognizes that a manager may use more than one style. A manager who can use a variety of more effective styles is said to have style flexibility. A manager who maintains a single style has style resistance. Some managers change styles to lower pressure on themselves rather than to increase effectiveness in the situation. This is called style drift. Managers who maintain an inappropriate, less effective style are demonstrating style rigidity.

The styles of three-dimensional theory are designed to give a clear and comprehensive picture of the managerial world. It is assumed that all the styles have an equal chance of occurring and, thus, if a sufficiently large number of managers in a sufficiently diverse number of organizations were tested, an equal number of each style would be obtained.[22]

---

[22]A comparative study of issues discussed in this and earlier chapters is provided by M. K. Badawy, "Styles of Mideastern Managers," *California Management Review*, Spring 1980, Vol. 22, No. 3, pp. 51–58.

SUMMARY OF CONTINGENCY LEADERSHIP THEORY

Tannenbaum and Schmidt's model shows the manager's style depends on three forces: those in the manager, in the subordinate, and in the situation.

The clearest summation of contingency factors to be considered by leaders is found in the writings of Tannenbaum and Schmidt. They present a range of leadership behavior from autocratic to democratic within the broader context of the organizational and societal environment. They then discuss forces in the manager, forces in subordinates, and forces in the situation that need to be considered when determining an appropriate style. The concept does not dictate to managers but helps them analyze their own behavior. Rather than offering a choice between two styles it suggests a range of appropriate behaviors. Figure 14-11 depicts the Tannenbaum and Schmidt continuum.

The manager's style depends on three forces: (1) those in the manager, (2) those in the subordinates, and (3) those in the situation.[23]

1. *Forces in the manager.* The manager's behavior in any given instance will be influenced greatly by the many forces operating within his own personality. Some of these forces include the following.
   (a) Value system: How strongly does he feel that individuals should have a share in making the decisions that affect them? Behavior is also influenced by the relative importance attached to organizational efficiency, personal growth of subordinates, and organization results.
   (b) Confidence in his subordinates: This depends on the amount of trust he has in people generally and his feelings about the subordinates' knowledge and competence with respect to the problem.
   (c) Personal leadership inclinations: Some managers seem to function more comfortably and naturally as highly directive leaders. Others seem to operate more comfortably in a team role where they are continually sharing many of their functions with their subordinates.
   (d) Feelings of security in an uncertain situation: The manager who releases control over the decision-making process thereby reduces the predictability of the outcome. Some managers have a greater need than others for predictability and stability in their environments. This "tolerance for ambiguity" is increasingly being viewed by psychologists as a key variable in a person's manner of dealing with problems.
2. *Forces in the subordinate.* Each employee, like the manager, is influenced by many personality variables. In addition, each subordinate has a set of expectations about how the superior should act in relation to him. Generally speaking, the manager can permit subordinates greater freedom if the following essential conditions exist.
   (a) The subordinates have a relatively high need for independence.

---

[23]An excellent discussion of the importance of the individual being managed when developing a leadership style is provided by William E. Zererden, "Leading Through the Followers Point of View," *Organizational Dynamics*, Spring 1980.

FIGURE 14-11

Continuum of Manager-Nonmanager Behavior

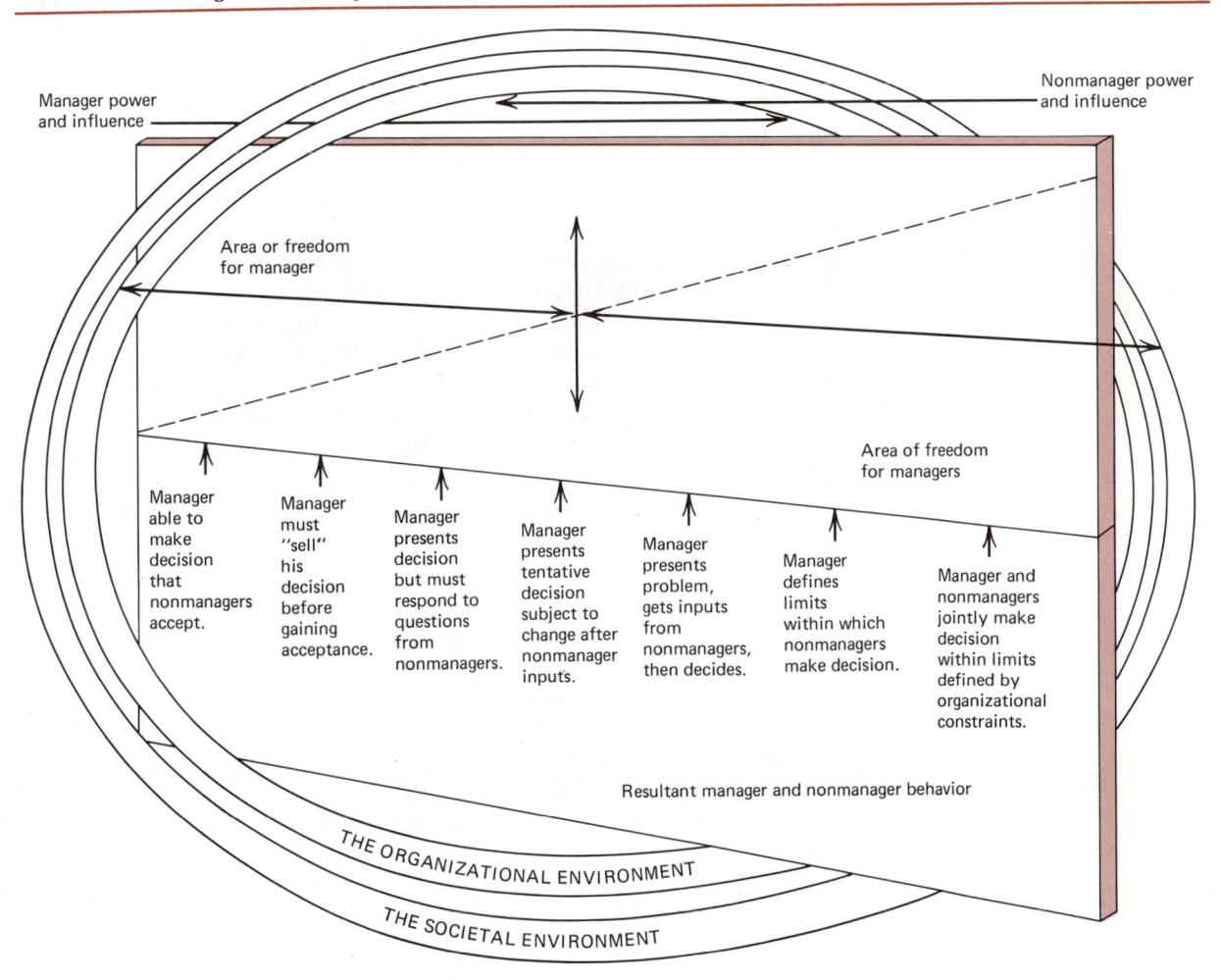

- Manager power and influence
- Nonmanager power and influence
- Area or freedom for manager
- Area of freedom for managers

| Manager able to make decision that nonmanagers accept. | Manager must "sell" his decision before gaining acceptance. | Manager presents decision but must respond to questions from nonmanagers. | Manager presents tentative decision subject to change after nonmanager inputs. | Manager presents problem, gets inputs from nonmanagers, then decides. | Manager defines limits within which nonmanagers make decision. | Manager and nonmanagers jointly make decision within limits defined by organizational constraints. |

Resultant manager and nonmanager behavior

THE ORGANIZATIONAL ENVIRONMENT

THE SOCIETAL ENVIRONMENT

Source: Robert Tannenhaum and Warren H. Schmidt, "How to Choose a Leadership Pattern," *Harvard Business Review,* May-June 1972.

(b) The subordinates possess a readiness to assume responsibility for decision making.
(c) They have a relatively high tolerance for ambiguity. (Some prefer to have clear-cut directives, others prefer a wider area of freedom.)
(d) They are interested in the problem and feel that it is important.
(e) They understand and identify with the goals of the organization.
(f) They have the necessary knowledge and experience to deal with the problem.

(g) They have learned to share in decision making. Persons who have come to expect strong leadership and are then suddenly confronted with the request to share more fully in decision making are often upset by this new experience. On the other hand, persons who have enjoyed considerable amounts of freedom resent the superior who begins to make all the decisions himself.

3. *Forces in the situation.* There are certain characteristics of the general situation which will also affect the manager's behavior. Among the more critical environmental pressures that surround them are those that stem from the organization, the work group, the nature of the problem, and the pressures of time.
(a) Type of organization: like individuals, organizations have values and traditions that inevitably influence the behavior of the people who work within them. These values and traditions are communicated through job descriptions, policy pronouncements, and public statements by top executives. For example, some organizations want their executives to be dynamic, imaginative, decisive, and persuasive. Others put more emphasis upon the executive's ability to work effectively with people. The fact that superiors have a defined concept of what the good executive should be will very likely push the manager toward one end or the other of the behavior range.

In addition, the amount of employee participation is influenced by such variables as the size of the working units, their geographical distribution, and the degree of inter- and intraorganizational security required to attain company goals. For example, the wide geographical dispersion of an organization may preclude a parochial system of participative decision making. Similarly, the size of the working units or the need for keeping plans confidential may make it necessary for the superior to exercise more control than would otherwise be the case. Factors like these may limit considerably the manager's ability to function flexibly on the continuum.
(b) Group effectiveness: this is perhaps the most clearly felt pressure on the manager. The more they feel the need for an immediate decision, the more difficult it is to involve other people. In organizations that are in a constant state of crisis and crash programming, one is likely to find managers using a high degree of authority with relatively little delegation to subordinates. When the time pressure is less intense, however, it becomes much more possible to involve subordinates in the decision-making process.

Therefore, successful managers can be primarily characterized neither as strong leaders nor as permissive ones. Instead, they maintain a high batting average in accurately assessing the forces that determine what their most appropriate behavior at any given time should be and in behaving accordingly. Possessing both insight and flexibility, such managers are less likely to be baffled by the problems of leadership.

Of course, perplexing questions will always remain. Should the leader constantly change to fit the situation? Give preference to the style employees want? Match the style desired by the organization? Pick the style she is most comfortable with? There are no absolute answers to these questions. Each of the approaches discussed, however, helps us to understand which style we are using and whether it will be effective for what we are trying to accomplish.

Contingency theory emphasizes the idea that a manager can choose a leadership strategy that will be effective in a given situation.

SUMMARY

This chapter has been devoted to the discussion of normative and contingency theories of leadership. Normative theories include Blake and Mouton's grid, Likert's four systems of management, and House's path-goal theory of leadership. All of these theories describe one best style of leadership for all occasions. Blake and Mouton's managerial grid is based on the fact that in any particular situation a manager has two basic concerns, for production and for people. The grid depicts the former on the horizontal axis and the latter on the vertical axis. Each axis is labeled 1 to 9. They then proceed to identify several different management styles based on where the manager places greatest emphasis. The grid suggests that a 9.9 style that emphasizes maximim concern for both people and production should be the ultimate goal for the leader to achieve.

Likert developed four systems of management to describe various management styles. The four systems that he identified were the exploitive authoritative, benevolent authoritative, consultative, and participative. Each of these systems is characterized by distinct conditions that exist in the management climate. Of the four systems, Likert feels participation holds the greatest potential for the long-

SUMMARY CHART

A Continuum of Organizational Patterns
Arranged by Design Principle and Logic

1. Normative theories.
   (a) Blake's grid (team management)—maximum concern for people and production.
   (b) Likert (participative management)—supportive relationships, group decision-making, and set high performance goals.
   (c) House's (path-goal theory)—establish rewards, increase assurance of forthcoming rewards, clarify the linkage between goal achievement and rewards.

2. Contingency theories.
   (a) Fiedler—task-motivated and relationship-motivated leaders can both excel if they match leadership style with the appropriate situation.
   (b) Hersey-Blanchard—within any task-relationship combination, certain leaders can exercise effective behavior while others will be ineffective.
   (c) Situational leadership theory—leadership style should change as one moves from low to high maturity organizations.
   (d) W. T. Reddin (tridimensional grid)—managers must be flexible and able to change style under stress situations, but should change styles only to improve effectiveness, not simply to lessen the pressure on themselves.
   (e) Tannenbaum and Schmidt—leadership continuum depicting range from autocratic to democratic. The appropriate leader behavior depends on forces in the manager, subordinates, and the situation.

range development of the human assets of the organization. The three distinguishing characteristics of the participation manager is that she exhibits supportive relationships, uses group decision-making techniques, and has high performance standards.

The manager is also seen as a linking pin between levels in the organization. To be effective she must be able to establish positive working relationships with both superiors and subordinates.

Contingency theories provide factors that must be considered in successful leadership, but presume that actual styles must be changed to fit the situation. Fielder's contingency model indicates that leadership style should vary with leader-member relationships, task structure, and the power of the leader's position.

The path-goal theory of leadership suggests that the leader can be successful by clarifying the path toward success for subordinates, showing them how they can be awarded for accomplishment and supporting goal-oriented behavior.

Reddin's tridimensional grid depicts a manager's task orientation, relationship orientation, and effectiveness. The grid then identifies eight styles of management behavior. Four are labeled as less effective styles and four as more effective styles. The eight styles result from eight possible combinations of task orientation, relationship orientation, and effectiveness. Each of the less effective styles has a complement of a more effective style. The purpose of the grid is to show managers how they can move from a plane of less effectiveness to one of more effectiveness.

Tannenbaum and Schmidt classified leadership as being either superior- or subordinate-centered, depending on the degree to which the manager uses authority or allows areas of freedom. Along a continuum they then identified and defined seven alternative positions. Finally, they pointed out that a manager's style depends on three forces: forces in the manager, forces in subordinates, and forces in the situation. Managers must assess each of these forces to determine their most appropriate behavior at any given time.

DISCUSSION QUESTIONS

1. One way of viewing leadership is from an overall style approach. Set forth the essential ingredients of Blake's and Mouton's managerial grid, describing each of the five basic positions. Discuss some of the significant observations about the grid that were made in the text and in class.

2. Discuss managerial leadership from the standpoint of Likert's four systems of management, being sure to thoroughly explore his System 4 approach and the idea of causal, intervening, and end result variables.

3. Explain in detail the linking pin concept. Why is it significant from a total organizational point of view?

4. Fully explain Reddin's tridimensional grid, being sure to distinguish between the planes of more and less effectiveness as well as distinctions between each of the eight styles.

5. Explain how the path-goal theory of leadership works from an operational point of view.
6. According to situational leadership theory, what is the appropriate task-relationship match for (a) the mature organization, (b) the immature organization? Explain the reasoning behind your answer.
7. Discuss the basic philosophy underlying Fiedler's contingency model of leadership. What are some of the major conclusions drawn from his work?
8. "If a person is an effective leader he or she can lead any group of subordinates." Discuss the wisdom of this statement.
9. "In the mature organizational world managers will need to spend most of their time reflecting on their superior's needs rather than their subordinates' needs." Do you agree with this statement? Why or why not?

APPLICATION EXERCISES AND CASES

IDENTIFYING LEADERSHIP STYLES

The following quotation is from a supervisor who is describing her leadership style. She supervises fifteen computer programmers in a fast-growing data processing company. The average age of these computer programmers is 21.

If a leader is going to be successful, she has to be respected by his subordinates. I've observed supervisors who are weak and are afraid to make decisions. Before they knew it, they soon discovered that there are enough "empire builders" around to quickly grab all the power they can. During the ten years I've been here, I've seen more than one superior squeezed out of her job either by another manager who reached into her area of authority or by subordinates who start as "do gooders" and then get permission from the "higher up" to maintain the authority which the supervisor once had.

Another thing a supervisor should keep in mind is consistency. Changing your leadership style, I think, is really bad. Subordinates would rather have a supervisor be tough all the time, rather than one who is lenient one minute and hard-nosed two minutes later.

Finally, there is the delicate matter of control. A supervisor who is not able to maintain tight controls in the work situation simply cannot do her job effectively. Tight controls assume proper discipline of the subordinate. Without these controls, you would soon have chaos. Also, keep in mind that, in spite of what they may say, subordinates really want you to provide discipline. They simply will not respect you unless you give them discipline and the best way to do that is close control.

Questions
1. Locate this manager with respect to the (a) Blake-Mouton managerial grid, the (b) Reddin tridimensional grid, the (c) leadership chart, Figure 14-12, and (d) Likert's four systems of management. Explain the reasons for your location.
2. What factors influence the leadership style which a manager develops?
3. In a paragraph summarize the leadership challenges that face this manager.

CAN ONE LEARN TO MANAGE SUBORDINATES?

Tom McAvoy was 27 and three years out of law school when he entered the legal department of Electro-Magnetic Induction Technology Industries as a legal researcher on an antitrust case. The company then had about $50 million in sales and operated almost exclusively in North America—and really only in the United States as the Canadian affiliate was barely more than a sales office. By the time McAvoy was 45, he was Associate General Counsel of a company—now renamed Emitco—with sales of $750 million and major operations in all developed countries, and especially in the European Common Market, where one-third of the company's sales now originated. McAvoy's father had been a diplomat, and Tom had spent much of his childhood and youth abroad before coming home to the United States for college and law school. He therefore was multilingual with excellent French, German, and Spanish and adequate Italian. Negotiations and legal work in Europe thus naturally had gravitated to him. He had become the company's mainstay in the development of the European network of Emitco subsidiaries and affiliates, was a member of the management committee of Emitco-Europe, and spent about half of his time in Europe and on European business.

It was no secret to any one in Emitco that McAvoy wanted to live in Europe. When he suggested establishing the company's European headquarters in Paris, more than one within the company commented that McAvoy's love for that city was the real reason for the choice. When therefore the company's vice president-European informed headquarters that he intended to retire on his sixtieth birthday, nine months hence, McAvoy's choice as his successor surprised no one. And it pleased the heads of the European companies who had worked closely with McAvoy over the years and had found him intelligent, well informed, and distinctly *simpatico*—whereas they often had difficulties working with some of the others in Emitco headquarters—most of them small-town midwesterners who had never lived outside their own country.

McAvoy was elated, but he also worried. He was conscious of the fact that he had never before managed people—he had always been a staff specialist. And now he was going to have reporting to him nine line managers and a total of 19,000 people in nine different European countries. He therefore requested a three-month leave—ostensibly to get his teenaged children into boarding schools and to move his home to Paris, but in reality to prepare himself for line operating responsibility. Being a conscientious man he got a list—a very long list—of books on personnel management and read them all. But the more he read, the more confused he became. The books were full of procedures, but McAvoy was fully determined to leave procedures to the personnel department. Otherwise they all talked of the kind of man he should be or should become. But what was he supposed to do? He knew that he had to establish himself fairly fast—he had seen enough men get a promotion to know that one had to establish himself in a new job within a few months or so. He knew that the only aspect of the job that was new to him was managing people—but it was *totally* new to him. And he felt strongly that he had to know in advance what to do and what not to do; he knew that improvisation wasn't his way of doing things.

Finally, with most of three months of his leave used up, he reluctantly went for advice and counsel to the retired chairman of the Emitco board, the man who had originally hired him. At the time Jonathan Forbes was an executive vice president. He had then soon become president and chief executive officer and the main architect of Emitco's growth and expansion. Forbes had never been the kind of "boss" the books recommended; he had been austere, aloof, demanding, critical, and rather distant. But McAvoy had respected him and so had many others in Emitco. And Emitco's growth and success, McAvoy believed, was primarily the result of Forbes' management of people—he seemed to be able to make the most diverse people perform and pull together.

Forbes was at first cool when McAvoy sought him out in his retirement retreat in Colorado Springs. But he warmed when McAvoy explained why he had come. "That you worry, Tom, is in itself a very good sign," Forbes said, "and perhaps it's the only thing needed to make you do a good job. Managing people isn't that hard—if you know that it is your job and that it is work. The only thing that is truly important is. . . ."[24]

Question
1. How would you finish the sentence? And what would you say to defend your choice of the one thing that is "truly important" in managing people?

---

[24] Peter F. Drucker, "Can One Learn to Manage Subordinates?," *Management Cases*, New York, Harper Row, 1977, pp. 49–50.

CHAPTER 15
HUMAN RESOURCE DEVELOPMENT AND QUALITY OF WORK LIFE

HUMAN RESOURCE PLANNING AND DEVELOPMENT—AN OVERVIEW
STAFFING
FORECASTING NEEDS
RECRUITMENT
SELECTION
ASSESSMENT CENTERS
HUMAN RESOURCE DEVELOPMENT—QUALITY OF WORK LIFE
BEHAVIOR MODIFICATION
PERFORMANCE APPRAISAL
AN INTEGRATED GOAL SETTING, APPRAISAL, AND COACHING SYSTEM
SETTING OBJECTIVES
ACTION PLANNING
REVIEWING AND APPRAISING PERFORMANCE
REINFORCING POSITIVE BEHAVIOR
MANAGEMENT DEVELOPMENT
KNOWLEDGE
EXPERIENCE
FEEDBACK
THE EFFECTIVENESS OF MANAGEMENT DEVELOPMENT PROGRAMS
DEVELOPING A CAREER PLAN
WHAT ARE CAREER GOALS?
GAINING SELF-AWARENESS
THE CAREER-LAUNCHING CHECKLIST
APPLICATION EXERCISE AND CASES
TALENT HUNT
A NOVEL APPROACH TO MANAGEMENT DEVELOPMENT

HOW GM STAYS AHEAD[1]

The critics might have had an easier time accepting the GM culture if its initials stood for General Motoru. For GM is essentially a tribal organization, and many of its traits are indeed those associated with the seemingly omnipotent Japanese automotive companies. GM has a singularly close-unit management. It boasts that it hires fewer people from outside than any other major U. S. corporation, and loses fewer to other companies. Two-thirds of GM's executives never worked for anybody else, and if last year's pattern continues to be typical, fewer than 1 per cent of the top 6000 executives will ever defect.

"GM loves to make low-risk appointments," says Fuller, "and the business of appointing managers here is low-risk because we're always looking solely at an established record of getting things done. There is no form of instant executive." Anyone who does the job well can be sure of moving up—"and the corporation has built-in ways of helping him do the job well." Moreover, GM has enough different types of jobs, at enough different levels, to honor loyalty with job security.

But how can the holder of an established record be confident that he or she will in fact get promoted? The answer lies in GM's management-appraisal system. Alfred Sloan used to insist that no use of his time was more important than picking the right people for the right jobs, and since the company's earliest years, top management has paid a lot of attention to people as far down the ranks as plant managers. In fact, today's senior executives may spend more time looking at some 35-year-old they've never met than at someone a few steps down in the hierarchy. "We've all known Alan Smith (GM's new executive vice president for finance) for some time, but we don't know a chief engineer or a general manager as well," Roger Smith points out. "And when you have to pick the best guy out of a dozen for a job, you have to take your time."

[1]Charles G. Burck, "How GM Stays Ahead," *Fortune*, March 9, 1981, pp. 48–56.

HUMAN RESOURCE DEVELOPMENT— AN OVERVIEW

Human resource planning and development (HRPD) looks at organizational needs and monitors the life cycle of new employees.

General Motors' long-run systematic planning for human resources is obviously one of the prime reasons for their success. Edgar Schein has emphasized the need for a planned, systematic linking of organizational and management development in a function that he calls *human resource planning and development* (HRPD).[2] Essentially this function looks at organizational needs on a continuous basis and monitors the life cycle of new employees as they move from beginning jobs to dealing with early career and midcareer choices.

[2]Edgar Schein, "Increasing Organizational Effectiveness Through Better Human Resources Planning and Development," *Sloan Management Review*, Fall 1977, Vol. 19, No. 1, p. 1.

The need for human resource planning and development is brought about for several reasons.[3] (1) Organizations are becoming more dependent on highly trained specialists. (2) Social values are changing and for many people less emphasis is being placed on long-term careers with the same organization. (3) There are increasing numbers of dual career families, which affects the organization's ability to move people geographically. (4) Research indicates that career crisis and the need for development continues throughout employees' lifetimes.[4]

Figure 15-1 conceptualizes the components of an effective HRPD system. On the left side organizational needs are shown. On the right, individual employee needs are itemized. Both of these are keyed to a long-term look at the employees of an organization. The center column suggests the processes that can be used to match organizational and individual needs. Note that all processes in the center column could become a part of a total human resource planning and development program.

This chapter examines the matching processes outlined by Schein as career of job choice and early career issues on the right merge with the need for organizations to plan for staffing on the left of Figure 15-1.

STAFFING

FORECASTING NEEDS

Human resource staffing begins with a forecast of the number of new personnel who will be needed because of growth, turnover, and retirement. Figure 15-2 illustrates how a personnel flow analysis portrays broad categories of management need requirements over a two-year period of time. It suggests to management that their attrition rate due to promotions, demotions, and separations is such that 150 lower-level managers must be hired or promoted from within in year 2 in order to allow a growth of only 15 new lower-level managers. Of course, in practice, the organization must develop a job analysis of each job to be filled and forecast specific needs job by job. Managers also would need to have a comprehensive picture of their present employees in order to decide how many of these jobs could be filled by promoting from within versus going to the outside.

Personnel flow analysis can assist in providing answers to such questions as the following.

- How many and what kinds of employees will we need to hire or develop over each of the next several years?
- What kinds of training programs will we need each year?

---

[3]Ibid., pp. 2–3.
[4]Ted Mills, "Human Resources—Why the New Concern?" *Harvard Business Review*, March-April 1975, pp. 130–131.

FIGURE 15-1

A Development Model of Human Resource Planning and Development

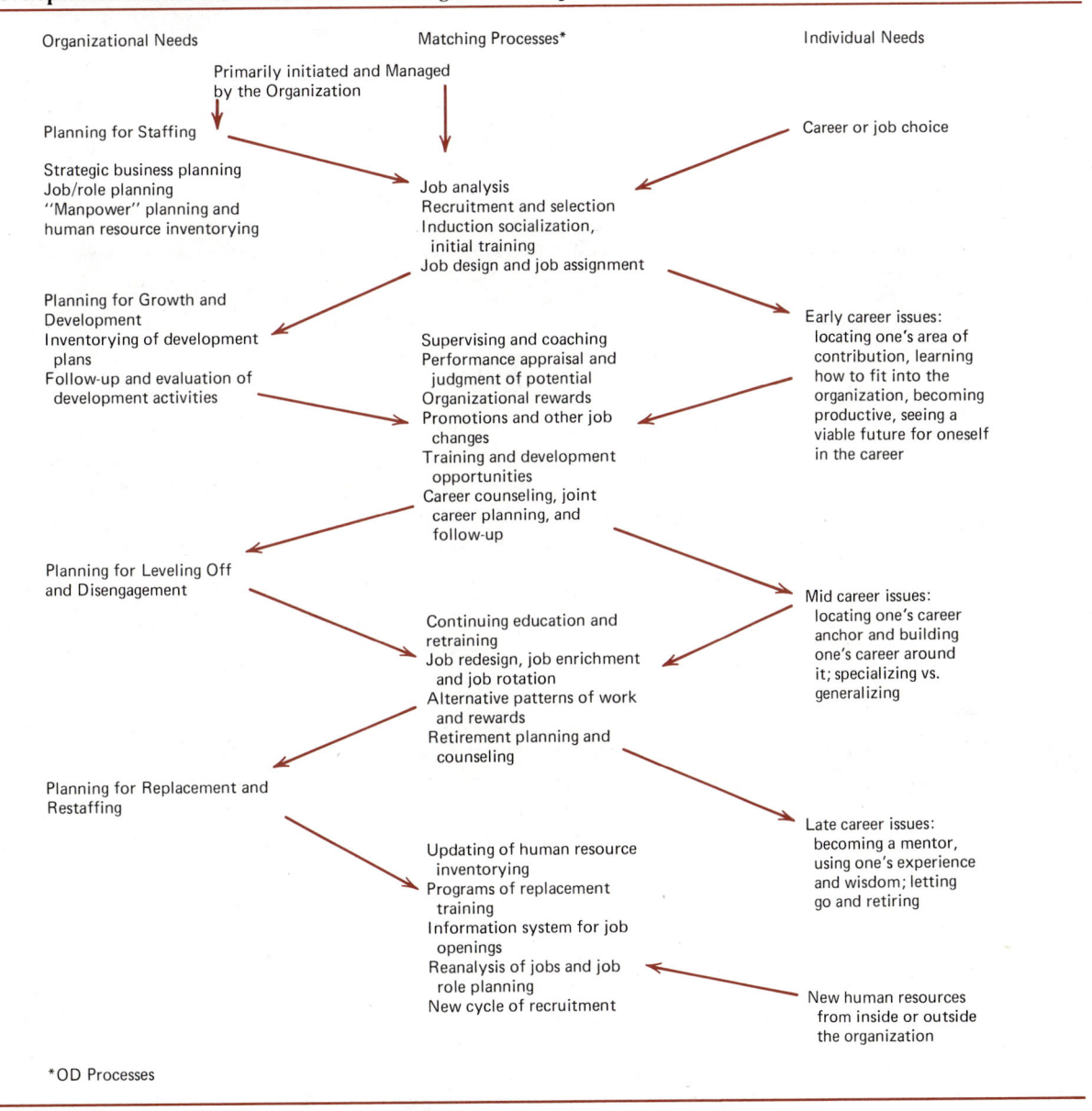

Organizational Needs	Matching Processes*	Individual Needs
	Primarily initiated and Managed by the Organization	
Planning for Staffing		Career or job choice
Strategic business planning Job/role planning "Manpower" planning and human resource inventorying	Job analysis Recruitment and selection Induction socialization, initial training Job design and job assignment	
Planning for Growth and Development Inventorying of development plans Follow-up and evaluation of development activities	Supervising and coaching Performance appraisal and judgment of potential Organizational rewards Promotions and other job changes Training and development opportunities Career counseling, joint career planning, and follow-up	Early career issues: locating one's area of contribution, learning how to fit into the organization, becoming productive, seeing a viable future for oneself in the career
Planning for Leveling Off and Disengagement	Continuing education and retraining Job redesign, job enrichment and job rotation Alternative patterns of work and rewards Retirement planning and counseling	Mid career issues: locating one's career anchor and building one's career around it; specializing vs. generalizing
Planning for Replacement and Restaffing	Updating of human resource inventorying Programs of replacement training Information system for job openings Reanalysis of jobs and job role planning New cycle of recruitment	Late career issues: becoming a mentor, using one's experience and wisdom; letting go and retiring New human resources from inside or outside the organization

*OD Processes

Source: Edgar Schein, "Increasing Organizational Effectiveness Through Better Human Resources Development," *Sloan Management Review,* Planning and Vol. 19, No. 1, Fall 1977 p. 1, author's note.

FIGURE 15-2

Management personnel flow analysis

	Year 1		Year 2				Year 2
Management level	Number in group	Don't move	Promote to next level	Demote	Separate from co.	Hired	Number in group
Lower	300	165	60	30	45	150	315
Middle	200	140	30	10	20	70	210
Upper	100	90	0	5	5	10	100

Source: Adapted from Neil Churchill, "Analyzing and Modeling Human Resource Flows," *Monitoring the Human Resource System*, ed. Ruth Shaeffer, New York, The Conference Board, 1976, pp. 19-29. Also cited in George Strauss and Leonard Sayles, *Personnel*, Englewood Cliffs, N. J., Prentice-Hall, 1980.

■ Given our present personnel policies, how likely are we to meet our Affirmative Action goals?[5]

In actual practice the staffing needs analysis, personnel inventory, and manpower development plans that large organizations develop are significantly more detailed and comprehensive than above. Indeed, the total process is many times more highly sophisticated and represents a major undertaking for firms committed to insuring that the organization has a long term supply of the best qualified personnel.

RECRUITMENT

In order to fill the forecasted manpower needs, an organization must make a decision; acquire personnel from outside or as is often the case "raise" and develop talent rather than "raid" for it. General Motors has carried this process of growing its own talent as far as almost any company, grooming many of its future leaders, at the General Motors Institute, a GM-owned university in Flint, Michigan. GMI's graduates do not have to work at GM, but many choose to do so.[6] It should be recognized however, that in rapid growth situations, where new skills or expertise are involved, when unforseen circumstances develop, or where it is deemed "new blood" needs to be introduced, it may be impossible to fully utilize a raise and develop your own strategy.

Organizations must decide whether to acquire personnel from outside the organization or "raise" and develop their own talent.

The recruiting and selection function in large companies is usually delegated to a personnel department. They recruit a pool of applicants from colleges, universities, trade schools, and employment agencies. From this pool, departmental managers and supervisors are usually allowed to make their choices. The lower the rank of the employee the more likely the selection process will be completely centralized in the personnel department.

---
[5]George Strauss and Leonard Sayles, *Personnel—The Human Problems of Management*, Englewood Cliffs, N.J., Prentice-Hall, Inc., 1980, p. 341.
[6]Op. cit., Burck, p. 52.

Well-known organizations with good salaries and company benefits often do very little recruiting for hourly employees except during start-ups of entire plants. Their personnel files bulge with applications. This has been especially true during the 1980s with unemployment at relatively high levels in many areas of the country. In such situations the organizations' favorable reputation plus the economic environment create a situation where the recruitment problem is minimal.

SELECTION

Once a pool of potential candidates to fill vacancies have been recruited, the process of selecting the most qualified begins. A total discussion of selection methods and their strengths and weaknesses can be found in personnel management texts.[7] The most common approach in managements' application of these methods is known as the "successive hurdles" approach. A view of how a total selection process might look is shown in Figure 15-3. Using this approach the organizations tries to eliminate candidates who do not fit the job specifications as early as possible. This saves time, energy, and money for the organization while also sparing the candidate's investment in the same type of things. In addition, the candidate is spared the disappointments that come from being turned down because too many false hopes have been built up.

Screening Interview. The initial screening interview is often very short. In the case of hourly, unskilled or semiskilled jobs, it may consist primarily of checking to make sure the applicant meets some of the most basic and obvious of the job requirements such as minimal experience or education requirements. Assuming the applicant's response to these is positive they will be requested to fill out an application blank. For higher-level or skilled jobs the screening interview maybe a somewhat lengthier process and in some cases may not take place until after the application blank (second step depicted in Figure 15-3) has been completed. The reason for changing the sequence for these types of jobs is that often much more background information must be gathered and documented in written form. Having this information in written form enables the person doing the interviewing (usually someone in the personnel department) to do a more thorough and higher-quality job at this phase of the selection process.

Application Forms. Application forms vary considerably in both length and depth of information sought and for different types of jobs within an organization. Along with the interview they are the most widely used of selection methods. Certain types of information contained in well-designed application forms can provide an interviewer with valuable initial insights regarding prospective employees. Included would be information that might offer clues regarding em-

---

[7]Edwin B. Flippo, *Personnel Management*, 5th ed., New York, McGraw-Hill Book Co., 1980, p. 511.

FIGURE 15-3

Summary of a Selection Procedure

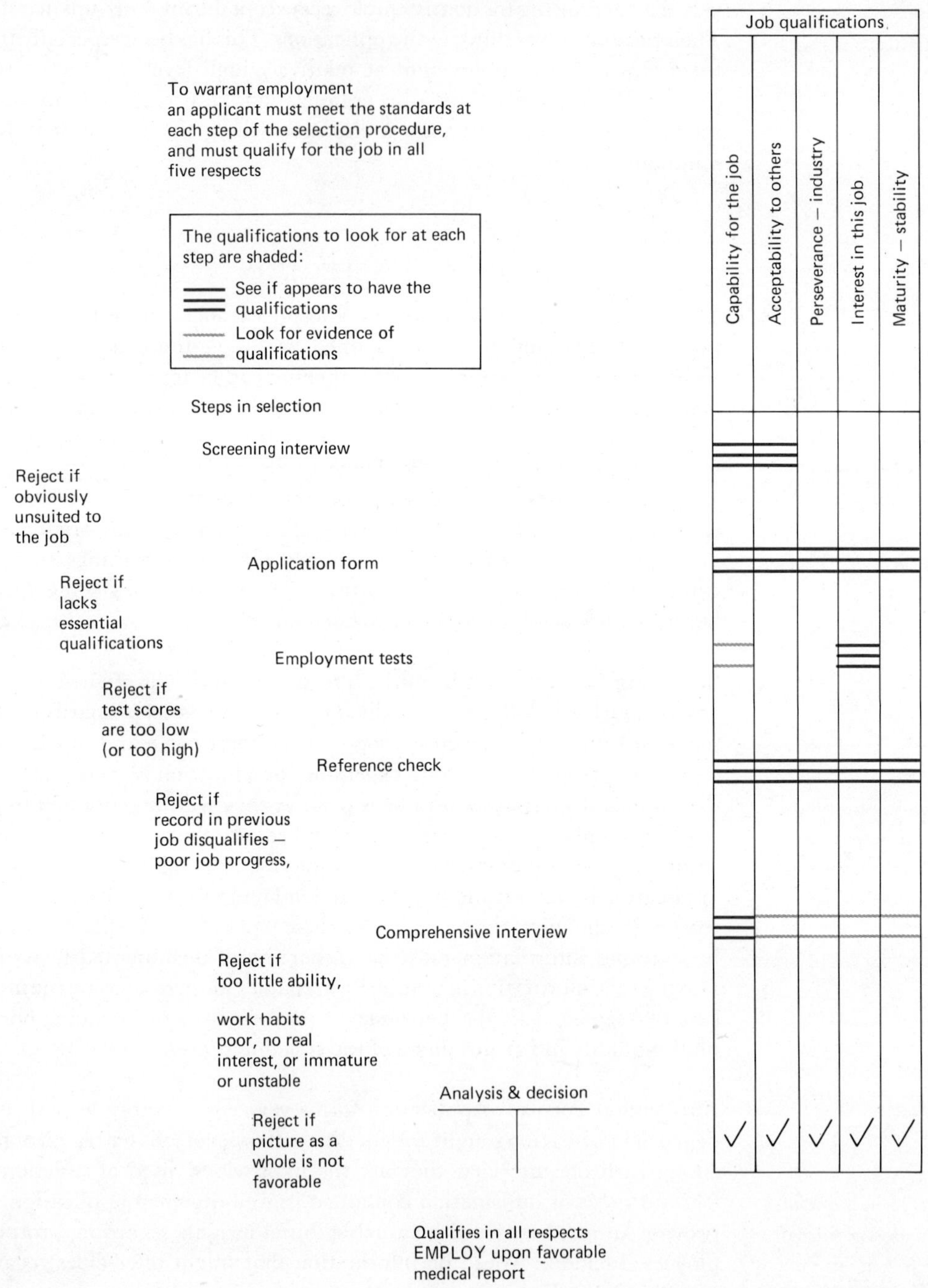

To warrant employment an applicant must meet the standards at each step of the selection procedure, and must qualify for the job in all five respects

The qualifications to look for at each step are shaded:
═══ See if appears to have the qualifications
─── Look for evidence of qualifications

Job qualifications
Capability for the job · Acceptability to others · Perseverance — industry · Interest in this job · Maturity — stability

Steps in selection

Screening interview
- Reject if obviously unsuited to the job

Application form
- Reject if lacks essential qualifications

Employment tests
- Reject if test scores are too low (or too high)

Reference check
- Reject if record in previous job disqualifies — poor job progress,

Comprehensive interview
- Reject if too little ability, work habits poor, no real interest, or immature or unstable
- Reject if picture as a whole is not favorable

Analysis & decision
✓ ✓ ✓ ✓ ✓

Qualifies in all respects EMPLOY upon favorable medical report

Source: Robert M. Fulmer, *The New Management*, New York: Macmillan, 1974.

ployment stability, compatability in working with others, depth of previous job experience, career goals, and others. However, those involved in the hiring decision process need to be trained and counseled regarding the purpose, value, and effective use of application blanks.

Some firms have had success in using weighted application forms. Weighted application blanks include certain items or categories of information, usually biographical in nature, given more weight in reaching the employment decision than are other items. The weightings are based on a statistical analysis which has shown that there is a high correlation between some items and such things as turnover, absenteeism or other performance-related factors that may be of particular importance to the employer.

Employment Tests. The third phase of the "successive hurdles" approach involves testing. A 1980 Prentice-Hall survey of 2500 companies revealed that 64.5 percent use testing in employment selection.[8] Tests fall into several categories including those designed to gain insight into (1) personality, (2) interests, (3) aptitude (potential to learn or perform in a given area,) (4) general intelligence or IQ, and (5) achievement or acquired ability. The latter are widely used in organizations hiring clerical workers (particularly secretarial jobs) or in jobs that require manual dexterity. Often a battery of tests is used by organizations considering people for management positions or making transfer and promotion decisions.

Employment testing has always been controversial and has become even more so as a result of equal employment opportunities legislation referred to previously. Although it represents an oversimplification of the issues involved, tests must be shown to be nondiscriminatory in nature. The burden of such proof falls on the employer.

In addition to the legal issues involved with the many types and variety of tests that are available for organizations to use, the matters of test validity and reliability have been historical concerns. Validity refers to how well a given test score predicts future job performance. In order to establish test validity one must decide which criteria will be used to judge eventual successful performance.

> Test validity refers to how well a test correlates with successful future job performance.

Reliability refers to the extent to which a test produces the same results each time it is utilized. In other works, if a person were to take a reliable test a first time and then retake it later, would the results be similar? One must be careful to design tests so that the responses cannot be faked by test takers. The probability of this happening will tend to increase as people become more familiar with tests through direct experience or through reading about tests.

> Reliability refers to the extent to which test results are consistent.

In summary, it is safe to observe that test administration and interpretation does not belong in the hands of "amateurs." If utilized properly, the tests just described can have significant value in selection, career counseling, determining training needs, making transfer or promotion decisions and in selecting candidates for

---

[8]Arthur A. Wilkin, "Commonly Overlooked Dimensions of Employee Selection," *Personnel Journal*, July 1980, p. 583.

management positions. Tests should be used as only one part of the selection process.

Reference Check. The reference check is a way of verifying information that the applicant has provided. If the person performing the reference check is skilled at interviewing procedures, they can often elicit valuable additional information from the individual being screened. Reference checks are usually more valuable if the investigator uses them to clarify and gather more facts about information on the application blank.

Comprehensive Interview. The interview is almost universally used as a part of the selection process and in many cases is a major determinant of eventual decisions regarding initial employment, particularly where several applicants have met or passed all other hurdles. Since it is such a key factor, it behooves organizations to invest the time and money that is necessary to train managers in the effective techniques and approaches to the interviewing process. Part of this training involves an awareness of some of the common problems of interviewing discussed next.

Stereotyping is the tendency to harbor predetermined opinions about broad categories of people such as someone who comes from the South or the East. These opinions may be either positive or negative. Similarly, the *halo effect* can operate in either a positive or negative way. It refers to the tendency to rate someone high or low on all or several characteristics based on single initial impressions in only one area.

Asking *leading questions* is a third common problem. For example: "I assume you enjoy working and interacting with other people on the job" is a leading question and in all probability will elicit a positive but perhaps an unreliable response.

Another problem is that of *overselling the job*. This is the tendency of the interviewer to present an inaccurate picture of the job including only its advantages. An effective interviewer will find out what is important to the applicant in the job climate: that is, what needs they are seeking to satisfy.

When a person accepts a job an unwritten psychological contract is formed between the organization and the individual.[9] Each party to the contract has a set of expectations with respect to the other. These expectations are very real and when at some subsequent time either the organization or individual employee finds that the expectations are not being met, problems relating to motivation and productivity inevitably occur.

Jobs have requirements and certain unchangeable characteristics just like people have needs. To promote a match between these fixed job elements and individual expectations, real candor is needed. At least part of the interview process should be devoted to investigating both sides of the matching up process.

---

[9] John Paul Kotter, "The Psychological Contract: Managing the Joining-Up Process," *California Management Review*, Spring 1973, Vol. XV, No. 3, pp. 91–99.

The interviewing method may follow a patterned or a nondirective approach. In the patterned interview the interviewer includes a specific set of questions that are asked of each candidate. In the nondirective approach the interview consists entirely of open-ended questions that leave room for a wide variety of responses. In practice, most interviews use a combination of the two approaches.

ASSESSMENT CENTERS

Often companies wish to fill supervisory positions from experienced employees already with the company. One promising technique for this type of selection is the assessment center. Today over 2000 businesses are estimated to be using assessment centers, among them some of the most prestigious companies in American business, plus several governmental agencies.[10]

The assessment center is a process in which individuals participate in a series of exercises most of which approximate what they would be called on to do in a future job. These are simulation or situational exercises. Assessors, usually selected from higher management levels in the firm, are trained to observe the participants and to evaluate their performance as fairly and impartially as possible. For example, Rouche Industries, a pharmaceutical firm, uses this assessment center to select sales personnel for sales management positions. When the assessment center is over the participants return to their jobs and the assessors discuss and evaluate each participant. A report outlining each participant's job strengths and weaknesses, as well as potential for future success, is completed including developmental recommendations. There is usually no pass or fail and the candidate is allowed to withdraw his or her name for a job previously applied for if he or she feels that as a result of the experience he or she is not qualified or is no longer interested.

The results of the assessment are used for promotional purposes, personal professional development, structuring of training programs, or identifying managerial potential, depending on the needs of the organization and the candidate.

The assessment center has the advantage of evaluating candidates for a position in an environment that extends over a period ranging from one to several days. The exercises and simulations worked through are similar or identical to problems to be found on the job, often including stress-related activities with such realistic, lengthy, and dynamic exercises, candidates have difficulty in faking other than their normal behavior. The candidates' real personalities and abilities show through.

Of course, assessment centers are expensive and they are usually more practical in evaluating employees already with an organization than in hiring new personnel.

---

[10]C. L. Jaffee and J. T. Sefcik, Jr., "What is an Assessment Center?" *Personnel Administration* February 1980, p. 40.

HUMAN RESOURCE DEVELOPMENT—QUALITY OF WORK LIFE

Once an individual becomes part of the organization human resource development (HRD) becomes important. Human resource development or quality of work life (QWL), terms often used interchangeably, is an area that is receiving a great deal of emphasis among operating organizations today. The issues surrounding this relatively new area of concern are summed up by the following quotation:

> It's at least possible, over the long haul, that there's a new day for American industry in general. A powerful movement is under way to reexamine and, as necessary, break with old managerial assumptions and formulas. Today's executives are confronting the knowledge that the business system they mastered is no longer the world-beater it used to be. They are considering options... that are more flexible and participative than the rigid hierarchies they grew up in. These alternative organizations take a long-run view of corporate self-interest, and are guided by a sense of common purpose that motivates all who work within them.
>
> By whatever name, and on whatever scale, this kind of effort is most broadly described as the process of expanding the responsibility and influence of rank-and-file employees. It assumes that people want to work together in common purpose, and it challenges the sharp distinction, inherent in classical Western industrial organization, between the actual work of producing goods, or services and the planning and coordination of that work. Today's employees, it holds, are able and willing to participate more fully in management decisions at all levels, and the organization that does not let them do so not only turns them off but also wastes valuable intelligence.[11]

HRD and QWL efforts are designed to improve how people work together.

The foregoing quote was taken from a very excellent lead article in a series recently published by *Fortune* magazine. In the same article Eastman Kodak chairman Walter A. Fallon observes that "you can't drive a good work force 30 percent harder but we've found we could often work 30, 50 or even 150 percent smarter. Working smarter means imparting a strong sense of teamwork and giving employees more say about how they do their jobs."[12]

Perhaps no area of management has been more neglected than improving the way people work together. Most HRD/QWL efforts address themselves to this concern. One of the best definitions of QWL comes from Charles Bisanz, a consultant to Northwestern Bell Company. He says, "It is not a solution devised by management so much as it is a decision by management to share responsibility with employees in devising solutions."[13]

Writers on the subject today are tending to lump together most of the behavioral programs in management under the general topic of Human Resource Development and Quality of Work Life. The programs most often noted are listed

---

[11]Charles G. Burck, "Working Smarter," *Fortune*, June 15, 1981, pp. 68–70.
[12]Ibid., p. 70.
[13]Ibid., p. 73.

as follows. Some have been discussed and others will be discussed later as noted in the chapter references.

	Chapter
Interpersonal Communication Development	8
Job Design	10
Group Dynamics and Teamwork Development	11
Participative Management	4
Quality Circles	17
Management by Objectives	7, 22

HRD or QWL concepts should not be embraced as a "fast fix" for an ailing or floundering operation. This will usually create greater problems than already exist.

The complexities involved in QWL as a long-term commitment on the part of the organization and for individual managers can be partially summarized as follows:

> Any executive who is contemplating a quality-of-worklife effort should be prepared for the possibility of fundamental, long-term changes in the entire organization—changes in traditional internal relationships and lines of authority. And, of course, the process will take time: GM has been at it for a decade and is barely halfway toward getting programs into all its plants.
>
> In the end, relatively few managers may be able to take the risks involved—or handle them. Yet it is hard to escape the sense that the principles underlying the many concepts of working smarter are right for the times. Certainly it seems far less likely that the system of industrial organization perfected at the end of the 19th century is still the best one for the end of the 20th.[14]

BEHAVIOR MODIFICATION

An approach to employee development that has received considerable attention recently is known as behavior modification or, as most practitioners refer to it, performance feedback and positive reinforcement. This system is derived from B. F. Skinner's experiments with animals, using positive reinforcement and operant conditioning. It avoids many of the problems inherent in analyzing the inner motivation of humans such as those encountered by Maslow or Vroom.[15]

Behavioral modification attempts to change only worker behavior that is observable and measurable.

Behavior modification attempts to change only worker behavior that is observable and measurable. Examples of such behavior would be worker tardiness or exceptional amounts of waste in a production process.[16]

---

[14] Ibid., p. 73.
[15] C. Ray Gullett and Robert Reisen, "Behavior Modification: A Contingency Approach to Employee Performance," *Personnel Journal*, April 1975, p. 206.
[16] Jim McAdam, "Behavior Modification: A Human Resource Management Technology," *Management Review*, October 1975, pp. 25–27.

You may wish to refer back to the discussion on reinforcement theory contained in Chapter 9 as part of your study at this point. An example will help clarify the approach:

If you ask a behaviorist human resource manager to do something about John, an employee, "because his morale is low," he will reply: "I don't know what 'morale' is. I can't measure it. Now, tell me something that John does that indicates his morale is low."

"Well," you say, "John is late to work at least three times a week."

"Ah," says the behavi orist, "here is a problem I can tackle. I can observe John being late. Count the number of times he is late. This is a problem I can do something about."

How do we decide that workers have low morale? Is it not through seeing what they do? Hearing what they say? Why, then, do we ignore this behavior, being late, and proceed to create programs to change John's thinking—often called motivation—or to provide him with more knowledge—training.

The behaviorist takes no such expensive detours. He concentrates on physical action, behavior. And he believes that the most important feature of behavior is frequency, how often it occurs. For if John is late only occasionally, he is just being human. But if he is late consistently, he is a human production problem. Rather than worry about why John is late, the behaviorist designs a program of behavior change to reduce the number of times he is late, even to zero if standards require it. The behaviorist operates on the theory that if the behavior is taken care of, John's attitude—or whatever name is being given to his mental behavior—will take care of itself.[17]

There are several principles inherent in behavioral modification.

1. Managers concentrate on observable behavior.
2. Providing people with feedback about their performance is a key ingredient of changing undesirable behavior or insuring the continuation of desired behavior.
3. Positive rewards such as praise and recognition are emphasized rather than criticism. (Where behavior is unsatisfactory, no reward is offered.)
4. Rewards are administered as close to the time of behavior as possible.
5. As behavior improves, reinforcement schedules are lengthened. When behavior deteriorates they are shortened.

The theory of behavior modification (performance feedback/positive reinforcement) is based on the idea that behavior is a function of its consequences and when as a result of a given behavior something good happens such as positive recognition, that behavior will tend to be repeated. Dr. Thomas K. Connellan of The Achievement Institute emphasizes that there are the following simple but important keys to making the performance feedback portion of a productivity improvement system work.

1. Use positive measurement rather than negative. People respond better to discussion of positives than to negatives. Change absence to presence, downtime up uptime, and scrap to yield when and wherever possible.

---
[17]Ibid., p. 25.

2. Direct feedback to natural work groups. When using group feedback, be sure the people who get it are part of the team that generated it. Crews are much more interested in crew feedback than in departmental feedback.
3. Give positive reinforcement to both the group and individual contributors. Giving strokes to individuals promotes individual performance and giving strokes to the group promotes group performance. People need both and it takes both to make a group go.
4. Train managers and supervisors in the use of the system. People can't just be turned loose with a positive reinforcement system and be expected to perform.
5. See that top management models the desired behavior for others. When top management changes its act, others take the effort seriously.
6. Follow up on the training. Don't just train 'em and run. New behaviors need to be supported and shaped.[18]

Like other efforts in the area of HRD, a behavior modification program cannot be installed overnight nor should one expect overnight magic in terms of results. Installation of such a program requires that the organization *or individual manager* (1) identify key areas of performance accountability for the department or individual job, (2) formulate standards of performance, (3) break down areas into small measurable segments, (4) determine how performance in each critical area of accountability will be measured, (5) develop an information feedback system that yields continuous and comprehensive output concerning performance in each area, and (6) provide specific feedback to both groups and individuals. The feedback system should adhere to the guidelines presented above. Also, the use of graphed data is invaluable in an effective system of working with people in a supportive capacity to stimulate positive and improved performance. With respect to the latter, if improvements in performance are recognized even though total performance may not be at standard, it is more likely that the upward trend will continue.

PERFORMANCE APPRAISAL

Performance appraisal is the systematic evaluation of an employee by the supervisor or some other qualified person who is familiar with the employee's work. The question is not whether to appraise or not, but rather whether to do so systematically or haphazardly and randomly.

A number of performance appraisal systems have been used throughout the history of personnel management. The more traditional ones include the graphic scale, ranking methods, and weighted and forced choice checklists. Insight into these traditional approaches can be gained by referring to any of several basic text in personnel management. More recently some organizations have turned to behaviorally anchored rating scales (BARS) and appraisal by objectives (MBO). At present we will focus on the behavioral anchored rating scale as an appraisal technique.

The question is not whether to appraise or not, but rather whether to do so systematically or haphazardly, randomly, and irresponsibly.

---

[18]"GM Exemplifies Productivity Gains—American Style," *Training/HRD*, November 1981, p. 82.

FIGURE 15-4

Example of BARS Scale

Absorb and Interpret Policies — learns new policies and procedures with a minimum of instruction.

Interviewers and claims deputies must keep abreast of current changes and interpret and apply new information. Some can absorb and interpret new policy guides and procedures quickly with a minimum of explanation. Others seem unable to learn even after repeated explanations and practice. They have difficulty learning and following new policies. When making this rating, disregard job knowledge and experience and evaluate ability to learn on the job.

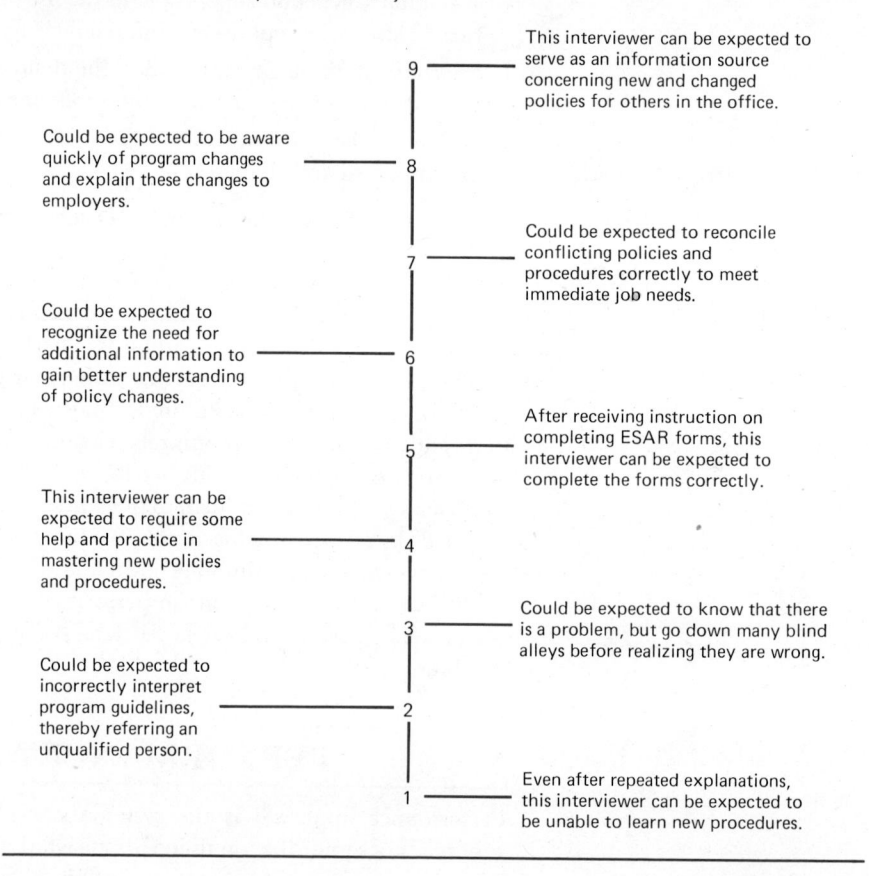

Left anchor	Scale	Right anchor
	9	This interviewer can be expected to serve as an information source concerning new and changed policies for others in the office.
Could be expected to be aware quickly of program changes and explain these changes to employers.	8	
	7	Could be expected to reconcile conflicting policies and procedures correctly to meet immediate job needs.
Could be expected to recognize the need for additional information to gain better understanding of policy changes.	6	
	5	After receiving instruction on completing ESAR forms, this interviewer can be expected to complete the forms correctly.
This interviewer can be expected to require some help and practice in mastering new policies and procedures.	4	
	3	Could be expected to know that there is a problem, but go down many blind alleys before realizing they are wrong.
Could be expected to incorrectly interpret program guidelines, thereby referring an unqualified person.	2	
	1	Even after repeated explanations, this interviewer can be expected to be unable to learn new procedures.

BARS represents an appraisal system that many think possesses superior qualities in terms of both appraising past performance and contributing to improved future performance. BARS is a scale with behavioral statements that relate to observable and job-oriented behavior in significant areas of performance. Figure 15-4 is an example of BARS scale.

The behavioral anchors are specific enough to be used as feedback in an appraisal interview to explain *why* employees received the rating they received. BARS are usually constructed through small group meetings of employees. This process causes employees to give more attention to the important aspects of their jobs because they have an input into determining what the critical elements of the job involve and correspondingly how their performance will be evaluated.

BARS are also useful because they produce a quantitative score that can be related to the wage and salary decisions as well as other purposes to which the appraisal process may be tied. In short, BARS has become an effective appraisal system because it is specific behavioral and job oriented enough to create standards that can be used for training and development, evaluations and rewards.

> BARS is a scale of behavioral statements that relate to observable and job-oriented behavior.

AN INTEGRATED GOAL SETTING, APPRAISAL, AND COACHING SYSTEM

Several authorities have suggested that the best employee development plans might combine the cognitive motivational concepts studied in Chapter 9 (need satisfaction, expectancy/valence theory, and goal setting or MBO) with the more applied behavioral modification approaches.[19] Such a process would include the following steps.

> The best employee development programs include both cognitive motivational approaches and behavioral modification.

1. Defining the work and major activities for which a subordinate is responsible and jointly setting performance objectives.
2. Action planning—determining jointly the factors on which performance will be judged and how performance will be measured.
3. Reviewing and appraising performance.
4. Reinforcing positive behavior.

SETTING OBJECTIVES

It is necessary for the manager and the subordinate to meet, discuss, and agree on *what the job involves specifically*, and why that particular work is important. This first area of mutual agreememt is similar to writing a job description. Job descriptions are formal statements of the responsibilities of a job and the abilities required to do the job. (This is discussed in Chapter 22.)

ACTION PLANNING

Assisting in developing their own objectives usually creates a greater degree of commitment on the part of employees. Furthermore, their own personal career goals are built into the system. A wise manager will also ask such questions as "What problems do you anticipate in accomplishing these goals? How can I support you?"

> Effective planning with subordinates should include both goal setting and a review of procedures.

Some MBO programs call for very little focus on the procedures for accomplishing objectives. However, it would seem prudent to discuss the guidelines within which acceptable behavior must fall. A system of appraisal such as BARS

---

[19]Donald B. Fedor and Gerald R. Ferris, "Integrating OB Models with Cognitive Approaches to Motivation," *Academy of Management Review,* Vol. 6, No. 1, 1981, pp. 115–123.

might be of value within an MBO-type system. For example, the anchors on BARS may call for the use of effective communications with subordinates. The dimension called "communicating skills could inform a job incumbent that effective communications would come about through such behavior as the solicitation of subordinates' views, holding frequent meetings, regular scheduled departmental meetings, and/or developing a system of memoranda sent to all staff members... .The BARS would tell job incumbents *how* to attain their objectives in behaviorial terms, while an MBO system would help decide what the objectives should be."

A "results at any price philosophy can be harmful to the organization." Ethical standards must be upheld. Personal relationships with other managers must be maintained.

REVIEWING AND APPRAISING PERFORMANCE

At the end of the period established (three months, six months, or a year) several questions should be asked. Has the employee accomplished his or her objectives? If not, why? Have conditions changed? Did I fail to support him or her enough? Is this a case of employee failure? If so, is it because of a lack of training, a lack of motivation, or a lack of discipline, and/or reward? Notice that these are cognitive questions, requiring a rather complex look at the *reasons* for performance.

Such questions help to determine the type of reinforcers necessary.

REINFORCING POSITIVE BEHAVIOR

Research done affirms the serious limitations of criticism as a means of affecting individual improvement. In their study, these researchers discovered the low tolerance of most individuals for criticism and the actual negative effect of too much criticism on employee performance in the period following the review session. Moreover, praise in this appraisal environment did not prove to be effective, inasmuch as it was viewed merely as a means of softening the preceding criticism.

Performance appraisal should concentrate on problem solving rather than individual shortcomings.

In contrast, the results approach emphasizes problem solving as the vehicle by which to discuss part performance and to plan future goals and development. The ability to make the transition from a concentration on individual shortcomings to objective problem solving may require extensive training and practice: it certainly requires more than mere intellectual assent to the concept.

The final and least definitive phase of the reinforcement format is the frequency of review. There seems to be no question that the traditional comprehensive annual review, with its laundry list of pros and cons stored up for a year, has had remarkably little positive effect on the recipient, and is a distasteful task for the manager conducting the review.

But the alternative is not as clear. Job objectives may or may not need much more than an annual review. The intent of these reviews is to provide the manager with an opportunity for downward and upward communication, as well as with occasions for meaningful coaching where the situation warrants. Therefore, the frequency of the reviews should be dictated both by the efficiency of other communications means and by the work cycles of those being supervised, but not by the need to make a salary decision or by the arrival of an anniversary date.

Review of performance should focus on positive factors.

In other words, reviews should follow a schedule tied to meaningful positive reinforcement as needed—not just a ritual of administration. Performance problems or exceptional behavior would both call for feedback to the employee.

One of the major problems of appraisal and reinforcement programs is the lack of control of pay plans. Pay could be a powerful reinforcer if it were directly related to performance and more immediate in reinforcing behavior.

One writer has suggested that each person's pay should include three parts: one for the job the employee is doing paid to everyone involved in a similar job, another determined by seniority and cost-of-living factors paid to everyone in the company. "The third part of the package, however, would not be automatic; it would be individualized so that the amount paid would be based upon each person's performance during the immediate preceeding period."[20] This last portion, of course, would be used for positive reinforcement.

MANAGEMENT DEVELOPMENT

Few companies are willing to leave the development of their management to learning through on-the-job experiences alone. Research supports the folly of such a choice. In Couch and Strother's review of management performance, they discovered that managers without formal management training tend to learn only from their mistakes, while managers who have studied formal management concepts utilize them to organize their experiences realistically, whether successes or failures.[21]

Managers without formal management training tend to learn only from their mistakes.

The more effective management development programs include three dimensions: (1) the teaching of knowledge or concepts, (2) opportunities to apply knowledge either on-the-job or in a simulated job environment, and (3) feedback and reflective information to accelerate learning.[22]

KNOWLEDGE

Most of the concepts taught in this text have, at one time or another been the subject of a management development program. The most popular programs have been ones dealing with *interpersonal relations*, such as Blake and Mouton's Managerial Grid program.[23] Other frequent areas of study include *problem solving* and

---

[20] Edward E. Lawler III, *Pay and Organizational Effectiveness, A Psychological View*, New York, McGraw-Hill Book Co., 1971, pp. 162–175.
[21] Peter D. Couch and George S. Strother, "A Critical Incident Evaluation of Supervisory Training," *Training and Development Journal*, Vol. 25, No. 9, 1971, pp. 6–11.
[22] Bernard Keys, "Toward the Complete Management Development Program," *Academy of Management Proceedings*, 32nd Annual Meeting, 1972, pp. 281–284.
[23] Robert R. Blake and Jane S. Mouton, *The Managerial Grid*, Houston, Texas, Gulf Publishing Co., 1964.

decision making, motivation, participative management, and additional behaviorally related topics.[24]

Many programs include accelerated coverage of *how-to approaches*, such as statistical quality control, materials management, zero-base budgeting, or management by objectives. Finally, management training often consists of orientation sessions that discuss organizational policies or objectives, operational techniques, and rules and regulations.

EXPERIENCE

On-the-job learning experience. This type of experience in a management position would seem to be the most realistic way in which developing mangers might try out acquired concepts. Unfortunately, such experience can have limitations. Often, the work being conducted is too critical for trial-and-error approaches. Furthermore, if more experienced managers on the job are utilizing other approaches, a recently hired or promoted person is likely to cast aside classroom ideas, and substitute instead the approach of the seasoned veteran. Perhaps the greatest limitation to on-the-job training is the lengthy time required to engage in a wide range of experiences.

Although valuable, on-the-job learning also has limitations.

Job Rotation. Rotating trainees through several jobs in succession can be effective if several elements are present. Experienced persons in the departments must have the time available to assist the trainees and observe their work closely to act effectively as a coach. Furthermore, jobs assigned must be meaningful, not trainee-made work. This latter qualification usually requires a long-enough period in each department to make rotational programs of value.

Job rotation involves moving a person through a series of jobs over a limited period of time.

The gains from experience on the job can be greatly improved by supplemental training, such as the Blake and Mouton "Criticube" which increases participant sensitivity to learning experiences.[25]

Experiential Techniques. *Business cases*, and other experiential techniques can provide accelerated experiences very similar to those that one would acquire on the job. Cases are to be found at the end of the chapters in this text as well as for each part. Cases allow participants to discover problems, identify alternative solutions, evaluate and select the wisest choice, and develop an implementation plan. Since these cases usually come from an actual organizational setting, they represent real situations that others have faced.

Experiential techniques can provide accelerated experiences similar to those one would encounter on the job.

---

[24]Publications such as the *Training and Development Journal* published by the American Society for Training and Development is a valuable source of information for the latest in training programs, techniques, and current issues.

[25]Robert R. Blake and Jane S. Mouton, "Criticube," *Training and Development Journal*, Vol. 30, No. 4, 1976, pp. 3–8.

Business games. These are dynamic exercises that include a background of a business setting similar to a case, but with decision elements that interact with the hypothetical economy and the decisions of other participants. In most games participants make decisions as to price, advertising, production, and other variables, which are punched on computer cards and fed into a computer. It then returns financial statements and other results to participating teams and they use this information in making another round of decisions.

In-basket Exercises. These allow participants to make decisions in response to a large number of interrelated letters and memoranda. Most of the exercises have as their goal the broadening of the manager's experience. Often companies discover that management and executive personnel have developed tunnel vision—the tendency to screen their view of the organization through their own specialty. For example, accountants may tend to view their problems as being initiated by marketing or production personnel who fail to comply with specified reporting procedures. Sales managers may attribute most of their woes to the failure of production in meeting shipment dates or failing to carry adequate inventories.

Participating in in-basket exercises can expose managers to a broad range of organizational problems.

By participating in games and other exercises managers may acquire a broad picture of total organizational problems in a compressed period of time. They can also experiment with new styles of management without undue fear of failure, as suggested by the following quote from a participant comparing his flight training to such a program.

> *In twenty years as a pilot, I suffered only two major crises from which to learn. I lost two engines. Over the years in the link trainers and more modern aircraft simulators, I have lost four engines, crashed twice, and died once. Simulations offer some distinct advantages as environments in which to learn from experience*[26]

FEEDBACK

The importance of feedback has been supported by extensive research. Reflective feedback by an instructor in an experiential training program is especially valuable. Experience alone is not a good teacher. The participant must be guided, corrected when mistakes are made, and rewarded by supportive comments. Feedback information can be provided in training programs through behavioral questionnaires such as File and Remmer's "How Supervise?"[27] or Marvin's "Management Matrix," which measures the personal leadership style of a manager on three action patterns: (1) working through others, (2) generating worthwhile results, and (3) generating usable ideas.[28]

---

[26] J. Bernard Keys, *Laboratories For Training and Development of Executives and Administrators*, Bureau for Business and Economic Research, University of Oklahoma, Norman, Oklahoma, April 1972, p. 10.
[27] Q. W. File and H. H. Remmers, "How Supervise? *The Psychological Corporation Test Catalog*, 1971, New York, The Psychological Corporation, 1971— pp. 16–17.
[28] Philip Marvin, *Management Goals*, Homewood, Ill., Dow Jones-Irwin, Inc., 1968, pp. 97–113.

THE EFFECTIVENESS OF MANAGEMENT DEVELOPMENT PROGRAMS

Most management training must develop managers for a variety of possible positions. Organizations are changing so rapidly that development must focus on problem solving or dealing with change rather than any mechanistic procedure for achieving goals. For these reasons it is not surprising that management programs have been criticized on several counts, as follows.

1. They fail to provide approaches that are relevant to the organization from which the participant comes.
2. They tend to deal with generalities and fail to provide concepts that can be applied.
3. While participants accept the information provided on an intellectual level, their behavior does not change—at least not for sustained periods after returning to the job.

Criticisms 1 and 2 may be best dealt with through total organizational development programs, to be discussed in the next chapter. In response to the third criticism, transfer of learning to the job has been most successfully accomplished in programs that apply a balanced approach.[29] The correct balance of knowledge, experience, and feedback will depend on the subect to be taught, the level of the managers, and previous concepts learned.[30]

The transfer of learning to the organizational environment is aided by programs using experiential methods.[31] Participating in realistic exercises and dealing with complex management problems with a new approach tends to unfreeze past behavior and allows new concepts to lock in.

DEVELOPING A CAREER PLAN

"Planning" and "doing" are both parts of the manager's job. Unfortunately, it's very easy for managers to get so tied up in day-to-day activities, so enmeshed in the many things they have to do, that they simply overlook the need to take time to plan their own careers. It's easy to overlook the need for conscious management of a career—some people seem to just drift with the tide.

It is easy for managers to get so tied up in daily activities that they overlook the need to plan their own careers.

Two very important benefits come from the career planning process. First, we develop an awareness of a specific set of targets that help us judge where we stand and help us keep our focus on the long term. The second benefit has been stated

---

[29] John L. Butler and Bernard Keys, "A Comparative Study of Simulation and Traditional Methods of Supervisory Training in Human Resource Development," *Academy of Management Proceedings*, 33rd Annual Meeting, 1973, pp. 302–305.

[30] Joseph Wolfe, "The Effects and Effectiveness of Simulations in Business Policy Teaching Applications," *The Academy of Management review*, Vol. 1, No. 2, 1976, pp. 47–56.

[31] Bernard Keys, "The Management of Learning Grid for Management Development," *Academy of Management Review*, Vol. 2, No. 2, April 1977, pp. 289–297.

succinctly by two researchers on managerial planning. Gilmore and Brandenberg[32] suggest that an important value of planning, to the manager, lies *not* in the final result (the plan) but in the *process* of developing the plan. That is, to develop a good *career plan*, we must develop a good understanding of ourselves, of our company, of our career opportunities. Career planning is a *learning* process as well as a goal-setting process. The next few pages will involve you in both of these processes.

WHAT ARE CAREER GOALS?

A goal is a clear statement of an end state to be accomplished. To the degree possible, career goals should be clearly and concisely stated, in unambiguous terms. For example, the goal "I want to succeed" does not provide direction, and does not help the person stating the goal *to* succeed. A better statement might be, "I will measure success by becoming an operations manager in the next ten years." This goal provides a sense of direction and definable accomplishment within a given time frame.

Obviously, career plans will have several career goals in them. Some goals will be general, with long-run "targets." The targets may involve salary, location, position, or other factors important to a given person's career. Targets supporting a long-term career goal might include the following:

- An annual income level of $60,000 by age 50.
- Job located at the corporate office in Atlanta by age 50.
- Position of vice president or higher by age 50.

These long-term targets are still helpful as guidelines. They provide some rather specific things to shoot for, and provide standards to measure progress against. Yet they are *flexible* in some areas. They do not specify just one position. They do, however, specify some constraints—some minimum standards to achieve in a definite amount of time. They also provide a framework for shorter-range career goals. If the supervisor is setting the above targets at age 30, he or she should be able to formulate some intermediate targets that need to be accomplished in order to move on to the higher-level career objectives. For example, the 30-year-old might set the following targets for age 40:

Career goals need to be established for every age level.

- Annual income of $40,000.
- Appointed to product manager position in Nashville Widgets Division.

These ten-year goals are more specific about the type of position, and provide guidelines for shorter-run planning. Shorter-run targets might include these:

- Complete master's degree in business by age 35.
- Complete company "advanced management" training by age 34.
- Complete company management rotation program by age 33.

---

[32]Frank F. Gilmore and R. G. Brandenberg, "Anatomy of Corporate Planning," *Harvard Business Review*, Vol. 40, No. 6, November-December 1962, p. 63.

In turn, the supervisor might want to "set things in motion" with a set of "very short-run" targets:

- Qualify for rotation program by this August.
- Talk to plant manager about career plans by July.

The idea involved in the above discussion is that career plans involve many goals and targets. The career plan contains a veritable *cascade* of objectives, with the longer-range goals providing the framework within which shorter range career goals are set. As Glueck has stated, "career development is the process of *creating a pattern* of jobs in a series of steps from the [current] job to retirement."[33] The really effective managers build a career plan that *takes advantage* of their strengths and *minimizes* or *compensates* for any weaknesses.

GAINING SELF-AWARENESS

Psychologists say that we should examine our "internal" strengths and weaknesses.

In addition to the obvious skills and aptitudes associated with a career path, psychologists suggest that an awareness of our "internal" strengths and weaknesses is important. A deep understanding of "who I am" helps define "where I should go." Because the supervisor and manager have to deal effectively with other people, part of this analysis must involve the perceptions other people have of us. It should also include the "personal" things we know about ourselves that others *do not* know.

A useful device for this stage in this evaluation in the Johari Awareness Window (Figure 15-5). The Johari Window provides four perspectives with which to view leadership and managerial personalities. In Quadrant 1 (the "open" window), one would place the characteristics that are obvious to oneself and others. Quadrant 2 (the "blind" window) emphasizes that other people may perceive some traits in oneself (good or bad) that are not perceived by that person. Then one must ask himself, "How do others see me? Do they see the same person I see?"

Quadrant 3 (the "hidden" window) categorizes those things that one knows about himself but that are hidden from view of others. Here arises the question of whether "higher" positions will cause some of the traits or skills to become publicly known. For example, one may not understand materials requirements planning (MRP). On the present job, this lack of understanding is not important to one's performance, and is not obvious to others. A move to a new position, however, may cause this "deficiency" to become known and may, in fact, hinder one's effectiveness in the position.

Finally, the "unknown" window" (Quadrant 4) reminds the person that he or she has certain leadership skills or aptitudes that are not recognized by oneself or by other people. Some people "blossom" in a new position, and people wonder why they didn't recognize that hidden potential previously. To reemphasize the point made earlier, a systematic self-analysis can contribute significantly to developing meaningful career plans.

---

[33]William F. Glueck, *Personnel: A Diagnostic Approach*, Dallas, Texas, Business Publications, 1974, p. 259.

FIGURE 15-5

The Johari Window

	Known to Self	Not Known to Self
Known to Others	Open Area	Blind Area
Not Known to Others	Hidden Area	Unknown Area

Source: Adapted from D. A. Kolb, I. M. Rubin, and J. M. McIntyre, "Interpersonal Perception," in *Organizational Psychology,* Englewood Cliffs, N.J., Prentice-Hall, 1971, p. 205

THE CAREER-LAUNCHING CHECKLIST

Some companies invest a great deal of time and effort to help their employees build career plans. Officials at Meridian Insurance Company, for example, began evaluating their company's career counseling and employee-development efforts in 1977. As a result of that analysis, they now train their managers and the staff of the Human Resources Department in career planning. To help their managers

Career counseling can be assisted by a good career-launching checklist.

FIGURE 15-6

A Checklist for Career Planning

_____ Do I know the things I do best? What are they? Why?
_____ Have I found some things I like to do very much? What are they? Why?
_____ Do I work better by myself or with other people? What kind of people? Why?
_____ Do I know what talents I do not have? What are they?
_____ Do I know the things I very much dislike doing? What are they? Why?
_____ Have I asked for and received professional advice about the fields of work I ought to consider for myself? What has that advice been?
_____ Has my education prepared me for these fields, or do I need further education, perhaps specialized courses or an internship, before making a full-fledged beginning? What kinds of continuing education?
_____ When do I want to accomplish each step in my career? What has to come first?
_____ How hard am I willing to work physically and mentally? Can I work long hours?
_____ What are my work habits? Do they consist of short bursts of very intensive effort, or do I work at a steady pace? Why?
_____ Have I talked with people who do the kinds of jobs I think I might or should be interested in so that I have first-hand information about what they do, and how they do it, and what a typical day is like for them? What have they said?

Source: Adapted from Ted R. Gambill, "Career Counseling . . . Too Little, Too Late?" *Supervisory Management,* April 1979, pp. 24–30 and Marion S. Kellogg, *Career Management*, published by AMACOM, a division of American Management Association, Inc. 1976.

hold effective career counseling sessions with employees, Meridian developed a *career-launching checklist*. A checklist similar to the one used at Meridian Insurance is contained in Figure 15-6. A checklist simply provides an *opportunity to learn more* about oneself and to match what he learns with what he plans to in his career.

SUMMARY

Human resources planning development (HRPD) looks at organizational needs on a continuous basis and monitors the life cycle of new employees as they move from beginning jobs to dealing with early and midcareer choices. It is the primary function that matches organizational and individual needs.

The matching processes include human resource staffing. This involves a needs forecast, recruiting, and selection. The process used by most companies is called successive hurdles. This allows the candidate to be rejected as early as possible with little of his or the company's investment of time and expense, if rejection is necessary. Assessment centers are often used to select persons already employed for promotion or supervisory jobs.

Once on the job the issue of human resource development (HRD) and quality of work life (QWL) come into sharper focus, and take an increased significance. HRD and QWL efforts are designed to improve how people work together, give a sense of teamwork, and lead to a better fit between the needs of individuals and the desire of the organization to gain maximum motivation and productivity from its human resources. HRD includes efforts designed to improve communications, performance feedback and positive reinforcement programs (behavior modification), job enrichment, and participation. Also involved may be changes in organizational design and management systems such as MBO.

An effective appraisal system is inherent in organizations. Behavioral-anchored rating scales (BARS) provide a means of appraising performance on a quantitative basis using behavioral statements that relate to observable job-oriented behavior.

SUMMARY CHART

Organizational Needs	*Matching Resources*	*Individual Needs*
Staffing		Career planning
Recruitment	Training and development	Developing career goals
Selection	Behavioral modification	Developing self-awareness
Assessment		
Performance Appraisal	Integrated goal setting and development	Building a successful career image

DISCUSSION QUESTIONS

1. What is human resource planning and development? Describe the concept in detail.
2. The selection process was divided into five different steps characterized as a successive hurdles approach. Identify and discuss the key elements and consideration involved in each of the five steps.
3. Discuss your understanding of what is involved and the issues surrounding current concerns with human resource development and quality of work life. Give some examples of the kind of things that are involved with HRD and QWL efforts.
4. Discuss the concepts of behavior modification. What are some of the important guidelines surrounding the implementation of an effective performance feedback and positive reinforcement program.
5. Describe the integrated development appraisal and coaching plan suggested in this chapter.
6. Discuss in detail the process and considerations involved in developing a career plan.

APPLICATION EXERCISES AND CASES

TALENT HUNT[34]

"We call it an early-identification program," says Douglas Yaeger, assistant vice president for management development. "We're trying to find people very early on who have strong potential for general management." Hardly any of the 18 men and 6 women know they have been singled out, but NCR makes a special effort to move them through a series of managerial jobs to broaden their experience.

Company officials say the program will remain small. They emphasize that it won't supplant older techniques of spotting high-potential managers. Meantime, NCR is testing another crop of top performers.

As the NCR program suggests, spotting potential superstars is an important activity at many companies these days. More big corporations are devising elaborate methods of finding executive timber in the forest of baby-boom recruits. And top management is paying much more attention to developing these candidates after they have been found.

---

[34]Bernard Wysocki, "Talent Hunt," *The Wall Street Journal,* Vol. 197, No. 38, Wednesday, February 25, 1981, p. 10.

"There's a lot more activity in this area," says Donald G. Carlson, a vice president of Booz, Allen & Hamilton Inc., management consultants. "It started picking up after the last recession and accelerated dramatically in 1979 and 1980."

The stepped-up search for talent comes at a time when it is terribly expensive to recruit managers outside, so companies are trying to groom more of their own executives. Also, "the higher-level jobs are more complicated" than ever, says William Byham, president of Development Dimensions International, a Pittsburgh consulting concern. "You must identify people early and move them through the hoops or they'll have big voids in their backgrounds."

A questionnaire asks how well you drive a car. A psychological test probes whether you have an adventurous personality. A mental-ability test, a two-hour interview with a psychologist, a simulation of an unfamiliar job reveal even more. It sounds a bit like a screening process for would-be astronauts.

NCR Corp. of Dayton, Ohio, doesn't need any astronauts, but the big computer company *is* looking for another type of highflier. It is continuously trying to spot young employees who can soar into the executive stratosphere. And two years ago, NCR officials used the questionnaire and other techniques to pick 24 high-potential employees from a field of 828 top young performers at the company.

Questions

1. What do you think of NCR's early identification program? Do you foresee any problems?
2. In a more comprehensive sense, what would you suggest they do in the area of human resource development?

A NOVEL APPROACH TO MANAGEMENT DEVELOPMENT[35]

The following display advertisement appeared in the newspaper of a suburban town located about 40 miles from the central city. It covered about one-quarter of a standard size newspaper page, had enough white space and a large-size typeface, so that it could be easily seen by even a casual reader of the particular issue of the paper. It represents a somewhat novel approach to management development.

ARE YOU A RECENTLY RETIRED TOP CALIBER VICE PRESIDENT—FINANCE AND ADMINISTRATION?

We are an exciting, active consumer goods company, located in _____, with annual sales over $50,000,000 and an excellent growth record that need you for not more than three years to give seasoning and training in broad gauge responsibilities to a brilliant 28 year oldster who will then take over. If you're looking for the enjoyment of being active and seeing a potential vice president "bloom and develop," please write in confidence to Box XYZ, _____ News.

---

[35]William J. McLarney and William M. Berliner, *Management Training Cases and Principles*, 5th ed., Homewood, Ill., Richard D. Irwin, Inc., 1970, p. 502.

Questions
1. Comment on the desirability of this approach for the development of a young executive.
2. What can the company do to help ensure the success of such an approach?
3. What disadvantages may be encountered by the company?
4. As an executive taking this job offer, what would you expect the company to do to effectively utilize your abilities?

CHAPTER 16
ORGANIZATIONAL DEVELOPMENT

THE MANAGEMENT OF CHANGE
TOTAL ORGANIZATIONAL DEVELOPMENT (OD)
ORGANIZATIONAL CLIMATE
MANAGERIAL PHILOSOPHY ABOUT PEOPLE
THE YB ORGANIZATION
CURRENT INSIGHTS INTO MANAGEMENT PHILOSOPHY
INITIATING CHANGES IN THE STRUCTURAL ENVIRONMENT
INITIATING CHANGES IN THE BEHAVIORAL ENVIRONMENT
METHODS OF BEHAVIORAL INTERVENTION
LABORATORY TRAINING
PROCESS CONSULTATION
SURVEY FEEDBACK
STEPS IN BEHAVIORAL INTERVENTION
THE GRID APPROACH TO ORGANIZATIONAL DEVELOPMENT
OBJECTIVES OF TEAMWORK DEVELOPMENT
APPROACHES TO ORGANIZATIONAL DEVELOPMENT BASED ON JAPANESE MANAGEMENT
AN INTEGRATED VIEW OF OD IMPLEMENTATION
APPLICATION EXERCISES AND CASES
PLANNING TO INTRODUCE CHANGE
A CASE INCIDENT FROM GERMANY

WESTINGHOUSE'S CULTURAL REVOLUTION[1]

At Westinghouse Electric Corp. something strange is going on: a sizable part of the company is converting to Japanese-style management. Westinghouse hopes to achieve dramatic improvements in productivity by trying a form of Theory Z, described by William C. Ouchi in a new handbook for American businessmen who want to follow the Japanese way. The effort is producing a cultural revolution at Westinghouse by overturning old-style boss-employee relationships.

The company's construction group, which represents 7% of the work force, offered itself up as guinea pig for the experiment last year. The new method rests on the theory that if labor and management work at achieving a Japanese-style consensus, Westinghouse will get better ideas, better decisions, and better execution. So today, in the black steel corporate headquarters in Pittsburgh's Gateway Center, bosses in the construction group don't simply issue orders; they seek consensus. Out in the factories, foremen don't bellow coarsely at workers—at least they aren't supposed to; they ask for suggestions. Everywhere new committees and councils are meeting on office time to discuss matters as nebulous as group synergy and as critical as next year's capital allocations.

Theory Z is a kind of "participative management," which is hardly novel. Social scientists have been advocating participative management for years and many American companies have tried it, up to a point. But to see it seep into a hierarchical old industrial company like Westinghouse, with its established chain of command and staff of tradition-minded engineers, is a bit like watching the U.S. Marines parade in blue jeans, long-haired and unshaven.

The experiment began as a drive to increase productivity. Westinghouse had gone through tough times in the 1970s; it made a series of bad acquisitions, got involved in a nasty bribery case, and lost a pile on consumer appliances before selling the business. Worst of all, Westinghouse agreed to supply uranium under fixed-price contracts—an appallingly risky decision that ultimately will cost the company nearly $1 billion. To recover lost ground and meet the escalating challenge of the Japanese, the company decided two years ago that it would have to increase productivity much faster than the 2 percent or 3 percent that U.S. industry achieves in a good year.

Participative management might seem a roundabout route to productivity; it certainly isn't a quick fix. Westinghouse expects to wait two years before seeing any results, ten years before the benefits take full effect. The corporation isn't betting all its marbles on participation; it's also testing a panoply of other devices ranging from a form of "matrix" management to heavy investment in automation.

Westinghouse executives think participation is a secret Japanese success. "When you visit Japanese factories and see everyone, but *everyone*, working like tigers to make that product more reliable at a lower cost, it's awesome," says William A. Coates, the executive vice president who runs the construction group. "They even come back early from their breaks. In factory after factory, everyone inside is trying to whip us. If we don't get that attitude, we literally won't survive."

---

[1]Abridged from Jeremy Main, "Westinghouse's Cultural Revolution," *Fortune*, June 15, 1981, pp. 74–103.

Since organizational life in the future is likely to be quite volatile as suggested by the Westinghouse example, organizations should learn to live with change. More organizations are finding the need to move toward improved performance, more effective relationships and more responsible and more highly motivated personnel. This is difficult to achieve, as noted by Kurt Lewin when he wrote the following:

> *A change toward a higher level of group performance is frequently short-lived, after a "shot in the arm," group life soon returns to the previous level. This indicates that it does not suffice to define the objective of planned change in group performance as the reaching of a different level. Permanency of the new level, or permanency for a desired period, should be included in the objective.*[2]

The change process consists of developing a need for change ("unfreezing"), working toward change ("moving"), and generalization and stabilization of change ("freezing").

The change process requires three general phases in order to arrive at the effective techniques and sustained change relationships:[3] development of a need for change ("unfreezing"), working toward change ("moving"), and generalization and stabilization of change ("freezing").

This chapter first discusses several representative approaches to organizational development that have been utilized in past years. Finally, some newer approaches to organizational development modeled after Japanese organizations will be reviewed.

THE MANAGEMENT OF CHANGE

The *unfreezing* phase in the change process develops when the top administration of the organization becomes aware of problems, develops a genuine desire to do something about them, and believes that the possibility for change exists. Often the need for change is noted because productivity is low, quality has slipped, turnover and absenteeism is excessive, or because of other deteriorating performance characteristics. The following situation illustrates the unfreezing phase.

In 1977 Cadillac was at the bottom of customer product satisfaction survey results and the costs of body repairs chargeable to 1924-built Fleetwood facility were 30 to 40 percent higher than at comparable Fisher Body locations. Moreover, quality of work life (QWL) survey results showed Fleetwood salaried employees 30 percent below other divisional employees in satisfaction, and it was an acknowledged fact that Fleetwood hourly employees weren't much happier. In short, the plant was in big trouble.

Determined to take an all-out crack at changing the situation, plant manager Les Richards and his staff went off-site and spent three days hammering out a plan of attack on Fleetwood productivity, quality, and QWL.[4]

---

[2]Kurt Lewin, "Frontiers in Group Dynamics," *Human Relations*, Volume 1, pp. 5–41.
[3]Ronald Lippitt, Jeanne Watson, and Bruce Westley, "The Phases of Planned Change" *Organizational Development: Values, Process, and Technology*, New York, McGraw-Hill Book Co., 1972, p. 71.
[4]From GM Exemplifies Productivity Gains—American Style", *Training Today*, November 1981, pp. 80–82.

ORGANIZATIONAL DEVELOPMENT 421

The second stage in the change process involves *moving* or working toward change. A systematic approach to Managerial Problem Analysis and Decision Making as discussed in Chapter 4 is critical at this point. During this phase data are collected and analyzed, and the problem begins to take on a visible shape. Often intense efforts are required for several years in order to bring about a sustained change in the organization. This means that management must be willing to settle for little evidence of results in the early stages.[5] The moving stage is illustrated by the following continuation of the Cadillac example cited previously.

In the early stages of change little visible results can be expected.

Cadillac's blueprint called for an ambitious three-pronged offensive:

- A goal-oriented management system that would function at all levels of the organization.
- A performance feedback system that not only would measure productivity improvement progress, but would also involve all employees in improving quality and reducing costs.
- A management style conducive to employee participation, including a labor/management team approach to tackling productivity and QWL problems.

A critical factor in the third phase, stabilization of change, is the spread of change to all departments of the organization. One author has called this last step of refreezing the *lock-in effect*; that is, the changing of organization structure so that organizational changes are supported and continued. Cadillac plant manager Les Richards comments as follows: "Organizational change is slow. You have to have faith in the people and the process. You can force some improvement out of an organization, but there is no way Fleetwood could have made such a dramatic improvement without the total involvement of everyone." Working simultaneously and jointly in the pursuit of such large goals as QWL and productivity improvement is a big, big effort. It requires hard work, trust, commitment, and perseverance.

Stabilization of change comes when the new approach to doing things are "locked in."

TOTAL ORGANIZATIONAL DEVELOPMENT (OD)

OD can be defined as an effort supported by top management, to increase the effectiveness of the total system (organization) through a series of planned interventions.[6]

In order to understand the goals of organizational development, one must first understand what we mean by organizational climate.

---

[5]Ibid., p. 78.
[6]John C. Aplin and Duane E. Thompson, "Successful Organizational Change," *Business Horizons*, August 1974, p. 62.

ORGANIZATIONAL CLIMATE

Organizational climate refers to a variety of possible variables that, when taken collectively, have an impact on eventual levels of job performance. It is important to note that the dimensions of organizational climate that carry the most significance and thereby have greater impact will vary from one group or classification of employees to another and also for individuals. Research is continually taking place that attempts to identify the significant climate variables in operation in a particular given situation.

One group of researchers has developed a model for studying organizational climate and its determinants.[7] They used this model to conduct a study of organizational climate as viewed by several hundred directors of research and scientists in twenty-one organizations. While the views of such an elite group of employees cannot be considered as those of the general work force, their findings were similar to those of several other studies.

The model consisted of factors considered important to organizational climate: the organization *structure, process, performance,* and *job satisfaction*. Each of these major factors was composed of several subelements as indicated by the following discussion. Figure 16-1 shows the model and the statistical correlation coefficients discovered in the study. (The higher the correlation coefficient, the stronger the relationships between the perceived effect of that item on total climate.)

Organization structure was measured by examining such properties as span of control, size of the organization, number of levels, and number of levels from the top management to the research and development department. No meaningful or

> Organizational climate is composed of structure, process, performance, and job satisfaction.

FIGURE 16-1

Factors Important to Organizational Climate

[Diagram: Organization structure connects to Organization performance (.15), to Organization climate (.12), and to Organization process (.09). Organization climate connects to Organization performance (.25) and Job satisfaction (.47). Organization process connects to Organization climate (.34) and Job satisfaction (.09).]

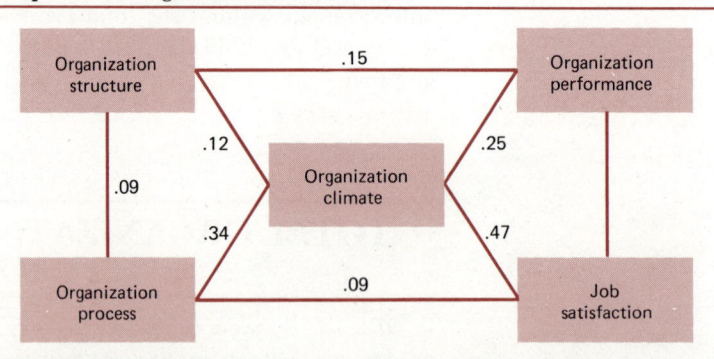

Source: Edward F. Lawler III, Douglas T. Hall, and Greg R. Oldham, "Organizational Climate: Relationship to Organizational Structure, Process, and Performance," *Organizational Behavior and Human Performance, II,* New York, Academic Press, Inc., 1974, p. 151.

---

[7] Edward E. Lawler, III, Douglas T. Hall, and Greg R. Oldham, "Organizational Climate: Relationship to Organizational Structure, Process, and Performance," *Organizational Behavior and Human Performance,* II, New York, Academic Press, Inc., 1974, pp. 139–155.

significant patterns were apparent as indicated by the .12 correlation coefficient. According to the researchers, "The organization's structure apparently has little relationship to the climate of the organization as perceived by research directors and scientists."[8] In other words structure and its subcomponents had little influence on their positive or negative reaction to the total climate.

Organization process includes such things as the frequency of performance reviews, the attention given to performance review and compensation, degree of professional autonomy, general versus specific assignments, and the support given personnel by management. The correlation coefficient of .34 indicates a reasonably significant relationship between these factors and the perceived favorableness of total climate.

Organization performance was measured by the number of contracts generated and completed, and by the adherence to time and cost schedules. This dimension showed only a slight relationship to perceived organizational climate favorableness as indicated by the .25 correlation coefficient.

Job satisfaction was measured on an attitude scale by such items as security, social satisfaction, esteem, autonomy, self-fulfillment, and pay. The .47 coefficient highlights job satisfaction as being the most important factor that leads to a perceived favorable climate.

The summary of the findings indicate that organizational climate is most influenced by things that directly affect a person's daily work experiences. The writers cite a number of similar studies, which "have shown that factors such as leadership, co-worker behavior, and tasks which have an immediate, meaningful effect on an individual's organizational life, have an impact on an organization's climate."[9]

> Organizational climate appears most affected by the job, the work group, and personal leadership.

While these research findings must be considered with some caution, organizational climate appears most affected by the job, the work group, and personal leadership.

MANAGERIAL PHILOSOPHY ABOUT PEOPLE

Most authorities agree that many of the crucial elements of organizational life are determined by the way managers view subordinates. Douglas McGregor made one of the most notable attempts to systematically describe alternative managerial philosophies about people and the approach to management they suggest.

In his book, *The Human Side of Enterprise*, McGregor sets forth two alternative sets of assumptions that a manager may have about people, summarized in Figure 16-2.

As the reader will note, the assumptions underlying what McGregor has labeled Theory X represents extremely negative viewpoints while those underlying Theory Y are very positive.

McGregor's thesis held that much of management practice in the past was based on a set of assumptions about people that were substantially open to question if

---

[8] Ibid., p. 149.
[9] Ibid., p. 155.

FIGURE 16-2

Assumptions About People and Their Reaction to Work

Theory X ←——— DIAMETRIC ———→ Theory Y

Theory X	Theory Y
1. The average person has an inherent dislike for work and will avoid it if he can.	1. Expenditure of physical and mental effort in work is as natural as play or rest—depending on controllable conditions, work may be either a source of satisfaction or dissatisfaction.
2. Because of this dislike for work, most people must be coerced, controlled, directed, threatened, punished to get them to put forth adequate effort toward the achievement of organizational objectives—even promise of reward is not enough. They will accept and demand more. Only threat will do the trick.	2. External control and the threat of punishment are not only means for bringing about effort toward objectives. Man will exercise self control in the service of objectives to which he is committed.
3. The average person prefers to be directed, wishes to avoid responsibility, has little ambition, wants security above all—mediocrity of the masses.	3. Commitment is a function of the rewards associated with their achievement.
	4. Under proper conditions, people will not only accept but seek responsibility. Avoidance of responsibility, lack of ambition, emphasis on security are consequences of experience, not human characteristics.
	5. Capacity to exercise imagination, ingenuity, creativity is widely, not narrowly distributed.

Source: Douglas McGregor, *The Human Side of Enterprise*, New York, McGraw-Hill Book Co., 1960.

used as generalizations. He contended that Theory X type methods of directing people were not conducive to motivating them, but instead actually caused antagonism.

The central principle of organization in the Theory X philosophy is the direction and control of subordinates through the exercise of authority with organizational requirements taking precedent over the needs of employees. Because this philosophy views people as motivated purely by economic rewards, it is presumed that enough pay or job security can be provided to cause people to accept close direction and control. Since potential is not recognized in people, there is no reason to devote time, effort, and money to encouraging them to tap such potential.

Theory X philosophy suggests that organizational requirements—direction and control—should take precedent over employee needs.

McGregor advocates that the assumptions underlying Theory Y represent a much closer approximation to the real situation and are therefore a much sounder base on which to structure a management approach to leadership.

The central principle of organization derived from Theory Y is that there must be an integration of individual and organizational goals. Management's job is to create an organizational climate that will challenge people to utilize their greatest potential and also one that provides the means by which this can become a reality. The following survey results would seem to support McGregor's contentions.

> The central principle of Theory Y is that there must be an integration of individual and organizational goals.

A major survey of U.S. workers' attitudes toward productivity conducted by the Gallup poll for the U.S. Chamber of Commerce in 1979 found "the overwhelming majority believe that if they are more involved in making decisions that affect their job, they would work harder and do better." A more recent international survey on productivity developed by Louis Harris and sociologist Amitai Etzioni and released in April echoed the point in some of its findings, and produced a striking complementary message about the kind of human resources that lie untapped. Asked what sacrifices they would make to "increase investment to achieve economic growth," nearly three-quarters of the employees surveyed said they were willing to be assigned to work wherever they were needed in their company, and nearly two-thirds would be happy to have their salaries linked to higher productivity.[10]

THE YB ORGANIZATION

Argyris has developed a technique for arriving at what he calls the "YB organizational climate" that parallels what McGregor envisioned in advocating Theory Y (depicted in Figure 16-3). In order to arrive at the position described, Argyris suggested that the interpersonal competence of management must be improved.

FIGURE 16-3

"YB" Organizational Climate

Organizational Variables	That Required
1. Leadership processes	1. High confidence and trust
2. Motivational forces	2. Economic rewards based on compensation system developed through genuine participation
3. Communication processes	3. Free and valid flow of information at all levels
4. Interaction-influence processes	4. High degree of mutual confidence and trust
5. Decision making	5. Wide involvement in decision making, and well integrated through linking process
6. Control processes	6. Wide responsibility for review and control at all levels

Source: Chris Argyris, *Management and Organizational Development*, New York, McGraw-Hill Book Co., 1971, p. 17.

---

[10]Charles G. Burck, "Working Smarter" *Fortune*, June 15, 1981, p. 73.

Theory YB depicts an organizational climate to which a Theory Y philosophy would lead.

By interpersonal competence Argyris was referring to how effectively we are able to interact with different people in a variety of settings. Argyris expected this improvement to come by "management developing more trust in people, concern for individual feelings and viewpoints, internal commitment, and more openness to and experimenting with new ideas in such a way that others could do the same."[11]

While Argyris' work is important in explaining how a leadership philosophy such as Theory Y can lead to an organizational climate such as YB, it does not necessarily depict the organizational climate that should exist in all circumstances. Our discussions in Chapter 10, Job Design, and Chapter 12, Contingency Approaches to Organizations, have made this point clear.

CURRENT INSIGHTS INTO MANAGEMENT PHILOSOPHY[12]

A number of management experts suggest that, by and large, there has been a gradual trend toward Theory Y acceptance over the last eighteen years.

Allen found that most managers espouse a philosophy between a pure Theory X and Theory Y.

Interestingly however, there have been few attempts to empirically determine the adherence of managers to those two opposing viewpoints. The only exception seems to be a solo piece of questionnaire research conducted by noted management consultant Louis Allen in 1973. The results of Allen's study will not surprise practicing managers. He found very few respondents espousing either a pure Theory X or Theory Y view of human nature. Instead, he discovered that the great majority fell somewhere in between.

Numerous researchers have found that changing attitudes on the part of lower level management in supervisory training programs seldom causes a change in behavior once the supervisors are back on the job in the same organizational environment. The same is true to a lesser extent of top level management development programs. The best situation for change is one in which all three elements of the organization (behavioral, structural, and technological) are changed to support the needed organizational development (OD) change. Technological changes were discussed in Chapter 10, Job Design. They will not be discussed further here except as they relate to structural or behavioral change.

INITIATING CHANGES IN THE STRUCTURAL ENVIRONMENT

The structure of an organization is based on technological processes and departmental boundaries. These become rather permanent over time, and major

---

[11] Chris Argyris, *Management and Organizational Development*, New York, McGraw-Hill Book Co., 1971, p. 17.
[12] Originally reported in the September 1978 issue of *Personnel Administrator*. Reprinted in *Training, The Magazine of Human Resources Development*, April 1979.

changes rarely occur in them. They are quite important, however, in implementing OD strategies. Consider the importance of structural changes on the total result of morale and motivation in the following incident.

> *(A) major insurance firm constructed a new building to house its headquarters. As in most organizations, placing the secretaries was a problem. The managers shared secretaries through a secretarial pool. Each secretary worked for several managers located throughout the building. A top administrator decided to place half of the secretaries on floor 3 and half on floor 5 of the 9 floor building. The secretarial supervisor was placed on floor 3. There was sufficient room for all secretaries to be located together, but proximity to managers was deemed to be most important in determining location.*
>
> *Although equipped in new movable cubicles with the latest equipment, the secretaries' morale dropped substantially after the move from the old headquarters to the new. The secretaries on the third floor felt too closely supervised and were envious of those on the fifth floor. There was much less sharing of work or helping out and turnover increased. . . . Subsequent interviews indicated that the managers were ambivalent as to the location of the secretaries since there were eight elevators serving the building. Had both the managers and the secretaries been consulted prior to the move, the situation could have been avoided. . . . Again, design, human resources, and efficiency were mistakenly felt to be separate constructs and unintended consequences of change arose, resulting in a loss of efficiency instead of gain.*[13]

Whenever changes are made in technical and structural environments the human needs must be considered.

Most changes are initiated by alterations in the structural environment such as organizational changes or new developments in the technical environment modifications of machinery, equipment, or the communication process. Whenever planned technical and structural change is made, the effect on basic human needs should always be considered. Two important basic needs often affected by this type of change are the needs for identity and intimacy. These needs are illustrated by a change that occurred when an insurance company moved from an old structure to a new modern facility with weight-supporting walls that did not require center posts and dividing walls. Unfortunately, the center posts in the old building, while much less attractive to uninitiated observers, afforded points of reference for various divisions within the office, allowed the office humorist to post cartoons and caricatures of various office workers, and generally provided flavor to the office environment. The psychological setting and cohesiveness of groups were never quite the same in the modern office to which the group moved.

Intimacy can be preserved during change by allowing and encouraging workers to add their own individual touches—a planter, a painting, or a throw rug to their work areas. Involvement in the planning, ordering, or selection of the various components of this setting can produce feelings of commitment, self-worth, and warmth.[14] It has been noted that intimacy or privacy does not necessarily mean closed doors. Instead it suggests freedom from distractions and constant interferences from those passing by, and from having to whisper to be confidential.[15]

---

[13]Ibid., p. 614.
[14]Ibid.
[15]Ibid.

When all three elements of the organizational system—technological, structural, and psychological—are considered in the change process, a successful OD strategy is more likely to be forthcoming.

INITIATING CHANGES IN THE BEHAVIORAL ENVIRONMENT

Figure 16-4 describes an action research model for organization development. Notice that it includes cycles of data gathering, diagnosis with the aid of a consultant, feedback of information to the client organization, and joint planning

FIGURE 16-4

Action Research Model for Organizational

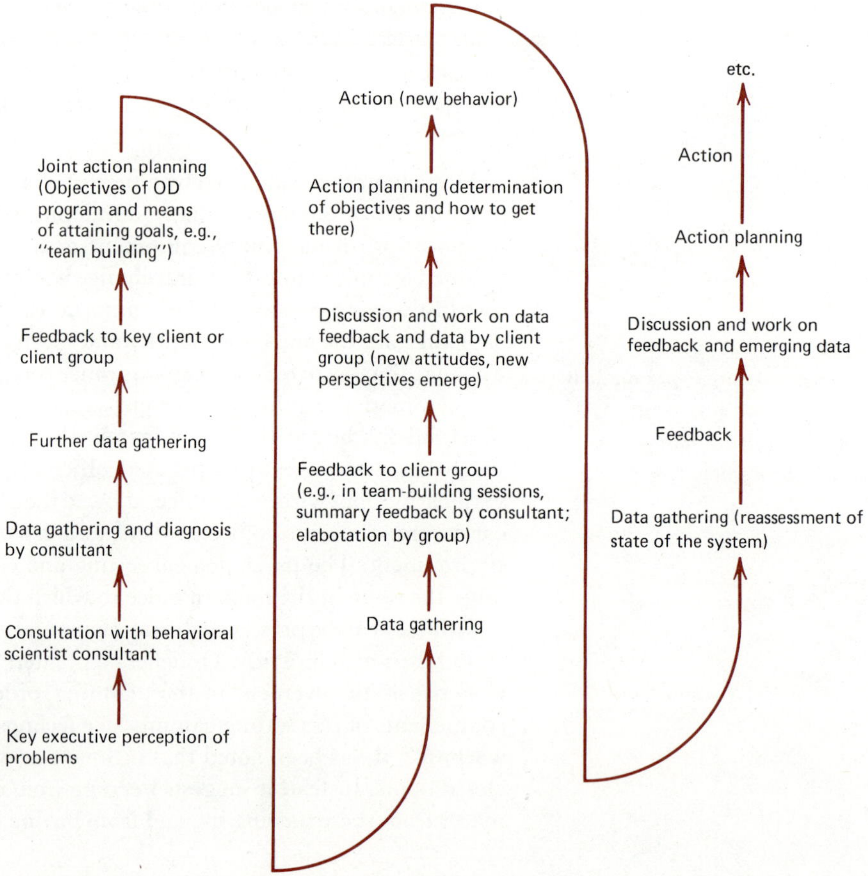

```
                                                                    etc.
                                                                     ↑
                                    Action (new behavior)          Action
                                           ↑                         ↑
Joint action planning              Action planning (determination   Action planning
(Objectives of OD                  of objectives and how to get         ↑
program and means                  there)
of attaining goals, e.g.,                 ↑
"team building")
       ↑                           Discussion and work on data     Discussion and work on
                                   feedback and data by client     feedback and emerging data
Feedback to key client or          group (new attitudes, new              ↑
client group                       perspectives emerge)
       ↑                                  ↑                        Feedback
Further data gathering             Feedback to client group               ↑
       ↑                           (e.g., in team-building sessions, Data gathering (reassessment of
Data gathering and diagnosis       summary feedback by consultant;  state of the system)
by consultant                      elabotation by group)
       ↑                                  ↑
Consultation with behavioral       Data gathering
scientist consultant
       ↑
Key executive perception of
problems
```

Source: Wendell L. French and Cecil H. Bell, *Organization Development: Behavioral Science Interventions for Organization Improvement,* Englewood Cliffs, N.J., Prentice-Hall, Inc., 1973, p. 86.

and team building with regard to the OD program. As opposed to some types of organizational research, OD is concerned with planning for immediate action on real organizational problems rather than hypothetical problems. This is the action component of OD. The process/maintenance component of OD includes an evaluation of the effectiveness of intervention by the consultant with the client organization. It attempts to answer the questions, "Are we solving problems effectively, managing against clearly understood goals, and achieving the interpersonal climate we think is desirable?"

METHODS OF BEHAVIORAL INTERVENTION

The types of intervention utilized by OD programs can be grouped into the following three general categories.[16]

1. Those relying on some form of laboratory training or growth group as the vehicle for change.
2. Those in which the major change role is vested in an external process consultant.
3. Those which use data feedback techniques.

LABORATORY TRAINING

This training technique, often called a *T-Group*, is used to increase the sensitivity of the individuals to those around them and to cause them to examine their own behavioral styles. Through self-analysis and feedback from participative members of the group, each person is encouraged to examine his actions, alter behavior, and adopt new ways of behaving likely to lead to increased organizational effectiveness.

T-groups are used to increase sensitivity of managers.

PROCESS CONSULTATION

This is a method in which a consultant works closely with a few decision makers in an organization. Usually small groups of the key executives talk with the consultant, attempting to clarify organizational problems and to arrive at viable solutions through free and open discussions. The skilled consultant uses such techniques as nondirective interviewing, probing, questioning, and other methods to stimulate a more intensive reflection on organizational developments by the process group.

SURVEY FEEDBACK

This is the method in which the consultants enter the organization at a high level and develop survey instruments for data collection. After the completion of the survey by the selected employees, the results are then fed back to members of the organization. Often the information collected from the survey will be presented at

---

[16]Ibid.

a series of meetings, beginning at the top of the organization and continuing throughout various subgroups. The survey information is used to elicit discussion and serves as a foundation for diagnostic assessment of organizational problems.

There is some indication that the use of survey techniques tends to move the organization away from dependency upon consultants much earlier. In addition, data gathered from a client/organization is often considered more credible than softer data gathered in consulting sessions, perhaps by tape recorder or by summaries from the consulting personnel. On the other hand, process consultation and laboratory training generally provide a greater depth of intervention than that of survey feedback. Deep intervention by consultants may be resented by the organization and may produce undue resistance, or cause undue dependency.

The use of survey instruments requires less intervention in the organization by consultants.

Another advantage of the survey feedback type of intervention is that it involves the management team in the construction of survey instruments, which provides effective means for building internal organization commitment. Added to this is the advantage that information obtained in the survey is "concrete, specific, and above all, in black and white."[17] It can be referred to later, and used as benchmarks for changing organizational styles.

Most OD specialists utilize all three techniques at the various stages involved.

STEPS IN BEHAVIORAL INTERVENTION

The first step in behavioral intervention is establishing a set of goals and objectives to which an organization is committed. Various OD specialists approach this first step in different ways. For example, Chris Argyris attempts to move organizations from a position that he terms XA to YB. These two patterns are based on McGregor's Theory X and Theory Y, which we discussed earlier. These patterns are similar to those outlined by Rensis Likert in his System IV type of management, which was summarized in Chapter 14, Leadership Styles.

The first step in behavioral intervention is establishing a set of goals such as those of Chris Argyris' YB organization.

Argyris' general approach is to try to move from a more closed, less expressive organization to an open, communicative organization by means of a series of meetings with management. While Argyris is likely to use many of the intervention approaches, the following is a typical pattern in which he follows. In the first meeting, he interviews top management and tries to promote unfreezing by suggesting that a useful program would include diagnosing potential problems such as the effectiveness of the personal leadership.

In Argyris's second meeting, a confrontation interview is held in which there is a discussion of issues not typically discussed in the organization. As his interviews progress with the OD group, communication becomes increasingly more frank and candid.

Tape recordings are kept of each session, and critical episodes are replayed from time to time to promote further discussion. Once preliminary interviews indicate that the top management is willing to work with the consultant on a long-term basis, an annual program is established, which might include the following steps.

---

[17]Ibid., p. 66.

1. The executives would be divided into groups.
2. Each group would explore the entire personnel evaluation program. They would raise any questions that they felt were important. They would also make recommendations for the final design and implementation.
3. The consultant would observe the dynamics of the small-group sessions as well as the substantive issues raised. During the afternoon they would present their views of the entire group.[18]

During the annual process, several OD techniques are utilized by this team. These processes can be described in an abbreviated form, as follows.[19]

1. *Identifying the restraining forces.* During this session, a series of questions are asked, which are intended to clarify the purpose of OD and define weaknesses in the understanding of the key executives. This process was particularly designed to discover the resisting key executives and to improve the unfreezing process.
2. *Exploring inconsistencies.* In this session, the consultant would help to clarify inconsistencies among the viewpoints and attitudes of the key executives.

By working through these inconsistencies early in the program, problems are headed off that could later become crucial if neglected.

THE GRID APPROACH TO ORGANIZATIONAL DEVELOPMENT

Blake and Mouton have built an OD program around the managerial grid described in Chapter 14, Leadership Styles. They have used a number of unfreezing processes, which are itemized and described in Figure 16-5. The implied objectives of OD in grid development involve a move of the organization from a closed, noncommunicative system to an open system in which feelings are aired. Figure 16-6 indicates the kinds of results produced by grid OD sessions. If there is any one point of difference which can be isolated between the Argyris and the Blake and Mouton approach, it is probably in the grid approach to developing teamwork. Argyris tends to focus on producing candor and open communications while Blake and Mouton tend to emphasize the development of teams at various points in the organization system. Blake and Mouton have produced some well-defined goals for teamwork and development.

Argyris tends to focus his OD on producing candor and open communications while Blake and Mouton tend to emphasize the development of teams.

OBJECTIVES OF TEAMWORK DEVELOPMENT

Teamwork development is designed to achieve the following five major objectives. See Figure 16-6.

Replacing Outmoded Traditions and Practices With a Problem-Solving Approach. This is an attempt to substitute routines, rituals, and long-established practices with

---
[18]Chris Argyris, *Management and Organizational Development: The Path from XA to YB,* New York, McGraw-Hill Book Co., 1971, p. 49.
[19]Ibid., pp. 73–77.

FIGURE 16-5

Results of Grid O.D. Sessions

Background reading	Gives an orientation as to how applied behavioral science is being used to strengthen organizations
Seeding	Provides a few organization members depth insight into Phase 1 and the Grid without the organization's being committed to doing more
Grid organization development seminar	Gives a few managers a bredth and depth of insight into the whole of Grid Organization Development as the basis for evaluation and possible recommendations for next steps.
Pilot grid seminar	Provides the organization a test tube trial of what would be involved were the organization to engage in Phase 1
Pilot teamwork development	Affords the top team direct understanding of how the Grid is applied to strengthening not only its team effectiveness, but also the effectiveness of individuals as the basis for assessing probable impact of Phase 2 applied on an organizationwide basis

Source: Robert R. Blake and Jane Srygley Mouton, *Corporate Excellence Through Grid Organization Development: A Systems Approach*, Houston, Texas, Gulf Publishing Company, 1968, p. 75.

updated ways of doing things. The new system focuses on what should be, and upon establishing a standard of excellence for the group.

2. *Increasing Personal Objectivity in Self-Assessment of Work Behavior.* Using the managerial grid as a framework for analysis, each member is encouraged to develop keener insight into his own personal work behavior. Associates are encouraged to discuss his patterns of behavior openly and frankly with him. The individual described "may not like all he hears but he can listen without defensiveness, that is, withour rationalizing, justifying, denying, or explaining away what others are saying about his performance and behavior."[20] Listening to the entire group rather than to one person whom he might consider prejudiced helps in accepting these kinds of views. Figure 16-7 represents one assessment of an individual, written by work team members, along with the corresponding suggestions for personal improvement opportunities identified during Phase 2 of the grid sessions. Notice the personal insight of Tom Gray after the session.

3. *Establishing Objectives for Team and Individual Achievements.* "Phase 2 is designed to Insure that what should happen does happen."[21] This is largely established by developing the objectives in a well-defined form, as indicated in Figure 16-7. The team works together to find the program for getting results and designates responsibility for this. A schedule for following up what has occurred among the team participants is then developed. After barriers in team culture are eliminated, a system of management by objectives (MBO) is suggested.

---

[20]Robert R. Blake and Jane Srygley Mouton, *Corporate Excellence Through Grid Organization Development: A Systems Approach*, Houston, Texas, Gulf Publishing Company, 1968, pp. 101–102.
[21]Ibid., p. 107.

4. *Increasing Teamwork Skills.* The following quote represents Blake and Mouton's strong feeling that the team approach is the ideal organizational style.

The effective work team is the key to individual and organization excellence. In any organization, every corporate member is a member of a work team. Few if any are organization hermits—those to whom no one gives directions, whose work is of no

FIGURE 16-6

Goals for Teamwork and Development

President of a Medium-Sized Electronics Firm	*Vice President, Marketing, Large Prepared Foods Firm*
We learned that conflict between individuals or within a group should not be suppressed, smoothed over, buried, or avoided.	Conflicts were apparent, but we were dealing with them in a new manner that was more constructive and creative. We were now becoming more concerned about the solution to the task or problem rather than fighting the person with the idea. We created the desire to foster productive solutions to our problems.
Managers and subordinates increasingly recognize that when opinions are wrapped in hierarchy, too often they are accepted as fact. Subordinates must learn to challenge such opinions.	Before these sessions we had had a conflict between a marketing group and a production group. Marketing felt they were not getting sufficient support from production. And production felt out in left field—uninformed, uninvolved, and more-or-less second class citizens. These different points of view are classic in organizations. Both groups got together at the labs and began to understand and work on their problems. The different points of view were examined. Plans for improving the situation were developed. So, an interdepartmental problem was solved.
My work team decided that the greatest barrier to our improved effectiveness was the lack of candor. In our work team and within the company there were certain subjects that were considered too delicate or sensitive to be discussed between us. We defined these as the "sacred cows" of the organization. During our 3-day seminar, the environment was created in which all of these sacred cows were flushed out. As a result, action decisions were made to deal with the sacred cows, whose demise will save the company nearly $1 million in operating costs in the next 12 months.	We see the need for listening to the soft voices and encouraging them to speak up. We recognize more dramatically our interdependence on each other and our need to work together.

FIGURE 16-6 continued

Goals for Teamwork and Development

President of a Medium-Sized Electronics Firm	*Vice President, Marketing, Large Prepared Foods Firm*
We have a better understanding of the importance of planning. We see that lack of time becomes an excuse that can be eliminated through better planning.	We now do a better job of planning—because we have a better flow of data upon which to base our decisions.
The organization development program to us, and I believe to many other companies as well, is turning out to be a very valuable method for harnessing the latent resources of many minds in the corporation. People are learning to think and behave differently and in so doing are achieving things they never believed possible either for themselves or for their companies.	I feel we also see job performance as more important. We understand the need to set tougher goals for ourselves. More people are now P & L conscious. We know we have to be experimental and innovative.
By integrating concern for production and concern for people in the right way, industry will be able to reach new heights of productivity and profitability. Even more important, individuals will obtain rewarding satisfaction and a sense of involvement and accomplishment in the production purpose not previously thought attainable in the traditional concepts of human endeavor in industry.	What we have learned has helped us immensely in improving the overall performance of the organization and developing greater skills and competence on the part of our managers. As a result, our decision making people are able to operate effectively under the heavy pressures involved in the running of a thriving, growing business today.

Source: Robert R. Blake and Jane Srygley Mouton, *Corporate Excellence Through Grid Organization Development: A Systems Approach*, Houston, Texas, Gulf Publishing Company, 1968, pp. 79–81.

consequence to anyone else, who need not communicate or coordinate with others. If this is individuality, it is a myth, at least in the modern corporation. People are bosses, subordinates, and colleagues. They have close interworkings, goals in common, and individual goals. They share the need for coordination and cooperation just as each shoulders solo responsibility and effort. A work team reflects the extent to which organization members are interdependent.[22]

The emphasis in teamwork is on spontaneity rather than structured problem-solving approaches.

5. *Using Critique for Learning.* One of the major purposes of grid organizational development is to increase the sensitivity of groups to the possibility of learning from experience. This requires increased effectiveness in critiquing experiences.[23]

---
[22]Ibid., pp. 112–113.
[23]Ibid., p. 116.

FIGURE 16-7

A Work Team Assessment and Suggestions for Personal Improvement

Tom Gray

My ability to produce sound decisions is reduced because of a combination of late starting and too much concern for detail. I back down because of pressure from above and because I try to maintain good relations.

I have a good grasp of detail and I use opinions of others to develop firm convictions which I often defend regardless of opposing views. I communicate my position poorly. When my convictions are not strong, I tend to accept the opinions and attitudes of others without probing in depth.

I avoid offending other people. I am able to communicate interest in the views of others and should use this more frequently to resolve conflict.

My feelings are always restrained, and I appear solid and dependable. The degree of emotional control reduces my effectiveness in a group.

Although my humor is retained under pressure, it is used too seldom.

I do not drive others but lead them. My production would be more effective if a better framework for problem solving were developed before I dealt with details.

Tom Gray

1. Communicate Clearly
   A. Be direct, cut the frills; give the main point as fast as possible with no extraneous material.
   B. Support communication with main facts.
   C. Do not waste time with bulky detailed support unless requested, particularly in verbal communications.

2. Organize and Plan More Thoroughly
   A. Set priorities for projects.
   B. Develop a plan of attack for major projects immediately.
   C. Disseminate plans for major projects to participating departments.
   D. Review and update projects weekly.
   E. Critique progress personally, with participants, and with the boss as necessary.

3. Express Emotions
   A. React honestly and candidly. Others will accept impatience with lack of progress on tasks.
   B. When faced with conflict, interact with others to resolve it by identifying its causes.

Source: Robert R. Blake and Jane Srygley Mouton, *Corporate Excellence Through Grid Organization Development: A Systems Approach*, Houston, Texas, Gulf Publishing Company, 1968, pp. 104, 109.

APPROACHES TO ORGANIZATIONAL DEVELOPMENT BASED ON JAPANESE MANAGEMENT

Recently American business literature has been flooded with articles referring to Japanese management and with good reason. Two recent best sellers outline approaches that the authors feel will help the United States. While neither approach can be accepted as a proven technique, nor can one be sure that either

Pascale and Athos suggest that American firms give more attention to the "soft Ss" than to the "hard Ss."

system will work in American companies, they do point the way many American companies are leaning in their organizational development.[24] Pascale and Athos conceptualize their approach by suggesting that American firms need to give more attention to the "soft Ss" than to the "hard Ss".[25] The Ss they speak of are actually seven elements of organization paralleling somewhat our conceptualization of Planning, Organizing, Leading, and Controlling. These elements are depicted in Figure 16-8.

The authors describe these with more descriptive examples in their book:

> **Strategy** *pertains to a firm's plan of action that causes it to allocate its scarce resources over time to get from where it is to where it wants to go.* **Structure** *refers to the way a firm is organized—whether it's decentralized or centralized, whether it emphasizes line or staff—in short, how the "boxes" are arranged.* **Systems** *refers to how information moves around within the organization. Some systems are "hard copy" types—computer printouts and other ink on paper formats that are used to keep track of what's going on. Other systems are more informal—like meetings. These three elements—strategy, structure, and systems—are probably quite familiar to most readers.*
>
> *The other four factors are what we call the "soft" S's.* **Staff** *pertains* not *to staff in the line/staff sense, but to demographic characteristics of the people who live in an organization. Are they "engineering types," "used car salesmen," "M.B.A.s," "computer jocks"?* **Skills** *refers to those things which the organization and its key personnel do particularly well—the distinctive abilities that truly set them apart from competition. For example, as an organization Procter & Gamble is skilled at marketing; its management is*

FIGURE 16-8

The Seven S's

Strategy	Plan or course of action leading to the allocation of a firm's scarce resources, over time, to reach identified goals.
Structure	Characterization of the organization chart (i.e., functional, decentralized, etc.).
Systems	Proceduralized reports and routinized processes such as meeting formats.
Staff	"Demographic" description of important personnel categories within the firm (i.e., engineers, entrepreneurs, M.D.A.s, etc.). "Staff" is *not* meant in line-staff terms.
Style	Characterization of how key managers behave in achieving the organization's goals; also the cultural style of the organization.
Skills	Distinctive capabilities of key personnel or the firm as a whole.
Superordinate goals	The significant meanings or guiding concepts that an organization imbues in its members.

Source: Richard Tanner Pascale and Anthony G. Athos, *The Art of Japanese Management,* New York, Simon and Schuster, 1981, p. 81.

---

[24] For example, see "Humanagement at Honeywell," *Industry Week,* July 27, 1981, pp. 23–24.
[25] Richard Tanner Pascale and Anthony G. Athos, *The Art of Japanese Management,* New York, Simon and Shuster, 1981, pp. 80–81.

skilled at sustaining the institution's vitality and maintaining an environment that continually provides new, viable consumer products to replace the older ones. It should be noted that skills apply on both the organizational and interpersonal level.   Two final factors require definition. Style *refers to the patterns of behavior of the top executive and the senior management team. For example, Geneen and his team had a tough, facts-oriented style. Style also refers to that of the organization as a whole. Clearly, Matsushita has a different style from ITT.* Superordinate goals *(which include the spiritual or significant meanings and shared values of the people within an organization) refer to the overarching purposes to which an organization and its members dedicate themselves. These are rarely bottom-line secular goals like growing x percent a year or obtaining y percent return on investment. Rather, this factor pertains to values or goals that "move men's hearts" and that genuinely knit together individual and organizational purpose.*[26]

Ouchi attempts a similar conceptualization in his *Theory Z*,[27] by citing first the contrasting differences in American and Japanese management (see Figure 16-9), then explaining thirteen steps to be utilized by corporations in moving from American (A) to Z (presumably an ideal).

First, top managers are urged to read and discuss the latest ideas on organizational design and Japanese management in order to promote reflection and dialogue. Next the company is asked to develop a statement of objectives—but objectives that are deeply rooted in a philosophy or culture. This statement should come out of an organizational audit. In order to be sucessful, of course, this philosophical statement of objectives must be supported by the chief executive officer. The company philosophy is to be implemented by creating both structure and incentives that support it. Ouchi would prefer to see organizations with no formal structure at all, operating much like a highly integrated basketball team or a "clan" of people on a communal farm or project, all of whom understand their roles and their relationships because of constant and widespread interaction. He

Ouchi recommends developing a "cultural" or "spirituallike" philosophy.

FIGURE 16-9

The Contrast

Japanese Organizations	*vs.*	*American Organizations*
Lifetime employment		Short-term employment
Slow evaluation and promotion		Rapid evaluation and promotion
Nonspecialized career paths		Specialized career paths
Implicit control mechanisms		Explicit control mechanisms
Collective decision making		Individual decision making
Collective responsibility		Individual responsibility
Wholistic concern		Segmented concern

Source: William Ouchi, *Theory Z—How American Business Can Meet the Japanese Challenge*, Reading, Mass., Addison-Wesley Publishing Co., 1981, p. 58.

---

[26]Ibid., pp. 80–82.
[27]William Ouchi, *Theory Z—How American Business Can Meet the Japanese Challenge*, Reading, Mass., Addison-Wesley Publishing Co., 1981, p. 58.

recognizes that this is idealistic, but he continues to emphasize "culture" or a spirituallike values as the foundation of success in Japanese management.

Like Pascale and Athos, Ouchi considers strong interpersonal skills to be critical to the implementation of Theory Z. He would prefer to see skills in developing interaction channels substituted for the many formal committees and delegated projects now common in American firms. He warns that a dependency on "working through problems" and allowing subordinates to criticize superiors' ideas may not be pleasurable to top executives at first. "In the short run, a manager in an autocratic company has more pleasures. No one below you questions your word, everyone defers to you, and you feel both powerful and capable. In the long run, of course, each person defers with equal certainty to a boss, feeling powerless, and the capacity for a coordinated company is low."[28]

While the suggestion for a substitution of skills for structure is not that new (Argyris, McGregor, and others have made this point), Ouchi's next suggestions are quite controversial and are not likely to be accepted easily by American businesspeople. These include a suggestion of lifetime employment and a very slow evaluation and promotion policy. Ouchi's argument here includes the notion that many firms in the United States are too quick to jump into ventures in which they have no experience and for which they must hire outside experts—often cutting back on employment of present personnel.

According to Ouchi "if actual costs of these workers were added up, fewer firms would undertake them. Should such a shift occur, the rate of innovation would not slow down, rather new ventures would be undertaken only by companies who already have some knowledge in the field."[29] Ouchi's argument is not convincing on this point and goes against the recent criticisms of the American automobile industry for its unwillingness to move away from long-established technology (the 350-cubic-inch engine) for fear of disrupting short-term financial reports. Nevertheless, Ouchi does point toward a close connection between personnel employment, their stability, and the overall philosophy of the business.

Ouchi's argument that America should settle for slower promotions and longer career paths seem equally doomed to fall on deaf ears. There are, he suggests, nonmonetary incentives such as challenging work and recognition for quality work that can stretch out career goals, but these alone are unlikely to turn around a nation of "fast-track" young people led by tens of thousands of MBA's. Ouchi's final argument dealing with revamping career paths does offer more hope. By broadening career paths to create generalists instead of specialists, Ouchi thinks we would see more capable executives develop and a tendency for less movement from company to company. There is no question but what families in the United States are opting for more stability and less movement. Some of this is due to high interest rates and inflation, making housing changes difficult. Some is due to the disruption in family life and the heavy "stress" burden that moving causes.

One thing stands out in the writings of the Japanese management advocates who seem to have the ear of the nation's business. The "wholistic" relationships

Some of Ouchi's arguments seem questionable for American industry, such as his advice that we offer slower promotions and longer career paths.

---
[28]Ibid., p. 113.
[29]Ibid., p. 119.

developed in Japanese industry have produced superior commitment to that of a fragmented lifestyle in the United States with loose attachments to the job. It is not likely that our culture will accept the company uniforms, company songs, and paternalism of Japanese industry, much of which was rejected by U.S. industry during the 1930s and 1940s. But many Americans seem to desire a change to a slower-paced, more stable life-style, based on commitment, loyalty, and emphasis on quality rather than simply quantity of production.

Ouchi's OD includes an emphasis on lifetime employment and stable and wholistic relationships rather than a fragmented life-style.

The next few years will probably bring many research-based studies of the suggestions of the two books reviewed above. For the meantime many major U.S. firms have hired Ouchi and other Japanese management type consultants and are proceeding to implement changes without the benefit of empirical research.

AN INTEGRATED VIEW OF OD IMPLEMENTATION

The rationale for organizational development rests heavily on the notion that there is no single best organizational approach. This notion rests on the success of contingency approaches to organizations, as discussed in Chapter 12.

The rationale for OD rests heavily on the notion that there is no single best organizational approach.

Another major qualification to OD has to do with the concept of equilibrium. Just as nature establishes equilibrium among the various plants and animals, there appears to be an equilibrium established in most organizations based on cultural frameworks, hierarchical structures, and managerial patterns. "Any change in the existing equilibrium of these role relations will create counterreactions that might outweigh the anticipated benefit, unless the change is effected within the framework of the total ecological system."[30] One writer indicates several illustrations of this phenomenon: for example, the implementation of job enrichment usually dictates the need for a change in supervisory styles. This suggests that supervisors develop a leadership quality we mentioned earlier; style flexibility. In one organization in Europe, where supervisors were very rigidly encased in hierarchical structures that dictated their roles, they became very unsure and reacted negatively to such a program.

The initiation of an MBO program usually requires a more generous delegation of authority and greater degrees of freedom of subordinates. It generally assumes that managers are motivated at the level of self-actualization and that control can be implemented through adequate measures of accomplishments for objectives. When an MBO system is implemented in a Theory X Plant with no cost accounting or budgetary systems, the equilibrium is upset and failure is likely to occur.

Finally, changes similar to those suggested by Ouchi, Pascale, and Athos require a complete turnaround in managerial styles, career paths, reward systems, and other important organizational elements.

---

[30]Eric C. Brightford, "How to Introduce Changes in Management Practices: Lessons From Europe," *Management Review*, June, 1975, p. 14.

The following five steps are suggested for preserving equilibrium while implementing change in organizations.

1. Study the history of the company in depth through interview and survey prior to implementing change. Do not assume that the management in all companies is a homogeneous group. Examine needs and motives of management in each major subgroup of the company. Try to discover underlying values and philosophies.
2. If change is necessary, implement it on a gradual basis, but simultaneously in the areas of leadership and management processes. Strive to promote an approach that allows people to feel competent, regardless of their need levels.[31]
3. Outline with management the necessary changes, emphasizing the interdependence between behavioral techniques and those based on other functions of the management process. Develop a strategy that modifies the organization so that it matches the major tasks to be performed.
4. Start with a goal-oriented system or a philosophically oriented system, such as MBO or Theory Z.
5. Expand forward into organizational development and job design, and backward into the management process. Figure 16-10 illustrates the integrative management method suggested by one consultant, using a behavioral approach.

FIGURE 16-10

The Integrated Management Method

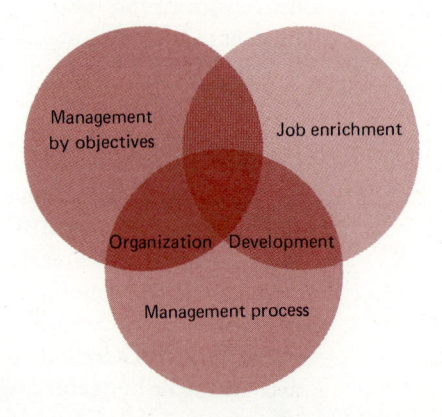

Source: Eric C. Brightford, "How to Introduce Changes in Management Practices: Lessons from Europe," *Management Review,* June 1975, p. 17.

---

[31]John J. Morse and Jay W. Lorsch, "Beyond Theory Y," *Harvard Business Review*, May-June 1970, p. 672.

SUMMARY

Organizations are being continually confronted with the need for change. The change process requires first that old habits and ways of doing things be *un*frozen. Next, some intervention technique must be used to work toward change ("moving"). Finally, groups and individuals must become accustomed to the new way of doing things ("freezing").

Organizational climate depends on organizational structure, process, performance, and job satisfaction. Organizational process is one of the most important elements of organizational climate and is determined largely by management action and philosophy.

Theoretically ideal organization climates can be depicted both by McGregor's Theory Y and Argyris's YB organization.

Theory Y represents a very positive philosophy about people in terms of their attitudes toward work, willingness to assume responsibility, capacity for self-control, creativity, and similar factors.

YB can be described as an organizational climate in which employees are treated with confidence and trust; rewards are based on a system developed through participation; and there is free and valid flow of information at all levels. Such a system produces a high degree of mutual confidence and trust. Decision making utilizes inputs from many persons within the organization. Control systems are the responsibility of many persons rather than a few. But, of course, different work situations call for different organizational climates.

In order to develop a sustained change in managerial behavior, management

SUMMARY CHART

Initiate Change Process	Implement Change in the:	Integrate Management Process and Organization	Consider Managerial Viewpoints	Determine Appropriate Organizational Climate
Develop a need for change ("unfreezing")	Technical environment	Management by objectives	Theory X	YB climate
Work toward change ("moving")	Structural environment	Job enrichment		
Generalize and stabilize change ("freezing")	Behavioral environment (a) Laboratory training (b) Process consultation (c) Survey feedback	Organizational development	Theory Y	Theory Z Climate
	Cultural environment			Soft Ss

development programs need to be coupled with overall development, including changes in technology, structure, and behavior. Behavioral intervention techniques include laboratory training, process consultation, and survey feedback. Two well-known behavioral intervention approaches are described in this chapter—one by Chris Argyris and the other by Blake and Mouton. Argyris focuses on producing open communications, while Blake and Mouton emphasize the development of teamwork.

Two new theories of OD utilizing Japanese management concepts are also discussed. Pascale and Athos recommend focusing on what they call the soft Ss—skills, style, and subordinate goals rather than strategy structure and systems. Ouchi proposes a totally new philosophy for American management based on lifetime employment with one company and wholistic relationships.

DISCUSSION QUESTIONS

1. Discuss each of the three phases of the change process. What are some of the problems related to implementing each phase?
2. What element of organizational climate is most important? Why?
3. Summarize the basic ingredients of McGregor's Theory X and Y. From an operational standpoint why are Theory X and Y assumptions important? How does Argyris's YB organization relate to Theory Y?
4. What are some of the issues involved relating to initiating changes in the structural environment? Discuss the various methods of behavioral intervention that are available.
5. Discuss in detail the process of team development as set forth in Blake and Mouton's approach to OD.
6. Summarize in organized form the basic elements of Ouchi's Theory Z. Do you think Ouchi's Theory Z has merit? Why? Why not?

APPLICATION EXERCISES AND CASES

PLANNING TO INTRODUCE CHANGE[32]

A top government executive was recently appointed head of his agency. The management of this agency had been performing its work well; in fact, this agency was frequently cited for the superior quality of its management. Still, the new head wants to introduce some major changes he hopes will improve an organization that

---

[32]Martin J. Gannon, *Organizational Change and Development*, Little, Brown, and Co., Boston, 1979, p. 338.

is already excellent. This is a regulatory federal government agency that employs a large number of professionals, many of whom possess advanced degrees.

Questions

1. Identify the various types and categories of changes this manager might have in mind.
2. Outline a general step by step approach the executive might follow in introducing any changes.
3. What kind of problems might be encountered in relation to the various types of changes?
4. What should he do if resistance is met from some of the key managers involved?

A CASE INCIDENT FROM GERMANY[33]

The company, a leading German automotive parts supplier, employs about 5000 workers. Owned by the same family for several generations, it has outstanding engineering know-how, modern plants, and good customer service, but it has been backward in terms of modern management techniques, particularly in areas of planning, organization, and cost control.

The chief executive officer (CEO) was aware of these deficiencies, but action was finally prompted by union pressure. The 1972 contract provided for job evaluation for white collar workers, which required that job descriptions be prepared. As this project progressed, management became aware of the need to streamline the organization structure and improve delegation.

As a first step in the change program, a series of in-plant management seminars was conducted for approximately 200 managers, including the CEO. These one-week seminars were behavior-oriented, highlighting MBO and OD, and had a strong motivating effect. It was, in fact, the pressure from middle management after the seminars that convinced top management to implement a major change program.

The entry point for this program was MBO, with initial emphasis on improving the process of management, particularly in areas of planning, organizing, and control. Management moved to complete the reorganization, establish a separate controller's department to introduce budgeting procedures, create improved feedback to managers regarding their production results, and improve sales forecasting as a start to medium-range planning.

To avoid slowing down the initial momentum—and because there were no corporate objectives—objective setting started with a "bottom up" approach. Interviews were conducted with lower-level employees based on the newly established job descriptions, and from those interviews, objectives based on jobs rather than corporate plans were developed.

---

[33]Eric C. Brightford, "How to Introduce Change in Management Practices. Lessons From Europe," *Management Review*, June 1975, pp. 15–16, reprinted with permission.

In one plant, which was particularly keen to move ahead more quickly with MBO, department heads jointly submitted a plant objective to top management dealing with improvement in production processes. Achievement of this objective resulted in savings after 10 months of nearly 2 percent of the value of the plant's annual production.

A number of personnel activities dealing with manpower and career planning, performance appraisal, and personnel policy were introduced during the second year of the program. Currently, company and divisional objectives, and associated control procedures, are being developed. Quantifiable individual objectives will follow.

During this year there were changes in the leadership styles of the company's managers as measured on the Likert questionnaire. The profile of the organization moved from System 2 (Benevolent-Authoritarian) to System 3 (Consultative-Participative) in the plant where the cost reduction was achieved. And other intangible Effects of organization development are recognized throughout the company. Management states that (1) conflict between divisions has been reduced; (2) morale has improved considerably; and (3) there is evidence of much greater delegation than previously and (4) of improved individual initiative and performance.

A number of roadblocks have not yet been fully overcome. As in many family businesses, there is still a reluctance to disclose profit and loss figures, but some operating results are now being released to middle managers. The group of managers who helped to rebuild the company after World War II can't see any need for change; retirement has helped here. One authoritarian manager is a major roadblock to bottom up participation in objective setting. His department is still lagging behind, but the success of other departments, and objectives from the top, will help to resolve this. Efforts to weld the top team into an integrated unit have not been fully successful. Old conflicts and jealousy die slowly, but T-group type meetings with the consultant have proved beneficial.

The beginning of the third year of the program coincided with the 1974 slump in the European automotive industry. The CEO has stated that his company is weathering the storm better than many of his competitors because of the change program. Cost reduction is being carried out effectively as part of objective setting from below rather than on orders from above.

Assignment
Diagram the change process being utilized here and outline the key steps. How does it compare with the behavioral models suggested by Argyris and Blake and Mouton? Ouchi?

PART FOUR

CASES

SOUTH PACIFIC HOTEL

HOTEL BACKGROUND

The South Pacific Hotel is wholly owned by World Wide Enterprises. The hotel is located in the scenic area of a south seas island about fifteen minutes from the tourist district. The South Pacific is unique, since it is the only resort hotel on the island.

The hotel's clientele is made up of foreign dignitaries, government officials, movie stars, business executives, and other V.I.P.'s—including the President of the United States. Because the hotel's profits rely heavily on continuous patronage by V.I.P.'s, much emphasis is placed on maintaining an image of being the "in" vacationing spot. An occupancy rate of 70 percent is needed to break even on hotel operations.

When the hotel first opened, the number of executive positions were held to a minimum to decrease costs. The personnel and housekeeping duties were handled by one manager. Also, there was no public relations director. After a year of operations, a manager was assigned to handle the duties of public relations director. An organization chart of the hotel follows as Exhibit 1.

As the number of management positions increased, meetings were set to help coordinate the departmental activities. The public relations director attended three meetings each week; 1) a staff meeting (including all executive staff members), 2) a sales meeting (including managers involved in selling of hotel rooms), and 3) a front-of-the-house meeting (including all those involved in servicing hotel guests.)

PUBLIC RELATIONS DIRECTOR

Julie Kennedy, the hotel's public relations director, was initially employed to fill a secretarial position. She graduated from a finishing school on the East Coast and later worked for several book publishing companies. Since she had always been intrigued with the tourist industry, she selected hotel work as a career. At the age of thirty-seven, she has earned the reputation of being one of the top P.R. women in the pacific islands.

Because of her training in finishing school, Julie has always been aware of all the do's and don'ts of social etiquette. She has always been a very meticulous person—most of the hotel workers call her a perfectionist. She examines all work to the minutest detail, making certain that nothing passes out of the hotel unless it has every comma in place.

As public relations director, Julie has always been concerned with building good community relations and establishing a favorable hotel image with visitors. She has always handled her public relations duties commendably and has been praised time and time again. She has an entire file for the "puff" letters she received, thanking her for all the courtesies extended.

Because of her preoccupation with the outside environment (guests and the local community), Julie has been blind to the behavioral problems within the hotel. It is ironic, therefore, that while being "tops" at public relations, Julie has problems with employee relations.

Source: Cyril P. Morgan, "The South Pacific Hotel." Reprinted by permission of Cyril P. Morgan, University of Colorado. This case was prepared as a basis for class discussion.

EXHIBIT 1.

Hotel Organization Chart

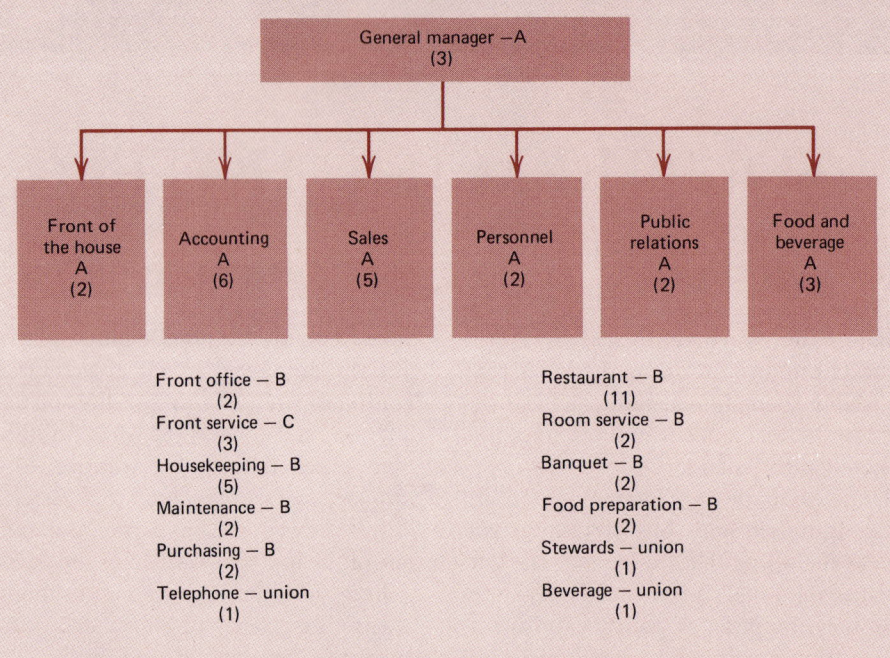

```
                          General manager — A
                                 (3)
        ┌──────────┬──────────┬──────────┬──────────┬──────────┐
   Front of    Accounting   Sales    Personnel   Public    Food and
   the house       A          A          A      relations  beverage
       A          (6)        (5)        (2)        A          A
      (2)                                         (2)        (3)
```

Front office — B	Restaurant — B
(2)	(11)
Front service — C	Room service — B
(3)	(2)
Housekeeping — B	Banquet — B
(5)	(2)
Maintenance — B	Food preparation — B
(2)	(2)
Purchasing — B	Stewards — union
(2)	(1)
Telephone — union	Beverage — union
(1)	(1)

A = Executive staff   B = Departmental heads   C = First-line supervisors

Numbers in ( ) denote persons in managerial capacities

INTERNAL RELATIONS

Julie's motto has always been, "Never assume that anything is done." Whenever the general manager delegates work to other department heads (who are designated by b's on the organization chart; see exhibit 1), Julie always finds it necessary to examine their work if it affects public relations in anyway. For example, if an important banquet is being planned, she finds it necessary to approve the menu and to inspect the silverware. Such interference usually results in friction with the banquet manger and the restaurant manager.

Although many of the managers resent Julie's interference, they have not brought their grievances to the general manager, since he is believed to favor the public relations director.

The sales, banquet, and front of the house managers have reached the point where they try to bypass Julie while doing their work. Rather than ask for her advice on publicity matters, the other managers prefer to rely on their own limited abilities. Therefore, Julie usually resorts to "snooping" tactics to see where her help is needed.

While in the sales office one day, Julie happened to read a letter dictated by the sales manager to his secretary. Because Julie felt that the letter contained a few inappropriate phrases, she took it upon herself to proofread and correct it. When she handed the letter back to the sales secretary, all of the sentences except one were crossed out. Annoyed by Julie's "interference," the sales secretary avoided Julie as much as possible in future situations.

Occasionally, Julie has exchanged a few harsh words

with some of the other managers in front of their subordinates. One such incident occurred at a hotel party. Julie had reserved four tables for her guests. One of the assistant managers mistakenly seated his guests at her tables. Enraged, she called him an idiot in front of the employees servicing the banquet.

Julie has always felt that the most priority should be placed on getting the work of the public relations director out on time. If she is under pressure, she will demand that a department head stop his work long enough to satisfy her needs. For example, Julie was submitting a recipe of a hotel dinner specialty to the local newspapers. The chef had to stop his own work on food preparation to write the recipe for her.

After the recipe was written, Julie needed a typewriter delivered to her office. She asked her assistant to phone the housekeeping department to have a boy deliver the typewriter. The housekeeping manager informed Julie's assistant that none of the boys were free then, but the typewriter could be delivered within the hour. When her assistant relayed the message, Julie was furious. She phoned the housekeeping manager and told her, "what do you mean by saying you're too busy? I'm busy too, and I've got deadlines to meet. I want that typewriter here now."

Although Julie usually riles a few tempers in the process of carrying out her duties as public relations director, she can always be depended on to get the job done. The local press and radio stations have always given the South Pacific preferential treatment, because they have had favorable encounters with Julie. Many movie stars have extended invitations to Julie to visit them as their guests in Hollywood. One even went so far as to write a letter to the senior vice-president of World Wide Enterprises, praising Julie's excellent handling of public relations. In his reply letter, the senior vice-president admitted that he considered Julie the best public relations manager in all of the World Wide Enterprises hotels.

Julie has received many job offers promising greater prestige and monetary compensation. However, she feels "at home" at the South Pacific. She will probably be the public relations director at the hotel for many years, since she thrives on the glamour of her job. Although she has made many friends outside the hotel, she has few friends among the other employees in the hotel.

The feelings of the other employees become evident after sitting in on a cafeteria conversation. Most of what is said about Julie in the cafeteria is derogatory. The other employees view Julie as a busybody perfectionist who would be impossible to work with. The employees often express their feelings to Julie's assistant.

Although her assistant has some problems working with Julie, she still finds her job satisfying. She realizes Julie is much more lenient toward persons working for the public relations department. She feels that Julie is "a wonderful person to work for."

Although Julie's assistant gets along well with her manager, she meets a lot of resistance when she tries to get help from other departments. If a favor is asked by the assistant, no one will offer any help if they suspect that their aid will benefit the public relations director. So Julie's assistant tries to get her work done through whichever channels offer the least resistance.

Questions

1. Write a summary paragraph that describes Julie's perception of her job as a manager. Include at least four major observations in your summary. Place yourself in an advisory capacity to Julie and describe the manager's job as you see it in general terms (refer to Chapter 13 in completing this assignment).

2. Identify examples of conflict in the case. What is Julie's approach to handling conflict and the results it yields? How should she approach handling conflicts and what positive benefits might result (Chapter 13)?

3. Using at least three of the frameworks for studying leadership style (Chapter 14) characterize Julie's approach giving examples to illustrate your reasoning. Suggest or describe what you feel would be a more effective approach and explain why. Be specifiic in your suggestions.

4. Utilizing some of the ideas, principles, and concepts contained in Chapter 16, describe the problems involved in how the hotel is presently functioning. Describe the characteristics and functioning of the hotel if it were operating in an "ideal" way. Set forth a step by step plan that you would follow in attempting to bring the hotel closer to the ideal you describe. How does your approach relate to or compare with those discussed in Chapter 16?

JOHN ANDERSON [35]

John Anderson was a man of 54. He had spent much of his working life as a personnel specialist with a number of large companies, usually in the area of training and development. His experience included jobs on both sides of the Atlantic, and he was familiar with many of the latest approaches to training and development in both the United States and Britain.

Anderson had returned to North America in 1971, after a four-year stay in England with a major manufacturing firm where he had occupied the post of Training Director. He had returned to accept a job with the Potterton Corporation, a large consumer durables manufacturer, as Manager of Management and Organizational Development for the Stag division.

Stag employed some 45,000 people and stretched across the country. Plants were either located near sources of supply, or close to major customers, and varied in size from 2000 to 8000 employees.

There were three levels of organization in the company. At the corporate level, Anderson reported to a vice-president of manpower development and industrial relations. There was a small corporate staff of eight specialists in the areas of management and organizational development.

At the divisional level, each division in turn had its own staffs. At Stag, management and organizational development, under Anderson, consisted of 20 specialists.

And finally, each plant had training and development people within the personnel function. These mangers reported directly to the plant personnel director, but also worked closely with the divisional staff. Their loyalties were often torn between the two. In the larger plants they tended to make themselves more independent of divisional influence, while in the smaller plants they were often loaded down with several other jobs and felt that the demands placed on them by divisional people were unrealistic.

When John Anderson took over as head of the Stag division training and development staff, morale was low. Of the twenty staff specialists, four were senior "career" people who had a broad range of experience in the training field. There were seven younger people who had university degrees and who saw themselves as "professional" trainers. The remaining nine staff positions were filled with people between the ages of 35 and 60 who had been moved into the management training function from other areas, for a variety of reasons. Several had been line managers in plants that had been reorganized, moved, or closed; a number had been timestudy men and skill trainers in the plants (i.e., they had been involved in teaching workers how to use machines, etc.); and two were ex-sergeants whose training experience had been in teaching trades or specific combat skills. There was little sense of cohesion among these groups. This problem was magnified by the fact that, with the exception of two older men, none of the training staff In the Stag division had been in their present jobs for longer than four years. Fifty percent had less than two years service with Stag.

Anderson called a meeting of the entire training and development staff of the Stag division on his third day on the job. At the meeting he introduced himself and gave a short resume of his background and experience. He asked each of the people at the meeting to introduce themselves and to describe their activities in training to date. Anderson then talked about his views on management and organizational development for about twenty minutes, and put forward his conception of the goals of the divisional staff. He then asked for comments and there was a discussion for another half hour. At the close of the meeting, Anderson said that his prime goal was to build an effective team within the Stag division. He stressed that he would be available for consultation at all times, and he encouraged every member of the staff to visit him in his office to discuss any problems they might be encountering.

Within the next few days, Anderson circulated a memo to all staff, listing his objectives for the group, and

---

[35] All names have been disguised. This case was prepared by Professor R. Stuart-Kotze as a basis for class discussion in the School of Business Administration, Acadia University. Copyright, R. Stuart-Kotze, 1975. Used with permission.

asking for comments, changes, additions or deletions, from anyone. He also converted an open area of the office into a lounge by bringing a number of coffee tables and easy chairs in. He made a point of appearing regularly at 10:45 A.M. and 3:15 P.M. for coffee, and usually stayed for about twenty minutes, chatting with whoever happened along. Within a week, almost everyone in the office came for coffee at these times. After a month on the job, Anderson invited the staff for a barbecue on saturday evening at his home. The party was informal and friendly and everyone seemed to enjoy themselves.

Three months after he had taken over, Anderson moved the divisional training staff to its own quarters, which included facilities for various training activities, and had a regular dining room, lounge, and small bar. The site also contained living accommodations for twenty-five people, and became used for a number of residential training activities. The daily coffee meetings continued, the staff all had lunch together in the dining room, and most of them stayed for a drink at 6:00 P.M., as the bar opened for people on residential courses. A number of social gatherings were organized by various members of the staff.

Sometimes these were held at private homes, and sometimes the facilities of the training center were used if no training activities were scheduled. At the suggestion of one staff member, a club tie was designed with the figure of a stag leaping in the air emblazoned on it. This became the "stag club" tie. It could be worn by members of the divisional training staff or by individuals who had attended training activities at the centre, and was a good seller at the bar. On any given day, 60 percent of the divisional staff could be seen wearing the "club" tie.

At the end of his first year as manager of management and organization development at Stag, John Anderson felt he had improved morale tremendously. He also felt he had increased the level of motivation and achievement to his staff. He noted that there was now a constant flow of ideas and suggestions from the staff on a wide variety of problems. They seemed to have organized themselves informally into a number of groups with common professional interests. Membership in these groups often overlapped. There was a great deal of informal communication on problems: suggestions and help were freely solicited and offered. The dichotomies of old/young, professional/nonprofessional, management training/skill training, management development/organization development, etc., all appeared to have been broken down. Anderson felt that he had, in fact, created a "team" at Stag.

However, problems began to occur in divisional relationships with both the plants and the corporate staff. The corporate group in an attempt to unify management development and organizational development policy throughout the company, began to set goals and objectives for adoption at all levels. The changes required were significant, and called into question much of what had been done in the company before. Corporate staff spent a large amount of time visiting the divisions, attempting to get agreement on the new policies. In a number of cases they reported back to the corporate vice-president that they were meeting with marked resistance from stag. They felt that anderson was blocking them on many occasions, and that he was being "uncooperative." The vice-president met with Anderson and talked the matter over with him. Anderson stated that he had no intention of being uncooprative, but that the corporate people expected too much too soon. He made the point that he had a very full program of activities on his own slate and that his people were overworked already. As soon as they could manage it, he said, they would begin to integrate their activities with the new corporate policy.

Late in 1972, the corporate vice-president was informed that the Stag division had not compiled the data for a government grant for training of minority groups. The potential loss to the company was approximately $500,000, as many of the Stag plants were located in areas where the labor force contained a high percentage of minority groups, and the company had been active in training and employing people from all these groups. Without data to back up their claim for assistance, they would not receive the government grants available for these activities. The vice-president immediately contacted Anderson who admitted it had been an oversight on the part of his staff.

Ten days later the data was on the vice-president's desk, and two of his own staff were in his office maintaining that the figures represented only about 60 percent of the actual training that had been done. They argued that there was another $200,000 of grant money not being claimed. As a result, the vice-president sent the two men into Stag to see if they could gather the missing data in the little time left. They managed to recover another $125,000.

This issue brought to light a number of complaints from the corporate staff. They maintained that Anderson was building an empire for himself at Stag and that he wanted to "go it alone" without the aid of the central staffs. The plants also began to complain. Several of the plant personnel directors contacted the vice-president and complained that various training and development packages were being shoved down their throats. They said they wanted their own plant people to have more autonomy, and questioned the usefulness of divisional staff. The vice-president pointed out that the reason for having divisional staffs was to try to unify the training and development program across plants, and to spread the overhead of specialists in a number of areas.

Privately, the vice-president was worried. While he could not be sure of the accuracy of the figure, he was informed by members of his own staff that stag had lost about $75,000 of federal grant money by poor administration and control procedures. He was also disturbed by the "club" atmosphere at Stag's training center. He wondered if it served as a unifying or divisive force for the company as a whole. And he noted that while anderson had a very close rapport with his subordinates, and they were very loyal to him, he adopted a very protective attitude towards them, and effectively screened them from other parts of the corporation. This had resulted in a number of other administrative problems, none quite as serious as the government grant, but otherwise annoying to the corporate group, and, to some extent, to the plants.

The vice-president decided that a tighter integration of the three levels of the company was needed. he saw the system of overall goals and objectives providing part of this linkage, but also decided to explore the idea of building interlocking teams within each functional area, using likert's "linking pin" approach. His basic idea is demonstrated by Figure 1, showing the linkage between the corporate level, divisional level, and plant level in the company.

In order to explore the idea more carefully, the vice-president arranged for a workshop where representatives from each level could learn about team building and could discuss its benefits and weaknesses in the light of the actual situation within the company. He asked that each division choose several representatives to attend the two-day meeting, and that some of the larger plants be represented by one or two people as well. The workshop was limited to training and development personnel, since they would ultimately be involved in any implementation of a program of team building within the company.

Stag division was represented by Anderson and one of his senior subordinates. It seemed to the vice-president that they stayed out of the discussions as much as possible for most of the two days, contributing very little overall. During the final session, however, which was

FIGURE 1

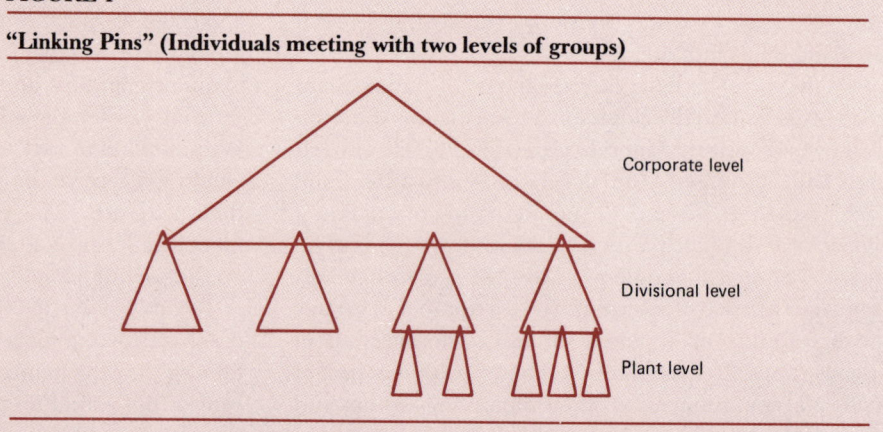

"Linking Pins" (Individuals meeting with two levels of groups)

Corporate level

Divisional level

Plant level

centered on sketching preliminary outlines for a plan of implementation, they both vigorously attacked the idea. It seemed to the vice-president that their arguments were not aimed at attacking the concept of team building, but rather that they were against the idea of the teams being built from the top level, downwards. They maintained that each division should maintain autonomy over how its training and development programs were designed and implemented. The workshop ended on a confused note, with some divisional people expressing interest in a corporate-initiated team building program, and others either remaining neutral, or going against the idea.

Questions

1. With respect to managing his own subordinates what organizational-leadership philosophy about people does John Anderson appear to be subscribing to? Cite examples from the case to illustrate your answer. In terms of his subordinates performance what have been the results of his approach? Evaluate its effectiveness. Present anderson with an alternative and justify your reasoning. Regarding the activities of a successful leader, how would you explain your perception of Anderson's job to him? (See Chapter 13 as background for handling this assignment.)

2. Set forth the several areas of the case where Anderson and his operation are coming into conflict. What are some of the negative consequences that are appearing as a result of these conflicts? What has been anderson's approach to resolving these conflicts? What approaches have others tried? Describe the approach to resolving the various conflicts you would suggest and what benefits would accrue to the parties involved? (See Chapter 13)

3. Using the material in Chapter 15 as a guide, set forth the ingredients of a plan for John Anderson and the organization as a whole to follow in providing for human resource development in the organization.

4. Using at least three different frameworks for examining leadership style, characterize John Anderson and explain the reasoning behind your response. What alternatives regarding leadership would you suggest to Anderson? Be specific in discussing the ingredients of your style suggestions. What do you think of the vice-president's idea for interlocking teams? Evaluate fully. (Chapter 15 will aid you in completing this assignment.)

5. Referring to Chapter 16 as a guide, undertake a complete analysis of the function of this organization in terms of the problems involved. How should the organization be functioning ideally? Describe in detail a plan for initiating the changes needed.,

PART FIVE
MANAGEMENT OF OPERATIONS

CHAPTER 17
OPERATIONS MANAGEMENT

CHAPTER 18
QUANTITATIVE DECISION MAKING AND OPERATIONS RESEARCH

CHAPTER 19
MANAGEMENT INFORMATION SYSTEMS AND THE COMPUTER

CHAPTER 20
CONTROLLING OPERATIONS

INTEGRATIVE CASES

McCALL DIESEL MOTOR WORKS

THE HOME EQUIPMENT COMPANY

This part presents a synthesis of the idea and management principles developed throughout the text as applied to the operations sections of organizations. It also provides an introduction to some of the methods being used to more effectively direct these production areas.

Chapter 17, Operations Management, describes the performance-related or production activities of the enterprise. These operations generate products or services which, when distributed and sold, provide the organization's revenues and, under skillful management, its profits. Chapter 17 also builds on the material studied earlier on planning and organizing, to realistically depict an example of an operations organization and its future-oriented planning activities.

Chapter 18 introduces various quantitiatve techniques for decision making that are being used in organizations today, and gives examples of their use in the management of operations.

Computers and management information systems have become primary supervisory tools of large-scale operations. Chapter 19 traces their growth, use, and the special problems which have developed from their use.

In Chapter 20, the control process is examined. Although the emphasis is on controls used in the production or operations area, this process is applicable to all areas of management. Techniques for scheduling and control of large-scale projects PERT, CPM, and simulation are discussed.

CHAPTER 17
OPERATIONS MANAGEMENT

AN OVERVIEW OF OPERATIONS OR PRODUCTION SYSTEMS
OPERATIONS MANAGEMENT ACTIVITIES AND DECISIONS
PRODUCT AND PRODUCTION DESIGN
PROCESS DESIGN AND EQUIPMENT CHOICES
LOCATION
FACILITIES LAYOUT
PRODUCT LAYOUT
PROCESS LAYOUT
PRODUCTION PLANS, SCHEDULING, AND DISPATCHING
PRODUCT LIFE CYCLE APPROACH
FRIENDLY AIRLINES
THE FOCUSED FACTORY
QUALITY CIRCLES
ISSUES IN OPERATIONS MANAGEMENT
APPLICATION EXERCISES AND CASES
SEBASTIAN's—LAYOUT OF A RESTAURANT KITCHEN
WORKERS ARE EXPERTS—QUALITY CIRCLES IN BREAKTHROUGH

BUSINESS REFOCUSES ON THE FACTORY FLOOR[1]

John F. Budd, Jr., and Emhart Corp. vice-president, calls it a "new pragmatism." David W. Wallace, chairman and president of Bangor Punta Corp., terms it the beginning of the "era of the manufacturing executive." Whatever the label, companies across the country are refocusing on one of the basics of business: making a better product faster and cheaper. They are recognizing that the best-conceived strategic plans or marketing analyses are useless if products are too costly to produce or too shoddy to sell. And they are putting in corporatewide programs aimed at spotting every quick and lucrative fix available to increase manufacturing productivity at the lowest cost.

Although the push is apparent in almost every industry, it is most dramatic in batch manufacturing, where setup times, materials flow, and the like require far more control than in continuous manufacturing. The batch plants are seeking techniques and concepts that may have slipped through the cracks in their own operations.

Clearly, top managers have realized that the nuts and bolts of business afford the best opportunities for savings. They are eliciting factory workers' ideas to increase quality and efficiency. And in companies as diverse as Emhart, TRW, Kellogg, Phillips Petroleum, and Westinghouse, they are hiring corporate vice-presidents for productivity to pull all the ideas together.

Perhaps the most formal productivity-improvement program is at Westinghouse Electric Corp., which in September started staffing a new productivity center. Its main goal, according to L. J. Hudspeth, vice-president for productivity, is to standardize as many productivity improvement tools as possible across the company's thirty-seven business units. Hudspeth is pushing for a "common data-base system"—already working in two transformer plants—that would force design engineers and manufacturing people to work with the same production criteria. Too often, manufacturing managers must waste time persuading designers to review their specifications to make them conform with the availability of parts and other manufacturing realities.

Hudspeth is also excited about the potential of a Japanese system called *kanban*, which represents a total reversal of U.S. conventional wisdom on production runs. Most U.S. plants aim for the longest fastest run on parts, even though it may mean increasing inventory carrying costs. They pay comparably little attention to the time costs of tooling up. *Kanban* concentrates on the other side of the equation, stressing short setup times, regardless of run length. Hudspeth notes that one Japanese auto company has designated ten minutes as the maximum setup time. It concentrates on short production runs and has been able to cut its parts inventory to one hour. "We think in terms of weeks of inventory," Hudspeth admits.

The Westinghouse center cost $10 million. It will eventually employ 250 people and operate with an annual budget of $30 million. Much of its focus will be on potential cost savings from avant-grade technology such as robotics. But in the area of streamlining existing operations alone, it hopes to increase productivity by 50 percent, although Westinghouse has not targeted a specific savings figure.

---

[1]"Business Refocuses on the Factory Floor," *Business Week*, February 2, 1981.

AN OVERVIEW OF OPERATIONS OR PRODUCTION SYSTEMS[2]

There are several common elements in an operations or production system. It involves *doing* something (transforming) to something (an input, a material item, or person to be processed) in such a way that it becomes something *else* (an output). In this latter form, it becomes useful to a customer. A manufacturing and distribution system for a grain processing company such as the Post Toasties Company involves materials flows and processes which quite literally can be diagrammed from field to table.

Sometimes it is clear that the output of one such system is the input to another. Argicultural grain harvesting becomes an input to the flour milling processes. Finished goods in railroad boxcars become an input to the marketing and distribution system, meeting customer demands for General Mills products. In each system, an input, a transformation, and an output can be identified, as illustrated in Figure 17-1.

The systems approach identifying the inputs (patients, tax dollars, etc.), the transformations (healing, road repairs, etc.), and the outputs (healthy people, good roads, etc.) are applicable to nonprofit and public sector operations situations as well. Such things as demand forecasting, purchasing planning, inventory management, and manpower planning are of concern to public as well as private enterprise. Thus, throughout this section, the issues and the examples apply to *operations*, other than strictly manufacturing. Effectiveness, rather than profit alone, is a guide to decision choices. *Efficiency* measures actual-to-ideal activity

Efficiency measures the actual-to-ideal activity performance. *Effectiveness* measures the balance of overall efficiencies to best attain organizational goals.

FIGURE 17-1

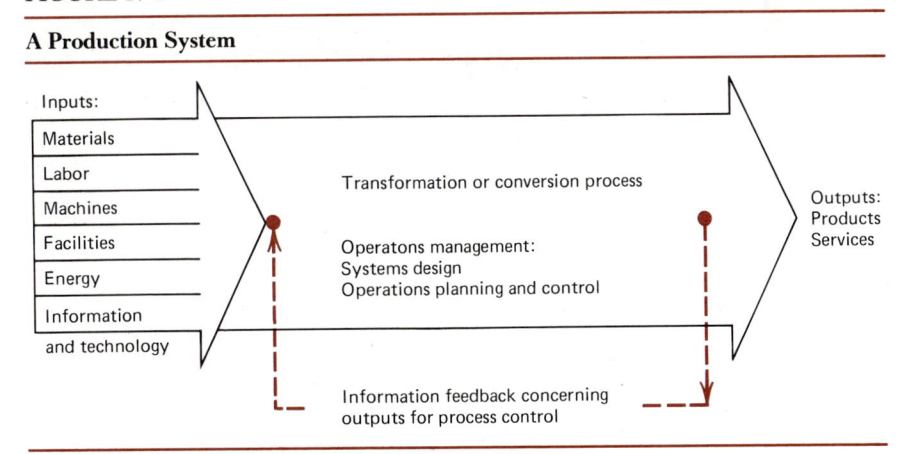

A Production System

Inputs: Materials, Labor, Machines, Facilities, Energy, Information and technology

Transformation or conversion process

Operatons management: Systems design / Operations planning and control

Outputs: Products / Services

Information feedback concerning outputs for process control

Source: Elwood S. Buffa, *Operations Management—The Management of Productive Systems,* New York, Wiley/Hamilton, 1976, p. 11.

---

[2] The authors gratefully acknowledge the assistance of John Burnham, Professor of MBA studies at Tennessee Technological University, Cookeville, Tennessee, who wrote this chapter.

performance. *Effectiveness* measures the balance of overall efficiencies to best attain organizational goals.

Operations management clearly extends far beyond the pure production aspects of the productive system. Individual purchasing, inventory, and distribution system decisions have aggregate effects on production. Overall *organizational effectiveness* depends on a balance among all of these elements—not only in their task performance, but in their planning and control as well.

Much of what has been learned about operations management comes from our knowledge of manufacturing, beginning in 1776 with Adam Smith's celebrated analysis of pin making. In more recent times, the scientific management studies and proposals of F. W. Taylor (1911) and the time-and-motion analysis of the Gilbreths (1921), have contributed greatly, as discussed in Chapter 2, Historical Development of Management Thought. These writers were among the pioneers in the field of industrial engineering, which has added so much to our ability to produce and distribute a wide variety of goods at low cost. Today's operations are becoming complex, as Buffa points out in the following quote.

> *"Current conditions and problems have focused attention and resources on new problems and have broadened considerably the range of productive systems. . . . In the past . . . health care, education, transportation, and retailing were carried on at almost the handicraft level. (But these have now grown) into huge systems and attracted attention (criticism) when their costs began to increase rapidly. As the productivity of the economy increased, a reallocation of personal expenditures was taking place.*[3]

Services have increased steadily, compared to durable goods, with considerable pressure being brought to bear in several sensitive areas: hospitals and medical care; postal services; and education, where the rising costs are a public concern.

Except for the variations resulting from producing different kinds of products, there are strong similarities in the production systems of the R. J. Reynolds cigarette plant in Winston-Salem, North Carolina, the Millikan Carpet Mills in Georgia, and the Proctor and Gamble Pringles plant in Jackson, Tennessee. Perhaps less obviously, we could be explaining the flow of patients through a hospital from admissions to the various specialty floors—operating, Xray, patient recovery, and patient's rooms. The final step in this service process would be the discharge of patients. A similar process would be that of moving letters and parcels through the local U.S. Post Office facility, goods to a big catalog store, or even the flow of bank checks through optical scanning equipment at the federal reserve bank.

In the latter example, another process is simultaneously taking place. Records are being created and classifications of check charges are being made so that a summary of these thousands of transactions can be sent to the member banks by computerized communication networks, without awaiting the physical arrival of the checks themselves. In all these cases, raw materials and human resources are being turned into finished goods or valuable services for either consumer or industrial use. These processes we call operations management.

There are strong similarities between the manufacturing plants and service organizations.

---

[3]Elwood S. Buffa, *Operations Management—The Management of Productive Systems*, New York, Wiley/Hamilton Publishers, 1976, pp. 4–5.

OPERATIONS MANAGEMENT ACTIVITIES AND DECISIONS

The following paragraphs deal with the many considerations, decisions, and procedures which must take place once the determination to create a productive system has been made. These factors include:

1. Product and production design.
2. Process design and equipment choices.
3. Location analysis and the distribution system.
4. Layout of facilities.

Once decisions about these matters have been made and implemented, the plant exists. Its characteristics may now be defined, the operations planning and control phases may be undertaken, and the production system may be brought "on-stream."

PRODUCT AND PRODUCTION DESIGN

The fewer the number of different parts and the simpler the product design, the less the cost to manufacturers.

Product Design. Although it is difficult to generalize about product design choices, certain guidelines can be given. The fewer the number of different parts, the lower the costs of manufacture. The cleaner and simpler the design, the lower the cost of employee training, assembly time testing, and maintenance.

> *"The obvious time to start thinking about basic modes of production for parts and products is while they are still in the design stage. This conscious effort to design for lower manufacturing cost is referred to as* production design, *as distinct from functional design. To be sure, the designer's first responsibility is to create something that functionally meets requirements, but once this is accomplished, ordinarily there are alternatives of design, all of which meet the functional requirements."*[4]

Production Design. There are various processes (chemical, forming, shaping, assembling, etc.) that may be applied to create a finished product. Production design seeks to match the product design with the most economical combination of processes, materials, and techniques. The existing facilities, equipment, assembly lines, and labor skills also must be evaluated so that costs may be minimized. Often the introduction of a new product offers the opportunity to acquire more modern equipment to perform the new product tasks and also deal more effectively with the existing products.

PROCESS DESIGN AND EQUIPMENT CHOICES

As can be seen, production design and production processes are virtually inseparable—and often several design stages are utilized in order to achieve the right mix for production. The total product consists of its functions, its appear-

---
[4]Elwood S. Buffa, *Basic Production Management*, New York, Wiley, 1975, p. 167.

ance, its quality, and its price. A Cadillac Eldorado and a Honda Civic both provide transportation, but there are very substantial differences along each of the other dimensions of *product*. These other details of product also are used to guide the designers in choosing production facilities.

Continuous processing includes an endless number or quantity of products.

Processes. In general, a process transforms inputs of materials, energy, and labor into a desired output. The choice of processes depends on the product designs. *Continuous processing* includes an endless number or quantity of products rather than a scheduled batch or number. The chemical process by which an oxygen blast furnace creates iron from inputs of fuels and ores is an example of continuous processing. Another example would be the refining of crude oils into gasolines and other petroleum products.[5] *Intermittent processing* requires the scheduling of a particular number of items to be formed to meet a stated production requirement for end items. Different products are usually produced using the same production line. An example would be the process of casting, by which iron or steel is molded into a particular form—for instance, as a pump casing—or that by which small parts are formed through injection molding of plastics.

Several things follow directly from these basic combinations of products and processes characteristics. (1) There is a very large size and high capital cost associated with most continuous processes. (2) In intermittent processes, creating single units or batches of similar products, the variety and complexity of the products to be made will affect the process choice. If a high volume and a narrow range of products are necessary, then fixed production lines and *special purpose equipment* will be chosen. For either a lower volume or wider products range (or both) the tendency will be toward less expensive, *general purpose* equipment—often organized into work centers which perform similar production functions.

Changes of Shape, Size, Form, Assembly. Incorporated into process are many transformations that are physical, such as the turning of metal stock on a lathe; the use of a saw to rough-form a chair leg; or the grinding and sanding of a piece to near-finished form; and the final polishing of the piece. Combining these with drilling and smoothing makes the workpiece capable of being assembled with other pieces into a finished product or larger component. For example, the finished chair frame would go on to an upholstery or caning operation, depending on the product.

Transportation Processes. Rather than being a *physical* change, the process may be designed to change *location*, as in the case of an airline. While not obvious at first, the transportation or distribution system completes the product by making it available to customers far from the plant. A critical element in the transportation process design is the location of productive facilities and warehouses. A variety of techniques, to be discussed later in this chapter, and in Chapter 18 may be used to optimize the transportation process for the company product.

---

[5]Sam G. Taylor et al., "Process Production and Inventory Planning Framework: A Summary," *Production and Inventory Management*, Vol. 22, No. 1, First Quarter 1981, pp. 15–33.

LOCATION

Sometimes there are a great many restrictions on acceptable locations. Consider the shipbuilding industry, where the production location must be on water navigable by the ship produced. In other cases, the cost of distribution of the finished product may suggest a processing location nearer the final consumer. Electric utilities, cement block manufacturers, and many baked goods producers fall into this category for essentially the same reason.

The Location Decision.   Johnson, Newell, and Vergin suggest that:

> *"Although revenue is relatively independent of location for manufacturing and wholesaling firms, . . . operating costs are strongly affected by facility location. . . . Factors such as the availability and cost of trained labor, power and water will affect transformation cost. For labor-intensive products, the wage rates may be the most significant in the location design. . . . At least in the early stages of the location decision process, the firm usually first determines the location that minimizes the cost of transportation. Once the firm has selected this area, it can make alterations to secure the necessary facilities for the conversion process. . . .*
>
> *In some cases, the production process requires several environmental conditions. Some processes produce disagreeable odors or other irritants and pollutants which require either the installation of expensive cleansing equipment or locations in an area where the pollutants do not create either short-term or long-run problems. . . . Still other processes require vast quantities of water or electricity, such as the production of aluminum, which usually is located close to inexpensive supplies of electrical power. Some special process requirements can be placed within the framework of operating costs; and others, such as vast requirements of electricity, must be placed in the category of transportation costs of raw materials. . . .*
>
> *Investments will also vary with the location, since the costs of land and construction will both be affected. For example, cold climates require more substantial construction than temperate climates. In addition, land values may vary by several hundred percent, depending upon whether an urban or a rural location is chosen."* [6]

The Japanese have made an intensive study of the entire vendor-manufacturer-distribution system, and, in most cases, vendor locations are very close to main assembly locations, in order to hold inventories to a minimum, and to maintain flexibility to changes induced by the customer.[7]

Multifacility Location—Allocation-size Problem.   When more than one location is involved, the problem takes on added dimensions. A new productive facility's nearness to raw materials or major markets will affect not only its own product

---

[6]Richard Johnson, William Newell, and Roger C. Vergin, *Operations Management*, Boston: Houghton-Mifflin, 1972, p. 130.

[7]David Nelleman, and Leighton Smith, "Just-in-Case vs. Just-in-Time Production Systems," Draft Article, Arthur Anderson & Co., Chicago Office, 1980. Also Robert Waterbury, "Kanban Cuts Waste, Saves $ With Minimum Effort" and "How Does Just-in-Time Work in Lincoln, Nebraska?" *Assembly Engineering,* April 1981, pp. 52–56.

delivery costs, but those of the best of the existing facilities as well. Fairly advanced mathematical methods have been employed to seek solutions to the problem—from which plant should we produce and ship? Approaches to this question will be suggested in Chapter 18.

Location decisions are long-term decisions and.

Long-term Consequences. Hopeman points out some of the long-term consequences of plant location decisions, after circumstances have changed. The first quotation illustrates why growth should be anticipated.

> *"One example involves a paper plant that is situated on an island in a river. At the time the plant-location decision was made, building on the island seemed reasonable, since logs were transported to the plant via water, a great deal of water was used in the process, finished paper was shipped via water, and waterfalls were available for power. Today, this company faces very difficult expansion problems. It has virtually reached the limits of possible expansion on the island. Buildings cover almost every square foot of available land. It is difficult to expand upward any further because of the nature of paper making and the machinery that is required.*

Unique location advantages may turn into handicaps in a rapidly changing market. An aircraft company located in the West

> *"acquired another aircraft plant nearby, which was used to manufacture amphibious aircraft, or seaplanes. The advantage of the seaplane operation was that the plant faced a large lake on which the new seaplanes were tested and from which the seaplanes were flown on their maiden flights. Today, however, the company does not manufacture seaplanes. It is faced with the problem of getting large jet airlines out of the plant with limited runway facilities. . . . Once the aircraft starts down the runway, it reaches a point at which it must take off and fly successfully, or land in the lake. Another possibility is to bring it down in the heavily populated city which surrounds the plant.*[8]

Site Selection. Once the location, city, or region has been selected, a specific site on which to locate the plant must be chosen. Just as there is more than one possible location, there will be various sites in the locale, and selection among them depend on such factors as the following.[9]

1. Size of the site.
2. Drainage and soil conditions.
3. Water supplies.
4. Utilities
5. Waste disposal and environmental considerations.
6. Transportation facilities.
7. Land cost and development costs.

---

[8]Richard J. Hopeman, *Production: Concepts, Analysis, Control*, 3rd Ed., Columbus, Ohio Bobbs-Merrill Book Co., 1975, pp. 113–114.
[9]Ibid., p. 125

OPERATIONS MANAGEMENT   463

These sites should have potential for expansion, tax advantages, convenience for commuting employees, local public transportation, and added considerations. But the special requirements imposed by the products, production design, and processes selection will be at the forefront of the site committee's thinking.

When both location and site have been chosen, the issue of materials flow becomes dominant, and the actual design of the building and its accesses can be completed. This step initiates the facilities management project, which will be discussed in Chapter 18, Quantative Decision Making.

FACILITIES LAYOUT

After a location is chosen, a site is selected and a facilities layout is constructed around the site.

Layout probably begins with the site selected—its roads, rail spurs, water and sewer line tie-ins, the direction of streams or rivers, wharfs, quays, etc. For it is the combination of the site, positioning of the building, and the ease of access which make for the best overall layout. First the layout is developed, then the building erected around it.

> *The primary objective of plant layout is to optimize the arrangement of machines, men, materials, and supporting services so that the value created in the production system is maximized.... The layout should also satisfy the needs of workers, managers, and other people associated with the production system. Beyond these general objectives, several specific objectives are strived for in the development of good layouts.*[10]

These objectives include (1) minimizing materials handling, (2) reducing hazards affecting employees, (3) providing balance in the production process, (4) minimizing interferences from machines, (5) increasing employee morale, (6) utilizing available space, (7) utilizing labor effectively, (8) and providing flexibility. The physical layout of the design puzzle is needed to show the great degree of interdependence among all of the facilities planning decisions. The choices of alternatives for the production design, and for the processes which will carry it out are used to make layout decisions.

PRODUCT LAYOUT

Product layout is the arrangement of machinery, equipment, and assembly lines in the chronological steps used.

Product layout is the arrangement of machinery or conversion equipment and assembly lines in the chronological steps used in the manufacture of the product. This form of layout is the dominant procedure for repetitive manufacturing[11] and continuous process[12] industries. A classical example in repetitive manufacturing would be an auto assembly plant where auto parts flow into a main line and several hundred identical model cars roll off the line each shift. It is an equally descriptive term for basic industries like chemicals, petroleum refining, or steelmaking. The key identifier of such a layout is sequential and balanced operations.

---
[10]Ibid., pp. 137–139.
[11]*Production and Inventory Management Review and APICS News*, April 1981, pp. 10–12; "Report on Detroit Conference and Workshop October 21–22, 1980, Repetitive Manufacturing Group."
[12]Taylor et al., op. cit.

Labor is applied using equipment and materials that are organized so that work flows smoothly through the plant to completion. While the plant may have responsibility for making several products, each will have its own product line with specialized machinery, materials handling equipment, and so forth, along which the product moves continuously. (See Figure 17-2.) Notice how the product's design dominates and determines the layout. Products move usually continuously, down a conveyor line and past successive work stations where workers or machines are stationed to perform one operation on each product.

The rate of completion of a single production unit is called the cycle time *of the line.*

The rate of completion of a single production unit is called the *cycle time* of the line. Thus, the *line design capacity* is the working hours for the line divided by its cycle time. The trick having a good product layout is to have balance, with each activity performing its tasks so that the same cycle time is met everywhere along the line.

Machines and equipment are arranged according to the sequence of operations required to fabricate and assemble. Machines and workers are specialized in the performance of specific operations, and the parts are almost continuously moving.[13]

Advantages of Product Layout. The principal advantage of product layout is that it allows continuous manufacturing and results in a low cost per unit. Special purpose equipment is used along fixed routes, allowing rapid movement of materials. "Materials handling costs, travel distances, inventory in process, and storage space are all reduced materially."[14] This type of layout is relatively simple to schedule and control. The use of semiautomatic special purpose machines reduces the necessity for skilled workers and shortens training periods for new employees.

Product layout allows continuous manufacturing and results in a low cost per unit.

Often the span of control of supervision can be large, since jobs are machine paced. Furthermore, the use of computer-controlled robots[15] is a reality and is prevalent in Japan[16] and, increasingly, in the United States. Here, the lack of meaningful work due to repetitive tasks, the advent of inexpensive microprocessors (small computers) and the need for consistent quality performance, have combined to give us "Robotics."

Disadvantages of Product Layout. The disadvantages of product layout derive chiefly from the high cost of initial investment for special equipment and conveyorization. Only products with high volume operations can be manufactured this way because the overhead must be spread over large numbers of individual units. The product layout is also quite vulnerable to work stoppages. When work on one part of the line stops the entire line is shut down.[17] Furthermore, if there is

Product layout requires special purpose equipment and expensive investment, but can result in low cost per unit.

---

[13] Buffa, *Basic Production Management*, p. 279.
[14] Franklin G. Moore, *Production Management*, 6th ed., Homewood, Ill., Richard D. Irwin, 1973, p. 187.
[15] Ibid., p. 188.
[16] W. Edward Deming, *On the Management of Statistical Techniques for Quality Control and Productivity*. In draft, February 1981.
[17] Deborah Churchman, "The Secret Weapon We Gave Japan," *Fort Lauderdale News/Sun-Sentinel*, Sunday, April 5, 1981, Section G, pp. 1, 7, and 8. The "Secret Weapon" is, of course, Dr. W. Edward Deming, a gifted statistician and recipient of the Medal of the Sacred Treasure from the Emperor of Japan

FIGURE 17-2

Layout for Two Different Products in One Plant

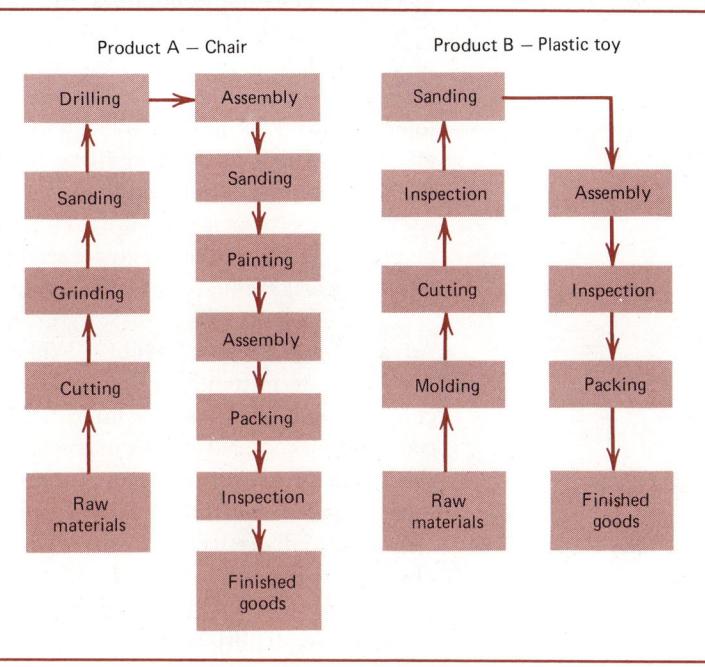

Product A — Chair

Drilling → Assembly
↑ ↓
Sanding Sanding
↑ ↓
Grinding Painting
↑ ↓
Cutting Assembly
↑ ↓
Raw materials Packing
↓
Inspection
↓
Finished goods

Product B — Plastic toy

Sanding ─→
↑ ↓
Inspection Assembly
↑ ↓
Cutting Inspection
↑ ↓
Molding Packing
↑ ↓
Raw materials Finished goods

a need to change over from one product to another, significant time and cost are involved in traditionally designed plants with conventional equipment. The Japanese, however, have made a virtue of necessity, concentrating on shortening the changeover time needed to achieve the required flexibility to meet changing demand for product.

Perhaps the greatest disadvantage springs from the boredom caused by workers engaged in monotonous tasks. The desire to "punish the system" for the uninteresting work environment leads to deliberate creation of defectives (sabotage) to test the quality control (QC) inspectors, to goldbricking if possible, and to the demand for increasingly high wages. Fortunately, there is progress being made in the development of work cells (the Swedish Volvo Plant, for example), and other group technology concepts; and in the use of "Quality Circles" where the detailed knowledge of workers is applied to improving the production process, leading to enriched jobs, higher productivity, and better quality.[18]

PROCESS LAYOUT

While the product or line layout is designed for continuous production of a single product, the process or functional layout is organized to be effective for inter-

---

[18] "Workers are Experts—Quality Circles in Breakthrough," *Herald Citizen*, Friday, June 19, 1981, pp. 1–2.

> Process layout is designed for intermittent or even one-of-a-kind jobs such as a custom machine shop.

mittent or even one-of-a-kind jobs—characteristic of a custom machine shop. For this type of layout, all activities of a similar type are grouped together—milling machines, for example, or lathes. All parts or products will be routed through the shop sequentially—by activity—and the physical flow will depend on the specific of the required end-product. Product differences call for routings toward completion which take into account the other work in the shop, manufacturing tolerances, and the materials of which the item is to be made. The classic case is "the job shop" which involves small-lot manufacturing of any product that can be fabricated on the existing equipment in the shop at a profit.

When the process layouts are evaluated, the rate of the mix of jobs expected will determine the success of the layout selected. Figure 17-3 traces the paths of the two different parts through a process layout.

Advantages of Process Layout. When a company needs to produce a variety of products intermittently, using similar equipment, a process layout is the best choice. General-purpose machines can be grouped together by function (a "work center") and changed over from product to product in accordance with the process sheet, and the machining/manufacturing steps specified. This means that process layouts are less vulnerable to shutdowns, and that when such interruptions occur, they are usually restricted to one or a few centers. General purpose equipment is also less expensive to buy, and is more or less standard within an industry (metal working, or furniture, for example.)

Since general purpose equipment requires more setup and operator ability, jobs often are richer in motivational properties. Furthermore since men and machines are somewhat independent of each other, the method lends itself to individual incentive systems.[19]

> Process layout utilizes general purpose equipment and is more flexible but more difficult to schedule.

Disadvantages of Process Layout. The disadvantages of process layout derive mainly from the slower operating speeds of the machines and the extra movement of materials required in processing. Notice in Figure 17-3 how the product must backtrack and crisscross its own path in order to get from one operation to another. Furthermore, routing, scheduling, and cost accounting are more difficult and therefore more costly in this method. Materials handling is expensive and inventories in process are always high. Still the process layout is better for small volumes on a wide variety of products.[20]

PRODUCTION PLANS, SCHEDULING, AND DISPATCHING

Product and production planning, process selection, location and site selection activities, and physical layout relate to the details of the physical facilities to be used by the company. Aggregate production planning, scheduling, and dispatch

---

[19] Moore, *Production Management*, p. 185.
[20] Ibid., p. 186.

FIGURE 17-3

Process Layout for Two Different Products

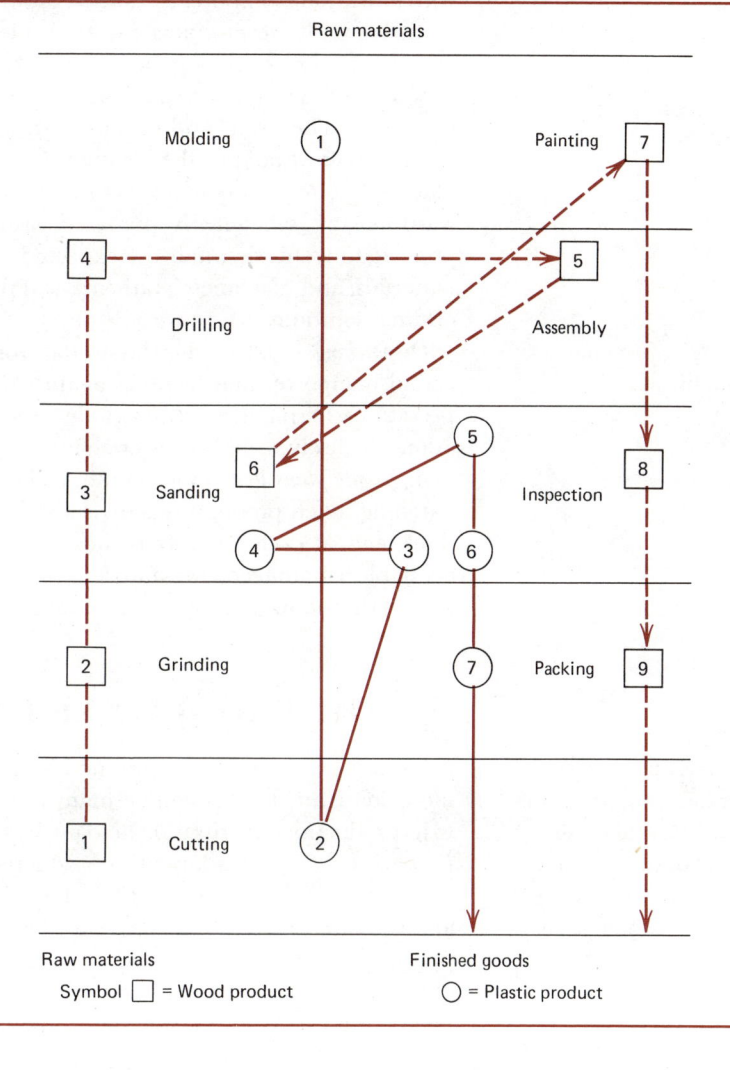

[Diagram: Process layout showing flow of Wood product (squares, solid line) and Plastic product (circles, dashed line) through stations: Molding, Painting, Drilling, Assembly, Sanding, Inspection, Grinding, Packing, Cutting. Raw materials enter at top and bottom; finished goods exit at bottom.

Wood product sequence (squares): 1 Cutting → 2 Grinding → 3 Sanding → 4 Drilling → 5 Assembly → 6 Sanding → 7 Painting → 8 Inspection → 9 Packing.

Plastic product sequence (circles): 1 Molding → 2 Cutting → 3 Sanding → 4 Sanding → 5 Inspection → 6 Inspection → 7 Packing.

Symbol □ = Wood product   ○ = Plastic product]

schemes are part of the *utilization* of the facilities that have been turned over for use by the productive system.

Aggregate production planning, often called master planning, is a description of the way that manufacturing will support the marketing plan. This marketing plan is a form of priority planning, since it phases the requirement for products over time in accordance with customer requirements or a forecast of this demand. Manufacturing then will "rough out" a schedule or master production schedule, and compare this with plant capacity. Generally the variables that management will be considering during this master planning phase will be manpower levels and numbers of shifts, the available support from vendors, suppliers, or subcontractors

Aggregate production planning (master plan) is a description of how manufacturing will support the marketing plan.

to reduce the demand for in-plant capacity, and the efficiencies needed for good plant performance. These procedures can be performed by experienced people with or without computer assistance. However, the ability to reach a good starting point for multiple products and multiple plant locations reaching over twelve months or more, usually requires large-scale linear programming packages.

Scheduling uses the aggregate plans as applied to a particular location (or set of locations). The input and output plans guide the quarterly, monthly, or even weekly commitment of the location's resources. A schedule spells out the time, place, personnel, and materials required to produce specific products. A forward-looking schedule is prepared, using the newest forecasts, actual and projected inventories, and the expected availabilities of short-term manpower, materials, and machines. Mathematical programming is frequently used to find optimal solutions.

Dispatching involves the day-to-day (or even hour-to-hour) commitment of actual manpower and facilities against the scheduled production based on expectations. Dispatch activities guide performance, using feedback from the operations themselves, and the ever-changing productive system environment.

Aggregate plans lead to general and detailed schedules, which then guide dispatching. Each program sets the stage for the performance of the actual operations; and, as each program is chosen, the facilities decisions govern the options available to management—and determine costs, backlogging, overtime, and other factors that show up only as operations take place.

THE PRODUCT LIFE CYCLE APPROACH

Another way to visualize a productive system is to trace it sequentially, from its inception as an idea through the many levels and decisions which are made leading to its production, distribution, and use by the public. Marketers call this *the product life cycle*. It has been adapted to productive systems in a "birth life, and death" appoach shown in Figure 17-4. Here the interdependence of many operations management decisions can be related to the characteristics of the production facility we are observing at the moment. The life cycle approach is especially helpful in explaining the time lags and accumulated investments which finally result in a new product reaching the market.

FRIENDLY AIRLINES

In order to demonstrate the product life cycle approach to the analysis of operations in an organization, a very different kind of enterprise, the mythical Friendly Airline Company, will be described.

Friendly Airlines is in the transportation service business, flying passengers, air cargo, and mail to the cities along their authorized routes. Friendly operates a fleet over 200 aircraft, 185 of which are jet powered. It serves over 100 United States cities, and makes over 1000 departures each day, principally in the eastern half of the country.

FIGURE 17-4

Key Decisions in the Life of a Productive System

BIRTH of the system	What are the goals of the firm?
	What product or service will be offered?
PRODUCT DESIGN and PROCESS SELECTION	What is the form and appearance of the product?
	Technologically, how should the product be made?
DESIGN of the system	Where should the facility be located?
	What physical arrangement is best to use?
	How do you maintain desired quality?
	How do you determine demand for the product of service?
MANNING the system	What job is each worker to perform?
	How will the job be performed, measured; how will the workers be compensated?
START-UP of the system	How do you get the system into operations?
	How long will it take to reach desired rate of output?
The system in STEADY STATE	How do you run the system?
	How can you improve the system?
	How do you deal with day-to-day problems?
REVISION of the system	How do you revise the system in light of external changes?
TERMINATION of the system	How does a system die?
	What can be done to salvage resources?

Source: Richard B Chase and Nicholas J. Aquilano, *Production and Operations Management*, Homewood, Ill., Richard D. Irwin, Inc., 1977, p. 14.

Like most carriers, Friendly has limited capital resources and must make difficult choices about the number, size, and characteristics of aircraft in their fleet, the cities they will seek authorization to fly into, and craft in their fleet, the cities they will seek authorization to fly into, and the variety and prices for services that they will offer. The airline business requires high capital investments for equipment. For example, each L-1011 Tristar cost over $15 million in 1973. Airlines also allocate about 20 percent of total revenues to salary payments. Furthermore, the variable costs of operations, such as payments for fuel, landing charges, maintenance, and meals, make up another 30 percent. The L-1011 consumes more than $4 worth of fuel each mile that it flies—with takeoffs costing much more. If a new route is approved, or additional cities are authorized on an existing route, a large number of other costs are added, including such things as: a counter and operations space, gates, fuel and baggage facilities at the airport, and a marketing reservations group to stimulate and sell space on Friendly's planes.

Birth of a Productive System. Consider the alternatives for serving an existing market such as the one in which Friendly is already operating. For the propeller aircraft still used, a conversion to jet power might be considered. Here both air speed and lifting capacity favor jets because of their much higher rate of available seat-miles daily. But different sizes of ships have different numbers of seats, therefore quantity of seats demanded per flight will influence the size of ship that is economical for Friendly. Also, the distance between cities served nonstop will affect aircraft choice because of operating costs.

But note some of the other factors implied by the birth element of this product life cycle approach: the product or services offered. In the aircraft puchase decision are included first class, tourist, baggage, mail, and cargo decisions as well as decor, lounge, galley, hand baggage, and lavatory outfitting—a highly complex "mix" of services. "Wide body" can be compared with "stretched" versions of conventional aircraft in terms of passenger revenues and capacities and variable costs.

The support required for new products in the product design and process selection stage is complex.

Product Design and Process Selection. Many of these factors must be considered when fleet purchases are contemplated. Many such purchases result from the capital investment decision. Remember that only a portion of the product is produced aboard the aircraft. Promotions, reservations, baggage and cargo facilities, check-in and lounges, meals, and other product marketing factors are distinct from the aircraft, yet must be compatible with it. For example, the present Friendly schedule out of Miami has five wide-body aircraft departing within a twenty-minute period. This has had a tremendous influence on the requirements of both product and process. In fact, it required a complete redesign of a whole Friendly concourse. Wide-body ships require more reservation data base for making and tracking customer reservations for a day and flight; more check-in and security screening capacity; and wider concourses and walkways. In addition, larger lounges, more space between docking positions, and longer lead-times on the actual loading process are needed, so that all five ships may still depart on time while each boards 150 or more passengers. Consider the complexity of this problem for the much larger Boeing 747, which seats 496 passengers.

Manning the System. In the airline business, the time table drives the airlines. This is especially easy to show when we start to develop manpower programs for the fleet. When a single ship is being evaluated, there are several factors which integrate equipment and flying ground personnel: the *ship* will fly an itinerary made up of flight segments between authorized departure stations and an arrival station, starting early in the morning and finishing late at night. The usual ship-operating day is from sixteen to twenty clock hours. The obvious conclusion is that there must be more than one crew assigned to the ship! This is complicated by the fact that the aircraft and the assigned work station is "on the move."

The problem is further complicated because both the crews and the aircraft have homes. Flight personnel have families and houses, and a stay overnight away from home is costly to both the airline and the personnel. The number of crews that must be added to the payroll is directly related to government regulations and the labor relations agreement covering working hours and other conditions of employment as well as the need to schedule so that most crews and most ships end up at "home" each work day.

As we consider the scheduling of the entire fleet of existing and new ships, the picture of how to plan transportation service is awesome in its complexity. Because service depends on the market, the first stage in Friendly's schedule development is done by market schedule planning. The available fleet is tentatively assigned to the various routes and services authorized. When the best marketing schedule has been developed, it is then coordinated with operations schedule planning. In this phase, the crew, maintenance, and terminal activities are added so that a good marketing schedule is then compared with the expected competitive timetables for relative attractiveness and published in the airline guide. At that point, travel agents and reservation clerks can begin to help customers in making travel arrangements. Complete new schedules may be generated three or four times a year.

System Start-up. After Friendly's new ships have been integrated into the flight schedule, flight crews are recruited and trained on the equipment. In order to bring the ships into operations a variety of other details must be looked after. Spare parts, special oils, maintenance training, cargo/baggage loading and unloading procedures, docking and maneuvering training, fueling and every-station ship checkouts must be provided. The first flights will require extra attention from high-level managers from operations, engineering, and flight supervision. Since the equipment is new to the company, Friendly's chief pilot will make the fiirst flights to check out all of the performance and safety aspects. The operational integration of the new equipment will take months. Much data will be gathered about speed, landing and docking times, clearances, inflight performance, fuel consumption, and average turn-around times from gate arrival to completion of passenger service. A stable and reliable timetable helps in marketing as well as in operations.

The start-up phase of introducing a new product is always full of difficulties.

The System in Steady State. With both flight and performance statistics established for the new aircraft, Friendly can return to routine scheduling, ground operations maintenance, and flight activities for the fleet. The material flow aspects include flight crews, passengers, meals, baggage, cargo, mail, and fuel. These depend on another flow—that of the ships through the air network from station to station. Preparation for the transportation service process takes place on the ground, as does completion of the service at the arrival station. Actual arrival times are not exact, but can be predicted statistically. Steady-state manning and facilities planning are based on these predictions. Baggage-handlers, gate agents, and security personnel are scheduled to keep arrivals and departures moving smoothly. On-line maintenance, personnel, emergency mechanics, and aircraft cleaning crews are set up to handle the ships moving through, as well as those doing overnight turnarounds at each station.

Revision of the System. Flight schedules are modified during the months between complete seasonal changes. Sometimes the changes result from customer feedback about demand. Sometimes the operations situation requires it. Changes can be initiated by gate congestion at peak times, difficulty in maintaining arrival and departure stability, high overtime or flight crew penalty hours, lower-than-expected ship utilization, or even some action on the part of the competition. The retirement of the remaining "prop" aircraft would also represent such a revision, as would ground facility changes at the larger stations manned by Friendly.

Termination of the System. There has been considerable debate in recent years about the ability of the airline industry to survive in its present form. The public interest has required a good bit of regulatory attention to safety and to prices charged and authority to serve routes. Both salary and operating costs have increased greatly, as has the price of replacement aircraft. A number of routes flown by Friendly have two or more strong competitors flying equivalent equipment and reducing the Friendly market share. But low-cost air travel is deemed in the public interest and profits are not high enough to accumulate the money needed for new ships, nor to attract lenders. Furthermore, the returns on investment available in other growth industries make equity financing unattractive.

Perhaps some of the airlines will follow the passenger trains into oblivion, completing the life cycle. In fact, a number of airlines have either gone out of business or merged with stronger companies for exactly these reasons. When this occurs, the company seeks to sell its aircraft and obtain jobs for its skilled employees, sell or lease its facilities, and return to its creditors and stockholders what can be salvaged. This has not happened with Friendly—in fact, they were active bidders when Northeast Airlines "bit the dust" a few years back.

THE FOCUSED FACTORY

Another example of an application of the product life cycle concept to manufacturing is the use of an approach called the focused factory, conceived of by Wickham Skinner of Harvard University.[21] Skinner criticizes our plants for operating with only one basic standard—cost efficiency and volume of production when the world is demanding higher quality products. He points out that American manufacturing plants have tried to become efficient at too many different things because of the wide range of products produced by most companies. Skinner suggests that companies would be more efficient if they concentrated on one product in each manufacturing plant, *focusing* the plant's layout and machinery on the most efficient type of manufacturing for that product.

Of course most companies would be unable to limit their production at any one plant to one product because of the economies of distribution, and because many multiline companies have only one plant for each line. Smaller companies may have only one plant and produce numerous products. For this reason, Skinner suggests that another alternative would be to create a *plant-within-a-plant* (PWP),

---

[21]Wickham Skinner, *Manufacturing in the Corporate Strategy*, New York, Wiley-Interscience, 1978, especially Chapter 6, "The Focus Factory" and Chapter 8, "Defining the Manufacturing Task." Also John M. Burnham, "The Operating Plant: Case Studies and Generalizations," *Production and Inventory Management*, Vol. 21, No. 4, Fourth Quarter 1980, pp. 63–94.

FIGURE 17-5

A Plant Within a Plant Organized by Product Life Cycles

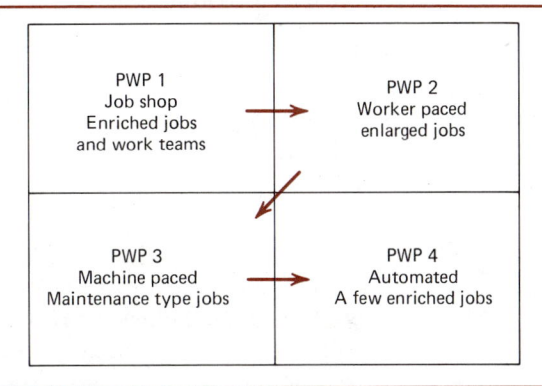

```
┌─────────────────────┬─────────────────────┐
│       PWP 1         │       PWP 2         │
│      Job shop       │    Worker paced     │
│    Enriched jobs    │    enlarged jobs    │
│   and work teams    │                     │
├─────────────────────┼─────────────────────┤
│       PWP 3         │       PWP 4         │
│    Machine paced    │      Automated      │
│ Maintenance type jobs│  A few enriched jobs│
└─────────────────────┴─────────────────────┘
```

by organizing the plant into three or four areas according to the volume and labor/machine ratio needed for *focus* in each PWP.

A fully developed PWP might include an arrangement such as that depicted in Figure 17-5. This approach can best be explained plant by plant.

PWP 1—The job-shop operation of the focused factory is easily adaptable and has highly enriched jobs.

PWP 1. New products typically require low-volume production until they are accepted nationwide. Some never justify high-volume operation. Therefore PWP 1 of the focused factory is designed using general purpose equipment and skilled labor. It is easily adaptable to highly enriched jobs and work team arrangements such as those discussed in Chapter 10. But machinery and employee training are not the only things which differ from PWP to PWP. The way in which efficiency is evaluated and the reward system for evaluating workers also varies. Usually quantity produced per man/hour will be low in this type of operation, but quality standards can be achieved much quicker by labor intensive production.

PWP 2 is an intermediate step which it is worker paced.

PWP 2. This PWP would be worker paced but would include more extensive use of conveyors and assembly line type work. It is an intermediate step between the job-shop process layout and the full-fledged product layout discussed earlier in this chapter. Employees in this plant would engage in work requiring rather long job cycles and might perform several operations before initiating the movement of the product along the line. Therefore, they could be trained for more enriched jobs in PWP 1 should they indicate an interest and aptitude for such. The product produced in PWP 2 may have begun as low-volume product in PWP 1 and moved to this stage as customer acceptance increased.

PWP 3 is the traditional assembly line.

PWP 3. This is the traditional assembly line with short job cycles—often less than one minute, and with a rapidly moving conveyor assembly line controlled by machines. For products that are simple to assemble, or where quality standards are not as great, this type of line is superior. It is very efficient at producing a high quantity of product per man/hour, although often at the expense of quality standards. Many employees find this type of job distasteful, but others may prefer it. Often young unskilled workers, employees who consider their job temporary (such as part-time college students) and employees with few skills and little education find such jobs suitable (if not desirable).

PWP 4 includes the fully automated line.

PWP 4. Not all product lines will lend themselves to the fully automated line of PWP 4. It is more applicable to fluid products such as petroleum and chemicals, which can flow with gravity and which will mold themselves to any configuration. Products requiring small delicate parts and ones requiring assembly of many solid parts usually must be assembled in PWP 1, 2, or 3. However, some portions of a product might be suitable for PWP 4.

Notice how the use of the PWP concept allows the continual evolution of products through the PWPs from left to right as they evolve through the product life cycle. Notice also how the workers tend to move from right to left as they become more skilled and are trained at more and more jobs. This type of flexibility is needed in a rapidly changing market requiring high quality and cost efficiency. It is also needed to accommodate a labor force many of whom are disenchanted with assembly line work.

A PWP allows flexibility in focused manufacturing and optional stages of job enrichment—all in one plant.

Many plants throughout the United States have implemented the PWP concept, among them the Fleetguard Division of Cummings Engines in Cookeville, Tennessee. Fleetguard has learned that having several PWPs also provides a good training ground for plant and general managers since the manager over each PWP can be delegated full profit responsibility with clean lines of accountability defined by the PWP.

QUALITY CIRCLES

Although the basic concept has been used in many ways for several years, a relatively new approach to improving productivity and promoting worker involvement on the job is the use of quality circles.[22] The concept involves the formation of a group of employees, usually but not necessarily led by a supervisor, that focuses on plant or office problems. The leader of the group is normally designated by the firm's management and the circle or group is typically limited to those employees that work closely together on a given task or process.

Quality circles are groups of workers meeting to discuss ways to improve productivity.

The concept is based on the premise that employees can best identify and solve problems that are related to increased efficiency and improved production effectiveness. Several assumptions are implied with this approach.

> Obviously, the group could not be expected to optimize a situation requiring linear programming if they could not use the technique. However, most companies provide engineering or other staff support in order to implement group ideas.

> Time must be available for the group to meet together. This has not been a

---

[22]One of the earliest and very frequently referenced articles on quality circles is J. M. Juran, "The Quality Circle Phenomenon," *Industrial Quality Control*, January 1967, pp. 335–341.

problem within the Japanese firms using this technique, but could well be a problem for American firms whose methods and history or way of operation has been different. The presence of labor unions is also a factor that impacts on the use of quality circles in U.S. industry.

3. Information regarding many facets of production must be available from the firm in order to provide a base for deliberation decisions. Without certain data the group's decision will certainly not be sound.

4. The firm must be willing to accept and or give serious consideration to suggestions made by the group.

5. The firm must be willing to financially support the group. Proponents of the quality circle concept cite several advantages that relate to their use. Additional minds can more effectively solve certain problems and those most closely associated with the task or process are in the best position to identify problems hindering accomplishment as well as formulate workable solutions. Direct involvement of the employee also leads to the advantages associated with participation. These include increased levels of commitment and motivation as well as the development of a certain amount of management mindedness. Of prime importance, of course, is the positive contributions quality circles make toward increasing productivity, reducing costs and improving the work place in general.

The quality circle movement is growing rapidly. The International Association of Quality Circles reports that 1000 organizations are using them, up from 150 a year ago[23] In many cases their formation has the blessing of labor unions.

The AFL-CIO's emerging strategy is to advise its unions to join the quality circles, rather than fight them. The federation is preparing a detailed manual that will suggest that, in unionized plants, labor should push for equal participation in the circles—and an equal share of the credit for any accomplishments.[24]

The following is an example of the corporate use of quality circles.

Honeywell has some 300 ongoing quality circles in operation, more than half organized in the past eighteen months. It also uses temporary task teams of workers to tackle certain problems. Recently, one of these ad hoc groups was presented with the job of finding a way to keep an aging but still successful product alive. The problem was that the company could no longer lower the labor costs of producing the product, and newer competitive models were beginning to eat into its market share. To the great surprise of management, the team proposed the installation of a robot on the production line, despite the prospect of eventually losing jobs for people. The company acted on the suggestion, introducing two robots, and says Joseph Riordan, director of corporate productivity services, "It has stablized the product's position in the market."[25]

---

[23]Robert S. Greenberger, "Quality Circles Grow, Stirring Union Worries," *The Wall Street Journal*, September 21, 1981.
[24]Ibid.
[25]Thomas J. Murray, "The Rise of the Productivity Manager," *Dun's Review*, January 1981, Vol. 117, No. 1. pp. 64–71.

Note that although the quality circle concept is presently enjoying a great deal of publicity and is a relatively rapidly expanding phenomena, we do not at present have enough results to be completely declarative in our absolute endorsement. As time passes, like many similar management programs we will know more about the advantages, disadvantages and requirements for effective implementation.[26]

ISSUES IN OPERATIONS MANAGEMENT

Perhaps much of traditional manufacturing is destined for "termination," to judge from current news releases and financial reports. The oil embargo and the literal end to abundant and cheap energy came in late 1973 and the problem has been with us since. Manufacturing was, and still is, for the most part, oriented toward meeting seemingly endless demand for products at any reasonable price—yet the increasing U.S. consumption of imported durables and high-technology products was apparent even in 1970. And the commitment of corporate resources toward manufacturing has lagged badly. The average age of machine shop equipment in the United States was almost twenty-three years, while in Japan the same equipment was but seven years old. The use of robotics in both Europe and Japan is much more intensive than in the United States. Japanese companies use *kanban* and other paperless systems to synchronize their production, attaining much higher efficiencies in manufacturing, yet with very little inventory, a high degree of flexibility and market responsiveness, and consistently high quality.[27] Furthermore, Japanese firms seem to have more effective labor relations, than American firms, with participation, productivity improvement from the shop floor, and company loyalty; all facts of life and important elements in the international competition for market share, which is currently placing severe pressures on many U.S. industries.

Japanese manufacturing efficiency has become a great competitive threat to American industry.

SUMMARY

In summary, operations management relates to productive systems in manufacturing, services, transportation, and governmental settings. It can be examined as (1) *inputs, transformations,* and *outputs* (the systems approach) or (2) as a series of sequential decisions and their consequent results and effects on the operations organization over the *product life cycle*.

In designing products one must anticipate the production processes which will be used to manufacture them. The cleaner and simpler the design the less complicated and expensive will be the production process required.

Production processes can be of the continuous or intermittent type. Continuous processing is usually made possible by product type layouts and special purpose

---

[26]This section of the chapter was prepared by Dr. R. Leon Price, Assistant Professor of Management, College of Business Administration, University of Oklahoma.
[27]Business Refocuses on the Factory Floor," *Business Week*, February 2, 1981.

equipment. This approach requires high volume operation and a comparatively heavy initial investment.

If the main product or service is changing rapidly and low volume is expected, intermittent processing will be required, necessitating general purpose equipment and a process type layout.

In selecting a location for a plant, long- as well as short-term consequences must be considered. The advantages of a site that matches product and process design perfectly must be weighted against changes expected in expansion, product line variation, work force needs, and other long-term changes.

Once the production process and plant layout are complete, problems of scheduling and dispatching arise. Many of the decision and control techniques discussed in the following chapters will apply themselves to this function.

Products, like people, have life cycles and provisions must be made for each different age when the initial operations plans are made.

The Japanese trend is calling for more flexibility in productivity and the introduction into our production system of concepts such as quality circles.

SUMMARY CHART

1. Operations management deals with the management of inputs, transformations, and outputs for business, nonprofit, and public sector organizations.

2. The sequence of operations management includes:
   (a) Product design—simplicity means lower cost.
   (b) Production design—matching processes with product.
   (c) Equipment choices—general vs. special purposes equipment.
   (d) Processes—continuous processing vs. intermittent processing.
   (e) Location analysis—considering short-term vs. long-term needs.
   (f) Facilities layout—use product layout for high volume continuous processes, use process layout for low volume intermittent processes.
   (g) Scheduling and dispatching.

3. The product life cycle approach was used to trace the operations management of an airline through its various phases.

4. The focused factory was suggested as a possible solution to lagging productivity and quality and disenchanted employees.

5. Quality circles, popular in Japan, are growing in the United States.

DISCUSSION QUESTIONS

1. Define the term *operations management*.
2. Match the following facility layouts with their most likely counterparts.

　　___ 1. Continuous processing　　　　Match either (a) or (b) with each number.

___ 2. Intermittent processing
___ 3. General purpose equipment   (a) Product layout
___ 4. Special purpose equipment   (b) Process layout
___ 5. Low volume production
___ 6. Expensive initial investment
___ 7. Large inventories in process
___ 8. Difficult scheduling and dispatching
___ 9. Monotonous tasks and boring jobs
___10. Vulnerable to work stoppages

3. Compare and contrast scheduling and dispatching activities.
4. Using the airlines example, explain what is meant by the product life cycle concept.
5. What is a PWP? Of what importance is it in focusing the factory?
6. Explain the concept of circles. What advantages do you see in their use and what problems might a firm encounter in attempting to introduce them? What are some of the conditions that would have to be met to insure their success?

APPLICATION EXERCISES AND CASES

SEBASTIAN'S[28]—LAYOUT OF A RESTAURANT KITCHEN

Sebastian's, a popular restaurant located in a large southern city, served luncheons and dinners throughout the year. During the winter, about 100 guests could be accommodated at one time; in the summer, the serving was done on the patio and terrace as well, increasing seating capacity by 50 percent.

The luncheon-serving cycle was as follows. Prior to arrival of the guests, glassware, silver, and napkins were placed on the table. When the guests arrived, glasses were filled and orders taken. The typical luncheon consisted of soup or salad, main course, dessert, drink, and rolls. The waitress first obtained the soup or salad. When the guests finished the first course, the waitress returned the dirty dishes to the kitchen and picked up the main course. The same process was repeated for dessert. Rolls were served with the main course, and drinks were served with the main course or dessert. Each girl served one to eight tables at one time.

In the kitchen the cook and two assistants prepared the food in the morning. Salad ingredients were prepared at the mixing table, then kept in the refrigerator until mealtime. During serving, salads were made up at the mixing table as required, the main course and soup were picked up by the waitresses at the main serving table, and desserts were prepared at the dessert counter. Ice cream was kept in the freezer and prepared for serving by the waitresses, coffee was kept in the

---

[28]Paul E. Holden, Frank K. Shalleberger, and Walter A. Diehm, *Selected Case Problems in Industrial Management*, 2nd ed., Englewood Cliffs, N.J., Prentice-Hall, Inc., 1962, p. 50.

coffee urn, and milk in the refrigerator. Water was served in pitchers. Silver, napkins, and tablecloths were kept on shelves below the serving table.

Dinners included both soup and salad and were served in the same manner as luncheons.

During meals, one of the assistants scraped and washed dirty dishes. The table across the aisle from the dirty dish stand was used to handle excess dishes during peak loads. After dishes were washed, they were placed on shelves above the dishwasher or above the dessert counter. Cups, saucers, and glasses were kept on shelves by the refrigerator.

Questions
1. Criticize the present kitchen layout and the procedures used at Sebastian's.
2. Prepare a new layout and set of procedures. Point out the merits of your plan.
3. What concepts presented in this chapter have you utilized in designing your new plan for running the restaurant?

WORKERS ARE EXPERTS—"QUALITY CIRCLES" IN BREAKTHROUGH[29]

The Japanese "quality circle" management technique used at the Murray, Ohio, manufacturing plant in Lawrenceburg since December, 1980, already has saved $90,000 and bigger savings are ahead, company spokesman Fred Pancoast told a Tennessee Tech audience.

Pancoast lectured on "Japanese Management and Quality Circles" for the university's Master of Business Administration Division.

"Quality circles," which were introduced in Japan in the 1950s, are made up of groups of assembly line workers, secretaries, maintenance workers, or others in the labor force of a business or industry who share common production problems. The employees make suggestions on how their jobs can be done better.

"The fellow who has run the same machine for 25 years is an expert," Pancoast said Wednesday. "He knows what can be done to improve things at his job."

"The most important aspect of the quality circle technique," Pancoast said, "is the impact it has on the self-esteem of blue collar workers who have not usually been consulted about how their work could be made easier and more productive."

"What they are saying is, 'Why haven't you asked us before?'" Pancoast said. Quality circles "break down barriers between management and labor," and workers take pride in telling management how to increase production and save money," he said.

Pancoast, a former head football coach at Vanderbilt University, spoke to about 200 TTU students, faculty members, and area businessmen. He joined Murray, Ohio, which manufactures bicycles, lawnmowers, and other items, about fifteen months ago and became director of ten quality circle groups at Lawrenceburg in December.

---

[29]*"Workers are 'Experts'—"Quality Circles" in Breakthrough,"* HERALD-CITIZEN, Cookeville, Tennessee, Friday, June 19, 1981, pp. 1 and 2.

The quality circle concept is a brainchild of quality control specialist Dr. W. Edward Deming and was first used in Japan in the 1950s to boost that country's floundering economy.

American industrialists, seeing the success of the concept in Japan, have established quality circles in U.S. plants.

Fundamental to the quality circle concept is the idea that mental and physical effort are natural to workers, an idea which Pancoast said contrasts with the all-too-common management assumption that people don't like to work.

Pancoast said the first quality circle project implemented at Murray, Ohio, in Lawrenceburg saved $90,000 and a future project will save over $200,000. Pancoast also recommended the hiring of consultants well versed in the quality-circle concept to train management, labor, and a director of such programs. The ideas are complicated and cannot be used successfully without proper training, Pancoast said. The cost of a consultant who charged $5000 would be quickly offset by improvements instituted by the workers, he said. The quality circle concept can be applied to any sort of company.

"Don't you think the offensive linemen will do a better job if TTU football coach, Don Wade, will let them tell him how to make an offensive play work. Of course they will," he said.

"And will workers who suggest an idea to improve their work do a better job? Of course." Some managers shudder to think that a machine operator might be an "expert," Pancoast said, but "Believe me, he is."

Questions

1. Critique the quality circle concept in terms of behavioral concepts that you have studied—group behavior, job enrichment, team approaches. How well does it fit these principles?
2. Do you think a football coach would make a good quality circle coach? Why?
3. Murray, Ohio, plans to put all 3000 employees into quality circles. What problems do you foresee? What benefits?

CHAPTER 18
QUANTITATIVE DECISION MAKING AND OPERATIONS RESEARCH

MODELS
THE MANAGEMENT DECISION ENVIRONMENT
DECISION SUPPORT AND THE COMPUTER
PRODUCT DESIGN AND DEVELOPMENT, USING COST-VOLUME-PROFIT MODELS
FORECASTING
FORECASTING DEMAND WITH CORRELATION ANALYSIS
FUTURE
RESOURCE ALLOCATION WITH LINEAR PROGRAMMING
PROGRAMMING SOLUTIONS
OTHER APPLICATIONS OF LINEAR PROGRAMMING
DECISION TREES
OPERATIONAL PLANNING ACTIVITIES
LINE BALANCING
WAITING LINES (QUEUEING)
MONTE CARLO TECHNIQUES
MAINTENANCE POLICY
THE MANAGERIAL ROLE
ADVANTAGES AND LIMITATIONS OF QUANTITATIVE MODELS
ADVANTAGES
LIMITATIONS
APPLICATION EXERCISES AND CASES
RETIREMENT HOTEL
LONG-TERM HEALTH FACILITY
CATCH A FALLING TRISTAR

THE MOST FAMOUS NAME IN JAPANESE QUALITY CONTROL IS AMERICAN[1]

His name is Dr. W. Edwards Deming, and he's a quality control expert. In 1950, the Union of Japanese Scientists and Engineers (JUSE) invited Dr. Deming to lecture several times in Japan, events that turned out to be overwhelmingly successful.

To commemorate Dr. Deming's visit and to further Japan's development of quality control, JUSE shortly thereafter established the Deming Prizes, to be presented each year to the Japanese companies with the most outstanding achievements in quality control.

Today, Dr. Deming's name is well known within Japan's industrial community, and companies compete fiercely to win the prestigious Demings.

Dr. Deming's advice to America is to rely heavily on quantitative techniques, particularly statistical quality control (SQC). He believes the basic concepts of SCQ should be taught to every plant employee.

While very few persons who study and master quantitative management techniques are likely to earn international honors, a record such as Deming's should impress us with the potency of the subject.

[1]"The Most Famous Name in Japanese Quality Control is American," *Business Week*, July 20, 1981, p. 30. Advertisement by Sumitomo Metals.

Today's manager is taking advantage of all the organizational, informational, and quantitative progress that has been made since the days of Taylor and the Gilbreths. We have learned a great deal about how organizations and planning systems can best be managed. We have developed formal decision analysis procedures. The computer has enabled us to capture data, and process and analyze it at very high rates of speed. And, as never before, the processing power of the computer has made numerical solutions to complex problems available for management evaluation.

The early efforts at establishing management sciences described in Chapter 2, Historical Development of Management Thought, have led to a modern approach known as *operations research* or *OR*, sometimes called management science. The OR approach includes the following steps or ingredients.[2]

*The authors gratefully acknowledge the assistance of John Burnham, Professor of MBA Studies at Tennessee Technological University, Cookeville, Tennessee, who wrote this chapter.

[2] Leonard J. Kazmier, *Principles of Management, A Programmed Instructional Approach*, 3rd ed., New York, McGraw-Hill Book Company, 1974, p. 110.

1. A systemwide or enterprisewide orientation
2. Specific identification and measurement of the goals of the system
3. Specific identification and measurement of all variables that affect goal attainment
4. Construction of a mathematical model to represent the situation being studied

In this chapter, you will be introduced to various models and the kinds of problems for which they have been used. *Cost-volume-profit analysis* is applied to investment planning, top management decision problem. *Correlation and regression analysis* is used in the development of product demand forecasts, which affects most levels of management. *Linear programming* can be useful in dealing with the resource allocation problem (i. e., how best to utilize limited facilities, manpower, or funds to gain the greatest efficiency for the organization). Linear programming is most often used at middle management levels. We will also discuss *decision trees*, frequently used by top level management in evaluating new products or investment alternatives. We will study four techniques that deal with operations activities planning: line balancing, waiting line analysis, and maintenance policy evaluation. Finally, the role of management in models development and use is presented.

While we are concentrating our attention on quantitative techniques for decision making in this chapter the important role of qualitative analysis should not be forgotten. In some cases qualitative factors will play a major role in the final choice. Even in these instances however, the astute manager will still use the techniques described in this chapter when they are applicable. These techniques can be used to sharpen whatever qualitative judgements we make.

Quantitative techniques can serve to sharpen whatever qualitative judgments we make.

MODELS

The word model is often used in conjunction with quantitative techniques. Almost all quantitative techniques can be classified as models. The actual definition of a *model* can be stated as *being anything that in some way represents something else*. A complex series of mathematical formulas representing the growth of the United States economy can be classified as a model. The model consists of mathematical equations. Following is a simple example of a mathematical expression which could be classified as a model.

A model is anything that represents something else.

It takes two units of raw material A and five units of raw material B to manufacture the final product C. The cost of A is $3.00 per unit, and the cost of B is $8.00 per unit. With the above information, a general cost model can be established to illustrate the relationship between A, B, and C, such that:

$$2A + 5B = C$$

The cost of producing C can be easily determined by substituting the cost figures of A and B into the model. Thus, the cost of producing C becomes $(2)(3) + (5)(8) = \$46$. The above model is established as a cost-predicting model for the production of C. If the cost of either A or B changes, or if the amounts of A or B required to produce the product C change, then the effect on the cost of C can be determined by substituting the changed variables into the model and performing the necessary calculations.

All the quantitative tools presented in this chapter are models and are of the same type as shown above since they predict information. The usefulness of models lies in their relatively low cost (as opposed to actually having to manipulate real-world occurrences), and their convenience. It should be noted that models only represent something and they can vary considerably in the degree to which they can actually be related to real-world occurrences. Although a given model may not be entirely accurate, it still may have widespread use because its predictive capabilities are often greater than alternative methods such as intuition, trial and error, or guesswork.

THE MANAGEMENT DECISION ENVIRONMENT

Management problems can be examined for complexity, futurity, and uncertainty.

Roland A. Howard has suggested that management problems can be examined for complexity, futurity, and uncertainty.[3] Even given a *certainty* situation such as that shown in Figure 4-1, the problems of *complexity* and *futurity* exist—and when risk (known events, and historical probabilities) or *uncertainty* (missing events, probabilities, or both) situations are also operating, then substantial sophistication is needed.

Uncertainty is present in such data as a sales forecast, a cost estimate, and production averages—all different ways to speak of an educated guess about the future. Where all of the future states of nature are known, and historical probabilities can be assumed to apply, we have the problem of *risk*. Choice will depend on the use of statistics and expected values—an area called *statistical decision theory*.

Futurity concerns the time lapse between the time an action is taken and the time it will pay off. For example, in the preceding chapter, recall the eighteen months to three years which elapsed between Friendly Airline's commitment to wide-bodied aircraft and their manufacture and delivery into operations.

The airline next faced a continuing cash outflow to bring the equipment into operation, without any accompanying revenues. Money has a time value—the amount it should earn while invested. Future cash flows are therefore worth less than present ones. This present value idea discounts future cash flows (both revenues and costs) to their current worth and thus handles this time (or futurity) dimension of decision problems. Note that as defined this is still a certainty situation.

Complexity is the problem of choosing among a number of feasible actions in response to a given situation. Mathematical programming or calculus may be used to identify the *optimal* action in a certainty situation. Think of the many different ways in which a fleet of aircraft may be routed among the cities served by Friendly Airlines.

---

[3]Roland A. Howard, "The Foundations of Decision Analysis," *IEEE Transactions on Systems Science and Cybernetics* SSC-4, September 1968, pp. 212–213.

Unfortunately, real life problems tend to combine these three fundamental ingredients: complexity (many choices), futurity (cash flows over an appreciable time horizon), and uncertainty (risk). Therefore, the kinds of analysis needed to provide good decision support to management also occur in combination, requiring a variety of quantitative skills and experience to apply them. This is the reason today's managers need business courses in statistics and operations research.

DECISION SUPPORT AND THE COMPUTER

Fortunately for both analysts and cost-conscious management, the computer has made possible at moderate cost the storage of data, models, and programs, and their easy retrieval. You may be aware of computer packages designed to provide support in recurring decision situations. There are also excellent supplementary textbooks which introduce such package programs in both operations management and operations research contexts. These programs are summarized in Figure 18-1.[4]

Because of the availability of computers, management's task has changed.

The programs listed in Figure 18-1, like many hundreds of similar packages presently available through commercial time-sharing and standard computer software, are designed for management's use. Because of the availability of high-speed and low-cost computers, management's task has changed from doing detailed calculations to performing problem analysis, formulation, and results interpretation. There will continue to be business analysts who choose to become trained in quantitative methods, and who will handle the more complex problems in support of management. This chapter is designed for management, not the analyst, and will concentrate on familiarization with selected problem types, the language of quantitative methods, and the usefulness of the results. Some models are especially useful in control situations, and these will be discussed in Chapter 20, Controlling Operations.

In addition, we will recommend some standard books and articles, which provide more details but are not necessary to formulate or run the program.

PRODUCT DESIGN AND DEVELOPMENT, USING COST-VOLUME-PROFIT MODELS

Quantitative techniques requires *models*. Quantitative models are symbolic, which means that symbols are used to describe essential relations among the things represented. An understanding of the model enables formulation for computer solution.

Cost-volume-profit (CVP) analysis will be used to illustrate how a model is developed, and its use for decision support in product development. CVP relates

---

[4]Roy D. Harris and Michael J. Maggard, *Computer Models in Operations Management—A Computer-Augmented Approach*, 2nd ed., New York, Harper & Row, 1977.

FIGURE 18-1

Package Programs for Operations Management and Research

Program Name	Purpose and Techniques
FUTURE	Statistical forecasting—mean (average), simple regression, seasonal average, seasonally adjusted regression lines, moving average, and exponentially smooth estimates
INSYS	A inventory system simulation for inventory levels and factory output for a simple distribution chain. Permits evaluation of reordering and lead-time policies on system performance
EOQ	Calculates the most economical quantity of an item to order when price discounts, storage limitations, and shortage costs exist in addition to the usual ordering and storage costs
DECIDE	Uses statistical decision theory to solve problems under both risk and futurity, and involves both probability and present value as applicable
CRIT	Solves project scheduling programs using PERT/CPM and critical path analysis
BALANCE	Uses heuristics to solve assembly line balancing problems for up to ninety-nine work elements
SQC	Uses statistics to develop control charts and evaluation of work samples of an ongoing process
MAINSIM	Simulates various maintenance policies and their effect on cost and reliability of an operating system
QUESIM	Simulates single-phase service system with from one to nine channels, with variable service and arrival rates, and costs
LINPRO	Linear programming package solves resource allocation problems up to twenty-four variables and twenty-four constraints
MRP	Materials requirements planning for depended demand, lumpy scheduling, and lead time for receipt of goods into a production system
DYNAM	A computer model that will handle general dynamic programming networks of up to nine stages and thirty states
NET	Provides minimum cost and or maximum flow solutions for networks of up to ninety-eight nodes

Source: adapted from R. D. Harris, M. J. Maggard, and W. G. Lesso, *Computer Models in Operations Research*, New York, Harper & Row, 1974.

> Cost-volume-profit (CVP) analysis is a model that relates fixed costs and variable production costs to the revenues generated by product sales.

fixed (FC) and variable (VC) production costs to the revenues [selling price (SP) times number of units sold (Q)] generated by product sales. A special break-even point Q(BEP) is that level of sales that exactly covers *all* costs. A lower volume of sales leads to loss (L), a higher volume, to profits (P). Using symbols,

$$P \text{ (or L)} = SP \times Q - VC \times Q - FC \quad \text{(a profit or loss model)}$$

$$BEP = \frac{FC}{SP - VC} \quad \text{(a break-even model)}$$

To use this simple model, we substitute known values for the symbols to obtain a numerical result. Note the very important simplifying assumptions involved here, as follows.

1. We know the exact selling price per unit (SP) for all units sold, and it is a *constant* (no elasticity).
2. We know the exact variable cost per unit (VC) for all units produced, and it is a *constant* (no economy of scale).
3. There will be no change in fixed costs (FC) over the feasible range of production.
4. All units produced will be sold in the present time period.

Suppose a firm can produce 800 units of a product during a year and incurs a fixed cost of $5000. The variable costs are $5 per unit and the firm can sell all these units for $10 per unit. What is the break-even point? Can the firm make a profit during the year?

$$\text{Break even} = \frac{\$5000}{\$10 - \$5} = 1000 \text{ units}$$

In the above example, if the firm sells 1000 units it will reach the break-even point; however, because it can only produce 800 units, it would be impossible for the firm to make a profit. The manager should now realize that in order to launch the product under study he must either reduce the fixed costs, increase the selling price, reduce the variable costs, or work on all three aspects. A graphical illustration of the above problem is given in Figure 18-2.

It would not be economical to use a computer package for such a straight forward application as that shown in Figure 18-2. But this model may not be useful for decision support because of its assumptions. We might design a model that would include demand elasticity (to stimulate higher sales, lower the prices). In

FIGURE 18-2

Break-even Analysis

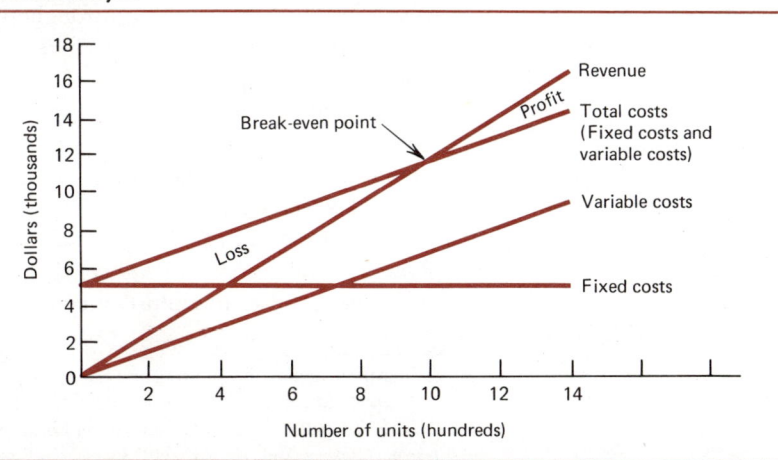

many productive systems, discussed in Chapter 17, Operations Management, larger production volumes can lead to lower average unit costs if either setup or learning factors are significant. Solutions to such problems generally requires calculus or numerical analysis. Other extensions which occur in practice include aspects of uncertainty (we have only a sales forecast to work with in estimating revenues) and futurity (we must make a large fixed investment now, but the revenues will be received only in later years). These more advanced forms of CVP analysis are used for planning and control purposes, which we will examine in Chapter 20, Controlling Operations. For supplementary information, the *Handbook of Operations Research* includes a chapter with eight variations of CVP analysis and a discussion of the models and techniques needed for solution.[5]

One particularly good example of CVP's use for product development is the study which led to Lockheed's decision to produce the Tristar airplane.[6] There were three distinct kinds of cost: Investment in know-how (technology) which was over three-fourth billion dollars; the usual capacity costs of roughly equal size; and the direct variable costs of aircraft production. While the selling price per ship was known for each booked contract and delivery position, the total revenues to be received, and their timing, were uncertain. Neither the total market for the airplane, nor Lockheed's share, could be more than estimated, and production and sale of the ships was at the rate of three to five aircraft a month. Further, production costs would clearly improve with learning while inflation would raise wage rates and equipment prices. The results of extremely sophisticated CVP analysis were presented in congressional hearings to obtain government guarantees for a $250 million loan to Lockheed.

CVP (Cost-volume-profit) analysis was useful in the congressional hearings that led to a $250 million loan to Lockheed Aircraft.

FORECASTING

Except in unusual circumstances the volume of future sales is uncertain. Unit sales volume estimates, therefore, are probably the most important set of data required by management. When the forecasts cover a long period of time they will affect facilities and capital investment planning. Forecasts affect manpower and aggregate production planning throughout the organization. And short-term forecasts, when compared with inventory levels, trigger the detailed plant production schedules and associated material requirements planning.

Organizations develop and apply forecasting techniques and constantly monitor and attempt to improve their usefulness. Some organizations pool the sales estimates of their marketing managers (consensus forecasting), and then both sales and production combine their efforts to make the forecast a reality. Others use market share and industry sales and forecasts to develop targets for their own planning. The more financially or competitively important the actions based on the forecast, the more sophisticated the techniques are likely to be.

---

[5] John M. Burnham, "Accounting and Finance Applications," *Handbook of Operations Research*, Volume II, Joseph J. Moder and Salah E. Elmaghraby, eds., New York, Van Nostrand/Reinhold, Inc., 1978.
[6] U. E. Reinhardt, "Break-Even Analysis for Lockheed's Tristar: An Application of Financial Theory," *Journal of Finance*, Vol. 28, No. 4, 1973.

QUANTITATIVE DECISION MAKING AND OPERATIONS RESEARCH   489

Correlation analysis is used for sales forecasting.

Even with very advanced techniques, management can develop only an estimate of expected volume and likely range for future sales. The accuracy of this estimate is influenced by the variability of demand—that is, the effect of the factors which act on buying behavior. The analyst is responsible for the detection of the most important of these factors and their inclusion in the model. *Correlation* strength is used to identify significant variables, and *regression* measures the variable's relative effect on sales.

The accuracy of the forecast is assessed when actual sales results are known—usually the amount of error in units or percentage, and its direction. Sometimes the forecast is too high, production exceeds demand, and unplanned inventory builds up, requiring cutbacks in employment, purchasing, and production. At other times demand exceeds the sales estimate, and the company is forced to abandon an orderly production strategy and chase the demand, causing higher costs due to overtime and hasty materials purchase.

FORECASTING DEMAND WITH CORRELATION ANALYSIS

The language of forecasting is in terms of *explanatory* or *independent* variables which describe the behavior or a *dependent* variable-predicted demand. To develop a symbolic model for this relationship (demand is a function of a group of explanatory variables):

$$X \text{ (demand)} = f(Y, Z, A, \ldots).$$

Although forecasting models can become very complex, the appropriate criterion of their usefulness is performance.

If analysis and evaluation show it to be reliable, the explanatory variables for demand may be *past sales*. These might be added together and divided by the number of observations to calculate the *average* demand. Or the most recent two or three periods might be used, with the sales results brought in as they are known, and the oldest observation dropped. This process is called a *moving average*. If sufficiently accurate, it is a very low-cost model to use. If greater accuracy is required, different *weights* can be placed on the sales data from particular past periods. Or another variation, *exponential smoothing*, can be used to adjust the next-period forecast by a fraction of the difference between predicted and actual results for the current period. To repeat, the appropriate criterion for the model is performance, not sophistication.

FUTURE

Standardized computer packages are available that will provide many services to organizations.

The objective of a forecasting package is to provide decision *support*, rather than decision *making*. FUTURE does this by furnishing a "family" of forecasts, using the same historical input data and different statistical techniques.[7] In addition to the mean, moving average, and exponential smoothing procedures mentioned elsewhere, the model will provide *seasonal* forecasts where cyclical sales patterns are evident from the data. The only inputs needed are the data pairs and the kinds of forecasts being requested. The computer does the rest.[8]

---

[7]Harris, Maggard, and Lesso, *Computer Models in Operations Management*, pp. 1–21.
[8]Ibid., p. 21.

RESOURCE ALLOCATION WITH LINEAR PROGRAMMING

When funds are limited and competing opportunities exist, top management must choose among investments. Upper middle management must decide on how best to use the limited productive capacity of its plants to meet the forecasted sales demand. Lower middle management must manage its funds and facilities to minimize the costs of meeting assigned products, volumes, and timing. Operational activities planning aims to attain the highest efficiency possible from the manpower, machines, and materials actually available each day. Each of these situations is a *resource allocation* problem, and in most cases the decision support needs are recurrent. What are the elements which identify such problems, and how may the problems be analyzed, solved, and evaluated for use?

Linear programming is a technique for handling resource allocation problems.

1. Limited resources may include investment capital, production capacity, labor or material, energy, or time.
2. Restrictions exist on acceptable solutions; mandatory projects; all-or-nothing situations; minimum plant volumes; delivery schedules; distribution restrictions; employee pay and working rules; pollution limits; bottlenecks; and demand restrictions. These are called *constraints*.
3. Complex relations describe profit; cost; materials consumption; labor use; machine time; production volumes; distribution costs; energy costs; and time. This is called the *problem technology*.
4. Many possible combinations exist: of products, volumes, timing, storage, shipment, new facilities, overtime. These will not violate any of the constraints or resource availabilities, yet each combination provides a different amount of profit, cost, or efficiency. The problem is one of complexity (and usually, certainty).

PROGRAMMING SOLUTIONS

One of the principal techniques for handling the resource allocations problem is *linear programming* (LP). The technique of linear programming is explained in the following paragraphs, using an example that could be found in a real life situation.

The Hand-Fashioned Shoe Company manufactures men's and women's shoes. The company uses a job enrichment program in which one worker performs all the processes necessary for making a pair of shoes. A time study was made of each of the processes for both types of shoes. The results of the time study are presented in Figure 18-3.

The contribution margin for a pair of women's shoes is $2.00. The contribution margin for a pair of men's shoes is $1.50. The company wants to determine what combination of men's and women's shoes should be produced per week by an employee to maximize the company's profits.

Solution: To maximize the company's profits, the combination of the two types of shoes that gives the greatest total contribution margin is the desirable mix. If X

FIGURE 18-3

Time Study of Shoe Production

	Process 1 Cutting (Minutes)	Process 2 Sewing (Minutes)	Process 3 Finishing (Minutes)
Women's Shoes (X)	10	20	16
Men's Shoes (Y)	16	10	15

represents the quantity of women's shoes produced and Y represents the quantity of men's shoes produced, then the formula for the total contribution margin would be: TCM = \$2.00X + \$1.50Y. This is the objective function, X and Y are the decision variables.

The constraints in this problem are the times required to perform each process and the total time each laborer has to perform them. Each laborer has 2400 minutes of work a week (40 hours x 60). Since it takes 45 minutes to produce a pair of women's shoes, the maximum number of shoes that could be produced would be 52 (2400/46). The maximum number of men's shoes that could be produced would be 52 (2400/41). Since there are three processes, the maximum amount of time that can be allotted to any one process would be ⅓ of the total time (2400) or 800 minutes. Using these constraints with the formula for a straight line, the following formulas can be derived from Figure 18-3.

$$10X + 16Y \leq 800$$
$$20X + 10Y \leq 800$$
$$16X + 15Y \leq 800$$

Using these formulas, a graph can be plotted. The graph is presented in Figure 18-4.

Because of the time restriction, the possible production combination must be in the shaded area of the graph. The possible production mix is found at one of the intersections of the constraint lines or the intersection of the X and Y axis. To determine the point where the company's profit will be maximized, these four points need to be substituted into the formula for the total contribution margin. Figure 18-5 presents these substitutions.

From this figure, the combination that gives the maximum contribution margin is at Point C. It is a fundamental proof of mathematical programming that one of these corners, A, B, C, or D, called *extreme points*, will always contain the optimal solution.

To conclude this procedure, we add to the graph the profit function described as \$2.00X + \$1.50Y. Profit is measured as the distance between the orgin ($X = 0$, $Y = 0$) and a plane perpendicular to the profit direction (\$2.00X + \$1.50Y). Clearly, the maximum profit is attained when the distance of this plane from the origin is maximized while staying within the solution space (the shaded area). This is attained at Point C, as before.

When the perpendicular plane is passed through this point ($X = 40$, $Y = 0$) the graph shows that more profit can be gained by introducing Y also. This is done

FIGURE 18-4

Graphs of Shoe Production Formulas

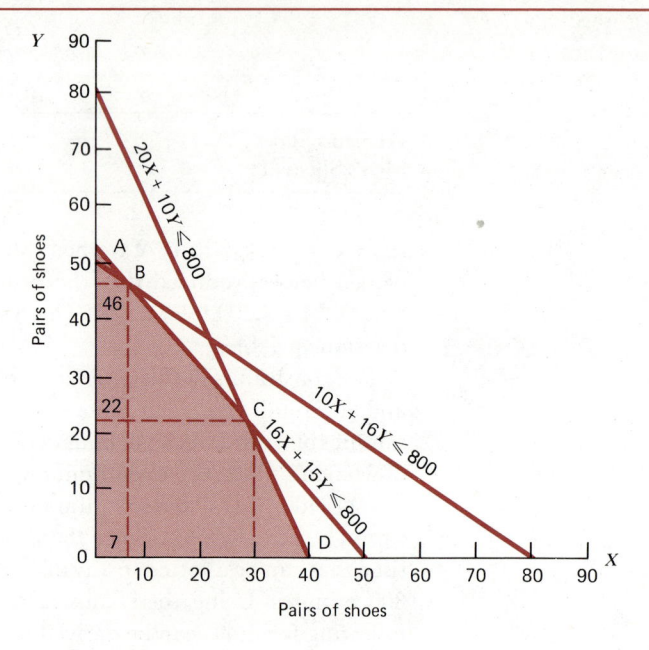

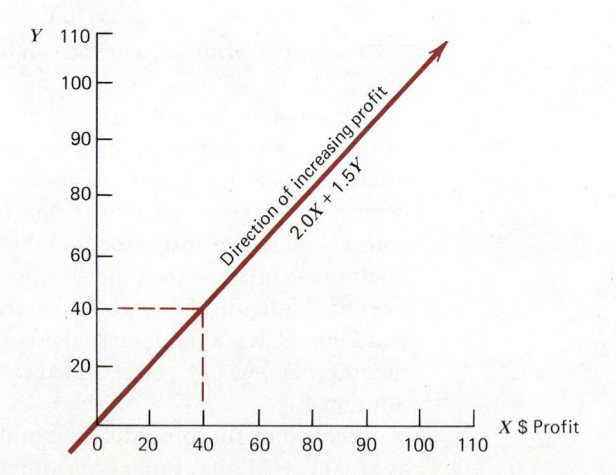

while keeping X as large as possible (visualize sliding the plane up the diagonal $20X + 10Y \leq 800$) up to corner C, where no further improvement can be achieved. The optimal solution is to let X take the value 30 (pairs of women's shoes) and Y take the value 22 (pairs of men's shoes). These choices of decision variables yield

QUANTITATIVE DECISION MAKING AND OPERATIONS RESEARCH 493

FIGURE 18-5

Table of Formulas for Calculating Profit

Point	X Coordinate		Y Coordinate		Total Contribution Margin
A	$2.00(0)	+	$1.50(50)	=	$75.00
B	$2.00(7)	+	$1.50(46)	=	$83.00
C	$2.00(30)	+	$1.50(22)	=	$93.00
D	$2.00(40)	+	$1.50(0)	=	$80.00

a profit contribution of $93, which is optimal for this situation. This example, if run with an LP package like LINPRO[9] would take about one second (YES! 1/60–minute!) to solve. A new package, LINDO, now on the market will handle up to 2500 decision variables and 800 constraints.[10]

OTHER APPLICATIONS OF LINEAR PROGRAMMING

Linear programming can be used to schedule products determine class size and schedules for a university, and determine complicated mixes of feed for livestock.

What are some of the uses of linear programming? A major Midwest university uses linear programming to determine class sizes, times of the classes, and who should teach the class by setting up a series of equations consisting of such variables as the students' desire to enroll in a particular class, number of students and professors, and hours available to hold the classes. The information is fed into a computer, and after a few hours of calculating, the entire enrollment for the university is determined.

DECISION TREES

A decision tree can be used to choose among several alternatives.

CPV and linear programming techniques can clarify the value of any particular decision, given the assumption of certainty about outcomes. But suppose several choices of products are available for capital investment. Or suppose that several combinations of products may be scheduled within given operational capacity. The answer to such questions call for a systematic, quantifiable approach to choosing among alternatives. Often a decision tree is used for this purpose.

Consider the decision tree developed by Emperor Products, a medium-sized electronics component manufacturer, to make a decision about purchasing some new equipment or meeting rising sales with overtime production (see Figure 18-6). Management was able to identify the alternatives, their costs, and the subjective probabilities of occurrence.

Using this approach the company multiplied probability of events times expected payout on each decision.

---

[9]Harris, Maggard, and Lesso; See Figure 18-1.
[10]Linus Schrage, *Linear Programming with LINDO and User's Manual*, Palo Alto, Cal., The Scientific Press, 1981.

FIGURE 18-6

A Decision Tree

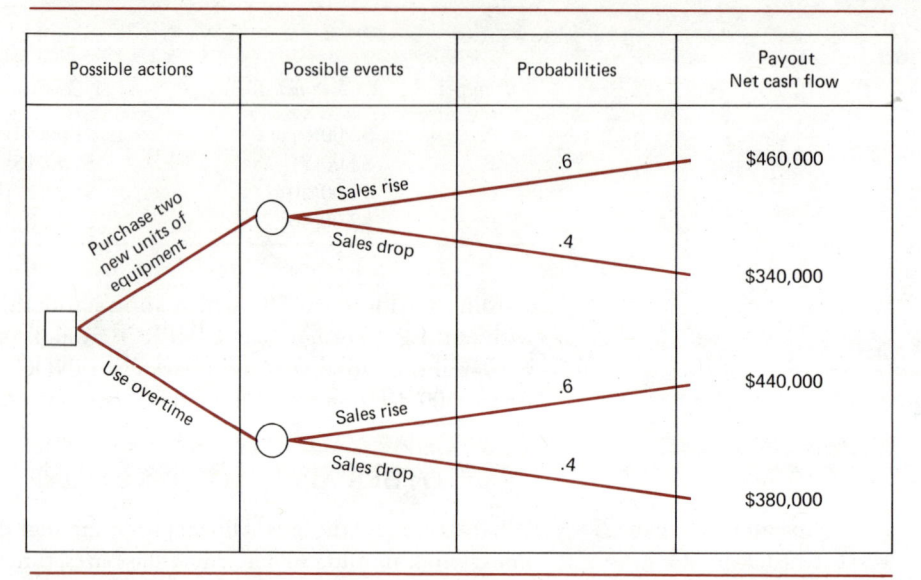

Possible actions	Possible events	Probabilities	Payout Net cash flow
Purchase two new units of equipment	Sales rise	.6	$460,000
	Sales drop	.4	$340,000
Use overtime	Sales rise	.6	$440,000
	Sales drop	.4	$380,000

Source: adapted from Edward A. McCreary, "How to Grow a Decision Tree," *Think Magazine,* IBM March-April 1967.

	Probability	*Payout*	*Expected Value*
Event Purchase Equipment	.6	$460,000	$276,000
	.4	340,000	136,000
Total Expected Value Event 1			$412,000
Event Overtime	.6	$440,000	$264,000
	.4	380,000	152,000
Total Expected Value Event 2			$416,000

By examining the two branches, it becomes clear that the best decision is to operate at overtime. In this particular case the odds and payouts were extended one year longer and the discovery was made that on a two-year or longer payout (more futurity) the new equipment would be a superior choice.

Although the decision tree does not provide a definitive answer, it does clarify the thinking of decision makers. Such trees are particularly useful in forcing managers to examine the risks and rewards of proposed projects and in helping to achieve consensus among top level decision groups.[11] Recently this technique has been combined with sales forecasting approaches to predict political instability of

---

[11] Edward A. McCreary, "How to Grow a Decision Tree," *Think Magazine,* IBM, March-April 1967, pp. 13–18.

QUANTITATIVE DECISION MAKING AND OPERATIONS RESEARCH

foreign countries. By extending patterns of uprising and turmoil and placing probability estimates on recurrences, firms can determine the wisdom of investing in certain countries.[12]

DECIDE is a computer program that can be used in decision tree analysis. DECIDE documentation includes an example of a decision tree and the needed probability, costs/benefits, and other inputs, as well as how to adjust future cash flows to their current expected worth, using present value and probability models. Suitable problem combinations are given to provide a clear description of the package's total capabilities and limitations, and to show how to prepare inputs and how to interpret outputs. DECIDE will solve a decision tree with up to 100 branches.[13]

> DECIDE is a computer package that will solve a decision tree with up to 100 branches.

OPERATIONAL PLANNING ACTIVITIES

By their nature, there are recurring situations in all operational planning in which some form of optimal solution will be a useful input to decision making. Three examples are presented: line balancing, waiting line service system design, and maintenance planning.

LINE BALANCING

A production line becomes economically attractive in any organization whose products are sufficiently standardized, provided volume is high enough and demand is stable. One of the measures of production line efficiency is *balance*. Balance is defined as the equalization of work assignments for all of the workers on the line. The procedures for balancing a line are as follows.

> Balance, is the equalization of work assignments.

1. Determine the number and content of the work elements to produce one complete item, and their times for performance.
2. Determine the number of units which must be completed in each work period (shift, day). Use the standard minutes per shift to calculate *cycle time*—the minutes allowed to produce each item.
3. Calculate the theoretical number of workers required to operate the line:

$$\frac{\text{time to complete one unit}}{\text{cycle time}}$$

4. Take note of the needed precedences (one job element must be done before another) and develop stations and numbers of workers per station to make tasks (group of elements to be performed by one worker) which are at the greatest, equal to, and preferably slightly less than the cycle time.

In all but the simplest cases, this last step is more easily said than done and is the

---

[12]R. J. Rummell and David H. Heenan, "How Multinationals Analyze Policital Risk, *Harvard Business Review*, January-February 1978, pp. 70–75.
[13]Harris, Maggard, and Lesso, *Computer Models in Operations Management*, pp. 55–57.

reason for the many package computer programs that have been developed commercially to handle line balance. BALANCE[14] will develop a feasible solution for up to ninety-nine work elements. It will also meet a specified cycle time and assign tasks so that a specified number of work stations is achieved.

WAITING LINES (QUEUEING)

In both production and service systems, lines form. People wait for banking service or to check out their groceries at a supermarket. Parts queue up for their turn at a machine center. Aircraft stack up at Kennedy Airport, awaiting their turn through landing traffic control. Because waiting lines affect both the service process and the customer, the operations manager must look at operating costs, efficiency, and customer satisfaction.

The problem in its simplest form is a tradeoff—the cost of keeping a customer waiting, on the one hand, and the cost of idle services on the other. Since an aircraft's time is worth perhaps $1200 per hour in the air and several hundreds of dollars per hour on the ground, customers are asked to come to airports early so that schedules may be maintained. However, there are usually a relatively large number of ticket and check-in agents at the airport counters so that even during peak hours, most customers wait less than five minutes. When the function is to provide flight information (or, hopefully, to sell space on a flight) the waiting time in most reservations systems is less than twenty seconds.

MONTE CARLO TECHNIQUES

Most queueing situations are examined using *simulation*—where the model devised behaves like, or simulates, the actual performance of the arrival and service system. We call the creation of simulated or artificial environments the *Monte Carlo technique*. If a complex system is being studied, special programs will probably have to be written. However, for a rather commonplace system which still is difficult to treat mathematically, a program like QUESIM[15] will help. For a variety of arrival characteristics (customers entering the system) and service times (distribution of time from commencing service until completion and departure of the customer from the system), QUESIM will print out samples from the simulated arrivals, waiting times and length of line, beginning and end of service, *and* the costs of waiting for both employees and customers combined, to find the lowest-cost number of servers to use for the system.

> Most waiting line problems (queueing) are examined using simulation, such as Monte Carlo techniques.

MAINTENANCE POLICY

Maintenance of equipment is an indirect variable cost. One manager might reduce her maintenance staff by following the policy, "If it works, don't fix it!" while another might use frequent periodic disassembly and inspection, with re-

---
[14]Ibid., pp. 112–135.
[15]Ibid., pp. 154–168.

Routinely replacing parts showing wear is called preventive *maintenance.*

placement of all parts showing wear. The latter approach is called *preventative maintenance.* A clear trade off exists. There are the *expected* costs caused by interruptions to production, such as lost labor hours; wasted raw materials, and disrupted distribution, possibly resulting in unhappy customers. On the other hand, the costs of maintenance staff, parts, downtime for service, and standby equipment are also substantial. An optimal maintenance policy is one in which the *sum* of the expected costs of interruptions (based on statistically valid history) and of maintenance activities or capabilities will be minimized.

MAINSIM[16] uses simulation to help management evaluate three policies: (1) replacement when a machine (or system) fails, (2) preventive maintenance, and (3) supplementary maintenance when failure requires shutdown for the failure rates and costs provided by the user. The simulation uses statistical history data on failure and allows selection of cutoff times for the third policy. The cost results are reported in dollars per hour of operation for each policy option.

This completes the discussion of activity planning models. Materials management (inventory) and project scheduling techniques will be presented in Chapter 20, Controlling Operations.

Making information available when and where needed, in useful form, has been called *management systems analysis (MSA).*[17] MSA provides decision support to management. That is, MSA methods can show how to give decision support to management questions so that good decisions can be made consistently.

THE MANAGERIAL ROLE

Sophisticated model building must be done by expert analysts, guided by management.

Sophisticated model building must be done by expert analysts. But management must also provide detailed guidance in a number of areas. The following questions summarize the viewpoint of a manager seeking good decision support, and are derived from a list of steps in management systems analysis, mentioned earlier.

1. What is the exact *problem* to be solved? What horizon (futurity) is involved?
2. What are *un*acceptable solutions? What constraints apply?
3. Who will be using the model? Management? Analysts?
4. For what level in the organization are the *results* intended? What levels provide the data? What levels do the manipulation? What levels can make effective use of the outputs (though perhaps in a different form)?
5. How often will such a model be used for decision support? How important are the results to management? How much cost in development will be justified by the benefits? How do model results compare with what is being done now?
6. What assumptions are acceptable for the sake of simplification? Which are *not*?
7. How much will (should) the model cost to run and maintain?

---

[16] Ibid., pp. 136–153.
[17] John M. Burnham, "Some Examples of Management Systems Analysis; in Finance, Manufacturing, and Transportation," Proceedings, *Eighth Annual Meeting of the American Institute for Decision Sciences,* San Francisco, Cal., November 1976.

8. When an "optimal" solution is reached, what *other* parts of the organization will be affected by implementation? How much error caused by input data or unrealistic assumptions will the *solution* tolerate before it is of no use to management?
9. Does the model offer results that correspond to common sense? Is competent management likely to develop confidence in the model and its results? Is it understandable?
10. What conditions prevailed when the model was solved? What data went into the model? How was it collected? What precautions should be observed when using the model solutions for management decision making?

ADVANTAGES AND LIMITATIONS OF QUANTITATIVE MODELS

The manager must be aware of the advantages and the limitations of the quantitative techniques in order to understand their application toward decision making.

ADVANTAGES

For those decisions that lend themselves to mathematical expression, quantitative techniques provide a means whereby a rational and systematic approach can be applied in solving problems. The use of quantitative techniques forces the formulation of explicit assumptions. Other approaches to decision making that rely on a large amount of judgment, whim, and caprice often produce inferior decisions. Quantitative techniques encourage disciplined thinking about many of the problems which a manager faces.

Another advantage of quantitative techniques lies in the fact that the human mind can evaluate only six or seven variables at one time. Quantitative techniques do not have this limit and in many cases can simultaneously evaluate the interrelationship of thousands of variables. Linear programming and correlation analysis are examples of techniques that are able to do this. As discussed at the beginning of the chapter, however, this does not imply that qualitative factors do not play an important role in many decisions and, in fact, these factors can be extremely important.

LIMITATIONS

Quantitative models are no stronger than the strength of the assumptions underlying them.

The most basic limitation of quantitative techniques has to do with the nature of the mathematical models. Assumptions are incorporated into the derivation of a mathematical expression and in many cases these assumptions may not realistically portray occurrences in the real world. A nicely presented formula allegedly showing the relationship among the variables in a problem can be rendered useless if the assumptions underlying the problem are false. Linear programming is a good example of this limitation. In many cases, some of the variables do not exist in a linear relationship. But if these variables are assumed to exist in a linear manner merely so that they will fit into the linear programming model, the effectiveness of the model will be reduced.

Many managerial problems involve intangible or nonquantifiable factors, many can greatly reduce the effectiveness of quantitative techniques. To illustrate this point, a large bank used queuing theory to solve its waiting line problem, and additional tellers were added to reduce waiting times. But the bank was heavily patronized by men who were content to wait in a long line in order to visit with a rather attractive female teller.

Many managerial problems involve intangible or nonquantifiable factors.

Finally, even if input data is quantifiable and of the order necessary, it may not be economical in many cases to gather and process data needed for quantitative techniques.

SUMMARY

The purpose of this chapter has been to introduce the student to several different quantitative techniques that can be valuable to management in their decision-making activities. Quantitative methods rely heavily on mathematics and model building. Each of the various techniques has unique value in solving particular types of problems.

Cost-volume-profit analysis is used to determine the number of units of a product that must be sold at a given price so that the firm will incur neither a profit nor a loss. Based on available information concerning the costs of producing a product, it can be determined how many units must be sold to break even. If anticipated sales at a given price will not generate sufficient revenue to cover the costs, the firm knows that it must either lower production cost, raise the price, or sell more units.

Correlation is a useful quantitative technique for statistical forecasting. Correlation analysis expresses the association of one variable with another. If, as one variable changes the other variable moves in the same direction, there is a high correlation. The opposite is also true. It should be emphasized that correlation analysis does not necessarily show a cause-and-effect relationship but only the degree of association between two variables.

Linear programming is a quantitative technique that has a variety of applications in terms of the types of problems it can be used to solve. One of the more common applications is that of determining how to allocate scarce resources between alternative uses. Given the proper background information, management can determine how to gain maximum benefit from the resources at its disposal.

A decision tree is a systematic quantifiable approach to choosing among alternative decisions when payouts can be computed and probabilities of occurrence can be assigned. Although decision trees do not provide definitive answers, they do clarify the thinking of decision makers and force the careful evaluation of alternatives.

In planning for operations, a number of specific models were discussed. Assembly line balancing deals with assignment of the workers to tasks on a production line. Dynamic process control will help to monitor the quality of the items being produced. Waiting line models use simulation to evaulate costs and effects of customer arrival patterns and numbers and capabilities of service personnel. Equipment maintenance policies affect both the cost and reliability of machines engaged in production. And these are but a sample of the kinds of models used in activity planning.

Throughout the chapter, recognition of the sort of problem (complexity, futurity, uncertainty) was shown to be a guide to selection and use of appropriate model(s) for decision support. The approach to management known as operations research was outlined. Advantages and disadvantages of quantitative methods have been presented.

SUMMARY CHART

1. *Operations Research* includes:
   (a) A systematic orientation.
   (b) Quantification of variables.
   (c) The use of mathematical models.

2. Management problems are examined for:
   (a) Complexity.
   (b) Futurity.
   (c) Certainty.

3. Most management models utilize computerized programs.

Problem	Model or Technique	Computer Program
Product design and development	Cost-volume-profit (CVP)	—
Forecasting	Correlation analysis	FUTURE
Resources allocation	Linear programming	LINPRO & LINDO
Choosing among alternatives	Decision tree	DECIDE
Line balancing	—	BALANCE
Waiting line queueing	Monte Carlo simulation	QUESIM
Maintenance policy	Simulation	MAINSIM

DISCUSSION QUESTIONS

A professor once stated that he thought the ideal student was one who was able to stay awake during one of his lectures. Is this an example of a model? Explain why or why not. Give two original examples of a model that include a mathematical formula and a drawing.

2. Discuss the concept of break-even analysis and correlation analysis. Give examples of the use of each in a decision-making situation.
3. Discuss the concept of linear pogramming. What kinds of decisions can it be used for?
4. Explain how queuing theory might be useful in a grocery store checkout counter. What conditions are necessary in order for queuing theory to be an effective model?
5. Give the major advantages and disadvantages of using quantitative decision-making techniques.

APPLICATION EXERCISES AND CASES

A RETIREMENT HOTEL

A retirement hotel has 120 rooms and employs three attendants who each work eight hours per day. Part of the cleaning duties include daily room makeups in which an attendant makes the bed and changes the towels. The time required to do this is seven minutes. Other cleaning duties include the weekly room changes in which the attendant changes the linen, vacuums, changes the towels, and performs general tidying activities that take seventeen minutes. The hotel manager wants the rooms to be changed as early in the week as possible so that the attendants can work at other duties.

Question

1. What is the optimum number of rooms that should be made up only and changed so that the attendants' time is spent as efficiently as possible?

A LONG-TERM HEALTH CARE FACILITY

A long-term health care facility has a total of 125 nonprofessional employees, such as nurse's aides, ward assistants, and dietary department workers. At present each is being paid an average of $10,000 per year. Recently many facilities in the area have been unionized. The administrator is considering granting an 8 percent increase in pay for all 125 employees, estimating that if the pay increase were given, the probability of their unionizing would be .30. However, if the pay increase is not granted, the administrator places a probability of .90 that they will vote for a union. Based on area agreements, the administrator feels that if he did not grant an 8 percent pay increase and if the employees unionized, they would bargain for and receive a 12 percent wage increase. Further, if he were to grant the 8 percent wage increase he is considering and the employees still unionized, they would obtain an addition 8 percent (total = 16 percent) wage increase on top of what he awarded previously.

Question

1. By examining the costs on an annual basis, recommend, by using a decision matrix, that the administrator either grant or not grant the 8 percent wage increase.

CATCH A FALLING TRISTAR[18]

In this chapter, the use of cost-volume-profit (CVP) analysis was cited as principal support for a $250-million loan guarantee by Congress for the Lockheed L-1011 TriStar aircraft. As this text was being revised, the following article appeared in *Time* magazine:

> "Business sense won out over pride last week, as the Lockheed Corp. announced that it was stopping production of its spectacularly unprofitable L-1011 TriStar wide-bodied jetliner. The California aerospace giant has lost $2.5 billion on the TriStar since 1968 and, with airlines currently mired in a three-year-long slump, it could see no relief in sight. Chairman Roy W. Anderson said that there was "no other choice but to begin now to phase the TriStar out in an orderly manner." The company will now concentrate mainly on defense production.
>
> Trouble struck Lockheed's TriStar just after the first of the 300-passenger jets rolled off the Palmdale, Calif., assembly line. Production temporarily stopped in February, 1971, when Britain's Rolls-Royce, the prime engine supplier, went bankrupt. The British government took over Rolls-Royce's aero-engine division, but demanded proof that Lockheed was financially sound before providing the equipment. Lockheed was indeed in trouble, but Congress approved a controversial $250 million loan guarantee for the company. The first TriStar was delivered to Eastern Air Lines in April, 1972, about six months later than scheduled. The delays and uncertainties caused by the Rolls-Royce bankruptcy gave Boeing and McDonnell Douglas an additional competitive lead in the wide-bodies market. Lockheed was never able to make up that disadvantage, even though airlines found the TriStar plane reliable and efficient. The largest TriStar customer was Delta Air Lines, which operates 35 of the 220 now in service, and is buying three of the remaining 24 on firm order.
>
> Lockheed flew into more turbulence during the mid-1970s, when it admitted making questionable overseas payments. The ensuing scandals rocked the Japanese and Italian governments, and in The Netherlands the then queen's consort was forced to give up virtually all his military and business positions. The jumbo jet even gave Lockheed headaches when times were good. Orders poured in so fast in 1978 and 1979 that the company was forced to pay premium wages and materials prices to meet the unanticipated demand. The result: Lockheed lost $199 million on the TriStar last year, and the company's overall earnings fell 51%.

Question

Does the above article indicate that quantitative techniques such as CVP are useless? Discuss.

---

[18] Excerpted from John Greenwald, "Catch a Falling TriStar," *Time*, December 31, 1981, p. 65.

CHAPTER 19

MANAGEMENT INFORMATION SYSTEMS AND THE COMPUTER

THE EVOLUTION OF MANAGEMENT INFORMATION SYSTEMS
THE DEVELOPING USES OF MIS
ELEMENTS IN AN EFFECTIVE MIS
THE USE OF COMPUTERS IN MIS
COMPUTER COMPONENTS
A LOOK AT COMPUTERIZED MIS
ORGANIZATIONAL PROBLEMS CREATED BY MIS
THE PROBLEM OF MISINFORMATION
PROBLEMS OF IMPLEMENTATION
BEHAVIORAL PROBLEMS IN MIS
NONCLERICAL WORKERS
CLERICAL WORKERS
TECHNICAL STAFF
OPERATING MANAGEMENT
TOP MANAGEMENT
PREVENTING DYSFUNCTIONAL BEHAVIOR IN MIS
APPLICATION EXERCISES AND CASES
NEEDED: BUSINESS-ORIENTED SYSTEMS ANALYSTS
WE HAVE PLAY-OFFS, RUN-OFFS, BAKE-OFFS; NOW A COMPUTE-OFF

WE HAVE PLAY-OFFS, RUN-OFFS, BAKE-OFFS; NOW A COMPUTE-OFF[1]

Building 857, a drab, windowless blockhouse here at Gunter Air Force Station, would seem an unlikely spot to decide who wins one of the biggest computer contracts ever.

But in September 1982 the gleaming computers—one made by Sperry Corp.'s Sperry Univac Division, the other by Burroughs Corp.—will be rolled onto the building's third floor to begin a 45-day, winner-take-all "compute-off." The prize: a contract worth some $500 million, and possibly much more eventually.

Separated by a drywall partition and operated by two Air Force test crews, the dueling prototype computers will gobble up identical data ranging from sales of sunglasses to inventories of jet-engine parts. Assuming that both machines spew forth immaculate printouts and sail past all technical hurdles, the company delivering the lowest bid will walk off with a contract for designing and installing the Air Force's "Phase IV" computer system. The system will keep track of such things as inventory, payroll, procurement and medical records at Air Force bases around the world.

By staging the compute-off, the Air Force has chosen to select its latest computer system in much the same way that it buys a new fighter plane. It hopes that thousands of tests preceding the main event will help it avoid embarrassing blunders like its purchase 10 years ago of computer hardware that its technicians couldn't program.

If it works, the compute-off could become routine in the awarding of other big government data-processing contracts. "Some people think compute-offs are the wave of the future, and some think we'll never see one again," says Robert Johnson, chief of Burrough's Air Force project team. "A lot depends on the success of this project."

The two bidders now vying to design the winning system have a formidable task. They must independently rewrite 1.3 million lines of existing Air Force programming to make it compatible with their machines—the Sperry Univac 1100/60 and the Burroughs 5930. Between 1983 and 1985, the winner must install about 150 computers, together with terminals, printers and other peripherals, at 105 Air Force bases.

The real challenge will be to give the Air Force what it says it wants—a "state of art" system—without straying from contract specifications. What makes that so demanding is that some of those specifications preserve longtime Air Force procedures that have been eclipsed by today's standards.

---

[1]George Anders, "We Have Play-Offs, Runoffs, Bake-Offs; Now A Compute-Off,," *The Wall Street Journal*, Monday, September 21, 1981, pp. 1 and 19.

---

*The authors gratefully acknowledge the assistance of John Burnham, Professor of MBA Studies at Tennessee Technological University, Cookeville, Tennessee, who revised this chapter.

The foregoing incident should indicate the rapidly developing complexity of management information systems and the computers that drive them. It is also a good example of the difficulty that large organizations are incurring as they try to adapt to rapid developments. This chapter will describe the evolution of management information systems, their operation, and the problems that they have solved and created for management. As noted in previous chapters, an organization consists of a number of elements—people who play various roles in the organization, the activities or tasks to be accomplished, the work place or physical location of the work, and the authority and communication relationships that tie the organization together.

Most organizations begin with very little in the way of objectives, plans, budgets, organizational charts, procedural manuals, or other formal paraphernalia. During the early life of an organization, the major ingredient may be only the entrepreneur and an *idea*. In this chapter we will learn how the need for formal management information systems develops in an embryonic organization and grows to become a larger system of interrelated elements.

Most organizations begin with very few formal systems.

First, we will look at the way in which management information systems have evolved as an answer to management's problems. Second, the role of computers in management information systems will be discussed. Next, we will examine management itself and the way in which conducting the organization's business is changed by the use of management information systems. Finally this chapter will reveal the way in which the management information systems have affected the human organization.

THE EVOLUTION OF MANAGEMENT INFORMATION SYSTEMS

As the organization develops, a manager hires assistants and subordinates to staff the various departments in the organization. Immediately a need for coordination and communication systems presents itself. Materials that the sole entrepreneur or manager ordered may now be ordered by a subordinate. One of his supervisors or managers may make commitments to the customer and fail to advise either the other departments or the entrepreneur himself. Obviously the organization needs a system of accurate, timely information. This need can be conceptually illustrated by the following example.

As one hires assistants and subordinates, the need for coordination and communication systems presents itself.

> Assume that there are only four managers in a given organization (Bill, John, Maureen, and Roberta). Each of these managers collects information relevant to his or her decision making from four general information sources (market, personnel, economy, and government). Each manager will collect information, process it (code it, store or file it, and later retrieve it), and deliver it for personal use or for others when needed.[2]

---

[2] Alan Dalton, "How Management Information Systems Work," *Supervisory Management*, January 1976, p. 15.

The communication relationships as well as several problems are depicted in Figure 19-1; as shown by the following list.

1. Each manager is expending a portion of his or her time collecting and processing data and information.[3]
2. There may be duplicate contacts to collect data.
3. Collection of data items may be needlessly duplicated.
4. There are diverse uncoordinated areas of data storage.

Figure 19-2 indicates an improved arrangement for determining information needs, collecting this information, and supplying it to the appropriate manager. After installing a system such as this one, the following advantages should accrue.[4]

1. Each manager can now spend more time in his or her own field of responsibility.
2. No duplicate contacts are made to collect data.
3. Data collection is not duplicated (although one data item may, of course, be applied to more than one manager).
4. A centralized (or, at least, coordinated) area for storing data is available—a setup that permits more combinations of data items.
5. Efficiency is increased. That is, an MIS unit's busines is the rapid handling of information—and an MIS can do it more effectively through automated means than individual managers can through conventional means.

Once an MIS is established, "formal, semiformal, and even informal reporting habits are standardized, proceduralized, and scheduled." Information flows are structured for early warning of problems, quick response to crises, and clear pathways for management directives to the critical action points of the organization. A viable management information systems is born! According to one writer, "The criterion for an effective Management Information System is that it provides accurate, timely, and meaningful data for management planning, analysis, and control to optimize the growth of the organization."[5] It is also important that this process be performed economically.

The criterion for an effective MIS is that it provide accurate, timely, and meaningful data for management.

THE DEVELOPING USES OF MIS

The more sophisticated organizations in our society could not be operated without computerized management information systems. This development has come about through a number of changes. Organizations have grown in size so that face-to-face communications and even written memoranda can no longer effect adequate communications. The number of interfaces between the public and private sectors has been increasing geometrically. Where firms once dealt with the federal government only in areas involving interstate commerce, most of the

The more sophisticated organizations in our society could not operate without computerized management information systems.

---

[3]Ibid., p. 15.
[4]Ibid., pp. 15–16.
[5]William A. Bocchino, *Management Information System: Tools and Techniques*, Englewood Cliffs, N.J., Prentice Hall, Inc., 1972, p. 4.

FIGURE 19-1

Relationships Resulting from individually collected information

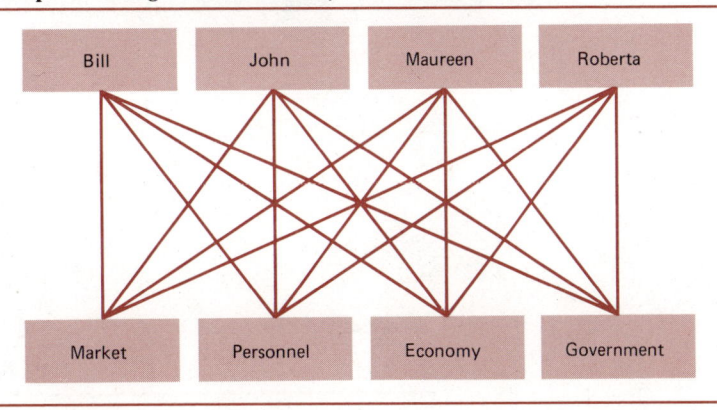

[Diagram: Bill, John, Maureen, Roberta connected with crossing lines to Market, Personnel, Economy, Government]

Source: Alan Dalton, "How Management Information Systems Work," *Supervisory Management,* January 1976, p. 15.

functions of business today require some governmental reporting and control procedures. Sophistication of decision-making techniques requires large-scale computers and data processing equipment.

The developing need for management information systems can be depicted in an hierarchial fashion, as shown in Figure 19-3. Notice that Level 1 is concerned primarily with the processing and sorting of information. As the complexity of organization grows, the need for systems that disseminate information to key decision-making centers is added to most organizations, as Level 2 depicts. Level 3 represents the additional element of statistical and mathematical decision-making techniques joined to the information systems previously developed.

FIGURE 19-2

Relationships Resulting From Use of a Management Information System

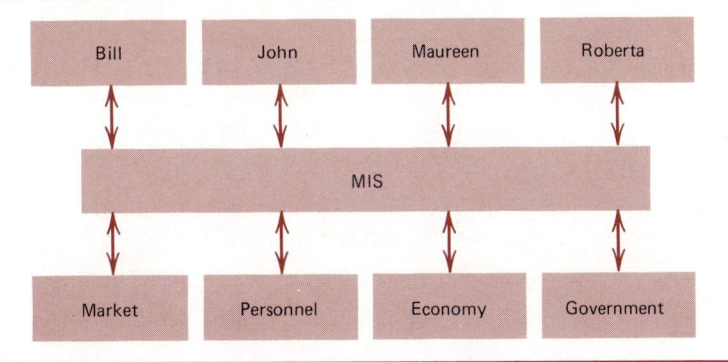

[Diagram: Bill, John, Maureen, Roberta connected via MIS to Market, Personnel, Economy, Government]

Source: Alan Dalton, "How Management Information Systems Work," *Supervisory Management,* January 1976, p. 17.

FIGURE 19-3

A Hierarchical View of MIS

Level	Area
1	Clerical systems
2	Information systems: 　Manual 　Mechanized
3	Decision systems: 　Independent 　Integrated
4	Interactive systems: 　Man-machine 　Man-man
5	Programmed systems

Source: Raymond Coleman and M. J. Riley, *MIS: Management Dimensions,* San Francisco, CAL., Holden-Day, Inc. 1973, p. 135.

Man-machine interactive systems are often called cybernated systems.

One of the most exciting and innovative developments in management information systems is the growth of level 4, interactive systems often called cybernated (man-machine) systems.

> A man-machine interactive system is one in which the decision maker is coupled to the information system by means of a remote console such as the typewriter, teletypewriter (TTY), or cathode ray tube (CRT) terminal. Through such a system, the decision maker may ask for information upon which to base a management decision or, if the system is integrated, he may even simulate the consequences of alternative courses of action.[6]

When the final decision responsibility is removed from human beings and turned over to an information-decision system, it is called a programmed system, (Level 5). Few fully programmed systems actually exist in ongoing organizations. Computerized systems for controlling viscosity and other dimensions of processing petroleum products, and auto pilot systems on such aircraft, as the Boeing 747 would be examples of completely programmed systems.

ELEMENTS IN AN EFFECTIVE MIS

In order to determine the effective network for a management information system the following questions have been suggested as pertinent.[7]

1. What data or information is needed?
2. When is it needed?
3. Who needs it?
4. Where is it needed?

---

[6] Ibid., p. 136.
[7] Ibid., p. 4.

5. In what form is it needed?
6. How much will it cost?
7. What priorities will be assigned various data?
8. What mechanics will be used for sorting the information, collating it, manipulating it into meaningful form, and presenting the synthesized information to decision makers for action?
9. How will a feedback control loop be provided for management?
10. What mechanism will be established for constantly evaluating and improving the management information system?

How does a management information system operate? Part of the answer is graphically shown in Figure 19-4. The system is also described vividly in the following thoughts:

> The lifeblood of any organization is the flow of intelligence, information, and data. This "plasma" moves along channels from point to point through the interrelated network of the operating elements of the organization. This flow of information includes data on supplies, operations, costs, customers, competitors, and, in fact, the total internal and external environment. The flow units may be in the form of telephone calls, memos, reports, forms, face-to-face encounters, electric or electronic signals, or any other medium that moves intelligible symbols from one place to another in the system.[8]

The lifeblood of any organization is the flow of intelligence, information, and data.

FIGURE 19-4

Anatomy of a Management Information System

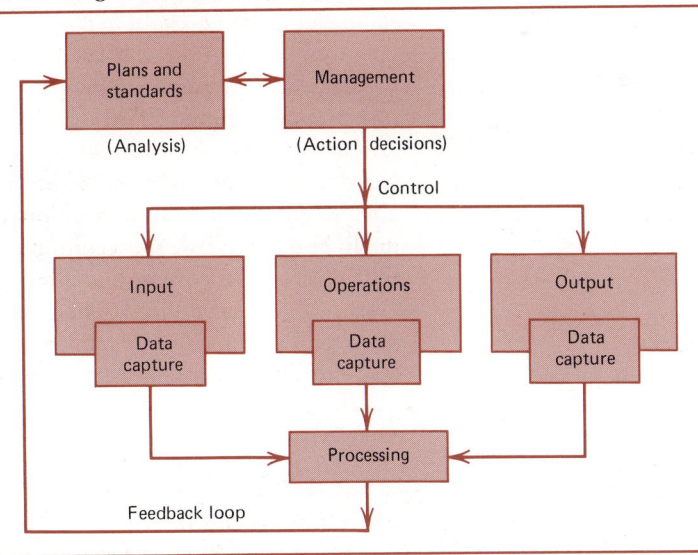

Source: William A. Bocchino, *Management Information Systems: Tools and techniques*, Englewood Cliffs, N. J., Prentice-Hall, Inc., 1972.

---
[8]Ibid., p. 6.

Modern systems include operations data *a* processing unit, *and* output data.

This flow of information is a continuous record of a tremendous number of pieces of information. To be effective, the management information system must capture data as close to its point of origin as possible and then channel it to the information processing stations where it will be utilized. In Figure 19-4, note the *input data* box, which will consist of such things as quantities of raw materials, delivery dates, prices of products, and labor costs.

Operations data will include such things as production rates, machine costs, and work in process. Data is transmitted along the communications channels to a *processing unit,* which, in the more sophisticated information systems consists of electronic computers and associated equipment. *Output data* will include such things as piece goods, ending inventory levels, and shipping dates.

The data capture input units will in some cases consist of the keypunching of data onto punched cards. Today, direct entry by keyboard terminal is the general rule, and in the extremely high-volume operations such as check clearing, completely automated optical character recognition devices "read" and imprint the dollar amounts onto checks, which are then scanned by magnetic ink character recognition devices. These read the preprinted data already on the checks and the dollar amounts. In this manner, millions of transactions may be summarized accurately and quickly for the variety of accounting and clearing operations that follow.[9] In any case, as data goes to the processing unit, it is organized into more useful forms and becomes an input into the planning and the problem-solving processes. The need for processing large amounts of information most often presents itself in the operations management and production sectors of enterprise.

The *feedback loop* consists of the information channels that transmit the processed input, operations, and output data to the *analysis* and *decision* steps so that plans and standards may be evaluated and *control* directives may be sent down to the operating levels of the organization.

Although the diagram in Figure 19-4 and the explanatory discussion may sound rather detached and unfeeling, the actual flow of information and its interpretation by the organizational role players becomes an emotional and highly subjective process at most points in any organization. Hence, while we are abstracting the flow of information in order to suggest the way in which systems might be designed, we must continually remember that human beings will initiate the collection, processing, and interpretation of data and that computer printouts must be read and utilized. The information system that we are discussing is not separate from the system of management which has been discussed throughout this text, but simply another way of viewing the processing of information.

THE USE OF COMPUTERS IN MIS

The computer has been defined "as an electronic device that processes data, is capable of receiving input and output, and possesses such characteristics as high speed, accuracy, and the ability to store a set of instructions for solving a

---

[9] John G. Burch, Jr., Felix R. Strater, and Gary Grudnitski, *Information Systems: Theory and Practice*, New York, Wiley, 1979, pp. 514–519.

problem."[10] Computers can do most of the types of processing of information that human beings can do and at a much more rapid rate with fewer errors. They can read data from hundreds of punched cards in a few seconds; type out information at the rate of hundreds of lines per minute; store millions of characters or numbers for instant retrieval; perform a variety of complicated mathematical calculations; print out whole paragraphs of text matter; sort checks and update accounts; write letters that have been programmed; draw pictures; plot curves and draw graphs. They are particularly adapted to sorting data, merging lists, searching files, and facilitating comparisons by rearranging data and comparing information. Today, we have an hierarchy of computers meeting specific user requirements and the cost of computing power is coming down rapidly.

A computer cannot originate thoughts, correct its own mistakes, or engage in processes that are considered to be creative in nature. However, error-detection routines can be programmed into computers so that they can give warning to their operator that mistakes are being made.

Most computers utilized in MIS are *digital computers*, which process data in the form of discrete *binary digits* (0, 1), using line printers, typewriters, card punches, or paper tape punches to produce standard typed reports and forms; and cathode ray devices for on-line visual display. *Analog computers* are used for processing data of a continuous form, such as temperature, pressure, and other engineering and production-type information. Often analog computer output is displayed on cathode ray tubes or graphical plotters.

COMPUTER COMPONENTS

Computers utilize components known as *hardware* and *software*. The basic hardware components of the computer consist of data entry equipment such as a card punch, terminal, cathode ray tube, tapes, or card reader, which is either automated or involves an operator; *a central processing unit* (CPU), which controls the sequencing and pacing of all operations; *storage units*, which are the memory of the computer ("core") or various auxiliary storage units (tapes, disks, drums, mass storage, etc.); and output devices such as terminals, cathode ray tubes, and line printers, some of which can print up to 3000 lines a minute.[11]

Translating human language and logic into machine language and logic requires software experts or ready-made software programs. This translation is a complicated process, requiring trained programmers who know languages such as COBOL and FORTRAN.

Management information systems experts *must* possess knowledge about the needs of the organization as well as computer language and the operation of the computer system itself.

Computers play an integral role in the processing of information both externally and internally for organizations. Figure 19-5 indicates how computers tend to centralize the information processing in both of these roles.

---

[10]Gerald A. Silver and Joan B. Silver, *Data Processing for Business*, New York, Harcourt Brace Jovanovich, Inc., 1973, p. 6.
[11]Burch et al., *Information Systems*, pp. 102–106, 109–111.

FIGURE 19-5

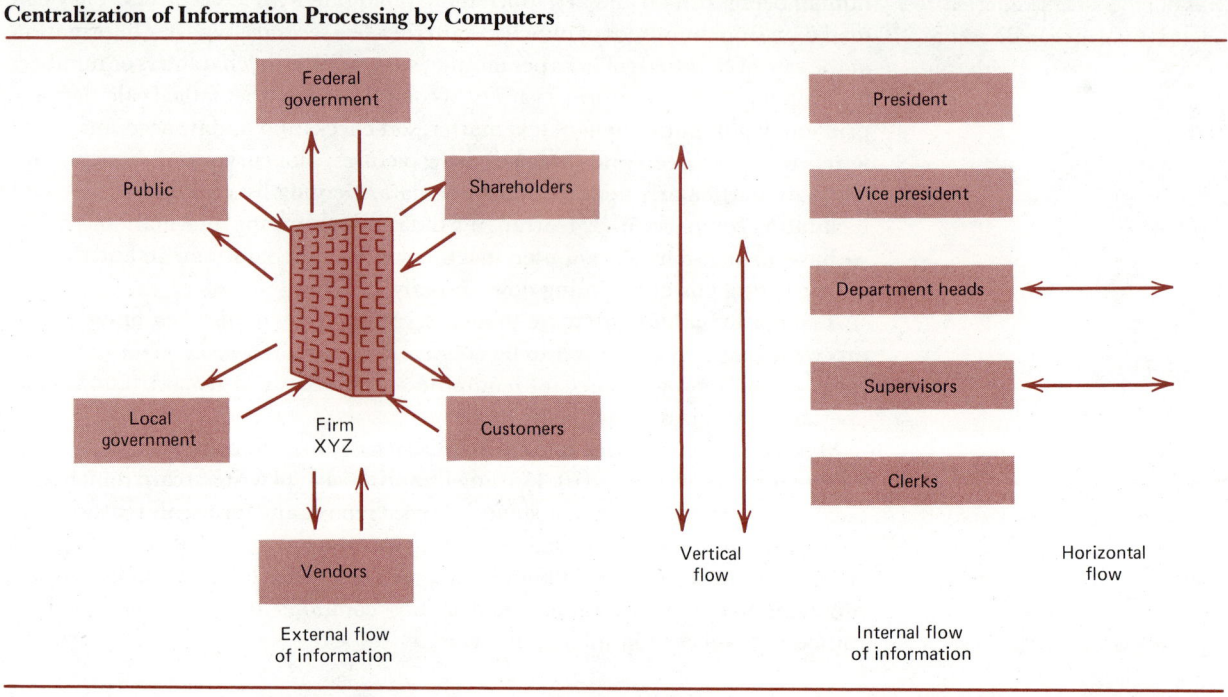

Centralization of Information Processing by Computers

Source: Gerald A. Silver and Joan B. Silver, *Data Processing for Business,* New York, Harcourt Brace Javanovich, Inc., 1973, pp. 20–21.

A LOOK AT COMPUTERIZED MIS

Computers have been well integrated into the functional areas of management for record-keeping in such departments as production control, accounting, and order handling analysis. Many of these functions could not operate today in large businesses without computers.

In Chapter 18, Quantitative Decision Making, several quantitative decision techniques were described. In Figure 19-3, systems operating at Levels 3 and 4 integrate quantitative decision making into the ongoing MIS process. For example, accounting reports can be transformed into decision-making reports by such installation. One large milling company has developed an information system to analyze cost-volume relationships as well as to provide other financial information in a decision-making form, as opposed to a traditional accounting report form.[12]

Today, we have active markets for a wide variety of distinctly different "computers."

Simulation techniques usually require computerized model building and often include the simulation of entire units or businesses. The airlines industry has

---

[12]Raymond Coleman and M. J. Riley, *MIS: Management Dimensions*, San Francisco, Cal., Holden-Day, Inc., 1973.

pioneered the use of this type of decision making. The Federal Aeronautics Administration has conducted simulations to determine the probability of an accident from extending structural hazards to various heights and distances in an airline approach path. Aircraft manufacturers have programmed computer flight characteristics so that various types of airplane characteristics can be programmed as input into the computer. A test pilot in the simulator can feel the movements that would occur from varying simulated design patterns.

Mathematical programming and other types of model building often require computer processing. But much work still remains to be done in making operations research reports suitable for review and use by top management. As one writer suggested several years ago, "Management must learn to crawl in the skin of the model builder and the model builder in the skin of the manager."[13]

> The closest computers can come to human problem solving is called heuristic programming.

The closest to human thinking that computers can come is the type of problem solving which requires heuristic programming. This is a process by which computers approach human learning by simulation, resimulation of data, and probability estimation.

In most MIS programs, a manager has remained the key link in the feedback loop, redirecting the execution of simulation models in accordance with her judgment and the results. At a higher level, the manager can provide *logical* models and *decision rules* by means of which the computer program can produce recommendations for action using the manager's logic and the decision rules and carrying out the simulations to determine the *best* results. The ability of management information systems to automatically revise concepts and models, however, has also been demonstrated in such areas as forecasting techniques, using exponentially-weighted moving averages, and in Bayesian analysis. The latter process is described by one writer as follows.

> *Subjective probabilities are provided to the MIS by the manager. These probabilities are his subjective estimates of the likelihood of specified future events such as "workers strike" or "sales over $2 million." Based on data obtained directly from the operating environment, these "prior" probabilities are revised by the MIS into "posterior probabilities," which are based on both the manager's prior judgment and the data from events in the real world.*[14]

> In order to complete the learning process in MIS, the system must be provided with real-world data.

In order to complete the learning process in MIS, the system must be provided with real-world data on events that have occurred more recently and the manager's evaluation of them. "Suppose the manager takes an action based on a prediction of the demand for his product, only to find that sales do not meet expectations. The system must be provided with a specification of the action taken, the prediction on which it was based, as well as performance data from the real world; the first two elements are provided by the manager and the last by the environment."[15]

It is interesting to note that in all of the many approaches to decision analysis

---

[13] Offershner Cross, Donald I. Lowry, A. R. Ziff, and others, *Computers and Management: The 1967 Leatherbee Lectures*, Boston, Mass., Harvard University, 1967, p. 14.

[14] William R. King, "Profiles of the Future: The Intelligent MIS—A Management Helper," *Business Horizons*, October 1973, p. 9.

[15] Ibid., p. 10.

utilized by MIS the creation of alternatives to be considered is left to the manager. Creativity must be developed by such processes as brainstorming and other approaches that we have discussed in previous chapters. Computers may rearrange data, update probabilities, and build new models; but they are unable to creatively submit new alternatives for the decision process.[16]

Computers are usually integrated into an MIS in an evolving nature.

Computers are usually integrated into MIS in an evolving manner. The following is an example of such development stretching over a long period of time. In 1954 Procter & Gamble created a data processing department. The system was built very carefully, beginning with such things as payroll, stock transfer, and dividend payments. By 1967, data processing had developed into a full-fledged management information system, as shown in Figure 19-6.

In 1957, P & G went to the test market with a subsystem for receiving orders and translating these two into various shipping papers, and also controlling and preparing invoices and accounts receivable. This was tried in one area of the country before the system went nationwide. After the completion of this first major building block, P & G then turned to other blocks. Notice how the system provides for more movement from basic data processing to more advanced analysis of data.

Building an integrated management information system requires a tremendous commitment by management.

Building an integrated management information system requires a tremendous commitment by management. At P & G this logical extension of the data processing system for rate making included twenty-three different departments, required many years of skilled systems analysis and programming time, and an investment of approximately a quarter of a million dollars. In spite of the amount of money spent by P & G in the sophistication of their system, the following final anecdote by one of their executives indicates the limitations of total system integration.

> *. . . shipping data which are processed in Cincinnati on a third generation 360–65 computer, transmitted in high speed (250 characters/second) sophisticated fashion via wire to Boston, printed out as a shipping paper and invoiced on a high speed printer at several hundred lines/minute, are then taken to the warehouse by taxicab. Why? Certainly, an electronic transmission system would be technically feasible—but the taxi is cheaper and meets the time requirement. In the sense of complete mechanization, we do not ever expect to have a "total system."*[17]

Since 1967, P & G has extended their system considerably and like many other companies is moving toward much more use of mini- and microcomputers for departments. The cases at the beginning and end of this chapter give a much more detailed look at developments in systems since the 1970s.

ORGANIZATIONAL PROBLEMS CREATED BY MIS

Although management information systems have assisted greatly in providing the needed communication and large quantities of data and facts necessary to operate sophisticated and complex organizations, they are not without problems.

---
[16] Ibid., p. 12.
[17] Cross, Lowry, and Ziff, *Computers and Management*, p. 41.

FIGURE 19-6

The Development of Data Processing Into a Management Information System

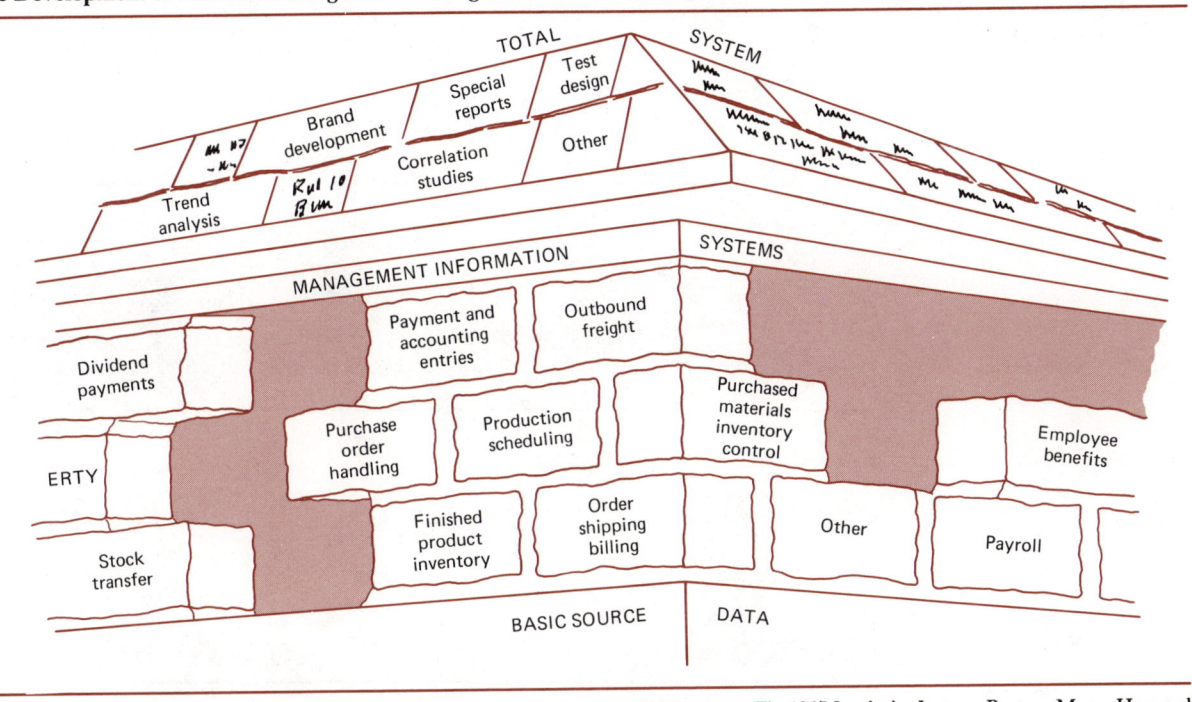

Source: Hershner Cross, Donald I. Lowery, A. R. Ziff, and others, *Computers and Management: The 1967 Leatherbee Lectures,* Boston, Mass., Harvard Universty, 1967, p. 38

THE PROBLEM OF MISINFORMATION

When managers complain that they have too little information, they may actually possess too much information.

There is a possibility that too much information will be provided executives. Or as one author suggests, when managers are complaining that they are suffering from a critical deficiency of relevant information, they may really be suffering from an overabundance of irrelevant information. This problem is further aggravated by the fact that top managers often do not know exactly what information they need. For example, marketing researchers in a major oil company once asked their marketing managers what variables they thought were relevant in estimating the sales volume of future service stations. Although the managers submitted seventy variables, the research team was able to learn by statistical analysis that a customer's perception of the amount of time lost by stopping for service was the major reason for the selection of a service station.[18]

MIS can eliminate useless data by using the filtering method.

Fortunately, the problem of too much data can be reduced by intelligent MIS design.[19] The first method which information systems utilize for eliminating useless data is the *filtering method*. Figure 19-7 demonstrates how information is

[18] Russell L. Ackoff, "Management Misinformation Systems," *Management Science*, Vol. 14, No. 4, December 1967, pp. 149–150.
[19] John G. Burch, Felix R. Strater, Jr., and Gary Grudnitski, *Information Systems: Theory and Practice*, 2nd ed., Santa Barbara, Cal., Hamilton Publishing Company, 1979, pp. 122–123.

FIGURE 19-7

Information Filtering Methods

President:				
Construction costs	7,200,000			
Manufacturing costs				

V.P. construction:	Airport projects	Highway projects	Building projects	Total
Prime costs	2,050,000	XXXX	XXXX	5,200,000
Overhead costs	700,000	XXXX	XXXX	2,000,000

Projects mgr:	Project-1	Project-2	Project-3	Total
Direct labor costs	250,000	XXX	XXX	850,000
Material costs	400,000	XXX	XXX	1,200,000
Overhead costs	220,000	XXX	XXX	700,000

Superintendent:	Concrete pipe	Excavation	Structures	Total
Direct labor costs	60,000	XXX	XXX	250,000
Material costs	100,000	XXX	XXX	400,000
Overhead costs	50,000	XXX	XXX	220,000

Source: John G. Burch and Felix R. Strater Jr., and Gary Grudnitski, *Information Systems: Theory and Practice,* 2nd ed., (Santa Barbara, Cal., Hamilton Publishing Company, 1979, p. 124.

filtered and screened so that the volume of detailed information going to the president is decreased, while the more detailed information needed at the lower levels of management is maintained. This filtering process reduces the amount of useless information provided each decision maker and conserves organizational resources.

Another method used to enhance the usability of data is the *monitoring method*. Consider the XYZ Company, which develops and maintains standard costs for 23,000 different products. A cost variance report for each product would require more than 1000 pages. Utilizing variance report monitoring, a much smaller report can be produced by assuming that only products varying more than ±5 percent from a standard require the attention of management.

MANAGEMENT INFORMATION SYSTEMS AND THE COMPUTER   517

Automatic notification is a monitoring system used to detect and report only predetermined information.

Another form of monitoring method is known as automatic notification. This process is used in a large hospital where the patients in a given area are the responsibility of many different doctors and nurses, and the information needs are as follows.

Each doctor has prescribed a definite schedule for administering medication, therapy, tests, and diets to each patient. Generally, a head nurse is in charge of monitoring these instructions and seeing that they are performed as scheduled in each area. In a twenty-four operation there are at least three head nurses involved. Moreover, patients are always coming and going, and doctors are continuously changing schedules.[20]

A monitoring system could input doctor instructions for each head nurse by way of a CRT or teletype device. This automatic notification would permit the nurse to spend time in other areas providing patient service rather than just keeping track of administrative details.

PROBLEMS OF IMPLEMENTATION

Information systems are not implemented without certain problems. Out of fear, managers may passively or actively resist the use of MIS. Often MIS systems distribute sets of facts, sometimes out of context, which show managers in an unfavorable light; and no amount of explanation is likely to remedy this initial impression.

It is very easy for the mechanized flow of information to evolve to the point where it becomes more important than the purpose for which it was designed. Since MIS systems tend to become staffed by highly influential supervisory directors, and since information is power, the other departments often are forced to conform to the procedures of the MIS department. Of course, some conformity will no doubt be necessary in order to use computerized and systematic processes. Nevertheless, top management should not allow the cart to get before the horse by allowing an MIS department to unduly alter the work of operations departments in order to make the job of processing information easier.

An MIS department needs to be flexible in terms of supplying needed data.

An MIS department needs to be flexible in terms of supplying needed data even when rapid change is necessary, and in supplying ad hoc information back to operating managers. In addition, a continuous study of operations by the users is necessary, with constant elimination of wasteful information.

During the review of a justification procedure for acquiring more expensive equipment, a consultant learned that the new computerized system already in existence was costing the company about $150,000 per month in excess inventories. He learned that several errors in the decision-making process were causing the overstocking of inventories. These overstocking problems were generated by easily detected errors, but because they were in a computerized system rather than a hand-operated inventory control system, middle and top managers did not feel confident to ask questions about them. "No MIS should ever be installed unless the managers for whom it is intended are trained to evaluate and hence control it rather than be controlled by it."[21]

---

[20]Ibid., p. 130.
[21]Ackoff, "Management Misinformation Systems," p. 153.

One of the ways in which control can be built in is by having the intended users play an active role in implementing the MIS system. This point is dramatically illustrated by the following conclusions in a recent research study.

Intended users neither intitiated nor played an active role in implementing 11 of the 15 systems that suffered significant implementation problems. Conversely, there were relatively few such problems in 27 of the 31 systems in which the users had a hand in initiating and/or played an active role in implementing.[22]

> The best long-term indicator of quality of an MIS is the degree to which managers utilize rather than circumvent the service.

Because it is difficult to evaluate the increased efficiency of MIS systems, a cost-output evaluation is very difficult to install. Although actual savings may accrue to an MIS, these are usually outweighed by the additional demands placed on the system which would not have been imposed on an informal system. The best long-term indicator of quality is the degree to which managers utilize rather than circumvent the service.[23]

One of the major feats of behavioralists in management has been that MIS would tend to centralize decision making once again and produce authoritarian management. As you will recall from Chapter 4, Managerial Problem Analysis and Decision Making, one of the major reasons for decentralization is to allow decision making to be made at the point where the facts are present. MIS does tend to allow management to circumvent middle and lower level management, and receive information directly.

For example, Phillip Morris automates the production of cigarettes for their plant in Richmond, Virginia. They expect ultimately to have a hierarchy of computers that feed summaries of data to a central computer at the end of each work shift. Top management receives financial summaries from these central computers.

The Southern Railroad Information System includes sensors in freight yards that keep close watch on what shipments are in each freight yard and the location of each car. As a result of the installation of this program, top management can take a sharp look at the location and utilization of "rolling stock," which was never before possible. Along with the increasing use of MIS, many top managers are increasing the size of their corporate staff—another indication of recentralization of management decision making.[24]

BEHAVIORAL PROBLEMS IN MIS[25]

Often workers look for ways to beat an MIS rather than looking for a payoff from it. One research group was investigating an information system in a complex organization designed to collect man-hours on a daily basis from different work

---

[22]Steven L. Alter, "How Effective Managers Use Information Systems," *Harvard Business Review*, November-December 1976, p. 103.
[23]Dalton, "How Management Information Systems Work," p. 23.
[24]Clair R. Miller, "Command and Control Replacement for Management Information Systems," *Data Management*, September 1975, p. 15.
[25]Much of the material in this section is based on G. W. Dickson and John K. Simmons, "The Behavioral Side of MIS," *Business Horizons*, August 1970.

stations. Workers frequently rotated from one work station to another. They learned that they could gang up on and punish unpopular foremen by punching in at their work station and spending the workday at another station. Such human problems must be anticipated when installing a management information system. Various organizational groups react differently to the installation of MIS, as noted in the following examples.

Often workers look for a way to beat an MIS rather than looking for a payoff from it.

NONCLERICAL WORKERS

These workers provide inputs to the system by punching time clocks, completing forms, entering prepunched cards, or serving as subjects for MIS studies. They, in turn, receive little output from the system other than a paycheck. As the MIS grows in complexity and in comprehensiveness, added responsibility is placed on the operative to provide accurate and timely input data. Often the reaction of personnel will be negative, although not usually as dramatic as the case encountered by one group of consultants.

> *An organization that had poor labor-management relations introduced an on-line management information system in one of its branches. Soon after, the discovery was made that source recorders were inoperable, because honey had been poured down them. Others were mysteriously run over by fork-lift trucks. In still others, paper clips had been inserted rather than badge cards. In addition, the system was being plagued continuously by errors in the input.*[26]

CLERICAL WORKERS

Operative and clerical employees often react negatively to the installation of a MIS because it changes and often limits their behavior.

This group of workers generally has to process input data and convert it to output. In other words, they become an integral part of the management information system itself. Perhaps this group more than any other must adapt to changes in their daily work routine and to more rigid work patterns. The type of behavior usually experienced when this change is brought about is acceptance of the change, accompanied by negative projections toward the new system.

TECHNICAL STAFF

The one group in the organization that is likely to exhibit no negative reactions to system installation is the technical staff programmers, system designers, and operations researchers. It is easy to understand their positive support of the system since they are highly involved in its installation and work with MIS in an operational sense on a day-to-day basis. Their reaction is further enhanced by the fact that they seldom use data from the system.

Technical staff persons are likely to react positively to the system.

But while positive in the support of the installation and operation of systems, the technical staff can be destructive in their interaction with operations management and clerical employees. In many cases they consider the line manager to be "an old fuddy-duddy, undereducated, flying by the seat of his pants, and getting in the way

---

[26]Ibid., p. 66.

of progress."[27] Furthermore, the fact that systems staff members tend to be younger, more highly educated, and less experienced than line managers does not enhance the rapport between the line and staff. Operating managers often view them as whiz kids who appear to think that they are ready to step into operating positions with little experience. To remove this conflict, MIS staff members should be experienced business-oriented systems analysts.

OPERATING MANAGEMENT

Operating management is the group that most often resists the installation of an MIS.

This group is greatly affected by management information systems since they are the principal users. Many of the operating decisions are made at this level, and the information systems are designed to provide the input to management decision processes. It is not yet clear what the effects of the installation of MIS will have in operating management. As suggested previously, many experts believe that the role of computerizing information systems will tend to centralize decision making and increase the ability of high-level managers to control their subordinates. Others believe that middle management jobs will be enriched by reducing the amount of time spent on routine tasks, thus allowing more emphasis on problems.

Although operating management should enjoy most of the benefits of MIS, this group most often resists the installation of the system. Several factors may account for this. First, systems are of such magnitude and so costly that top management seldom shares with lower level operating management the decision to install them. Second, systems specialists, operations researchers, and other specialists in this area tend to speak languages foreign to the operating manager and they often control information formerly controlled by this manager. Consequently it is very easy for operating management to react negatively by fighting the system through inadequate support or by failing to use information or suggestions provided by the system. Probably the most negative reaction engendered by operations management is that of blaming the system for operational failures, especially during the shakedown period when the system is new.

TOP MANAGEMENT

Top management is usually uncomfortable with the new MIS.

Top management has typically played a negative role with management information systems—one best described as avoidance and noninvolvement. As one moves from lower levels of management to top management, decision making becomes more intuitive. Output delivery systems seldom accommodate themselves to top management languages, as was pointed out in the beginning of Chapter 4, Managerial Problem Analysis and Decision Making; and only the most complex and sophisticated systems are able to assist at the policy making level. Top managers, by virtue of their ages and types of education, are the group most removed from background similarities to the systems people. For this reason MIS has typically been used by top management for control rather than policy making and objective setting.[28]

---

[27]Ibid., p. 66.
[28]Dickson and Simmons, "The Behavioral Side of MIS," p. 67.

MANAGEMENT INFORMATION SYSTEMS AND THE COMPUTER

One writer emphasizes this point with the following statement.

Since top management does not receive computer printouts directly except in a few cases, the effect of MIS on decision making is negligible. However, this is not to say that their decisions have not been influenced by MIS through the intercession of middle management. . . . I have never encountered a company where the computer analysis provided the final decision of an issue that was top management. . . . Automated management information systems can make decisions on lot sizes and length of production runs, but they cannot make final decisions on the introduction of new products, the site of a new warehouse, or the need for an additional factory.[29]

PREVENTING DYSFUNCTIONAL BEHAVIOR IN MIS

The key to preventing dysfunctional behavior on the part of line groups vis-á-vis systems groups rests with top management and the system people themselves.

The key to preventing dysfunctional behavior on the part of various line groups vis-a-vis systems groups rests with top management and the systems people themselves. The following considerations might prevent serious conflict and smooth the installation and operation of MIS.

1. Top management should set an example of full support for the system and a desire to see it fully integrated into decision making and information processing as soon as possible. When practical, top management should make every attempt to equip themselves to utilize the system in their own decision making.

2. Systems personnel should realize that they are dealing with a change situation that is likely to be highly threatening to existing operating, clerical, and top management personnel, many of whom possess an entrenched high-status position in the company. They should also realize that it is much more likely that they will be able to learn to speak the language of operating personnel than will be the reverse. It is also important that the systems analyst and staff make every effort to show line personnel the way in which MIS can help to obtain their personal goals and self-advancement.

3. The overall purpose and characteristics of the MIS should be clarified to those who must interface with it. This communication must take place before, during, and after installation. Usually what system staff people consider to be adequate information will be grossly inadequate. One writer has suggested that as much as 25 to 30 percent of the time of the systems analyst should be reserved for communication with users of the information.[30]

4. Sufficient time should be scheduled for "debugging" and shakedown so that errors may be recognized and eliminated before the installation of the on-going system. Error-free operation before the implementation can do much to prevent the undermining of a system.

5. The humanity of the system should be preserved. Managers often exhibit great reluctance to admit that the computer system in any way can tell them what to

---

[29] Jerome Kanter, *Management-Oriented Management Information Systems*, Second edition, Englewood Cliffs, N.J., Prentice-Hall, 1977, P. 274.
[30] Dickson And Simmons, "The Behavioral Side of MIS," p. 69.

do. Therefore some areas of human control for operating management should be preserved solely in the name of maintaining the human dignity and self-respect of the line organization. "Acceptance of the system is not likely if the individual has the feeling, rightly or wrongly, that the computer has usurped his position."[31]

6. Performance evaluation must be explained as it relates to MIS. As was mentioned earlier, twenty-six departments played a role in the integrated scheduling and billing system of Proctor & Gamble. Obviously some autonomy for each department was relinquished when this system was installed. The new concept of *appraisal by objectives*, which has been discussed earlier, suggests that managers should have control of the areas for which they are held responsible. However, MIS tend to take control from operating departments and make them dependent on the processing of information and integrated decisions by many departments. Effective reward systems in these complex situations will require appraisal on the basis of groups. Thus the use of MIS becomes a major reason for using team type organizations. (See Chapter 12, Contingency Approaches to Organizations.)

7. A management information system must continually be examined to make sure that it is user oriented. This means that proper information should be supplied to each level of management, that information overload should be avoided, and that the user should not be forced to maintain her own parallel system in order to understand the information being presented to her. During the installation of a new system its personnel must recognize that great burdens are placed on operating managers, who must maintain old systems in order to process day-to-day work, to assist in the transfer to the new systems, and to anticipate new ways of utilizing the system. The failure of systems personnel to realize that these three burdens have been imposed simultaneously upon the operating personnel has often caused the failure of an MIS installation.

SUMMARY

A MIS is a formal system of reporting, classifying, and disseminating information to the appropriate stations in an organization. The more advanced systems not only duplicate clerical functions but also provide decision-making assistance to management. Programmed systems, although rare, are able to monitor and direct certain operations unassisted by human beings.

MIS data consists of input data, operations data, output data, and a feedback loop. This data is transmitted and processed by a processing unit, usually consisting of electronic computers and associated equipment.

MIS systems must continually be evaluated to make sure they supply relevant information to the users.

---

[31]Ibid., p. 70.

Special care is required in the implementation stage of MIS. Often employees react negatively to the centralized control of information. Furthermore, the nature of the daily work of operations and clerical workers is altered by the installation of a MIS. Smooth installation and resolution of conflict can be assured by the following actions.

1. Top management should support and utilize the system fully.
2. Systems personnel should learn to speak the language of operating personnel and attempt to educate these employees regarding ways to utilize the system and perform their own work more satisfactorily.
3. Sufficient time for shakedown and explanation should be allowed in the implementation of MIS.
4. Finally, areas of human control should be preserved in order to maintain the human dignity of the system. A successful MIS must be user oriented.

In this brief overview of MIS, considerably more emphasis has been placed on management, on information, and on the people who must make it work than on the technology of the computer system. As important as that may be to the result, it can be demonstrated that very few MIS projects fail because of a lack of the technical capabilities. From the early beginnings of efforts to manage information, the hardware, software, and systems support have always been available at a much higher level of technical sophistication than that required for the project. The major constraint has always been the ability and willingness to participate on the part of the people involved: managers, supervisors, or workers. Problems of fear or of perceived threat, problems of education and of motivation, problems of communications and of involvement, and problems in implementation of the program have been the stumbling blocks to successful MIS development and use. The future of MIS is only limited by people's ability to plan and to control its use, to capture the benefits from its use, and to make those benefits their own.

SUMMARY CHART

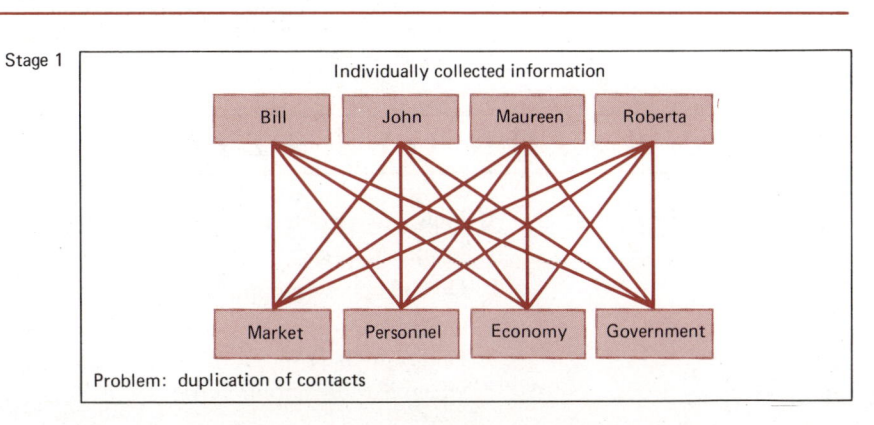

Stage 1 — Individually collected information

Bill, John, Maureen, Roberta

Market, Personnel, Economy, Government

Problem: duplication of contacts

524 MANAGEMENT OF OPERATIONS

Stage 2 — Noncomputerized MIS

Bill, John, Maureen, Roberta ↔ MIS ↔ Market, Personnel, Economy, Government

Problem: human processing of information difficult

Stage 3 — Computerized MIS

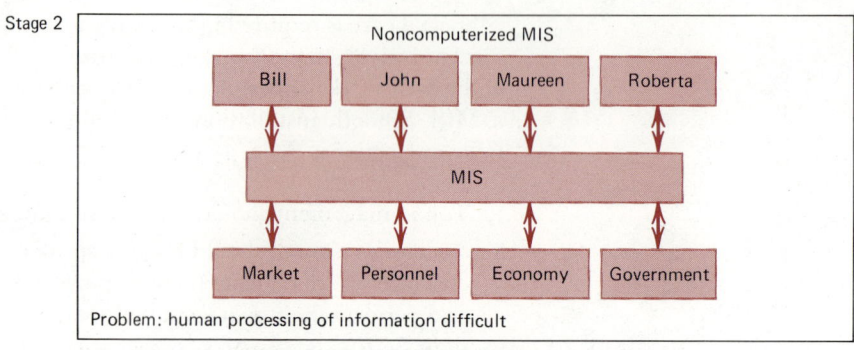

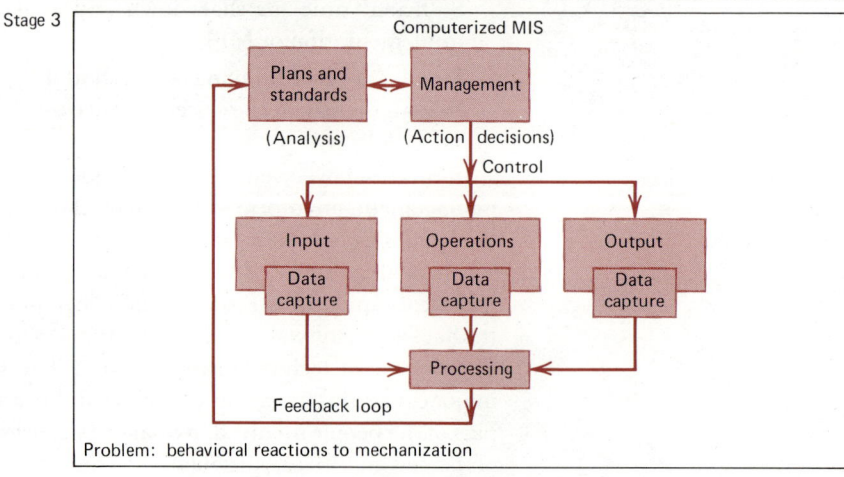

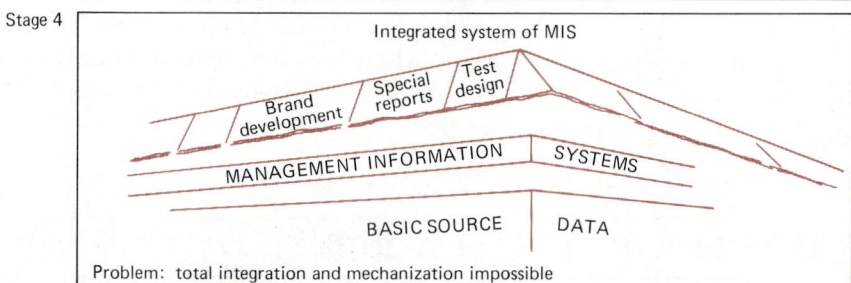

Plans and standards (Analysis) ↔ Management (Action decisions) → Control → Input (Data capture), Operations (Data capture), Output (Data capture) → Processing → Feedback loop

Problem: behavioral reactions to mechanization

Stage 4 — Integrated system of MIS

Brand development / Special reports / Test design
MANAGEMENT INFORMATION SYSTEMS
BASIC SOURCE DATA

Problem: total integration and mechanization impossible

DISCUSSION QUESTIONS

1. How can we determine when an organization has grown to the point where a formal MIS is desirable?
2. Do you believe computerized MIS will ever manage total organizations? Why or why not?
3. Diagram the process of MIS. What is the most important determinant of effective information flows?

4. Can MIS operate without computers? Discuss.
5. What stage of decision making do computers perform effectively? Ineffectively?
6. Why do various organization role players react differently to the installation of MIS? What is the greatest determinant of MIS acceptance?
7. As an MIS manager, how would you insure satisfactory relationships with operating personnel?

APPLICATION EXERCISES AND CASES

NEEDED: BUSINESS-ORIENTED SYSTEMS ANALYSTS[32]

> **WANTED**
> Systems analyst—Must have BAL and COBOL experience. Familiarity with CICS and IMS helpful. 360-30, 360-40 DOS shop converting to OS. Salary to 18 K.

The above ad is rather typical of many of the ads we have seen in the past for many jobs falling under the glamorous heading "systems analyst."

Unfortunately, such ads have tended to lead many of our future systems talent to believe that a systems analyst must be a person with strong programming experience and an in-depth knowledge of computer operating systems as well as a host of other software. It is true that we desperately need the type of background just described, but we do the title of systems analyst a disservice if we only associate it with programming and computer hardware knowledge.

. . .

True system analysis consists of determining what is needed to accomplish some necessary improvement in the way a job is performed so that it may be done faster, more efficiently, at less cost and/or with more accuracy and reliability.

. . .

Recent examples of system analysis at work are easy to find if we look around us. The cloverleaf, traffic circles and jug-handle exits on our highways certainly show system ingenuity at work. For years bus commuters to New York City from New Jersey had been faced with a very discouraging traffic tie-up as their bus left the New Jersey Turnpike to travel the approximate five miles to the Lincoln Tunnel which connects New Jersey to New York City.

Thousands of cars and buses in a bumper-to-bumper, five-mile-long traffic jam caused most bus schedules to be so unreliable that the average commuter would have to start out a half hour early just to compensate for the fact that the bus

---

[32]Ralph J. Morrison, "Needed: Business-Oriented Systems Analysts," *Info-Systems—America's Leading Systems Magazine for Management*, September 1975, pp. 48–49.

schedule could not be relied upon. The return trip was just as unreliable, since traffic would be backed up for miles as each car and bus stopped to pay the tunnel fee during the late afternoon rush hour.

Some smart systems analyst (probably with the title of traffic engineer) was put to work solving the problem. There were multihighway lanes going into and coming out of the city toward the New Jersey Turnpike entrance. The solution was to convert one of the several lanes leaving the city to a bus lane for use during the early morning rush hour. The systems analyst recognized the fact that the lanes leaving the city were barely used in the mornings, since most of the traffic went into New York at that time of day.

Today, the system works to perfection. The exclusive bus lane now allows hundreds of commuter-laden buses to zip along at normal highway speeds while thousand of cars still limp along at a snail's pace in the other inbound lanes. But commuters can now believe in the bus schedule and leave their homes at a more reasonable hour.

The other problem, mentioned earlier, of the massive pileups at the toll booths near the tunnel entrance during the late afternoon rush hour, was also solved by someone using the systems approach. Since the great majority of buses and cars entering the city in the morning also leave the city at night, it was decided to collect tolls only on the New Jersey (morning entrance) side.

Double tolls are collected on the way in, but no toll is collected on the way out of the city. This has now allowed the departing traffic to proceed through the tunnel without stopping and traffic now moves in a fairly smooth, unhampered fashion (if you can ever call New York traffic smooth). It has also allowed the utilization of more toll collectors on the New Jersey side since they were not needed on the New York side, with the additional benefit of speeding up the collection of tolls inbound.

The point of all this discussion on analytical solutions (without the use of the computer in this instance) is to demonstrate that systems analysts have many tools available to them in improving an existing operation. The most useful of these tools is an analytical mind coupled with a great deal of creativity.

Questions
1. What does this case suggest analysts possess?
2. How important is programming language to systems analyst work? Discuss.

WE HAVE PLAY-OFFS, RUNOFFS, BAKE-OFFS; NOW A COMPUTE-OFF[33]

In a field where many businesses trade up to the latest equipment every two or three years, the Air Force is still hobbling along with computers nearly 20 years old.

"You could go to Radio Shack and get bigger capacity from a personal computer

---

[33]George Anders, "We have Play-Offs, Runoffs, Bake-Offs; Now a Compute-Off," *The Wall Street Journal*, Monday, September 21, 1981, pp. 1 and 19.

than what we've got here to handle billions of dollars of inventory," says Robert Majors, deputy manager of the Phase IV program for the Air Force.

Though the lucrative job of bringing the system up to date was dangled before eight major computer makers, only Sperry and Burroughs came forward as serious bidders last December. Some would-be contenders—International Business Machines Corp., for one—were put off by the Air Force's reluctance to make changes that the manufacturers considered necessary to fully modernize the system.

Somewhat defensively, Air Force officials trot out documents to rebut charges that they too-narrowly specified such minor details as the size of data discs. But they concede that sweeping changes in some existing Air Force computer procedures were ruled out.

The Air Force chose, for example, to retain a large, autonomous computer at each base rather than consolidate operations at several regional centers connected to base terminals. And most notably, it will use punch cards, rather than discs or magnetic tapes, to feed some data into the computers.

"Except for the New Jersey Turnpike, I can't think of anywhere that you still see punch cards," says an official at a computer company that declined to go after the contract.

The Air Force says that it plans to gradually phase out punch cards. Meanwhile, officials say, it must make the new Phase IV computers at individual bases compatible with the punch-card-based computers that keep track of the same data on an Air Force-wide basis. The officials also say that they are hampered by the limitations of their own operators, who they fear couldn't adapt to vast procedural changes.

Even Sperry and Burroughs officials grumble privately about the difficulty of displaying a system that, as one of them puts it, will be operated by "an average Air Force recruit with an IQ of 90." (The Air Force says it doesn't give its recruits IQ tests, but a spokesman says that 88% of the recruits are high-school graduates.) John Gioia, a former Air Force Phase IV project manager who has since gone into industry, says that some Air Force computer operators have "grade-school reading ability" and require instruction manuals to match. He is quick to distinguish the operators from Air Force programmers, who, he says, "often have Ph.D.s and can be as innovative as the best."

The stodgy ways of the Air Force should come as no surprise to either Sperry or Burroughs, for it is their 1960s-vintage machines that are now being replaced. In fact, their status as incumbents was enough to discourage some competitors from bidding. "We thought our chance of winning was very slight," says a spokesman for Honeywell Inc.

The absence of other contenders has only intensified the rivalry between Sperry and Burroughs. So far, they both claim to be comfortably on schedule, though they concede that keeping pace has entailed some punishing workdays.

The Six-Hour Drive
To complete its first equipment test a week or so ahead of Burroughs, Sperry employes worked as late as 2 A.M. when deadlines loomed. And to avert an unnecessary delay, its software subcontractor, Computer Sciences Corp., once sent

an employe on a six-hour drive to pick up a certain magnetic tape needed that afternoon. Burroughs's software subcontractor, Planning Research Corp., has kept its computers running seven days a week, and has installed a telephone system that allows the 150 employes it has assigned to the project to continue working at home.

The winner won't be announced until February 1983, after the Air Force has evaluated the compute-off results and the bids. Air Force officials expect that cost and software differences will influence their choice more than differences in hardware. But the hardware, of course, is the most expensive item: The Air Force expects it to cost more than $500 million. Most of the software is already being paid for in the prototype contracts of about $50 million for each company.

Once the computers are all in place, the Air Force says, it will consider further upgrading of the system. In any case the winning contractor, barring any serious problems with the system, may get a six-year renewal contract for equipment and maintenance. Thus, the final stake may be well above the $500 million mark.

Questions
1. What mistakes has the Air Force made in their development of MIS?
2. Do you think they will make similar mistakes in the future? Discuss.
3. Based on your reading in this chapter what suggestion would you make to them regarding MIS and computers?

CHAPTER 20
CONTROLLING OPERATIONS

DEFINITION AND PURPOSE OF CONTROL
ELEMENTS OF CONTROL
STANDARDS
MEASUREMENT PROCESSES
COMPARISON OF STANDARDS AND RESULTS
CORRECTIVE ACTION
EVALUATIVE CONTROLS
EXTERNAL ENVIRONMENT
AREAS WHERE CONTROL IS NECESSARY
CONTROL IN THE OPERATIONS OF PRODUCTIVE SYSTEMS
QUALITY CONTROL AND INSPECTION
PRODUCTION PLANNING AND CONTROL
INVENTORY CONTROL
BUDGETING
NATURE OF BUDGETS
FLEXIBLE (VARIABLE) BUDGETS
RESPONSIBILITY ACCOUNTING
STANDARD COSTS
ZERO-BASE BUDGETING
PROJECT AND SCHEDULING CONTROL DEVICES
PROJECT CONTROL
PERT AND CPM
HUMAN ASPECTS OF MANAGERIAL CONTROL
**FUNDAMENTAL GUIDELINES OF
EFFECTIVE CONTROL ADMINISTRATION**
APPLICATION EXERCISES AND CASES
THE SIROCCO COMPANY—INTRODUCTION OF A BUDGETARY CONTROL PLAN
HELL WEEK
FAULTY LIGHT BULBS

HOW ROGER MILLIKEN RUNS TEXTILES' PREMIER PERFORMER[1]

Roger Milliken, the 65-year-old owner and president of Milliken & Co., a Spartanburg (S.C.) textile manufacturer with sales nearing $2 billion, is one of the nation's most powerful but unpublicized industrialists. He wields an influence in textiles that is probably unparalleled by an individual in any other industry. It stems from mangerial and technological innovations that he has introduced, his success in building a giant corporation in a highly fragmented industry while remaining privately owned, and his 33-year, one-man rule as its chief executive officer.

Roger Milliken enjoys visiting textile machinery shows, where he can often be seen on his hands and knees inspecting a new piece of equipment, attended by a platoon of executives taking notes. He is usually among the first to buy a new type of textile machine. As a fierce competitor, he has been known to place a big order for new machinery simply to tie up the manufacturer's capacity and delay delivery to rival textile producers.

Roger Milliken has an obsession about inventories. In the early 1960s he hired Arthur Andersen & Co. to conduct a study that showed that textile profits rose and fell inversely with inventories. The industry was then dominated by manufacturing-oriented men who paid little heed to the marketplace. Their pattern was to keep up production even when demand slackened, to pile up goods in warehouses, and then to dump them.

What Roger Milliken wants to do is achieve the most efficient production. He has strived for this by investing heavily in new technology and by assiduously avoiding marginally profitable operations. Another factor has been his fetish-like interest in the latest tools of management. He was among the first in textiles to engage in long-term planning and forecasting—concepts that old-timers scoffed at because of the industry's volatile markets. He was quick to set up a computerized management information system, which allowed him to analyze production costs and return on investment more meaningfully and to improve inventory controls.

But not everyone is impressed by Milliken's people. The company's preoccupation with quantitative management techniques, some critics say, has produced many executives whose marketing instincts are underdeveloped. "Some of their people are not quite as much belly-to-belly sellers as they should be," says one industry consultant. "They tend to have too many eggheads." In 1967, suddenly deciding that the company was saddled with excessive overhead, he fired 60 middle-management personnel without warning. "He decided that Parkinson's Law had been in effect long enough," says a former executive.

---

[1]"Roger Milliken—Running Textiles' Premier Performer," *Business Week*, January 19, 1981.

*The authors gratefully acknowledge the assistance of Harold O. Wilson, Professor of MBA Studies, Tennessee Technological University, Cookeville, Tennessee, who revised this chapter.

CONTROLLING OPERATIONS 531

Obviously effective controls can make a difference in an industry like that in which Roger Milliken competes. A classic writer on the subject of control explains the basic reason it is needed.[2]

> *Most of the manager's problems today, as well as his opportunities, are the outgrowth of either society's complexity or its propensity to change. Thus if our economy were static, or if a firm could be assured of a predetermined share of its market, the subject of executive control would only be of casual concern . . . Therefore the manager is left with two alternatives: to suppress or discourage change, or to create the sort of environment in which change can take place with minimum disruption. In brief a manager must be able to coordinate diverse influences and activities if he is to control rather than be controlled by them.*

For these reasons Jerome visualizes executive control as a *catalyst*, rather than a rigid constraining element in the management process.

DEFINITION AND PURPOSE OF CONTROL

Accountability is getting things done in accord with objectives.

A manager's job is to achieve results in specific key areas of accountability—that is, to get things done in accord with objectives. The manager must develop and use a control system that will demonstrate at all times whether or not the progress toward objectives is effective and being accomplished efficiently and on schedule. Control and coordination are mutually beneficial for this purpose.

Managerial control of operations involves pinpointing key operational weaknesses or accomplishments and taking corrective actions or rewarding performance. The kind of control used should take into consideration the individuals or groups who will be employing the control system.

Control systems are usually designed and administered by staff departments assigned to a monitoring function. It is only natural that points of conflict will develop, as suggested in our earlier discussion of line and staff conflict. There is a danger that the control system may become an end in itself, rather than a means to an end. The staff department may forget it exists to aid the achievement of results. And departments subject to the system attack its inadequacies and rigidities. In this connection there may be tendencies to gather and report much more data than is needed to really control—resulting in an expensive and involved system which is counterproductive. In general, however, the cost of quality controls is exceeded by the benefits.[3]

ELEMENTS OF CONTROL

The primary aim of control is to assure that the results of operations conform as closely as possible to established goals.[3] In its simplest form, control compares the

---
[2] William Travers Jerome III, *Executive Control, The Catalyst*, New York, Wiley, 1961, pp. 4–5.
[3] It has been estimated that the average factory spends perhaps 20 percent of its effort making and correcting errors. See Jerry Main, "Toward Service Without a Snarl," *Fortune*, Vol. 103, No. 6, March 23, 1981, p. 58.

The primary aim of control is to insure results of operations conform to established goals.

results of operations with the desired results established by plan or standard, and provides the comparison data to management for evaluation and action if needed. The control system consists of the following four essential elements.

1. Establishment of a standard or plan for desired results.
2. Measurement of performance over time.
3. Comparison of the results with the plan, and evaluation.
4. Direction of needed corrective actions.

Figure 20-1 depicts a simple control system.

STANDARDS

Standards and specifications are usually determined by engineers in cooperation with the sales, manufacturing, inspection, and purchasing departments. *Standards* define the measurable characteristics of products, including such things as performance, weight, composition, and permissible variations. Chance variations are called *tolerances*, with anything beyond those assumed to be assignable to a specific removable cause. A good set of standards and their accompanying tolerances must be definite, reasonable, understandable, and achievable.

Standards established in a participative manner result in self-control.

When standards are established in a participative manner using MBO, they often become a means of self-control as noted in Chapter 22, MBO—An Integrative System of Management.

Planning is a precontrol. That is, the generation and revision of operations plans keep a current and relevant standard available. Examples of precontrol include a production schedule, a machine preventive maintenance plan, a manpower budget, and the assignments for nursing personnel.

Sometimes the standard is in the form of a rule for action (a so-called *decision rule* designed to faciliate operations. The procedure used by credit personnel in deciding to grant or deny credit to applicants is an example of control by rules. These rules are designed to control risk—in this case, the risk of noncollection for goods sold on credit. Mehta[4] has shown that decision tree analysis (Program DECIDE—see Figure 18-1) can be used to develop such control rules, both for new customers and for clients seeking to extend or to enlarge credit already established. A company can adjust these rules to influence the total of credit sales and the probable reduction in revenues due to uncollectible accounts. A number of other good examples of this sort of control system are given in the *Handbook of Operations Research*.[5]

Standards in the form of a rule for action are called procedures.

Figure 20-2 depicts several control variables that are usually monitored in each of the functional areas of business.

---

[4]Dileep Mehta, "The Formulation of Credit Policy Models," *Management Science*, Vol. 15, No. 2, 1968, pp. B30–50; and Dileep Mehta, "Optimal Credit Policy Selection: A Dynamic Approach" *Journal of Financial and Quantitave Anaylsis*, December 1970, pp. 421–444.
[5]John M. Burnham, "Applications in Accounting and Finance," *Handbook of Operations Research*, Vol. II, Joseph J. Moder and Salah E. Elmaghraby, eds., New York, VanNostrant/Reinhold, 1978.

FIGURE 20-1

Elements of a Control System

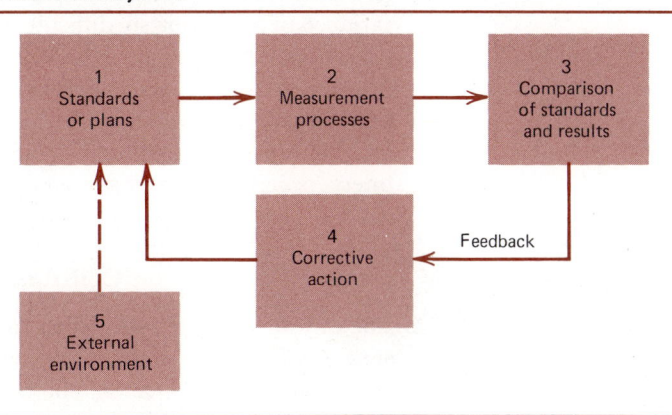

```
1 Standards or plans → 2 Measurement processes → 3 Comparison of standards and results
                                                              ↓
        ↑         ↑                                    
        |         └─── 4 Corrective action ←── Feedback
        |                    ↑
        └─── 5 External environment
```

MEASUREMENT PROCESSES

Resource accounting and social responsibility auditing are being added to traditional controls.

In the past control has been viewed largely as a financial process, thus financial measures were stressed. Nowadays many measures of human resource accounting and social responsibility auditing are being added to corporate activities. While the burgeoning of control measures carries some risk, there is strong reason to believe that goals and objectives that are not measurable will always be overlooked in favor of those that can be measured. In such areas as labor relations and social responsibility, at least some subjective measure of success seems warranted.

FIGURE 20-2

Standards of Control

Production
1. Quality
2. Quantity
3. Cost
4. Machine
5. Individual job performance

Personnel Management
1. Labor relations
2. Labor turnover
3. Absenteeism
4. Wage and salary administration labor costs)
5. Safety

Finance and Accounting
1. Capital expenditures
2. Flow of capital
3. Liquidity
4. Inventories
5. Costs

Marketing
1. Sales volume
2. Sales expenses
3. Credit
4. Advertising costs
5. Individual salesperson's performance

COMPARISON OF STANDARDS AND RESULTS

Most standards do not call for perfect agreement. Almost all of them allow some variance. This is not so difficult a process when dealing with machine tool tolerances or the number of days of credit outstanding. But when managers begin to evaluate the more subjective areas of human relations and supervisory ability, trouble often ensues. Principles of nondirective interviewing and transactional analysis can be of assistance at this point (see Chapter 8, Organizational and Interpersonal Communications).

CORRECTIVE ACTIONS

A control system should focus on deviations from objectives.

The control system should focus on deviations from objectives so that problem areas can be quickly spotted. The idea behind focusing on deviations is not aimed at chastising the manager, but rather at helping him to be able to quickly pinpoint where some type of corrective action needs to be taken. If the control system does not specifically pinpoint deviations, the manager must spend a considerable amount of time analyzing and trying to interpret the reports with which he is being furnished. Also, there is the danger that some potential problem areas will be overlooked.

When a feedback data is compared with the standard, the control may send a signal that automatically adjusts the process.

Management sets the standard, the amount of allowable deviation or tolerance, and the adjustment desired. The control does the rest.

Controls are *concurrent* or *dynamic* when feedback data is being collected while the process is going on, and evaluation action follows immediately. Statistical sampling techniques in quality control accomplish *dynamic process control* in manufacturing. The sample measurements are compared with a standard, the sample variation computed, and a test applied (decision rule) to see whether or not the process is in control.

Production representatives often make minute-to-minute adjustments called operational control.

Another type of concurrent control takes place through dialogue between FAA personnel in an airport control tower and the pilot of an aircraft approaching for a landing. Direction of flight path, speed and rate of descent, runway designation, and so forth, are provided in the exchange of communications between ground and air. The activities of a production supervisor when making minute-to-minute adjustments on the shop floor is also operational control. In this case, it consists of comparing results with the dispatch plan for the shift, taking actions based on progress, and reporting on the labor, equipment, and materials actually on hand.

EVALUATIVE CONTROLS

Evaluative controls take place after the operation has been completed. Such postcontrol is intended to improve operations, or planning, or both, when similar activities are to be done again.

It is important that deviations be reported to the employee himself. By making progress reports available to those who are actually doing the work, a climate is

Evaluative controls following the completion of operations are used to improve future operations.

created where they can adjust their own performance instead of being told to do so. Also there is less need for the manager to act in a policing capacity. Rather, he can function as a coach. The only time he needs to step in is when adjustments are not being made or if the performance gap is such that he wants to make sure that it has been spotted and something is being done. This represents the more positive approach to control called *management by exception.*

EXTERNAL ENVIRONMENT

Realistic control systems collect data for both internal and external activities.

One of the caveats mentioned earlier—that of a rigid staff-designed control plan—will be explained further here. The plan for flying Friendly aircraft throughout the system in mid-1973 included a fuel cost budget (Chapter 17, Operations Management). During the Arab oil embargo, fuel prices skyrocketed. The only way to meet the preembargo fuel budget was to reduce considerably all future Friendly flights, causing major revenue losses, idle ships, and crew layoffs. This reminds us of the words that Robert Burns made famous: "The best laid schemes o' mice an' men gang aft a-gley." Of course plans are only as good as their assumptions about the future. A realistic control system collects data from both the internal operating activities and the external environment. This means that uncontrollable variations are not charged to operations error and that improper corrective actions are not taken. In this light, a fuel budget revision and the selective cancellation of Friendly flights show a most important managerial response to changed conditions.

AREAS WHERE CONTROL IS NECESSARY

As with the managerial function of planning, control is of concern to both the total organization and the individual manager in his particular department. It is therefore possible to talk about areas of control in a broad general sense as well as in a very specific sense as it relates to such functions as personnel management, marketing, research and development, production, finance and accounting, or any other functional specialties. It is not our purpose to treat control in great detail, but rather, to develop an overall insight into some areas where control is exercised.

Before specific examples from production, marketing, and accounting/finance are presented, a guideline must be mentioned. The *principles* of control for the various levels of operations will be similar whether we refer to *production* operations, *sales* operations, or *credit* operations.

CONTROL IN THE OPERATION OF PRODUCTIVE SYSTEMS

The following three major topical areas will be discussed.

1. Quality control and inspection.
2. Production planning and control.
3. Inventory control.

The quality is defined by a set of specifications. Quality can be too high or too low.

QUALITY CONTROL AND INSPECTION

The quality of a product is defined by a set of specifications governing the functional performance, composition, strength, shape, dimensions, workmanship, color, and finish of that product. Good quality is attained when a product or a service fully satisfies the purpose for which it is designed. The better the quality, the greater the cost of production. Moreover, there will always be some upper quality limit that, when surpassed, would require the consumer to pay a price for something which in her judgment she does not need.

Quality Control. Quality control is the recognition and removal of identifiable causes of defects and variations from set standards. Various techniques can be used for the systematic observation of quality and interpretation of the causes of variability. But the objective of quality control goes beyond the identification of defects to discover what is causing them. Then, once quality control has pinpointed the *why* of defects, corrective action can be taken.

Inspection is the testing of products to compare them with specified standards.

Inspection. This is the application of test and measuring devices to compare products and performance with specified standards. Inspection determines whether a given item falls within specified limits of variability and therefore is acceptable. Inspection can aid in identifying the causes of defective work. Some of the tangible benefits of quality control and inspection include a higher degree of customer satisfaction, the uniform quality necessary for interchangeable parts, and prevention of waste of labor and machine time by interrupting out-of-control processes for adjustment.

Determination of Points of Inspection. Where and when to inspect is determined by analyzing the stages in the manufacturing of the product. Generally, lower-priced products require fewer points of inspection than will higher-priced products. If a fountain pen, upon completion, is found to be defective, it can be scrapped with a very minimum loss in labor and material costs. In contrast, if a television set is carried through to completion and then found to be defective, the loss would be considerable. In determining points of inspection it is therefore necessary to weigh the cost of inspection against the potential savings in terms of scrap reduction and reduced labor costs. Defective items should be rejected at points which will result in the lowest production costs. As far as work in process is concerned, inspection may be required at any of the following points.

1. Before or after key operations where there is a high probability of defects, that is, at each major machine.
2. Before costly operations, where checking the accuracy of fabricated parts will prevent trouble and delay in assembly.
3. Where succeeding operations could conceal defects.
4. At the last step of any logically grouped series of operations.
5. After each setup of a job on a machine.

6. Anywhere along a single assembly line where inspectors may sample work.
7. At the close of departmental responsibilities.

Layout of Inspection Activities. Inspection may take place either on the floor as production is in process, or products may be transferred to some centralized location for inspection. In the former case, quality is checked at the machine or where the operation is being performed. In the latter case, goods are moved to the central inspection point after they are complete.

Inspection may take place on the floor or in a centralized area.

The advantages of floor inspection include these: (1) defects are quickly discovered and corrected, (2) the handling of materials is reduced, and (3) line layout of machinery need not be disrupted. The principal disadvantages of floor inspection are that (1) costs are higher because of the need for more skilled inspectors and tools and (2) the inspectors are frequently under pressure to accept work in order to avoid delays and interruptions of production.

Centralized inspection has a number of advantages: (1) there is no pressure on inspectors, (2) the flow of the production process is not interrupted, and (3) larger quantities of work can be checked. The principal disadvantage of central inspection is that defects may not be detected until considerable labor and material costs have been incurred.

Closely related to the decision of whether floor or central inspection is most appropriate is the decision as to whether each piece is to be inspected or if there is to be inspection by samples. Sample inspection means that at certain intervals a small percentage of the total product being produced is subject to inspection. Statistical techniques allow one to predict that all products will meet the same quality requirements that the items selected for inspection meet.

PRODUCTION PLANNING AND CONTROL

Production planning and control systems coordinate the use of manpower machines and materials efficiently.

The purpose of a production planning and control system (PPC), is to integrate and coordinate the use of manpower, machines, and materials for efficient output of goods to meet sales requirements. The production planning and control department is usually organized separately from the manufacturing function to relieve supervisors from certain nonoperating responsibilities.

Production planning and control (PPC) was discussed in some detail in Chapter 17, Operations Management, and is comprised of a series of related activities, each predetermined and timed to coordinate the total manufacturing program. It guides production by preparing and issuing manufacturing orders which direct the use of facilities, materials, and labor to the output of the required quantity of goods. It regulates the how, when, and where work is to be done. As noted in Chapter 18, Quantitative Decision Making, linear programming models are often used to develop production plans and schedules.

Benefits of the Production Planning and Control System. Every organization needs some type of system to plan and control production. How elaborate and detailed the system is will depend on the nature and size of the operation.

Effective production control systems can promote steady production, eliminate confusion, and reduce investments in inventory.

Tasks of Production Planning and Control. There are four primary tasks that every production planning and control system must accomplish. These include routing, scheduling, dispatching, and follow-up.

Routing refers to the designation of the processing methods and the sequence of operations for the manufacture of each part, assembly, or product. Routing is therefore concerned with the sequential flow of the product through the total manufacturing process, and receives most emphasis in the job shop or mixed process-production organizations. An analogy would be an individual who planned to travel by car from New York to Los Angeles. Before commencing the trip, he would probably procure a highway map of the entire country and then mark the roads he proposed to take.

> Routing refers to the sequential flow of the production throughout the total manufacturing process.

Scheduling deals with the time element and is concerned with establishing the rate of output and the beginning and end dates for the various phases of production. Any deviation from schedule will throw the entire manufacturing process off balance. It can prove costly since some departments or work stations may have to shut down because of unavailability of parts or subassemblies. Using the travel analogy cited previously, once the route to be followed was determined, it would then be necessary to block out the trip in terms of time segments. Usually this would take the form of specifying the number of hours to be driven each day and the number of miles to be covered.

> Scheduling establishes the rate of output and the beginning and ending times for production.

Dispatching represents the paper control of production planning and control. It involves the preparation of manufacturing orders and the clerical control of work in the plant. Depending on the nature of the operation, these manufacturing orders may be very involved. They specify which machines are to be used for which jobs, contain detailed engineering data, information for machine setups, and other technical data. At a minimum, the manufacturing order will contain all pertinent data with respect to routing and scheduling. Continuing our analogy of the traveler, dispatching would correspond to the making of motel reservations at the beginning of each day for that evening, compiling gasoline and mileage records, and keeping track of expenses for lodging, food, and miscellaneous items. All of the foregoing are planning activities, and thus are *pre*control.

> Dispatching is the preparation of manufacturing orders and clerical control of the working plant.

The final task of PPC is *follow-up*, which is designed to assure the achievement of output goals. Follow-up will require that the PPC department receive constant feedback on the status of production throughout the entire operation. What is actually happening must be monitored on a continuous basis and if deviations from plans exist, they must be pinpointed and corrective action taken. In a large plant, this will necessitate a very elaborate reporting system, using an on-line real time MIS. This follow-up is *concurrent* control.

Factors Influencing the Design of the Production Planning and Control System. As noted in Chapter 17, Operations Management, there are two basic ways to set up productive systems: *production line* for continuous manufacture or assembly and *process* setup for a work center layout. The high volume, interchangeable parts, and continuous materials flow of product lines are very different from the job order and work center routing of a process layout.

In production lines for single products, the path to success starts with good process design. Programs like BALANCE, (see Figure 18-1) are used to develop an efficient assembly line. If there will always be a single product running through the line, then a PPC is really a facilitator for *materials flow* into and away from the production line, and is a relatively simple system.

If multiple products use the same line or facilities, and if the rates of consumption of the raw materials or finished goods is uneven, detailed production scheduling is required to keep utilization high. Models like Program LINPRO are often used for more complex scheduling. The schedule then becomes the *pre*control for the line or lines, involving both timing and quantity of production, batch by batch. This is called *intermittent continuous flow* and is typical of all but the largest production organizations.

> Job shops are used for small independent production jobs.

In job shops, where the size of individual production jobs is small and specifications vary from customer to customer, or where the materials and production processes changes with the job, a production line would be inefficient if not impossible. Job shops are organized into work centers, and high-volume production planning and control is very complex.

The Warner and Swasey Turning Machine Division in Cleveland, Ohio, is a *job shop* that has a large computer exercising shop floor control over their numerically controlled machine tool production. The Ingersoll-Rand plant at Mocksville, North Carolina, has an equivalent system for manufacturing the components for its compressors and controlling parts through to final assembly. These are large organizations with hundreds of millions of dollars of revenues annually. There are small machine shops doing work to customer order that are also classical job shops. In each case, the problems of routing, scheduling, dispatching, and follow-up are the same, although the size of the task is obviously different.

The design of a PPC, then, depends on the *kind* of production system, the *variety* of products, the overall *scale* or size of the operation, and the *value* of the individual items being produced.

INVENTORY CONTROL

Controlling inventories means deciding at what levels inventories can be economically maintained and then holding them at these levels. Inventory is found in three forms: raw materials, goods in process, and finished products. Each of these stages must be controlled, because with every unit of inventory, there are certain cost advantages and disadvantages.

Functions of Inventories. If inventories cost money to maintain, why carry them? First, inventories serve to offset errors in forecasting. Whether it be raw material, purchased parts, or manufactured parts, it is virtually impossible for the firm always to predict exactly what its needs will be. Rather than face the

> Inventories serve to offset errors in forecasting and avoid potential loss from cutback.

possibility of incurring the tremendous costs which would be involved in shutting down the operation because of a lack of necessary production parts, it is more feasible to carry a safety stock, or buffer inventory as a form of insurance. Similarly, the firm cannot predict exactly what customer demand for its own product will be. To avoid a potential loss in sales due to shortages, it becomes necessary to carry inventories of finished goods.

A second function of inventories is to permit more economical utilization of equipment, buildings, and manpower when the nature of business is such that fluctuations in demand exist. The demand for many types of products is seasonal in nature. This means that perhaps as much as 70 to 80 percent of annual sales may occur within a period of only two or three months. Rather than producing enough to meet the projected demand all at once and then completely suspending operations for a period of time, it is often more economical for the firm to even out its production over the entire year. To realize the labor cost advantages of a level production schedule requires the building up of inventories.

Inventories allow for the leveling of production.

Third, inventories enable the company to purchase or manufacture in economic lot sizes. Every time a particular item is purchased or manufactured, certain fixed costs are incurred. In the case of manufacturing something, the machine(s) must be set up or prepared, and this costs money in the form of labor. The setup cost is the same whether 10 or 100 items are produced. If, within every two-week period, 20 of the items are needed, it does not make sense to keep incurring the same setup cost over and over again every two weeks. Similarly, in purchasing, suppliers offer quantity discounts and large shipments often have lower freight costs. It becomes much more eocnomical to produce a three-month supply and thereby spread the fixed cost over more items. This is what is meant by purchasing or manufacturing in economic lot sizes. It is the quantity of goods that balance the fixed costs of purchasing or manufacturing something against the cost of carrying the inventory.

Inventories enable the company to purchase in lot sizes.

Finally, inventories serve to minimize the adverse effects of ahead-of-schedule or behind-schedule production. If production is ahead of schedule and an inventory of needed parts is available, it can continue without interruption. If production is behind schedule, then inventories can be drawn on to meet requirements.

Having inventories available to perform these functions involves a price. The price is the cost of maintaining inventories. The goal of inventory control is to establish levels of inventory that will serve to minimize the company's cost and maximize its revenues. Although the relevant costs will vary, there are some more likely to be relevant in most situations.

Relevant Costs Involved in Inventory Control. The relevant costs associated with inventories can be divided into three major categories: (1) those concerned with the lot sizes a firm should produce or purchase, (2) those suggesting an inventory buildup, and (3) those that discourage an inventory buildup. Each of these categories will be discussed separately.

1. Relevant Costs Relating to Lot Sizes. Quantity discounts are the first of the relevant costs associated with lot sizes. Lower unit purchase prices are usually available if items are purchased in larger lots. Quantity discounts tend to encourage purchase of large lot sizes and hence larger inventories.

Direct material costs are a second factor in determining the proper lot size. There are cases where a relatively fixed number of units are scrapped every time a piece of equipment is set up for production purposes. If three units are scrapped before the correct adjustments can be made and then three good units produced, there is an average of two units of raw material used per unit of output. If, however, 10 units are produced, the average raw material used is only 1.3 units. This yields a lower average direct material cost, and therefore encourages larger lot sizes and inventories.

As discussed previously, setup costs are fixed and are incurred every time a production run is inaugurated. Larger lot sizes mean few production runs per year and consequently, lower setup costs. Again, however, as lot sizes increase the average inventory also increases. This element encourages larger inventories.

Another relevant cost is that of direct labor. Labor efficiency will usually increase after a warm-up period, leading to a higher average efficiency as lot sizes increase. This tends to promote larger lot sizes and inventories.

Finally, procurement costs are also a factor. The cost of preparing an order is usually independent of the size of the order, or else increases but at a relatively lower rate. As lot sizes increase, fewer orders will be processed and average annual procurement costs will decrease. As with quantity discounts, therefore, procurement costs tend to encourage the purchases of larger lot sizes and hence also larger inventories.

2. Costs Suggesting an Inventory Buildup. If a company is caught short in terms of being able to meet the demand for a particular product, they will be forced to work overtime or add additional shifts.

Both overtime and additional shifts require that some premium be added to the regular wage. Hiring, training, and layoff costs are also factors of importance. If the firm is unable to supply current market demand, more people may have to be added to the payroll and this will necessitate additional expenses. After the firm catches up with demand, layoffs will occur, and this also entails such costs as unemployment compensation.

Owning sufficient equipment to meet peak demand also means that a portion of the plant will be standing idle during other times. These higher fixed costs mean a higher total production to cover all costs (BEP). A final factor that encourages inventory buildup is the possibility of lost orders, production delays, and customer dissatisfaction. Inventories enable firms to meet delivery dates and eliminate delays due to material shortages.

3. Costs that Discourage Inventory Buildup. Inventory buildup and a level production strategy, then, are favored by labor cost savings, higher productivity, a better balance between capacity and demand, and improved customer service levels. Costs that tend to discourage inventory include deterioration and obsolescence; taxes; interest or investment opportunity loss; and storage costs for insurance, handling, and security.

In summary, there are two forces at work, one encouraging and one discouraging the purchase and production in larger lot sizes. These relationships are graphically depicted in Figure 20-3. What the firm must do is find the lot size or reorder quantity that results in the minimum cost. A number of techniques are available for making the necessary cost comparisons.

An economic order quantity (EOQ) of 400 units can be illustrated by the low point in the total cost curve shown in Figure 20-3.

Economic Order Quantity. The model for ordering and controlling inventory is often called a sawtooth inventory curve because of its slope. For example, suppose that we assume an annual requirement (R) of inventory of 2400 units or an average of 200 units per month. The inventory model would appear as in Figure 20-4.

From previous derivations the formula to derive the economic order quantity (EOQ) has been found to be:

$$EOQ = \sqrt{\frac{2RS}{C}}$$

where R equals the yearly requirement,

S equals the procurement or setup costs per order,

and C equals carrying costs per order.

Therefore, in the example, if we know that S is $20 and C is $.60 per unit, we can compute EOQ.

$$EOQ = \sqrt{\frac{2 \times 2400 \times 20}{0.60}} = 160,000 = 400 \text{ units}$$

FIGURE 20-3

Graphical Model of EOQ

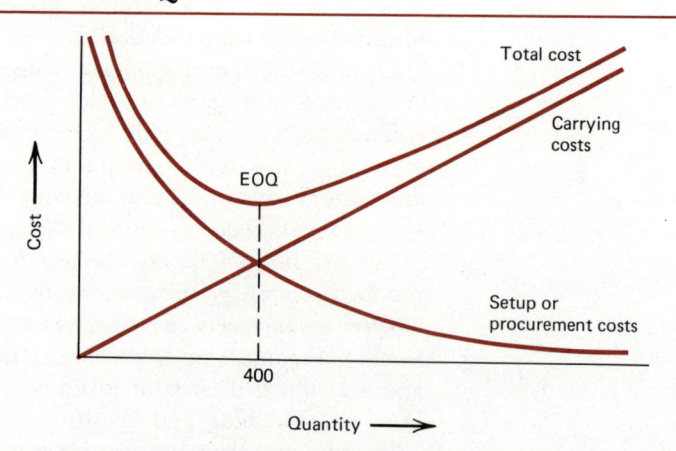

CONTROLLING OPERATIONS 543

EOQ formulas can be used to solve for the proper economic order of quantity.

A computer package, Program EOQ, will solve for the optimal quantity of an item to purchase for conditions where setup costs, carrying costs, and demand are known with certainty, and when there are price breaks for larger volume purchases.[6] EOQ will also choose purchase quantities when warehouse space is limited—a not unusual situation. A very large proportion of manufacturers in the United States uses inventory models in everyday management, because of the large investments and the complexity of the problem.

Many inventory management problems may be corrected by common sense.

Many problems such as inventory management problems may be corrected by common sense and listening to plant employees. For example, one of the first suggestions made by a "quality circle" group at a plant producing lawnmowers related to the placement of oxygen tanks for a welding job. It seems that these tanks were kept at the far end of the production line and every time the welder ran out of oxygen the line was shut down for an hour or two. Employees suggested that the storage cage be brought to the point in the line where welding was done. The projected yearly savings was $200,000 in line down time. Management was amazed and asked the employees, "Why did you not tell us this years ago?" To which the employees replied, "You didn't ask."

BUDGETING

NATURE OF BUDGETS

Budgets are prepared as a part of management's planning function. The firm's objectives and goals are considered when budgets are being prepared. But budgeting is more than planning; it is a control device. A comprehensive operating budget presents a plan for the future expressed in dollars. Continuous comparisons between the budget and actual results are made, and significant variances point to the need for corrective action. Thus, the budget becomes a yardstick or standard for measuring actual performance.

A comprehensive budget is a plan for the future expressed in dollars.

A comprehensive operating budget includes a sales budget, a production budget, an expense budget, a cash budget, and a capital expenditures budget.

From the various budgets, a comprehensive operating budget can be prepared which estimates the firm's earnings and financial position in the future. The individual budgets and the comprehensive operating budget become the standard against which actual performance can be compared.

Budgets are frequently prepared for the following year. Since conditions frequently change, however, a yearly budget often becomes outdated. Budgets for shorter time periods, a quarter or a month, are less likely to become outdated due to changing conditions.

---

[6]Roy D. Harris and Michael J. Maggard, *Computer Models in Operations Management,* 2nd ed., New York, Harper & Row, 1977, pp. 41–54.

FIGURE 20-4

Simplified Model of Inventory Fluctuations

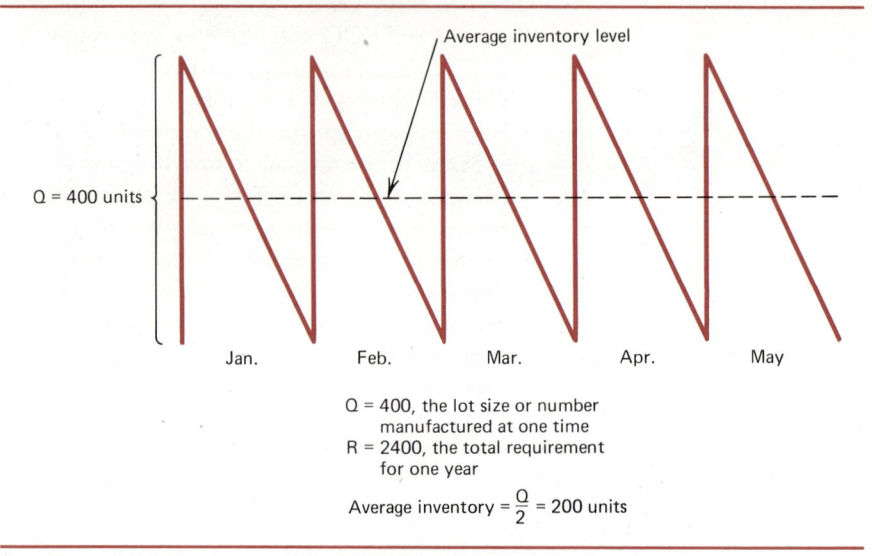

Q = 400, the lot size or number manufactured at one time
R = 2400, the total requirement for one year
Average inventory = $\frac{Q}{2}$ = 200 units

Source: Elwood S. Buffa, *Basic Production Management,* New York, Wiley, 1975, p. 463.

FLEXIBLE (VARIABLE) BUDGETS

Since operating budgets, production budgets, expense budgets, and so forth, depend so much on the volume of sales or output of the firm, and since output is an estimate and subject to variance, companies frequently use a flexible budget. This provides a standard by which to measure performance at varying levels of output. Budgets are prepared for different levels of output and when actual output is known, a budget for that level is available. The preparation of a flexible budget centers around the division of costs between fixed costs and variable costs. Some costs (such as the president's salary) will remain about the same regardless of the firm's volume of output. Other costs (such as sales commissions) vary with the volume of sales. Still other costs vary with output but not necessarily in direct proportion with the volume of output. For example, the more electricity one uses the less per kilowatt hour it costs. In preparing a flexible budget, costs are budgeted for varying levels of output, considering what the different cost (fixed variable or semivariable) should be at each budgeted level of output. The use of flexible budgets enables management to control costs more effectively at different levels of output.

> Flexible budgets provide a standard by which to insure performance at varying levels of output.

RESPONSIBILITY ACCOUNTING

To better enable management to control operations, responsibility accounting is frequently employed. In responsibility accounting, costs are budgeted for responsibility centers and actual costs are assigned to the responsibility centers. A

STANDARD COSTS

Standard costs are management's best estimates of what it should cost to efficiently manufacture products.

Flexible budgets are often difficult to devise for a manufacturing concern that makes a number of products. A different method of budgeting, utilizing *standard costs*, is frequently used in such cases. Standard costs are costs based on management's best judgment as to what it should cost to efficiently manufacture a product, rather than calculations of actual costs after production. Standard costs have the advantage of being assignable to production before the product is made. If variances from standard are not minimal, they must be analyzed for causes.

A standard cost system is of particular importance to manufacturing control for it is a valid and meaningful yardstick by which actual performance can be measured in dollar terms, assuming quality control standards are also being maintained.

In a standard cost system, the costs of manufacturing the various products of the firm are determined before production occurs. All elements of manufacturing costs are included in the standard cost of a product. Actual cost of producing the product is later determined and the two are compared. The comparison of standard and actual costs indicates areas that may require management attention. A detailed breakdown of the difference between standard and actual costs, which are called *variances*, allows management to pinpoint the area requiring attention.

The difference between standard and actual costs are called variances.

To illustrate, assume that the Head Company has established the following standard costs per unit for its Product X-2.

Materials—18 lb. per unit at $1 per lb.	$18.00
Direct labor—4 hr. per unit at $3.50 per hr.	14.00
Overhead—$2 per standard direct labor hr.	8.00
Total standard cost per unit	$40.00

During July, the Head Company produced 10,000 units of product X-2. The company used 190,000 lb. of material costing $.95 per pound or a total material cost of $180,500. To product the 10,000 units the company incurred 41,000 hr. of direct labor at a cost of $3.60 per hour, or a total direct labor cost of $147,600. During July, the company incurred $85,000 of overhead costs.

Under these assumptions a comparison of standard and actual costs reveals the following.

	Standard		Actual	
Materials	(18 lb at $1 x 10,000)	$180,000	(190,000 at $.95)	$180,500
Direct Labor	(4 hr at $3.50 x 10,000)	140,000	(41,000 hr at $3.60)	147,600
Overhead	(4 hr at $2 x 10,000)	80,000		85,000
Total	(10,000 units at $40)	$400,000	(10,000 units at $41.31)	$413,100

The total difference between standard and actual cost for July is $13,100, an unfavorable variance. Knowing this, however, does not help to pinpoint the person or persons responsible for the variance. A further breakdown of the variance is more helpful. Material and labor variances can be identified and broken down between quantity variance and price variance. For example, a quantity variance is determined by calculating the difference between standard quantities which were used and multiplying this difference by the standard price.

During July, the Head Company's material and direct labor variances would be calculated as shown below.

Material:
  Quantity Variance—
    Standard quantity (10,000 units x 18 lb)   180,000 lb
    Actual quantity   190,000 lb

      Excessive use of materials   10,000 lb
      Stand material price $ 1.00

        Unfavorable material quantity variance $ 10,000

The breakdown of material variances enables management to locate problem areas and then take whatever corrective action is indicated.

ZERO-BASE BUDGETING

Zero-base budgeting means that every department's budget should be built from the ground up every year.

Another budgeting technique growing out of the increased demands for accountability is *zero-base budgeting*. It can be defined as the concept that every department or agency's budget should be built from the ground up every year. Programs and tests already conducted should be reevaluated to see if they can be done more cheaply or eliminated.

This approach was pioneered at Texas Instruments, Inc. and subsequently implemented in the state of Georgia by former governor Jimmy Carter. As president, Mr. Carter required implementation of zero-base budgeting throughout the major agencies of the federal government.[7]

Not all agencies are pleased with these developments. To many managers, evaluating programs already established is an undue burden appended to the administrative work load. Furthermore, most agencies and businesses have grown accustomed to thinking in terms of adding more funds to existing programs rather than cutbacks. Under President Reagan, even more federal budget trimming is taking place. Zero base budgeting should assist in this endeavor.

PROJECT AND SCHEDULING CONTROL DEVICES

In this section brief discussions will be given of *Project Control* (PERT/CPM); (PPBS); uses of *simulation* for training and decision making; and finally, analysis of an organization's *control structure* as a means of effective system design.

---

[7]"Zero-Base Budgeting: A Way To Cut Spending or a Gimmick," *U.S. News and World Report*, September 20, 1976, pp. 79–82.

PROJECT CONTROL

The effective management of complex and nonrecurring capital requires all of the precontrol and current control procedures set forth in this chapter—but *without* the existing standards. That is, while management can communicate the desired *results* and even specify how the final facility should look, or perform, the real difficulty comes when seeking ways to plan and currently control progress *toward* the specified end item. Large-scale, high technology industrial plants, major shipbuilding activities, and aerospace engineering and development projects, are one-of-a-kind activities presenting these control problems.[8]

Critical path techniques trace through the network of tasks that must be completed in order to finish a complex project.

Although not a panacea, critical path techniques have been found useful in the analysis and planning for such projects. The goal is to dissect thoroughly the completed building (or plant, or space system) into its various component *physical* parts; then analyze each element for the design, development, building, and test phases to complete it, then to install, check out, and test with the rest of the jobs. The result is a network of purchasing, design, and physical tasks, each of which must be completed in order to finish the entire project. Program CRIT solves such a project network for its longest path.[9]

PERT AND CPM

PERT (program evaluation and review technique) and CPM (critical path method) are two closely related techniques that are often used in project control. CPM was developed in 1957 by Morgan Walker of Dupont and James Kelly of Remington Rand. PERT was developed in connection with the Polaris weapons system. Both have been widely used in aerospace work.

Although each of these techniques has its unique terminology, they conceptually differ only in that CPM attempts to systematically determine the expected times of completion of the total project and subprojects (tasks) that comprise the total project, whereas PERT goes further and attempts to estimate the *time variances* associated with these expected times of completion. PERT deals more directly with the problem of *uncertainty with respect to time* than does CPM.

Figure 20-5 illustrates how a PERT chart is drawn to represent the tasks that must be completed before the total project (represented by 1) can be completed. The critical path is illustrated by the heavy line that runs through the sequence of tasks that has the longest expected time of completion. In Figure 20-5 the unique terminology of CPM is not used, but is adapted to show how closely CPM relates to PERT.

The total expected time to complete a given task is determined by examining all the Te alternatives beforehand and selecting the largest total leading to that task. For example, task 3 cannot begin until tasks 4 and 5 have been finished. No matter how early task 4 is completed, the project must still wait until task 5 is completed before task 3 can begin.

---

[8]Harris and Maggard, *Computer Models,* pp. 78–98.
[9]For a detailed review of a number of techniques available, see L. A. Digman and Gary I. Green, "A Framework for Evaluating Network Planning and Control Techniques," *Research Management,* January 1981, pp. 10–17.

FIGURE 20-5

PERT and CPM Flow Diagram for a Five-Task Project

O = Task number that must be completed before the next task can begin
Te = Earliest expected time to complete the task (days, hours, weeks, etc.)
TE = Total expected time to complete a given task
V = Variance in time associated with the completion of task

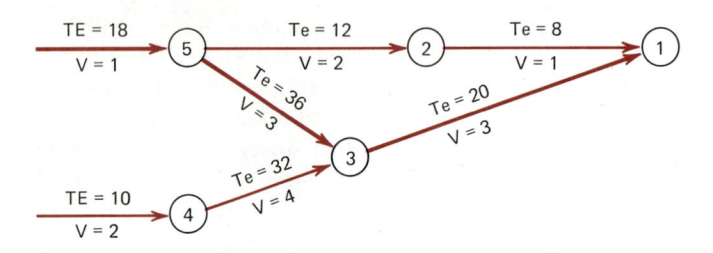

According to expected times, it will take longer to complete task 5 than task 4. Thus task 5 is selected as the critical task leading to task 3, and the total expected time to complete task 3 is 54 because 18 + 36 is larger than 10 + 32. This method is continued until the total project 1 has been reached. The total expected time to complete the project is 74 (18 + 36 + 20), and the time variance associated with the completion of the project is 7(1 + 3 + 3). The critical path is 5, 3, 1, 20, the longest path through the project. The time variance in this example means that the project could be completed 7 days earlier (74 - 7 = 67) or seven days later (74 + 7 = 81) than the total expected time. The critical path method, however, is concerned only with the total expected time to complete the project and not the time variances associated with the project. Thus, PERT is broader in scope than CPM.

The critical path is the longest path throgh a complete project.

HUMAN ASPECTS OF MANAGERIAL CONTROL

Control is not only an important but a necessary function for the individual manager and the organization as a whole. It is important to note, however, that it is people and their performance who become the subjects of control, and when this human element is introduced problems invariably result. The problems are a reflection of the emotional response of those being controlled to the control system.[10]

In the past, management's approach to installing control systems has often been based on a negative set of assumptions about people. As a result many control systems have been either structured or administered in a negative sense. That is, consciously or unconsciously they have been used to exert pressure, both

---
[10]This section of the chapter draws very heavily from Douglas McGregor, *The Professional Manager*, New York: McGraw-Hill Book Co., 1967.

as a basis for disciplining people and as a way to force compliance with externally imposed standards.

UNINTENDED CONSEQUENCES OF CONTROL

Where such negative control systems exist, several unintended consequences of control have developed. Douglas McGregor has delineated them as follows.[11]

1. Widespread antagonism to the controls and to those who administer them.
2. Successful resistance and noncompliance, not just by a few people, but by many, and not alone at the bottom of the organization, but at all levels up to the top.
3. Unreliable performance information because of 1 and 2 above.
4. The necessity for close surveillance. This results in a dilution of delegation that is expensive of managerial time as well as having other poor consequences.
5. High admininstrative cost.

The following example illustrates all five of these consequences.

> *Not long ago, the Boy Scouts of America revealed that membership figures coming in from the field had been falsified. In response to the pressures of a national membership drive, people within the organization had vastly overstated the number of new Boy Scouts. To their chagrin, the leaders found something that other managers have also discovered: organizational control systems often produced unintended consequences. The drive to increase membership had motivated people to increase the number of new members reported, but it had not motivated them to increase the number of Boy Scouts actually enrolled.*[12]

McGregor further notes that these consequences are readily observable inside any large organization, and to varying degrees are characteristic of all management control systems. This should not be interpreted to mean that negative consequences are the inevitable result of all attempts at exercising the control function.

The key to a successful system lies in how it is administered. Some principles of effective administration of control systems will be pointed out and discussed shortly, but first the reasons why these consequences sometimes develop must be considered.

REASONS FOR THESE UNINTENDED CONSEQUENCES OF CONTROL

The reason for the occasional negative reaction to control systems is explained by how people react to perceived threat. If people feel that the system represents a threat to their overall security, they will adopt a pattern of behavior that in their

---

[11] Ibid., p. 117.
[12] Cortlandt Cammann and David A. Nadler, "Fit Control Systems to Your Managerial Style," *Harvard Business Review*, January-February 1976, p. 65.

estimation will defeat the system and thereby eliminate, or at least temper, the threat.

McGregor lists the primary conditions under which threat is likely to be perceived.

1. Where punishment, as opposed to support and help in meeting standards and objectives is emphasized.
2. Where trust is lacking in the relationships involved.
3. Where feedback negatively affects the individual in terms of his employment relationship and career expectations.[13]

FUNDAMENTAL GUIDELINES OF EFFECTIVE CONTROL ADMINISTRATION

If a control system is to accomplish its purpose it must not only be structurally sound from a technical standpoint, but it must be properly administered. The objective of effective administration is to prevent or minimize the human problems which might otherwise arise. There are four important guidelines to effective control administration.

First, the manager must communicate, discuss, and gain the highest possible degree of commitment among his people to the goals and objectives of the unit or department and their individual jobs. The greater the extent to which people are committed to a particular objective, the higher their level of job performance tends to be. The team members must be convinced that the objective is important and that accomplishment will be recognized and awarded.

Subordinates must be educated in the purposes of control.

Second, emphasis should be placed on educating subordinates with respect to the purpose of control. The control procedure does not exist for the purpose of finding out who made mistakes and who should be disciplined and subject to various types of pressure. It should be clearly communicated that the control system is a tool to help the individual perform at her full level of capability. Rewards must be specific when corrections or improvements are made. Cost accountants and quality control personnel should be viewed as those gathering valuable data, rather than as watchdogs in the event of emergencies.

Third, in day-to-day dealings with subordinates, and in particular those dealings involving aspects of control, the manager must establish a climate of help and support and must create a climate where employees are convinced that he or she is truly concerned about helping them to do the best job possible.

Fourth, in order to gain commitment and to reinforce the true purpose of control, managers should continually provide feedback on the status of achievement and progress toward objectives.

Successful performance of the control function goes far beyond the designing of a control system that is technically sound. Like all other aspects of management, the human element must also receive consideration if the desired results are to be achieved.

---

[13]Ibid., p. 119.

SUMMARY

Controls help organizational members achieve desired results, in terms of quality, quantity, timing, cost, or combinations of these elements. Plans or standards indicate the target; performance is measured over time; the measurements are compared with the standard and evaluated; and corrective actions may be taken to change the activity—or to change the plan if indicated. Standards, in quantifying goals, help to increase efficiency, conserve assets, improve quality, safety, performance, and costs, and, when completed organizationwide, help achieve balance.

Planning is a form of precontrol, and guides actual performance. Current or dynamic controls operate with the activities themselves. Postcontrol, or evaluation, takes place after the fact, and aims at future improvement. Principal issues in all control systems are the choice of standards in essential key result areas, and the choice and frequency of measurements to verify performance. The management-by-exception principle applies to control reporting, since management is more concerned with significant deviations from standard than long reports of goal achievement.

The control principles studied in this chapter were applied to the area of quality control, production control and inventory control. Production control consists of routing, scheduling, dispatching, and follow-up. Linear programming is often used in production control projects. Quality control is a system for identifying and removing causes of defects in products and materials. Statistically quality control is used in maintaining assurance of quality standards. Inventory control is primarily concerned with maintaining an adequate supply of materials or products on hand while keeping storage and other inventory costs to a minimum. An economic order quantity can be computed to assist in this area.

Budgeting is a control device used in every function of business and government. Flexible budgets allow one to determine financial needs at different possible levels of operation. Standard costs can be computed to check actual costs, to see if they are reasonable. Planning-programming-budgeting is an integrated system of goal setting, planning, and budgeting used by the federal government.

Zero-base budgeting is a recently developed system of budgeting based on the principle that every department or agency's budget should be built from the ground up.

Project control needs such as those in aerospace have given birth to scheduling control techniques such as PERT and CPM. Both are systematic processes for determining the expected times for completion of projects.

Simulation is often used for control purposes by simulating a portion of an organization and examining control problems that arise.

Technically sound control systems must also be administered properly. This requires gaining commitment, educating people regarding the reasons for control, and establishing a climate of helpfulness and support.

SUMMARY CHART

Elements of Control Systems

1. Standards or plans
2. Measurement processes
3. Comparison of standards and results
4. Corrective action

Key Control Points in Production	*Control Devices*
1. Quality Control	Statistical Quality Control (SQC)
2. Production Planning and Control	Linear Programming (LINPRO) or Simulation
3. Inventory Control	EOQ

Budgeting

    Flexible budgets: For different forecasts

    Standard costs: To determine what it should cost

    Zero-Base Budgeting: Budgets should be evaluated from the ground up.

Project Control

CPM: Expected times and critical path

PERT: Expected times of completed project and time variances

Simulation: Experimentation with decision variables and control effects

Human Aspects of Managerial Control

Fundamentals of Effective Control Administration

1. Communication
2. Education
3. Supportive Climate
4. Feedback

DISCUSSION QUESTIONS

1. Describe the four factors that can inhibit the effective functioning of a control system.
2. Briefly describe the four essential elements of a control system.
3. Describe the factors involved in determining whether a product should be

inspected by floor inspection or centralized inspection. What general factor is involved?
4. Describe each of the four primary tasks of production planning and control.
5. What should a company do in order to minimize its inventory costs, but still maintain the advantages of having an inventory on hand?
6 "The main objective of a quality control system is to assume the highest possible quality." Do you agree with this statement? Explain why or why not.
7. Why do companies use flexible budgets?
8. Standard costs systems allow companies to check for out-of-line costs. What is the difference between actual and standard costs called?
9. Explain the purpose of a responsibility center.
10. Why are corporations and the federal government moving toward zero-base budgeting?
11. Discuss some of the unintended consequences that may arise as a result of control systems and why they arise. What are the guidelines to effective control administration?

APPLICATION EXERCISES AND CASES

THE SIROCCO COMPANY—INTRODUCTION OF A BUDGETARY CONTROL PLAN[14]

The Sirocco Company, located in a large Midwestern city, manufactured and sold hot-air heating equipment for residential installations. Since its incorporation the company had experienced a steady and satisfactory growth. About two years ago several new designs and sizes of both oil and gas furnaces were added to the rather restricted product line that had been adhered to previously. Concurrently, distribution was extended to the Eastern seaboard and the Southeast, as well as to a wider coverage of the Middle West market.

As a result of these two moves, sales volume increased rapidly until it reached a level about double that of any prior year. Net profits, however, moved in the opposite direction. The president of the company, who was also its principal stockholder, was deeply concerned about this poor showing and set out to determine the reasons for it. He was convinced that, while increased taxes and higher wage rates had some bearing on the lower profit margins, there were other more fundamental causes.

The president asked his son to undertake an investigation of the situation and make recommendations. The son had been with the company six years following his graduation from college. During this time he had been successively in the

---
[14]Paul E. Holden, Frank K. Schellenberger, Walter A. Diehm, *Selected Case Problems In Industrial Management*, 2nd ed., Englewood Cliffs, N.J., Prentice-Hall, 1962, p. 329.

Engineering, Manufacturing, Sales, and Accounting Departments, learning something of the major phases of the company's operations with a view toward taking over some of the administrative burden from his father.

In the course of his investigation the son discovered the following conditions, which he believed were primarily responsible for the recent period of "profitless prosperity":

Although the company had established broad company policies and objectives, it had never instituted any set method of systematic planning and control of company operations. No attempt had ever been made to control expenditures or determine financial requirements for the fiscal periods of the business. There was little or no coordination between any of the departments except that which could be accomplished personally by the president. This problem had not been too serious previously because the company's operations had been small enough for the president to coordinate the activities of the departments on a personal basis through conferences with the various department heads. However, the operations of the company had now grown so large that it was impossible for one man to provide this coordination effectively.

An analysis of the cost-accounting system in use showed that only historical costs were provided. Standard costs were considered by the controller to be the lowest costs ever incurred. Therefore, any measurement of current results involved nothing more than a comparison with records of prior periods. The controller agreed that, because of the many variables which could enter the picture, this type of comparison was not an adequate measure of performance.

It was discovered that expenditures for administrative expenses, such as officers' salaries, office expense, credits and collections, accounting, personnel, and the like, were taking ten cents out of every sales dollar. Administrative expenses had increased over 200 per cent during the period that profits were declining.

Sales estimates had been made in the past by the sales manager on a very unscientific basis. As a matter of fact, his estimates of sales consisted of little more than what he thought his salesmen should sell. Since his estimates had consistently been too optimistic, the head of the Production Department paid little attention to them and produced what he deemed necessary in the light of past experience. As a result, there was little tie-in between sales and production. On several occasions, production of one product had to be discontinued to make way for a customer's order which could not be filled out of stock.

Each year, the sales manager had appropriated a round amount for advertising. Last year, this amount was $150,000. Advertising expense was allocated to sales branches on the basis of past sales. The sales manager reasoned that advertising should be directed to those branches which were doing the best job.

Because of the poor coordination between production and sales, the purchasing program of the company had always been largely on a hand-to-mouth basis. For example, when it was decided to undertake the manufacture of oil burners, no accurate estimate of sales had been made. As a result, the purchasing agent had held up on his purchase of materials at the request of the production manager until sufficient orders for burners had been received to warrant a production run. Because materials then had to be purchased quickly, top prices were paid for them. This procedure had been one cause of the low profit-margin on oil burners.

The personnel manager had frequently been burdened with the task of hurriedly hiring many new workers in order to speed up production on a certain line for which the demand was larger than had been anticipated by either the sales manager or the production manager.

In the report to his father, the son recommended that a system of budgetary control be established. He explained that a sound system of budgetary control would alleviate the company's main problem, namely, that each department head had been working for the good of his own department, irrespective of the effect upon the other departments.

Upon this strong representation, the father decided to accept the recommendation and asked the son to proceed immediately to install a budget. After the figures had been obtained, an estimate of the results for the next twelve months revealed a net loss of $14,000. Thereupon the father suggested that all budgetary procedure be discontinued, with the remark, "We do not need a budget to put us into the red; we can find the way ourselves. Instead of sitting around trying to figure out what may or may not happen, instead of dreaming about the future, let's get rid of all this red tape and go to work and get business."

Questions

Put yourself in the position of the son.

1. What reasons beyond that mentioned in his final recommendation would you have advanced in support of a plan of budgetary control? In other words, what other benefits should accrue to the company?
2. In order that a proper perspective be obtained, what would you have pointed out as the limitations of budgetary control?
3. What steps, preferably in chronological order, would you have taken to set up the budget?
4. What recommendations, in addition to the installation of a budget, would you have made?

HELL WEEK[15]

The Navy has a jet pilot training station at Kingsville, Texas. About half the Navy's fighter and attack pilots must complete their training there before receiving their Navy wings. These symbols of completion of flight training are earned after approximately 350 hours of training in the air and countless hours of ground school and military training.

The other half of the Navy's fighter and attack pilots complete their formal training at nearby Beeville, Texas. Other types of training, such as antisubma-

---

[15] Charles E. Summer, David R. Hampton, Ross A. Webber, "Hell Week," *Organization Behavior and the Practice of Management*, 3rd ed., New York, Scott-Foresman and Co., pp. 588–589.

rine warfare training, take place at Naval Air Stations in Corpus Christi and New Iberia, Louisiana. The headquarters for advanced training is located on the Naval Air Station at Corpus Christi.

One Tuesday morning each month, the commanding officers from the eleven advanced training squadrons are invited (command performance) to attend the admiral's conference. This conference covers general subjects of interest to the groups and progress reports on the status of each squadron in the production of naval aviators, with heavy emphasis placed on the previous week's statistical figures, shown in graphic and chart format. Various formulas are used—some complicated and confusing—to depict the amount of training performed in relation to several factors, such as the type of flying weather, aircraft availability, student and instructor availability, the number of students who completed flight training during the period, and use of flight simulators, and other things. Running totals are depicted, as are comparisons with the same periods of previous years.

Searching and detailed questions are asked the commanding officers of the squadrons whose charts show discrepancies and shortcomings that are not self-explanatory. Questions on any phase of the squadron's operation are asked. Those that cannot be answered by the commanding officer cause him great embarrassment and discomfort in front of the admiral who must sign his personal evaluation report. Very few questions are asked concerning squadron training of those squadrons that have high production figures for the week preceding the meeting. Therefore, it becomes important to have high figures for at least this one week of the month, and so avoid questions.

Since the formula by which the graphs and charts are made is known to the squadrons, steps can be taken to beat the system. The graphs having the most variables are the easiest to manipulate. Even the figures for the weather can be controlled, since this is a variable used to reflect the differences in squadron training—that is, 100 percent good flying weather for an instrument training phase might only be 20 percent good flying weather for a fighter tactics flight. The weather percentage is turned in by each squadron training officer, based on his own best judgment.

The number of flying days per week, when weather is not a factor, can be adjusted by subtracting time taken to perform military drills or inspections. Since the official work week is a five-day period, weekend flying does not add flying days to the figures although it does add flight hours. Thus, problems during the week can be remedied by working six- or seven-day weeks. For example, a squadron having flown only 300 hours during the official five-day week might add 200 hours to the total by flying Saturday and Sunday, thus getting credit for 500 hours for the five days.

The number of aircraft available for flight is an easy one to adjust. Aircraft that are out of commission awaiting parts at the beginning of the period and not counted as available can be put into commission by exchanging parts from other grounded aircraft. Extra aircraft above the normal squadron allowance are also assigned as a pool of replacements, and these have to be flown periodically. Instructors can combine instruction flights with minor test flights. All of these methods make aircraft available that are not chargeable against the squadron's use figures, but that improve the reported figures.

Other measures used in determining the squadron's standing on the graphs and charts can also be manipulated, and are not illegal, unsafe, or unrecognized by the admiral's staff. In fact, some of the maneuvers are condoned and recommended. The loophole provided by the Saturday and Sunday flying, for example, was intentional. It provides an incentive to work overtime to get the job done.

The week preceding the monthly conference attended by the commanding officers is appropriately called "hell week" by some instructors. No matter how bad the weather is or what the aircraft and personnel situation might be, this week is usually a six- or seven-day work week. The flight day starts before sunrise and ends late at night, and all sorts of finagling takes place to improve the statistical figures. Since none of the personnel wants to work Saturdays and Sundays when it can be avoided, all of them contribute their part in boosting the figures that have to be reported. The mechanics work harder with fewer breaks for personal business; aircraft availability seems automatically to be higher. The line personnel refuel the aircraft and make minor adjustments and repairs more quickly, and more flights are flown. Fewer flights are cancelled for any reason. Instructor and student availability are improved with less illness, and more of the "can do" spirit prevails. More students are graduated during this particular week. The weather is always less than 100 percent.

The statistics used to produce the charts and graphs assume great importance. Squadron personnel tend to concentrate on those items that are reported and pay less attention to unreported ones. It becomes more important in some minds to have aircraft reported up and flyable than to be certain that aircraft meet rigid quality control inspections. Since the quality control people work for the men responsible for high aircraft availability, a relaxation of quality standards sometimes results. Some of the best qualified inspectors are transferred to head production units, with less qualified inspectors assigned to quality control units.

Students are often held over from the previous week so that student completions during "hell week" will be higher. Scheduling is arranged so that students who could have been completed the previous Friday are actually completed early in the following week. This sometimes fouls up their travel arrangements and lengthens their time in the squadron. Other students will be rushed to completion at an unnecessarily fatiguing pace.

Questions
1. What are the advantages and disadvantages of the system of measurement and evaluation described in this case?
2. Why does finagling with the numbers occur?

FAULTY LIGHT BULBS

Dave Williams is quality control inspector for the Ra Light Bulb Company. His job is to take a sample of light bulbs from the production line and run various tests on these bulbs to determine whether they have met the buyers' specifications. The final test involves a "severity test" in which the bulb must burn for at least 12 hours under an overloading of electricity. If a significant number of light bulbs does not meet the buyer specifications, then Dave notifies the superintendent of the problem. The production line is then immediately shut down and is not started up again until the condition producing the faulty light bulbs has been corrected.

At the end of each day, Dave prepares a summary of his day's activities and submits them to his supervisor, the president of the corporation. Dave's daily reporting stemmed from some complaints by a few buyers that their light bulbs were not meeting specifications. The president felt that more inspections of the product would reduce these complaints, but she wanted to be certain that these inspections actually took place. The daily summaries submitted by Dave include the name of the buyer for whom the product was being produced and the lot number in the warehouse. If the buyer complaints continued, the president felt that another inspector would be needed to make an even closer inspection of the production process.

Question

1. Can you identify each of the elements of the two control systems described in the above case?

PART FIVE
CASES

McCALL DIESEL MOTOR WORKS[16]
Need for a Complete System of Production Control

The McCall Diesel Motor Works has been a pioneer in the manufacture of this type of internal combustion engine. The plant is located on tidewater in the state of New Jersey because the company originally built engines for the marine field, chiefly fishing boats and pleasure craft. Subsequently, its activities were extended to the stationary type of engines, used primarily for the production of power in small communities, in manufacturing plants, or on farms.

During the earlier years of the company's operation, its engines were largely special-order jobs. Even at the present time about 60 percent of the output is made to order. There has been in recent years, however, a trend toward standardization of component parts and reduction in the variety of engines produced. The Engineering Department has followed the principle of simplification and standardization in the case of minor parts—such as studs, bolts, and springs—giving a degre of interchangeability of these components among the various sizes and types of engines. Sizes of marine engines have been standardized to some extent, although customer requirements still necessitate some designs. In the small engines for agricultural use there has been a genuine effort to concentrate sales on a standard line of engines of three sizes—twenty HP, forty HP, and sixty HP.

The company has always been advanced in its engineering development and design. The production phase, on the other hand, has not been progressive. The heritage of job-shop operation persists, and despite the definite trend toward standardization, manufacture continues largely on a "made-to-order" basis. The increasing popularity of diesel engines has brought many new producing companies into the field, with a consequent tightening of the competitive situation.

High manufacturing costs and poor service have been reflected in the loss of orders. Customer complaints, together with pressure from the Sales Department, prompted the management to call in a consulting engineer to make a survey of the Manufacturing Department and recommend what action should be taken. The report of the engineer submitted the following findings:

1. *Manufacturing methods*, while still largely of the job-shop character, are in the main good, and no wholesale change should be made. As production is still 60 percent special, a complete shift to line manufacture or departmentalization by product is not feasible.
2. *Machinery and equipment* is for the most part general-purpose, in line with manufacturing requirements. Some machine tools are approaching obsolescence, and for certain operations high production single-purpose machines would be advisable. Extensive

---
[16]Paul E. Holden, Frank K. Shallenberger, and Walter A. Diehm, *Selected Case Problems in Industrial Management*, 2nd ed., Englewood Cliffs, N.J., Prentice-Hall, 1962, pp. 293–295.

replacement of machine tools is not a pressing need, but an increased use of jigs and fixtures should be undertaken immediately. There are many bottlenecks existing in the plant, but contrary to your belief, as well as that of your foreman and other shop executives, there is no serious lack of productive equipment. The trouble lies in the improper utilization of the machine time available.

3. *Production control* is the major element of operating weakness, and improvement is imperative. The lack of proper control over production is evidenced by the following:

   (a) high in-process inventory as indicated by piles of partially completed parts over the entire manufacturing floor areas;

   (b) absence of any record concerning the whereabouts of orders in process from their initiation to delivery at assembly;

   (c) inordinate number of rush orders, particularly in assembly but also in parts manufacture;

   (d) too many parts chasers who force orders through the shops by pressure methods;

   (e) piecemeal manufacture—a lot of twenty parts usually is broken up into four or five lots before it is finished; not infrequently the last sublot remains on the shop floor for months and, in a number of instances, is lost in so far as records are concerned; subsequent orders for the same part are issued and new lots pass through to completion while the remains of the old lot lie in partially fabricated condition;

   (f) excessive setup costs resulting from the piecemeal methods mentioned in (e), as well as failure to use proper lot sizes, even when lots are not broken up during manufacture;

   (g) failure of all necessary component parts to reach assembly at approximately the same time; the floor of the assembly department is cluttered with piles of parts awaiting receipt of one or more components before engines can be assembled;

   (h) lack of definite sequence of manufacturing operations for a given part; responsibility for the exact way by which a part is to be made rests entirely on the various departmental foremen; these men are able machinists but, burdened with detail, their memories cannot be relied upon to insure that parts will always be manufactured in the best, or even the same, sequence of operations; moreover, they have the responsibility for determining the department to which a lot of parts should be sent when it has been completed in their department;

   (i) in the case of certain small standard parts, shop orders have been issued as many as six or eight times in a single month;

   (j) information is lacking from which to estimate, with any degree of close approximation, the overall manufacturing time for an engine; the result is failure to meet delivery promises or high production cost due to rush or overtime work;

   (k) parts in process or in stores, and destined for imminent assembly, are frequently taken by the Service Department to supply an emergency repair order; the question here is not the academic determination of priority between the customer whose boat may be lying idle due to a broken part and the customer who has not yet received his engine; the question is why there should be any habitual difficulty in rendering adequate repair service and at the same time meeting delivery promises;

   (l) virtually all basic manufacturing data resides in the heads of the superintendent, departmental foreman, assitant foremen, and setup men;

   (m) delivery dates are set by the Sales Department and generally are dates which customers arbitrarily stipulate.

The state of affairs found by the consultant was, he realized, due to two main causes:

1. The strong influence of the original job-shop character of manufacture and the very slow evolution to large-scale operation.
2. The fact that the top management of the company was essentially sales minded.

His recommendations, therefore, had to be made with the idea of presenting a simple, straightforward program to provide adequate control over production and to enable this control to be instituted gradually and logically.

Questions
1. Outline the essential features of a production-control system for this company.
2. What data must be compiled before your system can become fully effective?
3. Enumerate the benefits that the company will derive when your production-control system is in operation.

THE HOME EQUIPMENT COMPANY [17]
Organization and Procedure for New Product Development

The Home Equipment Company produces and sells a line of electric stoves, dishwashers, and clothes washers. The company, from its outset, placed primary emphasis upon the engineering design and styling of its products. The soundness of that policy has been reflected in a steady growth of business and profits.

Market acceptance of a given model has never been permitted to relax the efforts or attention of the Engineering Department and other departments in developing improved models. Along with excellence of design, the company has consistently adhered to a simplified line of each of its product groups. This policy has enabled development and research to be concentrated on a few models, has kept down the investment in tooling, and has permitted the manufacturing department to produce at low cost.

These two fundamental policies have been largely responsible for the management's decision to establish a standard procedure for the consideration, development, and adoption of a new model or any significant modification of an existing model. The chronological steps in this procedure, which incidentally applies to all three product lines, are shown in chart form as Figure 1. What actually occurs at each step is set forth in Figure 2.

The Home Equipment Company is one of the older firms in the appliance manufacturing business. The procedure by which a product change is processed from the point of suggestion to full-scale production has evolved over a number of years. It thus represents what the management regards as an effective means of providing coordination and control over one of the most important phases of the company's operation.

Questions
1. What is your opinion of the procedure? Point out the good and bad features.
2. With respect to Step 1 of the procedure, what would you regard as "sufficient data" which top management should have to justify a project?
3. Likewise, in Step 9 top management is called upon to make a vital decision. At this point in the procedure, what information should these executives have before authorizing the first production quantity?
4. In Step 4C, what information would you expect each of the sources to provide? Present this in outline form.
5. Top management has a further decision to make and one not specifically mentioned in the procedure. The decision has to do with the timing of a new model supplanting an existing one. What factors should this group take into consideration in determining just when to stop production on the old model and to start full-scale production on the new model?
6. What policies, in addition to the two fundamental ones mentioned in the problem, should the company adopt with respect to its products?

---
[17] Ibid., pp. 11–15.

FIGURE 1

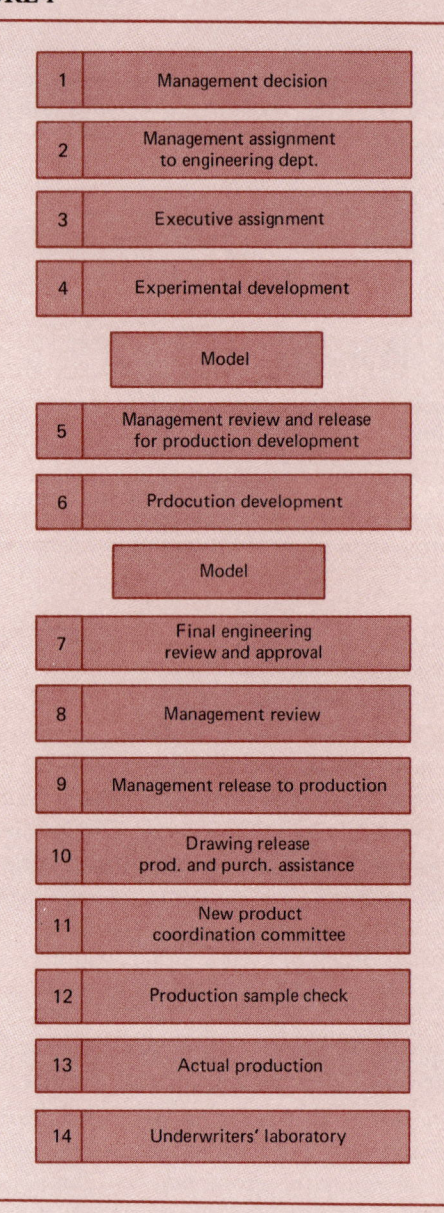

1	Management decision
2	Management assignment to engineering dept.
3	Executive assignment
4	Experimental development
	Model
5	Management review and release for production development
6	Prdocution development
	Model
7	Final engineering review and approval
8	Management review
9	Management release to production
10	Drawing release prod. and purch. assistance
11	New product coordination committee
12	Production sample check
13	Actual production
14	Underwriters' laboratory

FIGURE 2

Procedure for Product Introduction

Step 1 is the decision of top management to start action upon a product development suggestion that may have been proposed by the Engineering Department, a salesman, a customer, or some other source. This decision is based upon sufficient data to justify the project.

Step 2 is the transmission of the management's assignment to the Engineering Department. In most cases this assignment is in the nature of a general request that a new model or product be developed for production. At this time, the management outlines its general requirements and gives the specific instructions that are required.

Step 3 is the specific interpretation of the management's assignment by the executive heads of the Engineering Department, and the formulation of a program covering the work to be done. It is needless to say that each of these steps may entail extended investigations by the individuals charged with the various responsibilities.

Step 4 is the stage at which the data to be used in the design of the new product is gathered. This step is carried out in five sub-steps:

  A. Formulation of tentative specifications—a group activity carried on by the various section heads of the Engineering Department in accordance with their interpretations of the engineering assignment.

  B. Collection of substantiating data—the specifications for a new model often include certain features for which the laboratories have not yet collected enough basic data to predict definite results. It then becomes necessary to push the resarch or tests on these particular features, and the laboratory work program is set up accordingly. As soon as the research has progressed far enough to indicate an acceptable design, models are rushed through the experimental shop and immediately tested, so that the new equipment can be evaluated. Other models are made of each functional part, allowing all performance data to be obtained by the laboratory at a date early enough for any necessary changes to be investigated and provided for before being incorporated into the final design.

  C. Collection of recommendations and governing data from various sources, such as:
  (1) Sales
  (2) Service
  (3) Advertising
  (4) Patent and legal
  (5) Production
  (6) Purchasing
  (7) Engineering Laboratories
  (8) Merchandising Council
  (9) Styling Council

The order of importance and the weight given to the data received are determined largely by the nature of the assignment. In certain instances, notably production and purchasing, it is necessary for the engineering department to release preliminary information in order to secure such help as tooling advice, preliminary quotations, and material data. Frequently the information concerning the new products is confidential, and in some instances it is necessary to restrict the dissemination of new product information to certain key men in associated departments, placing upon them the responsibility for departmental opinions used as a basis for future engineering action.

D. Actual design work—sometimes the design passes through several evolutionary phases before it is released as an operating model.

E. Model construction and test—the final step in experimental development is the building and testing of experimental models. This activity requires close cooperation with the Production and Purchasing Departments, so that they may eliminate, as much as possible, the differing viewpoints with respect to employment of production processes, materials, design features, and so forth. To this end the Production Department is called in to review and approve the various component parts and their associated production problems. The Purchasing Department is requested to secure semifinal quotations when production suggests certain pieces be secured from external suppliers. The suggestions of these suppliers with respect to minor design changes to facilitate production are incorporated whenever possible.

Step 5 is top management's review pf experimental models, performance characteristics, tentative cost estimates, and the like. If the experimental model fulfills expectations and requirements, the Engineering Department is authorized to proceed.

Step 6 is the development of the experimental design into final production shape. When the Engineering Department has made the usual compromises and fulfilled to a reasonable extent the requirements of various associated departments, a group of tentative production models is built. These machines are tested for such characteristics as performance, resistance to abuse, and life of various parts. The design is submitted to the Service Department for the final review, and a production release is requested from the Patent Department to make certain it has approved the design to be produced. Models are submitted to the Sales Department for criticism, to secure at an early stage opinions that might not otherwise arise until a later date from individuals not associated with the development. Changes are incorporated in accordance with the validity of the suggestions received. Final styling conferences are held with representatives of the Sales and Advertising Departments, and with any necessary merchandising counsel.

Step 7 is the final review by the Engineering Department, at which time the results of tests and other departmental reviews are analyzed. If the design and performance are satisfactory, the Engineering Department gives final approval to the model.

Step 8 is the submission of the model to top management. At this time, various other departments are called upon to contribute information that will assist the management in the formulation of its decisions. Typical items of information may be listed as follows:

(a) Performance data from the Engineering Department.
(b) Estimated cost data from the Cost Department.
(c) Plans from the Advertising Department.
(d) Tentative Sales Department schedules and merchandising plans.
(e) Tooling program data from the Production Department.

Step 9 is the decision of top management to proceed with the manufacture of the new product and the authorization of an initial production quantity.

Step 10 is the release of production drawings and the cooperation of the Engineering Department with the Production, Purchasing, and Inspection Departments.

Step 11 takes place during the production tooling interval, and is a review to see that all departments of the company are prepared for the advent of a new model. This is the function of the Products Coordination Committee, which is composed of representatives from the Engineering, Production, Inspection, Sales, and Service Departments.

Step 12 is a production run of about 100 units for the purpose of testing the tooling and manufacturing methods and of providing samples for engineering examination and test. Normally about one month is allowed for this step.

Step 13 is the launching of actual production on a scheduled basis.

Step 14 is the submission of samples taken out of regular production to the Underwriters' Laboratories for test and certification.

PART SIX
GOAL-ORIENTED MANAGEMENT SYSTEMS

CHAPTER 21
SOCIAL RESPONSIBILITIES OF MANAGEMENT

CHAPTER 22
MBO—AN INTEGRATIVE SYSTEM OF MANAGEMENT

CHAPTER 23
INTERNATIONAL MANAGEMENT AND MANAGEMENT IN THE FUTURE

INTEGRATIVE CASES

UNION CARBIDE AND VIENNA, WEST VIRGINIA
CONSOLIDATED INSTRUMENTS-B

This part integrates concepts and ideas from the entire text. Chapter 21 examines the management of social responsibility. The many facets of this growing area of concern are explored. Chapter 22 presents a model of the total management process, using an MBO approach. Finally, in Chapter 23 many of the changes taking place in society are discussed. The management practices which are likely to result from these changes are examined. The growing use of the multinational organization is explored in depth.

CHAPTER 21
SOCIAL RESPONSIBILITIES OF MANAGEMENT

WHAT IS CORPORATE SOCIAL RESPONSIBILITY?
DEMANDS FOR BUSINESS RESPONSIBILITY
THE CLASSICAL VIEW
THE MANAGERIAL VERSION OF BUSINESS RESPONSIBILITY
THE PUBLIC AND RADICAL VIEWS

RESEARCH FINDINGS REGARDING SOCIAL RESPONSIBILITY OF BUSINESS

DEVELOPING A STRATEGIC POSTURE TOWARD SOCIAL RESPONSIBILITY

AREAS OF MANAGERIAL RESPONSE TO SOCIAL RESPONSIBILITY
COMPANY SOCIAL POLICY
ORGANIZATIONAL CHANGES

PATTERNS OF SOCIAL ACTION PROGRAMS
URBAN AFFAIRS
CONSUMER AFFAIRS
ENVIRONMENTAL AFFAIRS

THE SOCIAL AUDIT: A STRATEGY FOR DEFINING AND IMPLEMENTING SOCIAL RESPONSIBILITY

APPLICATION EXERCISES AND CASES
A MATTER OF PRIORITY
THE XEROX EXPERIMENT

SOCIAL RESPONSIBILITY—A REAL CONCERN

On February 3, 1975, the 53-year-old chairman of the board of United Brands, Incorporated, entered his offices in the forty-fourth floor of the Pan American Building in New York City. He instructed his secretary that he was not to be disturbed, then locked the door to his executive office. Using his briefcase, he smashed the window behind his desk and jumped to his death on the streets below.

The next morning, *The Wall Street Journal* quoted a statement issued by United Brands, which said that the chairman had been under "great strain during the past several weeks because of business pressures."[1] United Brands had been widely acclaimed as an excellent corporate example of social responsiveness. The Chicago Daily News had recently said "it may well be the most socially conscious American company in the hemisphere."[2] The chairman, in turn, was known for his commitment to positive social change. In 1970, for example, he had personally negotiated with Caesar Chavez and the United Farm Workers Union, and United Brands was the first major lettuce grower to sign with the union.[3]

The "pressures" referred to in *The Wall Street Journal* stemmed from public disclosure that $750,000 in bribes to Italian officials had been paid by the company. Later, on April 8, the company also admitted that its chairman had authorized well over $1 million in bribes to officials of the government of Honduras. The "bribes" were payments that allowed the company to continue profitable operations in the country.

---

[1] *The Wall Street Journal,* February 4, 1975, p. 15.
[2] *United Brands Annual Report,* 1972.
[3] "United Brands" in F. D. Sturdivant and L.M. Robinson, *The Corporate Social Challenge,* Homewood, Ill., Richard D. Irwin, 1977, pp. 290–301.

Social responsibility means taking initiative in meeting needs of society and problems.

In this chapter we are shifting to a subject area that reflects a level of concern that, although very strategic, especially in today's world, is not always given a great deal of thought by students and, in some cases, practitioners of management. The reason for this may be that most of us are removed from the level of mangement that initiates decisions and actions related to social responsibility. Although we are using these terms somewhat interchangeably, social responsiveness implies reacting positively to pressures imposed on the firm by various segments or elements in the environment. Social responsibility would imply that an organization takes initiative in meeting societies' needs and problems before they are pressured to do so.

In any case, remember that this chapter deals with much broader issues than much of the previous material. The comparison of the American corporate system to a total ecology system discussed as follows illustrates this. Specifically,

---

*The authors gratefully acknowledge the assistance of Robert Bell, Assistant Dean, College of Business, Tennessee Technological University, who helped to prepare this chapter.

SOCIAL RESPONSIBILITIES OF MANAGEMENT 569

organizations do not operate in a vacuum. Organizations have an impact on society in general and society in turn has an impact on organizations. For this reason social responsibility is a key issue and concern in the modern world.

WHAT IS CORPORATE SOCIAL RESPONSIBILITY?

The United Brands experience brings the dilemma of social responsibility into clear focus. What is the responsibility of the corporate executive? Is there a corporate responsibility separate from the responsibilities of its executives? This chapter examines some of the views that attempt to answer these questions.

Socially responsible behavior reflects action in providing necessary amounts of goods and services at minimum financial and social costs, distributed equitably.

Socially responsible behavior has been defined as actions taken by a corporation "that, when judged by society in the future, are seen to have been of maximum help in providing necessary amounts of desired goods and services at minimum financial and social costs, distributed as equitably as possible."[4] The same writers who presented this definition explained that defining social responsibility is a difficult problem, since socially responsible actions necessarily reflect moral values; and these are very difficult to determine in an absolute sense—that is, apart from specific or particular situations. This problem is made much clearer by Farmer and Hogue as they ask the questions:

> What are society's needs? In what order or priority? Who will pay the costs of meeting them? Just because one group wants a particular action taken does not mean that others do, nor even that the action is socially responsible. In the end someone has to establish a corporate goal system that makes social as well as economic sense.[5]

Ecologists dealing with nature have understood for some time that all systems in nature are interrelated and interlocking. They can be defined as *ecosystems*, meaning that if changes are made in one of them, reactions are felt by the other systems. For example, if the temperature of the water is changed in a fresh-water stream, the type of wildlife that can exist there will change also.

In the corporate ecosystem, solving a problem for one group may reduce satisfaction for other groups.

The corporate environment consists of an ecosystem in which changes for various interest groups existing within or affected by the system produce interrelated changes for other groups. Usually solving a problem for one group, such as minority unemployment, reduces the satisfaction or increases problems for other groups such as majority groups. Since corporations are supported by the profits of the business system and can only rarely call on governments for subsidies or support when losses are incurred, there is an absolute limit to the trade-offs that can be made when and if costs are incurred by the firm.

The interrelated nature of interest groups in the managerial ecosystem and the tendency for all social goals to require trade-offs in monetary costs point to a need for a well-defined system of social responsibility for the firm. Figure 21-1 represents a simplified system of goal orientation, defining one dimension of trade-

---

[4]Richard N. Farmer and W. Diverson Hogue, *Corporate Social Responsibility,* Chicago, Science Research Associates, Inc., 1973, p. 6.
[5]Ibid.

FIGURE 21-1

GOAL SYSTEMS OF FIRMS

I	II	III	IV
Profit maximization: social goals incidental	Profit growth: social goals also important	Social goals: break even on money	Social goals: money losses acceptable

Source: Richard N. Farmer and W. Dickerson Houge, *Corporate Social Responsibility*, Chicago, Science research Associates, Inc., 1973, p. 7.

offs—that of profit maximization versus social goals and responsibilities. Even though overly simplified and not representing trade-offs between parties within the managerial ecosystem, this figure is useful as a starting point in understanding social responsibility.

Most of the small businesses in the United States operate at Position 1 (profit maximization) on the scale in Figure 21-1. This does not necessarily mean that they have no interest in social goals, although this may be the case for some; but rather that the revenues and profits of the firm are not large enough to absorb any appreciable expenditure on social goals. Any attempt on the part of a small manufacturer or retailer to change appreciably the pollution problem or unemployment problem in a local community is likely to be met with minimal results, unless the efforts of the firm are coordinated with other similar businesses.

A few large corporations still operate at Position 1 in Figure 21-1. For the most part, however, most larger American firms tend to fall on the continuum at Position 2. The reason is obvious. As firms move from Position 2 to Position 3, social goals are becoming more important than profits. Only publicly owned businesses such as transit systems, the Tennessee Valley Authority, and the post office can afford such goal orientation. Privately owned companies must continually exert great efforts in order to maintain a reasonable profitability and to satisfy their stockholders in terms of dividend payouts and the accrual value of stock.

> Most large corporations operate at Position 2—profit growth: social goals also important.

Rarely will a firm be found operating at Position 4 in Figure 21-1. Such a firm must have a wealthy financial sponsor to provide operating funds, since productivity has been traded for social orientation. Only governments are likely to have enough resources to subsidize such enterprises, and even with strong government support we tend to see ineffective allocation of social resources.[6]

Even if a firm decides to operate at Position 2 or 3 on the continuum in Figure 21-1, certain basic questions still must be answered.

DEMANDS FOR BUSINESS RESPONSIBILITY

What percentage of corporate profit should be spent on socially responsible actions that contribute little or nothing to future corporate profit? Who in the

---

[6]See, for example, "How Sweden's Middle Road Becomes a Dead End," *Forbes*, April 27, 1981, pp. 35–38.

corporation can be trusted with deciding how to spend the money? When a manager is appointed by a small group, such as stockholders, to manage their property, does he have the right to dispose of it in ways not approved by them? Finally, and perhaps most important, do large corporations have the right to spend monies on social goals that influence a large portion of society, or should such expenditures be left to government, whose leadership is more democratically determined?

Business firms have historically been active in politics.

Should corporations be actively involved in politics? S. Prakash Sethi, in his article "Corporate Political Action Strategies for the 1980's," argues that the question is largely rhetorical, since business firms have historically been quite active in politics. Campaign financing, Sethi suggests, has been a "time-honored method for influencing public policy decisions."[7] Lobbying and coalition building are also mentioned as "traditional" methods of political influence.

Should the public accept corporate involvement in public affairs? Sethi suggests that "the style and substance of corporate political involvement and the contributions of business to the public interest will largely determine the degree to which the public will accept the corporation as a political participant."[8] These and other basic questions have caused management to look at social responsibilities as a controversial area generating a great deal of frustration and uncertainty. The viewpoints taken by management over the years can be rationalized in a polarized sense by the following examples.

A review of the literature reveals four major philosophies concerning business responsibility. These philosophies might be called the *classical view*, the *managerial view*, the *public view*, and the *radical view*.[9]

THE CLASSICAL VIEW

The classical view says that the primary criteria of business performance are economic efficiency and growth.

According to the classical view, the primary criteria of business performance are economic efficiency and growth in the production of goods and services, all of which are exemplified by the acquisition of profits. The classical view is in essence described by Adam Smith's "invisible hand." His theory contended that the pursuit of self-interest by a business was the most effective way to enhance the public good.

The simplified classical view of business responsibility can be summarized as follows.[10]

(1) Economic behavior is separate and distinct from other types of behavior, and business organizations are distinct from other organizations even though the same individuals may be involved in business and not in business affairs. Business organizations do not serve the same goals as other organizations in a pluaralistic society.

---
[7]S. Prakash Sethi, "Corporate Political Action Strategies for the 1980's," *Management Review*, March 1981, p. 9.
[8]Ibid., p. 8.
[9]James W. McKie, *Social Responsibility and the Business Predicament*, Washington, D.C., The Brookings Institution, 1974, pp. 18–19.
[10]Ibid.

(2) The primary criteria of business performance are economic efficiency and growth in production of goods and services, including improvements in technology and innovations in goods and services.

(3) The primary goal and motivating force for business organizations is profit. The firm attempts to make as large a profit as it can, thereby maintaining its efficiency and taking advantage of available opportunities to innovate and contribute to growth. Profits are kept to reasonable or appropriate levels by market competition, which leads the firm pursuing its own self-interest to an end that is no part of its conscious intention: enhancement of the public welfare. It need not recognize any responsibility to the public to accomplish this result.

Milton Friedman, the renowned conservative economist from the University of Chicago, has eloquently expressed a contemporary version of this philosophy as follows.[11]

Few trends could so thoroughly undermine the very foundations of our free society as the acceptance by corporate officials of a social responsibility other than to make as much money for their stockholders as possible. This is a fundamentally subversive doctrine. If businessmen do have a social responsibility other than making maximum profits for stockholders, how are they to know what it is?

The contemporary classical view on business responsibility is supported by the following arguments. A business cannot pay less than competitive prices for labor and other factors of production in the market system, and it should not be forced to pay more—even for minority and underprivileged labor sectors. To interfere with the profit system is to interfere with the ownership of firms and the rightful returns to stockholders and proprietor's equity. If such a distribution of income is to be altered, it is up to the government to make the change. Even in these cases, the government should alter income in such a way as to interfere the very least with the efficiency of the market system. It is better to make direct taxation and direct payments to underprivileged groups in the form of lump sum transfers than to alter the business system itself by forcing various types of hiring, employment, and pay practices that are not competitive in nature.[12]

Furthermore, in regard to such problems as national stability of employment, income and prices, as well as such global problems as nationwide pollution, the individual firm is too small in relationship to the total economy to have much impact. These arguments have been supported over the years with a legal philosophy that said that the firm was an extension of the personal property of its owners, and therefore had the right to use or dispose of its property as the owners so desired, as long as it did not infringe on the legal rights of others.[13]

THE MANAGERIAL VERSION OF BUSINESS RESPONSIBILITY

The classical view of business responsibility generally has been softened with some benevolent viewpoints. When pressures such as eonomic downturns were

---

[11] Milton Friedman, *Capitalism and Freedom*, Chicago, University of Chicago Press, 1962, p. 133.
[12] McKie, *Social Responsibility and the Business Predicament*, pp. 20–21.
[13] Ibid.

SOCIAL RESPONSIBILITIES OF MANAGEMENT

on, however, the primary preoccupation of businesses turned to profits and costs savings. The managerial viewpoint of business responsibility was fostered by several things. First, the rise of large-scale corporations, with their permanent nature, presuming to have a life and purpose of their own, caused professional management to recognize other interest groups besides stockholders as absentee owners. "Employees, customers, suppliers, and other parties began to be recognized as having rights in the organization that were not merely contractual claims."[14] Second, most modern corporate managers can be better described as professional managers than as entrepreneurs whose management training arose out of a proprietorship. They have been trained in professional schools of management and oftentimes have a strong orientation toward labor problems, social problems, and other problems of society. They often have been taught to welcome a partnership between business and government; and to attack social problems, when possible, with the resources of the corporation. Legal codes have also been changing, allowing more social responsibility.

In 1935, corporations were given the legal right to make donations of the "stockholder's property" and to charge them as a business expense, up to five percent of pretax income. Though corporate giving has never approached the maximum deductible rate, the five percent amendment of 1935 gave official sanction to the use of corporate income for nonbusiness contributions and, thus, established business as an independent source of support.[15]

The managerial view of business responsibility was articulated by Francis S. Sutton in the 1950s.[16] This view depicts the manager of a large corporation as being responsible for balancing the claims and rights of many diverse groups, among them, employees, customers, suppliers and the local community, rather than enhancing the wealth of shareholders. It encourages a conscious effort by business managers to promote the public good.

THE PUBLIC AND RADICAL VIEWS

The move to professional management and the orientation and legal changes mentioned above have been the result of voluntary business actions. On the other hand, there has been a strong impetus for change in business responsibility, brought about by the formation of power blocks within society. Labor unions, group blocks such as NOW (the National Organization for Women), the NAACP, and the consumer advocate organizations have caused business to change its orientation by what might be called the "shock effect."

This more recent position concerning business responsibility (which could be called the public view) is perhaps best illustrated in the writings of Ralph Nader and John Kenneth Galbraith.[17] They depict large corporations as institutions

---

[14]Ibid., p. 30.
[15]Ibid., p. 29.
[16]Frances S. Sutton et al., *The American Business Creed*, Cambridge, Mass., Harvard University Press, 1956, pp. 57–58.
[17]See, for example, "Whistle Blowing," *The Report on the Conference on Professional Responsibility*, Ralph Nader, ed., New York: Peter J. Petkus and Kate Blackwell Grossman, 1972; John Kenneth Galbraith, *The New Industrial State*, Boston, Houghton-Mufflin, 1967; Robert L. Heilbroner and others, *In the Name of Profit*, New York: Doubleday, 1972.

exercising enormous power over society—power so great that it must be counterbalanced by whatever is required to protect the public interest—whether it be public ownership of certain industries, federal chartering of corporations, or more stringent government regulation of private enterprise.[18]

The radical view is one which depicts corporate executives as being incapable of exercising social responsibility and, therefore, implies a need for public ownership and control of all business enterprise.[19]

RESEARCH FINDINGS REGARDING SOCIAL RESPONSIBILITY OF BUSINESS

In an effort to uncover trends and attitudes toward the social role of the corporation, Holmes conducted a questionnaire study asking a sample of 180 to 200 top executives from large corporations to select the one statement they believed to describe their firm's philosophy regarding social responsibility in the years 1970, 1975, and projecting it for 1980. As shown in Figure 21-2, Part (2) of the third statement best described the executives' attitudes: "In addition to making a profit, business should help to solve social problems whether or not the business helped to create those problems—even if there is probably no short-run or long-run profit potential."[20] Although this category was characteristic of the largest single category taken as a group, most executives preferred positions that included some profit. There was found to be a significant change in view by the respondents in favor of a more overt social opinion over the five-year period from 1970 to 1975. They did not anticipate equally significant changes during the next five-year period, from 1975 to 1980. Although this was an attitude survey and not a survey of results, it should be noted that the largest percentage of these executives is suggesting a position similar to Position 2 of our corporate goal scale depicted in Figure 21-1.

"In addition to making a profit, business should help to solve social problems."

In an attempt to determine the motives behind executives' reactions to social responsibilities, this same group was asked what positive and negative outcomes they expected from involvement in social activities. There was considerably more agreement on positive outcomes of corporate social involvement than on negative outcomes.[21] Almost every respondent believed that corporation reputation and goodwill would be enhanced, and a large percentage also believed that the social and economic system would be strengthened by corporate social involvement. But more tangible results were thought to be less likely.[22] Finally, the researchers in this study attempted to determine how a corporation selects from

---

[18]Sandra L. Holmes, "Executive Perceptions of Corporate Social Responsibility," *Business Horizons*, June 1976, p. 35.
[19]McKie, *Social Responsibility and the Business Predicament*, p. 34. For a summary discussion of many of these criticisms, see Charles Perrow, *The Radical Attack on Business: A Critical Analysis*, New York, Harcourt Brace Jovanovich, 1972, pp. 220–222.
[20]Holmes, op. cit., p. 37.
[21]Ibid., p. 38.
[22]Ibid., p. 37.

FIGURE 21-2

Executives' Opinions and Firms' Philosophies about the Social Responsibilities of Business: 1970, 1975, and 1980

	Percent of Executives Who Selected Statement to Describe Their Opinion			Percent of Executives Who Selected Statement to Describe Their Firm's Philosophy		
	1970	*1975*	*1980*	*1970*	*1975*	*1980*
Business is responsible for making a profit and abiding by legal regulations.	13.2	.1	.6	17.4	2.2	1.7
Business is responsible for making a profit and helping to solve social problems which business may directly create (such as pollution).	23.1	16.1	9.6	27.5	17.1	7.8
In addition to making a profit, business should help to solve social problems whether or not business helps to create these problems:						
1. As long as there is at least some short-run or long-run profit potential.	24.2	23.5	21.9	21.3	26.5	26.7
2. Even if there is probably *no* short-run or long-run profit potential.	31.3	46.4	46.6	28.1	41.5	(Change 1975-80) 46.1
3. Even though doing so may *reduce* short-run profits and no long-run profit returns are possible.	8.2	13.9	21.3	5.7	12.7	17.7
Number of responses	*182*	*188*	*180*	*178*	*181*	*180*

Source: Sandra L. Holmes, "Executive Perceptions of Corporate Social Responsibility," *Business Horizons,* June 1976, p. 36.

The most highly influential factor on social behavior was corporate reputation and goodwill.

among the various social demands cited earlier, when it begins to respond. Executives in the survey were asked to rank the factors that most heavily influenced their firm's selection of areas for social involvement. Figure 21-3 shows the ranking of this survey. The most highly influential factor was corporate reputation and goodwill. Social needs tended to rank a close second.[23]

---

[23]Ibid., p. 39.

FIGURE 21-3

Factors in the Selection of Areas for Social Involvement, as Ranked by Executives

Factor	Percent Ranking Factor 1-3	Percent Ranking Factor 4-10	Percent Reporting Not a Factor
Matching of a social need to corporate skill, need, or ability to help	70.7	12.5	16.8
Seriousness of social need	53.4	22.0	24.6
Interest of top executives	47.6	30.9	21.5
Public relations value of social action	20.9	44.0	35.1
Government pressure	20.9	28.8	50.3
Pressure of general public opinion	20.4	35.6	44.0
Pressure from special interest groups	13.1	33.5	53.4
Amount of corporate effort required	12.1	36.1	51.8
Measurability of results, or some form of cost/benefit analysis of social effort	12.0	29.8	58.2
Profitability of the venture	9.4	17.3	73.3

Source: Sandra L. Holmes, "Executive Perception of Corporate Social Responsibility," *Business Horizons,* June 1976, p. 39.

Most of the executives in the study believed that business possessed the ability and means to be a major force in the alleviation of social problems. In summarizing, it could be said that:

> *A significant change in executive opinions and corporate philosophies of social responsibility has occurred over the past five-year period. Executives anticipated more positive than negative outcomes from the social efforts of their firms, and almost all executives believed that corporate reputation and goodwill would be enhanced through social endeavors. Factors relating to the special competencies of the corporation and the seriousness of a social need were believed to be the most influential in the selection of areas for corporate social involvement. The majority of executives were optimistic about the ability of business to alleviate social problems and believed that the level of corporate social efforts was only partially determined by the general economic conditions.*[24]

A significant change occurred from the early to the middle 1970s, in favor of socially responsible behavior.

DEVELOPING A STRATEGIC POSTURE TOWARD SOCIAL RESPONSIBILITY

The perceptive student will note that in most of the scales and research questions so far, there is an implied notion that socially responsible action necessarily requires a trade-off in profits. Although this is a very difficult question to research, some evidence is available that sheds light on the question. The same

---
[24] Ibid., p. 40.

study suggests the manner in which businesses might go about establishing reasonable strategy in the area of social responsibility.

Bowman and Haire evaluated the annual reports of a number of matched groups of corporations. One group was selected because it was noteworthy in outstandingly responsible social behavior. For each of these premier firms, another firm of approximately equal size was chosen at random in the same industry. This yielded a comparison group of neutral firms to match the premier group. Two studies were conducted. In the first investigation the authors, in a very closely controlled sample, simply counted the lines of narrative material in the companies' annual reports that were devoted to discussion of social responsibilities.

More socially responsible firms tend to discuss their responsibility more in their annual reports.

The researchers found a significant difference in the number of lines of annual reports devoted to a discussion of social responsibiilty, in favor of the premier firms. This simply meant that firms that had better reputations for social responsibility allocated space in their annual reports to discussing it. From this test alone, the direction of the causality could not be determined. Next, the authors investigated the mean and median return on equity obtained by the two groups of firms. The results of this study are shown in Figure 21-4.

Their reason for conducting this study was to answer the question, "Does responsible activity come, net, out of the stockholder's pocket?" Although the researchers found that firms that discussed corporate responsibility tended to make higher return on equity, no direct conclusion could be made from this. In the authors' own words, "at the same time, it is perfectly clear that more corporate social responsibility is not associated with less profits."

More corporate social responsibility is not associated with less profit.

By refining their study a bit further, to look at firms who were moderate in their mention of and devotion to corporate social responsibility, the authors found a clearer distinction (see Figure 21-5).

In this case, firms in the median range of corporate social responsibilty clearly tended to have a higher return on equity. "Medium activity in corporate responsibiilty is clearly more closely associated with high profitability than is either little or much activity."[25]

Moderate activity in corporate responsibility is more closely associated with high profitability.

The conclusions of the researchers are important in each of these studies. After evaluating comparable studies of subjective data and external operating strategy of firms, the authors conclude:

FIGURE 21-4

Profitability and Corporate Responsibility

	Mean ROE	*Median ROE*
Some discussion of CRS (31 firms)	14.3%	14.7%
No discussion of CRS (51 firms)	9.1%	10.2%

Source: Edward H. Bowman and Mason Haire, "A Strategic Posture Toward Corporate Social Responsibility," *California Management Review,* Vol. XVIII, No. 2, Winter 1975, p. 52.

---

[25]Edward H. Bowman and Mason Haire, "A Strategic Posture Toward Corporate Social Responsibility," *California Management Review,* Vol. 18, No. 2, Winter 1975, p. 52.

FIGURE 21-5

Profitability and Corporate Responsibility

	Low Mention	Medium Mention	High Mention*
Number of firms	51	18	13
Percent devoted to CR	0	0.1–9.9	10 or more
Median ROE	10.2%	16.1%	12.3%

*Mention.of CR x = 3.63%

Source: Edward H. Bowman and Mason Haire, "A Strategic Posture Toward Corporate Social Responsibilty," *California Management Review*, Vol. XVIII, No. 2, Winter 1975, p. 53.

> *From both of these studies . . . we begin to see a picture of a firm being active, balanced, sensitive, responsive, and coping with pressures in the environment that are intangible, perhaps inchoate, and hard to identify. Does this kind of managerial behavior have any relationship to more conventional measures of business activity, for example, profitability?*[26]

The answer by the researcher is an implied "yes." Proceeding further with their conclusions, the writers state the following.

> *We would argue that the presence of a discussion of corporate responsibiilty, or indeed the activity itself, is not a cause of higher profits. Rather, it is a sign of the presence of a* tertium quid *which lies behind and is a causal factor. That is a sensitivity to a variety of facets in the external world, of which such things as pollution control or affirmative action are only a part. The sensitivity, responsiveness, flexibility, on one hand, are part of the requisite strategic posture. The adaptive readiness to cope proactively with the signals from the outside world make up the other part. Finally, in terms of a decision rule coefficient, the data seem to suggest neither too much nor too little . . . . Corporate socially responsible behavior, not by itself and not uniquely, is a signal of good, sensitive, informed, balanced, modern, negotiating, coping management. For many issues it is good neither to underrespond to them, nor to overrespond to them.*[27]

Corporate socially responsible behavior is a signal of good management.

The authors suggest further that this is comparable to the economist's theory or concept of equilibrium. It is a rational approach, since in terms of external information the norms about what other firms are doing in the area of social responsibility provide the only guideline available to organizations. In light of our earlier discussions about the conflicting demands of external interest groups and the difficulty of establishing social or moral values for society, it is not surprising that the central strategy used by the most successful firms is one of moderation. It is, however, a moderation that poses an increasing attention to social responsibility and a stronger approach than many of the critics have thus recognized.

---

[26] Ibid., p. 55.
[27] Ibid., p. 57.

The research regarding the relationship between social responsibility and profitability of firms is mixed.

But these findings are clouded by a more recent study, which found the most responsive firms, not the moderately responsive ones, to be the most economically superior. Conclusive research is yet to be conducted on this issue.[28]

AREAS OF MANAGERIAL RESPONSE TO SOCIAL RESPONSIBILITY

Thus far, our investigation of social responsibility practices has dealt with the pressures of interest groups on various types of social responsibility, and the general reaction and degree of intervention by firms. We have yet to discuss the specific areas that to which firms are beginning to respond. One research study has examined this question by surveying 1,250 firms on Fortune's list of the largest United States industrial and nonindustrial firms, listing responses from 232 of the companies. Three areas of intervention were examined: urban, consumer, and environmental affairs. In turn, three levels of response were investigated: levels requiring the establishment of company policies, the creation of new organizational elements or upgrading the existing ones, and the election of special interest groups as representative to the board of directors. Since a control study was developed to determine the differences to responding and nonresponding companies with no significant difference discovered, only the nature of the respondents will be reported. Figure 21-6 summarizes the findings of the study.

The greater number of firms had established social policies in the urban affairs areas.

COMPANY SOCIAL POLICY

As indicated by Figure 21-6, a significantly greater number of firms had established corporate social policies in the urban affairs areas. Despite increased public and government pressure, however, many of these companies have not yet formally established policies for action in this category.

ORGANIZATIONAL CHANGES

The most common organizational change cited by companies was that of the establishment of a social responsibility department with specialized full- or part-time personnel. Since one of the major complaints regarding social responsibility is that outside interest groups are not protected, a number of proposals have been made in recent years to represent these groups on boards of directors. No more than eight percent of the surveyed companies had actually elected board members whose major responsibility was to represent interest groups. The urban affairs and consumer affairs areas have received almost equal attention on boards of directorships. Most of the environmental area action has occurred since

A few companies have organized social responsibility departments.

---

[28]Frederick D. Sturdivant and James L. Ginter, "Corporate Social Responsiveness," *California Management Review*, Vol. 19, No. 3 (Spring 1977): 30–39.

FIGURE 21-6

Nature and Timing of Selected Structural Changes

Percent of Companies Reporting (N = 232)

Structural Changes	Year of Adoption 1969 and before	1970-72	Companies with no changes
Established company policies			
Urban affairs	55	13	32
Consumer affairs	40	16	44
Environmental affairs	42	21	37
Created new organizational elements upgraded existing ones			
Urban affairs	49	14	37
Consumers affairs	38	15	47
Environment affairs	37	23	40
Elected special interest group representatives to the board			
Urban affairs	5	2	93
Consumer affairs	5	3	92
Environmental affairs	2	1	97

Source: Vernon M. Buehler and Y. K. Shetty, "Managerial Response to Social Responsibility Challenge," *Academy of Management Journal*, Vol. 19, No. 1, 1976, p. 69.

1970. By contrast, urban affairs was favored in 1969 and before, probably reflecting the city riots in the mid-1960s and the 1964 passage of civil rights legislation.

Further investigation revealed that a relatively higher proportion of large-size firms than small-size firms has made structural changes. This is to be expected from the fact that only larger organizations can afford to dedicate portions of their activities and assign positions to such responsibilities. More manufacturing than nonmanufacturing firms had introduced structural changes—probably reflecting antipollution requirements.

Peter Drucker has recently suggested another, much more far-reaching organizational change. "Managers cannot and will not be able to maintain their control unless they build the employee into the power structure and control of an enterprise."[29] The real owners of big business in America, according to Drucker, are the employees. Their employee pension funds alone "own" between 40 and 50 percent of all of Americas equity capital. He argues that management will be

> Peter Drucker says the real owners of American big business are the employees.

---
[29]Peter F. Drucker, "Managing in Turbulent Times," *Industry Week*, May 12, 1980, p. 47.

able to gain support and continued control only by integrating the worker-capitalist into the decision-making process.

PATTERNS OF SOCIAL ACTION PROGRAMS

In order to learn which specific programs were being utilized for social action, companies were asked to rank their activities within the programs in terms of their degree of involvement. Figure 21-7 presents a summary of this ranking.

URBAN AFFAIRS

Employment and training of the disadvantaged attracted the most active involvement in this area. This is probably due to the fact that inadequate employment in training opportunities constitutes the heart of the urban affairs issues, and also because of the economic advantages inherent both in an improved labor force and in the expanding markets that result from increased incomes. These types of activities are highly visible and relatively simple to administer compared to other programs.

Within urban affairs, companies were more deeply involved with employment and training of the disadvantaged.

FIGURE 21-7

Patterns of Corporate Social Actions

Activities	Average Ranking[a]
Urban affairs	
1 Employment and training	2.1
2 Contribution to education	2.6
3 Medical assistance	3.1
4 Contributions to culture and arts	4.0
5 Urban renewal	4.0
Consumer affairs	
1 Quality control	1.9
2 Design improvement	2.2
3 Customer service	2.7
4 Marketing improvement	3.0
5 Customer information & education	3.2
Environmental affairs	
1 Water pollution	2.1
2 Air pollution	2.2
3 Waste disposal	2.6
4 Noise abatement	3.2
5 Radiation abatement	4.2

Source: Vernon M. Buehler and Y. K. Shetty, "Managerial Response to Social Responsibility Challenge," *Academy of Management Journal*, Vol. 19, No. 1, 1976, p. 76

An emerging challenge to traditional employee training and development is the changing work ethic in America. David Cherington has demonstrated the dramatic differences between the work ethics of young and older workers.[30] The trend in the United States, according to Cherington, is toward a four-day work week, the elimination of "dirty" jobs, early retirement, and automation. These changes may significantly affect the type of developmental efforts corporations undertake for their employees.

CONSUMER AFFAIRS

Companies' first choices here tend to be those of quality control, design improvements, and better customer service. These types of activities have probably been fostered by the high cost of recalling and modifying defective products, as well as by the damaging legal exposure from product liability. Again, a major reason for willingness of companies to engage in the activity is the predictable nature of quality control, utilizing quantitative models, statistical techniques, and other computer routines.

Companies' first choice of consumer affairs activity included quality control, design improvement, and better customer service.

ENVIRONMENTAL AFFAIRS

Water and air pollution control received the major emphasis in this area. In spite of the fact that air pollution was generally considered a more serious problem to health impairment, companies indicated they were doing more with water pollution control. As in the other cases, this probably is due to a number of reasons, such as increased visibility, ease of implementation, and the ability to see results accrued to an immediate community or company georgraphical area.

Under environmental affairs, water and air pollution received the most attention.

A further study of these companies, as shown in the quotation following, indicates that problems associated with the implementation of social action programs generally cluster around three basic and interrelated issues: (1) changing prices, (2) adjusting to legal requirements, and (3) developing required technology. Within the urban area category, however, the problem of justifying increased costs to shareholders is rated as more difficult than developing required technology.

> *The responding companies doubted whether they could adjust the price of their products to meet the costs of social action programs without substantially reducing the demand for and/or the quality of their products. Furthermore, they perceived regulatory rules or standards, especially those relating to pollution control and to a lesser degree those relative to product safety, as being unnecessarily servere and inflexible and therefore difficult to satisfy. The companies also claimed that, even though techniques for determining acceptable standards appeared to be inadequate, government agencies were setting arbitrary and conflicting standards and wanted unrealistically quick action. It was further stated that the standards were often applied without sufficient attention to variables such as size, capability, locality, and industrial structure. Finally, the available*

---

[30] David J. Cherington, *The Work Ethic: Working Values and Values that Work*, New York, Amacom, 1980.

technology could not, according to many companies, meet the standards within the specified time.[31]

Perhaps the major pressure on the environment in the coming decades will be caused by another environmental factor—the need for food created by the population explosion. This massive increase in population will be covered in more detail in Chapter 23, but some of the effects will be treated here. In 1979, for example, it was estimated that more than 1.4 billion people received less than their minimum daily requirements for food. In the next twenty years, world population will grow by another 3 billion people. Pressures to feed these people will be enormous, and pressures for more efficient means of food production will also be great. These pressures may indeed include efforts to relax environmental control standards on pesticide treatments unless acceptable substitutes for pesticides are found. Pressures for newer types of high-yield fertilizers may also appear, as may pressures for greater use of land resources.[32]

THE SOCIAL AUDIT: A STRATEGY FOR DEFINING AND IMPLEMENTING SOCIAL RESPONSIBILITY

The social audit is a means by which the corporation takes stock of its social performance.

Because of the difficulties discussed in the preceding section, firms and governmental agencies alike have been searching for tools that can be adapted to the management of social responsibility. The corporate social audit has been suggested as a useful step in this direction. The social audit is basically a mechanism by which the corporation takes stock of its social performance and reports it to the public.[33] Because it is administered by the corporation, it reflects the firm's view of its role in society and its social responsibility problems.

Dr. Clark Abt, of Abt Associates, Inc., has presented a comprehensive discussion of the role of the social audit in corporate decision making. This approach to the audit uses cost/benefit analysis to evaluate the company's actual and potential social programs. In essence, Abt proposes that the company construct "a balance sheet of company current and long-term social assets and liabilities and a statement of the social gains and losses in the current year."[34] In this way, the company would define the dollar values associated with corporate programs and the results they achieve. This leads to a relatively objective (and comparable) assessment of the impact of all of the actions of the corporation on its environment.

---

[31] Vernon M. Buehler and Y. K. Shetty, "Managerial Response to Social Responsibility Challenge," *Academy of Management Journal*, Vol. 19, No. 1, 1976, pp. 75–76.
[32] F. Luthans, R. Hodgetts, and K. Thompson, *Social Issues in Business*, New York, Macmillan, 1980, pp. 197–201.
[33] Raymond A. Bauer and Dan H. Fenn, *The Corporate Social Audit*, New York, The Russell Foundation, 1972, p. 90.
[34] Clark Abt, "An Annual Social Audit," *Congressional Record*, January 20, 1970, pp. E111, E112.

584 GOAL-ORIENTED MANAGEMENT SYSTEMS

The auditing approach suggested by Abt utilizes actual costs incurred in company programs, but does not stop there. The audit also incorporates opportunity costs of programs not undertaken by the company. The heart of the audit is a *social and income statement*. This statement measures all costs and values associated with corporate activities in areas like *social benefits* (in-house and external recreation, education, health programs, etc.), *quality of life other than fringes* (working conditions, air quality, privacy at work, adequate parking for workers, etc.), *career advancement* (equal opportunity, decreases in voluntary terminations, net promotions), *environment* (improvement in building, landscaping, public awards, contributions to knowledge, social impacts of contracts, etc.). The resultant of these calculations is a statement of net social income or loss for the company.[35]

FIGURE 21-8

A Social Auditing Matrix

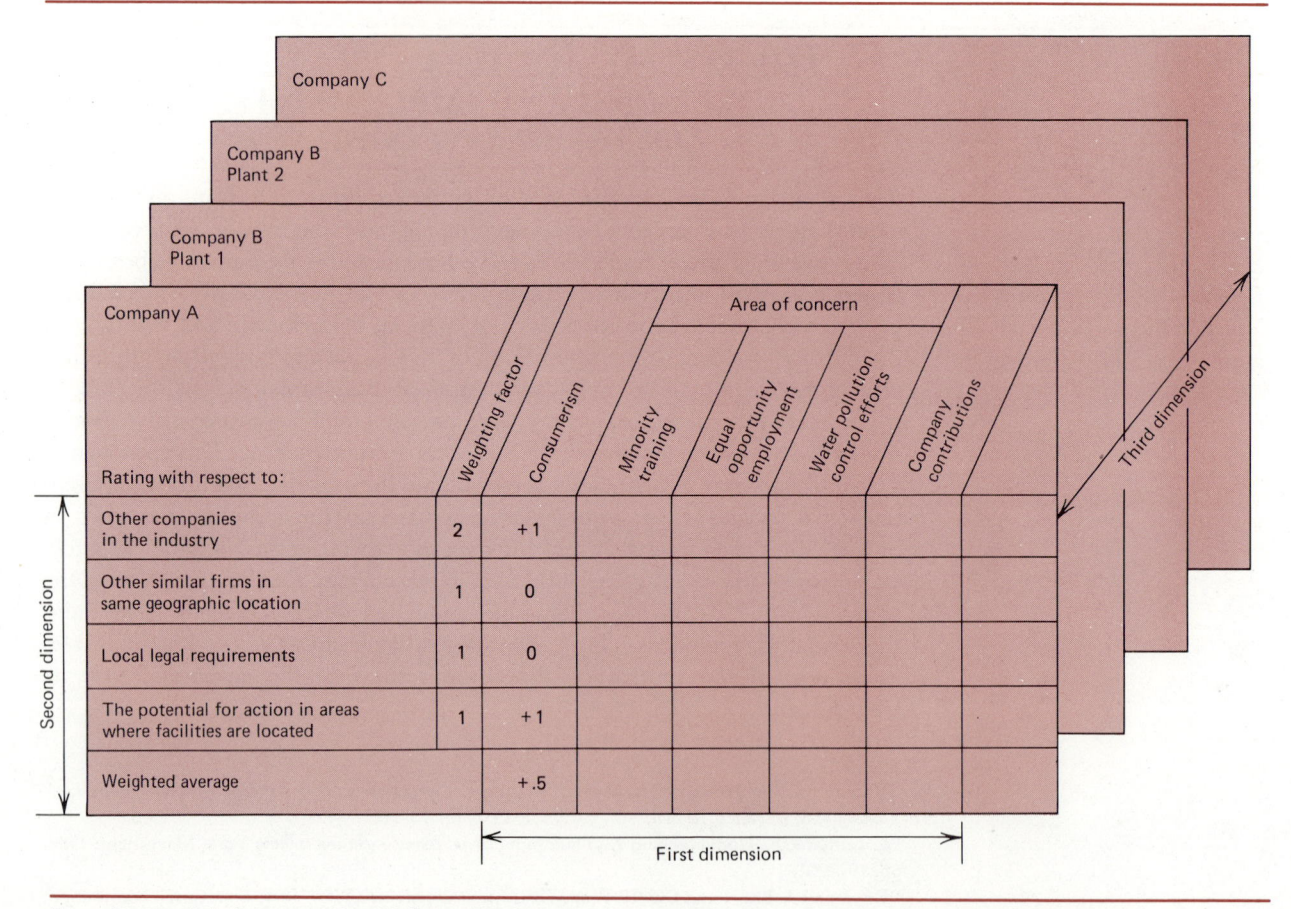

Rating with respect to:	Weighting factor	Consumerism	Minority training	Equal opportunity employment	Water pollution control efforts	Company contributions
Other companies in the industry	2	+1				
Other similar firms in same geographic location	1	0				
Local legal requirements	1	0				
The potential for action in areas where facilities are located	1	+1				
Weighted average		+.5				

Source: Raymond A. Bauer and Dan H. Fenn, *The Corporate Social Audit,* New York, Russell Sage Foundation, 1972, p. 20.

[35]Bauer and Fenn, *The Corporate Social Audit*, pp. 22–24.

Another approach recommends that an external agency conduct the social audit.

Another, somewhat simpler, proposal for the social audit has been made by Claire W. Sater, account adviser with Fields, Grant, & Company, investment advisers. This proposal represents a major change in emphasis from the Abt approach, because it recommends that an *external agency* conduct the audit of firms on a comparative industry-by-industry basis. This audit would be supplied to potential investors to give them an indication of relative corporate social responsibility. Rather than a balance sheet, Sater proposes a three-dimensional matrix which rates firms or plants relative to others in their industry. Figure 21-8 shows an example of the rating matrix.

The Abt and Saber poposals present many operational problems which must be solved before industry can implement them. They also point out the dilemma of *internal* versus *external* evaluation of social responsibility. If we accept the views expressed by Professor Friedman, quoted earlier in this chapter, the measurement and ranking methods used as input to the social audit will be quite different (and much simpler) than if we do not accept the Friedman position. The focus on judgments made by the firm, rather than those made by an outside observer or agency, also must be reconciled with these findings, in most curcumstances, the answer to this question is that *both* internal and external evaluations should be made. Whether or not we call them "social audits," it is important to recognize that systematic procedures such as those described previously will contribute to the effectiveness with which the firm defines and meets its social responsibility.

SUMMARY

As was implied in the studies of attitudes of executives and their statements in annual reports, the actions of companies indicate that more and more of them are committing their organizations to a variety of social action programs through *structural changes*. More than half of the responding firms in one research study of 1250 corporations indicated the existence of programs designed to meet the challenge of corporate responsibility. These companies generally had policy support from top mangement and usually had given a high-level executive definite responsibility in a social action area. But more than one-third of the firms sampled had not effected *internal* changes. This seems to be due to the fact that the firms are not prepared to make well-planned and integrated responses to the corporate responsibility challenge, but does not indicate a lack of desire to respond.

More companies are involved in employment, training, and contributing to education under the urban affairs category; in quality control, design improvements, and improved customer service under the consumer affairs grouping; and in air and water pollution control, under the environmental designation. Companies find the most difficulty in implementing social action programs in the areas of changing prices, adjusting to legal requirements, and developing the required technology. Just as was the case in the annual report survey, the data suggested that the response of a given corporation to perceived social demands depends upon its own organization's resources and skills. The studies described in

SUMMARY CHART

Views of Social Responsibility:

Classical—The pursuit of self-interest will best promote economic efficiency and public welfare.

Managerial—The manager of the large corporation is responsible for balancing the claims and rights of many diverse groups, such as employees, customers, suppliers, and the local community.

Public—Large corporations exercise such enormous power that it must be counterbalanced by government to protect the public interest.

Radical—Corporate executives are incapable of exercising social responsibility; therefore, there must be public ownership and control of all business enterprise.

Areas of Social Responsibility Chosen by Management:

Urban Affairs—Employment and training of disadvantaged

Consumer Affairs—Improving customer service

Environmental Affairs—Improvement of water and air pollution

Methods of Implementing Social Responsibility:

Establish Policy

Establish Social Responsibility Department

Use the Corporate Social Audit

   Internal Agency

   External Agency

this chapter give general support to a contingency perspective of corporate responsibility and show the possible value of such analysis to those formulating corporate strategy and public policy.[36] The corporate social audit, in turn, provides management with a starting point for making decisions which affect that strategy.

DISCUSSION QUESTIONS

1. Define social responsibility. Is your definition workable or idealistic? Discuss.
2. Would social responsibility be more easily met if ecosystems did not exist? Explain.

---

[36] Beuhler and Shetty, "Managerial Response to Social Responsibility," pp. 77–78, reprinted with permission.

3. Which goal system do you think is most appropriate for the larger blue chip corporations today? (See Figure 23-1.) Where are most firms operating?
4. Explain the classical, managerial, and public or radical views on social responsibility.
5. Are executives willing to sacrifice profits in order to meet social responsibilities? Explain.
6. Discuss the relationship, to be found in research, between profits and social responsibility.
7. In which area do corporations intervene most heavily: urban affairs, consumer affairs, or environmental affairs?

APPLICATION EXERCISES AND CASES

A MATTER OF PRIORITY[37]

The Acme Steel Company was located in a medium-sized (population 50,000) Midwest city. It was the largest employer in the area. Acme's president, Richard Yettar, Jr., aged 61, had inherited the business from his father. Richard, Sr., who founded the company in 1900 and managed it until his death in 1947.

Acme had never been a very profitable firm. A 1 to 2 percent annual return was considered quite good. Because of this low ROI, little money was available to replace or modernize the plant. Most of the equipment was badly out of date and inadequate. Mr. Yettar felt helpless. He could not justify paying 6 percent for a long-term loan to buy new equipment when the most he could derive from the investment would be 2 percent. He reasoned that it was better to continue operating with the poor equipment.

In February Mr. Yettar received a telephone call from the mayor, Mr. Anthony Grouber. The mayor abruptly told Mr. Yettar that a group of irate citizens, calling themselves the Committee for Clear Air (CCA), was in his office demanding that Acme cease polluting the air and install special antipollution control devices. The CCA felt that pollution coming from the plant was intolerable. The group was especially angry with Acme because Mr. Yettar's secretary had told them the week before that he was too busy to be bothered by them. The mayor suggested that perhaps it would be best for all parties if a meeting was held the next day. Mr. Yettar reluctantly agreed to attend.

The following afternoon all parties gathered in the mayor's office. After the CCA presented its case Mr. Yettar took the floor. He very quietly but deliberately outlined Acme's profit picture. He explained that although he appreciated the committee's suggestion, it was nevertheless impossible for the firm to implement them at this time. After answering a few questions regarding the company's

---

[37]F. Luthans and Richard M. Hodgetts, *Social Issues in Business*, 2nd ed., New York, McMillan, 1976, pp. 495–496.

profit position, Mr. Yettar kindly thanked them for allowing him to speak. The meeting adjourned shortly thereafter.

The following Monday the mayor called again. "Listen, Richard, you'd better do something about that pollution problem and fast. The CCA attorney, Bob Fairfax, was just here and he informed me that the committee intends to take your company to court. They're going to ask that you either immediately install antipollution equipment or pay damages to the committee." Mr. Yettar immediately called his attorney, Frank Hopper. The two men were in conference the rest of the day. The company lawyer, Mr. Hopper, offered the following advice.

This approach is being used by a number of similar groups around the country. In almost all instances the companies have backed down and made the necessary costly changes. However, some firms have chosen to fight the action. My personal feelings are that there is little to be gained by a court fight, and much to lose. Not only would it be expensive, but if you should win the case you would still create much hostility in the town. For instance, you might have a lot of husbands working here who will support you initially, but their wives may have a different view. Few husbands are going to back you over their wives' objections. Did you count how many women are on the CCA? Why, most of them are females. Furthermore, the leader is none other than Connie Ferguson, the wife of one of our own foremen. I think you should compromise with them now before this emotionally packed issue gets out of hand. Of course, if you choose to fight it, I'll back you all the way. It's all up to you.

The following morning Mr. Yettar called in Les Henderson, the head of his finance department. After relating the events of the last few days, Mr. Yettar asked, "What do you think we should do, Les?" Les answered,

"Well Mr. Yettar, I've gone over our finances very carefully and I estimate that it will cost about $100,000 to install antipollution equipment. We just don't have that kind of money available. Conditions are extremely tight, and the way the economy is moving, things will probably get worse before they get better. If we go to court, we might win or, or least, delay any action. This would give us some needed time to put aside some earnings for the new equipment. I realize that sooner or later will probably have to install the antipollution equipment, but belive me, from a financial standpoint it isn't possible within the next five years. We're in a very tight financial pinch. It's easy for the CCA to ask for changes, they don't have to meet a payroll and pay suppliers. If we are forced to install this equipment right now, we will have to cut back our work force immediately.

Mr. Yettar thanked him for his analysis of the situation. The president then sat down and began sketching out a list of the company's objectives. When he was finished, he went back over the list and assigned priorities. In this way he hoped to determine whether or not he should agree to the demands of the CCA or pursue a court fight.

Questions
1. What objectives do you think are on the list being put together by Mr. Yettar? Be specific and include at least five objectives on your list.

2. Assign the priorities you believe Mr. Yettar would give each. What would be your priorities?
3. What should Mr. Yettar do now? Explain in detail.

THE XEROX EXPERIMENT[38]

XEROX CORPORATION
Memorandum to Corporate Executives

To	See Distribution	Date	August 7, 1970
From	J. M. Wainger	Location	HR 2
Subject	Xerox Social Action	Organization	Corporate Personnel

We have decided to institute, as promptly as possible, a program for Xerox employees which we think will have substantial positive impact internally and externally, both now and for our future.

We will offer to twenty Xerox employees, regardless of level in the Corporation, (though excluding all of you) the opportunity to work for a year out of Xerox in some position that has high social value. As examples, the jobs might be with some community organization attacking urban problems, or some Federal Government agency, or a school, etc.

We plan to use the following approach. Through appropriate Xerox communications media, we will publicize the program and ask all those employees who are interested in submit a short description of the project they wish to work on and their reasons for choosing it. As part of their submission, they must include assurance that they have agreement from the prospective employer to take them on if they are freed up. We hope to receive many submissions.

All of these submissions will be screened by an impartial, outside board of prestigious men who will choose the twenty they consider to be most worthy according to the social criteria we've established.

The twenty selected employees will then be given a year to work at their chosen task. We assume they will return to Xerox at the end of that time, though no guarantee can be exacted. We will require that the projects they select be in or near their present communities. In other words, this program should not carry with it relocation subsidies for attractive long-range trips to such places as Los Angeles, Washington, or Hawaii.

Xerox will maintain the employees' total compensation at the rate prevailing at the time they left Xerox by paying them the difference between whatever they receive from their outside job and their then Xerox salary.

We need to set up our outside screening board as soon as possible. I need your help. Would you please submit to me as soon as possible the names of one or more people you deem suitable to serve. The names you submit should be of people you feel fairly confident you can "deliver" if asked to contact them directly. I

---

[38] C. Roland Christensen, Kenneth R. Andrews, and Joseph L. Bower, *Business Policy, Text and Cases,* "Exhibit 3, Xerox Corporation," Homewood, Ill., Richard D. Irwin, Inc., 1973, p. 663. Reprinted with permission.

anticipate a board of perhaps five men, disparate in background but uniform quality.

I recognize that there are problems inherent in this program, and I'm sure you do too. However, the results will more than justify taking the problems on. We will benefit and, by leading, we will influence.

You will, of course, be apprised of the details of the program as it is shaped up. May I have your nominees for the selection board as soon as possible.

JMW/sd

Distribution: D. J. Curtin   A. R. McCardell
                J. B. Flavin   C. P. McColough
                J. E. Goldman   J. W. Rutledge
                S. Kaplan   J. C. Wilson

Questions

1. In light of your studies regarding social responsibility in business, how would you view the project of Xerox to pay twenty employees to work exclusively on projects with social value?
2. Would you consider this project to fall exclusively in Section IV of Figure 21-1, Goal Systems of Firms? Why or why not?
3. What dangers would you see for the general public in such a project? To Xerox?

CHAPTER 22

MBO—AN INTEGRATIVE SYSTEM OF MANAGEMENT

A SYSTEMS APPROACH TO MBO
SETTING OBJECTIVES AND DEVELOPING STRATEGIC PLANS
ASSESSING THE EXTERNAL ENVIRONMENT
DEVELOPING ACTION PLANS
ASSIGNING PRIORITIES AND RESPONSIBILITIES
DEVELOPING DEPARTMENTAL OBJECTIVES
IMPLEMENTING PLANS THROUGH LEADERSHIP AND DELEGATION
EMPHASIZING WELL-WRITTEN OBJECTIVES
INSURING GOOD TIMING
MEASURING AND REWARDING PERFORMANCE, IN VIEW OF THE OBJECTIVES
THE MBO APPRAISAL
MBO AND JOB ENRICHMENT
BUDGETING AND CONTROL
EXTERNAL INPUTS FROM MANAGERIAL AND ORGANIZATIONAL DEVELOPMENT
GROUP PROCESS AND MBO
MATCHING ORGANIZATION STYLE WITH OBJECTIVES
LIMITATIONS TO MBO
WHAT DISTINGUISHES MBO FROM NON-MBO?
APPLICATION EXERCISES AND CASES
MBO OR SOMETHING ELSE?
CHOOSE A LEADERSHIP STYLE

THE WORKINGS OF A JAPANESE CORPORATION[1]

In an interview with the American vice-presidents, I asked how they felt about working for this Japanese bank. "They treat us well, let us in on the decision-making, and pay us well. We're satisfied." "You're very fortunate," I continued, "but tell me, if there were something that you could change about this Japanese bank, what would it be?" The response was quick and clearly one that was very much on their minds: "These Japanese just don't understand objectives, and it drives us nuts!"

Next I interviewed the president of this bank, and expatriate Japanese who was on temporary assignment from Tokyo headquarters to run the United States operation, and asked about the two American vice-presidents. "They're hard working, loyal, and professional. We think they're terrific," came the reply. When asked if he would like to change them in any way, the president replied, "These Americans just don't seem to be able to understand objectives."

With each side accusing the other of inability to understand objectives, there was a clear need for further interviewing and for clarification. A second round of interviews probed further into the issue. First the American vice-presidents: "We have a nonstop running battle with the president. We simply cannot get him to specify a performance target for us. We have all the necessary reports and numbers, but we can't get specific targets from him. He won't tell us how large a dollar increase in loan volume or what percent decrease in operating costs he expects us to achieve over the next month, quarter, or even year. How can we know whether we're performing well without specific targets to shoot for?" A point well taken, for every major American company and government bureau devotes a large fraction of its time to the setting of specific, measurable performance targets. Every American business school teaches its students to take global, fuzzy corporate goals and boil them down to measurable performance targets. Management by objective (MBO), program planning and evaluation, and cost-benefit analysis are among the basic tools of control in modern American management.

When I returned to reinterview the Japanese president, he explained, "If only I could get these Americans to understand our philosophy of banking. To understand what the business means to us—how we feel we should deal with our customers and our employees. What our relationship should be to the local communities we serve. How we should deal with our competitors, and what our role should be in the world at large. If they could get that under their skin, then they could figure out for themselves what an appropriate objective would be for any situation, no matter how unusual or new, and I would never have to tell them, never have to give them a target."

---

[1] William Ouchi, *Theory Z—How American Business Can Meet the Japanese Challenge*, Reading, Mass., Addison-Wesley Publishing Co., 1981, pp. 39–41.

---

*The authors gratefully acknowledge the assistance of Robert R. Bell, Assistant Dean, College of Business, Tennessee Technological University, Cookeville, Tennessee, who revised this chapter.

The management system, which includes the establishment of specific goals and agreement on goals is called management by objectives.

Does management matter? Do managerial actions have an effect on bottom life performance? The answer to both of these questions, according to most researchers, is an unequivocal yes![2] But the impact of managerial action varies considerably with circumstances, as we saw in Chapter 12, Contingency Approaches to Organizations. At the individual level, most research has found that performance usually improves when specific goals are established and with mutual agreement between the superior and the subordinate as to how the goals are to be accomplished.[3] The managerial process typically used to create this type of environment is called management by objectives (MBO), and many managers believe it is a quite effective tool.[4]

However, a systematic approach to management, utilizing unambiguous goals, is not as highly regarded in Japan as suggested by the incident at the beginning of this chapter. Nevertheless, this chapter presents an integrated system of management utilizing MBO, which represents a typical system used by American firms today. For an alternate approach receiving much attention, the reader should refer to Ouchi, cited earlier.

While there have been many books and articles written on techniques of implementation, perhaps the classic approach to MBO remains that of Peter Drucker, as presented in his description of the manager's letter.[5] This procedure for generating the letter follows a six-step process in which the subordinate writes a "letter" to his or her manager specifying what he believes to be the objectives of the boss, his own objectives, performance criteria, subobjectives needed to be accomplished to reach each objective, and the organizational resources and requirements that will hinder or help in accomplishing goals.[6] The subordinate also gives the specific activities that will lead to the completion of overall job objectives.

Once the manager's letter is written, the subordinate and the boss discuss it.

Once this letter is written, the subordinate and the boss discuss it in order to discover and correct any misunderstandings as to what is expected from each within a specified time frame. If the subordinate has misinterpreted what is supposed to be accomplished in the job, the boss has a unique opportunity to erase misunderstandings about what the subordinate should be doing, what activities will lead to the objectives, and how the subordinate feels he is being evaluated. It is at this point where superior-subordinate communications are clarified.

---

[2] See, for example, R. T. Lenz, "Antecedents of Organizational Performance: An Interdisciplinary Review," *Proceedings*, 1980 Academy of Management National Meeting, pp. 2–6.

[3] H. H. Meyer, E. Kay, and J.R.P. French, "Split Roles in Performance Appraisal," *Harvard Business Review*, January-February 1965, pp. 123–129.

[4] See R. C. Ford, F. S. McLaughlin, and J. Nixdorf, "Ten Questions about MBO," *California Management Review*, Winter 1980, Vol. XXIII, No. 2, pp. 88–94.

[5] The introductory material in this chapter draws heavily from Robert C. Ford and Robert R. Bell, "MBO: Seven Strategies for Success," *Advanced Management Journal*, Vol. 42, No. 1, Winter 1977, pp. 14–24.

[6] Peter Drucker, *The Practice of Management*, New York, Harper and Brothers Publishers, 1954.

Once the letter has been agreed to by both the boss and the subordinate, it becomes a performance "contract" for a specific time period. At the end of this time, the contract is reviewed by the manager and the subordinate to determine how well the latter met or failed to meet goals. This review session allows the subordinate to find out, in a relatively objective way, his areas of weakness that need development, and his strengths. The result should be a clear idea of what everyone's job is and how that job relates to the accomplishment of the overall organizational goals.

The process of implementation is based on the simple notion that the manager and the subordinate can reach agreement in what needs to be accomplished. This idea assumes that most people like knowing what they are supposed to achieve in their jobs, and do not like expending effort on the wrong or inappropriate tasks. Consequently, if top management can define and communicate the overall goals and objectives of the organization, lower-level managers should be able to develop appropriate objectives for coordinating their units' activities with organizational expectations. This breaking down of overall goals into smaller pieces should allow everyone in the organization to know where and how specific tasks fit into the overall goal. While this may seem a bit utopian, the implementation of the process is quite likely to bring revelations to many managers about what they are actually expected to accomplish. At the very least, some subordinates may find out, perhaps for the first time, what their boss is expecting from them, both in the scope of their job activities and the level of accomplishment. As the subordinate and higher manager reach consensus on goals, research shows that employee goal attainment tends to rise.[7] Furthermore, because MBO is a planning tool, both managers and their subordinates can shift their focus from worrying about what yesterday meant to preparing for the problems of tomorrow.

The MBO approach also recognizes that people become more committed to organizational objectives when they see how these goals tie into their own personal goals and aspirations. MBO is a system that allows each worker to relate her personal needs to her job and, where possible, even to incorporate personal development goals into the attainment of objectives. In doing so, MBO provides a communications link between the impersonal goals of the firm and the very personal aspirations each worker and manager brings to the job.

Douglas McGregor also advocated the use of MBO; but, primarily as an appraisal process. In his well-known article, "The Human Side of Enterprise," he suggested that people will exercise self-direction and self-control in the attainment of organizational goals to the degree that they are committed to them.

His emphasis on MBO became oriented toward the need for integration of individual and organizational goals, leading to self-control. Appraisal based upon such integrated goals, McGregor argued, would be superior to traditional

---

[7] R. A. Martin and James C. Quick, "The Effect of Job Consensus on MBO Goal Attainment," *MSU Business Topics*, Winter 1981, pp. 43–48.

performance appraisal methods because is shifted the emphasis from identification of weaknesses to an analysis of performance and strengths.[8]

A SYSTEMS APPROACH TO MBO

MBO is a system that integrates the organization with its environment and the key management activities.

Since the advent of MBO, it has become more than simply an objective setting process, an appraisal tool, or a budgeting device. MBO has "become a system of managing that integrates the organization with its environment and the various key managerial activities, so that the whole is more than simply the sum of its parts."[9]

The major components in the MBO system are depicted in Figure 22-1. They can be viewed as an operational approach to the systems model discussed in Chapter 3, Managerial Planning and Strategy. The major components in the MBO system—setting objectives, developing action plans, leadership and others described in blocks 1 through 7—are very similar to the subjects discussed throughout this text. This is no coincidence. If MBO is an integrative approach to the total management process, it must include all of the basic functions of management. These various components will now be discussed as they are normally implemented in an MBO mode.

SETTING OBJECTIVES AND DEVELOPING STRATEGIC PLANS

An old axiom states that the best fertilizer ever invented was the footsteps of the farmer. Similarly, the best assurance of effective planning in an organization is active support, participation, and guidance of the chief executive.[10] The process of setting objectives, formulating plans and designing systems to implement them becomes a cascading process. It was described more fully in Chapter 3.

But when MBO is used, a new and unique element is added to the goal-setting process. Rather than simply becoming an autocratic management system, successful MBO programs include upward and downward communications.

Peter Drucker's clarification of the importance of well-defined top objectives is enlightening.

To manage a business is to balance a variety of needs and goals.

> *To manage a business is to balance a variety of needs and goals . . . What should these objectives be, then? There is only one answer:* Objectives are needed in every area where performance and results directly and vitally affect the survival and prosperity of the business. . . . *Objectives in these key areas should enable us to do five things: To organize and explain the whole range of business phenomena in a small*

---

[8] D. M. McGregor, "An Uneasy Look at Performance Appraisal," *Harvard Business Review*, 35, May-June 1957, pp. 89–94.
[9] Heinz Weihrich, "MBO—Quo Vadis?" *Management Review*, January 1977, p. 43.
[10] Anthony P. Raia, *Managing by Objectives*, Glenview, Ill., Scott Foresman and Co., 1974, p. 29.

The MBO System

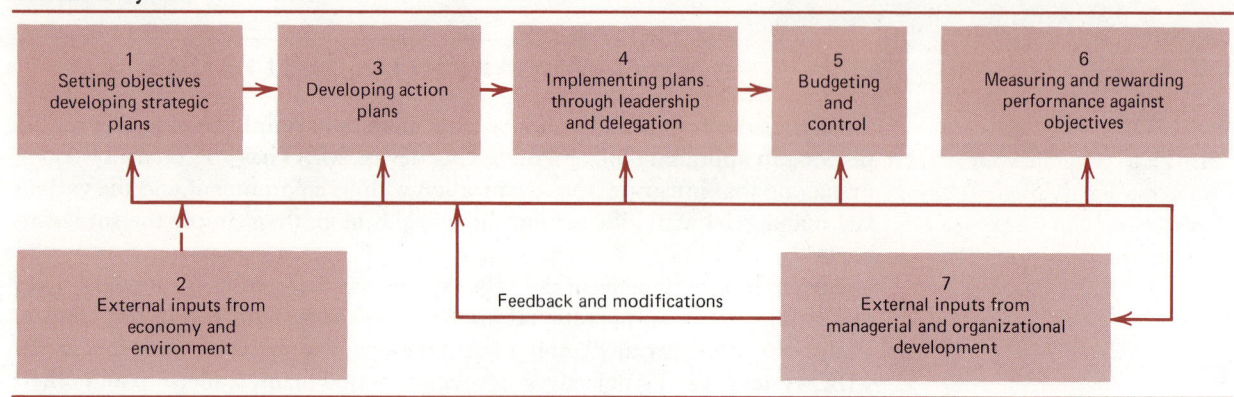

```
1                    3                    4                      5              6
Setting objectives → Developing action → Implementing plans  → Budgeting    → Measuring and rewarding
developing strategic  plans               through leadership     and            performance against
plans                                     and delegation         control        objectives
   ↑                    ↑                                          ↑              
   │                    │                                          │              
   2                         Feedback and modifications        7
External inputs from                                           External inputs from
economy and                                                    managerial and organizational
environment                                                    development
```

Source: suggested by Anthony P. Raia, *Managing By Objectives* (Glenview, Ill., Scott Foresman and Company, 1974), pp. 20–21, and Heinz Weihrich, "MBO—Quo Vadis?", *Management Review,* January 1977.

number of general statements; to test these statements in actual experience; to predict behavior; to appraise the soundness of decisions when they are still being made; and to enable practicing businessmen to analyze their own experience and as a result, improve their performance.[11]

Drucker proceeds to cite the following eight areas as being crucial to business success.[12]

1. Market standing.
2. Innovation.
3. Productivity.
4. Physical and financial resources.
5. Profitability.
6. Manager performance and development.
7. Worker performance and attitude.
8. Public responsibility.

Objectives and goals are needed for nonprofit- as well as profit-oriented organizations.

Such all-encompassing objectives and goals are needed for nonprofit organizations as well. Often in governmental organizations, there is the additional difficulty of having goals established at the federal level and implemented by states or lower-level organizations. For example, the statement of mission, or purpose, cited by the U.S. Department of Health, Education and Welfare for state vocational rehabilitation administrations of 1975 was as follows: "To serve

---
[11]Drucker, *Practice of Management*, pp. 62–63.
[12]Ibid., p. 63.

1,860,000 persons and to rehabilitate 338,000 of these persons of which 115,000 are to be severely disabled."[13] Later, this goals was broken down into subobjectives and goals.

ASSESSING THE EXTERNAL ENVIRONMENT

As goals and objectives are formulated, the external environment must be assessed. For the corporation, major threats to existing markets and product lines must be examined. Trends and changes in consumer needs should be analyzed. Resources should be reviewed; and areas for their deployment, in order to exploit new opportunities, should be investigated.[14] One major area of inquiry is social responsibility and environmental consequences of management actions, which we discussed in Chapter 21, Social Responsibilities of Management.

DEVELOPING ACTION PLANS

Objective setting often suffers from the static sound of its name. Action is much more likely to result when objectives are spoken of as change or improvement plans. Thinking of *improvement* helps us break our psychological set and move on to different approaches. For example, a company with a major objective of 15 percent earnings per share could pursue several strategies as depicted in Figure 22-2, and described as follows.

Thinking about improvement objectives or plans is much more likely to lead to action.

FIGURE 22-2

Three Strategies for Achieving Earnings of Fifteen Percent per Share

Target	High Volume	Approach High Asset Utilization	Aggressive Financing
Sales growth	15.0	7.0	10.0
Profit before income tax/sales	4.0	4.0	4.0
Inventory turnover	3.5	4.0	3.5
Dividend payout	60.0	60.0	40.0
Debt/equity	50.0	50.0	60.0

Source: Frank T. Paine and William Naumes, *Strategy and Policy Formation. An Integrative Approach*, Philadelphia, Pa., W. B. Saunders Company, 1974. Adapted from L. V. Gerstner, Jr., "Can Strategic Planning Pay Off?", *Business Horizons*, Vol. 15, No. 6, December 1972.

---

[13] State Vocational Rehabilitation Agency, *Program and Financial Plan*, Washington, D.C., State Department of Health, Education, and Welfare, 1975.
[14] Raia, *Managing by Objectives*, p. 35.

The alternatives are: (1) a high volume policy, (2) a high asset utilization policy, and (3) an aggressive financing policy. Each of the alternatives implies a fundamentally different way of operating the company, yet, each set of objectives is internally consistent and may allow the organization to achieve an identical overall earning per share target. In the high volume approach, emphasis may be placed on lower prices and heavy promotion. For high asset utilization approach, emphasis may be placed on eliminating slow-moving products. In the aggressive financing approach, dividend payout may be held back, the percentage of debt to equity increased and new products added.[15]

ASSIGNING PRIORITIES AND RESPONSIBILITIES

Many users of MBO quickly discover that they have a number of things they must accomplish as well as other things they would like to accomplish in order to be effective in their job. It becomes difficult when confronted with seven to ten good things to do, to decide which good thing to do first. A useful method for assigning priorities to various objectives is a simple ranking of objectives. Other more elaborate systems may include a series of priority categories (A 3 must do; B 3 should do; and C 3 nice to do).[16] The choice of the particular priority ranking system will depend upon the number of objectives the manager is responsible for and the extent to which the objectives compete with one another.

The number of objectives a manager is working toward must be manageable.

DEVELOPING DEPARTMENTAL OBJECTIVES

The cascading process continues throughout each department of an organization. First, key result areas are identified. Next, these are further broken down for assignment to lower-level units. "For example, sales volume and market penetration might be further broken down by product, and assigned to regions, to districts, and eventually to individual salesmen while share of the market and customer acceptance might also be developed for each product and be further defined in terms of national and foreign market places."[17] In this manner, objectives for one level of the organization become action plans for another.

The cascading approach into the regional and local levels of the Rehabilitation Administration can be seen by the following statements in the 1975 *Program and Financial Plan*.[18] (Note their overall mission statement cited earlier.)

The cascading process continues; objectives for one level to become action plans for another.

(a) Carry out intensive short-term training efforts focused on (1) acquainting all levels of state agency staff with the purpose of the Rehab Act of 1973, and (2) helping states improve their evaluation capability.

(b) Mount a series of Program Administrative Reviews focusing primarily on the severely disabled being served and rehabilitated, and on state systems.

---

[15]Frank T. Paine and William Naumes, *Strategy and Policy Formation. An Integrative Approach*, Philadelphia, Pa., W. B. Saunders Company, 1974, pp. 145–150.
[16]Raia, *Managing By Objectives*.
[17]Ibid., p. 14.
[18]State Vocational Rehabilitation Agency, *Program and Financial Plan*, p. 4.

(c) *Convene key regional office staff for the purpose of planning a coordinated approach to identifying and attempting to overcome barriers to the achievement of quality rehabilitations in acceptable numbers.*
(d) *Work with directors of state vocational rehabilitation agencies for the purpose of establishing a national strategy leading toward improvement of administration and management of the system.*

IMPLEMENTING PLANS THROUGH LEADERSHIP AND DELEGATION

Participative goal setting between superior and subordinate is one of the most unique elements in the MBO process. In MBO, the goal setting, leadership, and appraisal functions become blended into one ongoing system. This is what Peter Drucker called managing by "objectives" rather than "drives" or "crisis". Drucker dramatizes the latter approach with the following quote.[19]

"For four weeks we cut inventories," a case-hardened veteran of management by crisis once summed it up. "Then we have four weeks of cost cutting, followed by four weeks of human relations. We just have time to push customer service and courtesy for a month. And, then the inventory is back where it was when we started. We don't even try to do our job. All management talks about, thinks about, preaches about, is last week's inventory figure or this week's customer complaints. How we do the rest of the job they don't even want to know."

We should recognize one key change in the superior-subordinate relationship that is caused by participative goal setting. When we encourage participation through delegation, we also give subordinates a great deal of freedom in making decisions. The subordinate, in a sense, can make the play as he or she sees it. Joseph Litterer comments:

Needless to say, this leaves the superior without a direct influence on what the subordinate will choose to do. It increases the superior's dependency on subordinates, which some superiors are philosophically or emotionally reluctant or even unable to accept.[20]

One of the best defined systems of leadership by objectives is outlines by George Odiorne. After discussing an overall MBO process similar to the one that we have been discussing, Odiorne develops a scheme for personal goal setting and leadership as follows.[21]

---

[19]Drucker, *Practice of Management*, p. 128.
[20]Joseph A. Litterer, "Elements of Control in Organizations," in M. Jelinek, J. Litterer, and R. Miles, *Organizations by Design: Theory and Practice*, Plano, Texas, Business Publications, Inc., 1981, pp. 429–440.
[21]George S. Odiorne, *Management by Objectives*, New York, Pitman Publishing Corp., 1965, pp. 70–73.

Step 1: Set objectives for the next budget year with each man individually. This is done in the following manner: Before meeting, list some objectives you'd like to see him include for the next year and have them ready. Note especially any innovations and improvements required of his function. Ask the subordinate to make notes on what objectives he had in mind for next year and set a date when you'd like to discuss these with him. Normally, these goals will fall into four categories: Routine duties, problem-solving goals, creative goals, and personal goals.

Step 2: In your personal conference, review the person's own objectives in detail, then offer your own suggestions or changes. Have two copies of the final draft of his objectives typed—give him one and keep one yourself. Working from the final agreement, ask him what you can do to help him accomplish his targets. Note his suggestions, keep them with your copy, and include them in your objectives, if pertinent.

Step 3: During the year, check each subordinate's goals as promised milestones are reached. Ask yourself if he is meeting his targets. Time, cost, quantity, quality and service should be measured here. Discuss whether his targets should be amended. Don't hesitate to eliminate inappropriate goals or add new ones.

Step 4: Near the end of the year, ask each subordinate to prepare a brief "Statement of Performance Against Budget" using his copy of his performance budget as a guide. Set a date to go over this report in detail. Search for causes of variance. At this meeting, also, you can cover other things that may be on his mind. Set the stage for establishing the subordinate's performance budget for the coming year. Here, of course, the manager finds himself back at Step One of the goal setting stage, but better equipped by reason of his experience, to set more realistic goals for the next budget period.

Although the process described above is often suggested as the ideal one, many styles of leadership behavior have been found workable within an MBO system. Furthermore, high levels of mutual involvement do not necessarily lead to high subordinate influence in the goal-setting process. One group of researchers found that when the subordinate prepares a set of goals and objectives that are later edited by the boss, without the boss preparing a separate set, subordinate-perceived influence is higher. Apparently, there is a cultural norm that says that the superior should have more to say about the subordinate's goals than the subordinate does. When the boss is physically present and involved, this feeling is heightened.[22]

Additional problems arise both in the assignment of priorities of objectives and in putting them in written form.

The contingency approaches to leadership reviewed in Chapter 14, Leadership Styles, suggest that the interaction of the superior and subordinate should vary, based on several considerations. Research in MBO systems indicates that subordinate influence is usually greatest in marketing departments, and least in engineering departments.[23]

> High levels of mutual involvement do not necessarily lead to high subordinate influence.

---

[22]Stephen J. Carroll, Jr. and Henry L. Tosi, Jr., *Management by Objectives—Applications and Research*, New York, Macmillan, 1973, p. 33.
[23]Ibid., p. 29.

EMPHASIZING WELL-WRITTEN OBJECTIVES

A major difficulty in implementing MBO programs rests in the inability of managers to write clear objectives. As Louis Allen observes, "To communicate effectively, a plan must do more than be read; it must *create* understanding."[24] Simply stated, an objective is a statement of a measurable end result. It is a plan stated in terms of a *single, desired, tangible, accomplishment.* The plan should communicate where the person is going, at what rate, and when they expect to get there.[25] Managers have a dual role to play in emphasizing well-written objectives. They must not only write their own objectives well but must also be able to coach their subordinates in arriving at appropriate statements of their own objectives. Many managers and scholars have suggested specific guidelines concerning the writing of objectives. Writing on "objective penmanship," for example, John B. Lasagna of Wells Fargo Bank has suggested that well-stated objectives possess the following characteristics.[26]

1. Start off with an action verb.
2. Identify a single key result for each of the objectives.
3. Give the day, month, and year of estimated completion.
4. Identify costs (i.e., dollars, time, materials, and equipment).
5. State verifiable criteria that signal when the objective has been reached.
6. Be sure the objective is controllable by the person setting the objective and if not totally controllable, at least isolate the part that is.

William Reddin suggests other guidelines to follow. Objectives, according to him, should be written so as to avoid commonly made errors.[27] The manager, for example, should question whether objectives are set too high or too low. He or she must be concerned with the number of objectives a subordinate has, because too many can cause dilution of error. Dale D. McConkey, for example, suggests that six to ten high-priority objectives are about right for most managers.[28] In addition, the time frame of objectives should be evaluated in terms of whether the review cycle is too long or too short. Cost estimates must be realistic and priorities must be properly assigned to the more important objectives. Finally, Reddin suggests objectives should not be overly complex or elegant and should be measurable if possible.

Another key to well-written objectives is the use of consistent terminology. One company, Ameron, Inc., has developed a companywide planning dictionary.

---

[24] Louis A. Allen, "Managerial Planning: Back to Basics," *Management Review*, April 1981, p. 20.
[25] William A. Denny, "Ten Rules for Managing by Objectives," *Business Horizons*, October 1979, pp. 66–69.
[26] John B. Lasagna, "Make Your MBO Pragmatic," *Harvard Business Review*, November-December 1971, pp. 64–69.
[27] William J. Reddin, *Effective Management by Objectives*, New York, McGraw-Hill, 1971.
[28] Dale D. McConkey, "Building Toward MBO," *Data Management*, January 1980, pp. 44–47.

The dictionary contains a glossary of standard terms, and all managers are trained in how to use it.[29]

INSURING GOOD TIMING

The last item in Drucker's management letter format is the area where many MBO programs fall apart. If it is assumed that the subordinate and the boss do have a sufficiently good working relationship so that they can agree on the job's objectives, the very difficult task of specifying the activities required to accomplish subobjectives becomes the immediate problem. Not only is the subordinate required to define the activities necessary to reach various subobjectives, he or she must also be able to define the expected time frame for accomplishing these activities. Even the best intentioned employees are not able to predict the course of events, and the less motivated members of the organization may not even try. The manager is, therefore, faced with the continued dilemma of determining what an appropriate time frame for activity/task accomplishment really is.

Specifying activities and determining proper timing is difficult.

Several familiar management techniques may offer some hope for solving the problem. One approach is to incorporate a modified network planning tool into the structuring of MBO activities. One such device is the Program Evaluation and Review Technique (PERT), described in Chapter 20, Controlling Operations.[30]

The network approach can provide several advantages when used with the MBO system. In a typical MBO program, a manager has to specify what actions he or she will undertake to accomplish a subobjective as well as estimate a completion time. All too often, the activities are merely listed with a rough guess estimate of completion time. Often, little effort is focused on interrelationships between activities and on their sequencing. The manager using the network technique is forced to to use MBO to its greatest advantage in the planning area. He must incorporate into his thinking the various activities that are required to reach a specific goal as well as their sequence of occurrence and interrelationships with other goals and activities.

A network approach to MBO includes the sequence and interrelationships of goals and objectives.

MEASURING AND REWARDING PERFORMANCE, IN VIEW OF THE OBJECTIVES

While this approach will insure a systematic and effective performance appraisal, several specific considerations are required in reviewing MBO performance. Since the focus of the review is on specified results, care should be taken in

---

[29]Louis A. Allen, "Managerial Planning: Back to Basics," *Management Review*, April 1981, p. 17.
[30]Robert W. Miller, "How to Plan and Control with PERT," *Harvard Business Review*, March-April 1962, pp. 93–104.

examining what caused the results. When things go amiss, the superior should ask herself the following.[31]

> Was it my fault?
> Was it some failure on the subordinate's part?
> Was it beyond anyone's control?

The appraiser must also be careful to consider objectives that are not quantifiable, and must not become overly preoccupied with short-term objectives. Finally, since MBO requires appraisal of accomplishments on the present job only, an additional consideration must be made for the potential of the subordinate to progress to more difficult jobs.[32]

MBO appraisers must be careful to consider objectives that are not quantifiable.

THE MBO APPRAISAL

MBO appraisal requires one of the most mature and frank discussions that is likely to be undertaken by the supervisor and subordinate. For this reason, the principles outlined in transactional analysis should be utilized. If both superior and subordinate operate from an I'm OK-You're OK position, the interview will most likely be successful. In such a case, the procedure can be described as follows.[33]

MBO appraisal requires one of the most mature and frank discussions that is likely to be undertaken by the supervisor and subordinate.

> *The employee evaluates his performance against preestablished, verifiable objectives. He knows and acknowledges whether or not he achieved them. He solicits the help of his superior (whom he considers OK) to develop plans for the future which are designed to build on strengths and to overcome weaknesses. He is not blind to his shortcomings but views them as a challenge. He is confident in his abilities and feels good about his accomplishments. Moreover, he trusts his superior who is not out to "get him" and collaborates with him in his own personal development which, in turn, contributes to organizational objectives.*

MBO AND JOB ENRICHMENT

What about personal goal setting in an MBO style as it relates to the satisfaction of the worker on the job? In Chapter 19, Job Design, we discussed job enrichment and its importance to productivity and the satisfaction of the worker. As suggested previously, job enrichment increases worker satisfaction but does not always increase productivity. Recent research findings of job enrichment studies within a firm using MBO provide additional information.

---

[31]Odiorne, *Management by Objectives*, p. 72.
[32]Raia, *Management By Objectives*, p. 118.
[33]Heinz Weihrich, "MBO: Appraisal with Transactional Analysis," *Personnel Journal*, April 1976, p. 175.

The researchers concluded as follows:

> *In summary, our predictions were confirmed—job enrichment had a major impact only on job satisfaction while goal setting had its major impact on productivity. Perhaps an even more important result is that setting specific goals did not cause satisfaction to decline. In fact, goals seemed to have some enriching effects on their own—setting goals seems to add interest to an otherwise very boring job.*[34]

Job enrichment tends to have its greatest impact on job satisfaction.

BUDGETING AND CONTROL

Budgeting poses a particular problem during the installation of an MBO system of management. Since all organizations already have some form of budgeting, the tendency is to establish dual channels of objective setting and budgeting. But, to be successful, there must be a careful integration of objectives and budgets. Plans and objectives without the strength of appropriate funding are meaningless. Conversely, budgets cannot be appropriately justified without plans and objectives.

The following guidelines should be followed in utilizing a budget with the MBO system of management:[35]

1. The formulation of objectives and plans should precede the preparation of the budget.
2. Objectives should be based on the priority of needs of the organization.
3. Each manager (and department) should be given the opportunity to compete for available resources by demonstrating what will be done with the resources awarded to them.

McConkey summarizes the relationship between in MBO and budgeting well, as follows.[36]

> *Thus, from an MBO viewpoint, budgets in their simplest form are the quantification in dollars and cents of what the objectives and plans of all managers viewed collectively mean in profit and/or loss for the target period.*

The motivational approach to MBO presumes that budgeting will be a consequence of objectives and plans.

Figure 22-3 illustrates the sequence of budgeting and planning. Note that the motivational approach presumes that budgeting will be a natural consequence of objectives and plans. On the other hand, the fiscal approach tends to allocate monies, often on the basis of existing programs; and plans and objectives are developed on a perfunctory basis to conform to the budgeting process. A number of organizations are moving toward zero base budgeting systems (see Chapter 20

---

[34] Denis D. Umstot, "MBO + Job Enrichment—How to Have Your Cake and Eat it Too," *Management Review*, February 1977, p. 26.
[35] Dale D. McConkey, "The Position and Function of Budgets in an MBO System," *The Business Quarterly*, Spring 1974, p. 48.
[36] Ibid., p. 47.

FIGURE 22-3

Position of the Budget in a Profit Plan

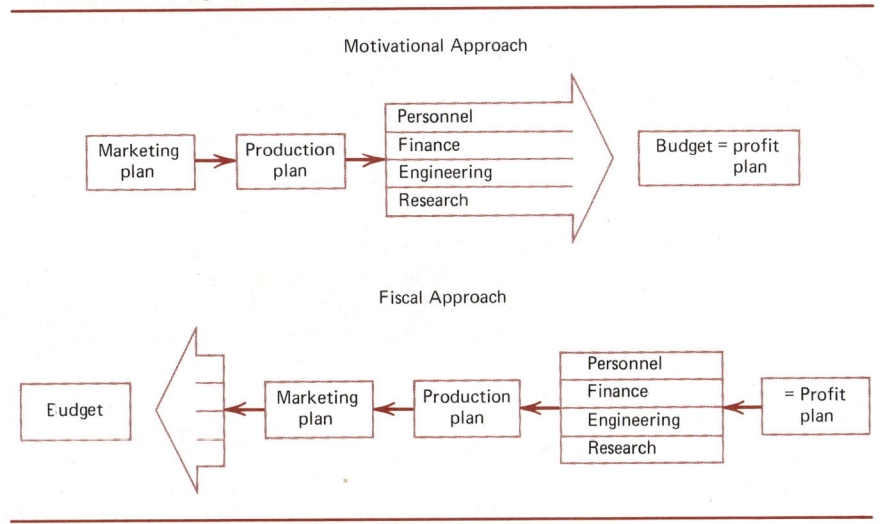

Motivational Approach

Marketing plan → Production plan → Personnel / Finance / Engineering / Research → Budget = profit plan

Fiscal Approach

Budget ← Marketing plan ← Production plan ← Personnel / Finance / Engineering / Research ← = Profit plan

Source: adapted from dale D. McConkey, "The Position and Function of Budgets in an MBO Systems," *The Business Quarterly,* Spring 1974, p. 48.

Controlling Operations). This approach calls for a total system of management similar to MBO but with a much less participative approach. Yezdi K. Bhada and George Minmier suggest that MBO and zero-base budgeting (ZBB) do not have to be conflicting and can be integrated effectively.

Some similarities between MBO and ZBB are the following:

1. Both systems emphasize establishing objectives and priorities.
2. The decision-making phase of ZBB is almost identical to one of establishing priorities and objectives.
3. ZBB's final budget represents a quantitative expression of mutually agreed-upon objectives.[37]

Some advantages of integrating MBO into ZBB are the following:

> ZBB includes how ends are to be achieved.

1. ZBB encourages a trade-off analysis at different levels permitting constant updating and integrating of goals.
2. MBO sometimes fails to provide methods for achieving results. ZBB eliminates this by formalizing an expression of "how" ends are to be achieved.[38]

---

[37]Yezdi K. Bhada and George Minmier, "Integrate ZBB Into Your MBO Framework," *Financial Executive,* June 1980, pp. 42–47.

[38]Ibid., p. 42. See also J. Bernard Keys and Robert R. Bell, "Integrated Planning and Control Using Zero-Base Budgeting and MBO," *Michigan Business Review,* November 1979, Vol. XXXI, No. 6, pp. 25–31.

EXTERNAL INPUTS FROM MANAGERIAL AND ORGANIZATIONAL DEVELOPMENT

The use of MBO processes does not guarantee an open participative organization. As is true with all leadership styles, the personal philosophy of the leader and the climate established by top management ultimately determine the nature of the MBO implementation. As shown in Figure 22-4, if management possesses a Theory X viewpoint, MBO will take a rigid, less participative approach. Similarly, a Theory Y philosophy will lead to strong participation interaction between subordinate and superior. Note that many possible combinations of styles lie between the Theory X and Theory Y positions. For example, zero-base budgeting calls for much less participation in goal setting, but it demands the consideration of alternative decision packages.[39]

GROUP PROCESS AND MBO

One element of the traditional MBO process poses a contradiction compared to previous theories of leadership. As was pointed out by Blake and Mouton, and also Likert's System 4 management, team management often provides superior results to individual superior-subordinate management. MBO's strong personal goal definition, evaluation, and reward processes can cause an overemphasis on competition, which is contrary to the best interests of the firm.

MBO can be converted to a group or team relationship by the following procedures.

1. Results and relevant past performance are disseminated on a group or departmental basis.
2. Objectives are established for appropriate time periods on a group or team basis.
3. The evaluation of achievement is performed on a group problem-solving basis.

The process continues as follows.[40]

> At the end of each period, the manager and his or her work group examine all relevant data and assess how well the specific goals and overall objectives have been achieved. In addition, they consider how well each member has achieved the objectives that were the reponsibilities of the particular individual. New goals and objectives are then set for the next period. Again, each member of the work group knows what is expected both over all and from each group member.

---

[39] Logan M. Cheek, *ZeroBase Budgeting Comes of Age*, New York, Amacon, A Division of American Management Association, 1977.

[40] Rensis Likert and M. Scott Fisher, "MBGO: Putting Some Team Spirit into MBO," *Personnel*, January-February 1977, p. 42.

FIGURE 22-4

MBO: Theory X and Theory Y—A New Perspective

	Theory X—People dislike work; people must be forced to work; people do not willingly assume responsibility	*Contingency Approaches to MBO*	*Theory Y—People like to work; people work best under self-direction; people like to assume responsibility*
1. Setting objectives	Autocratic approach. Superior sets objectives. Little participation by subordinates. Low commitment to objectives by subordinates. Few alternative objectives considered. Rigid organization. Little coordination.		Subordinate sets own objectives. Superior as a coach. Objectives as a challenge. Contribution to higher levels. Organizational objectives are coordinated. Personal development objectives included. Integration of individual and organizational objectives. Flexible and adaptable organization.
2. Developing action Plans	Superior determines tasks. Few alternatives explored. Superior sets time frame. Problems with uncertain tasks. Low creativity. Superior defines responsibilities.	Combinations of X and Y	Subordinates develop action plans. Many alternatives are explored. Coordination may be a problem. Teamwork emphasized. People seek responsibility and are accountable for results.
3. Implementation	Rigid, mechanistic program. Paperwork and policy manuals emphasized. Little coaching. People resist MBO. Philosophy of MBO not taught.		MBO flexible and adaptable. Active participation. Possibly pilot program. People are prepared for MBO. MBO philosophy taught. Opportunity for growth. Integration of organizational demands and individual needs. Team approach.
4. Control and appraisal	External, rigid controls. Superior as a judge. Inappropriate standards may be pursued. Team performance may suffer. Low trust. Focus on past. Minimum feedback and information. Little self-control and self-development.		Utilizing people's potential and creativity. Internalized self-control. Commitment to performance. Frequent review of standards. Superior as a helper. Considerable trust. Necessary information available. Focus on future opportunities and improvement. Feed forward control. Self-development. Problem-solving attitude.

Source: adapted from Heinz Weihnich, "MBO: Theory X and Theory Y," *The Personnel Administrator,* February 1977, p. 55.

The MBGO (group MBO) process has been used successfully by a team of foremen in an assembly plant. The foremen meet weekly to discuss mutual problems and manage regular production activities. The team represent interfunctional teams—production, quality control, maintenance, material handling, stores and engineering, using *the linking pin concept*.[41] A similar approach has been used with the regional and local managers of a retail sales division of a firm making consumer products.[42]

MATCHING ORGANIZATION STYLE WITH OBJECTIVES

Recalling our studies of the functional organization from Chapter 7, Organizational Dynamics, one will quickly note its limitations or use in MBO. In the functional oganizations, MBO will usually include *functional performance objectives*. That is "reponsibility for meeting a given objective would probably be assigned to a particular individual and job. Maintaining a planned product standard would probably be assigned to the manufacturing manager; an objective for returns and allowances would be assigned to the quality control manager," and so forth.[43] But in actuality, many of the functional areas must cooperate to maintain a standard rate of production, reduce returns and allowances, and other such goals. This can best be accomplished through the use of a responsibility chart, often called "an objective grid."[44]

Responsibility charts (objective grids) may provide an effective tool for portraying the relationships among differing components of the organization. This is a technique that lays out in a pictorial format the managerial responsibilities and relationships among various jobs in an organization, as shown in Figure 22-5.

Raia provides an example of this procedure for charting the responsibilities associated with an MBO activity:

> *The major activities and tasks required to achieve an objective or a set of objectives are listed on the left side of a matrix . . . . The names of individuals (or management positions) who are in some way concerned with a given activity or task are entered along the top of the matrix. The coded relationship that each manager or position has with regard to an activity or task is then determined and entered at the appropriate intercept.*[45]

Melcher developed a useful coding system to implement his approach to linear responsibility charts.[46] He defines the codes as follows.

A General Responsibility. The individual guides and directs the execution of a function through the person to whom he has delegated operating responsibility and over which he retains approval authority.

B Operating Responsibility. The person is directly responsibile for the execution of the function.

C Specific Responsibility. The person is delegated the responsibility for a specific portion of the function.

---

[41]Ibid., p. 46.
[42]Ibid., p. 45.
[43]Douglas S. Sherwin, "Management by Objectives," *Harvard Business Review*, May-June 1976, pp. 149–160.
[44]Ibid., p. 152.
[45]Raia, *Managing By Objectives*, p. 76.
[46]R. D. Melcher, "Roles and Relationships: Clarifying the Manager's Job," *Personnel*, May-June 1976, pp. 33–41.

Responsibility charts clarify the extent of responsibility for each of several managers working on the same project.

FIGURE 22-5

Responsibility Matrix for Sales Volume Objective

Objective: to increase sales volume by 10 percent by the end of next year. Major Activities/Tasks	President	V.P. marketing	Sales manager	V.P. manufacturing	Production manager	Engineering	Quality control	R and D	V.P. finance	Personnel manager	Regional sales manager	Responsibility Codes
1. Increase the rate of delivery of products X and Y.		A B	C	D	D	F	F				F	
2. Revise the price structure of existing products.	A	B C	D						F		F	A = General responsibility B = Operating responsibility C = Specific responsibility D = Must be consulted E = May be consulted F = Must be notified G = Must approve
3. Upgrade the effectiveness of sales personnel in the northeastern and southern regions.	A		B							D	C	
4. Release the new product.	G	A F		D	D	C		B				

Source: Anthony Raia, Managing by Objectives, *Glenview, Ill., Scott Foresman and Company, 1974. p. 77.*

D Must be Consulted. The person, if a decision affects his area of responsibility, must be called in prior to any decision being made to render advice or relate information but does not make the decision or grant approval.

E May be Consulted. The person may be called in prior to a decision being made to confer, render advice, relate information, or make recommendation.

F Must be Notified. The person must be notified of a decision once it is made.

G Must Approve. The person (other than persons holding general and operating responsibility) must grant approval.

The responsibility chart in Figure 22-5 shows how this technique could be used by a marketing vice president for a sales volume objective. The major activities appropriate for meeting his sales objectives are listed along the side of the form. The managers involved in the activities necessary to meet the objectives are listed across the top of the form. Responsibility charts should be developed for each of the major managerial objectives.

Responsibility charts benefit the manager by showing who is going to be involved, and how.

These charts can be used both by the manager and her superior at the evaluation interview. The manager will benefit by preparing this plan showing who is going to be involved, and how, prior to the inception of the task or activity. This may be useful for clarifying in advance the extent of responsibility of each concerned manager. It will also serve as a self-check device to ensure that appropriate people are brought into the decision process in relation to each activity.

From the superior's point of view, this chart will be useful at evaluation and review time to show the location of impediments to the accomplishment of objectives. If, for example, some people on the chart refused to take appropriate or timely action, this can be noted and perhaps documented. On the positive side, outstanding cooperation or assistance by those involved in an activity may also be pinpointed and noted in other performance appraisals.

This technique will also facilitate the acceptance of the philosohy of participation in the MBO program. As the manager becomes aware of the scope and nature of these interactions with others, he or she becomes more concerned with the quality of coordination and communication existing in the department.

The functional organization is used primarily to perform repetitive tasks. But when change and improvement are needed, two different strategies have been employed. On the one hand, appendages have been added, such as product managers, project engineers, and market development groups, to assist in bringing about change. On the other hand, separate organizations such as the project group discussed in Chapter 12, Contingency Approaches to Organization, have been created.

Appended Groups. Product managers, project engineers, and other change agents have difficulty in operating with the functional organization. Often they have only staff authority. An objective grid can assist in showing functional groups how their objectives must contribute to an overall change objective.

Project Teams. Project teams, matrix organizations, and other new forms of organizations suffer from the problem of dual authority. They report to the functional oganization, but are on loan to the project or team type organization. Using an objective grid can assist these teams in clarifying project goals and administrative goals.

It should be obvious by now that the objective grid is an approach to assigning objectives on a team or group basis, which is precisely the approach needed to make MBGO work. The chief weaknesses in the MBGO and objectives grid approach are in individual performance appraisal. An equitable system of performance appraisal would be based upon the following two things.

1. Results of objectives that are within an employee's own scope.
2. The effectiveness of the employee in making his contribution to the multiperson objectives of the organization.[47]

An objective grid assists in defining goals in the product manager and project manager type organization.

---

[47]Sherwin, "Management By Objectives," p. 154.

It is often difficult to establish objectives on a team basis without clouding individual responsibility. In the case of operating employees, group incentives and rewards may be established. When dealing with management, team objectives need to be further refined as individual objectives.

LIMITATIONS TO MBO

While this chapter presents a rather positive view of MBO as a total system of management, several limitations to its use need to be considered. First of all, different organizations will find MBO useful only in certain stages of the management system. Some will use it as basically a managerial planning approach, and others as primarily an approach for evaluating performance. While most MBO systems have produced positive attitudes toward the work situation, managers still complain of the excessive paper work generated by the system. Furthermore, the measurement of performance is a difficult process in areas where goals are not easily quantifiable.[48]

Different organizations find MBO useful only at certain stages of the management system.

Failures in the implementation of MBO systems have been most frequent when organizations are involved in rapid technological changes. Success is also much less likely when MBO is not adequately integrated into other organizational systems, such as budgeting processes.

But perhaps the number one reason for failure of MBO programs has been the lack of (or perceived lack of) top management commitment to MBO. Part of that commitment must include *authenticity*. "In an authentic relationship both parties listen to one another and can display a sense of caring and empathy for each other. Each one tries to 'step into the other's shoes' to know how the other feels."[49] Finally, research results indicate that the more successful MBO programs do not follow a set formula, in any organization or at any level, but rather are tailored to fit the leadership style of the managers in the organizations.[50]

Research indicates that successful MBO programs do not follow a set formula.

WHAT DISTINGUISHES MBO FROM NON-MBO?

There are many goal-oriented systems of managing. Many of the components of the MBO process, in turn, embody several of the functions of managing. A fair question, then, is "What distinguishes MBO from Non-MBO?" Dalles T. DeFee suggests the following:

> *What separates MBO from non-MBO is the attempt to make goal setting routine, to develop structured methods of participation, and to consistently apply a particular methodology of performance appraisal.*[51]

---

[48]Carroll and Tosi, *Management by Objectives*, p. 15.
[49]Linda Smircich and R. J. Chesser, "Superiors' and Subordinates' Perceptions of Performance: Beyond Disagreements," *Academy of Management Journal*, 1981, Vol. 24, No. 1, p. 201.
[50]Carroll and Tosi, *Management by Objectives*, p. 45.
[51]Dallas T. DeFee, "Management by Objectives: When and How Does It Work? in K. R. Rowland, M. London, G. R. Ferris, and J. L. Sherman, *Current Issues in Personnel Management*, Boston, Allyn and Bacon, Inc., 1980, p. 151.

SUMMARY

Management by objectives (MBO) is a total system of management incorporating clearly established objectives at every level of an organization. It is an attempt to produce commitment on the part of subordinates by participative goal setting and the delineation of a clear path of success for the subordinate. Through this process, objectives are converted to action plans, priorities are assigned, and delegation is carried out in a cascading participative manner throughout the organization.

Objectives are usually written in action form, including innovation and improvement goals. Individuals are appraised on how well they accomplish the same objectives to which they have agreed. The emphasis is on accomplishments and constructive criticism in a TA style. Budgeting is aligned so as to support

SUMMARY CHART

1. Set objectives and develop strategic plans
   (a) Establish objectives in every important area
   (b) Consider inputs from the external economy and environment

2. Develop action plans
   (a) Consider alternatives
   (b) Assign priorities
   (c) Develop departmental objectives, using the cascading approach

3. Implement plans through leadership and delegation
   (a) Set objeties with each employee individually
   (b) Ask subordinate to make a list of his objectives
   (c) Consider innovations and improvements
   (d) Agree on objectives jointly
   (e) Check on accomplishments throughout the year
   (f) At end of period, ask employee to prepare a statement of performance against budget

4. Remember to state objectives in terms of measurable results that are controllable

5. Align the budgeting process with MBO

6. At year end, measure and reward performance in view of the objectives
   (a) Consider variances
   (b) Ask why things went right or wrong
   (c) Use TA

7. Consider using external inputs and group approaches to MBO

8. Consider the effect of organizatioinal arrangement on MBO

9. Use objectives grid to align organization and MBO

10. Adapt methodology to fit the existing philosophy and style of management.

goals and objectives. Self-direction and self-control are encouraged, based on clearly stated objectives.

An objective grid can be used to align interlocking objectives of various departments both horizontally and vertically. Group MBO is a natural extension of the individual goal setting process and possesses several advantages. However, group MBO (MBGO) poses some additional problems in appraisal and evaluation.

MBO, like all management systems, suffers from several limitations. Its weaknesses are found largely in the implementation stage, and in the frequent failure of top management to support the system once it is established.

DISCUSSION QUESTIONS

1. Peter Drucker says "to manage a business is to balance a variety of needs and goals." Explain what he means by this statement.
2. State the basic premise behind MBO. Do you agree with it? Discuss.
3. Enumerate the four stages of MBO as suggested by Odiorne. Which stage distinguishes MBO from traditional objective setting?
4. How would you define a well-written objective? What are the characteristics of one?
5. As a subordinate, would you favor being evaluated by an MBO appraisal system? Why or why not?
6. In utilizing a budget with an MBO system what are the guidelines that should be followed?
7. Does an MBO process guarantee participative decision-making?
8. What is the purpose of a responsibility chart or objective grid?
9. What do you consider the most serious limitation of MBO?

APPLICATION EXERCISES AND CASES

MBO OR SOMETHING ELSE?[52]

A large agency in the federal government decided to introduce a management-by-objectives system. Both employees and managers were involved in the development of the goals their particular units would seek to attain, although top management eventually made the final decisions. Top management decided there were 305 goals that the organization and its subdivisions should seek to

---

[52]Martin J. Gannon, *Organizational Behavior, A Managerial and Organizational Perspective*, Boston, Little, Brown and Co., 1979, p. 116.

achieve. Then they established a department whose sole function was to track the completion of these goals.

Questions

1. Does this approach carry out the concept of MBO? Explain in detail your understanding of MBO as a systems philosophy of management.
2. If MBO was, in fact, going to be implemented outline and explain the procedure that would be followed.
3. What benefits would accrue to the organization from a true MBO approach? What limitations are there to MBO? Would it tie into other elements of the organizations functioning such as budgeting?

CHOOSE A LEADERSHIP STYLE[53]

The following leadership processes represent styles chosen by various managers around the nation for implementing an MBO system. Read them carefully and respond to the questions that follow.

Four Methods for Initiating an MBO System

Process 1. Generally, the superior would first hold a department meeting during which the unit goals and projects for the coming operating period were discussed. The subordinate would then, using the information from his general meeting, prepare a set of personal goals. At the same time, the boss would independently prepare a set of goals and targets for the subordinate. Later they would meet to discuss these and arrive at some mutual agreement on the subordinate's goals.

Process 2. Goal setting usually began with an informational meeting in which the general department and organizational objectives were discussed. Later the subordinate prepared a set of goals and target dates, which he gave to his boss. Rather than preparing a set of goals for the subordinate, the boss edited and altered those prepared by the subordinate. When a meeting was held to discuss the goals, the basis for discussion was the subordinate's edited and revised goal statement.

Process 3. First, the boss called a general meeting to discuss departmental objectives. From this, subordinates prepared individual goal statements, which they sent to the boss. However, contrary to processes 1 and 2 these goal statements were accepted without any meeting or discussion. The subordinate did not have the oppotunity to determine whether or not the goals were acceptable to his boss. He could only assume that they were so by the superior's silence.

---

[53]Stephen J. Carroll and Henry L. Tosi, *Management by Objectives*, New York, Macmillan, 1973, pp. 31–32. Adaption.

Process 4. The subordinate was simply informed about the objectives program. The boss and the subordinate met, at which time the subordinate was given a set of goals that the boss had prepared. The subordinate had little to say about the goals and the target dates set for them.

Questions
1. Which process most clearly parallels Odiorne's suggested approach?
2. As a subordinate, which would you prefer? As a superior?
3. In which process would you think the subordinate would have the greatest influence on the planning process? The least? Why?

CHAPTER 23
INTERNATIONAL MANAGEMENT AND MANAGEMENT IN THE FUTURE

MULTINATIONAL CORPORATIONS
CORPORATE PLANNING
MARKETING
ORGANIZATIONAL STRUCTURES
HUMAN RESOURCES
POLITICAL AND LEGAL ENVIRONMENT
THE PRODUCTIVITY CHALLENGE
THE ORGANIZATION AND THE MANAGER IN THE TWENTY-FIRST CENTURY
LONG-RANGE PLANNING WILL BE MORE FORMAL
NATURAL RESOURCES
CHANGING SOCIAL NEEDS
CHANGING VIEWS OF AUTHORITY
WOMEN IN MANAGEMENT
CROSS-CULTURAL SENSITIVITY
MANAGEMENT PRACTICES OF THE FUTURE
TOP MANAGEMENT DECENTRALIZATION, AND INFORMATION SYSTEMS
THE ORGANIZATIONAL CHART AND MIDDLE MANAGEMENT
ORGANIZATIONAL AND MANAGEMENT DEVELOPMENT
MANAGEMENT STYLES
PLANNING AND DECISION MAKING
MBO IN THE FUTURE
APPLICATION EXERCISES AND CASES
SUCCESS IN THE SMALL MULTINATIONAL CORPORATION
THE NONCONFORMISTS

INSIDE EXXON: MANAGING AN 85 BILLION DOLLAR A YEAR EMPIRE[1]

The Exxon Corporation is almost incomprehensibly big. Last year, its revenues totaled $84.8 billion—a figure slightly higher than the gross national product of Sweden and somewhat less than that of Spain. The net income from those 1979 revenues came to $4.3 billion, more than the profits of Eastman Kodak; Du Pont; Sears, Roebuck; Proctor & Gamble; Xerox; and RCA combined. In the first three months of 1980, Exxon made a profit of $1.9 billion, more than any other enterprise has ever earned in a single quarter.

What may be most awesome about the Exxon empire is its scope. It operates, for examle, in nearly 100 countries. Its 195 oceangoing tankers, owned and chartered, constitute a private navy as big as Britain's. Even with the latest in computer-controlled, satellite-directed communications, how is it possible to keep so mammoth an enterprise running smoothly, to fit all the far-flung bits and pieces of this empire into a profitable pattern?

The Exxon Corporation doesn't really sell oil, chemicals, electronic typewriters, and motors; rather, it owns an array of companies that sell those things. It is, in effect, a fabulously wealthy investment club with a limited portfolio. Each year, it makes investments in 13 affiliated companies that are expected to return that money plus a suitable profit. Those that can show they can make more with more, get more. Those that cannot, do not. It is just that simple, and just that complicated.

[1]A. J. Parisi, "Inside Exxon: Managing an 85 Billion Dollar a Year Empire," *New York Times Magazine*, August 3, 1980, pp. 18–25.

The fundamentals that pertain to Exxon today pertain to most of today's enterprises. But all institutions live and perform in two time periods: that of today and that of tomorrow. Tomorrow is being made today, irrevocably in most cases. Managers therefore always have to manage the fundamentals both today and tomorrow. In turbulent times, managers cannot assume that tomorrow will be an extension of today. On the contrary, they must manage for change; change is both an opportunity and a threat.[2]

MULTINATIONAL CORPORATIONS

International business operations will figure prominently in the economic picture of the 1980s and 1990s. Many American companies will truly earn the title of

---

*The authors gratefully acknowledge the assistance of Robert R. Bell, Assistant Dean, College of Business, Tennessee Technological University, Cookeville, Tennessee, who revised this chapter.
[2]Peter F. Drucker, *Managing in Turbulent Times*, New York, Harper & Row, 1980, p. 41.

multinational corporation (MNC),[3] and more will enter into ventures in the international market. At the same time that American firms venture abroad in increasing numbers, firms from other nations will continue to be active in United States markets.[4] Prasad and Sherry have described the MNC as follows:

International business has evolved from the simple ideas of trade—the importing and exporting of the products of various areas—into a complex system in which multinational corporations (such as the American-based IBM, the Japan-based Matsushita, or the Canada-based Massey-Ferguson) play a major economic role in a worldwide context, often with far-reaching political and social implications. This economic role, more precisely stated as manufacturing and marketing, stems from direct investment in a number of countries.

The multinational corporation (MNC) has now become a household word. Although its definition is still the subject of debate, what distinguishes an MNC from its predecessors, companies with foreign subsidiaries or affiliates, is direct investment abroad and direct interest in the business environment in which it has such investments . . . the hallmarks of an MNC are control *and* integration *of affiliates.*[5]

> The distinguishing characteristic of the MNC is the control and integration of foreign affiliates—not just ownership.

Multinational corporations differ from domestic companies in that their effectiveness stems from operating effectively under several different national sovereignties. In addition, the MNC must cope with wide variations in economic conditions, different value and cultural systems, and wide geographic separations.[6] The MNC must operate from a base in an industrial nation, but with operations in areas ranging from highly industrialized to preindustrial revolution economies.

The multinational corporation operates in a unique role. Working in a diversity of national environments, allocating resources, and making decisions in the light of worldwide alternatives, the MNC must not only cope with a more complex organizational structure, but also with a far more elaborate and sensitive array of environmental variables than a domestic operation has. The sheer size of the MNC, relative to some of the national economies in which it functions, often demonstrates the important economic consequences of its decisions. The political impact of these decisions and the burden of responsibility on the decision maker may be heavy, especially in countries where nationalistic spirits are high.

> The MNC must cope with a more complex organizational structure and environment.

CORPORATE PLANNING

Multinational corporate planning must be responsive to sets of conditions quite differ from those of the domestic firm. Expansion into international boundaries is much more than a step across a geographical line—it is an entrance into a quite

---

[3] Ideas in this section are taken from S. B. Prasad and Y. K. Sherry, *An Introduction to Multinational Management*, Englewood Cliffs, N.J., Prentice-Hall, 1976.
[4] See for example, R. T. Johnson and W. G. Ouchi, "Made in America (Under Japanese Management)," *Harvard Business Review*, September-October 1974, pp. 61–69; and James Cook, "A Tiger By the Tail," *Forbes*, April 13, 1981, pp. 119–128.
[5] Prasad and Sherry, *Multinational Management*, p. 1.
[6] R. D. Robinson, *International Management*, New York, Holt, Rinehart and Winston, 1967, p. 3.

FIGURE 23-1

A Comparison of Domestic and International Planning

Domestic Planning	*International Planning*
1. Single language and nationality	1. Multilingual/multinational/multicultural factors
2. Relatively homogeneous market	2. Fragmented and diverse markets
3. Data available, usually accurate, and collection easy	3. Data collection a formidable task, requiring significantly higher budgets and personnel allocation
4. Political factors relatively unimportant	4. Political factors frequently vital
5. Relative freedom from government interference	5. Involvement in national economic plans; government influences business decisions
6. Individual corporation has little effect on environment	6. "Gravitational" distortion by large companies
7. Chauvinism helps	7. Chauvinism hinders
8. Relatively stable business environment	8. Multiple environments, many of which are highly unstable (but may be highly profitable)
9. Uniform financial climate	9. Variety of financial climates ranging from over-conservative to wildly inflationary
10. Single currency	10. Currencies differing in stability and real value
11. Business "rules of the game" mature and understood	11. Rules diverse, changeable and unclear
12. Management generally accustomed to sharing responsibilities and using financial controls	12. Management frequently autonomous and unfamiliar with budgets and controls

Source: adapted from W. W. Cain, "International Planning: Mission Impossible?" *Columbia Journal of World Business*, July-August 1970.

different arena of political, social, economic, and technological forces. Figure 23-1 demonstrates some of the planning challenges involved. Multinational planning thus entails scanning a worldwide environment, assessing a wider range of variables, and coming up with a strategy that increases the effectiveness of the multinational business.

Every corporate planning effort requires accurate information about the corporate environment. In the multinational company, this requirement is made more difficult because of the lack of accurate, readily available market intelligence in many countries. Yet knowledge of the national environments in which it operates is crucial to the sound and profitable development of the enterprise. This fact constitutes a major challenge of the abilities of MNC corporate leaders in the coming years.

Multinational corporations differ in the kinds of planning systems they use. Some use centralized planning, with headquarters setting global objectives and

Gaining accurate market and environmental information is more difficult for the multinational company.

assigning subobjectives to national subsidiaries. Other firms favor decentralized planning, wherein the operating units are responsible for formulating objectives for their operations, with these objectives then being combined for the company as a whole. Another approach combines both centralized and decentralized planning. In this system corporate headquarters and the subsidiaries continuously interact throughout the planning process. This approach allows the company to plan from the vantage point of specific markets, while simultaneously integrating strategy to promote overall corporate goals.

In almost all cases, the planning process involves a "cascade" approach similar to the following.

> *The* strategic plan *envisions the kinds of business in which the company will engage in its various national environments, defines the role it expects to play in the countries where it operates, and sets forth its long-range objectives.*
>
> *Within the framework of the strategic plan, which may extend from ten to twenty years ahead, an* interim plan *specifies more detailed targets and goals for the years immediately ahead. Depending on the nature of the business and the practical reliability of the forecasts for the various host economies, the interim plan may extend from three to ten years ahead; five years is probably close to the mean.*
>
> *Finally, within the context of the interim plan, an annual* operating plan *sets forth precise, detailed objectives for the years immediately ahead, designed to bring the company the first part of the way toward its interim and long-range goals. Translated into financial terms, this operating plan often becomes a budget for the ensuing year.*[7]

Multinational companies usually start with a strategic plan *that defines its role.*

MARKETING

Peter Drucker believes that the future key to success for multinational corporations will lie in their ability to market.[8] And in this area, Drucker feels that the medium-sized company will have distinct advantages over the larger multinational. Multinational marketing efforts differ significantly from those aimed at domestic marketing. In order to understand foreign markets and effectively penetrate them, it is necessary to understand the differences in these markets. Factors such as income levels, attitudes toward selling and promotional efforts, education and culture, currency valuations, and legal restrictions all may be different in different cultures. People throughout the world differ in their values and respond differently to promotion and selling strategies. So diversity is an important challenge to multinational marketing. Foreign markets usually must be treated as entirely separate target markets. Product development, pricing, and promotional appeals must be designed to fit specific cultural and social values of individual countries.

Peter Drucker says that the significant challenge of the MNC is marketing.

ORGANIZATION STRUCTURES

Multinational operations add new challenges to the task of designing organization structures. The environmental diversity shown in Figure 23-1 poses unique

---
[7]Gilbert H. Klee, "Guidelines for Global Business," *The Economist*, October 17, 1964, p. 271.
[8]Peter Drucker, *Managing in Turbulent Times*, New York, Harper & Row, 1980, p. 106.

organizational problems not normally found in domestic corporations. The sheer physical distance between headquarters and the operating units also creates a need for special organizational mechanisms. Most structures for multinational operations evolve. Size of operations, company history, top management philosophy, product-market diversification, and several other factors influence the organization. According to Prasad and Shetty, the degree of the diversity of involvement in multinational operations usually plays the most significant role in determining the final structure of the organization.[9] Most companies start with some type of export division, which eventually evolves into a complete international operations division. After this, larger multinational firms adopt a global structure, with functional, product, or geographic divisions within this structure.

No matter which form of organization evolves, as a multinational firm's foreign operations grow, it becomes very difficult for top management to make all decisions involving foreign activities. The growing size of the operation and the ever-increasing complexities of managing place severe burdens on corporate executives. The demands on their time, energy, and resources cannot be met by any manager or small group of managers. To overcome this problem, many companies have moved to decentralized forms of decision making. Well-known multinationals like Massey-Ferguson are examples of firms that moved in this direction. Management in each division of Massey-Ferguson operates relatively independently of corporate headquarters. Each division is reponsible for earning adequate profits and meeting other company performance measures.

Drucker suggests that many companies will become "transnational" organizations:

> Transnational confederations will instead increasingly organize production across national boundaries and across markets, so as to optimize both labor resources and market resources. Stages of production that are labor-intensive will increasingly be done where the labor is, and increasingly not by "subsidiaries" and "branches" but by subcontractors. And the cohesion of the enterprise will come from its control of marketing rather than from its control of capital.
>
> This will require new structures. Instead of the present pyramid, in which a central top management commands a large number of units, each of them engaged in very much the same activity, top management will act as an integrating force. Its control will be through marketing rather than through legal authority. It will lead an orchestra rather than an army.[10]

HUMAN RESOURCES

The management of human resources in multinational operations also presents unique challenges. Initially, the MNC brings into the host country a group of home-based managers and technicians whose skill and training are transferred to the domestic nationals whom they train. In most cases, these nationals will

---
[9]Prasad and Shetty, *Multinational Management*, pp. 84–103.
[10]Peter Drucker, Ibid., p. 107.

Major problems facing MNC's are training and compensating managers.

ultimately assume managerial responsibilities for local operations, in turn training a new generation of managers and technical workers.

Most MNC's provide several types of on- and off-the-job training programs for their expatriate managers. Most firms, for example, provide training in language skills, and knowledge of the culture and people of the foreign country before managers are assigned abroad. Multinationals also provide training and development programs for host country employees. Each is designed to fit the needs of the particular country and the particular group of employees. Because outside facilities are generally limited in many countries, most multinational companies do most of the management development training within their own organizations. However, many universities are adding international management training to their executive development programs.[11]

A particularly difficult problem for the multinational corporation involves compensation of its employees. According to R. D. Robinson,[12] the choice of basic strategies relating to remuneration of international management usually involves the following two options.

(1) dual (American personnel on an American salary scale, all others on the local scale), or (2) an international base plus a variety of extras. Commonly included among such extras are a cost-of-living differential, an expatriate bonus to compensate for being away from home, and a number of personal adjustment payments (language training, moving allowance, children's education, home leave, entertainment, special health and accident insurance).

Insofar as United States nationals are concerned, a special problem arises in the international area due to the need (1) to provide inducement to leave the United States, (2) to maintain an American standard of living, (3) to facilitate re-entry into the United States (through maintenance of a United States home, professional updating), (4) to meet the requirements of children's education, (5) to maintain social obligations vis-a-vis friends and family. The obvious cost of these many payments to already highly paid American managers constitutes pressure toward the localization of management, or the employment of third-country nationals.[13]

POLITICAL AND LEGAL ENVIRONMENT

To a large degree, the political and legal environment of the host country defines much of the behavior of foreign corporations. The foreign investment law of a

---

[11] Alfred G. Edge, Bernard Keys, and William F. Remus, *The Multinational Management Game*, Dallas, Business Publications, 1980.

[12] R. D. Robinson, "Selection, Promotion and Remuneration of Overseas Managers" in John M. Hutchinson, *Readings in Management Strategy and Tactics*, New York, Holt, Rinehart and Winston, 1971, pp. 420–431.

[13] For further examples of the challenges of personnel management in MNC's, see Y. Zeira, "Overlooked Personnel Problems of Multinational Corporations," *Columbia Journal of World Business*, Summer 1975, pp. 96–103; E. L. Miller and J. L. Cheng, "Circumstances That Influenced the Decision to Accept an Overseas Assignment," *Proceedings, Academy of Management Annual Meeting*, Kansas City, 1976, pp. 336–339.

country is perhaps the most important, since it provides the framework for operations. In general, however, the legal environment facing the multinational corporation is a complex, almost incomprehensible, maze of regulations and guidelines. No two countries have the same laws and, it seems, no two local officials interpret a given country's laws in the same way. In the past, the political risk of multinational operations has usually centered around expropriation, the takeover of the firm's assets by the host country. Many authors believe that expropriation will not be a serious threat in the future, largely because of new financial laws and new joint venture methods of operating in host countries.[14]

THE PRODUCTIVITY CHALLENGE

The world dominance of American multinational businesses has eroded dramatically in the last few decades. Today, multinational corporations in Japan and several other countries are openly challenging, and often beating, American competitors in the marketplace. There are a number of possible reasons for this decline, among them industrial and social maturity in the United States, with better productivity occurring in the countries with developing economies (like Japan).

Many American firms are trying to adopt the more useful parts of the Japanese management system for use in American plants. Traditional Japanese business organizations tend to be highly paternalistic, for example, and tend to use a great deal of participative management. The "quality circle" concept so widely attributed to the Japanese management system is one example of a system that involves line workers in weekly suggestion circles, often making presentations to vice presidents.[15]

Part of the productivity challenge for American corporations will lie in the attitudes of workers and management. One of the most successfully innovative companies is 3M Corporation of St. Paul, Minnesota. Writing in *Fortune* magazine, Lee Smith suggests that 3M has cultivated "a distinctive corporate culture" that underlies their success at innovation.[16] This culture must not only spur innovation, but must also stimulate worker productivity at the individual level.

"If we're going to improve productivity in this country," says President James Treybig of Tandem Computer, Inc., "workers have got to care about their company."[17] This may be the biggest productivity challenge young managers face in the next two decades.

---

[14]See, for example, Earl Rodney, "Financial Controls for Multinational Organizations, *Financial Executive*, May 1976, pp. 26–28; and Prasad and Sherry, *Multinational Management*, pp. 192–194.

[15]Robert R. Rehder, "What American and Japanese Managers are Learning from Each Other," *Business Horizons*, Vol. 24, No. 2, March-April 1981, pp. 63–70. See also, W. Ouchi and A. Jaeger, "Type Z: Organizational Stability in the Midst of Mobility," *Academy of Management Review*, April 1973, pp. 305–314.

[16]Lee Smith, "The Lures and Limits of Innovation," *Fortune*, October 20, 1980, p. 21.

[17]Quoted in G. C. Lubenow, "The Silicon Valley Style," *Newsweek*, June 8, 1981, p. 83.

THE ORGANIZATION AND THE MANAGER IN THE TWENTY-FIRST CENTURY

Mark Twain once remarked that he was concerned about the future because he was going to spend the rest of his life there. Today, with the rapidity of technological and social changes, Mark Twain might be too busy to even think about the future—but think and plan we must! Before we consider this important topic we will first discuss some trends in society that are likely to affect management. Next we will discuss the management practices which are apt to result from these trends.

In 1967, F. J. Borsch, then chairman of the board of General Electric Company, suggested that we can view the development of mankind by looking at the life spans of 800 people. Each person would form a link between life today and life centuries ago. The first 650 people, Borsch suggested, spent their lives as nomads. Except for stone tools or cave paintings, only the last 70 or 80 persons in this chain left any kinds of records of their existence. Only the last 8 in the chain would have known printing; only 5 could measure temperature. Only the last person would know most of the applications of science and technology we have today.[18]

Today's business executive manages a world of change. Imagine, if you can, the manager's world back in 1900. Place yourself in the manager's position, enjoying all of the conveniences of the successful business executive—eight-hour work days, telephone, electricity, hot and cold running water. Could you have predicted the manager's job of fifty or eighty years later?

The challenge of the future is the ability to manage change.

Imagine yourself in 1950—have things changed much from then? The contemporary manager in 1950 had never seen or used a computer, had never witnessed live coverage of a moon landing, and did not have the capability to communicate by satellite with any place in the world. The manager had never heard of heart pacers, Xerox machines, or organ transplants, and he or she had never had visual/voice conferences with managers all over the country (television was a new thing then).

It has been predicted that more advances will be made in the next thirty years than were made in the past thirty. Today's manager, before his or her career ends, will experience even more mind-bending changes in the practices of management. This chapter will try to forecast some of the changes in the work world of the 801st person—the manager of the twenty-first century.

Dr. Richard Farmer suggests that the future changes relevant to management lie in four general areas: changes in the operating environment; in basic sciences; in applied sciences; and in management tools, techniques, and methods.[19] Perhaps the best approach to looking at the future is to start with the present. At the

---

[18]F. J. Borsch, "The 801st Man: Or a Man for the 21st Century," in John M. Hutchinson, *Readings in Management Strategy and Tactics,* New York, Holt, Rinehart and Winston, 1971, pp. 552–559.
[19]Richard N. Farmer, *Management in the Future,* Belmont, Cal. Wadsworth Publishing Co., 1967, pp. 17–24.

> Most major crises in the past were natural disasters or created by bad intentions of government.

present time, mankind is faced with an astonishing number of crises—the population crisis, the environmental crisis, the energy crisis, the world food crisis, the raw materials crisis, to name a few.[20] These problems derive from ecosystems, and attempts to solve any one problem by itself obviously affects others. The energy crisis, for example, caused the construction of the Alaskan Pipeline. The pipeline, in turn, has drastically affected the Alaskan tundra and the migration/living patterns of many animals in the Alaskan environment. The energy crisis has also caused great concern over the potential for increased pollution levels in the Northeastern United States.

When we look at many of the problems confronting us today, we see a major difference between them and various problems faced in the past. In the past, most major crises were either natural disasters or had negative origins—that is, they were created by aggression or other bad intentions of governments.[21] Many of the crises of today, on the other hand, have been the result of actions that were well intentioned. Pollution and ecology crises, for example, were caued largely by efforts to increase productivity capabilities of industry or to increase the availability of recreational activities for people. The population crises may have been partly created by the idea that the strength of the family, the community, and the nation lies in large numbers of children. These problems, then, are consequences of programs started by man's better intentions.

It can be argued that some of the basic values ingrained in societies must be changed before these problems are solved. Affirmative action programs, forced school busing, and other civil rights legislations in the 1960s and 1970s were attempts to force changes in certain basic value structures related to civil rights of minorities. The manager of tomorrow will be faced with continued changes of this type. For example, attitudes relating to the role of women in management and in American society are now being changed. The expectations that the female's role is to "stay home and raise kids" has a quite different effect on population level than does a definition of the female role as an equal partner in the work force. Perhaps even more important for the future practice of management is the challenge to the basic values of the American free enterprise system—the profit motive, the concepts of individualism, free competition, private property, and limited government. Some respondents to a recent *Harvard Business Review* survey, for example, saw the free enterprise idealogy as a "cowboy" economy—suited to the frontier, which no longer exists.[22]

> The United States is in a period of major cultural and economic transition.

There is no question that the United States is in a period of major transition. In addition to the changes we will discuss, future changes may involve movement from: a united nation into a divided one; a two-party political system to a three- or four-party system; a nation of younger people to a nation of relatively older

---

[20]The Club of Rome, *Mankind at the Turning Point, The Second Report to the Club of Rome*, New York, E. P. Dutton & Co., Inc., The Readers' Digest Press, 1974, p. 1.
[21]Ibid., p. 11.
[22]W. F. Martin and G. C. Lodge, "Our Society in 1985—Business May Not Like it," *Harvard Business Review*, November-December 1975, pp. 143–152.

people; a three-class to a two-class society.[23] The environment in which tomorrow's manager operates will be greatly affected by these transitions. The decisions made by future administrators will hopefully, cause changes to occur in an orderly and effective manner. The challenge of the future is in the management of the significant changes which will occur.

LONG-RANGE PLANNING WILL BE MORE FORMAL

As the business environment grows more complex, it appears that the long range planning function will become more formalized. The planning process deals with risk and uncertainty, and increased complexity typically means more risk, more uncertainty. To handle this, small firms will undertake long-range planning *earlier* in their life cycle, and larger firms will evolve even more formal long-range planning departments and procedures.[24] A number of studies have shown that businesses are attempting to "fit" their long-range planning processes to their perceived environmental condition. To do this, many corporations develop sophisticated techniques for integrating change into company operations. Ian Wilson, corporate planner for General Electric Corporation, has described a framework for planning used by G.E.[25] This model, outlined in Figure 23-2, defines the managerial job of predicting the future in terms of four types of forecasting—economic, technological, social, and political. In order to demonstrate how trends in these areas affect management, we will review some representative changes in natural resources, multinational corporations, and social needs, after which resulting changes in patterns and styles of management will be considered.

NATURAL RESOURCES

American industry was shaken in the early 1970s by an oil embargo imposed by OPEC, the Organization of Petroleum Exporting Countries. This embargo literally altered the way of life in America. Universities closed their doors. Gasoline was rationed in many areas. In Florida, a state dependent upon tourism and travel, economic disaster plans were built. This action by OPEC may have been the forerunner of a period of international conflicts for control of scarce natural resources.

Twenty-five years ago, the United States was virtually self-sufficient in its possession of the raw materials needed for industrial production. Twenty-five years from now, however, it is estimated that we will depend on importation for

---

[23]D. S. Morris, Jr., ed., *Perspectives for the 70's and 80's*, New York, National Industrial Conference Board, 1970.

[24]See, for example, W. M. Lindsay and L. W. Rue, "Impact of the Organization Environment on the Long Range Planning Process: A Contingency View," *Academy of Management Journal*, 1980, Vol. 23, No.3, pp. 385–404.

[25]Ian Wilson, "What One Company is Doing to Appraise Today's Demands on Business," Conference on Business and Its Environment, University of California at Los Angeles, July 26, 1977.

FIGURE 23-2

General Electric Corporation's Framework for Corporation Forecasting

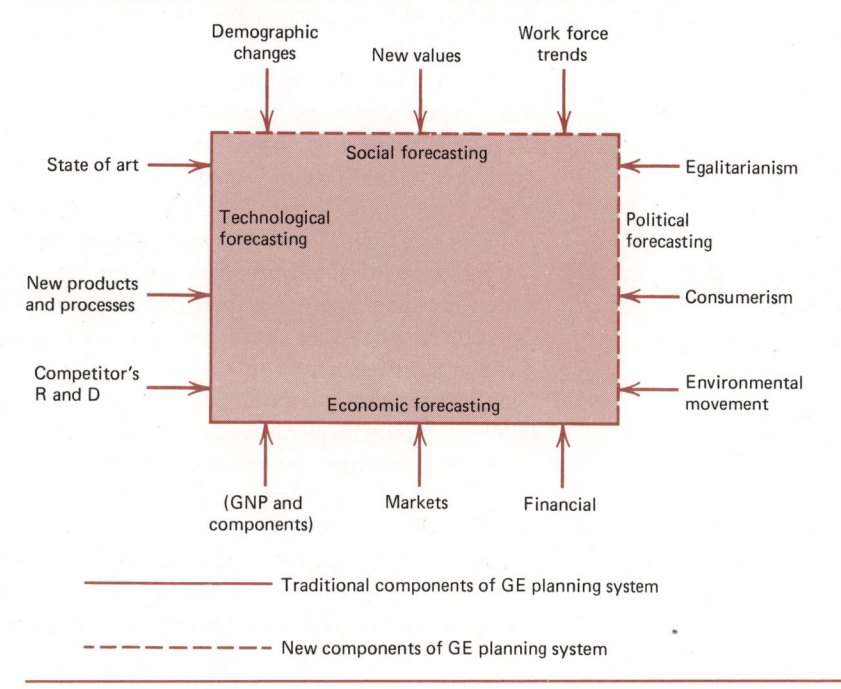

Inputs to the framework:
- Demographic changes
- New values
- Work force trends
- State of art → Social forecasting → Egalitarianism
- Technological forecasting / Political forecasting
- New products and processes → Consumerism
- Competitor's R and D → Environmental movement
- Economic forecasting
- (GNP and components)
- Markets
- Financial

——— Traditional components of GE planning system
– – – – New components of GE planning system

Source: Ian Wilson, "What One Company is Doing to Appraise Today's Demands on Business," paper delivered at the Conference on Business and its Environment, UCLA, July 26, 1977.

over 80 percent of industrial raw materials. At the same time, other nations of the world will have just as great a dependence on the United States for other (primarily agricultural) resources.[26] Much research is being done in American firms to try to continue U.S. leadership in agricultural production. The statistics are staggering. In 1970, the United States exported approximately six million tons of food. Just ten years later in 1980, the export figure had jumped to 170 million tons annually. The head of agricultural research for E.I. DuPont de Nemours and Company says, "Soybeans and feed grains would have to increase from 150 million metric tons a year to 500 million by the year 2000 if the world is to keep eating meat."[27] It is also estimated that all of the world's known supply of recoverable petroleum liquids and natural gas will be consumed within fifty years. Conventional methods of utilizing nuclear fuel will also deplete the supplies of uranium 235 within a very few decades.[28]

---

[26] National Materials Policy Commission, estimated in The Club of Rome, *Mankind at the Turning Point*, p. 84.
[27] Bob Tamarkin, "The Growth Industry," *Forbes*, March 2, 1981, p. 80.
[28] P. W. Barkley and D. W. Seckler, *Economic Growth and Environmental Decay: The Solution Becomes the Problem*, Harcourt Brace Jovanovich, 1972, pp. 25–26.

> **In the last decade of the twentieth century population will be the least stable element of society.**

Part of the reason for this tremendous consumption of resources can be seen in Figure 23-3. The world population is growing exponentially, and the Malthusian theory may be realized. The rate of growth has caused a concerned National Academy of Sciences to prepare estimates of precisely how many people our earth can hold. The Academy estimates that the maximum carrying capacity of the Earth, with projected technological change, is about thirty billion people. At this level, however, the great majority would be compelled to immigrate to less populated lands, and forced to exist at near starvation all their lives. On the positive side, the National Academy estimates that population controls will level off the numbers of people in the world to a little above ten billion around the year 2050. The Academy ends this estimate with a strong statement, however: "It is our judgment that a human population less than the present one (emphasis added) would offer the best hope for comfortable living of our descendants, long duration of the species, and the preservation of environmental quality."[29]

Peter Drucker echoes these thoughts, stating that in the last decade of the twentieth century, "population structure will be the least stable and most drastically changing element in economics, society, and world politics, and probably the single most important cause of turbulence."[30]

The long-term planning and administration of resources on a multinational systems basis offer one of the greatest challenges ever known to management. Many managers in government and industry will confront this problem in the near future. The successes and failures they achieve will surely affect the lives (and jobs) of most managers in the coming years.

CHANGING SOCIAL NEEDS

In a work prophetically titled *The Doomsday Book*, Gordon Rattray Taylor gives a chilling description of everyday life in the industrialized areas surrounding Osaka and Tokyo, Japan:

> *Along this strip 34 tons of dirt a month fall on every square kilometer . . . coastal vessels collide regularly or run aground, because they cannot see each other's navigation lights in daylight . . . traffic policemen go back to the police station after four hours on duty and breathe pure oxygen from cylinders . . . in cafes and arcades coin-in-the-slot machines disperse oxygen to shoppers . . . in school, children wear facemasks while they do their lessons on smog-warning days.*[31]

Works such as these, published in the late 1960s and the 1970s, shocked societies into realizing that even positive actions which increase productivity have side effects. Perhaps the most important contributions of the 1960s and 1970s (even beyond achievements in space exploration) may be the era's growth

---

[29]National Academy of Science, National Research Council, Committee on Resources & Man; *Resources and Man: A Study and Recommendation*, San Francisco, W. H. Freeman & Co., 1969, pp. 5–6.
[30]Peter Drucker, *Managing in Turbulent Times*, New York, Harper & Row, 1980, p. 77.
[31]Gordon Rattray Taylor, *The Doomsday Book,* London, Book Club Associates, 1970.

FIGURE 23-3

World Population Growth

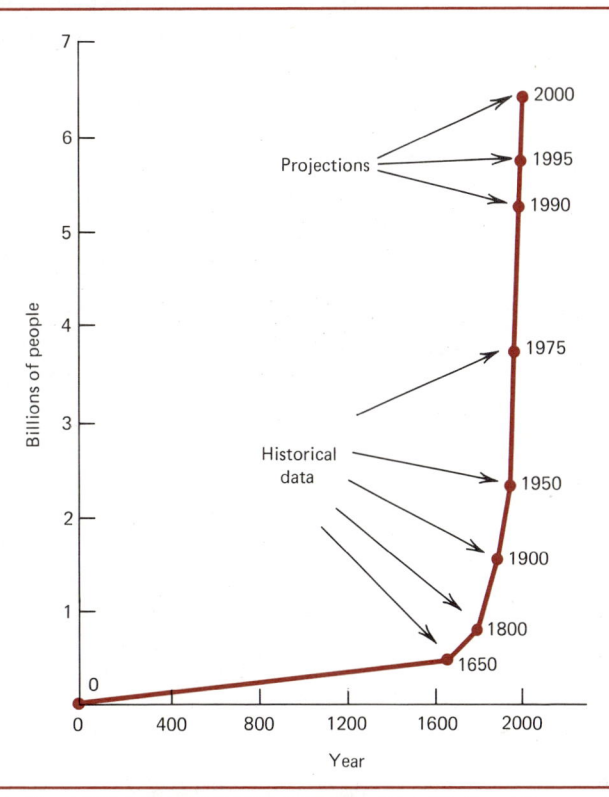

Source: M. Mesarovic and E. Pestel, *Mankind at the Turning Point: The Second Report to the Club at Rome*, New York, E. P. Dutton & Co., The Reader's digest Press, 1974, p.73.

in awareness of social needs and responsibilities. This awareness will continue to develop as time passes, and will reshape the thinking and the values of coming generations. It will affect, not only large-scale projects involving pollution control, equal employment, and social accounting, but will also transfer down to each individual in society.

Peter Drucker believes that, for some time now, America has been in what he terms an Age of Discontinuity.[32] These discontinuities, or changes, will be the major forces reshaping the business environment of the future, according to Drucker. First among the major changes, he believes, are the new technologies resulting from space research, atomic energy, chemistry and biology, psychology, etc.—technologies which will render obsolete many existing industries and businesses. The second major discontinuity is the emergence of a worldwide economy instead of a whole series of national economies. The multinational inter-

> The Age of Discontinuity includes developing technologies, emergence of a worldwide economy, institutionalization of social and economic life, and education.

---

[32]Peter F. Drucker, *The Age of Discontinuity*, New York, Harper & Row, 1969, p.i.

dependencies discussed earlier in the chapter emphasize the importance of this factor. The third major discontinuity lies in what Drucker calls the "political matrix of social and economic life." He notes that "every single social task of importance today is entrusted to a large institution organized for perpetuity . . . yet . . . everywhere there is a rapid disenchantment with . . . modern government."[33] Education is the fourth major discontinuity, rapidly changing our knowledge of the sciences and arts, changing the labor force and work expectations.

Drucker suggests that our modern technologies must drastically change in order to avoid stagnation, as follows.

In their ability to provide the thrust for future substantial growth of the developed economies, they are mature, if not stagnant . . . . They will increasingly lose the capacity to contribute to rising national incomes, to increased employment and career opportunities. They will increasingly be unable to provide economic dynamics for the developed countries.[34]

The drastic changes that will create new industries involve technologies in information handling, oceanography, materials, and urbanology (the management of cities). They will be based on different scientific techniques, logic and perceptions than those of today. They will also involve a drastically different work force, one comprised of *knowledge* workers rather than manual laborers.[35]

To accompany these changes, the manager will also see a somewhat illogical development in American society: an expansion of government activities along with a growing distrust of authority, government, and big business.

CHANGING VIEWS OF AUTHORITY

The 1960s and 1970s brought significant change to American society. Perhaps the major vehicle of this change was the communications industry. For the first time ever, Americans witnessed live television coverage of open challenge to the traditional way of life and to traditional authority in the United States. Civil rights protests, antiwar demonstrations, disruptions of political conventions, and ecology strikes brought widespread disenchantment and rebellion into the living rooms of most Americans. Civil disobedience and violence were used increasingly to promote change.

> The manager of tomorrow may possess a very different view of authority.

The clear implication of these movements is that many persons in society distrust legal and political channels as instruments of change. During the period mentioned above, the groups apparently most involved were the young and members of minority groups. Since these two groups are significant parts of today's managerial and nonmanagerial work force, the manager of tomorrow may be faced with an *institutionalized* view of authority and regulation that is quite different from the traditional views of the 1950s and 1960s.

---

[33]Ibid., pp. x–xi.
[34]Ibid., p. 12.
[35]Ibid.

WOMEN IN MANAGEMENT

Several demographic changes in the work force will also affect business in the future. The last fifteen years have been marked by increasing concern that all persons in America have the opportunity to pursue desired educational, social, and career goals without reference to their race, sex, religion, or other demographic characteristics. One recent effect of this concern for equal opportunity involves the occupational opportunities for women.

The past decade saw a tremendous increase in the number of women who are demanding interesting, challenging, and well-paying careers. Several factors have contributed to this trend. Perhaps the most important is a change in cultural values concerning woman's role in society. This in turn has stimulated new federal laws banning sex discrimination in employment practices, and has created better opportunities for women to acquire specialized education in fields related to business. Increasing numbers of women with significant experience, and larger numbers of unmarried women who have no family ties, have also contributed to the trend.

The assimilation of women into managerial positions represents a challenge for business.

The assimilation of women into managerial positions represents a challenge and opportunity for businesses. Several corporations have recently come under strong legal pressures to compensate for past inequities in their employment practices. In 1973, for example, the American Telephone and Telegraph Company agreed to an out-of-court settlement of approximately $15 million to compensate minorities and women for past discriminatory practices. This case has been interpreted by many organizations as a clear warning that personnel policies affecting female employees will come under close evaluation in the future.[36]

Obviously, not all the blame for past discrimination against women workers rests with business. Much of the reasoning behind sex discrimination stems from our history. In the early 1900s, it was unusual to find women working outside the home. When they did work, it was in jobs considered appropriate to the feminine role—teaching school, for example, or selling in a clothing store. With the invention of the typewriter, women moved in large numbers into the realm of big business, although in most cases still in a role restricted to secretarial duties.

Changes in the roles of women in the working world are interesting to study statistically. In 1900, approximately one-sixth of all women worked. Today, over one-third of all women are in the work force. Around the turn of the century, about half of all women worked at some point in their lives; today over ninety percent of all women work for pay at some time in their lives. In 1900, women worked an average of eleven years; today that figure is around twenty-five years of work. The number of women working in managerial positions was approxiamtely 8900 in 1950; just ten years later, that number had almost tripled.[37]

---

[36] Benson Rosen and Thomas H. Jerdee, *Becoming Aware*, Chicago, Science Research Associates, 1976, p. 13.

[37] Lawrence C. Hackamack and Alan B Solid, "The Woman Executive," *Business Horizons*, April 1972, p. 90.

632 GOAL-ORIENTED MANAGEMENT SYSTEMS

In spite of antisex discrimination laws considerable difference in the pay for men and women on similar jobs still exists.

Statistics also point out some of the inequities which caused sex discrimination laws to be written. In 1967, only 3.3 percent of all fully employed females had annual incomes of $10,000 or more, while over 24 percent of all employed males made more than $10,000. Among professional and technical workers, men earned an average of $3,460 more per year than women, according to a 1968 survey.[38] According to more recent data, almost 96 percent of all jobs paying an annual wage of more than $15,000 are held by white male employees, even though women comprise almost 40 percent of the work force.[39] Further evidence of past inequality comes from a survey of top personnel in 1220 large American corporations taken by *Fortune* magazine in 1973: among approximately 6500 officers and directors earning annual salaries of more than $30,000 only 11 were women.[40]

Equal opportunity for women can be enforced.

The federal government has been actively enforcing equal employment opportunity for women in the past decade. Several vehicles are used for this enforcement. Title VII of the Civil Rights Act of 1964 is a very broadbased piece of legislation, prohibiting discrimination in any type of employment or employee development activity. The Equal Employment Opportunity Commission (EEOC) is the federal agency responsible for enforcing the act. The Equal Pay Act of 1963, an amendment to the Fair Labor Standards Act, prohibits sex discrimination in determining wages. Presidential executive orders (particularly Executive Order 11246, revised Order 4, 1972) prohibit sex discrimination among federal contractors, and require these contractors to initiate affirmative action programs that ensure equal (or in many cases preferential) treatment for women and minorities.[41]

Prompted by the women's rights movement, the practice of appointing women to corporate boards began in 1972, and has increased tremendously since. Only about one-third of these women come from the corporate world. There are well over 400 women directors of major corporations today, and the number is steadily growing as more companies respond to governmental pressures.

CROSS-CULTURAL SENSITIVITY

Leaders cannot afford to be ethnocentric.

As leaders we cannot develop an effective interpersonal competence if we continue to be ethnocentric—"To notice and appreciate only our own culture and values." Culture is changing rapidly in this country and industry is rapidly becoming multinational in its orientation.

Schein illustrates blind spots regarding cross-cultural differences by relating a story about a trip to Australia, a country that he describes as "superficially and historically similar to the United States."

---

[38]Ibid.
[39]Rosen and Jerdee, *Becoming Aware*, p. 35.
[40]Ibid.
[41]Barbara Boyle, "Equal Opportunity for Women is Smart Business," *Harvard Business Review*, May-June 1973, P. 86.

It took me quite a while to discover that while Australians (like Americans) are achievement oriented, they also have the "tall poppy syndrome": one must not stand out above the crowd; one must accomplish things without seeming to work too hard at them; and one must not take too much personal credit for one's accomplishments. The son of a friend of mine told us how, after waiting all day for the perfect wave, he had finally succeeded in having a brilliant ride on his surfboard. When he hit the beach, he told his watching friends—as he knew he had to—"Boy that was a lucky one.[42]

It is interesting to note that the public image of the Australian businessperson is that of a complacent security oriented employee; yet Schein observed many tough aggressive managers among them.

In the United States managers are often ambitious climbers and power seekers.

In the U. S. counterpart image, managers are ambitious climbers and power seekers. Schein again notes many exceptions, such as a "Growing number of allegedly ambitious managers who admit in private that they are not motivated to continue the "rat race," that they would like early retirement, or that they are considering another career altogether."[43]

Schein continues to emphasize the importance of these relationships, especially in what he calls *face work*. "At the minimum, we nod and say 'uh huh' when someone is talking to us, or we try to laugh politely at a joke that is not really funny, or we ignore embarrassing incidents." We must practice detecting the subtleties of how others perceive situations and what their expectations are for us—given such perception.

Cultural/moral humility is the ability to appreciate other cultures and value systems.

Schein is proposing the development of what he calls "cultural/moral humility—the ability to see our own culture and values as *different*, not necessarily as better." He explains his argument with a thought-provoking example.

A few years ago, a group of American students teased one of their German peers about his heel-clicking, head-nodding, hand-shaking formality. After some nine months of being teased, he stopped them one day with the statement, "When I go to work in the morning, I go to my boss's office, click my heels, bow my head, shake his hand, and then tell him the truth." The teasing stopped.[44]

The following principles are suggested as approaches to the many interpersonal problems that you will encounter each working day.

1. Develop a keen self-insight and sense of your own identity.
2. Develop cross-cultural sensitivity—the ability to decipher other people's values.
3. Improve your cultural/moral humility—the ability to see one's own values as *not* necessarily better or worse than another's values.
4. Assist others in protecting their "self" in face-to-face situations.
5. Work toward an I'm OK—You're OK life position in all relationships.

---

[42]Schein, op. cit., p. 45.
[43]Ibid., p. 46.
[44]Ibid.

MANAGEMENT PRACTICES OF THE FUTURE

TOP MANAGEMENT, DECENTRALIZATION, AND INFORMATION SYSTEMS

Chief executive officers in organizations will spend more and more time on external relations:

> *The chief executive officer of the future will work with an increasing proportion of outside directors, spend more time on 'outside' societal affairs, and concern himself or herself with broader and longer-range objectives. Willingness and ability to communicate with and relate to others will distinguish the CEO of the 1980's from many of his predecessors.*[45]

This means that there is likely to be increased decentralization at least in terms of decision making at the top management level.

However the research on the subject (and the crystal-ball gazing) has been mixed. In a now classic study of the 1950s, Harold J. Leavitt and Thomas L. Whisler argued that information technology, or what we might now call the computerized MIS, would have a considerable impact on the upper levels or organization.[46] Specifically, they forecasted that middle management planning would be moved upward and taken over by operations researchers and organization analysts. This recentralization would cause middle management jobs to move downward in status and compensation. This programmed assistance provided to top management was predicted to allow them to become more creative and innovative.

In a 1971 Delphi study of this question, using a panel consisting of management experts, the opinions were mixed. About half of the panel members thought that the use of computers would lead to decentralization and half of them saw more centralization ahead.[47]

Perhaps the best explanation of this phenomenon is suggested by J. G. Hunt and P. F. Newall in a more recent study.[48] They argue that it is possible to have a high degree of centralization of facilities, such as computer systems, accompanied by a high degree of decentralization of decision making. The type of decision making is frequently determined not by the computer but by the personal preferences of the chief executive.[49]

The trend appears to be toward centralization of physical facilities and decentralization of authority.

---

[45]Perry Pascarella, "The CEO of the Eighties," *Industry Week*, January 7, 1980, Cleveland, Ohio, Penton/IPC, p. 75.

[46]Harold Leavitt and Thomas Whisler, "Management in the 1980's," *Harvard Business Review*, November-December 1958, pp. 41–48.

[7]Robert M. Fulmer, "The Management of Tomorrow," *Business Horizons*, August 1973, pp. 7–8.

[48]J. B. Hunt and P. F. Newall, "Management in the 1980s Revisited," *Personnel Journal*, January 1971, pp. 35–39.

[49]John Diebold, "What's Ahead in Information Technology," *Harvard Business Review*, September-October 1965, p. 82.

Hunt and Newall solidify their argument by quoting a study by Earnest Dale in which he found that of the thirty-three largest users of computers, fourteen reported no computer impact on their organization structure, thirteen reported more centralization, and six reported more decentralization. The trend appears to be toward centralization of physical facilities and decentralization of decision making.[50]

THE ORGANIZATIONAL CHART AND MIDDLE MANAGEMENT

If the ranks of middle management are indeed thinned by the use of the computer, new organizational forms might appear on the horizon. Leavitt and Whisler foresaw an increasing number of staff specialists working at the top management level and fewer middle managers, because of the programming of the middle management functions. Thus they concluded that:

> *The organization chart of the future may look something like a football balanced upon the point of a church bell. Within the football (the top staff organization), problems of coordination, individual autonomy, group decision making and so on should arise more intensely than ever. We expect that they will be dealt with quite independently of the bell portion of the company, with distinctly different methods of remuneration, control, and communication.*[51]

The football and bell substitute for the organizational pyramid was vividly portrayed in a later journal article, as reproduced in Figure 23-4.

Fulmer cites other predictions of the 1960s, which suggest that the organization of the future will evolve into a wheel or an inverted pyramid.[52] Although there is little agreement about the future shape of the organization, all writers agree that it will have to be capable of dealing with increased complexity and more rapid change. Fulmer's panel of experts believed that the basic pyramid form of organization would continue in use past year 2000, with some adaptations of the football-on-the-bell configuration. This view is supported by the trends reviewed by Hunt and Newall. These writers think the future pyramid will be designed as a system with continuous flow of information and materials from department to department.[53]

The organization of the future will have to be more capable of dealing with change.

Several changes in the age composition of the managerial work force will also be felt in the next decades. Recent federal legislation has moved the "mandatory" retirement age to 70 for many workers. With inflation eating away at retirement savings, many more workers may elect to stay on the job longer. Changes in the birthrates from the 1950s to the 1960s also mean that relatively fewer workers and managers are now entering the work force. As older workers

---
[50]Earnest Dale, "The Impact of Computers on Management," unpublished manuscript, pp. 42–46.
[51]Leavitt and Whisler, "Management in the 1980's," p. 47.
[52]Fulmer, "The Management of Tomorrow," p. 8.
[53]Hunt and Newall, "Management in the 1980s Revisited," p. 41.

636 GOAL-ORIENTED MANAGEMENT SYSTEMS

FIGURE 23-4

The Football and Bell Concept of Organization

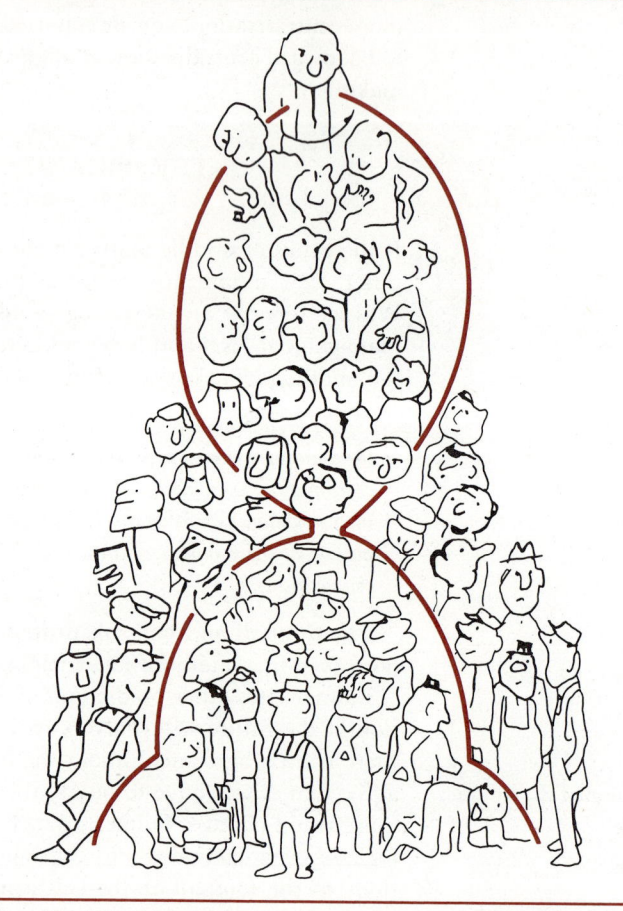

Source: Hak Chong Lee, "The Organizational Impact of Computers," *Management Services,* May-June, 1967, p. 41.

stay longer (including those in top management positions) and with fewer younger workers, middle-aged managers may experience extreme competition for career-related job changes.[54] Such competition is unlikely to assist the lifetime employment guarantee being suggested by current bestselling books that laud Japanese management. Mandatory retirement for most workers in Japan is at age 55.[55]

---

[54] Donald L. Lunda, "Personnel Management: What's Ahead?" *Personnel Administrator,* April 1981, p. 54.
[55] William Ouchi, *Theory Z, How American Business Can Meet The Japanese Challenge,* Reading, Mass., Addison-Wesley Publishers, 1981, p. 17.

Numerous studies indicate that the nature of the middle manager's job is changing for the better, with less clerical work to do and more time to interpret and explain conditions to higher management. Trends since the 1950s do not indicate a reduction in the number of middle managers nor of organizational levels, but the increase in these areas does seem to have been slowed or aborted.[56]

ORGANIZATIONAL AND MANAGEMENT DEVELOPMENT

In 1969, Peter Drucker predicted that, "We will, within another ten years, become far less concerned with management development (i.e., adapting the individual to the demands of the organization), and far more with organization development (i.e., adapting the company to the needs, aspirations, and potentials of the individual)."[57] Although there is some tendency for designing organizations around key people, Fulmer found general agreement that his panel of experts expected very few organizations to design organizational structure around individual needs or abilities. One of Fulmer's panel summarized the issue as follows.

> *Fundamentally, no mattter what shining short-range cause seems to show the contrary, man is seeking order, especially for feasible teamwork. Individuals come and go. All the hundreds of thousands within institutions should not, either on human or economic grounds be upset . . . to suit individual whim.*[58]

Although organizations are not likely to be designed around people, work rules and job design may be more flexible.

In spite of these predictions, corporations do seem to be moving toward more flexibility for employees by adding flexible and sometimes optional working hours, optional enriched or assembly line jobs and other such alternatives.

MANAGEMENT STYLES

Over ten years ago in his presidential address to the Academy of Management, George Steiner categorized some predictions about the changes which management was likely to take in the future.[59] Steiner introduced these changes as largely ones deriving from a change in emphasis on quantity (of production) to quality of life.

Steiner clarified the changes enumerated in Figure 23-5, with a number of rather far-reaching explanations. We have already discussed some of the shifts toward social responsibility by some of the larger firms. But what about management styles? Steiner sees a change not only toward the flexible, permissive, and democratic management style, but in the areas of top mangaement, a shift

---

[56]Ibid., pp. 42–43.
[57]Peter F. Drucker, "Management's New Role," *Harvard Business Review*, November-December 1969, p. 69.
[58]Fulmer, "The Management of Tomorrow," p. 10.
[59]George A. Steiner, "The Redefinition of Capitalism and Its Impact on Management Practice and Theory," in *The Proceedings of the 32nd Annual Meeting of the Academy of Management*, Minneapolis, Minnesota, August 13–16, 1972, pp. 2–11.

FIGURE 23-5

Recent Past vs. Future Managerial Practices

Recent Past	Toward Future
Assumption that a business manager's sole responsibility is to optimize stockholder wealth	Profit still dominant but modified by the assumption that a business manager has other social responsibilities
Business performance measured only by economic standards	Application of both an economic and social measure of performance
Emphasis on quantity of production	Emphasis on quantity *and* quality
Authoritarian management	Permissive/democratic management
Short-term intuitive planning	Long-range comprehensive structured planning
Entrepreneur	Renaissance manager
Control	Creativity
People subordinate	People dominant
Financial accounting	Financial *and* human resources accounting
Caveat emptor	Ombudsman
Centralized decision making	Decentralized and small group decision making
Concentration on internal functioning	Concentration on external ingredients to company success
Dominance of solely economic forecasts in decision making	Major use of social, technical, and political forecasts as well as economic forecasts
Business viewed as a single system	Business viewed as a system of systems within a larger social system
Business ideology calls for aloofness from government	Business-government cooperation and convergence of planning
Business has little concern for social costs of production	Increasing concern for internalizing social costs of production

Source: The Proceedings of the 32nd Annual Meeting of the Academy of Management, Minneapolis, Minnesota, August 13–16, 1972, p. 4.

from the enterpreneurial to what has been called statesmanship, or what Harold Johnson calls the *renaissance man*.[60] The move toward multinational corporations magnifies the need for corporate statesmen.

Steiner suggests that the new orientation on people is causing a "shift away from emphasis on control to stimulating creativity, from a focus on objects and things to concentration on people, and from subordinating people to business

---

[60]Harold L. Johnson, *Business in Contemporary Society: Framework and Issues*, Belmont, Cal., Wadsworth Publishing Co., Inc., 1971, p. 134.
[61]Steiner, "Redefinition of Capitalism," p. 6.

ends to viewing their interests as being of dominant concern."[61] Thus far Steiner's predictions have tended to be quite accurate.

If the general trends suggested by Steiner continue to be correct, the effectiveness required of the future manager will be greater than ever before. Greater burdens will be placed on selection of managers with personalities that fit a specific organization. This will require the use of sophisticated management models such as those presented in this text rather than simply dividing all persons into categories X and Y.

Future managers must be selected with personalities that fit a specific organization.

"The Eskimo has thirteen words to describe snow in various states; he needs them to talk about, explain, and deal with the dominant element in his situation."[62] Management styles may become even more subtle than snow!

One management development expert describes the manager of the future as follows.

> *By the 1980s, the truly professional manager will emerge, change will be his stock in trade. The qualities that differentiate him will be those of intellect and behavioral flexibility. Managers will be selected for intellectual capacity, not knowledge, because the latter is out of date in three years.*[63]

The social responsibility and multinational trends have led one futuristic writer to caption the manager of the future a public manager. Referring to the growth and influence of multinational firms, bank holding companies, and conglomerate corporations, the writer concludes:

> *Managers of these organizations have the opportunity to influence the peace of the world and the living standards and life styles of the peoples of less developed nations because the influence of their operations can transcend national boundaries more readily than that of governments or religious orders.*[64]

Although the effective manager's style will depend on the contingencies of the situation, the trend is toward a more informal, fluid way of bargaining, brokerage, advice, and consent. Roger Talpaert, Secretary-General of the European Institute for Advanced Studies in Management, suggests that the most important qualification for this manager will be political skills and moral credibility.[65] This trend is expressed by William Backie, the past Chairman of Caterpillar Tractor Company, as follows.

The trend of the effective manager's style is toward a more informal way of bargaining, brokerage, advice, and consent.

> *Insofar as authority has meant the power to order or command, its definition will be modified by the addition of some such qualifications as "but expect or deserve to be obeyed or followed only if you can satisfy those being ordered or led.*[66]

---

[62]W. J. Reddin, "Management Effectiveness in the 1980s," *Business Horizons*, August 1974, p. 8.
[63]Ibid., p. 9.
[64]John F. Mee, "The Manager of the Future," *Business Horizons*, June 1973.
[65]Roger Talpaert, "Management in the Twenty-first Century," *Management Review*, March 1981, p. 25.
[66]Reddin, "Management in the 1980s," p. 10.

PLANNING AND DECISION MAKING

Steiner predicts a greater emphasis on long-run planning and social as well as technological forecasting. Urban and social problems will encourage joint business-government planning. Businessmen who wish to improve the environment or the quality of products must often petition government to do so. Otherwise, they would end up in a noncompetitive position if they were to sink millions of dollars in a project on which competitors spent nothing.[67]

Since Steiner predicts that people will be viewed as the most valuable asset of companies, he suggests that human resource accounting may become as important as financial accounting. This means that emphasis will probably be given to the psychological contract between corporate and people expectations regarding work. Employees will be searching for meaningful work, an opportunity for self-expression and chances to make worthwhile contributions, while business will be searching for individuals who can discover new methods of performing tasks, so as to work productively with others, and to use time and energy for the benefit of the company.[68]

It should be noted that Fulmer's Delphi panel predicted only a 25 percent probability for social accounting by the year 2000.[69] Perhaps Steiner is too optimistic about such a change.

MBO IN THE FUTURE

What about the total system of management described in this text—MBO? Certainly this approach has led the way in focusing on results-oriented management as opposed to process-oriented management. With MBO, managers and employees alike are less inclined to go through the motions on the job, but will be motivated because they know their work goals and objectives.

Reddin predicts that "MBO will change in the way that life itself will change."[70] It will become less a structured, paper shuffling delegation process and become more of a basis for interaction, involvement, and participation. "It will be used less for accuracy or for answers and used more for understanding methods and consequences."[71]

One can only hope that Reddin's faith in favorable behavioral change will take place. Recent shifts to zero-base budgeting in the federal government, Texas Instruments, Consolidated Edison, and numerous other firms indicate that management emphasis, at least at the top levels, may not be moving toward more participative approaches. On the other hand, a number of Fortune 500 firms are trying to adopt the Japanese management technique that includes an emphasis on interpersonal skills, philosophy, and open leadership styles, as opposed to an

---

[67]Steiner, "Redefinition of Capitalism," p. 7.
[68]Ibid.
[69]Fulmer, "The Management of Tomorrrow," p. 11.
[70]Reddin, "Management in the 1980s," p. 10.
[71]Ibid., p. 10.

emphasis on structure, strategy, and systems. Perhaps the pattern will be an alternating one with participation emphasized during economic upturns and control emphasized during downturns.

In conclusion, we are glad to observe that the ingenuity, resourcefulness, adaptability, and overall productivity of both American management, and our entire labor force are unparalleled in history. We are also confident that the challenges to come will be met as successfully as were those in the past.

The productivity achievements of some modern nations stand as a challenge to others, including the United States. We are beckoned to find ways to help employees to produce more and to find ways that managers can employ to harmonize and unify the efforts of all—in short, to manage better.[72]

SUMMARY

According to a Chinese proverb, "It is very difficult to make predictions, especially about the future." Consequently, the summary to this chapter is fraught with uncertainties. However, the experts predict that the following changes are most likely.

Multinational corporations will figure prominently in the economic picture of the 1980s and 1990s, and may even rise to domiante world business. Their operation and management will present special complexity and difficulties and present unusual risks.

The problems of diminishing supplies of natural resources and increasing population put great pressure on the manager of the future to be effective in his job. The responsibility incumbent upon large multinational firms that can affect the future of nations will necessitate even greater social and diplomatic obligations. Changing social needs will create a climate of rapid change perhaps even greater than that which managers of the last decade have faced.

Our management system will need to integrate within it a large number of well-qualified and well-educated women. It will also need to accommodate itself to the demands of workers for more satisfying jobs.

Technological change, especially the change in computers toward large-scale systems, will tend to centralize physical facilities. On the other hand, the desired prompt reaction to the needs of society will tend to decentralize managerial decision making. Organizations will become more complex and perhaps, at least at higher levels, will tend to accommodate themselves to individual behavior rather than expecting conformity.

There will be some movement toward social and human resource accounting rather than merely a financial accounting. Finally, the management system of the future, while it may not be highly participative and interactive, will probably remain a modification of MBO. The effect of zero-base budgeting on management systems is yet to be determined.

---

[72] James Gatza, Insurance Institute of America.

SUMMARY CHART

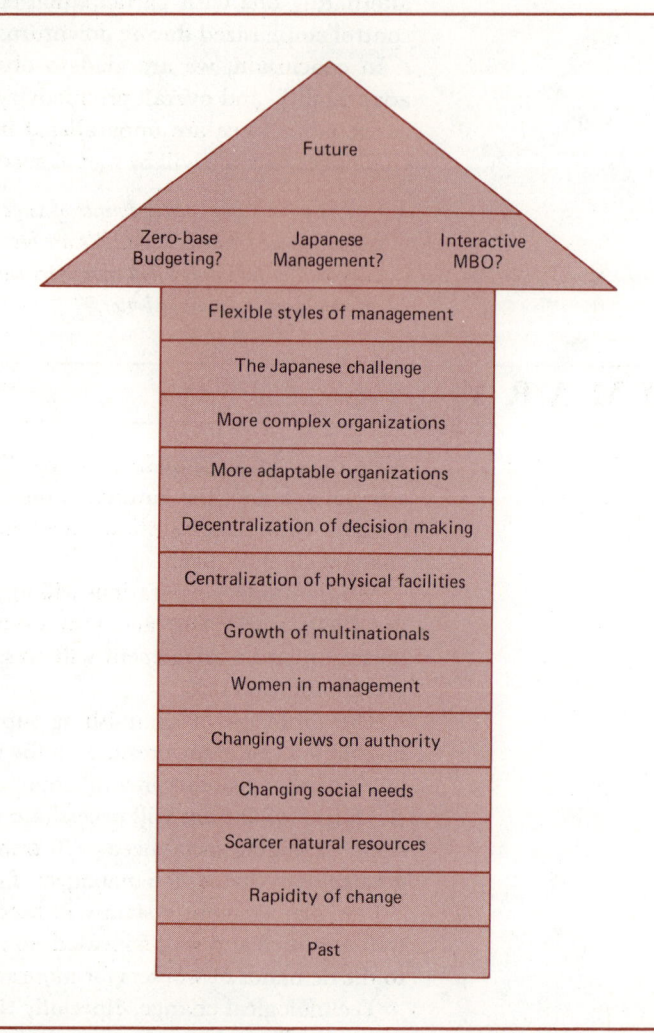

Arrow pointing upward from Past to Future, showing progression through:

- Future
- Zero-base Budgeting? | Japanese Management? | Interactive MBO?
- Flexible styles of management
- The Japanese challenge
- More complex organizations
- More adaptable organizations
- Decentralization of decision making
- Centralization of physical facilities
- Growth of multinationals
- Women in management
- Changing views on authority
- Changing social needs
- Scarcer natural resources
- Rapidity of change
- Past

DISCUSSION QUESTIONS

1. What are the major trends occurring in society that will most likely affect future management?
2. How can management prepare for the rapid changes with which it is faced today?
3. Is a multinational corporation truly different from domestic companies other than in its market to be served? Explain.
4. What organizational and management changes are likely to result from the following trends?

(a) Social awareness.
(b) Changing views of authority.
(c) Women in management.
(d) The multinational corporation.

5. Draw the organizational chart of the future as you see it.
6. Describe the oeprations profile of the ideal manager of the future. Explain your description.

APPLICATION EXERCISES AND CASES

SUCCESS IN THE SMALL MULTINATIONAL[73]

A good example of the small and highly successful multinational company is a small Swiss company, Urania A.G., located in the small town—hardly more than a village—of Glarus in eastern Switzerland. Its history is a very peculiar one; twenty years ago, Urania was on the point of liquidation, totally unsuccessful, and indeed practically bankrupt.

The story actually begins with a man, Christian Bluntschli, now in his early seventies. Bluntschli, who had been educated as an engineer in Zurich, came in the 1920s to Philadelphia's Wharton School as an exchange student. He stayed long enough to get a Master's degree and then a Doctorate. When he went back to Switzerland, he was promptly hired by that country's first business school, the Commercial University in St. Gallen. He became a very successful and popular Professor of Finance and stayed until the late 1950s. Then he went to one of the big Swiss banks as an economist. But he found himself rather bored by the work. When the Wharton School approached him with the suggestion that he come to Philadelphia and join the faculty, he was on the point of accepting.

But before he could resign, the bank's president called him in and said: "I wonder, Bluntschli, whether you would take on a special assignment? We have lent a lot of money to a small company which makes precision gears in Glarus, Urania A.G. We now own about 35 percent of the stock. The company seems to be in terrible trouble; in fact, I strongly suspect that it is completely bankrupt. It seems we should liquidate, but the company is the largest employer in a poor rural area, and we are rather worried about the public relations aspect of letting it go out of business. Could you go down to Glarus and look into the affairs of the company and tell us whether you think that salvage is worth trying?"

When Bluntschli went to Glarus, he found things much worse than anything he had been prepared for. Early in the century, the company had been the world's leading supplier of gears for the then-fashionable cog railways. But cog railways had gone out of fashion, replaced by cable cars and rope tows. And

---

[73]Peter F. Drucker, *Management Cases*, New York, Harper's College Press, 1977, pp. 10–12.

although the company had the right products needed for the manufacture of these replacements, it had never tried to sell them. Instead, it built tremendous service staffs and spare part inventories to service old cog railway customers everywhere. In Japan alone, it had twenty-eight trained people on its payroll to supply spare parts and service to only twelve customers—all of them themselves losing money and going out of business. The people who ran the company had spent all their time and all the company's money on inventing in a wide variety of fields. However, they had never done anything with the patents. Their policy was not to license, but to manufacture. Where they could not manufacture—and in few of the areas in which they had taken out patents did they have any manufacturing capability—they simply did nothing. The more Bluntschli saw, the more depressed he became. But also he was excited by the worldwide service capability the company had built up. Finally—and he himself says, "in a fit of temporary insanity"—he decided that managing Urania was what he wanted to do. He went to his associates in the bank and said: "The company is hopeless. How much do I have to pay you for its ownership?" And before he could recover from his temporary insanity, he owned 100 percent of a bankrupt company with no business, no working capital, and no assets, except for an excellent worldwide service staff.

That was twenty years ago. Today, Urania is one of the most profitable small businesses in the world. It employs only about 900 people. But it is the leader in precision gearing—in specialized transportation such as cable cars, ski tows, mining gondolas, and in the special gearing needed for the equipment to put containers on ships and so on. It actually has manufacturing facilities in about thirty countries, but it only makes one or two parts of each of the patented pieces of equipment it sells. Whatever is standard is contracted out to be made on the spot. It still focuses on service, and especially on design service. But it now charges for service, and makes enough profit on service to cover its entire worldwide payroll. Whatever it gets for selling equipment, minus what it has to pay to its own suppliers, is in effect net profit.

When you ask Bluntschli how he got there, he smiles and says: "I did only the obvious things, the things you find in each textbook."

Question

What do you think Bluntschli did that neither his predecessors in the ownership and management of Urania nor his associates in the bank did?

THE NONCONFORMISTS[74]

Many of today's young managers can best be described by the term "nonconformist." Consider the case of James W. Hughes of the Equitable Life Assurance Society. Recently he was offered a transfer from Dayton to New York.

---

[74] The data in this case can be found in Roger Ricklefs, "Young Managers Today Less Eager to Adapt, So Firms Alter Policies," *Wall Street Journal*, May 16, 1973, pp. 1, 34.

In addition to a big raise, the move would have eventually been worth $5000 a year. However, Mr. Hughes turned down the offer because he felt commuting to and from work in New York City would take him away from his family more each day. In the past, such a decision might well have meant the end of a young manager's career with the firm. However, in this case:

> *The people at Equitable weren't too surprised by the decision. More than half of its workers today reject proferred transfers, compared with about 10% a decade ago—even though practically every move involves both a raise and a promotion, says Patrick J. Scollard, vice president and personnel director. Young managers "aren't willing to accept the company above all else," he says.*

Other executives echo these sentiments. The national sales manager at Pet Foods division of General Foods Corporation, for example, says, "Today, many people are less willing to move—and more willing to tell the company how they feel." Furthermore, refusal to accept a transfer is no longer the end of the line. At the Exxon Corporation, a young executive refused a transfer overseas and his father, a retired company executive, told him that his career was "as good as dead." Since that time, however, the man has had two promotions.

This nonconformity carries over to the work itself. Today many firms are finding that they are having to cut their training periods and get the individual started on his career. The young manager wants meaningful work and responsibility, not training. As a vice president at First National City Bank in New York explained, "Shortening our training program gave us a real selling point. Good people want responsibility early." A young employee at the bank, who turned down offers from two competitors to join Citibank, agreed, "At the other two banks, it would have been at least a year before I could get into a line position. Here, I was working on a real problem by 2 P.M. of the first day."

Questions
1. Are the trends described in this case going to continue throughout the 1980s? Explain.
2. Are these trends dangerous for business? Are the managers getting too powerful with their nonconformist attitude?
3. What advantages do you see accruing to business by allowing managers to refuse assignments and putting people into positions of responsibility early in their career? Explain.

PART SIX

CASES

UNION CARBIDE AND VIENNA, WEST VIRGINIA [75]

West Virginia, never one of the more prosperous areas of the United States, went into rapid economic decline in the late twenties as the coal industry, long the state's mainstay, began to shrink. The decline of the coal industry was hastened by rising concern with mine accidents and miners' diseases. For many of the coal mines of West Virginia were small and marginal and could not afford modern safety precautions or adequate health protection.

By the late 1940's the leading industrial company in the state became alarmed over the steady economic shrinkage of the region. Union Carbide, one of America's major chemical companies, had its headquarters in New York. But the original plants of the company had been based on West Virginia coal, and the company was still the largest employer in the state, together with a few large coal mining companies. Accordingly, the company's top management asked a group of young engineers and economists in its employ to prepare a plan for the creation of employment opportunities in West Virginia, and especially for the location of the company's new plant facilities in areas of major unemployment in the state. But for the worst afflicted area—the westernmost corner of the state on the border of Ohio—the planners could not come up with an attractive project. In and around the little town of Vienna, West Virginia, there was total unemployment, and no prospects for new industries. There was, however, also considerable unrest in the area, great bitterness, and a good deal of feeling against "big business" from "outside the state". Indeed, whenever a tax measure came up in the State Legislature, the representatives of the Vienna area asked for high taxes for business—and in a few instances they had blocked and defeated tax bills of considerable importance to Union Carbide's plants in other areas of the state.

Top management was keenly aware of the situation. The whole idea of a strategic plan for new plants in West Virginia had started with a question by the president, himself originally a miner's son from a small town not far from Vienna: "What can we do to help Vienna's economy and employment?" But the only thing the study would find as even a remote possibility for Vienna was a ferroalloy plant using a process that had already become obsolete and had heavy cost disadvantages compared to more modern processes such as Union Carbide's competitors were using.

Even for the old process, Vienna was basically an uneconomical location. The process required very large amounts of coal of fair quality. But the only coal available within the area had such high sulfur content that it could not be used without expensive treatment and scrubbing. Even after this heavy capital investment, the process was inherently noisy and dirty, releasing large amounts of fly ash and noxious gases.

The only rail and road transportation facilities were not in West Virginia but across the river, on the Ohio side. Putting the plant there, however, meant that the prevailing winds would blow the soot from the smokestacks and the sulfur released by the power plants directly into the town of Vienna, on the other bank of the river.

---

[75] Peter F. Ducker, *Management Cases*, New York, Harper's College Press, 1977, pp. 86–89.,

Yet the Vienna plant would provide 1,500 jobs in Vienna itself and another 500 to 1,000 jobs in a new coal field not too far distant. In addition, the new coal field would be strip mined, so the new jobs would be free from the accident and health hazards that had become increasingly serious in the old worked-out coal mines of the area. Union Carbide top management came to the conclusion that social responsibility demanded building the new plant, despite its marginal economics.

The plant was built with the most up-to-date antipollution equipment known at the time. Whereas even big-city power stations were then content to trap half the fly ash escaping from their smokestacks, the Vienna plant installed scrubbers to catch 75 percent—though there was little anyone could do about the sulfur dioxide fumes emitted by the high-sulfur coal.

When the plant was opened in 1951, Union Carbide was the hero. Politicans, public figures, educators, all praised the company for its social responsibility. But ten years later the former savior was fast becoming the public enemy. As the nation became pollution-conscious, the citizens of Vienna began to complain more and more bitterly about the ash, the soot, and the fumes that floated across the river into their town and homes. In 1961 a new mayor was elected on the platform "fight pollution," which meant "fight Union Carbide." Ten years later the plant had become a "national scandal." Even *Business Week*—hardly a publication hostile to business—chastised Union Carbide (in February 1971) in an article entitled "A Corporate Polluter Learns the Hard Way."

Yet this is not the basic lesson of this cautionary tale. Once the decision had been made to employ an obsolescent process and to build an economically marginal plant in order to alleviate unemployment in a bitterly depressed area, the rest followed more or less automatically. This decision meant that the plant did not generate the revenues needed to rebuild it. There is very little doubt that on economic reasoning alone the plant would never have been built. Public opinion forced Union Carbide to invest substantial sums in that plant to remedy the worst pollution problems—though it is questionable whether the technology exists to do more than a patch-up job. Publicity also forced Union Carbide to keep the plant open. But, once the spotlight shifts elsewhere, most of the jobs in the Vienna, West Virginia, plant are likely to disappear again, if indeed the plant remains open at all. And there is still no other employer in the area.

Questions
1. Discuss in detail your idea of what social responsibility involves. For all of the questions be sure to explain and defend your position.
2. Was it "socially responsible" to build to plant in the first place?
3. Was it "socially responsible" to keep it running once changing concepts of the balance between pollution and jobs created an environmental problem?
4. Would it have been "socially responsible" to pour additional millions in to clean up the plant when it could never hope to become a competitive producer?
5. And would it be "socially responsbile" for Union Carbide to close the plant?

CONSOLIDATED INSTRUMENTS—B[76]

Consolidated Instruments (CI) begans as a producer of precision control devices for the petroleum industry. During World War II its president, Homer Peake, successfully developed several important control

---
[76]William H. Newman, Charles E. Summer, and E. Kirby Warren, "Consolidated Instruments—B," *The Process of Management,* 3rd ed., Englewood Cliffs, N.J., Prentice Hall, 1972, pp. 674–682. Reprinted by permission of Prentice-Hall, Englewood Cliffs, N.J.

648 GOAL-ORIENTED MANAGEMENT SYSTEMS

devices used in aircraft and by 1970, through internal developments and acquisitions, Peake and his successor, David Meyers, had broadened CI's market still further. With its most recent acquisition of the PCD (Pollution Control Devices) Company, CI found itself listed in *Fortune* magazine's list of the five hundred largest corporations in the United States. The company now designs and produces control devices and markets them not only to the oil and chemical industries, but also to the food processing, aircraft, space, and missile industries.

The newly acquired PCD Company differs from other parts of CI in that it is the only business that manufactures the end-products in which control devices are used. When acquired, there was considerable debate as to how PCD should be integrated into the existing organization, and it was finally decided to permit it to remain a separate division reporting directly to the president. Given its sales of only $28,000,000, PCD might more properly have been made a part of one of the three existing divisions (see Exhibit 1).

There was a double reason for maintaining PCD's separate identity. First, although PCD sold products in all the markets served by the other divisions, none of the existing divisional general managers wanted to

EXHIBIT 1.

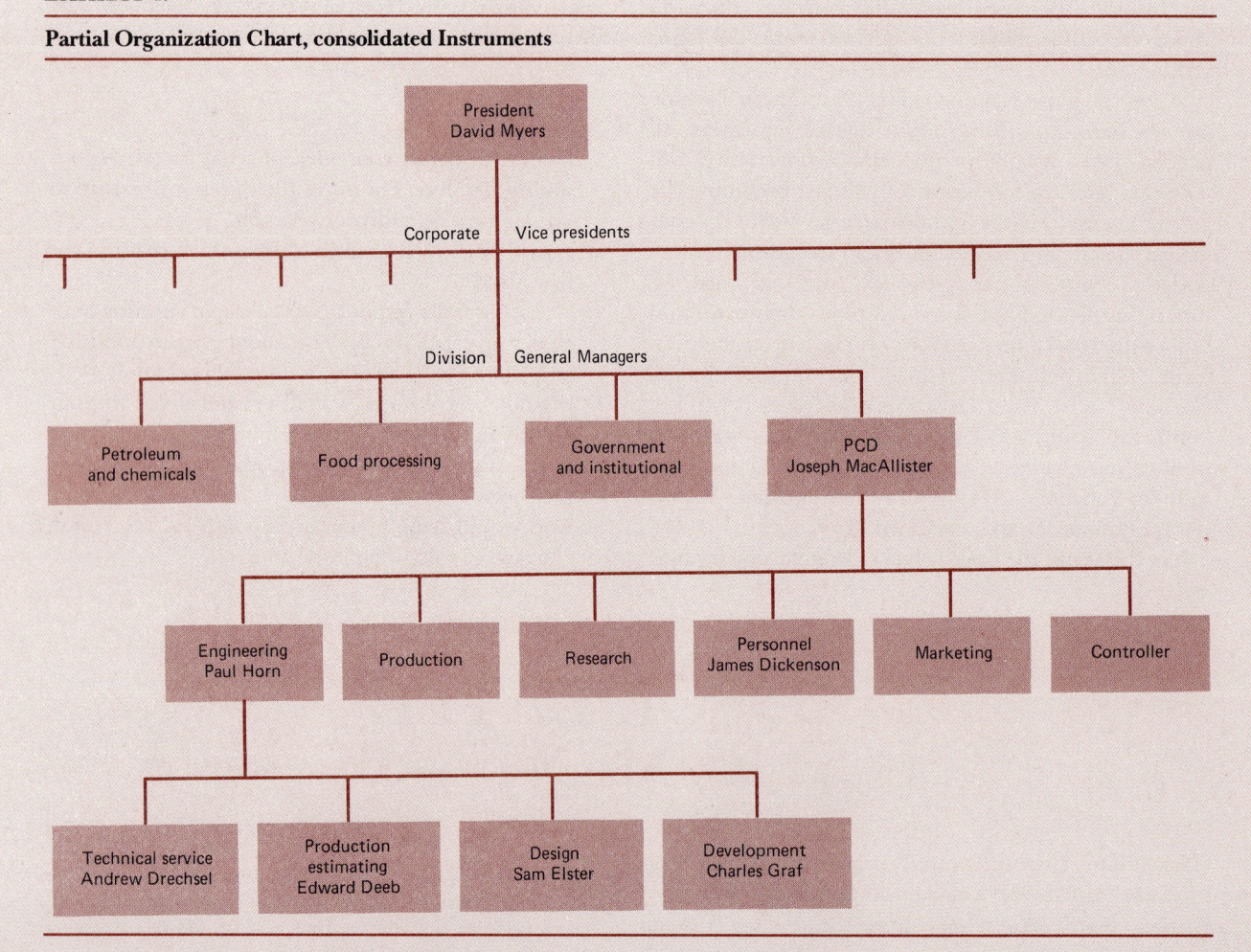

Partial Organization Chart, consolidated Instruments

```
                          President
                          David Myers
                              │
          ┌─────┬─────┬─────┼─────┬─────┬─────┐
          │     │     │  Corporate Vice presidents
          │     │     │     │     │     │     │

                     Division General Managers
          ┌───────────┬───────────┬───────────┐
     Petroleum    Food processing  Government    PCD
   and chemicals                  and institutional  Joseph MacAllister
                                                    │
            ┌──────────┬──────────┬──────────┬──────────┬──────────┐
       Engineering  Production  Research   Personnel   Marketing  Controller
       Paul Horn                          James Dickenson
            │
   ┌────────┼────────┬────────┐
 Technical  Production  Design   Development
  service   estimating Sam Elster Charles Graf
Andrew Drechsel Edward Deeb
```

take on the responsibility for the PCD business. Each argued that PCD fit better in another's division. Underlying this disinterest were the low margins and high risks associated with work in the pollution-control area. Many companies in recent years had sought to establish themselves in the pollution abatement market but despite growing concern by industry and government alike, very few companies were able to earn a profit in this market. When acquired, PCD had shown a $2,000,000 loss on $28,000,000 sales in its last fiscal year.

President Myers' second reason for keeping the PCD company intact as a separate division reporting to him was to facilitate its sale if in five years the division failed to satisfy him that it could meet at least minimum profit standards as well as contribute to technology in other divisions. "I'm eager to do my part to deal with our ecological problems," he told his Board," and we will not expect any miracles from PCD, but within five years it will either be in the black or on the block."

He assigned several capable executives from other divisions of CI to key posts in PCD but kept Joseph MacAllister, PCD's founder and president, as president of the new division. Myers states:

MacAllister knows the business. He is only fifty-one and although he may be a little too much of the Tom Swift inventor-type, he is an adequate coordinator. By backing him up with a new man in the top engineering post, a new controller, and two of our good marketing service men, I think we have the makings of a good team. Because MacAllister took most of his equity in PCD in the form of CI stock and options, I'm sure he is as anxious as we to see things work out.

Finally, we have assigned one of our best personnel people, James Dickenson, as his new director of personnel. Jim will see to it that we bring their salary and benefit programs into line with ours as smoothly as possible, and more important, he will get them working with our management by objectives and related programs.

The new division director of engineering is Paul Horn. He is 56 years old and has been with CI for over twenty years. Before moving to the PCD division in Pittsburgh, Horn held several key posts in other parts of CI. Trained initially as a mechanical engineer, Horn gained both bachelor's and master's degrees in electrical engineering by attending night school for eleven years. After holding the second highest engineering post in first the oil and chemical and then the food processing divisions, he served as the director of engineering estimates and then divisional director of the government products division. A drop in government sales led to a reorganization of that division and for sixteen months Horn served as manager of the corporate engineering review department and reported to the corporate vice-president of engineering.

Horn at first resisted the move to PCD, but was eventually persuaded that he was needed there to put the new division on the road to profitable operations.

Myers himself spoke with Horn, telling him, "I would not ask this of you, Paul, if I didn't think it important. We need your experience, good business sense, and knowledge of our practices to help get them out of the red."

Myers informed the casewriter that

Horn had some fool notion that we were unhappy with him for being a little hard-nosed in his corporate review job. Heck, that's why I wanted him in that post to help Shel Thayler [vice-president of engineering] sift through requests for new projects and get rid of the old ones that hadn't worked out. Paul Horn may not be the easiest man to work with, but technically he is first-rate and he's experienced enough and energetic enough to take on a tough assignment like this.

Horn accepted the new post, but he made it abundantly clear to Jim Dickenson, PCD's new personnel director, that he had a different understanding about the reasons behind his transfer.

I know why I'm here, Jim, regardless of what Myers and Thayler say. They are all excited about your human relations ideas and these new organization development concepts. I've done a lot of tough jobs for this company over the years when we didn't have the time or resources to pussyfoot around. But times change; nowadays maybe the people-problems are more important than the technical ones. I've still got what I hope are eight to ten good years to go before retirement and I found when they sent me off to that six-week management course[1] that I adapted to, and handled, the new material and cases as well as men twenty years my junior.

Although I was plenty upset about this transfer at first, I don't intend to go around sulking for the next ten years. Neither do I intend to make the same mistakes I've made before. If it's "develop people" and a "healthy climate" that they want, whatever that means, then I'll develop people and climate. But I'm going to need your help, Jim.

Dickenson explained to the casewriter that he had been pleasantly surprised by Horn's words. "I had expected that Paul would be something of a problem," Dickenson said. "I had heard that he was upset about the move and I had him down as a potential trouble spot in installing our management-by-objectives program in PCD. But he seems genuinely interested in working with me and proving that he can be more than a hard-boiled engineering manager."

The management-by-objectives program that both Myers and Dickenson spoke of involved working with all key managers to develop new techniques for dealing with their subordinates in the planning, decision-making, and review phases of their work. Dickenson explained the program further:

It is difficult to summarize the M.B.O. approach because it deals with intangibles like climate as well as specific procedures. In essence, a manager sits down with each of his key subordinates and they establish a few key objectives which then serve as targets. Most of the targets will be for a six- to twelve-month period but some will be larger-range. There are four main points to keep in mind during the target, or objective-setting, stage:

1. Regardless of who initiates the objectives, the manager and the subordinate should discuss them until they are jointly satisfied that they can be reached.

2. Wherever possible, objectives should be formulated in measurable terms.

3. Where objectives might take a year or more to achieve, measurable checkpoints should be agreed to.

4. The objectives, wherever possible, should be few and on the broad, integrated, end-result level. The department managers should not get into the numerous procedural steps to accomplish end-result objectives; these will be worked out by their subordinates. If managers interfere they will remove much of the challenge and commitment the subordinate should feel for the objective.

Periodically, these objectives should be reviewed as required. Unless significant failures to achieve key objectives take place, or appear imminent, the superior should not involve himself in the means by which his subordinates seek to accomplish their objectives.

This approach involves an entire network of corollary systems. In order to make it work, you have to build recruiting, training, career development, and compensation programs that reinforce the M.B.O. approach. Communications, including management information systems, budgetary systems, and planning procedures have to fit too, and a climate of mutual respect and trust must be built. The total system, which is designed to more fully tap human resources by meshing individual and organizationl goals, is often called O.D., or Organizational Development.

The casewriter asked Dickenson whether he felt Horn was sincere and if so, would be able to learn and use these concepts. Dickenson's response was:

I think he is sincere, and despite his history of being a driver I think he can learn. You know, the only time when you can't teach an old dog new tricks is when the dog thinks he is too old to learn. Paul can learn but is likely to be impatient with himself as well as with the system. One thing that will help is that he will be managing quite a few departments headed by people who are far more knowledgeable than he is in the specific areas in which they work. At least, I think this will help. His inability to plunge in with both feet and show them a "better way" may force him to learn how to manage a process rather than make a series of technical decisions.

Horn, in fact, seemed anxious to get started when interviewed by the casewriter just after his appointment was announced.

There are some people in this company who think I can't adjust to new management techniques. At first, I was angry about this move but now I see it as a good opportunity to try something new.

Two years ago, when they first asked me to install the M.B.O. program in my corporate engineering review department, I talked Dickenson's former superior out of it. I explained that mine was an unusual department with a very tough, dirty job to do at that time and that it would be better to leave us alone for awhile. That was a mistake on my part. I am sure that it is one of the reasons why I am in Pittsburgh now. At that time, I was more interested in immediate results than in trying to understand and institute what seemed like the latest in an unending stream of management fads.

Furthermore, many of my friends at division level who were trying to install M.B.O. didn't like it one bit. They complained that it often left them with an uneasy feeling that they were losing control of the work they supervised and that by focusing on results they were overly dependent on their subordinates. Fred Biggs, whom I worked with in Houston, said, "Paul, this is the gol-dangest approach I ever saw. It's like playing poker, Only now my subordinates play all the hands—with my money—and according to the rules they don't even have to show me their cards. They just call me up twice a month and tell me how much they won or we lost."

I guess my biggest objection, though, was that instituting a new system like M.B.O. takes time and I wasn't prepared to invest it. Judging by what happened I made a poor decision. I won't make the same mistake twice, though!

For the next six weeks Horn spent almost all of his time trying to familiarize himself with the work done by the four departments under his control and the men who managed them.

I found [Horn said] that I was really in over my head on much of the work they are doing. With all of my experience I know very little about the technical aspects of their work. Only in production estimating do I have a good feel, and this is based on my knowledge of good procedures and practices. This knowledge helps some in the technical service group but as far as the design and development departments, it would take me at least a year to feel qualified to make technical judgments in those areas. As I understand this M.B.O. approach, I shouldn't be terribly concerned about this.

At the end of the first six weeks, Horn requested that each of his department managers develop a plan for the next twelve months showing how they would increase their efficiency by at least 10 percent during that period. Horn did not give them any specifics on how this was to be accomplished but indicated that this efficency must be achieved without deterioration of service or cutbacks in development of key personnel.

I told them that it was up to them to show the initiative and imagination required to give as good or better service for less money. I don't know enough about their work to know how they can do it, and I might interfere with their personal development if I did know enough to try. The one thing I do know, after more than twenty year's experience, is that there are almost always ways of improving efficiency. What you need are good men and a little pressure from above.

A month after making his request, Horn set up a meeting with each of his subordinates. He spent less than an hour alone with each man in the morning and then at a general meeting in the afternoon he allocated one hour for each man to present his plan to the others.

The tone of the meeting was described by one of the department managers as "firm but friendly." Andy Drechsel, manager of the technical service group, said:

I explained to Mr. Horn that it was difficult for me to forecast cost or efficiency, because so much of our work was tied to requests from the marketing people. We have several measures of productivity that we use but they are rough and involve a number of intangibles. I tried to explain some of these to Mr. Horn, but he indicated that he didn't feel he should get into them. He asked me to give him my honest estimates of how much I could do to meet his 10 percent increased efficiency goal.

Frankly, I came into the meeting prepared to hedge a bit and give him something a little more conservative, by way of targets, but he made me feel that he was counting on me and that I owed myself as well as him the best I could do. I ended up by giving him rather optimistic estimates and I am going to have to work like the devil to meet them. Judging from the afternoon meeting my overall target of 18 percent increase is the highest, but we can make it if Mr. Horn helps when marketing puts too much pressure on.

Edward Deeb, manager of production estimating, agreed with Drechsel that his meeting with Horn had been friendly.

Even though he understands my department better than the others [Deeb said], he made no attempt to get into the details I worked out to support our annual plan. All he wanted to know was could I do it? I came away feeling that he didn't even keep a copy of my department plan; just a one-page summary of our overall budget. I promised him the 10 percent he wants and I think we can do it.

Sam Elster and Charles Graf, managers of the design and the development departments respectively, were more mixed in their reactions to the day's meeting.

> I spent a full month with my people [Elster said] working up a very detailed plan. It is very difficult to be precise about cost and efficiency in our design work but we tried. We made the best estimates we could of what kinds of things would come out of development and production and how we would tackle them. I developed several PERT diagrams to work out schedules and costs, but as near as I can tell, Mr. Horn never even looked at them.
>
> When I asked him this morning what he thought of our plans he said, "We're not here today to talk plans, Sam: we have to agree on targets—objectives. I'll leave the plans to you. All I want to know is what objectives we can set down now and count on you reaching by next year."
>
> When it became clear that he was not going to let me go into any detail on the many imponderables that I had to face in my plan, I was glad I had been a little cautious with my summary targets for departmental operations. If I thought he would be willing to dig in with me to understand why I may or may not succeed, then I might have revised my targets upward a little. Overall, I showed what amounts to a 7.5 percent improvement in efficiency. Mr. Horn went over the six key targets that will be the basis of this improvement and tried to get me to increase them to bring the total up to 10 percent, but I stood fast. I said, "Mr. Horn, if you want me to change the totals then you have to show me where we disagree in my plans." He laughed and said, "Sam, you know I don't know enough about the operation of your department to win a debate with you. I'm sure you can figure out how to get to 10 percent. Everybody else has."

Elster maintained, however, that he had given Horn the most accurate and aggressive objectives he could and Horn begrudgingly accepted them. On several occasions during the afternoon session, however, Horn made reference to the lower than 10 percent target for the design department.

Charles Graf, or "Doc" as he was known in his department, was a brilliant engineer himself and had built a very strong group of development people. His department was highly regarded for the quality and dependability of its work, but it also exceeded budget more frequently and by larger amounts than the other three. Graf gave his reaction to what had happened at the meeting.

> I feel like the man who had a magician pull a tablecloth off the table without disturbing the food. I came in this morning with a plan that I felt supported my claim that is was impossible for our department to show any tangible evidence of improved efficiency and I left agreeing to a 15 percent improvement. The nature of development work and its heavy dependence on inputs from research and production makes planning virtually impossible. We must be able to do creative work under time pressure and do it well. If I get everyone overly budget conscious, I will lose more than I gain.
>
> I told Horn this from the first day he arrived and I told him again this morning. I tried to show him why we should be evaluated in a different way. He had leafed through my plan but apparently only in search of budget or output summaries. When it became apparent that I wasn't getting anywhere I decided it would be wiser to go along with him. We went over the four major elements of cost in my department and for each of my targets he would ask, "How about it Doc, can't we tighten up a little here?" Before I knew it, we had "agreed" to objectives that show me improving overall efficiency by 15 percent.
>
> It wasn't until this afternoon, when I had to present my "revised" plans to the others, that I realized what I had agreed to. Well, Mr. Horn made it clear that we would review our progress each month, and so now I have to figure out how I can gradually move his expectations back to a more realistic level.

Paul Horn was pleased with the meetings and told Jim Dickenson so the next day.

> Jim, you have no idea how much I appreciate your help on this management-by-objectives approach. I have just gotten my people to agree on some good, ambitious objectives for the year and I think I can bring in a much better cost-effectiveness ratio as a result.
>
> By staying away from details with them, Jim, I not only kept them from getting me to make the tough decisions for them, but I'm in a much better position to hold them fully accountable for results. The ones who deliver will be

rewarded and if anyone doesn't, I'll have more time to help them out. I doubt that we will reach all our targets this year but it is healthy to try. Three of my men will probably come very close. There is only one about whom I am worried, but I will leave him alone for at least six months and give him a chance to prove me wrong.

Finally, Jim, by staying out of details, I will have time to work more closely with production, marketing, and research and better coordinate our overall efforts.

Dickenson was somewhat taken aback by Horn's comments and a little concerned.

I think Paul is sincere but I'm not sure he is fully aware of what it takes to make a management-by-objectives system work. I had no idea he would move this quickly, because I thought he would take a few more months to get a feel for operations. As a result, I haven't worked very closely with him on some of the wrinkles that have to be ironed out of this approach.

Question
1. What do you think of Myers' comments that he is eager to do his part to deal with ecological problems but that PCD in five years' time would either be "in the black or on the block"? How far should a business go in sacrificing profits for such things as contributing to major areas of social concern?
2. Write a paragraph summarizing Horn's apparent view of MBO as an integrative process. Based on your reading of Chapter 22 write another paragraph summarizing your view and understanding of what MBO involves.
3. In what respect is Horn's view of MBO deficient? Be specific.
4. Comment on the process of reaching decisions on key goals that Horn used. How would you suggest he should have proceeded?
5. Describe the kind of problems and conflicts that your foresee might be forthcoming between Horn and each of his subordinates.
6. If you were to advise Horn regarding how he should have proceeded what would you tell him? Outline a step-by-step plan.

INDEX

Abt, Clark, 583
Acceptance theory, 36
Accountability, 153, 531
   creation of, 153
Achievement motivation, N(ACH) 232–235
   dynamics of, 233–234
   managerial implications and, 234–235
Adult data processing, 207
Advisory staff, 122
AFL-CIO, 475
Age of Discontinuity, The, 628–630
Alderfer, Clayton, 227–228
Allen, Louis, 601
Allhiser, Norman, 141
American workers, work week of, 261
Application exercises and cases:
   Adelson Sales, 219–220
   Analyzing Motivational Patterns, 250
   Central High School, 165
   Can One Learn to Manage Subordinates?, 388–389
   Case Incident from Germany, A, 443–444
   Catch a Falling Tristar, 502
   Choose a Leadership Style, 614–615
   C.I.T. Financial Corporation: Merger and Morale, 218–219
   Communications at the James River Plant, 360
   Dr. Holt's Dilemma, 251
   Efferson Associates, Consultants, 45–46
   Douglas Fowler's Dilemma, 137
   Faulty Light Bulbs, 557–558
   Forming a New Company, 136–137
   Foster Chemical, Inc., 108–109
   Hell Week, 555–557
   Identifying Leadership Styles, 381
   Implementing Concepts for Job Design, 277–278
   Importance of the Management Job, 21–22
   Importance of Management Philosophy, 164
   Industrial Scale Company, 107
   Long Term Health Care Facility, A, 501–502
   Matter of Priority, A, 587–589
   MBO or Something Else, 613–614
   Naylor Corporaton, 189–190
   Needed: Business-Oriented Systems Analysts, 525–526
   Nonconformist, The, 644–645
   Novel Approach to Management Development, A, 416–417
   One out of Three, 358–359

   Pitt Foundry, 83
   Planning for Home Improvements, 82
   Planning to Introduce Change, 442–443
   Plating Room Group, The, 301–302
   Research Coordination in the Pharmaceutical Industy, 188–189
   Retirement Hotel, A, 501
   River Glen Manufacturing Plant, 302–303
   Sebastians—Layout of a Restaurant Kitchen, 478
   Sirocco Company–Introduction of a Budgetary Control Plan, 553–555
   Success in the Small Multinational, 643–644
   Talent Hunt, 415–416
   Turning People On, 278–279
   Utilizing Management Concepts, 45
   Utilizing Your Understanding of Management, 20–21
   We Have Playoffs, Runoffs, Bake-offs: Now a Compute-off, 526–528
   Workers are Experts—"Quality Circles" in Breakthrough, 479–480
   Xerox Experiment, The, 589–590
Argyris, Chris, 39, 352, 425–426, 430–431
   XA to YB movement, 430–431
   YB organizational climate, 425–426
Assembly line, Volvo and, 253
Assessment centers, 399
"Assistant to," purpose of position, 120–121
Athos, Anthony G., 436
Authority:
   Barnard's view of, 36
   decentralization of, 179–184
   delegation of, 139–140
   effective use of, 146, 148–151
   flow of, 147
   future views of, 630
   hard approach, 150
   line, 314–315
   power and, 143–148
   primary, 314
   project, 314
   soft approach, 149
   steps for granting, 152
   uses of, 150
   vs. power, 144–147
   views of, 143–144
   see also Delegation; Decentralization

656 INDEX

Automatic notification, 517
Automation continuum, 271, 272

Babbage, Charles, 26
BALANCE program, 496, 539
Barnard, Chester, I., 36–37, 64, 143, 147–148, 347
BARS Scale, 404
Basic Leader Behavior Styles, 376–377
Behavior modification, 243–244, 401–403
Behavioral sciences, management and, 39–40
Behavioral scientists, free form organization and, 320–321
Berne, Eric, 205–211
   application of TA theory, 206–211
Bhada, Yezdi K., 605
Binging, 292–293
Bisanz, Charles, 400
Blackie, William, 639
Blake, Robert R., 38, 363, 366, 367
Blanchard, Kenneth H., 38, 374, 375
Bonus system, origin of, 29
Boredom, workers and, 258–259
Borsch, F. J., 624
Boulton, Watt and Company, 25
Bradshaw, Thornton F., 54
Brainstorming, 102
Break-even analysis, 487
Bribery, 568
Brown, Alvin, 143, 171
Budgeting, 543–546
   flexible (variable), 544
   nature of, 543
   responsibility accounting and, 545
   standard costs, 545
   zero-base, 546
Bureaucracy, 174–178
   advantages of, 177
   characteristics of, 174, 176
   disadvantages of, 177–178
   enterprise and, 178–179
Business functions, 114
Business responsibility, 420–421, 573–576
   classical view of, 571–572
   managerial view of, 572–573
   public view of, 573–574
   radical view of, 573–574
   research findings, 574–576

Cadillac, change process, 420–421
Career goals, explanation of, 411–412
Career planning, 410–414
   checklist for, 413
Cascading approach, 62, 598
Center for Creative Leadership, 14
Central processing unit (CPU), 511
Champion Paper Company, 356

Change process, 420–421
Chart, organization, 114–115, 132–133
Cherington, David, 582
Chief executive, function of, 47–48
Chief of staff, origin of, 30
Church, 65–66, 73
   communion policy, 73
   objectives for establishing a, 65, 66
Classical management era, 35
COBOL, 511
Collegial organization, 314, 320–322
Communication, 112, 198–216
   barriers to, 212–216
   definition of, 201
   development of, 203
   good program for, 200
   grapevine and, 215–216
   human barriers to, 213–214
   importance of, 199–200
   "I'm OK You're OK," 206–211
   inadequate, 199, 200
   information side of, 202–204
   interdepartmental, 205
   interpersonal behavior and, 205–206
   linkages, 112
   listening and, 211–212
   manager's role and, 201–202
   organizational barriers, 214–215
   people as barriers to, 215
   technical barriers to, 212–213
   two-way process of, 202
Computer competition, 504
Computer programs:
   BALANCE, 496, 539
   DECIDE, 495
   FUTURE, 489
   LINPRO, 539
   MAINSIM, 497
   QUESIM, 496
Computers:
   analog, 511
   binary, 511
   components of, 511
   decision support and, 485
   definition of, 510
   digital, 511
   forecasting package, 489
   management information systems and, 510–514
   package programs, 486
   see also Computer programs
Conflict, 352–355
   handling of, 355 (chart)
   resolution of, 353–355
   types of, 352–353
Contingency approaches to leadership, 373–384

INDEX

Fred Fiedler, 373–375
Hersey-Blanchard Studies, 375–378
Least Prefered Coworker Score (LPC), 373–374
Reddin's tridimensional grid, 378–381
situational leadership theory, 376–378
Contingency theory of management, 13
Control, 530–550
   administration of system, 550
   budgeting, 543–546. *See also* Budgets
   concurrent, 534
   definition of, 531
   dynamic, 534
   elements of, 531–535
   evaluative, 534–535
   inventory, 539–543
   managerial, 548–550
   measurement process, 533, 534
   Project Control (PERT/CPM), 546–548
   production planning and, 537–539
   productive systems and, 535–543
   quality, 536–537
   realistic systems, 535
   standards of, 532, 533, 534
Controlling executive, 11
Controlling operations, 530–550
   function of, 8
   supervisory, 11
   see also Managerial control
Control staff, 123
Corporate goals, 60
   range of, 63
Corporate planning, 69, 78–79
   major steps, 79
   multinational, 619–620
Corporate policies, examples of, 72
Corporation, multinational, 617–623
Cost-volume-profit (CVP) analysis, 485–488
Couch, Peter D., 407
Country club manager, 364–365
Creative Organization—A Japanese Experiment, 329–333
Criticube, 408
Customer departmentation, 128
Cybernated systems, 508

Decentralization, 179–184
   advantages of, 182–183
   definition of, 179
   delegation of authority, 279–280
   disadvantages of, 183
   implementation of, 180
   organizational, 179–184
   profit center concept, 180
   reasons against, 181–182
   reasons for, 180–181
   trends in, 183–184

DECIDE program, 495
Decision rule, 532
Decision rules, 99–100
Decision styles, 98
Decision support:
   computers and, 485
   forecasting and, 489
Decision-making:
   acceptance priority rule, 100
   acceptance rule, 100
   analyzing alternative solutions, 94–95
   barriers to, 104
   as behavioral decision model, 87
   brainstorming, 102
   case studies, 88–89, 91, 92, 93, 94, 97
   communication of, 96–97
   conflict rule, 100
   developing alternative solutions, 93
   fairness rule, 100
   future and, 640
   goal congruence rule, 99
   group, 100–104
   implementing decisions, 95–96
   information rule, 99
   intuition and, 87
   negative influences, 101–102
   participation in, 97–100
   phases of, 88–97
   problem analysis, 89–93
   problem attributes, 99
   quantitative, 482–499
   role of manager in, 85–86
   scalar chain of command and, 117–118
   span of control and, 157
   states of decision, 86
   techniques of, 86–87
   unstructured problem rule, 99–100
   see also Group decision-making; Quantitative decision-making
Decision-making system, 86 (chart)
Decision trees, 493–495
Delegation, 139–154
   advantages of, 141–143
   authority and power, 143–148
   definition of, 143
   effective, 140–141
   managerial authority and, 139–153
   managers and, 140–141
   motivation and, 142–143
   phases of, 151–153
   subordinates and, 141–143
   what it is not, 153–154
Delphi Technique (DT), 103–104
Deming, W. Edwards, 482
Departmentation, 125–128
   customer, 128

658 INDEX

Departmentation *continued*
   functional, 125–126
   geographical, 128
   levels of, 126 (chart)
   means of, 125–128
   product, 126–128
Design logic, organizational, 313–314
Design principles, 312–313
   functional organization, 312
   system organization, 313
   team organization, 313
   types of, 312–313
Differentiation, organizational, 307, 310–311
Directing, 7–11
   executive, 10
   function of, 7, 8
   supervisory, 11
Direct pressures, 101
Discipline, chief elements of, 169
Doomsday Book, The, 628
Drucker, Peter, 68–69, 184, 580, 595–596, 602, 620, 628–630, 637

Economic order quantity, 542–543
Educational Testing Service (ETS), executive effectiveness of, 347–348
Efficiency, principles of, 30–31
Elements of management, 34
Emergent behavior, 288–294
   early study, 291–294
   groups and, 288–290, 291–294
Emerson, Harrington, 30–31
Enterprise, and bureaucracy, 178–179
Enterprise, characteristics of, 175
Environment, organizational structure and, 309–311
Equity theory, 231–232
E.R.G. Theory, 227–229
Ethnocentricity, 632–633
Etzioni, Amitai, 425
Executive, 9–11, 347–348
   controlling and, 11
   directing and, 10
   effectiveness of, 348
   functions of, 9
   organizing and the, 10
   role of top, 347–348
   social responsibility and, 574–576
   see also Communication; Decision-making; Leader; Managerial Authority
Exxon, 617

Fayol, Henri, 34–35, 168–170
Fayol Bridge, 170
Fayol's elements of discipline, 169
Fayol's gangplank, 170, 312
Fayol's General Principles of Management, 169

Feedback loop, 510
Fiedler, Fred, 38, 373–375
File, Q.W., 408
Filtering method, 515–516
First-line supervisor, role of, 344–345
Fiscal approach, planning and, 55–56
Fixed costs, 486, 487
Florida Test Facility, 315
Focused factory, The, 472–474
Follett, Mary Parker, 36, 37
Football and Bell Concept of Organization, 636
Forecasting, 488–489
   correlation analysis, 489
   decision support and, 489
   model of, 489
FORTRAN, 511
Four systems of management, 367
Free form organization, 314, 320–322
Friedman, Milton, 572
Functional departmentation, 125–126
Functional organization, 311–313
   weaknesses of, 311–312
Functional performance objectives, 608
Functional principle, 35
Functional staff, 123–124
Future, 626–642
   authority in the, 630
   decision-making in, 640
   long range planning in, 626
   management by objectives, 640–641
   management practices in, 634–641
   management styles in, 637–639
   natural resources and, 626–628
   organization and manager in, 624–641
   womens' role in management, 631–632
FUTURE program, 489

Galbraith, John K. 573
Gantt Chart, 30
Gantt, Henry L. 29–30
General Electric Co., restructuring process, 111
General Mills, product managers of, 305, 318
General staff, 121–122
Geographical departmentation, 128
Geographical organization design, 129
Gilbreth, Frank, 28–29
Gilbreth, Lillian, 28–29
Goal setting, 62, 245
   cascading approach to, 62, 598
Graicunas, V. A., 154
Griffiths, Edgar H. 54
Group decision-making, 100–104
   Delphi Technique (DT), 103–104
   nominal group techniques (NGT), 103
   techniques of, 102–104

Groups:
    cliques, 294
    cohesiveness of, 285–287
    consequences of intragroup behavior, 293–294
    definition of, 282
    effect on motivation, 235
    emergent behavior, 288, 290, 291
    formal, 283
    formation factors, 284–288
    function in organization, 281–300
    groupthink, 100–102
    Herzberg's theory and, 293
    informal, 283–284
    intergroup behavior, 294–298
    intergroup competition, 295–296
    intergroup conflict, 296–298
    intragroup behavior, 285, 288–294
    isolates, 291
    managerial implications, 298–300
    Maslow's theory and, 293
    norms and, 288, 290, 292, 293
    process approach, 36
    required behavior, 289, 290
    resolving intergroup conflct, 297
    small, 282–283
    training, 39
    types of, 283–284
    work, 291
    work-group behavior, 289
    see also Group decision-making
Groupthink, characteristics of, 100–102

Halo effect, 398
Handbook of Operations Research, 530
Hard approach, 150
Harder Company, 193–194
Hardware, computer, 511
Harris, Louis, 425
Hawthorn studies, 32–34
Hersey, Paul, 38, 374–375
Herzberg, Frederick, 38, 235–237, 264, 293
    dual factors, 236–237
    theory of work groups, 293
Heuristic programming, 513
Hewlett-Packard Corp., 198
Hierarchy, of objectives, 62
Horizontal organization growth, 118–120
House, Robert J., 372
Howard, Roland A., 484
Human relations era, 32–34
Human resource planning and development, 391–414
    assessment centers, 399
    behavior modification and, 401–403
    charts, 393–394
    General Motors, 391–392
    integrated system of, 405–407
    management development, 407–410
    performance appraisal and, 403–405
    personnel recruitment, 394–395
    personnel selection, 395–396, 397–399
    quality of work life (QWL), 400–401
    staffing, and, 392–394
Hunt, J.G., 634, 635
Hygiene factors, 236

Illusion of invulnerability, 101
Illusion of unanimity, 101
Impoverished management, 365
Input data, 510
Institutionalization, definition of, 176
Integration, organizational, 307–308, 310–311
Integrative Cases:
    Consolidated Instruments-B, 647–653
    Creative Organization—A Japanese Experiment, 329–333
    Function of the Chif Executive, The, 47–48
    Harder Company: Development of a Safety Program, 193–194
    Home Equipment Company, The, 561–563
    John Anderson, 448–451
    Kentown Corporation, 326–329
    McCall Diesel Motor Works, 559–561
    South Pacific Hotel, 445–447
    Stellar Steel Products Company: A Plan to Provide Staff Assistance for Manufacturing, 191–192
    Union Carbide and Vienna, West Virginia, 646–647
    Wilson Bindary—Application of Scientific Management to a Small Business, 48–49
Intermediate-range plans, 74
International Association of Quality Circles, 475
Interpolation, 345
Interview, job, 398–399
Intragroup behavior, 285
Intuition, decision-making and, 87
Investment planning, 68
Isolates, 291

Japanese corporations, workings of, 437–439, 461, 482, 592, 623
Japanese management system, 623
Japanese productivity, kaban, 456
Japanese quality control, 482
Japanese study, vendor locations, 461
Japanese-style management, 419, 435–439
    Theory Z of, 437
Jennings, Eugene, 338
Job design, 254–274
    contingency approach, 270–273
    economics in, 271
    enlargement of job, 262–264
    historical approaches to, 254–257
    impact of historical approach, 256

Job design *continued*
    motivation and, 259–264
    operation chart, 255
    personality and, 272
    related research, 272–273
Job enlargement, 262–266, 268–270
    ability utilization, 263
    meaningful work modules, 262–263
    performance feedback, 263
    research on, 269–270
    task variety, 262
    worker-paced control, 263–264
Job enrichment, 264–269
    experiments in, 264–265
    Herzberg and, 264
    job nesting and, 266–268
    office layout after nesting, 269
    Office layout before nesting, 267
    organizational audit format, 273-274
    research on, 269–270
    versus enlargement, 266
    vertical job loading, 265
    work modules, 265–266
Job nesting, 266–269
Job redesign, 260–262, 270
    attempts at, 260–262
    current research, 270
Job shop, 539
Johari Awareness Window, 412–413
Johnson, Harold, 638
Johnson, Robert, 504

Kaban, 456
Kahn, Irving Berlin, 362
Kentown Corporation, 326–329
Koontz, Harold, 184

Labor, as active participant, 24
Labor-management participation teams, 24
Lasagna, John B., 601
Law of situation, 36
Lawler, Edward E., 260
Lawrence and Lorsch, study of, 309–310
Leader:
    activities of successful, 349–355
    conflict arbitration and, 352–355
    delegating authority, 350–351
    objectivity of, 349–350
    rewarding subordinates, 351
    skills of, 348–349
    subordinates and, 351
    work of, 344–348
    see also Decision-making; Managerial authority
Leadership:
    contingency approaches to, 373–384. *See also*, Contingency

    approaches to leadership
    developing philosophy for, 337–356
    Fiedler's theory of, 38
    normative theories of, 363–372
    path-goal theory of, 372
    situational theory of, 38
    skills of, 348–349
    theory of, 38
Leadership skills, 348–349
    managers, 349
Leadership styles, 362–384
    chart, 378
    managerial grid and, 363–367
Learning groups (L-groups), 39
Leavitt, Harold J., 634, 635
Legitimacy, 145
Legitimate power, 145
Lewin, Kurt, 420
Likert's four systems of management, 38, 367–372
Likert, Rensis, 38, 367–372
Line balancing, 495–496
Line functions, 113–114
Line managers, 118, 119
Line organization structure, 118
Linear programming, 491–493
    applications of, 493
    charts, 491–493
    extreme points, 491
"Linking Pin" concept, 371, 372
LINPRO, 539
Listening skills, 211–212
    importance of, 211–212
    nondirective interviewing, 211–212
Litterer, Joseph, 599
Long range planning, future and, 626
Long-range planning, positive payoffs, 76–77
Luce, Charles, 338

McClelland, David, 149, 232–235
McConkey, Dale D., 56, 601, 604
McGregor, Douglas, 37, 184, 423–425, 430, 549, 594
Machine bureaucracy, 313
MAINSIM, 497
Maintenance, preventative, 497
Man-machine interactive system, 508
Management:
    acceptance priority rule, 100
    acceptance rule, 100
    achievement motivation N(ACH) and, 232–235
    alternative solutions to problems, 94–95
    authority and, 36, 143–151, 314–315
    barriers to communication, 212–216
    behavioral science findings, 39–40
    budgeting and, 543–546
    bureaucracy and, 174–178

business responsibility, 420–421, 573–576
by objectives, 184–185, 592–611
case studies in decision-making, 88–89, 91, 92, 93, 94, 97
change processes of, 420–421
communication of, 112, 198–216
conflict, 352–355
contingency approaches to leadership, 373–384
contingency theory, 13
control and, 530–550
controlling function, 8
corporate goals and, 60
decentralization, 179–184
decision-making and, 86–87
decision styles chart, 98
definition of, 6
delegation, 139–154
departmentation, 125–128
development, 11–12
directing function, 7, 8
early development of, 25–26
Fayol's elements of, 34
four era's of, 24
functions of, 6–11
future and, 634–641
hard *vs.* soft approach, 150
historical development of, 24–43
human element in, 12–13
human relations era, 32–34
"I'm OK You're OK," 206–211
importance of job, 21–22
international and future, 617–641
Japanese-style, 419, 435–439
listening and communication, 211–212
management by objectives (MBO), 184–185, 592–611
management information systems (MIS), 504–522
modern era, 37–42
Mooney's principles of, 35–36
organization and management theorists era, 34–37
organizational decentralization, 179–184
organizing function, 7
participative, 97–100, 350, 367
people as approach to management, 339–349
planning function, 7
principles of, 159–161, 168–171
scientific era, 26–32
social responsibility of, 568–585. *See also* Social Responsibility
as specialized area, 11–12
strategy with groups, 298–300
technical barriers to communication, 212–213
two-way process of communication, 202
utilizing an understanding of, 20–21
Management by objectives (MBO), 184–185, 592–611
budgeting and control, 604–605
elements of, 184
future and, 640–641

group process and, 606, 610
measuring and rewarding performance, 603–604
objective setting, 595–597
participative goal setting, 599–602
priorities and, 598
responsibility charts and, 608–610
Theory X and Theory Y, 607
writing objectives well, 601
zero-base budgeting and, 605
Management development, 407–410
Management information systems (MIS), 504–522
automatic notification, 517
behavioral problems and, 518–522
elements of effective, 508–510
evolution of, 505–506
filtering method, 515, 517
monitoring method, 516
organizational problems and, 514–518
uses of, 506–508
Management philosophy, current trends in, 426
Management science, 40–41
approaches to, 40–41
definition of, 40
Management style, diagnosis of, 368–369
Management style, future and, 637–639
Management systems analysis, 497
Management systems, Likert's, 38, 367–372
Manager:
career plan development, 410–414
decision-making role of, 85–86. *See also* Decision-making
delegation and, 140–141
dependencies of, 148
development of, 410–414
effective *vs.* ineffective, 5–6
executive level performance of, 9
goal setting of, 245
granting authority, 152. *See also* Managerial authority
listening and, 211
management system analysis and, 497–498
manager development, 410–414
"Manager-Nonmanager Behavior," 383
middle, role of, 345–347
MIS programs and, 513
motivation and, 13–14
nature of job, 14–15
performance differences, 8–11
performance expectations of, 245
philosophy about people, 423–425
plans and, 74
problem analysis and, 89–90
program effectiveness, 410
role in organizing, 112–113
role of, 5, 11–13. *See also* Leadership
span of control and, 154
styles of, 380–381

Manager *continued*
  supervisory level performance, 9
Managerial authority:
  Barnard's view of, 36
  delegation of, 139–153
  effective use of, 146, 148–151
  flow of, 147
  future views of, 630
  hard approach, 150
  line of, 314–315
  power and, 143–148
  primary, 314
  project, 314
  soft approach, 149
  steps for granting, 152
  uses of, 150
  vs. power, 144–147
  views of, 143–144
Managerial control:
  administration of system, 550
  budgeting, 543–546. *See also* Budgets
  concurrent, 534
  definition of, 531
  dynamic, 534
  elements of, 531–535
  evaluative, 534–535
  human aspects of, 549–550
  inventory, 539–543
  managerial qualitities of, 548–550
  measurement process, 533, 534
  production planning and, 537–539
  productive systems and, 535–543
  Project Control (PERT/CPM), 546–548
  quality, 536–537
  realistic systems, 535
  standards of, 532–533, 534
Managerial delegation:
  advantages of, 141–143
  authority and, 139–148
  definition of, 143
  effective, 140–141
  managers and, 140–141
  motivation and, 142–143
  phases of, 151–153
  subordinates and, 141–143
  see also Authority; Management.
Managerial grid, 38, 363, 364–367, 407, 431–435
  organizational development program and, 431–435
Managerial planning and strategy, 54–79
Managerial problem analysis and decision-making, 84–104
Managerial styles, managerial grid and, 363–367
Managerial talent, need for, 4
Manufacturing plants, study of, 308
Marketing, 67–68, 620

  examples of strategy, 67–68
  multinational business and, 620
  scientific forecasting, 67
Marquand, William, R., 362
Marvin, Philip, 408
Maslow, Abraham, 37, 224–227, 293, 372
  need hierarchy of, 224
  work and group theory of, 293
Matrix organization, 314, 317–321
Mayo, Elton, 32
Means-end chain, 175
Mechanistic pattern, organizaional form, 306
Merger, 181
Middle manager, role of, 345–347
Middle-of-the-road-management, 365–366
Milliken, Roger, 530
Model:
  cost-volume-profit (CVP) analysis, 485–488
  definition of, 483
  quantitative, 485
Modern management era, organizational behavior, 37–40
Monitoring method, 516
Monte Carlo technique, 496
Mooney, James D., 35–36, 171
Motivation:
  achievement, N(ACH), 232–235
  behavior modification and, 243–244
  comparison of theories, 229
  content theories, 224–229
  delegation and, 142–143
  equity theory, 231–232
  E.R.G. Theory and, 227–228
  Herzberg's concepts of, 38, 236–240, 261
  hygiene factors, 236
  impact of objectives on, 62
  incentives to, 235
  job design and, 259–264
  leadership and, 246
  Maslow's theory and, 37, 224–227
  money and, 239–240
  overview, 222–223
  Porter and Lawler model, 241–243
  process theories, 229–235
  reinforcement theory, 243–244
  supervision and, 245
  Vroom's theory, 229–231
Motivation-hygiene theory, 238–239
Motivation-to-manage, 13–14
Motivational approach, planning and, 55–56
Motivational factors. *See* Motivation
Mouton, Jane Srygley, 38, 363, 366–367
Multinational corporations, 617–623
  human resources and, 621–622
  marketing and, 620
  organization structure and, 620–621

planning and, 618–620
political climate and, 622–623
productivity challenge and, 623
Multiplicity, definition of, 63
Murray, Philip, 24
Myers, Scott, 351

Nadar, Ralph, 573
Natural resources, future and, 626–628
Network, of objectives, 62
Newall, P.F., 634, 635
Nichols, Ralph, 211
Nominal group techniques (NGT), 103
Nondirective interviewing, 211–212
Norms, definition of, 288, 290, 292, 293

Objective grids, 608–610
Objectives:
  accomplished by plans, 73, 74
  church, 65
  constraints to, 63
  establishing business, 64–65
  formation of hierarchy, 62
  formation of network, 62
  individual motivation and, 62
  multiplicity of, 63
  organizational effectiveness and, 60–64
  personal, 64–65
  policy and, 69, 71
  profit, 64
  social responsibility, 64
  volunteer service organization, 66
Objective setting, 60–62
  process, 60–61
OD programs. *See* Organizational development
Odiorne, George, 184, 599
Operations data, 510
Operations management, 40, 456–477
  activities and decisions, 459–463
  equipment choices, 459–460
  facilities layout, 463–465
  issues in, 476
  location, 461–463
  package programs, 486 (chart)
  process design, 459–460
  process layout, 459, 465–466, 467 (chart)
  product design, 459, 470
  production plans, scheduling, dispatching, 466–468
  product life cycle approach, 468–474. *See also* Product life cycle approach
  quality circles, 474–476
Operations systems, 457–458
Organic pattern, organizational form, 307
Organization:
  authority in, 128–130

changes in behavioral environment, 428–429
changes in structural environment, 426–426
characteristics of, 307
definition of, 343, 344
development of, 115–116, 117–118
differentiated departments, 125–126
differentiation of, 307, 310, 311
elements and functions of, 112–115
expansion of, 116
functional approach, 311–312
functional type of, 312
growth of staff, 118–120
horizontal growth, 118–120
integrated functions, 126
integration of, 307–311
life cycle of, 171–172, 173–174
line structure, 118
management theorists era, 34–37
means-end chain, 175
principles of, 159–161
process of organizing, 130–132
responsibility in, 128–130
results gained through people, 343–344
staff types, 120–124
system type, 313
team type, 313
vertical growth, 117
Organization chart, 114–115, 132–134, 316
  limitations of, 132
  missile control department chart, 316
  value of, 133
Organization of Petroleum Exporting Countries (OPEC), 626
Organization structure, 308–322
  multinational business and, 620–621
  review of, 159–161
  study of, 155–157
  tall structure, 155
Organizational behavior, 37–40, 128–130
  accountability and, 128–130
  principles of, 39–40
Organizational climate, 422–423
  job satisfaction, 423
  organization performance, 423
  organization process, 423
  organization structure, 422
  YB, 425–426
Organizational development, 419–440
  action research model, 428
  behavioral intervention methods, 429–431
  grid approach to, 431–439
  integrated method, 440
  integrated view, 439–440
  Japanese *vs.* American companies, 435–439
  total type, 421–426
Organizational forms, 306–308

Organizational malaise, causes of, 173
Organizational philosophy, 342–343
Organizational policies, 72, 73
Organizational structure, 308–322
    collegial type, 314, 320–322
    design logic, 313–314
    design principles, 312–313
    environment and, 309–311
    free form type, 314, 320–322
    matrix type, 314, 317–320
    project type, 314–317
    study outcomes, 310
    technology and, 308–309
    types of, 312–313
Organizations:
    contingency approaches, 305–322
    external changes and, 76
    motivational theory and, 233–234
    see also Organizational development; Organizational structure.
Organizing:
    executive, 10
    function of, 7
    mechanistic patterns, 306
    organic patterns, 307
    patterns of, 306–307
    steps in, 130–132
    supervisory, 11
Ouchi, William C., 419, 437–438
Output data, 510
Overselling the job, 398
Owen, Robert, 25–26

Participative management, 97–100, 350, 367, 419
    Theory Z, 419
Pascale, Richard T., 436
Patent policy, University, 75–76
Path-goal theory of leadership, 372
People, motivations-as-management approaches, 339–340, 341–342
People, organizational results and, 343–344
Personal staff, 120–122
Personality states, 206
Phillips, Tom, 362
Physical factors, productivity and, 32–33
Planning, 54–77
    business, 68–69
    corporate, 69, 78
    domestic vs. international, 619
    executive, 8–9
    fiscal approach, 55–56
    function of, 7
    historical approach, 55–56
    importance of, 55–56
    integrative view of, 77–78
    investment, 68
    long-range, 54, 76–77
    managerial orientations toward, 54–55
    motivational approach, 56
    performance approach, 56
    "Planning is Not", 57
    requirements for successful, 77
    strategic, 57
    supervisory, 9, 10
    see also Plans
Plans, 73–75
    accomplishing objectives and, 74
    development of, 74–75
    intermediate-range, 74
    procedures for implementation, 75–76
    short-range, 74
    statistical quality control, 75
    strategic, 73
    timing of, 74
    types of, 73–74
Policy, 69–73
    corporate, 72
    definition of, 69–70
    development of, 70–71
    formation, 71–72
    objectives and, 69, 71
    organizational, 72–73
    sound advantages of, 70
    statements of, 71
Porter and Lawler:
    automation continuum, 271–272
    motivation model, 241–243, 242
    study, 158–159
Power, 145–151
    bases of, 146
    effective use of, 148–151
    implication of, 145
    legitimate, 145
    socialized, 149
Principle of Staff, 35
Problem analysis, 89–93
Problem attribute, 99
Problem technology, 490
Procedures:
    planning and, 75
    University patent policy, 75–76
Process flowcharting, 29
Processing unit, 510
Process setup, 539
Product departmentation, 126–128
Production line, 495–496, 538–539
    balancing, 495–496
Production planning and control, 537–539
Production system, 457–458, 467–471
    decisions about, 469
Productivity:
    improvement of, 456

Japanese, 455–457
multinational business and, 623
physical factors and, 32–33
quality circles and, 474–476
workers' attitudes toward, 222, 425
Product life cycle approach, 467–474
case, 468–472
focused factory, 472–474
plant within plant, 472–474
Product organization, 127
Professional bureaucracy, 313
Profit centers, 180
decentralization and, 180–181
Program Evaluation and Review Technique (PERT), 30
Project Control, (PERT/CPM), 546–548
Project organization, 314–315 (chart), 316–317

Quality circles, 474–476
Quality control, 536–537
Quantitative decision-making, 482–499
cost-volume-profit models, 485–488
decision trees, 493–495
forecasting, 488–489
linear programming, 490–493. *See also* Linear Programming
managerial role in, 497–498
operational planning activities, 495–497
pros and cons of quantitative model, 498–499
Quantitative model, 485
Quantitative techniques, 41
QUESIM program, 496
Queuing, 496

Range of Corporate Goals, 63
Rationalization, 101
Reddin, William T., 378–381, 601
Remmers, H.H., 408
Renaissance man, 638
Resource allocation problems, 490
Responsibility charts, 608–610
Richards, Les, 420
Riordan, Joseph, 475
Robertshaw Controls Company Corporate Goals 1977, 60
Roethlisberger, Fritz, 32

Sater, Claire W., 585
Satisficing, definition of, 87
Scalar chain of command, 117–118
Scalar chain principle, Fayol's, 170
Scalar Principle, 35
Schein, Edgar, 39, 341, 343, 344, 391
Scientific forecasting, 67
Scientific management, 26–32, 168
application to small business, 47–48
history of, 27–28
results of, 31–32

Sears Roebuck and Co., reorganization of, 167
Self-actualization, 225
Self-censorship, 101
Service staff, 123
Sethi, S. Prakash, 571
"Seven Expressions of Executive Effectiveness," 348
Sheperd, Clovis, 283
Short-range plans, 74
Simon, Herbert, 87
Situational Favorableness Dimension Scale, 374
Skinner, B.F., 243, 401
Sloan, Alfred, 391
Small business, growth of, 115–117
Smith, Adam, 458, 571
invisible hand, 571
Smith, Alan, 391
Smith, Lee, 623
Smith, Roger, 391
Social audit, 583–585
Social responsibility, 568–585
business and, 570–576. *See also* Business Responsibility
corporate, 569–574
managerial response to, 579–581
research findings, 576–579
social action programs, 581–583
social audit, 583–585
Socialized power, 149
Social systems school, 39
Soft approach, 149
Software, computer, 511
Span of Control, 154–159
chart, 155
decision-making and, 157
size of, 157–159
studies of size, 158–159
wide and narrow, 154–157
Specialist staff, 122–124
Staff:
advisory, 122
"assistant to," 120–121
control, 123
functional, 123–124
general, 121–122
organizational positions, 120
personal, 120–122
role of, 118, 119
service, 123
specialist, 122–124
types of authority, 120–124
see also Authority; Delegation; Manager
Staiger, John G., 179
Standards, 532
Steiner, George, 637–640
Stellar Steel Products Co., The, 191–192
Steno pool, 281

Stereotyping, 101, 398
Storage unit, 511
Strategic business planning, 68–69
Strategic plans, 73
Strategy:
   marketing examples, 67–68
   selection of, 66–68
Stringer, Robert A., 233
Strokes, 207
Strother, George S., 407
Subordinates:
   delegation and, 141–143, 152
   leader and, 351
   reward system and, 351
   superiors and, 147–148
Summary of Quantitative Techniques, 41
Supervisor, 9–11, 344–347
   control and, 11
   directing and, 11
   first-line, role of, 344–345
   functions of, 9
Sutton, Francis S., 573

Talpaert, Roger, 639
Task manager, 364–365
Taylor, Fredrick 27–28, 34, 124, 458
Taylor, Gordon Rattray, 628
Taylor's Functional Organization, 124
Team management, 366
Teamwork development:
   goals for, 433–434
   objectives of, 431–434
   personal improvement suggestions, 435
Technology, organizational structure and, 308–309
Tests, employment, 397

T-group, 429
Theory X and Theory Y, 37, 423–426
Theory Z, 437–438
Therbligs, 29
Tolerances, 532
Top executive, role of, 347–348
Training groups (T-groups), 39
Transactional Analysis (TA), 208–211
Treybig, James, 623
Tridimensional grid, 378–382
Twelve Principles of Efficiency, 30–31

Unity of command, Fayol's, 171
Universality, definition of, 16
Urwick, L.F., 113

Variable production costs, 486, 487
Vertical job loading, 265
Vertical organization growth, 117
Volvo, 253
Vroom, V., motivation theory, 229–231
Vroom's Motivational Equation, 230

Wages, as motivation, 239–240
Waiting line problems, Monte Carlo technique, 496
Wells Fargo, 198
Westinghouse Electric Corp., 419
Whisler, Thomas L., 634, 635
Williams, Whiting, 231–232
Women, future role of, 631–632
Woodward, J. 308–309
Woodward Study, 159
Work environment, 112
Work modules, 262, 265–266
   definition of, 265